85
MB

PAKISTAN'S FOREIGN POLICY

An Historical Analysis

PAKISTAN'S
FOREIGN POLICY
An Historical Analysis

S. M. Burke

and

Lawrence Ziring

Second Edition

OXFORD UNIVERSITY PRESS

KARACHI

Oxford University Press, Walton Street, Oxford OX2 6DP
OXFORD NEW YORK TORONTO
DELHI BOMBAY CALCUTTA MADRAS KARACHI
KUALA LUMPUR SINGAPORE HONG KONG TOKYO
NAIROBI DAR ES SALAAM CAPE TOWN
MELBOURNE AUCKLAND MADRID
and associated companies in
BERLIN IBADAN

OXFORD is a trade mark of Oxford University Press

First published in 1973 by Oxford University Press, Oxford.
This second edition published in 1990
by Oxford University Press, Karachi.

ISBN 0 19 577407 8

Second Impression 1994

Printed in Pakistan at
Civil & Military Press (Pvt.) Ltd., Karachi.
Published by
Oxford University Press
5-Bangalore Town, Sharae Faisal
P.O. Box 13033, Karachi-75350, Pakistan.

Respectfully dedicated to the memory
of Charles Lesley Ames,
Founder of the Ames Library of South Asia

Preface to the Second Edition

The first edition of this book was well received and soon ran out of print and there has been a general demand for an updated new edition. My own facilities for research have been greatly reduced since retirement from the University of Minnesota in 1975 but I am glad my friend Dr. Lawrence Ziring kindly agreed to undertake the task.

The text as written by me for the First Edition forms Chapters 1 to 16 of the present edition (developments during the period January 1971 to July 1972 which had appeared as the postscript in the first edition have been incorporated as Chapter 16). Professor Ziring has written Chapters 17 and 18 and the Epilogue and brought the subject-matter up to the summer of 1989.

S. M. Burke

Great Bookham
5 June 1990

Preface to the First Edition

This history of the development of Pakistan's external relations since independence is the first of a series of books I am preparing on India and Pakistan, as a result of several years of research and reflection, for which the opportunity has been provided by the University of Minnesota, the Hill Family Foundation, and the Ford Foundation.

The review has been brought up to the end of the year 1970 which marked the passing of an era in Pakistan. With the first-ever national elections under universal suffrage, held at the close of the decade, the country entered a new phase of which the full implications are not yet apparent.*

My outlook is necessarily Pakistani but I submit to the reader that the rationale for Pakistan's foreign policy deserves to be better known than it is, and also that anyone wishing to study Pakistani foreign policy must begin by trying to understand what the world looked like to Pakistanis themselves and why, at crucial moments, those at the helm of affairs in Pakistan chose certain courses in preference to others which were also open.

However, I have not failed to state what non-Pakistanis have said, and have fully documented this version. The sources indicated here should enable the more serious student to pursue his investigation further if he so wishes.

S. M. Burke

University of Minnesota
January 1971

---

* For developments during the period January 1971–July 1972, see the Postscript.
July 1972   S. M. Burke

Acknowledgements

The following persons assisted me in research over varying periods:

At the University of Minnesota—Rhoda Copeland, Lyle Frost, Craigh Morton, Wilma Kennedy, Cheryl Lee Luger, and Rosemary Anne Ruffenach.

In Lahore, Pakistan—Hayat Feroze, Zafar Asim, Munawar Alam, Murad Gill, and Abdul Majid.

In London—Gillian King.

My friend and former colleague, B. A. Khan, has kept me constantly supplied with material from Pakistan.

The largest amount of patience and industry has been contributed by my secretary, Esther Schwartz; and my wife, Louise, provided helpful counsel at times when I needed it most.

Contents

Part 1
The Non-Aligned Years
(1947-1953)

I Partition and Indo-Pakistani Disputes

I. Hindu-Muslim Differences and the War of Succession

Ask any Indian or Pakistani and he will tell you in all sincerity that it is imperative for the security and welfare of both India and Pakistan that the two neighbours should bury the hatchet and settle down to a friendly and co-operative relationship.

Prime Minister Jawaharlal Nehru had said:

> Their geographical position being what it is, India and Pakistan cannot help playing an important role in Asia. . . . If India and Pakistan follow a contrary policy and are opposed to each other, they will obviously be neutralizing each other and cannot play that role. . . . This conflict and wasteful effort will wipe us out from the face of the earth.[1]

Pakistan's first, and most distinguished, Foreign Minister, Sir Zafrulla Khan, expressed a similar view:

> Pakistan and India . . . if they stood together, could play in world affairs an almost decisive role. . . . [But] from what might have been a position of positive and constructive beneficence for the human race, they have been pushed into one that threatens the peace and prosperity of the whole of South Asia and in its turn constitutes a grave menace to international security.[2]

What dark force, then, propels these intelligent peoples along the path of mutual destruction, in contravention of their own good sense?

Nehru said the question of Indo-Pakistani relationship was difficult to deal with because it was a 'psychological thing', resulting from the way the subcontinent was divided between India and Pakistan. There was 'a complete emotional upset of all the people in India and Pakistan because of this'.[3]

---

[1] Jawaharlal Nehru, *Speeches*, II, p. 446.
[2] M. Zafrulla Khan, *Pakistan's Foreign Relations*, p. 8.
[3] J. Nehru, *Speeches*, I, p. 251.

The Indian statesman was wholly right in describing the malaise which afflicts India and Pakistan as a psychological ailment. But by limiting his diagnosis to the bloody and destructive character of the partition he was telling only the last part of a much longer story. The traumatic days of partition undoubtedly left behind deep scars on both sides, but an explanation of Indo-Pakistani hostility limited only to that short period in the life of an ancient land at once begs a broader and more fundamental question. What deep-seated compulsion caused Hindus and Muslims to split a subcontinent, which geographically forms a single unit, when, at the termination of British rule, they clearly had the option of realizing the fascinating dream of a united, prosperous, and powerful India, after a lean and humiliating period of foreign rule?

Once one has grasped the nature and depth of the differences between South Asia's two major communities, it is easier to understand why India and Pakistan follow different foreign policies and are perpetually feuding with each other.

Though the leaders of the Indian National Congress, who stood for a united India, spoke lightly of Hindu-Muslim differences and ascribed them solely to the British policy of 'divide and rule', Jinnah believed Pakistan had 'started the moment the first non-Muslim was converted to Islam ... [because] as soon as a Hindu embraced Islam he was outcast not only religiously but also socially, culturally and economically ... throughout the ages Hindus ... and Muslims ... had not merged their entities—that was the basis for Pakistan.'[1]

A good seven centuries before Clive laid the foundation of Britain's Indian empire by winning the battle of Plassey, Alberuni, the noted Central Asian scholar, who studied Hindu religion and civilization in India for several years, had found that the Hindus entirely differed from the Muslims 'in every respect ... we believe in nothing in which they believe, and *vice versa* ... their fanaticism is directed against ... all foreigners. They call them *mlecca*, i.e., impure, and forbid having any connection with them, be it by intermarriage or any other kind of relationship, or by sitting, eating, and drinking with them, because thereby, they think, they would be polluted.'[2] R. C. Majumdar, the well-known Hindu historian, affirms that Alberuni's words 'were almost equally true in A.D. 1800'.[3]

[1] Jamil-ud-Din Ahmad (ed.), *Recent Speeches and Writings of Mr. Jinnah*, I, p. 64.
[2] *Alberuni's India*, pp. 19, 22.
[3] R. C. Majumdar, *History of the Freedom Movement in India*, I, p. 52.

Indeed, it is difficult to think of any two religions more anti-thetical to each other than Islam and Hinduism. Islam is the youngest of the universal religions. Its basic doctrine is brief and explicit: belief in one all-powerful God, in Muhammad as his messenger, and in the Quran as the message. Hinduism, on the other hand, is an ancient religion and has no central dogma .or agreed scripture: 'Hinduism, as a faith, is vague, amorphous, many-sided, all things to all men. It is hardly possible to define it, or indeed to say definitely whether it is a religion or not, in the usual sense of the word.'[1]

Mahatma Gandhi defined the Hindu creed simply as 'search after truth through non-violent means'.[2] Many Hindus, however, do not consider non-violence an essential part of Hinduism. 'We thus have truth left by itself as the distinguishing mark of Hinduism. That, of course, is no definition at all.'[3] While belief in one supreme God is the central theme in Islam, the Hindu pantheon comprises some 330 million gods and Radhakrishnan explains that all the gods stand for some aspect of the Supreme.[4] Hinduism is also heavily caste-ridden. For a person to belong to a caste in the Hindu society he must be born in it. 'A convert is not born in a caste,' said Ambedkar, the well-known leader of 'untouchables', 'therefore, he belongs to no caste.'[5]

Islam, too, sets up a strong barrier of its own. It divides all humanity into two watertight compartments, Muslims and non-Muslims. All the Muslims, according to the Quran, belong to one 'brotherhood'.[6] It follows, to use poet-philosopher Muhammad Iqbal's words, that 'there is only one *millat* [community] confronting the Muslim community, that of the non-Muslims taken collectively'.[7] Quaid-i-Azam Muhammad Ali Jinnah pointed out that Islam imposes a duty on its followers not to merge their identity and individuality in any alien society.[8]

As a result of the unbridgeable gulf between Hinduism and Islam, their followers existed together in the same land for hundreds of years like two streams, which continue to run parallel to each

[1] J. Nehru, *Discovery of India*, p. 63.
[2] Quoted by S. Radhakrishnan, *Eastern Religions and Western Thought*, p. 312.
[3] J. Nehru, *Discovery of India*, p. 63.
[4] S. Radhakrishnan, 'Hinduism', *Legacy of India*, p. 268.
[5] B. R. Ambedkar, *Pakistan or the Partition of India*, p. 119.
[6] Quran, 49:10.
[7] Shamloo, *Speeches and Statements of Iqbal*, p. 234.
[8] Jamil-ud-Din Ahmad, *Some Recent Speeches and Writings of Mr. Jinnah*, II, p. 64.

other indefinitely, without ever becoming one body of water. Nehru called them 'closed systems'.[1]

When the British began to consolidate their position in India the Moghul empire was in decay and the country was divided into countless princedoms. So numerous were these units that, even when the British relinquished power in 1947, no less than six hundred autonomous princedoms .still honeycombed the map of India. It is clear, therefore, that had the British not come to India, unsettled conditions and strife would have continued for an indefinite period. But what would have happened in the end?

After all, the eighteenth and nineteenth centuries did witness many far-reaching changes all over the world. Several states in North America joined together to form the United States of America; national states emerged in Germany and Italy, which previously were geographical expressions only; France entered the modern phase, following a revolution; and Japan rapidly shed her medievalism.

The peoples of the Indian subcontinent could have developed in either of the two following directions. Their nationalism could have followed the lines of the main civilizations, resulting perhaps in a Muslim national state in the northern parts and a Hindu national state comprising the central and western areas and the southern peninsula.[2] Or they could have imbibed the philosophy of modern nationalism based on ties of geography, language, history, and composite culture. In the latter case India could have seen the emergence of a Punjabi, a Hindi-speaking (corresponding in area roughly to the province called the 'United Provinces of Agra and

---

[1] J. Nehru, *India and the World*, p. 11.

[2] In the course of a discussion following a lecture entitled 'Reflections on the Transfer of Power' by Alan Campbell-Johnson at the East India Association on 27 March 1952, Lord Birdwood made the interesting observation that the accusation of 'divide and rule' against the British was a complete misapprehension because often the mistake had in fact been to 'unite and rule'. 'Would it not have been better', he continued, 'if some British statesman 100 years ago had said to himself that as in the north-west there was a Muslim majority, should not this great sub-continent be organized into two administrative units? One thought today of the case of the Sudan where there was the Nubian pagan south and the Muslim-Arab north. Once again we committed the old mistake of "unite and rule".'

As a matter of fact at least one British observer of the Indian scene did suggest precisely what Birdwood thought would have been a wise move. Wilfred Scawen Blunt, while in Calcutta in 1883, outlined 'pretty clearly the Pakistan demand.of the future. He said the subcontinent should have two separate Governments, a Muslim one in the north, and a Hindu one in the south.' (For Birdwood's remarks see *Asiatic Review*, July 1952, p. 178, and for Blunt's suggestion see Ian Stephens, *Pakistan*, p. 70.)

Oudh' in British times), a Bengali, a Mahratta, and a Dravidian state.

But the British did come and they influenced Indian politics in two ways. First, by administering the entire country as a single unit, making communications between the different parts easier, and giving the intelligentsia a common language—English—they created and strengthened the idea of a united India. Secondly, they nourished and perpetuated the existing tendency in India for nationalism to follow religion; and, in the end, this traditional conception prevailed over the newer idea of an all-India nation.

As soon as the British Government started India on the road to constitutional advance, there was a demand that Muslims should vote separately from Hindus to elect their own representatives. This happened when Local Boards were being established in pursuance of Lord Ripon's Resolution on Local Self-Government. Speaking on the Central Provinces Local Self-Government Bill in 1883, Sir Syed Ahmad warned against the danger of introducing representative institutions in India modelled on those in England. India, he said, was a heterogeneous continent in which 'in one and the same district the population may consist of various creeds and various nationalities'. It was not like England where 'the distinctions of race no longer exist, [and] . . . the differences of sectarianism in religious matters have been mitigated by tolerance'. The larger community in India would 'totally override the interests of the smaller community'.[1]

Under Muslim pressure, the Indian Councils Act of 1909 gave definite recognition to the claim of the Muslim community that it formed a political entity, distinct from the Hindus. Muslims were given separate constituencies and their representatives were to be elected by purely Muslim voters. This principle of 'communal representation' henceforth became a necessary part of all constitutional enactments and culminated in the recognition of the Muslims as a separate nation.[2]

After the First World War the demand for the transfer of greater power to Indians became increasingly insistent and with it the

---

[1] R. Coupland, *The Indian Problem, Report on the Constitutional Problem in India* Part I, pp. 155–6.

[2] When the demand for Pakistan was growing in 1945, Jawaharlal Nehru said that 'all' the communal troubles in India were due to separate electorates. J. S. Bright (ed.), *Before and After Independence*, p. 78. He was not right in placing the entire blame for communal differences on separate electorates but there was a large element of truth in his remark.

rivalry between the Hindus and the Muslims for the fishes and loaves of political power also sharpened, leading to an intensification of Hindu–Muslim rioting. As the Simon Commission said, it was 'a manifestation of the anxieties and ambitions aroused in both communities by the prospect of India's political future'.[1] After detailing the communal violence of the years 1920–40, Ambedkar labelled it 'twenty years of civil war between the Hindus and the Muslims of India, interrupted by brief intervals of armed peace'.[2]

By far the darkest period of Hindu–Muslim antagonism followed Prime Minister Attlee's announcement in February 1947 that the British would definitely leave India not later than June 1948. The fighting now took on the character and proportions of a war of succession. At issue was the question whether power should be transferred to India as one unit, which was the Congress standpoint, or to two independent countries, which was the Muslim demand.

After trying hard to avoid the division of existing India, the Viceroy, Lord Mountbatten, concluded that the movement for Pakistan was irresistible, and, on 15 August 1947, the two sovereign states of India and Pakistan came into being. The latter comprised the two predominantly Muslim areas of the subcontinent, one in the north-west and the other in the north-east.

The Pakistanis, having got their wish, had a sense of fulfilment and were mentally better conditioned to let bygones be bygones. Practical good sense also demanded that Pakistan should try to turn down the heat. She was the weaker of the two parties, and dependent on Indian mercy for her share of the joint assets. Jinnah, on entering the Government House at Karachi as the Governor-General of independent Pakistan, said, 'I never expected to see Pakistan in my lifetime. We have to be very grateful to God for what we have achieved.'[3]

But the Hindus of India accepted partition only as a temporary necessity. In his broadcast of 3 June Nehru said, 'It may be that in this way we shall reach that united India sooner than otherwise.'[4] Similarly, the All-India Congress Committee, in its resolution agreeing to Pakistan, stated: 'The picture of India we have learnt to cherish will remain in our minds and our hearts. The AICC earnestly trusts that when the present passions have subsided,

[1] *Report of the Indian Statutory Commission*, I, p. 29.
[2] B. R. Ambedkar, *Pakistan or the Partition of India*, p. 175.
[3] Hector Bolitho, *Jinnah*, p. 195.
[4] Quoted by H. V. Hodson, *The Great Divide*, p. 315.

India's problems will be viewed in their proper perspective and the false doctrine of two nations in India will be discredited and discarded by all.'[1]

Azad has written that Sardar Patel was 'convinced that the new State of Pakistan was not viable and could not last. He thought the acceptance of Pakistan would teach the Moslem League a bitter lesson. Pakistan would collapse in a short time.'[2]

Subsequently, both Nehru and Krishna Menon conceded that Congress had accepted partition to get rid of the British.[3] Acharya Kripalani, then President of the Congress party, frankly declared, 'Neither the Congress nor the nation has given up its claim of a united India', and Patel confidently prophesied: 'Sooner than later, we shall again be united in common allegiance to our country.'[4]

This deep-seated reluctance on the part of Hindu leaders to accept the separate existence of Pakistan has been a principal factor in hindering reconciliation between India and Pakistan. Almost till his dying day Nehru nursed the wish for India and Pakistan to come 'constitutionally closer ... [because] there is no other way for India and Pakistan'.[5]

The war of succession continued at a mad pace for several months after independence. With its horrible loss of life and property, and the migration of millions of dazed and destitute men, women, and children on both sides, it left lasting scars on the minds of all Pakistanis and Indians. Some half a million persons were mercilessly slaughtered, and no less than fourteen million crossed the international border. Smaller Pakistan, having received 1.7 million more refugees than India, had a much greater problem of rehabilitation. She was, at the same time, faced with the overwhelming task of setting up a new administration from scratch, amidst conditions of utter confusion. An American writer was amazed to find in 1947 that the entire Pakistani Foreign Office had only one typewriter.[6]

The early years after independence, when the wounds of partition were still raw, were specially difficult. Even Gandhi, normally the apostle of non-violence, could not escape the evil spell of those furious days and added to the prevailing tension by some of his

[1] V. P. Menon, *The Transfer of Power in India*, p. 384.
[2] M. A. K. Azad, *India Wins Freedom*, p. 242.
[3] *Jawaharlal's Discovery of America*, p. 144; *Statesman*, 14 Oct. 1947.
[4] Quoted by M. Ayub Khan, *Friends Not Masters*, p. 115.
[5] *Lok Sabha Debates*, 13 April 1964, col. 10717.
[6] Vincent Sheean, *Nehru, The Years of Power*, p. 93.

prayer-meeting pronouncements. On 26 September 1947, for instance, he threatened that, 'If Pakistan persistently refuses to see its proved error, and continues to minimize it, the Indian Government would have to go to war against it.'[1]

Governor-General Jinnah complained: 'It is very unfortunate that vigorous propaganda has been going on ... that Pakistan is ... merely a temporary madness [and] that Pakistan will have to come into the Union as a penitent, repentant, erring son. ... It is now clear beyond doubt that it was well-planned, well-organized, and well-directed and the object of it all ... was to paralyse the new-born Dominion of Pakistan.'[2]

II. Indo-Pakistani Disputes

Premature Closure of Supreme Commander's Headquarters

A circumstance that specially placed Pakistan at a disadvantage in all her disputes with India was that the latter withheld Pakistan's share of military supplies. As Liaquat said, 'an army without equipment is as much use as tin soldiers'. The responsibility for the movement of ammunition, stores, equipment, and installations from one Dominion to the other had been entrusted to Field-Marshal Sir Claude Auchinleck, erstwhile Commander-in-Chief of the British Indian Army, redesignated the Supreme Commander. It was intended that his Command should last till 1 April 1948. However, as personally reported by Auchinleck to Attlee, 'the present India Cabinet are implacably determined to do all in their power to prevent the establishment of the Dominion of Pakistan on a firm basis. ... The Indian leaders persistently tried to obstruct the work of partition of the Armed Forces ... so that the one impartial body remaining in this country shall be removed. ... If we are removed, there is no hope at all of any just division of assets.'[3] When the question of the abolition of the Supreme Command was considered by the Joint Defence Council, Liaquat opposed its closure but the Indian Defence Minister, Baldev Singh, said, 'I pledge myself, on behalf of my Government, to take upon myself the full responsibility of delivering to Pakistan her share of stores.'[4] The headquarters of the Supreme Commander

---

[1] Alan Campbell-Johnson, *Mission With Mountbatten*, p. 206.
[2] *Statesman*, 25 Oct. 1947.
[3] John Connell, *Auchinleck*, p. 921.
[4] ibid., p. 928.

having closed down on 30 November 1947, it was Auchinleck's prediction—that Pakistan would not get her share—which was eventually fulfilled, and not India's pledge to deliver to Pakistan whatever rightfully belonged to her.[1]

Evacuee Property

When millions of people fled in haste across the new international borders in search of a new homeland, they left behind all their urban and agricultural property and carried only such movable belongings as the distressing circumstances permitted. Both India and Pakistan were thus faced with the dual problems of having to rehabilitate the millions of refugees who had poured in and take care of the innumerable houses and millions of acres vacated by evacuees who had streamed out. The obvious solution was to utilize the property which the outgoing evacuees had abandoned to rehabilitate the incoming refugees, and in the end this is what was actually done.

In the opening years of independence, with hordes of distraught and destitute refugees on both sides pressing their respective governments hard, the differences over evacuee property generated much heat and ill-will and were the subject of frequent exchanges and a large number of conferences but, with the gradual settlement of the refugees on both sides, the excitement died down and the matter has not been raised by either side for several years.

The Indus Waters[2]

Of all Indo-Pakistani disputes, that relating to Kashmir is the most substantial; but in immediate terms the most intolerable for Pakistan, and therefore the most explosive, was the question of sharing the waters of the Indus basin. 'No army with bombs and shellfire', wrote David E. Lilienthal, 'could devastate a land as thoroughly as [West] Pakistan could be devastated by the simple expedient of India's permanently shutting off the sources of water that keep the fields and the people of [West] Pakistan alive.'[3]

[1] For details of Pakistan's share, as well as what she actually received, see Major-General F. M. Khan, *The Story of the Pakistan Army*, p. 40.

[2] For details of this dispute see Chaudhri Muhammad Ali, *The Emergence of Pakistan*, Columbia University Press, 1967, ch. 15.

[3] David E. Lilienthal, 'Another "Korea" in the Making?' *Collier's Magazine*, 4 August 1951. This article was the result of Lilienthal's visit to India and Pakistan where *Collier's* had sent him for a first-hand report. Lilienthal had formerly headed the Tennessee Valley Authority and the Atomic Energy Commission.

On 1 April 1948, just one day after the life of the Arbitral Tribunal, set up to decide those questions relating to the division of joint assets which the joint committee of officials could not settle, had come to an end, India cut off the supply of water from the two headworks under her control. A Pakistani delegation had to rush to Delhi and sign an agreement at India's bidding before the flow was resumed.[1]

Luckily for the parties, Eugene Black, President of the International Bank for Reconstruction and Development, offered the good offices of the Bank for the solution of the water problem, which both governments accepted in 1952. Moving at a snail's pace, the negotiations were not finalized till 19 September 1960 when President Ayub Khan and Prime Minister Nehru signed the Indus Waters Treaty and the Indus Basin Development Fund Agreement at Karachi.

The treaty allowed for a transitional period of ten to thirteen years, after which the three eastern rivers would fall exclusively to India's share and the three western rivers to Pakistan's, except for certain limited uses in upstream areas in Kashmir. During the transitional period, Pakistan would construct a system of replacement works consisting of two dams, five barrages, and seven link canals. As the cost of financing these extensive works was far beyond the capacity of India and Pakistan, the Bank set up an Indus Development Fund totalling more than a billion[2] dollars to which India was to contribute about $174 million. Other contributors to the fund were several friendly countries anxious to promote peace and prosperity in the subcontinent. With a pledge of $177 million, the United States, as usual in such cases, was the largest single contributor to the Fund. On 6 April 1964 a Supplemental Agreement provided an additional $315 million to complete the programme which was to be the largest of its kind ever undertaken anywhere in the world.

To ensure implementation of its terms, the Treaty set up an Indo-Pakistani Permanent Indus Commission composed of one nominee from each country. Provision was, wisely, made for

---

[1] Sir Patrick Spens, former Chief Justice of India, who had presided over the Arbitral Tribunal, affirmed at a meeting in London afterwards that the Attorneys-General of both India and Pakistan had assured the Tribunal that 'there would be no interference whatsoever with the then existing flow of water' and added that he was 'very much upset' that within a day or two of the closure of the Tribunal 'there was a grave interference with flow of water'. *Asian Review*, April 1955, p. 152.

[2] Billion is used in the US sense of 'a thousand million'.

differences to be resolved by reference to a 'neutral expert' or a Court of Arbitration.[1]

Cash Balances

At the time of partition, the cash balances of undivided India stood at about 4,000 million rupees. At first the question was among those referred to the Arbitral Tribunal for a ruling. At the beginning of December 1947, however, India and Pakistan mutually came to an agreement that Pakistan would get Rs.750 crores as her share. The case was, thereupon, withdrawn from the Arbitral Tribunal. Rs.200 crores had been paid to Pakistan as an interim instalment; Rs.550 crores, therefore, remained outstanding. Soon afterwards, however, Sardar Patel threatened that the implementation of the agreement would depend upon the settlement of the Kashmir issue.[2] In a rejoinder the Pakistani Finance Minister pointed out that 'at no stage of the discussions, which led to the signing of the agreement, was the question of Kashmir ever mentioned'.[3]

In the meantime Gandhi had been becoming increasingly concerned with the continuing communal bitterness and Indo-Pakistani tension. Finding no better way to influence the situation, he announced at his prayer meeting on 12 January 1948 that he would start an indefinite fast on the following day. When Sardar Patel sent word that he would do anything Gandhi might wish, the latter insisted that the first priority be given to the question of Pakistan's share of cash balances.[4] A harassed Indian cabinet, meeting at Gandhi's bedside, hurriedly decided to comply with the Mahatma's demand. On 17 January the Reserve Bank of India was authorized to pay Pakistan Rs.500 million, retaining the balance of Rs.50 million to adjust some claims against Pakistan. Indian elements which were already angry with Gandhi for his alleged softness towards the Muslims became even more infuriated with him. 'The fast created much discontent,' comments Patel's biographer, 'and ultimately led to tragic results ... the Hindu Mahasabha and its offshoot, the RSSS [Rashtriya Swayam Sewak Sangh], were sore that Gandhiji should use the bludgeon of the fast to finance Pakistan for the destruction of Indian soldiers and to secure unconditional protection to even rowdy Muslim elements.'[5] Before the month was

[1] For text of Treaty see A. A. Michel, *The Indus Rivers*, p. 559.
[2] J. B. Das Gupta, *Indo-Pakistan Relations (1947-1955)*, p. 46.
[3] ibid.
[4] D. G. Tendulkar, *Mahatma*, VIII, pp. 246-7.
[5] K. L. Panjabi, *The Indomitable Sardar*, p. 174.

out, a member of the RSSS shot Gandhi dead when the latter was walking to his daily prayer meeting.

Devaluation of the Indian Rupee

Indo-Pakistani trade was virtually halted when, following the devaluation of the British pound sterling vis-à-vis the American dollar by 30.5 per cent in September 1949, India similarly devalued her rupee and Pakistan did not. The Reserve Bank of India announced that it would not quote any rate for the purchase of Pakistani rupees.

To India, the political and economic implications of the Pakistani decision were both equally painful. Indians were shocked that a country which they had expected to collapse under the weight of her own problems had dared to be the only one in the sterling area to defy the pressure for devaluation and, to add insult to the injury, they faced the prospect of having to pay a 30 per cent higher price for Pakistani jute, upon which the jute industry in Calcutta was then so dependent, and for Pakistani cotton and foodgrains.

Alleging that Pakistan had failed even to deliver the jute paid for by Indian merchants before devaluation,[1] India, in the last week of December, shut off the urgently needed supply of coal to Pakistan. By the end of 1949 trade between India and Pakistan had thus reached an almost complete standstill. The deadlock was ultimately broken when negotiations were opened, at India's request, and a new Indo–Pakistani trade agreement was signed on 25 February 1951, on the basis of the acceptance of the Pakistani rate of exchange by India.

Though in the end the par value of the Pakistani rupee had prevailed, the outcome had been far from certain. The strongest single factor which rescued Pakistan from possible disaster was one which no one could have foreseen at the time when the currency crisis erupted. In the summer of 1950 the Korean War suddenly broke out and gave an unexpected boost to the price of raw materials which Pakistan produced, and saved the situation. 'By now it is fairly obvious', commented the *Economist*, 'that a good fairy must have attended the birth of Pakistan.'[2]

The battle of the rupee had three repercussions. In the first

[1] The Pakistani version is that these contracts were between private parties and payments were to be made in Pakistani rupees. Because of the refusal of the Reserve Bank of India to allow any transactions in Pakistani rupees, deliveries of jute had to be suspended. G. W. Choudhury, *Pakistan's Relations with India*, p. 148.

[2] *Economist*, 27 Jan. 1951.

place, the pattern of trade between India and Pakistan was permanently affected. Both countries took vigorous steps to reduce their dependence on each other, Pakistan by taking urgent measures to develop the port of Chittagong as an alternative to Calcutta and by spurring on her efforts to set up jute and cotton mills of her own, and India by taking steps to become self-sufficient in the supply of raw cotton and jute. 'Between 1950 and 1954, an index covering the output of seventeen major industries in Pakistan showed an increase of nearly 200 per cent.'[1] Secondly, the devaluation issue contributed to the communal flare-up in West Bengal and East Pakistan which nearly resulted in full-scale war between India and Pakistan in the early part of 1950. The cessation of trade naturally caused hardship on both sides—in India most of the jute mills had to close down and in East Pakistan cultivators suffered hardship when the traditional outlet for the sale of their raw jute was suddenly closed—and economic distress soon expressed itself in the form of increased communal passion. Thirdly, there was a sudden spurt in Pakistan's trade with China, and this was not without significance for their future political relations. In 1949–50 Pakistan had sold 47,000 bales of cotton to China; in 1950–1 the figure rose to 109,000 bales. China also supplied coal to Pakistan which was badly needed for running the railways and industry and had been denied by India. In 1948–9 imports from China, if any, had been insignificant; in 1949–50 they were valued at Rs.8.4 crores.

[1] *Economist,* 2 Dec. 1961.

2 The Kashmir Dispute

I. The Constitutional Position of the Princely States at the Time of Transfer of Power

Besides the issue whether 'British India' was to become one independent unit or two after the British Government had relinquished power, there was the question of the future of the princely states, numbering about 600,[1] spread over 712,508 square miles, and containing an aggregate of 93.2 million souls.

These units varied in size from 84,471 square miles (Kashmir) to 0.29 square miles (Vejononess). They were internally autonomous but the British Government, as the paramount power, was responsible for defence and foreign affairs, and could also intervene in internal affairs in cases of gross misgovernment.

The constitutional position of the states, upon the transfer of power to Indian hands, was first enunciated by the Cabinet Mission in paragraph 14 of their Statement dated 16 May 1946: 'Paramountcy can neither be retained by the British Crown nor transferred to the new Government.' Section 7 of the Indian Independence Act of 1947 declared that 'the suzerainty of His Majesty over the Indian States lapses'. The legal position, therefore, was that the states became completely independent, and were under no obligation to join India or Pakistan. However, what the British Government had given with one hand they took away with the other. In the House of Lords, Lord Listowel, Secretary of State for India, plainly announced: 'We do not, of course, propose to recognize any states as separate international lentities.' This was equivalent to telling the princes: 'As the British Government will not recognize your independence, no one else will. You have no choice but to opt for either India or Pakistan.' As to the criteria for deciding which

[1] The exact number of the Indian states varies from source to source. I have here taken the round figure of 600 from the *Report of the Indian Statutory Commission*, II, p. 193, where the number is given as 'nearly 600'.

of the two new Dominions a state should join, Lord Mountbatten said, 'Normally geographical situation and communal interests and so forth will be the factors to be considered.'[1]

By 15 August 1947 every one of the 600 princely states, with three exceptions, had acceded to either India or Pakistan, on the same basis as the principle underlying the partition of British India, namely non-Muslim majority states joined India and Muslim majority states chose Pakistan. The three which stood out were Junagadh, Hyderabad, and Kashmir. In addition to these three, another state, Jodhpur, is also relevant to our discussion.

II. Junagadh, Hyderabad, and Jodhpur

Junagadh's ruler was a Muslim but his subjects were 80 per cent Hindu. On 15 August 1947 the Government of Junagadh announced that the state had acceded to Pakistan and, exactly a month later, Pakistan accepted the accession. But Mountbatten, now Governor-General of India only, telegraphed to Governor-General Jinnah that Pakistan's acceptance of Junagadh's accession was 'in utter violation of principles on which partition of India was agreed upon and effected'.[2] On 17 September the Indian Cabinet decided to deploy troops around Junagadh 'with a view to insuring the security of the country and to maintaining law and order in Kathiawar'.[3] After the administration of the state had been taken over by India, a plebiscite was conducted and it was announced that the majority of the population had voted for India. Pakistan's complaint against India, claiming Junagadh as Pakistani territory, is still pending before the Security Council.

With a population of 16 million and an annual revenue of Rs.26 crores, Hyderabad was by far the most viable state in India. Its population was 85 per cent Hindu but the ruler (Nizam) was a Muslim. The ruler desired to assume the same status as India and Pakistan, i.e. Dominion status, or to join Pakistan, but he was dissuaded by Mountbatten from adopting either of these courses.[4] Sardar Patel, the Indian Minister for States, 'saw no alternative but to insist on the Nizam's accession to India'.[5] V. P. Menon, Secretary of the Indian Ministry of States, warned that 'if Hyderabad stood out of the Indian Dominion the Hindus of the State would

[1] Earl Mountbatten of Burma, *Time Only to Look Forward*, p. 42.
[2] *Security Council, Official Records, 250th Meeting*, 18 Feb. 1948.
[3] V. P. Menon, *The Story of the Integration of the Indian States*, p. 125.
[4] ibid., pp. 303, 304.
[5] ibid., p. 306

have a justifiable grievance'.[1] On 24 August Hyderabad appealed to the Security Council against Indian threats but on 13 September, before the Council could hear the case, the Indian army invaded Hyderabad and subdued all opposition. An Indian official pleaded that 'there was a real danger that communal disorders, spreading over Hyderabad, might break out all over India'.[2]

Yet another prince, the Mahàraja of Jodhpur, expressed a wish to join Pakistan but Mountbatten warned him that, his subjects being predominantly Hindu, his accession to Pakistan 'would surely be in conflict with the principle underlying the partition of India on the basis of Muslim and non-Muslim majority areas'.[3] Accordingly, Jodhpur, too, acceded to India.

Thus: (a) 599 states out of 600 acceded to India or Pakistan, in accordance with the religion professed by the majority of the population in each case; and (b) in all three cases in which the rulers had indicated their wish to go against the principle of partition, India compelled them to abandon the idea on the ground that their action would violate the principle on which the division of the subcontinent had been effected. Furthermore, the Muslim League had desired to include the whole of the predominantly Muslim provinces of Bengal and the Punjab in Pakistan but, at Congress insistence, they were divided so that the Hindu parts could join India.

The trouble over Kashmir arose from the fact that India laid claim to every single Hindu majority area on the ground that partition of the subcontinent was effected on communal lines but, at the same time, she denied Muslim Kashmir to Pakistan.

III. Recent History of Kashmir

At the time of partition the State of Jammu and Kashmir, popularly called simply Kashmir, had an overall Muslim majority of 78 per cent. In its most desirable part, the Vale of Kashmir, the Muslims numbered 93 per cent. Other factors, too, linked Kashmir closely with West Pakistan. N. C. Chatterjee, a Hindu member of the Indian Parliament, pointed out that

The geographical situation of the State was such that it would be bounded on all sides by the new Dominion of Pakistan. Its only access to the outside world by road lay through the Jhelum Valley road which ran through Pakistan, via Rawalpindi. The only rail line connecting the

---

[1] ibid., p. 316.
[2] 'India as a World Power', by an Indian Official, *Foreign Affairs*, July 1949.
[3] V. P. Menon, *The Story of the Integration of the Indian States*, pp. 112-13.

State with the outside world lay through Sialkot in Pakistan. Its postal and telegraphic services operated through areas that were certain to belong to the Dominion of Pakistan.

The State was dependent for all its imported supplies like salt, sugar, petrol and other necessities of life on their safe and continued transit through areas that would form part of Pakistan.

The tourist transit traffic which was a major source of income and revenue could only come via Rawalpindi. The only route available for the export of its valuable fruit was the Jhelum Valley route. Its timber could mainly be drifted down only in the Jhelum River which ran into Pakistan.[1]

However, by a comparatively recent accident of history, the ruler of Kashmir at the time of partition happened to be a Hindu. From the fourteenth century onwards Kashmir had been ruled by Muslims but in 1819 Ranjit Singh, the Sikh ruler of the Punjab, conquered it from the Afghans. Gulab Singh, a Dogra Rajput, who was a scion of the ruling family of Jammu, had won Ranjit Singh's favour by entering his service. Ranjit Singh rewarded Gulab Singh by acknowledging the latter as Raja of Jammu. Gulab Singh extended his dominions till they comprised all the areas which collectively came to be known as the State of Jammu and Kashmir. He acquired all the parts by conquest except the Vale of Kashmir, which he purchased from the British in the following circumstances. After the death of Ranjit Singh in 1839 his kindgom had fallen into a state of chaos, leading to its conquest by the British in 1846. Gulab Singh, having assisted the British, was allowed by the latter to take the Vale in return for a payment of Rs.75 lakhs in cash plus a nominal tribute to signify British paramountcy.

During the century that followed, the Hindu Dogras ruled their hapless Muslim subjects with the greatest cruelty and callousness. Until 1934, for example, the slaughter of a useless cow was a capital offence.[2]

But not even the placid politics of Kashmir could for ever remain unaffected by the agitation launched in India by Gandhi from 1920 onwards. Spearheaded by Sheikh Abdullah, a young man recently returned from Aligarh Muslim University, the movement in Kashmir at first took the form of demands by Muslims for a better life in their own country. By 1931 the agitation had become serious enough for Maharaja Hari Singh to order Abdullah's arrest and

---

[1] Quoted by Sheikh Mohammad Abdullah in 'Kashmir, India and Pakistan', *Foreign Affairs*, April 1965.
[2] Lord Birdwood, *Two Nations and Kashmir*, p. 31.

declare martial law. Upon his release in the following year, Abdullah resumed his political activity and founded a political party called the All-Jammu and Kashmir Muslim Conference.

Broadly, politics inside Kashmir in the ensuing years followed the same course as politics next door in the North-West Frontier Province. Just as, in their efforts to win autonomy from the British, the Khan brothers had turned for help to the Indian National Congress as the only effective political party in India at the time, Abdullah, too, turned to Congress for assistance in his fight for liberation from the oppressive rule of the Maharaja. In 1939 he converted the Muslim Conference into the National Conference, opening its doors to both Muslims and non-Muslims. A year later, the Muslim League having passed the Pakistan Resolution, one of Abdullah's right-hand men, Ghulam Abbas, separated from his chief and revived the Muslim Conference (1941). Kashmir politics thus assumed virtually the same shape as Indian politics. The National Conference was already an appendage of the Congress Party of India; the Muslim Conference now became that of the Muslim League. During this period Abdullah also formed a close personal friendship with Jawaharlal Nehru.

As the movement for Pakistan gathered momentum, Abdullah's popularity correspondingly diminished among his Muslim compatriots, just as that of the Khan brothers had slipped in the adjoining territory. 'As Muslims in British India became more and more pronounced in their support for an independent Pakistan,' writes Korbel, 'the Muslims in Jammu and Kashmir began to return to the Muslim Conference led by Ghulam Abbas, abandoning the ranks of the National Conference of Sheikh Abdullah.'[1]

Though Abdullah and Abbas were pursuing different ends, the Maharaja, as the sole repository of power, was their common target. In his eyes, therefore, they were both equally reprehensible. On 20 May 1946 Abdullah was arrested and sentenced to nine years' imprisonment for treason. In September Abbas also was apprehended for launching a 'direct action' campaign against the ruler. Thus when the Congress and League leaders accepted the partition plan in India on 3 June 1947, both the topmost Kashmiri leaders were prisoners of the Maharaja.

It remains to mention one more important fact: that Prime Minister Jawaharlal Nehru, who exercised untrammelled control over India's external affairs till his death, happened to be of Kashmiri

[1] Josef Korbel, *Danger in Kashmir*, p. 22.

descent and was deeply attached to his ancestral home. 'Everyone who was of Kashmir', he wrote about a visit there in 1940,
'reminded me that I, too, was a son of this noble land and owed a
duty to it . . . it pleased me to be welcomed everywhere as a brother
and a comrade who, in spite of long absence, was still of Kashmir.'[1]
The visit was over 'but Kashmir calls back. . . . How can they who
have fallen under its spell release themselves from its enchantment?'[2]
On another occasion he said, ominously anticipating his role in the
Kashmir dispute with Pakistan, 'My partiality for it [Kashmir]
occasionally leads me astray.'[3] A year after independence, when the
dispute over Kashmir had resulted in an undeclared war between
Pakistan and India, he confessed before the Constituent Assembly:
'I was intensely interested [in Kashmir] . . . for emotional personal
reasons.'[4]

IV. Origins of the Kashmir Dispute

Indian spokesmen single out two events as the 'basic facts' in the
Kashmir dispute and wish the rest of the world to infer from them
that Pakistan has been the 'aggressor' in Kashmir. The first is the
tribal invasion of Kashmir, which began on 22 October 1947, and
the second is the intervention of the Pakistani army inside Kashmir
in the first week of May 1948. They completely ignore India's
provocations that led to these developments and also that, first, the
United Nations have never pronounced Pakistan an aggressor and,
second, that these occurrences notwithstanding, India agreed in the
United Nations that the people of Kashmir should decide their own
future by a plebiscite, thus making the holding of a plebiscite the
central issue in the dispute. A brief outline of the early history of the
Kashmir problem will make the position clear.

A direct approach by India for getting Kashmir was clearly
impossible because, at that very time, she was insisting upon the
accession to herself of Junagadh, Hyderabad, and Jodhpur, on the
ground that they had a Hindu majority—by which criterion Muslim
Kashmir obviously belonged to Pakistan. India, therefore, did not
demand Kashmir's accession openly through the Ministry of States
but employed political pressure behind the scenes to create a
situation in which the appearance would be that the majority of the
people of Kashmir wished to join India of their own volition.

[1] J. Nehru, *Unity of India*, pp. 221, 222.
[2] ibid., p. 240.
[3] J. Nehru, *Discovery of India*, p. 571.
[4] J. Nehru, *Speeches*, I, p. 195.

In May 1947, several months before the first tribesman was seen inside Kashmir, Acharya Kripalani, President of the Indian Congress Party, visited Kashmir but 'failed to persuade the Maharaja to join the Constituent Assembly [of India]'.[1] In commenting on Kripalani's visit, a leading Congress newspaper revealed Congress strategy: 'If the Maharaja evolves a new democratic constitution and holds fresh elections under it, enabling Sheikh Abdullah's party to have its legitimate share in the administration, the co-operation of Kashmir with the Constituent Assembly and its marriage with the Indian Union will be facilitated.'[2]

Kripalani was followed into Kashmir by the Maharajas of Patiala, Kapurthala, and Faridkot, and the rulers of the Punjab Hill States, all of whom were intent upon discharging the 'noble mission'—to use the *Tribune's* phrase—of persuading the Maharaja of Kashmir to follow their own example and join India.

In June 1947 Mountbatten went to Kashmir and advised the Maharaja to join either India or Pakistan, after ascertaining the wishes of his subjects. Nehru had asked Mountbatten to obtain Abdullah's release from prison. As Mountbatten had not been able to do anything in the matter, Nehru expressed the wish to go to Kashmir personally. Mountbatten thought Nehru should not leave his post as the head of the Interim Government at that critical juncture and it was agreed that Gandhi should go instead.[3]

Gandhi made a two-day visit to Kashmir in early August and saw Prime Minister Kak, the Maharaja, and National Conference workers.[4] On returning to Delhi he sent a report to Nehru in which he stated that Bakshi Ghulam Muhammad was 'most sanguine' that the people of Kashmir would vote for India, 'provided, of course, that Sheikh Abdullah and his co-prisoners were released, all bans were removed and the present Prime Minister was not in power'.[5]

Prem Nath Bazaz, the well-known Kashmiri Hindu writer, sums up the 'real nature' of Gandhi's visit in these words: 'The Congress leaders were ready to help the Maharaja but on two conditions.

---

[1] Sisir Gupta, *Kashmir*, p. 95.

[2] *Tribune*, 29 May 1947.

[3] This part of the story has been related to me by a person who had direct knowledge of the facts. See also Pyarelal, *Mahatma Gandhi, The Last Phase*, II, p. 353 and H. V. Hodson, *The Great Divide*, p. 442.

[4] Pyarelal, *Mahatma Gandhi, The Last Phase*, II, p. 355.

[5] ibid., p. 357. Bakshi, at that time, was Abdullah's close associate in the National Conference.

First, Ram Chandra Kak, who was for his own reasons in favour of the State remaining independent, was to be replaced by a new Prime Minister acceptable to the Congress leaders and secondly, the State was to accede to the Indian Union.'[1]

Within a week of Gandhi's visit to the state, Kak was replaced as Prime Minister by Janak Singh, a Dogra, and on 29 September Abdullah was released and conferred with the Congress leaders at Delhi.

Five years later Nehru revealed the advice given to Abdullah and his colleagues: 'This matter [accession to India] must not be hurried and it was our idea that a Constituent Assembly should be elected in Kashmir quickly and as soon as possible decide these and other questions.'[2]

The scenario was now complete: a Constituent Assembly in Kashmir should be set up and it should be left to Abdullah to pack it with his own followers who would rubber-stamp a verdict in favour of joining India.

However, the tribal invasion precipitated matters and it was then conveniently asserted that Abdullah and his National Conference represented the majority in Kashmir and their option for India was a sufficient declaration of the popular will. A plebiscite was promised to pacify the outside world but the plan of using the Constituent Assembly to ratify accession to India was not abandoned. In subsequent years the undertaking to hold a plebiscite was gradually buried and the device of accepting accession by a vote of the Assembly was again brought to the fore.

In the middle of October 1947 the pro-Indian forces inside Kashmir were further augmented by the appointment as Prime Minister of Kashmir of Mehr Chand Mahajan, a judge of the Punjab High Court, who, in Sardar Patel's words, 'was released for Kashmir for strategic and tactical reasons'.[3] Mahajan, who subsequently became India's Chief Justice, has revealed that, upon his appointment to the Kashmir post, he was assured by the Indian authorities that he would be given 'military aid whenever I wanted it'.[4]

In the meantime the members of the Muslim Conference had been pressing the Maharaja to join Pakistan and, on 19 July, passed a

---

[1] Prem Nath Bazaz, *The History of Struggle for Freedom in Kashmir*, p. 318.
[2] *Lok Sabha Debates*, 26 June 1952, col. 2587.
[3] M. C. Mahajan, *Looking Back*, p. 188.
[4] ibid., p. 150.

2

resolution to that effect. Trouble started towards the end of July when the Maharaja ordered his Muslim subjects to surrender their arms to the police. The Muslims responded by organizing themselves as guerrillas in the hills of Poonch, an area abounding with demobilized ex-servicemen who had fought in the Second World War in the ranks of the British Indian Army. While the tough warriors of Poonch held their own against the Maharaja's forces, the Muslims in Jammu province, where Hindus formed a considerable portion of the population and where Sikhs and other militants from India had infiltrated, were slaughtered by the thousand. Almost the entire Muslim population of 500,000 was eliminated: some 200,000 were killed and the rest fled to West Pakistan.[1]

At a press conference on 15 October Mahajan alleged that raids from West Pakistan into Kashmir were being organized and that Pakistan was preventing essential supplies such as petrol, cloth, and food from reaching the state. However, the state administration backed down from their own proposal for an impartial inquiry when it was accepted by Pakistan.[2]

The Tribal Invasion
By this time the tribesmen of the frontier, whose feelings had long been inflamed by the atrocities in East Punjab and the massacre of fellow Muslims next door to them in Kashmir, lost their patience. On 22 October a large band of tribesmen crossed the border into Kashmir to wage a holy war (*jihad*) against the Dogra forces.

'There are sound reasons to believe', observes Bazaz, 'that if the Congress leaders had not made repeated and vigorous attempts to influence the Maharaja to function in a partisan spirit and take the fatal step of making preparations for joining India there would have been no incursion of tribesmen into Kashmir.'[3]

Advancing rapidly, the forward units of the tribesmen captured the power house near Srinagar on 24 October. They could have taken the capital and its airport had their main body not lingered behind for pillage. On 27 October a battalion of Sikhs was flown to Srinagar from India and saved that city. To explain how this happened we must pick up another thread of the story.

[1] Ian Stephens, *Pakistan*, p. 200.
[2] K. Sarwar Hasan (ed.), *Documents on the Foreign Relations of Pakistan, The Kashmir Question*, p. 68.
[3] P. N. Bazaz, *The History of Struggle for Freedom in Kashmir*, p. 338.

The Maharaja Accedes to India

On 24 October, when Srinagar was threatened, the Maharaja appealed to India for help. In response the Government of India sent V. P. Menon to Srinagar to study the situation at first-hand. Menon found the Maharaja totally unnerved with practically no state forces left.[1] At night the Maharaja collected his family and valuables and fled to Jammu. On the following morning (26 October) Menon flew back to Delhi. The Government of India, acting on Mountbatten's advice, decided that Indian troops could be sent to Kashmir only if the Maharaja first acceded to India and, further, that, since Kashmir had a Muslim majority, accession should be conditional on the will of the people being ascertained by a plebiscite after the raiders had been expelled.[2]

Menon then flew to Jammu and brought back a letter for the Governor-General from the Maharaja as well as the Instrument of Accession, in standard form, bearing the ruler's signature. The Maharaja's letter[3] (26 October) had two notable features. It did not accuse the Government of Pakistan of giving direct assistance to the tribesmen, as India was to allege later, but simply mentioned that the infiltration of the tribesmen into Kashmir could not have taken place without the 'knowledge' of the Pakistani authorities. Secondly, it granted India's standing wish that Abdullah should be installed in a place of power in the state government. 'It is my intention', the letter ran, 'at once to set up an interim government and to ask Sheikh Abdullah to carry the responsibilities in this emergency with the Prime Minister.' Mountbatten's reply (27 October) stated that India had decided to accept accession 'in the special circumstances' described by the Maharaja and that

In consistence with their policy that in the case of any State where the issue of accession has been the subject of dispute, the question of accession should be decided in accordance with the wishes of the people of the State, it is my Government's wish that, as soon as law and order have been restored in Kashmir and its soil cleared of the invader, the question of the State's accession should be settled by a reference to the people.[4]

Though India made much of Pakistan's alleged complicity in the tribal invasion, the truth seems to be that the Government of Pakistan at that time was tottering under the weight of millions of

[1] V. P. Menon, *The Story of the Integration of the Indian States*, p. 380.
[2] ibid., p. 381.
[3] J. Korbel, *Danger in Kashmir*, p. 82.
[4] ibid., p. 83.

refugees and other partition problems and was in no position to organize intervention in the conflict. Sir William Barton assessed the situation in these terms:

> If an attempt had been made to drive them [the tribesmen] back, the whole border from Chitral south to Quetta would have burst into flame, and at that time Pakistan forces were still disorganized and largely un-equipped, thanks to India's refusal to hand over Pakistan's share of the military supplies left by the British. They could not have held down a tribal rising and might have been driven across the Indus. This would have given the Afghans an opportunity of taking territory as far as the Indus, which they look on as Afghanistan irredenta. In such an event Pakistan would either have been absorbed in India, or have become a satellite of that country.[1]

At popular level, of course, there was much sympathy and support in Pakistan for the Kashmiris, and many West Pakistanis crossed the border as volunteers to help fellow Muslims in distress. Furthermore, many Poonchis, from among those serving in the ranks of the Pakistani regiments, left their posts to fight beside their kinsmen.

In another development the National Conference, which had already passed a resolution on 19 July 1947 that Kashmir should accede to Pakistan, on 24 October set up its own government in areas already liberated from the Maharaja, and assumed the name 'Azad [Free] Kashmir'.

Indo-Pakistani Negotiations
Mountbatten was in favour of a meeting between the Indian and Pakistani leaders at Lahore on 1 November to resolve the problem amicably but Nehru 'fell suddenly ill'[2] and Mountbatten had to go alone. Jinnah proposed that the two Governors-General should jointly conduct a plebiscite in Kashmir while Mountbatten said a plebiscite should be held by the United Nations, and the meeting ended inconclusively. Campbell-Johnson has explained that 'Jinnah's objection, which he made quite clear at the Lahore meeting, is not to the idea of a plebiscite as such, but to the presence of Indian troops in Kashmir while it is being held, which he claims likely to prejudice any chance of its being impartial.'[3]

---

[1] Sir William Barton, 'Pakistan's Claim to Kashmir', *Foreign Affairs*, Jan. 1950.
[2] J. Connell, *Auchinleck*, p. 931.
[3] A. Campbell-Johnson, *Mission With Mountbatten*, p. 233.

The respective positions taken up by Prime Ministers Nehru and Liaquat in the ensuing months have some interesting features.

In striking contrast with India's later assertion, that Kashmir was strictly a domestic matter for India, Nehru's telegram to Liaquat dated 30 October made this bold promise: 'Our assurance that we shall withdraw our troops from Kashmir as soon as peace and order are restored and leave the decision about the future of the State to the people of the State is not merely a pledge to your Government but also to the people of Kashmir and to the world.'[1]

Another telegram from the Indian Prime Minister belied India's future contention that the Maharaja's signature on the Instrument of Accession had concluded the question and Mountbatten's letter of 27 October to the Maharaja was of no consequence: 'Here let me make clear that it has been our policy all along that, where there is a dispute about the accession of a State to either Dominion, the decision must be made by the people of that State. It was in accordance with this policy that we added a proviso to the Instrument of Accession of Kashmir.'[2]

Nehru also clearly held out the promise that the referendum in Kashmir would be 'held under international auspices like the United Nations'.[3] However, when Liaquat proposed that an impartial administration be set up in Kashmir to ensure freedom of voting Nehru barefacedly claimed that 'Sheikh Abdullah's administration . . . is impartial.'[4]

With regard to the Maharaja's accession to India, Liaquat emphatically stated that Pakistan could never accept it because 'accession' was fraudulent inasmuch as it was achieved by deliberately creating certain conditions, with the object of finding an excuse to stage the 'accession'. It was based on violence because it furthered the plan of the Kashmir Government to liquidate the Muslim population of the State. The accession was against the well-known will of an overwhelming majority of the population and could not be justified on any grounds whether moral or constitutional, geographical or economic, cultural or religious.[5]

Pakistan pointed out, further, that the Maharaja had no authority left to execute the Instrument of Accession because his subjects

[1] K. Sarwar Hasan (ed.), *Documents on the Foreign Relations of Pakistan, The Kashmir Question*, p. 67.
[2] ibid., p. 74.
[3] ibid., p. 75.
[4] ibid., p. 93.
[5] ibid., p. 100.

had overthrown his government by a successful revolt and forced him to flee from the capital.[1]

V. The Security Council and the Kashmir Dispute

Under Mountbatten's pressure India ultimately decided to refer the question to the United Nations and, on 1 January 1948, filed a formal complaint against Pakistan in the Security Council.

It is noteworthy that India, who was later to place the utmost emphasis on her allegation that Pakistan was the 'aggressor' in Kashmir and also to deny that the Kashmir issue constituted a 'dispute', filed her petition in the Security Council under Section 35 of Chapter VI which relates to 'Pacific Settlement of Disputes', and not under Chapter VII which deals with acts of aggression. She prayed that Pakistan be called upon immediately to cease assisting the raiders as otherwise India might be 'compelled' to enter Pakistani territory to take action against the invaders. Accession to India was defended because the request had come not only from the Maharaja but also 'from the largest popular organization in Kashmir, the National Conference, headed by Sheikh Muhammad Abdullah . . . on behalf of the people of Kashmir'. It was promised once more that, after the raiders had been expelled, the people of Kashmir 'would be free to decide their future by the recognized democratic method of a plebiscite or referendum . . . under international auspices'.

Pakistan responded by denying that she was assisting the raiders and, in turn, accused India of genocide of Muslims and of forcible possession of Junagadh, which had joined Pakistan. She prayed that the Security Council appoint a commission to assist in the solution of the 'various problems' between India and Pakistan because friendly relations were possible only by the elimination of 'all differences'.

Opening for India on 14 January 1948, Gopalaswami Ayyenger emphasized that the expulsion of the invaders and the stoppage of the fight were the 'only tasks' to which the Council should address itself. He reiterated the Indian promise that: 'The question of the future status of Kashmir vis-à-vis her neighbours and the world at large, and a further question, namely, whether she should withdraw from her accession to India, and either accede to Pakistan or remain independent, with a right to claim admission as a Member of the United Nations—all this we have recognized to be a matter for

[1] *Security Council, Official Records, Fourth Year, Special Supplement No. 7, UNCIP Third Report, S/1430,* 9 Dec. 1949.

unfettered decision by the people of Kashmir, after normal life is restored to them.'

On behalf of Pakistan Zafrulla Khan asked for more time than till the following afternoon to prepare a reply because the issues were not as simple as the representative of India had tried to make out, but Ayyenger vehemently opposed the request because 'the situation does not brook delay'. Some members of the Security Council were later to twit Ayyenger about this when, finding that India was not getting her own way, Ayyenger himself insisted upon a long adjournment.

Zafrulla said Pakistan was woefully short of military supplies and in no condition to help anyone. Nor did the tribesmen, who were well known for their fighting prowess and their capacity to acquire or manufacture guns and rifles, or the Poonchis, 70,000 of whom were ex-servicemen, need any help. He said the situation demanded that 'everyone' who had gone into Kashmir from outside should be made to go out and the Kashmiris should then freely 'express the way in which they want to go'.

While the lengthy debate was in progress the Security Council passed two resolutions. That of 17 January asked the parties not to aggravate the situation but to do everything in their power to improve it. It also requested both governments to inform the Council immediately of any 'material change' in the situation. The resolution of 20 January established a mediatory commission, which eventually came to have five members and was called the United Nations Commission on India and Pakistan (UNCIP).

Matters came to a head on 6 February when the President of the Council for that month, General McNaughton of Canada, tabled a resolution which evidently reflected the views of the majority at the time. It called for a withdrawal of all irregular forces from Kashmir; the establishment of law and order jointly by Indian and Pakistani forces followed by the withdrawal of regular forces; the setting up of an interim administration commanding the confidence of the people of Kashmir; and the holding of a plebiscite, under the 'authority' of the Security Council.[1]

Ayyenger found the suggestions relating to the replacement of Abdullah's administration by a neutral one and the withdrawal of the Indian armed forces unacceptable. He insisted that the plebiscite must be organized and conducted by the existing administration

---

[1] Text in Sarwar Hasan (ed.), *Documents on the Foreign Relations of Pakistan, The Kashmir Question*, p. 162.

in Kashmir with the role of the Council limited to sending observers 'to see how that plebiscite is conducted'. Finding the majority out of tune with him, he asked for an adjournment till a date between 15 and 20 March to enable him to fly to India for instructions Several members reminded Ayyenger of his earlier opposition to the short adjournment requested by Zafrulla, and one of them, the representative of Colombia, turning round Ayyenger's own words, said that if the proceedings were interrupted the Indian delegation would be travelling 'while Jammu and Kashmir burns'.[1] The Indian delegate angrily complained that the 'great country' which he represented had not elicited at the hands of the Security Council the consideration to which she was entitled.[2] The Council had to give way and the hearing was adjourned.

There is no direct evidence concerning the Indian moves during the period between 12 February, when Ayyenger left New York, and 10 March, when the Council took up the Kashmir question again, but the circumstantial evidence shows that the Indian Government was able to enlist the powerful support of its Governor-General, Mountbatten, to have the instructions to the British representative in the Security Council modified to mollify India. As the US and most other members of the Council in the early years had little experience of Indo-Pakistani questions, they held Britain's views in special respect. Britain's change of front, therefore, had far-reaching consequences, and greatly reduced the chances of a Kashmir settlement on a reasonable basis.

An entry in Campbell-Johnson's diary under 17 February reveals how anxious Mountbatten was that the Indian viewpoint should prevail in the Security Council:

Mountbatten is worried because he feels that Attlee [Prime Minister] and Noel-Baker [Secretary of State for Commonwealth Relations who was personally acting as the British representative in the Security Council] do not seem to be showing themselves sufficiently alive to the psychological influences of this dispute and that their attempt to deal out even-handed justice is producing heavy-handed diplomacy. The crux of the problem as seen in London is India's unwillingness to recognize that a plebiscite carried out under the auspices of Abdullah and with the sole support of Indian troops, even with Security Council backing, would not be regarded as fulfilling the condition of its fair conduct. In Mountbatten's opinion the United Kingdom delegate could with advan-

[1] *Security Council Official Records, 243rd Meeting*, 10 Feb. 1948.
[2] ibid., *245th Meeting*, 11 Feb. 1948.

tage take a less unfriendly line towards India by supporting the view that the first step should be for Pakistan to stop helping the raiders. The question of superintending the plebiscite without interfering with the legally constituted Government deserved, he felt, more sympathetic discussion and treatment than it has yet received.[1]

Evidently, Mountbatten began by winning the support of Gordon Walker, Under-Secretary of State for Commonwealth Relations, who happened to visit India in the last week of February. On 23 February Campbell-Johnson recorded in his diary: 'He [Gordon Walker] has, I think, been able to see for himself that Mountbatten is not exaggerating the bad impression caused here by the British attitude at the United Nations.'[2]

Zafrulla says in his unpublished 'Reminiscences' that Noel-Baker personally told him that just when he, Noel-Baker, was feeling hopeful that India might accept the Security Council proposals, the 'disastrous telegram' arrived from Attlee and 'upset the whole business'.[3]

Resolution of 21 April 1948
Instead of the proposed resolution of 6 February which India had found so objectionable, the Security Council, after another debate, passed a watered down resolution permitting India to retain her forces in Kashmir in 'minimum strength required for the support of civil power' and stating that the Secretary-General of the United Nations would appoint a Plebiscite Administrator who would act 'as an officer of the State of Jammu and Kashmir'.[4]

The UNCIP arrived in the subcontinent on 7 July, landing at Karachi on that day.

Intervention of Pakistani Forces in Kashmir
Meanwhile, with the advent of spring and the melting of mountain snows, the Indian Army had mounted an offensive in Kashmir. On 13 April 1948 The Times correspondent cabled from Srinagar that 'the long-awaited spring offensive in Jammu and Kashmir has begun'.[5] A week later General Douglas Gracey, Commander-in-Chief of the Pakistani Army, reported to the Pakistani Government

[1] A. Campbell-Johnson, Mission With Mountbatten, p. 287.
[2] ibid., p. 290.
[3] Reminiscences of Sir Muhammad Zafrulla Khan, pp. 338-9.
[4] K. Sarwar Hasan (ed.), Documents on the Foreign Relations of Pakistan, The Kashmir Question, p. 162.
[5] The Times, 14 April 1948.

the grave consequences for Pakistan if the Indian Army pursued its objective unhindered. On crossing the Ravi and the Chenab the Indian forces would come right up to the Pakistani border, 'thereby sitting on our doorsteps, threatening the Jhelum bridge' controlling the Mangla headworks, and having the irrigation in Jhelum and other districts at their mercy. The occupation of Poonch by the Indians would adversely affect the morale of the Pakistani troops, many of whom were Poonchis. The loss of Muzaffarabad or Kohala would 'enable the Indian Army to secure the rear gateway to Pakistan through which it can march in at any time'. It would also encourage Afghanistan[1] and the subversive elements within Pakistan. Gracey stated that, if disastrous consequences to Pakistan were to be avoided, it was 'imperative that the Indian Army is not allowed to advance beyond the general line Uri-Poonch-Naoshera'.[2]

In the circumstances described by Gracey the Pakistani Government had no option but to order units of the Pakistani Army to move into Kashmir and hold defensive positions. As Zafrulla put it later, 'Anyone responsible for the security of Pakistan who did not at least do that should have [been] impeached and executed.' On 8 July, as soon as Zafrulla met the members of the UNCIP, he informed them that Pakistan had been compelled to deploy her forces inside Kashmir. To the Indian charge that the participation of the Pakistani Army in the Kashmir fighting constituted a 'material change' in the situation which Pakistan was bound immediately to convey to the Security Council under the terms of its resolution of 17 January, Zafrulla replied that the 'material change in the situation' had first been caused by India who mounted a big offensive in Kashmir. 'Did the Government of India, in mounting their offensive, notify the Commission?' he asked.[3]

Resolutions of 13 August 1948 and 5 January 1949
After talking to leaders on both sides and studying the situation, the Commission passed a resolution on 13 August 1948 which had three parts. Part I asked India and Pakistan to order a cease-fire and Part III called upon them to reaffirm that Kashmir's future status would be determined by the Kashmiris themselves.

[1] Afghanistan was at that time agitating for the setting up of an independent state under the title of 'Pakhtunistan' in the north-western frontier areas of Pakistan.
[2] K. Sarwar Hasan (ed.), *Documents on the Foreign Relations of Pakistan, The Kashmir Question*, p. 174.
[3] ibid., p. 136.

Part II proposed that both governments accept these principles as a basis for a truce agreement: (1) As the presence of Pakistani troops in Kashmir constituted a material change in the situation, Pakistan should withdraw her troops. (2) The tribesmen and Pakistani nationals not normally resident in the state should also withdraw. (3) Pending a final settlement, the territory vacated by the Pakistani troops would be administered by the local authorities under the surveillance of the Commission. (4) When the Commission notified the Government of India that the tribesmen and the Pakistani nationals had withdrawn and the Pakistani forces were being withdrawn, the Government of India would begin to withdraw the bulk of her forces. (5) Pending the acceptance of the conditions for a final settlement, the Indian Government would maintain, within the lines existing at the moment of the cease-fire, minimum forces necessary to assist the local authorities in the observance of law and order.[1]

India accepted the resolution but Pakistan objected that it did not contain detailed guarantees for a free plebiscite.[2]

After another round of negotiations the Commission was able to get the two governments to agree to a cease-fire from 1 January 1949, and also to certain proposals which were embodied in the Commission's resolution of 5 January. By spelling out the arrangements for a plebiscite, this resolution was meant to supplement that of 13 August 1948 which Pakistan had deemed inadequate. A plebiscite would be held after the Commission had found that the cease-fire and truce agreement set forth in the resolution of 13 August had been carried out. The Secretary-General of the United Nations would, in agreement with the Commission, nominate a Plebiscite Administrator who, though formally appointed to office by the Government of the state, would be given 'the powers he considers necessary' for ensuring the impartiality of the plebiscite. After the requirements of the truce agreement had been fulfilled, the Commission and the Plebiscite Administrator would determine the final disposal of Indian and state armed forces as well as the forces in Azad Kashmir. Provision was made for the expulsion of persons who had entered the state since 15 August 1947 and also for the return of citizens who had left the state on account of disturbances.[3]

---

[1] ibid., p. 180.
[2] Josef Korbel, *Danger in Kashmir*, p 144.
[3] K. Sarwar Hasan (ed.), *Documents on the Foreign Relations of Pakistan, The Kashmir Question*, p. 212.

The resolutions of 13 August 1948 and 5 January 1949 form the basic resolutions for the settlement of the Kashmir dispute but there has been no movement towards their implementation all these years, except that a cease-fire came into force on 1 January 1949, a cease-fire line was established by mutual agreement on 27 July 1949, and the Secretary-General of the United Nations nominated Fleet Admiral Chester W. Nimitz, an American, as the Plebiscite Administrator on 22 March 1949.

Each side has blamed the other for the impasse, but India has consistently refused to have recourse to arbitration or adjudication to determine which side is to blame and what can be done to move forward.

UNCIP Proposes Arbitration

Having failed to obtain the agreement of the parties to a programme of demilitarization, the Commission suggested that all questions raised by both sides, regarding the implementation of Part II of the resolution of 13 August 1948, be submitted to binding arbitration.[1] This proposal was backed by President Truman and Prime Minister Attlee and was accepted by Pakistan but rejected by India.

Accepting the Commission's view, that a single person may prove to be more effective to carry on further negotiations than a five-member Commission, the Security Council asked its own President for the month, General McNaughton of Canada, to try and resolve the deadlock. McNaughton based his proposals for demilitarization on the 'basic principle' that the reduction of the armed forces on either side should be 'in such stages as not to cause fear at any point of time to the people on either side of the cease-fire line'.[2] Pakistan accepted the McNaughton proposals, India rejected them.

On 14 March 1950 the Council passed a resolution disbanding the UNCIP and replacing it by a United Nations Representative to assist towards demilitarization.

The Dixon Mission

The Council's choice for the role of UN Representative fell on Sir Owen Dixon, a judge of the High Court of Australia and afterwards Chief Justice of Australia. He arrived in Delhi on 27 May 1950, and laboured till his departure from Karachi on 23 August to obtain

---

[1] ibid., p. 231.　　　　[2] ibid., p. 240.

the agreement of the two governments to a programme of demilitarization, but in vain.

Faced with India's persistent demand that Pakistan be declared
an aggressor, Dixon, in order to move forward, assumed, for argument's sake, that Pakistan contravened international law when she
sent her army across the cease-fire line. Indian commentators
frequently quote the last part of the relevant passage in Dixon's
report[1] to support their contention that Dixon gave a definite
finding that Pakistan had offended against international law, but a
reading of the entire text places Dixon's *obiter dictum* in proper
perspective:

Upon a number of occasions ... India has advanced not only the
contention to which I have already referred, that Pakistan was an aggressor, but the further contention that this should be declared. The Prime
Minister of India, at an early stage of the meeting made the same contention and he referred to it repeatedly during the conference. I took up
the positions, first that the Security Council had not made such a declaration; secondly that I had neither been commissioned to make nor had I
made any judicial investigation of the issue; but thirdly that, without
going into the causes or reasons why it happened, which presumably
formed part of the history of the subcontinent, I was prepared to adopt
the view that when the frontier of the State of Jammu and Kashmir was
crossed, on I believe 20 October 1947, by hostile elements, it was contrary to international law, and that when, in May 1948, as I believe, units
of the regular Pakistan forces moved into the territory of the State, that
too was inconsistent with international law.

However, Dixon was unable to get India's agreement to any
reasonable terms:

In the end I became convinced that India's agreement would never be
obtained to demilitarization in any such form, or to provisions governing
the period of the plebiscite of any such character, as would in my opinion
permit of the plebiscite being conducted in conditions sufficiently guarding
against intimidation and other forms of influence and abuse by which the
freedom and fairness of the plebiscite might be imperilled.

Dixon also gave it as his own view that: 'The question whether
Pakistan had or had not been an aggressor had, to my mind, nothing
to do with the ... fairness and freedom of a ... plebiscite.'

He believed that if there was any chance of an agreed settlement
it lay in the partition of the state and 'in some means of allocating
the Valley' because it was not possible to break up the Valley; and

[1] ibid., pp. 251–79.

he added: 'No method of allocating the Valley . . . is available except a poll of the inhabitants.'

VI. Mediation by Commonwealth Prime Ministers

Liaquat threatened to boycott the Commonwealth Prime Ministers' Conference, scheduled to convene in London on 4 January 1951, unless his colleagues agreed to include the Kashmir problem in their discussions. The Conference opened without the Pakistani Prime Minister but he joined his colleagues on 7 January after being assured that Kashmir would be discussed outside the Conference. Accordingly, the Kashmir question was discussed at two informal sessions. Liaquat disclosed afterwards that, in order to meet India's objection that she could not remove her troops from Kashmir for security reasons, the other Prime Ministers had suggested that a Commonwealth force, a joint Indo-Pakistani force, or a United Nations force could be stationed in Kashmir for the duration of the plebiscite. Pakistan had accepted all three alternatives; India had rejected all of them.[1]

VII. Security Council Resumes Consideration of Kashmir Dispute

Resolution of 30 March 1951

At Pakistan's request the Security Council took up the Kashmir question again on 21 February 1951 and, after another lengthy debate, passed a resolution on 30 March 1951 under which it decided to appoint another United Nations Representative in place of Dixon, and declared that any action which the proposed Constituent Assembly of Kashmir might take regarding the state's future affiliation would be ineffective. If the parties failed to achieve agreement in their discussions with the UN Representative, they would be required to accept arbitration on 'all outstanding points of difference reported by the UN Representative'.

Sir Benegal Rau for India assured the Council that the Constituent Assembly of Kashmir was not intended 'to prejudice the issues before the Security Council'.[2] This promise was reiterated by Indian spokesmen before the Council on 9 March 1951, 29 March 1951, and 29 May 1951, and by Prime Minister Nehru in Parliament on 28 March 1951 and at a press conference on 11 June 1951. Ultimately, however, these assurances were conveniently forgotten

---

[1] Patrick Gordon Walker, *The Commonwealth*, p. 176; Sisir Gupta, *Kashmir*, p. 227.

[2] K. Sarwar Hasan (ed.), *Documents on the Foreign Relations of Pakistan, The Kashmir Question*, p. 281.

both by the Kashmir Assembly and by the Government of India.

However, India rejected the resolution of 30 March because of its prescription that the parties should submit their differences to arbitration. Nehru said that the United Kingdom and the United States, who had sponsored the resolution, had 'completely lost the capacity to think and judge anything. . . . The whole thing is a fantastic nonsense.'[1]

Frank P. Graham's Mediation

Pakistan accepted the 30 March 1951 resolution in its entirety. India, despite her formal rejection of the resolution, said she had no objection if the Council sent another representative to the sub-continent to try his hand at mediation.

On 30 April 1951 the Council appointed Frank P. Graham, a former US Senator from North Carolina, as the new UN Representative. Altogether, the indefatigable Graham submitted six reports to the Council, on 15 October 1951, 19 December 1951, 22 April 1952, 19 September 1952, 27 March 1953, and 31 March 1958.[2] In the end Graham's efforts came to naught because India did not agree on the number and character of forces to be left on either side of the cease-fire line after demilitarization.

After receiving Graham's fourth report the Security Council passed a resolution on 23 December 1952, mainly embodying the proposals which Graham had unsuccessfully laid before India and Pakistan. It urged the parties to enter into further negotiations under Graham's auspices in order to reach agreement on the number of forces to remain on each side after demilitarization, this number to be between 3,000 and 6,000 on the Pakistani side of the cease-fire line and between 12,000 and 18,000 on the Indian side.[3] Graham's further efforts also having failed to bear fruit, he submitted his fifth report to the Council recommending that India and Pakistan be left to negotiate the dispute bilaterally and report 'an agreement on Kashmir and thereby light a torch along the difficult path of the people's pilgrimage toward peace'.[4]

Before following the thread of the story further we must pause here to take note of a new development which took place in the

---

[1] *Hindu*, 12 June 1951, quoted by Josef Korbel, *Danger in Kashmir*, p. 182.
[2] For texts of Graham's reports see *Reports on Kashmir by United Nations Representatives*, Govt. of Pakistan, 1958.
[3] K. Sarwar Hasan (ed.), *Documents on the Foreign Relations of Pakistan, The Kashmir Question*, p. 310.
[4] Paras. 57 and 58 of Report dated 27 March 1953.

Security Council in January 1952, when Graham's second report was being discussed.

The Soviet Union Takes a Stand in the Kashmir Dispute

The Soviet Union at first had taken no substantive stand on Kashmir during the Security Council debates. On 17 January 1952 the USSR representative, Jacob Malik, took the floor, and suddenly launched a bitter attack on the UK and the US for their alleged imperialist designs in Kashmir. He said the two Western powers wished to introduce Anglo-American troops into Kashmir under the guise of a United Nations force and to turn that territory into a military base. The Kashmir question, he asserted, 'can be re solved successfully only by giving the people of Kashmir an opportunity to decide the question of Kashmir's constitutional status by themselves, without outside interference. This can be achieved if that status is determined by a Constituent Assembly democratically elected by the Kashmir people.'[1]

Malik's strong participation in the Kashmir debate under the roof of the Security Council was something new, but the content of his remarks was not surprising. He was merely voicing inside the Council what Soviet spokesmen had all along been saying elsewhere. It was the Soviet belief that Britain had divided the Indian peoples into two in order to keep them weak so that she could perpetuate her own domination in the subcontinent. Though both Indian and Pakistani leaders were criticized for playing into British hands, 'in Pakistan the reactionary elements are stronger than in Hindustan ... Pakistan is being converted into a British bridgehead in the East, into a second Trans-Jordan of enormous dimension'.[2] About Kashmir, 'the Anglo-American strategists felt that, if they were to retain Kashmir as a strategic military base, they must get it included in Pakistan.'[3]

The Soviet Union could hardly fail to notice that Pakistan's foreign policy was distinctly biased in favour of the Western powers. In 1950 Liaquat had given precedence to the invitation to visit America over an earlier invitation to visit the USSR, and afterwards Pakistan had given diplomatic support to the Western position in the Korean question as well as in the matter of signing the Japanese Peace Treaty.[4]

[1] *Security Council Official Records, 570th Meeting*, 17 Jan. 1952.
[2] A. Dyakov, 'Partitioned India', *New Times*, no. 3, 1948.
[3] O. Orestov, 'The War in Kashmir', *New Times*, no. 40, 1948.
[4] For details see ch. 5 and 6.

VIII. Direct Negotiations

Three weeks after Graham had proposed that India and Pakistan should have recourse to direct negotiations over Kashmir, internal developments in Pakistan facilitated just such a course. Governor-General Ghulam Muhammad dismissed Nazimuddin and appointed Muhammad Ali Bogra as Prime Minister. The new Prime Minister had been a successful Ambassador to Burma, Canada, and the US and had a certain amount of boyish charm and optimism. He was conscious of Pakistan's lack of weapons and economic weakness and believed that she could best be strengthened by allying herself with the US. At the same time he was aware that it was essential for Pakistan to establish good neighbourly relations with India, and he was genuinely anxious to work towards that goal. He saw no contradiction between his two objectives because it was his conviction that a healthy relationship between India and Pakistan could only be built up if the existing wide margin between India's strength and Pakistan's weakness could be reduced.[1]

Ten days after he had taken office, Bogra said he looked upon Nehru as 'an elder brother' and would like to meet him 'soonest'. The two Prime Ministers first met informally in London in June 1953 on the occasion of Queen Elizabeth II's coronation where they were fellow guests.

Bogra and Nehru met for serious negotiations at Karachi on 25 July. Nehru was spontaneously cheered by the people on arrival and thought his reception was 'very remarkable' and 'not a put-up job'. A joint press note issued on 28 July said the two leaders had talked together cordially but that the discussions had necessarily been of a preliminary nature and would be resumed in Delhi.

Before Bogra and Nehru could meet in Delhi the political cauldron inside Kashmir, which had been bubbling for some time, boiled over.[2] Abdullah, who had been denying the finality of Kashmir's accession to India, was dismissed from the premiership on 9 August and clapped in jail, being replaced by Bakshi Ghulam Muhammad, who had been affirming Kashmir's affiliation with India. *Dawn* strongly advised Bogra not to undertake the expected journey to Delhi but to pursue the Kashmir question in the United

---

[1] He often spoke to me on these lines on the eve of his appointment as Prime Minister in 1952, when he was Ambassador in Washington and I was the Minister. Interestingly, in the context of Sino-Indian relations Nehru also said, 'Natural friendship does not exist if you are weak and if you are looked down upon as a weak country.' Quoted by Neville Maxwell, *India's China War*, p. 120.

[2] See the next section for details.

Nations. If Nehru could not tolerate even his 'dear friend' Abdullah 'expressing views which he [Nehru] does not like, how can he be expected to tolerate the ordinary man in Kashmir going to the polls and voting against accession to Bharat in a plebiscite?'[1]

At Bogra's insistence Nehru agreed to receive him at short notice and he arrived in the Indian capital on 16 August. A joint statement of the two Prime Ministers reiterated that the Kashmir dispute should be settled according to the wish of the Kashmiri people 'with a view to promoting their well-being and causing the least disturbance to the life of the people of the State'. The most feasible method of ascertaining the people's choice was an impartial plebiscite and this method had been agreed to some years previously but progress could not be made because of lack of agreement on certain 'preliminary issues'. The Prime Ministers agreed that these issues should be resolved by them 'directly'. The next step would be the appointment of a Plebiscite Administrator. It was decided that he should be appointed by the end of April 1954. On the Plebiscite Administrator's appointment and induction into office by the Jammu and Kashmir Government, he would examine the situation and report on it.[2]

A number of commentators have suggested that this communiqué showed that India and Pakistan were well on the way towards a settlement of the Kashmir question and that Pakistan foolishly upset the whole arrangement by accepting US military aid and angering India. This view overlooks certain important implications contained in the communiqué. First, though it agreed that the Kashmir dispute should be settled in accordance with the wish of the people of Kashmir, the basic objectives were stated to be to promote the 'well-being' of the people and to cause 'the least disturbance to [their] life'. A favourite Indian interpretation of these goals was that India being a progressive secular country, and Pakistan a bigoted backward one, the well-being of Kashmiris lay in joining India; also that, if the vote went in favour of Pakistan, the life of the Hindus and Sikhs in the state would be disturbed, setting off a fresh wave of communal frenzy in the subcontinent, and this had to be avoided. Secondly, the joint declaration totally omitted any mention of the United Nations resolutions on Kashmir. The two Prime Ministers were now required to resolve differences

[1] *Dawn*, 10 August 1953.
[2] K. Sarwar Hasan (ed.), *Documents on the Foreign Relations of Pakistan, The Kashmir Question*, p. 328.

directly but it was not spelled out what would happen if the customary deadlock between them took place. The role of the United Nations, on which weaker Pakistan had relied so much, was totally eliminated. Thirdly, the Plebiscite Administrator, who was previously a nominee of the Secretary-General of the United Nations, was now to be solely a creation of the Government of the state. Fourthly, the important question of conditions under which a plebiscite was to be conducted was not even touched on in the statement. It soon became clear from the Bogra–Nehru correspondence that followed[1] that India remained adamant, first, that the pro-Indian regime in the state should remain in power while the plebiscite was being conducted and, second, that no neutral troops should replace Indian troops to ensure freedom of the vote (Nehru's letter of 3 September 1953). Nehru also said publicly that Nimitz should be replaced as Plebiscite Administrator by a person from a small neutral country. Nimitz thereupon resigned, and this turned out to be the only concrete result of the Bogra–Nehru effort.

Nehru blamed the receipt of US arms by Pakistan for the breakdown of the Indo-Pakistani negotiations over Kashmir but Prem Nath Bazaz, an astute observer of the Kashmir scene, says that, in fact, 'by this time the Hindu revivalists and reactionaries had been able to exert sufficient baneful influence on the policies of the Central Government', as exemplified by Abdullah's dismissal and imprisonment, and 'blame for the basic change in policy was irrelevantly laid at the door of Pakistan for entering military pacts with Western powers'.[2]

It should not be difficult at this juncture to perceive the double standard employed by Nehru towards the Kashmir dispute on the one hand, and towards other international conflicts in which India had no direct interest, on the other. In the case of Kashmir he incessantly pressed the allegation that Pakistan was an aggressor, and consistently refused to allow a UN force in Kashmir or to submit the issue for mediation or arbitration, completely disregarding the following facts:

(a) that he had condemned those who wished to brand China an aggressor in Korea on the ground that this would only increase the tension and reduce the chance of a peaceful settlement;[3]

---

[1] For this see *Negotiations Between the Prime Ministers of Pakistan and India Regarding the Kashmir Dispute, June 1953–September 1954*, Govt. of Pakistan, 1954.

[2] P. N. Bazaz, *Kashmir in Crucible*, p. 69.

[3] See 'The Korean War' in chapter 6.

(*b*) that he had claimed that Indian representation on the proposed Political Conference on Korea would have helped because the
intervention of neutral countries helps in toning down differences
and tensions;[1]

(*c*) that India had sent her own troops into Korea under the
banner of the United Nations;

(*d*) that not only does the UN Charter recommend arbitration
as a method of solving disputes but it is also one of the 'Directive
Principles' of India's own Constitution that 'the State shall endeavour
to encourage settlement of international disputes by arbitration'
(Article 51d).

IX. Internal Developments in Kashmir

A politician's utterances over the years seldom form an even pattern,
and Abdullah's statements are no exception to this rule. On the
whole, however, it would appear that he would have preferred the
Valley to become independent even if the remaining parts of the
state broke away and joined India or Pakistan. Because of his personal friendship with Nehru, close association with the Congress
Party, and known antipathy to Jinnah, he had no option, in the
emergency created by the tribal invasion, but to declare for India.
And once the Indian Army had marched into Kashmir it was
not easy to get rid of it. Abdullah's hope now lay in securing autonomy for Kashmir within the Indian Union, but the agitation of
Kashmiri Hindus, backed up by other Hindus of India, for the
complete integration of the state with their country, not only dashed
Abdullah's hopes for an autonomous status for his homeland but
also showed him that Hindu India's veneer of secularism had a very
thin coating. It was too late and too dangerous for him now to turn
round and talk about joining Pakistan. He therefore revived his
idea of a Kashmir free from the control of both India and Pakistan,
and paid for it by dismissal from office and imprisonment. A brief
review of Abdullah's own statements, and the developments
inside Kashmir, will make this clear.

A month after taking over the Administration in Kashmir,
Abdullah told the Maharaja that 'it would be a good thing if India
and Pakistan were made to recognize the state as an independent
unit like Switzerland'.[2] In an exclusive interview with Michael

---

[1] ibid.
[2] M. C. Mahajan, *Looking Back*, p. 162.

Davidson of the *Observer* in May 1949, Abdullah said accession to either India or Pakistan could not bring peace to Kashmir. If Kashmir joined India, Pakistan would fight; if she went to Pakistan a 'ghastly' exodus of Hindus from the state would take place.[1]

In the Constitution of India, inaugurated on 26 January 1950, Article 370 had accorded Kashmir a special status. According to Nehru this provision 'made clear that any change in, or addition to, that position would depend upon the wishes of the people of the State as represented in their Constituent Assembly. The subjects of accession were three, namely Foreign Affairs, Defence, and Communications.'[2]

On 27 October 1950 the National Conference proposed that a Constituent Assembly be summoned to determine 'the future shape and affiliations of the State'.[3] In the elections to the Assembly that autumn all the 75 seats were captured by Abdullah's National Conference, 73 of them without contest. The Praja Parishad of Jammu, which stood for complete integration of the state with India and the preservation of the rights of the Dogra dynasty, boycotted the polls, alleging that the state Government had brought undue pressure, and rejected the Parishad nomination papers 'wholesale'.[4] Noting the entirely one-sided result of the election, Korbel comments: 'No dictator could do better.'[5]

In his opening address to the Constituent Assembly (5 November 1951) Abdullah argued that Kashmir could not become independent because she was a small country and could not join Pakistan because of that country's 'reactionary' politics. He declared his preference for India because she had respected Kashmir's 'internal autonomy' for the previous four years and because she was a 'secular democracy' which negated the fear that Kashmiri Muslims could not feel secure in India with its Hindu majority.[6] Critics of Abdullah, who accuse him of having gone back on his professions, would do well to recall the reasons which led him to opt for India in the first instance. They would discover then that Abdullah did not change his mind perfidiously but was forced to do so because India belied the expectations on which he had originally acted.

---

[1] P. N. Bazaz, *The History of Struggle for Freedom in Kashmir*, p. 424.
[2] *Lok Sabha Debates*, 10 August 1953, Part II, col. 440.
[3] Lord Birdwood, *Two Nations and Kashmir*, p. 104.
[4] Sisir Gupta, *Kashmir*, p. 366.
[5] J. Korbel, *Danger in Kashmir*, p. 222.
[6] Sisir Gupta, *Kashmir*, pp. 367–70.

Abdullah–Nehru Agreement of July 1952
To clarify the constitutional relationship between Kashmir and India, discussions were held in Delhi as a result of which Nehru and Abdullah reached a broad agreement. Abdullah explained the nature of this understanding to the Kashmir Constituent Assembly on 11 August 1952:

> ... the fact that Article 370 has been mentioned as a temporary provision in the Constitution [of India] does not mean that it is capable of being abrogated, modified, or replaced unilaterally. In actual effect, the temporary nature of this Article arises merely from the fact that the power to finalize the constitutional relationship between the State and the Union of India has been specifically vested in the Jammu and Kashmir Constituent Assembly. It follows that whatever modifications, amendments or exceptions that may become necessary either to Article 370 or any other Article in the Constitution of India in their application to the Jammu and Kashmir State are subject to the decisions of this Sovereign Body.

He warned that 'any suggestion of altering arbitrarily this basis of our relationship with India would not only constitute a breach of the spirit and letter of the Constitution, but it may invite serious consequences for a harmonious association of our State with India'.[1]

The Rise of Hindu Communalism and Dismissal and Incarceration of Abdullah
The decline in the power of the Dogra ruler and the corresponding rise in the power of Abdullah was watched with apprehension by Hindus in Kashmir as well as in India. Early in 1948 the Hindus organized themselves under the banner of Praja Parishad in Jammu, the Dogra homeland, where the Muslims were being forcibly transformed from a majority into a minority. In 1949 Abdullah's administration apprehended a large number of Dogra workers, including the seventy-year-old Parishad President Prem Nath Dogra. At the time of the elections to the Constituent Assembly, the Parishad agitation once more raised its head and the Parishad boycotted those elections on the ground that Abdullah's government was indulging in malpractices. Nehru said publicly that by trying to bring down Abdullah, the Praja Parishad, Jan Sangh, and RSS 'were doing Pakistan's work'.[2]

Despite Nehru's criticism, the Parishad continued its demand for

---

[1] For text of Abdullah's statement see *Indian Press Digests for the period 1 Aug. to 30 Oct. 1952*, vol. II, no. 1, pp. 125–36.

[2] *Indian Press Digests for the period 16 Nov. 1951 to 15 Jan. 1952*, vol. I, no. 3, p. 11.

a complete integration of Kashmir with India and on 20 April 1952 passed a formal resolution to that effect. 'During the course of this agitation,' writes Bazaz, 'Hindu nationalism threw aside the mask of secularism and came out in its true colours. All differences between Congressmen and non-Congressmen as well as between Hindu nationalists and Hindu communalists were virtually obliterated. It is true that officially both the Government of India and the Congress organization deprecated the agitation but there is no manner of doubt that Hindu India, which includes Congress rank and file, sympathized with the aims and aspirations of the Praj Parishad.'[1]

Renewed demonstrations in Kashmir and India were set off on 11 May 1953 when S. P. Mukerjee, President of Jan Sangh, was arrested on entering Jammu in defiance of a ban. In some places Abdullah's effigy was burned.

Abdullah was greatly upset at the intensity of the agitation and declared that, if they so desired, Jammu and Ladakh could integrate with India and leave the Valley free to maintain a limited accession.[2] On 18 May 1953 he said the time had come for re-examining the entire question of Kashmir's relations with India.[3] In his Id broadcast in the following month he wished success for the Bogra–Nehru talks because, so long as tension prevailed between India and Pakistan, nobody in Kashmir could live in peace. This emphasis upon Indo-Pakistani harmony as a *sine qua non* for Kashmir's welfare henceforth became a recurring theme in Abdullah's policy.

After the ugly anti-Abdullah demonstrations, following Mukerjee's death in prison of a heart attack in June 1953, Abdullah felt convinced that everybody in India, except Nehru, was a communalist. He said experience had 'made the Kashmiri Muslims aware of India's real intentions. India has thrown her net around us and we are in fear of being enslaved as in old days . . . I have . . . come to the conclusion that our relationship with India has been harmful to Muslims.'[4] Addressing an 'enthusiastic gathering' on Martyrs' Day the Sheikh declared that Kashmiri martyrs had not sacrificed their lives for India or Pakistan. The purpose for which they had

---

[1] P. N. Bazaz, *The History of Struggle for Freedom in Kashmir*, p. 659.

[2] ibid., p. 573.

[3] *Indian Press Digests for the period 1 Apr. to 31 July 1953*, vol. II, no. 5, p. 20.

[4] From a letter to Lohia from an unnamed correspondent in Kashmir, dated Martyrs' Day (13 July 1953) and published in *Janata*, 16 Aug. 1953. *Indian Press Digests for the period 1 Apr. to 31 July 1953*, vol. II, no. 5, pp. 38–9. Ram Manohar Lohia was General-Secretary of the Praja Socialist Party of India.

shed their blood was independence. Why must Kashmiris be compelled to join either India or Pakistan? Why should they not have good relations with both?[1]

Evidently, even Nehru thought Abdullah by now had gone too far because the Sadar-i-Riyasat (Head of State) of Kashmir, Karan Singh, could not have dared to act against Abdullah in the harsh manner he did without the Indian Prime Minister's approval. By a communiqué, issued at 4.30 a.m. on 9 August 1953, Karan Singh dismissed Abdullah from office and installed Deputy Premier Ghulam Muhammad as Prime Minister. The new Premier asserted that Abdullah had been dismissed to avert the 'national disaster' of 'an independent Kashmir under the influence of an imperialist power'. Everyone took the unnamed 'imperialist power' to mean the USA, and US Ambassador George V. Allen had to issue a statement, denying that his country was interfering in Kashmir. By a twist of history India in 1962 had to solicit arms from the same 'imperialist power' to fight China, whom India for many years had courted as a fellow anti-imperialist.

Frank Moraes, editor of the *Times of India*, who happened to arrive in Karachi on the day of Abdullah's arrest, found that 'every single Pakistani high and low' was confident that Pakistan would now win the Valley.[2]

[1] ibid., pp. 40-1.
[2] *Indian Press Digests for the period 1 Aug. to 31 Oct. 1953*, vol. II, no. 7, p. 7.

3 Indo-Pakistani Crises and Efforts at Conciliation

I. Inter-Dominion Conferences

With a view to reducing the overwhelming flow of destitute and dispirited refugees into both countries, Nehru and Liaquat published a joint statement on 24 March 1948 which said, 'Both governments hope and trust that the minority communities will remain in their homes. . . . They are convinced that this is in the best interests of all concerned.'[1] This was followed by a ministerial conference at Calcutta resulting in an Agreement on 20 April 1948, affirming that 'the responsibility for protecting the lives and property of the minority communities . . . rests on the Government of the Dominion in which the minorities reside'. It was promised further that 'any propaganda for the amalgamation of Pakistan and India, or portions thereof, shall be discouraged'.[2]

Another Inter-Dominion Conference between India and Pakistan was convened at New Delhi from 6 to 15 December 1948 and made a fresh agreement on the lines of the Calcutta Agreement. A more concrete achievement of the new accord was the decision to set up a tribunal, consisting of one judge each from India and Pakistan and a mutually acceptable presiding judge from a third country, to resolve the boundary disputes between East Bengal and West Bengal, and between East Bengal and Assam. The tribunal was duly set up and, the Indian and Pakistani judges having gone through the usual ritual of registering disagreements with each other, the final award was given by the President of the tribunal, Justice Bagge of Sweden.

II. Pakistan Appeals to the United Nations and the Commonwealth

Though India associated herself with Pakistan in bilateral joint

[1] K. P. Karunakaran, *India in World Affairs, Aug. 1947–Jan. 1950*, p. 151.
[2] *Hindu*, 21 Apr. 1948.

appeals and Inter-Dominion Conferences, she declined all suggestions for third-party mediation and teams of observers. Towards
the end of September 1947 Governor-General Jinnah approached
the sister nations of the Commonwealth, through the Government
of the United Kingdom, for 'help in ending the murderous raids on
the trains and columns of refugees' in both India and Pakistan. 'In
Hindu India', reported *The Times*; 'the Pakistani approach has
been strongly criticised in the newspapers.'[1] Jinnah recognized that
Britain and the other Dominions could use only moral persuasion
to help settle differences between members of the Commonwealth
but complained that His Majesty's Government were shirking
their responsibility in this respect.[2]

It was also reported from Karachi on 28 September 1947 that
India had rejected a Pakistani proposal that the two governments
should jointly approach the United Nations and request that twelve
observers be immediately flown to the subcontinent, six of them to
station themselves in disturbed areas in India and six in any part of
Pakistan they chose.[3]

III. India's Proposal for a No-War Declaration
At the end of November 1949 India invited Pakistan to join her in
a no-war declaration. After an exchange of letters between Prime
Ministers Jawaharlal Nehru and Liaquat Ali Khan, that phase ended
inconclusively with Liaquat's letter of 27 November 1950. But the
Indian offer of a no-war declaration, resurrected several times since,
has become a continuing feature of Indo-Pakistani diplomacy.

At times Indian spokesmen have mentioned the recurrent Indian
offer and, without saying anything about Pakistan's stand on the
question, have alleged that Pakistan has always rejected India's
offer to subscribe to a no-war pact. An examination of the record,
however, makes it quite clear that neither Liaquat nor his successors
have ever 'rejected' India's offer of a no-war pact out of hand as the
Indian pronouncements imply. Pakistan, in fact, has uniformly
welcomed the offer, provided the slogan of no-war was given real
meaning by adding to it an agreed formula ensuring the fair settlement of the disputes between the two countries which could erupt
into war if allowed to fester too long.

The drafts of a declaration put forward by Nehru and Liaquat

[1] *The Times*, 29 Sept. 1947.
[2] M. Rafique Afzal, *Selected Speeches and Statements of the Quaid-i-Azam Mohammad Ali Jinnah*, p. 451.
[3] *The Times*, 29 Sept. 1947.

during their correspondence show the precise position taken up by
each side:

Indian draft:

The Government of India and the Government of Pakistan . . . hereby
declare that they condemn resort to war for the settlement of any existing
or future disputes between them. They further agree that the settlement
of such disputes between them shall always be sought through recognized peaceful methods such as negotiation, or by resort to mediation or
arbitration by special agency set up by mutual agreement for the purpose,
or by agreed reference to some appropriate international body recognized
by both of them.

Pakistani draft:

The Government of India and the Government of Pakistan . . . hereby
declare that they will not resort to war for settlement of any existing or
future disputes between them. They further agree that settlement of
such disputes shall always be sought through peaceful methods of negotiation and mediation and, if these should fail to bring settlement, by
resort to arbitration of all points of difference including those relating to
the procedure for arbitration. They undertake that they will abide by the
award of an arbitral Tribunal, which shall consist of ***** for the
settlement of all existing disputes. In the event of their not being unanimous, the decision of the majority shall be binding. Negotiations for
the settlement of all such disputes shall begin as early as practicable, and
such of them as are not settled by negotiation within two months from
the date of this declaration shall be referred to mediation, for which a
further period of two months shall be allowed. Any matters remaining
unsettled at the expiry of this period shall be referred to arbitration.[1]

As to the composition of the arbitral tribunal, Liaquat proposed
that the governments of three friendly countries should be asked to
nominate one member each (letters dated 14 February and 26
September 1950).

To Nehru's objection that political disputes are not justiciable,
Liaquat replied that there was no reason for refusing to accept the
decision of an impartial statesman. The solution to Indo-Pakistani
problems, Liaquat went on, would come when each side accepted

---

[1] For texts of the two drafts see *No-War Declaration and Canal Waters Dispute,
Correspondence between the Prime Ministers of India and Pakistan*, Govt. of Pakistan,
1950. This publication also contains texts of letters exchanged by Nehru and Liaquat
from 18 January 1950 to 27 November 1950.

adjudication of all issues that were justiciable and arbitration on all other issues (Nehru's letter dated 27 October and Liaquat's dated 20 November 1950). Liaquat pointed out, further, that India's and Pakistan's membership of the United Nations itself constituted a declaration that they had renounced force as a method of settling disputes. A bare no-war declaration by them would add nothing new to that commitment.

The closest Nehru came to accepting any machinery for the settlement of disputes was in respect of canal waters and evacuee property. He suggested that these two disputes be referred to a tribunal 'of the highest standing, consisting of two judges from India and two judges from Pakistan'. 'I am perfectly prepared', he added, 'to extend this principle to any other justiciable issue' (letter dated 8 October 1950). Liaquat commented that Nehru's proposal 'permits of endless delay' because a tribunal consisting of two Indian and two Pakistani judges would be hopelessly dead-locked (letter dated 21 November 1950), but the Indian Prime Minister refused to accept even the addition of a neutral judge to the tribunal proposed by himself.[1]

Four years later, when Pakistan accepted United States military assistance, Nehru expostulated with Bogra that Pakistan had 'ruled out' a no-war declaration with India and had chosen instead to rely on military aid. 'A no-war declaration', he asserted, 'brings more security than military preparation.' He drew Bogra's attention to the Nehru-Chou En-lai joint declaration of five principles and said that such a declaration gave far greater assurance of security than military pacts or military preparations.[2] Bogra resented Nehru's assertion and reminded him that Liaquat had 'wholly welcomed the proposal' and that it had fallen through only because Nehru had declined Liaquat's suggestion that the declaration should embody

---

[1] *India's Threat to Pakistan, Correspondence Between the Prime Ministers of Pakistan and India (15 July-11 August 1951),* Ministry of Foreign Affairs and Commonwealth Relations (Pakistan), 1951, p. 27.

[2] However, when the real test came India unhesitatingly assumed the same down-to-earth attitude towards foreign military assistance for which Nehru earlier had so loftily reprimanded Pakistan and the United States. After the rout of the Indian forces at the hands of the Chinese, in the border clashes of 1962, India, feeling threatened by a stronger neighbour, herself became a supplicant for American military hardware. During a State visit to the USA President Radhakrishnan said at the Press Club in Washington, D.C., on 5 June 1963, that it was possible at any time for the Chinese to invade India through the Himalayas and that that was why 'we are anxious to increase our military strength.... Military weakness is a temptation. Military strength may prove a deterrent ... India would be able to settle the problem only by having strength with which to back her bargaining power.' *Asian Recorder,* 1963, p. 5332.

also an effective procedure for the peaceful solution of all Indo-
Pakistani disputes.[1]

Pakistani leaders have on occasion actually taken the initiative
and called upon India to agree to an impartial arrangement for
solving Indo-Pakistani disputes and simultaneously subscribe to a
no-war declaration with Pakistan, as instanced by Prime Minister
Chaudhry Muhammad Ali's statement in Parliament on 19 March
1956, and Presidents Ayub Khan's and Yahya Khan's offers in the
General Assembly on 13 December 1965 and 22 October 1970.
But Pakistani leaders from Liaquat onwards have believed that a
settlement of the Kashmir problem would be a far more powerful
contribution to peace and friendship than any no-war declaration.
Bhutto declared on 20 June 1963, 'Let India arrive at an equitable
and honourable settlement with Pakistan over Kashmir. We can
then have not one but a dozen no-war pacts with her.'[2]

The well-established pattern of exchanges continues to this day.
In 1969 Prime Minister Indira Gandhi suggested to Yahya
Khan the 'normalization and improvement' of Indo-Pakistani
relations on the basis of easing travel between the two neighbouring
countries, encouraging cultural exchanges, and improving commerce. 'If you agree,' she said, 'we could set up a joint Indo-Pak
body for this purpose at any level acceptable to you. I have already
suggested a no-war pact between Pakistan and India.'[3] But these
proposals were scarcely different in substance from the numerous
previous Indian offers to Pakistan to subscribe to a no-war declaration. They omitted mention of the two most serious disputes
plaguing Indo-Pakistani relations, Kashmir and Farakka Barrage,
and made no provision for compulsory and binding non-partisan
arbitration in case direct negotiations remained indefinitely dead-
locked, as they often had in the past.

Not surprisingly, therefore, Yahya in his reply to Mrs. Gandhi
said: 'It is our sincere conviction that amity and friendship will
continue to elude India and Pakistan if our two Governments run
after the shadow that the peripheral issues are and evade the reality
that our two outstanding disputes regarding Jammu and Kashmir
and the Ganges waters represent. . . . We have explained . . . our

---

[1] *Negotiations Between the Prime Ministers of Pakistan and India regarding the Kashmir
Dispute, June 1953–September 1954*, Govt. of Pakistan, 1954, pp. 85 and 89.

[2] *Dawn*, 21 June 1963.

[3] For text of Indira Gandhi's letter dated 22 June 1969, see *India News*, 1 August
1969.

ideas of the type of self-executing machinery that would be a necessary concomitant of a no-war pact.'[1]

It is noteworthy that, while India was reluctant to take her differences with Pakistan to the International Court of Justice or to submit them to arbitration, these were precisely the methods she repeatedly proposed to China after losing territory to the latter in border clashes. On 10 December 1962 Nehru declared in Parliament, 'I am prepared . . . even to refer the basic dispute of the claims on the frontier to a body like the International Court of Justice at the Hague.'[2] Again, 'We would be perfectly prepared to refer the matter [of differences between India and China] to the International Court of Justice or to arbitration if it was agreed to.'[3] Yet again (5 March 1963), 'We have suggested that we are prepared to refer these frontier disputes to the International Court of Justice at the Hague or to arbitration.'[4] And, with the balance of physical power and the *status quo* in her favour, China's response to India was strikingly similar to India's own policy towards Pakistan all these years. In a letter to Nehru on 20 April 1963, Prime Minister Chou En-lai wrote: 'The Chinese Government is of the opinion that complicated questions involving sovereignty, such as the Sino-Indian boundary question, can be settled only through direct negotiations between

---

[1] For text of Yahya Khan's letter, dated 26 July 1969, see *Pakistan Affairs*, 30 August 1969.

[2] J. Nehru, *Speeches*, IV, p. 254. When Liaquat repeatedly pressed Nehru at least to agree to submit the canal waters dispute to the International Court of Justice, Nehru declined the proposal on grounds which contrast sharply with the reason he advanced in his letter of 5 March 1963 to Chou En-lai for proposing that Sino-Indian differences be referred to that court. To Chou En-lai he represented that 'there could be no fairer and more reasonable approach than this proposal for peaceful resolving of our differences'. To Liaquat he protested: 'To think, ab initio, of a third party will lessen the sense of responsibility of the [Indian and Pakistani] judges and will also be a confession of our continued dependence on others. That would hardly be becoming for proud and self-respecting independent nations' (letter dated 8 October 1950). Liaquat wrote back that the International Court of Justice 'is our Court. India and Pakistan by accepting the statute of the Court and agreeing to the jurisdiction, far from impairing their sovereignty, [would exercise] it in aligning themselves with those nations that have freely chosen to live under the rule of law' (letter dated 21 November 1950). But Nehru thought that a hearing by the tribunal, consisting of an equal number of Indian and Pakistani judges as proposed by him, would make settlement easier and more expeditious than reference to 'a tribunal sitting thousands of miles away' (letter dated 24 November 1950). Liaquat on the other hand believed that a tribunal of undoubted standing, 'sitting thousands of miles away', would be in a better position to 'decide the question dispassionately and without getting entangled into the barbed wire of political controversy' (letter dated 27 November 1950).

[3] ibid., p. 260.

[4] ibid., p. 408.

the two parties concerned, and absolutely not through any form of arbitration.'[1]

If recent history is any guide, Pakistan's scepticism regarding the efficacy of a mere declaration to eradicate war is not without foundation. Neither the Kellogg–Briand Pact of 1928 nor the notorious German–Soviet Non-Aggression Pact of 1939 was able to ensure peace between those who had so solemnly subscribed to those documents. A suggestion to renounce force, moreover, is a well-known diplomatic ploy to ensure the preservation of the *status quo* in a given situation. Two examples of this strategy in recent years have been the United States exhortation to the People's Republic of China to renounce force as a method of enforcing her claim to Formosa, and the Soviet Union's suggestion of a non-aggression pact between the NATO powers and the Warsaw Pact powers. If accepted, the former suggestion would increase the chances of survival of the United States-backed Chiang Kai-shek regime and the latter would improve the prospects of a continuation of the division of Germany and of Russian hegemony over Eastern Europe. Israel's insistence on direct negotiations, after she occupied further Arab territories in the summer of 1967, is yet another instance of a country in possession of the subject matter of a dispute wishing to perpetuate the existing state of affairs under the cover of bilateral talks with a weaker opponent.

Liaquat Ali Khan's observation, after his exchanges with Nehru had ended fruitlessly, seems to Pakistanis as valid today as it was when their first Prime Minister made it in 1950. 'A declaration as suggested by him [Nehru],' Liaquat had concluded, 'would be utterly useless and would not carry us any further. It might possibly have served as a good basis for international propaganda but it could not have contributed to the solution of the problems in the least.'[2]

IV. Pakistan's Offer of Joint Defence
Almost as regularly as India asked Pakistan to make a no-war declaration, Pakistan, till 1962, invited India to enter into an arrangement by which they could jointly defend the subcontinent against all outsiders.

[1] *Notes, Memoranda and Letters exchanged between the Governments of India and China, White Paper No. IX*, p. 11. The text of Nehru's letter of 5 March 1963 to which Chou En-lai refers also appears in *White Paper No. IX*, pp. 5–7.

[2] *Constituent Assembly (Legislature) of Pakistan Debates*, 28 Nov. 1950, p. 829.

To make this story complete it is necessary briefly to refer to the relevant historical background. The Hindus of India, understandably, found it difficult to forget the successive invasions by Muslim conquerors from Central Asia or centuries of Muslim overlordship in India. It was therefore not surprising that many of them should have wondered whether history would repeat itself when the British departed from India. In a letter to C. R. Das, written in the nineteen-twenties, Lajpat Rai, a respected Hindu leader who was president of the Hindu Mahasabha for some time, said, 'I am not afraid of the seven crores of Mussalmans. But I think the seven crores in Hindustan plus the armed hordes of Afghanistan, Central Asia, Arabia, Mesopotamia, and Turkey will be irresistible.'[1]

That Pakistan singly, or in conjunction with one or more Muslim countries, would embark upon the conquest of India seems fantastic in the realities of today.[2] In fact it has been the Hindus who have thought of Pakistan as a part of mother India which must come back to her. Several Indian political parties such as the Hindu Mahasabha, the RSSS, and the Jan Sangh thrive mainly because they stand for militant Hindu nationalism and for Hindu supremacy in South Asia. But no leader or political party of any consequence in Pakistan has ever called for a reconquest of India by the Muslims.

Indeed, from the poet Iqbal onwards, Muslim leaders have uniformly recognized the need for Hindus and Muslims to combine against all outsiders who may threaten the Indo-Pakistani subcontinent. In the same presidential address, at the December 1930 session of the All-India Muslim League, in which Iqbal put forward the conception of a consolidated Muslim province in the north-west of India, he also envisaged that such an arrangement 'will intensify their [the Muslims'] sense of responsibility and deepen their patriotic feeling. Thus possessing full opportunity of development within the body-politic of India, the North-West India Muslims will prove the best defenders of India against a foreign invasion.'[3]

[1] Quoted by Jinnah in his presidential address at the annual session of the All-India Muslim League at Lahore on 22 March 1940. For text of address see Syed Sharifuddin Pirzada, *Evolution of Pakistan*, p. 290.

[2] It is amazing that a person of Krishna Menon's calibre, talking in the middle nineteen-sixties, should say that 'In Pakistan's view the Partition [of India, 1947] is only the beginning. Her idea is to get a jumping-off ground to take the whole of India. Their minds work in this way—that it was from the Moghuls that the British took over. Now, the British having gone, they must come back.' Michael Brecher, *India and World Politics*, pp. 170–1.

[3] Syed Sharifuddin Pirzada, *Evolution of Pakistan*, p. 125.

After the Pakistan resolution was passed at Lahore in 1940, the Hindus began to speculate once more whether the setting up of Pakistan would facilitate the conquest of India by a foreign Muslim power. Jinnah pointed out how illogical such fears were:

Why must you assume that when the Muslims have established their own independent sovereign state in the North-West zone, somebody else will be allowed to come over and rule over us, because he must rule over us before he rules over Hindu India? Therefore Muslim India will guard so far as the frontier is concerned and I hope the Hindus will guard so far as the South and Western India is concerned. (Cheers) We join together as good friends and neighbours and say to the world, 'Hands off India.'[1]

On 14 October 1944, and again on 15 November 1946, Jinnah said India and Pakistan will proclaim a 'Monroe Doctrine' of their own for the defence of the subcontinent against all outsiders.[2]

After independence, Jinnah, as Governor-General of Pakistan, visualized the future course of Indo-Pakistani relations in terms which remained the standard Pakistani policy till 1962: 'It is of vital importance to Pakistan and India as independent sovereign states to collaborate in a friendly way jointly to defend their frontiers both on land and sea against aggression.'[3] Some of the Pakistani overtures for joint defence made to India by Jinnah's successors were:

1. On 21 April 1949 Governor-General Nazimuddin stated in an interview that he foresaw defence arrangements between India and Pakistan.[4]

2. On 30 August 1952 General Ayub Khan contributed a letter to the India Cricket Souvenir published in Kanpur (India) in which he said, 'Realism demands that if Pakistan and India wish to retain their independence, so dearly won, the first thing they must do, and quickly, is to learn to live in peace with each other to meet jointly the impending dangers.'[5]

3. On 27 April 1953 Muhammad Ali Bogra, newly appointed Prime Minister of Pakistan, said in a public statement that once

---

[1] Jamil-ud-Din Ahmad (ed.), *Speeches and Writings of Mr. Jinnah*, Vol. I, p. 234.
[2] Jamil-ud-Din Ahmad (ed.), *Some Recent Speeches and Writings of Mr. Jinnah*, Vol. II, pp. 225, 474.
[3] M. Rafique Afzal (ed.), *Selected Speeches and Statements of the Quaid-i-Azam Mohammad Ali Jinnah*, p. 459.
[4] *New York Times*, 22 April 1949.
[5] Col. Mohammad Ahmed, *My Chief*, p. 26.

3

Indo-Pakistani disputes were settled, they could think of joint defence of India and Pakistan.[1]

4. On 8 September 1957 Foreign Minister Feroze Khan Noon stated that Pakistan would consider an attack on India as an attack on Pakistan provided Prime Minister Nehru honoured his international commitments with regard to the holding of a free and fair plebiscite in Kashmir.[2]

5. From 24 April 1959 onwards President Ayub Khan repeatedly offered joint defence to India provided the basic disputes between the two countries were resolved on fair terms.

Ayub appeared to have withdrawn the offer in April 1963 after the Sino-Pakistani border agreement, concluded the previous month, had signalled a marked improvement in Sino-Pakistani relations, while the Indo-Pakistani talks on Kashmir, then in progress under Anglo-US pressure, were proving fruitless as usual. In an interview at that time he said, 'A lot of water has flowed down the bridge [since his first offer of joint defence to India] and, unless the situation changes completely, the question of offering joint defence does not arise.'[3]

Those in India who never tire of criticizing Pakistan for joining the Western system of defence alliances and for improving her relations with China, as moves hostile to India, would do well to recall that Pakistan's first thought had been to seek the co-operation of neighbouring India for ensuring the safety of both countries against all outsiders. Pakistani leaders from Jinnah to Ayub were all realistic enough to realize that India, more than any other country, is Pakistan's natural partner for the defence of the subcontinent. It was India who spurned the Pakistani suggestion and, instead of inculcating a sense of security in the mind of her smaller neighbour, so that both countries could forget the unhappy past, continued to be the greatest source of danger to Pakistan, forcing the latter to look for protection elsewhere.

While the fate of the Pakistani idea of joint defence has now got involved with the question of China's relations with Pakistan and India, it is apparently still open to India to get her own proposal for a no-war declaration accepted by agreeing to arrangements ensuring the final settlement of the disputes which continue to estrange the two sister countries.

---

[1] Sisir Gupta, *Kashmir*, p. 258.
[2] *Dawn*, 9 Sept. 1957.
[3] *Pakistan News Digest*, 15 May 1963.

V. The Crisis of 1950 and the Liaquat-Nehru Pact

While the Prime Ministers of India and Pakistan were exchänging letters on the question of a no-war declaration, war nearly broke out between the two countries as a result of rioting against minorities in West Bengal, Assam, and Tripura in India, and in East Bengal in Pakistan, resulting in large-scale migrations in both directions.

It was only natural that each side should blame the other for the tension but it is amply clear that there was nothing comparable in Pakistan to the pressure in India for invading Pakistan and ending her separate existence. In the course of his presidential address to a Hindu Mahasabha conference in December 1949, B. N. Khare declared that Pakistan should be reabsorbed in India.[1] Deputy Prime Minister Sardar Patel said at Calcutta on 14 January 1950, 'If we can express sympathy with the people of South Africa and run to their assistance, it is easier to do so in the case of people in East Pakistan. Do not forget that important limbs of your mother India have been cut.'[2] Prime Minister Jawaharlal Nehru threatened in Parliament on 23 February 1950 to use 'other methods' against Pakistan to rectify her erring ways. This caused the *New York Times* to comment: 'What is surprising about Mr Nehru's somber threat is that it should be made by a leader who . . . insisted during his visit to this country that peace between East and West could be achieved without show or threat of force. Evidently he is not so convinced of the power of persuasion and negotiation on the home ground.' So strong was the movement for the invasion of Pakistan that even J. P. Narain, usually an advocate of Indo–Pakistani amity, suggested 'police action' in the Eastern wing of Pakistan,[3] raising in Pakistani memories the ghosts of similarly described Indian actions to annex Junagadh and Hyderabad.

These were not the utterances of irresponsible rabble-rousers but of respected leaders of public opinion and of the Deputy Prime Minister and the Prime Minister of India. Pakistanis were far from blameless but at responsible level they were all genuinely for curbing the disturbances, if for no other reasons than that Pakistan was in no condition to withstand an armed onslaught by India, and had far fewer resources and less territory than her bigger neighbour to cope with a new rush of destitute refugees.

The key figure in the tense situation was Prime Minister Nehru.

---

[1] Quoted by Liaquat in the Constituent Assembly on 28 March 1950.
[2] Quoted by G. W. Choudhry, *Pakistan's Relations with India*, p. 188.
[3] Speech at Nagpur, 7 March 1950, quoted by Sisir Gupta, *Kashmir*, p. 212.

He more than anyone else was in a position to decide the issue of war or peace. In the end his basic abhorrence of war prevailed over his flashes of anger. Not only did Nehru conclude an agreement with Liaquat against the wishes of a large body of his inflamed countrymen but he also stoutly defended it afterwards.

Liaquat arrived in New Delhi on 2 April 1950 and the Liaquat–Nehru Agreement was announced to the anxious millions in the subcontinent on 8 April. As Nehru himself put it, 'We have stopped ourselves at the edge of the precipice and turned our back to it.' The agreement promised to the minorities in both countries complete equality of citizenship, a full sense of security, and equal opportunity.

In Pakistan, militarily at the mercy of India, the agreement was welcomed with a great sense of relief. In India generally it was well received but in the crucial area of West Bengal the pact was bitterly denounced. Both the Bengali Ministers in Nehru's Cabinet handed over their resignations in protest. These were Shyamaprasad Mukerjee, Minister for Industries and Supply, and K. C. Neogy, Minister for Commerce. In its issue of 22 July 1950 the *Economist* said that, by the end of its first two months, the agreement had succeeded in completely stopping the net flow of Hindus from East Bengal to West Bengal but the flow of Muslims in the reverse direction, though very considerably reduced, had not stopped. 'The truth is', it commented, 'that many West Bengalis do not want the agreement to work.'

A paper agreement could not very well provide a ready cure for the disputes which were poisoning the relations between the two neighbours, nor for the deep-seated prejudices in people's minds. It stopped the drift towards war in 1950 but it could not prevent the numerous other crises that followed. In theory it subsists today.

VI. The Crisis of 1951

On 15 July Prime Minister Liaquat Ali Khan announced at a press conference in Karachi that heavy concentrations of Indian armed forces were massing in East Punjab and in Jammu and Kashmir.[1] At the same time Liaquat sent a telegram to the Prime Minister of India, alleging that the main reason for the existing state of

[1] For the text of Liaquat's statement to the press on 15 July 1951 and texts of telegrams exchanged by Liaquat and Nehru, beginning with Liaquat's telegram of 15 July and ending with his telegram of 11 Aug. 1951, see *India's Threat to Pakistan, Correspondence between the Prime Ministers of Pakistan and India, 15 July–11 Aug. 1951*, Ministry of Foreign Affairs and Commonwealth Relations (Pakistan), 1951.

tension was the persistent refusal by the Government of India to settle disputes between the two countries by peaceful means. He urged Nehru to remove the threat to Pakistan's security created by the forward move of the Indian forces.

In reply Nehru asserted that the armed forces of Pakistan had been largely massed on Indian frontiers and that an intensive campaign for *jihad* against India had been carried on in Pakistan. The Government of India could not ignore this and had ordered troop movements in defence (telegram dated 17 July 1951).

The real causes of the crisis of 1951 lay in the background against which the drama was enacted. The United Nations representative, Graham, was due to arrive in the subcontinent that summer to mediate the Kashmir dispute. On 20 April 1951 Yuraj Karan Singh, as Head of State in Kashmir, issued a proclamation calling for elections to a Constituent Assembly. Preparations for the elections continued throughout the summer and the polling took place early in autumn. Though India had given numerous assurances before the Security Council that the proposed Constituent Assembly would not determine the question of the accession of Kashmir, the National Conference in its resolution on 27 December 1950, proposing the setting up of the Assembly, had stated that the purpose of the Assembly was to determine 'the future shape and affiliations of the State'.

The *Manchester Guardian* observed that 'the most plausible explanation [for Indian troop movements against Pakistan] is that India is putting herself in an advantageous position before the meeting of the Constituent Assembly'.[1] A few weeks later the *Economist* said the same thing: 'Indian troops have been massed on the frontiers in order to keep Pakistan overawed while the Kashmir Constituent Assembly plays its preordained part of formally voting for accession to India.'[2]

The threat of Indian invasion caused considerable alarm within Pakistan and ordinances were promulgated to activate civil defence and air-raid services. On the Indo-Pakistani borders the Indian and the Pakistani Armies faced each other and any chance incident could have started an explosion which the politicians would have been powerless to control. As on all such unhappy occasions, the minorities on both sides were the worst sufferers. According to

[1] *Manchester Guardian*, 19 July 1951, quoted by G. W. Choudhury, *Pakistan's Relations with India*, p. 204.
[2] *Economist*, 25 Aug. 1951.

Indian estimates, 30,000 Hindus migrated from East Pakistan to West Bengal from 11 June to 24 June, while Pakistani sources said they had received an influx of 30,582 Muslims into East Pakistan during August.[1]

When Defence Day was celebrated on 27 July 1951, a two-mile procession, organized by the Karachi Provincial Muslim League, made its way to the residence of Prime Minister Liaquat Ali Khan. At the end of his speech, which was punctuated with cheers and slogans, the Pakistani Prime Minister said, 'From today onwards our symbol is this'. He then raised his clenched fist and stood in that position for a full three minutes. The crowd, numbering about 150,000, responded by clenching their fists.[2] President Ayub Khan, who was Commander-in-Chief of the Pakistani Army at the time, has disclosed that Liaquat told him, 'I am tired of these Indian threats. If this business is to be settled by war, then we shall have to take to war even though everyone of us is killed in the process.'[3]

In the end the danger of war, so grave while it lasted, just receded without any apparent exertion by either side. First the monsoon rains at the end of the summer made any deployment of heavy armour impossible. Secondly, with Graham's departure from the subcontinent on 12 September to prepare his first report, the spotlight on Kashmir was for the time being reduced in intensity. Thirdly, Pakistan was plunged in grief when Liaquat Ali Khan was shot to death on 16 October as he rose to address a public meeting at Rawalpindi.

VII. Turning Point in Pakistani Foreign Policy

Though the crises of 1950 and 1951 had mercifully passed without the outbreak of war between India and Pakistan, the traumatic experience through which Pakistanis had lived in those anxious days left a deep impression on the minds of the leaders as well as the people. Coming on top of the continuous tension of the preceding

---

[1] *Statesman*, 11 July 1951 and *Pakistan Times*, 17 Sept. 1951, both quoted by J. B. Das Gupta, *Indo-Pakistan Relations, 1947–1955*, pp. 229, 230.

[2] It would appear that Liaquat's symbol of the mailed fist was a reply to the leading article in the *Hindustan Times* of 23 July 1951 which had referred to the mailed fist directed by India against Pakistan. Liaquat mentioned that article in his telegram to Nehru dated 20 July. For a description of the demonstration at Liaquat's residence in the course of which he raised his fist see *Dawn*, 28 July 1951, and Government of Pakistan *Handout E. no. 2720* dated 27 July 1951.

[3] *Dawn*, 18 Oct. 1964.

years, the threat of invasion for two successive years made most
Pakistanis realize that they needed a powerful friend to support
and strengthen them against their much bigger neighbour. When
Liaquat told Commander-in-Chief Ayub Khan in 1951 that he was
tired of the constant threat and was prepared to accept India's
challenge to war, Ayub warned him that Pakistan had only thirteen
tanks with about forty to fifty hours' engine life in them to face the
Indian Army. 'Not only politicians but our troops were itching to
settle accounts with India', Ayub recalls. 'It was my job to hold them
back which, thank Heavens, I did.'[1]

By 1951, therefore, Pakistan had begun seriously to look around
for a protector. Her overtures to the Commonwealth and the
Muslim countries for special ties had failed to elicit the desired
response and Pakistan was not yet prepared to turn to the Communist countries because of ideological differences with them and
also because neither new China nor war-ravaged Russia at that stage
was in a position to render any substantial help to others. This left
the USA as the obvious, indeed the only, choice. By August 1951
Ayub, for one, was 'definitely thinking' in terms of requesting
military aid from the USA.[2]

By a coincidence it was in the same year of 1951 that any hope
the US may still have entertained that India might join the West
in its confrontation with the East, was extinguished by the Indian
role in the important questions of the Korean War and the Japanese
Peace Treaty. Pakistan, on the other hand, proved herself a good
friend of the Western powers on these and other issues. All the
signs had thus begun to point towards a closer relationship between
Pakistan and the US.[3]

---

[1] M. Ayub Khan, *Friends Not Masters*, p. 40.
[2] Major-General F. M. Khan, *The Story of the Pakistan Army*, p. 154.
[3] For details see 'Pakistan and the United States of America' in chapter 6.

4 Pakistan and the Muslim World

The poet Muhammad Iqbal said that the ultimate purpose of the prophetic mission of Muhammad was to create a form of society which followed that divine law which the Prophet Muhammad received from God. In other words the object was to purify the nations of the world of the abuses which go by the name of time, piace, land, nation, race, genealogy, country, etc.[1] In Islam God and the universe, spirit and matter, church and state, are organic to each other.[2] If one begins with the conception of religion as complete other-worldliness, then what has happened to Christianity in Europe is perfectly natural. The universal ethics of Jesus has been displaced by national systems of ethics and polity.[3] But the construction of a polity on national lines, if it means a displacement of the Islamic principle of solidarity, is simply unthinkable to a Muslim.[4] Iqbal thought there was an historical reason for the separation of the Church from the State in European political thought. Primitive Christianity, he argued, was founded not as a political or a civil unit, but as a monastic order in a profane world, having nothing to do with civil affairs, and obeying the Roman authority in all practical matters. The result of this was that, when the State became Christian, State and Church confronted each other as distinct powers with interminable boundary disputes between them. Such a thing could never happen in Islam, for Islam was from the very beginning a civil society, having received from the Quran a set of simple legal principles which, like the twelve tables of the Romans, carried great potentialities of expansion and development by interpretation. The nationalist theory of State, therefore, is misleading inasmuch as it suggests a dualism

---

[1] Shamloo, *Speeches and Statements of Iqbal*, p. 236.
[2] ibid., p. 5.
[3] ibid., p. 5.
[4] ibid., p. 9.

which does not exist in Islam.[1] These views led Iqbal to say in one of his poems, '*Muslim hein hum wattan hai sara jehan hamara*' (We are Muslims, our motherland is the entire universe). After independence, a Pakistani writer, summing up the Pakistani conception of Islam, stated that Islam itself is a nationality.[2]

Until 1924 the symbol of universal Islamic unity for the Indian Muslims was the Sultan of Turkey in his capacity as the Khalifa of Islam, and the fate of Turkey, therefore, deeply stirred their emotions. During the Russo-Turkish war of 1877 religious services were held in the mosques in Calcutta and subscriptions were collected for the Turkish wounded. All subsequent Turkish causes similarly evoked Muslim sympathy in India. Notable amongst these were the wars against Greece (1897), Italy (1911), and the Balkan League (1912). During the Balkan War the Muslims of India sent a medical mission to Turkey, under Dr. M. A. Ansari. When the Bulgarians approached Constantinople, Maulana Muhammad Ali was so overcome with grief that he seriously contemplated suicide.[3]

After the First World War, in which Turkey had been on the losing side, the Muslims of India tried their utmost to ensure that the territorial and spiritual status of the Sultan should remain intact. 'About the middle of 1920,' noted Subhas Bose, 'anti-British feeling was stronger among the Moslems than among the rest of the Indian population.'[4] A Khilafat movement was inaugurated in India, and two delegations, one led by Maulana Muhammad Ali and the other by the Aga Khan, journeyed to London to plead on behalf of the Sultan.

It so happened that at that very time the Congress Party, hitherto a loyal organization, was also contemplating rebellion against the British because, instead of rewarding Indians with greater freedom for their co-operation in the war effort, the British Government

---

[1] Iqbal's doctrine, that religion and the State are inseparable, was not, however, acted upon by Mustafa Kemal, the maker of modern Turkey. When the Aga Khan sent Kemal a message in 1923 adjuring him not to weaken the moral hold of the Khilafat by divorcing it from politics, Kemal, while not repudiating Islam, held that it was 'indispensable, in order to secure the revival of the Islamic faith, to disengage it from the condition of being a political instrument'. *Economist*, 13 Feb. 1954.

Iqbal thinks 'the Turkish Nationalists assimilated the idea of the separation of the Church and the State from the history of European political ideas'. Muhammad Iqbal, *The Reconstruction of Religious Thought in Islam*, p. 155.

[2] Aslam Siddiqi, *Pakistan Seeks Security*, p. 160.

[3] R. A. J. Nadvi, *Selections From Muhammad Ali's Comrade*, p. 40.

[4] S. C. Bose, *The Indian Struggle*, p. 41.

passed the notorious Rowlatt Bills, which authorized the continuation in peace time of certain special powers the Government
of India had assumed during the First World War. The most
serious incident during the agitation was the horrible massacre of
Jalianwalla Bagh in Amritsar (Punjab), in April 1919, when General
Dyer ordered his troops to fire at a meeting of over 20,000 men,
women, and children, in an almost enclosed space, killing 379 and
wounding 1,500 others. Martial law was imposed in all the important
towns in the Punjab and the movement was brutally suppressed.

Realizing that such an opportunity of uniting Hindus and Muslims
'will not occur for another hundred years',[1] Gandhi placed himself
in the forefront of the Khilafat movement as well as the agitation
for the repeal of the Rowlatt Act and the redress of the Punjab
atrocities, and he launched the first of his famous non-cooperation
movements.

The *raison d'être* for Hindu–Muslim unity, however, ceased to
exist in March 1924 when the Turks themselves abolished the
institution of the Khilafat. Instead of bringing the Muslims closer
to the Hindus, the Khilafat movement, by inciting the pan-Islamic
feeling of the Muslims, in the long run served to widen the gulf
between them. The fanatical feelings roused by the Khilafat
movement, in fact, led to the ugly Moplah Rebellion in 1921, at the
very time when Hindu–Muslim unity was supposed to be at its
zenith. The Moplahs, who are Muslims and mostly peasants and
fishermen by vocation, started with the aim of replacing British
rule by a Khilafat kingdom, but they soon fell upon the Hindus,
who were near at hand and represented the more prosperous land-
owner and moneylending classes. 'By the middle of 1923,' observed
the Simon Commission, 'communal riots, marked by murder,
arson and looting, were almost monthly occurrences. In 1924 fierce
outbursts occurred in many of the greater cities of the North.'[2]

The abolition of the Khilafat by Turkey formed a watershed in
the evolution of Muslim politics in India. Muslim hopes, having
lost their outside focal point, turned inward. In his famous presidential address to the Muslim League at Allahabad, in 1930, Iqbal
stressed that seventy million Muslims in India constituted 'a far
more valuable asset to Islam than all the countries of Muslim Asia
put together'.[3] A few years later he wrote to Jinnah that 'the whole

---

[1] Quoted by R. Coupland, *India, A Re-Statement*, p. 122.
[2] *Cmd. 3568*, 1930, p. 253.
[3] Shamloo, *Speeches and Statements of Iqbal*, p. 34.

future of Islam as a moral and political force in Asia rests very largely on a complete organization of Indian Muslims'.[1]

The unification of a part only of the Muslims of the world under the flag of Pakistan was thus not viewed by the founding fathers of Pakistan as the culmination of their efforts but merely as a necessary milestone on the journey towards the ultimate goal of universal Muslim solidarity. Prime Minister Liaquat Ali Khan eloquently expressed the true aspirations of all Pakistanis when he stated that Pakistan came into being as a result of the urge of the Muslims of the subcontinent to secure territory where Islamic ideology could be practised and demonstrated to the world and, since a cardinal feature of this ideology is to make Muslim brotherhood a reality, it was a part of her mission to do everything in her power to promote fellowship and co-operation between Muslim countries.[2]

However, the issues facing Muslims in the predominantly Muslim countries of the world were different from those confronting the Indian Muslims. The latter were surrounded by a non-Muslim majority which subscribed to a highly receptive faith, and Islam was their only defence against the threatened loss of identity. In Iqbal's words, Islam furnished them with 'those basic emotions and loyalties which gradually unify scattered individuals and groups and finally transform them into a well-defined people. . . . India is perhaps the only country in the world where Islam, as a people-building force, has worked at its best.'[3]

But Islam was not an issue in the politics of other Muslim lands. As the age of imperialism approached its end, nationalism in those countries took the familiar form of territorial, racial, and linguistic nationalism, for the problem there simply was how to get rid of European domination. The task before the Indian Muslims, however, was uniquely complex. Like all other peoples who were struggling to be free, they wished to get rid of the foreigner. But how were they, at the same time, to escape the yoke of the more numerous Hindus, whose claim to the same homeland was even more ancient than their own, except by claiming a separate share of the territory on the basis of Islam? Luckily for them, although the Hindus commanded the majority on an all-India basis, the Muslims predominated in the western and eastern parts of the

[1] *Letters of Iqbal to Jinnah*, p. 11.

[2] From Liaquat's inaugural speech at the Motamar-e-Alam-e-Islami session at Karachi on 9 Feb. 1951. Government of Pakistan, *Handout E. no. 484* dated 9 Feb. 1951.

[3] Shamloo, *Speeches and Statements of Iqbal*, p. 4.

country. They therefore pressed that these wings be separated from the rest of the subcontinent and constituted into the Islamic State of Pakistan.

While the device of dividing the country provided the only means of real freedom to the Indian Muslims, the very word partition was anathema to Muslims elsewhere. For the latter it conjured up the example of Ireland, the spectres of the proposed partition of Palestine, and the separation of the Sudan from Egypt; and they viewed the partition of India as yet another manifestation of the same imperialistic strategy of divide and rule. Finding direct control of the subcontinent no longer feasible, Britain, they thought, was now resorting to the trick of divide and quit so that the new nations of India and Pakistan would remain weak and at loggerheads with each other, enabling the erstwhile ruling power to continue its overall domination. It seemed to them that the Muslim League, by demanding a division of the motherland, was playing into the hands of British imperialism, while the Congress Party was putting up a genuine fight for freedom, just as they themselves were doing.

Though the approach of the Pakistani Muslims to the task of achieving the solidarity of Islam is now less naïve than it was in the early years of Pakistan, and they have increasingly begun to realize that there are important differences of outlook between themselves and fellow-Muslims of other lands, their desire to serve the cause of Islam is as ardent as ever. Muslims of other countries, for their part, have also learned, with the passage of time, to view the Indo-Pakistani problem with greater understanding, and Pakistan's genuine concern for their welfare with increasing appreciation. Pakistan's relations with Muslim countries, in fact, have passed through three distinct phases.

The earliest period (1947–54) was marked by Pakistan's efforts to forge closer links between Muslim countries by playing host at various conferences. In retrospect these moves seem to have been over-optimistic and amateurish but those were the heady days of newly won independence and it needed time and experience to develop the capacity to view matters in perspective. There were references then to Pakistan being the largest Muslim state and the fifth largest country in the world. Such talk from a country the rationale of whose creation was little understood at the time, and whose capacity to survive bore a large question mark, naturally was not well received by other countries, proud of their own heritage. If the matter had rested with the various conferences staged by Pakistan, she would have earned little respect for her endeavours to build up the solidarity of Islam. What, however, did win Pakistan a measure of esteem was her consistent and effective advocacy of Muslim causes, many of which happened to come before the United Nations during her early years. But just as Pakistan was beginning to gain ground in the Muslim world she joined the Baghdad Pact, and with it began the second phase (1955-7) during which her relations with the Arab countries, the heart of the Muslim world, reached their lowest ebb. The third phase began in 1958 when Pakistan became emotionally estranged from her most powerful ally, the USA, and, on the rebound, once more began to look towards her first and greatest love, the Muslim countries. Both Pakistan and the other Muslim nations now looked at each other with better understanding and their relations registered a growing improvement.

With two important Muslim countries, Egypt and Indonesia, Pakistan's relations in the early years were less than satisfactory. In November 1951 the Egyptian Foreign Minister, Salah el Din Pasha, told an Indian correspondent in Cairo that Egypt looked to India for moral support in her struggle for national liberation.[1] King Farouq was reported to have ridiculed Pakistan's over-zealous devotion to Islamic causes by saying to his courtiers, 'Don't you know that Islam was born on 14 August 1947?'[2]

When the Dutch took police action against Indonesia in December 1948, Pakistanis demonstrated their genuine concern in various ways. In Parliament Foreign Minister Zafrulla Khan called it 'an affront to the soul of Asia' and Pakistan immediately suspended the licence of the Dutch airline, KLM, whose aircraft were being used to aid the Dutch military action. When Indonesian independence was recognized Pakistan celebrated the event by declaring a public holiday. Indonesia, however, at this time felt much closer to India because, like the latter, she had made secularism, non-alignment, and socialism the main pillars of her policy. During Nehru's visit to Indonesia in December 1950, President Soekarno publicly said Nehru politically was his 'father'.[3]

Pakistan's relations with Turkey and Iran, however, were cordial from the first day, foreshadowing the formal co-operation between the three countries first in the Baghdad Pact and later in the Regional Co-operation for Development (RCD). The deep agony with which

[1] *Indian Press Digests for the period 16 Sept. to 15 Nov. 1951*, vol. I, no. 2, p. 29.
[2] *Dawn*, 27 Sept. 1956.
[3] *Statesman*, 9 June 1950.

Indian Muslims had viewed the decline of the Ottoman empire and the demise of the Khilafat was transformed into admiration for the way the new Republic of Turkey emerged as a vigorous, modern state from the ashes of the Sultanate. Pakistan's abiding love for Iran arises from the fact that not only is Iran an immediate neighbour but also the mother of Pakistani culture.[1]

I. Relations with Afghanistan

One of the most painful experiences of Pakistan has been the almost continuous hostility of the neighbouring Muslim State of Afghanistan. With the threat of India perpetually looming from the east and north-east of West Pakistan, Afghan pressure on the western flank greatly added to Pakistan's already heavy burden of anxieties. As Ian Stephens has pointed out, if, on Pakistan's birth, 'co-ordinated movements opposed to her could be produced in Kashmir and Afghanistan, both of them predominantly Muslim territories near to one another, the new State [of Pakistan] might be still-born, crushed by a sort of pincer movement'.[2]

Pakistan's problem with Afghanistan has resulted from Afghan ambitions in respect of certain areas in the north-west and west of West Pakistan which, for a brief period, formed a part of the territories conquered by Ahmad Shah, the first native-born king of Afghanistan who reigned from 1747 to 1773. Ahmad Shah's successors, including the present king of Afghanistan, all Durranis like Ahmad Shah, have considered themselves natural heirs to the transitory empire of their illustrious kinsman and have fondly cherished the dream of recovering its lost parts.

Towards the middle of the nineteen-forties, when it began to appear that Britain would soon have to relinquish her Indian empire, the Government of Afghanistan represented to Britain that the people of the frontier lands be given the choice of becoming independent or reuniting with their 'motherland' (Afghanistan). But this move failed to create any enthusiasm among the people of the area for joining Afghanistan. Thereupon Afghanistan, at least outwardly and for the time being, gave up her irredentist claims and began to devote her energy to playing the seemingly more altruistic role of champion of the cause of independence for the Pakhtuns,

---

[1] So pervasive is Irani culture in northern India that Jawaharlal's father, Motilal Nehru, though a Hindu, 'had grown up in an Indo-Persian cultural atmosphere'. J. Nehru, *An Autobiography*, p. 169.

[2] Ian Stephens, *Horned Moon*, p. 108.

with a state of their own to be called 'Pakhtunistan'. This state
would come into being by detaching the following parts from West
Pakistan: the frontier states of Dir, Swat, Chitral, and Amb;
Baluchistan and the Baluchistan states of Kalat, Kharan, Makran, and
Las Bela.[1] It will be helpful at the outset to recall how the various
lands just named became a part of Pakistan in the first instance.

On the eve of partition 'a bastard situation'[2] prevailed in the
North-West Frontier Province.[3] A Congress Ministry under Khan
Sahib was still holding office in that 92 per cent Muslim province
though the majority of the people had gone over to the League, now
that a Muslim homeland was definitely within sight.[4] The difficulty
was resolved by inserting a provision in the partition plan that the
question whether the Frontier Province should belong to India or
Pakistan would be decided by the electors of the provincial Legislative Assembly in a referendum.

Realizing that the proposed referendum in the changed atmosphere
of the Frontier would result in a victory for Pakistan, 'Congress
tried a little sleight of hand ... by suggesting that the referendum
which was to take place under the terms of the plan should not be
simply to decide whether the population should choose Pakistan
or Hindustan, but also whether it should become an independent
State.'[5] But the proposed independence was simply a stratagem to

[1] For fuller details see the next section which is devoted to a discussion of 'The
Afghan Case'.

[2] Lord Ismay's phrase. Alan Campbell-Johnson, *Mission With Mountbatten*, p. 54.

[3] Strictly speaking, the North-West Frontier of British days consisted only of the
five 'settled' or 'administered' districts but, as the charge of the 'unadministered'
Tribal Agencies, or Tribal Areas, was also held by the Chief Commissioner (in his
capacity as Agent to the Governor-General), it was common to refer to both parts as
though, together, they constituted one province.

[4] That the Muslim League had become the favourite was unmistakably demonstrated by the local population during Nehru's and Mountbatten's visits to the frontier
in October 1946 and April 1947 respectively. For a description of what transpired see
M. A. K. Azad, *India Wins Freedom*, p. 200, and Campbell-Johnson, *Mission With
Mountbatten*, p. 74.

Abdul Ghaffar Khan, elder brother of Khan Sahib, started his Red Shirt movement
in 1920 because of Pathan resentment against the British Government for denying to
their province the representative institutions given to other provinces in India under the
new reforms. The Congress being the only really effective political party in India at the
time, the Red Shirts joined forces with it against the British. They were popularly
called *Surkhposhan* (Red Shirts) because of the colour of the shirts they wore as a
uniform. Their official designation was *Khudai Khidmatgaran* (Servants of God). In the
course of a day-long discussion at his village, in 1939, Khan Abdul Ghaffar Khan told
me that he had affiliated his movement with the Congress Party mainly to ensure its
survival. As a purely local organization the British Government could have easily
crushed it without the knowledge of the outside world.

[5] Leonard Mosley, *The Last Days of the British Raj*, p. 131.

tide over the immediate problem of preventing the Frontier from joining Pakistan. In his report to London Mountbatten stated, 'Nehru quite openly admitted that the NWFP could not possibly stand by itself, and it became clear to me that this was a device to free Khan Sahib's party from the odium (in a largely Muslim province) of being connected with Congress during the referendum period, since Nehru spoke about Khan Sahib wishing to join the Union of India at a subsequent stage.'[1] Failing to have the option of independence included in the questionnaire of the referendum, the Khan brothers called upon their followers to boycott the poll. Nevertheless, the referendum in the North-West Frontier Province (the five settled districts) was duly held from 6 to 17 July 1947. To meet the Congress objection, that the Governor and his senior officers were siding with the Muslim League, it was arranged by Mountbatten that the Governor, Sir Olaf Caroe, should proceed on leave and the poll be conducted by a specially appointed military regime with Lieut.-General Sir Rob Lockhart as acting Governor and Brigadier J. B. Booth as the Referendum Commissioner.

Out of a total electorate of 572,798, just over 50 per cent took part. Pakistan received 289,244 votes and India 2,874. Pakistan thus secured an absolute majority of the total number of votes cast.[2]

But a plebiscite such as the one held in the Frontier Province could not possibly be arranged for ascertaining the wishes of the inhabitants of the Tribal Agencies for the simple reason that the latter had no legislature and, therefore, no electoral roll. The

[1] ibid., p. 132.

[2] V. P. Menon, *The Transfer of Power in India*, p. 389. Some writers have stated that more than half the total number of voters refrained from exercising their right in response to Ghaffar Khan's appeal and must be presumed to have favoured independence, but the figures show that more than half the electorate positively voted for Pakistan. Moreover, at no election do 100 per cent of the electors ever turn out to register their opinion and it is anybody's guess why a particular person fails to show up. In the 1946 election in the North-West Frontier Province no more than 68 per cent of the electorate had voted. Finally, it should be remembered that many of the absentees must have been Hindus and Sikhs who constituted 13 per cent of the voters' list (though not of the population).

Pakistan and India differed from each other on most matters, but it is noteworthy that neither of them questioned the impartiality of the frontier referendum. Though the result overwhelmingly favoured Pakistan against India, India signified her confidence in Lockhart's integrity by afterwards appointing him the first Commander-in-Chief of the Army of independent India. There is thus no substance in the repeated Afghan allegation that the vote was 'rigged'. The Congress suspicion, that the Governor was not impartial, was also without foundation. Mountbatten was convinced of Sir Olaf's 'straightforwardness' and desire to act impartially, but did not wish to take up any position which might stand in the way of a smooth transfer of power to Indian hands. H. V. Hodson, *The Great Divide*, pp. 282-8.

representative institution in the Tribal Agencies was the *jirga* of each tribe and it was through their *jirgas* that the tribesmen governed themselves and expressed their preferences. Britain was content simply to exercise political sovereignty. There was no civil police or organized magistracy and no taxes of any kind were levied. The British connection was based on special agreements with the various tribes negotiated through their respective *jirgas*. The underlying motive for utilizing this simple traditional constitutional machinery, as will be explained later, was not so much to allow 'independence' to tribesmen as to save the Central Government from having to deal with an internationally important and highly sensitive frontier area through a provincial government whose direct responsibility did not extend to matters of foreign policy. And of course the tribesmen did not at all mind being left alone to regulate their daily life in accordance with their own age-old usages. So the partition plan of 3 June 1947 laid down that fresh 'agreements with the tribes of the North-West Frontier of India would have to be negotiated by the appropriate successor authority'. This was done on behalf of Pakistan, in November 1947, by Sir George Cunningham, then Governor of the North-West Frontier Province, in the only manner known to the tribes. 'I interviewed the *jirgas* of all the big tribes from end to end of the frontier', explained Sir George afterwards. 'Without exception they stated and confirmed in written statements that they were part of Pakistan, and wished to preserve the same relations with Pakistan as they had with the British. This agreement was ratified by the Pakistan Government.'[1]

The rulers of the four frontier states of Dir, Swat, Chitral, and Amb also led their subjects into Pakistan by executing Instruments of Accession in favour of that Dominion.

Baluchistan's constitutional position was similar to that of the Tribal Areas of the north-west. The ties with the ruling power there, too, consisted of agreements with the tribes. In the 3 June official pronouncement it was stipulated that the province would be given an opportunity to choose between Pakistan and India and it was stated that the Governor-General was 'examining how this can most appropriately be done'. Ultimately it was decided by the British Government to entrust the responsibility for the decision to the Shahi Jirga and the non-official members of the Quetta municipality who unanimously opted for Pakistan. This was followed

[1] 'Pakistan's North-West Frontier and the Tribes', *Statesmen*, 28 May 1949 (reproduced in *Pakistan Affairs*, 23 June 1949).

by accession to Pakistan by the Baluchistan States of Kharan, Makran, and Las Bela. The Khan of Kalat harboured the idea of independence for some time but in the end he, too, declared for Pakistan.

Afghanistan's earliest formal move was made in November 1944 when it had become fairly obvious that Britain could not long deny independence to India. The Afghan authorities approached London for an assurance that, in the event of India becoming independent, the people of those frontier areas which had been annexed by Britain during the previous century would be given the choice of becoming independent or reuniting with their 'motherland'. A representation was simultaneously made that Afghanistan be given a corridor to the sea through Baluchistan in order to improve her economic position.

After the announcement of the partition plan on 3 June 1947, Afghanistan mounted a vigorous public and diplomatic campaign that all tribes living between the Indo-Afghan frontier, called the Durand Line, and the river Indus be allowed to say whether they wished to become completely independent or revert to Afghanistan. His Majesty's Government in London took up the position that the territories claimed by Afghanistan were an integral part of India, having been recognized as such by the Anglo-Afghan treaty of 1921, and that Afghanistan, therefore, had no *locus standi* to interfere in the arrangements concerning their future. The British Government could deal with the situation only as it existed at the time of transfer of power. An historical investigation of the Afghan claim, they pointed out, could very well end up with India claiming the whole of Afghanistan instead of Afghanistan claiming a part of India.

Afghanistan soon realized, also, that there was no desire among the Pathans on the Indian side of the Durand Line to join Afghanistan. Even the Khan brothers, who represented the extreme opposition to Pakistan, did not entertain union with Afghanistan as one of the acceptable alternatives. When they realized that there was no chance whatever of the referendum going in favour of India, their organization resolved 'that the issues should be amended on the basis of Pakistan and free Pathan State'.[1] There was no mention in the resolution of joining Afghanistan. On 2 July 1947 Dr. Khan Sahib wrote to Pandit Nehru, 'We assure you that we have never thought of joining Afghanistan. . . . We have also learnt for the first time

[1] Ghaffar Khan's letter of 11 June 1947 to Gandhi. Pyarelal, *Mahatma Gandhi: The Last Phase*, II, p. 273.

that the Afghan Government have officially approached the Government of India. We having been placed in an unenviable position, naturally, the Afghan Government are taking advantage of it and exploiting the situation.'[1] After the referendum had gone in favour of Pakistan, Ghaffar Khan further adjusted his position in the light of the new reality. He declared, at a meeting of his followers, that all they demanded was 'full freedom for the Pathans to manage their internal affairs as a unit within Pakistan State'. One of the resolutions adopted at the meeting ran: 'This new State will comprise the present six settled districts of the NWFP and all such other contiguous areas inhabited by the Pathans which may wish to join the new State of their own free will. This State will enter into agreement on defence, external affairs, and communications with the Dominion of Pakistan.'[2] Once again, though there was still a desire for local autonomy, there was no suggestion of any constitutional links with Afghanistan. Unable to find any supporters for union with Afghanistan, the Afghan authorities thought it wiser not to press irredentist claims directly but to concentrate upon the apparently selfless issue of independence.

Afghan pressure on Pakistan has been almost continuous and at times has resulted in a state of high tension between the two neighbours. When Pakistan's application for admission to the United Nations came up in the General Assembly on 30 September 1947 the Afghan representative, Hosayn Aziz, cast the only opposing vote, because 'we cannot recognize the North-West Frontier Province as part of Pakistan so long as the people of the North-West Frontier have not been given an opportunity free from any kind of influence—and I repeat, free from any kind of influence—to determine for themselves whether they wish to be independent or to become a part of Pakistan.'[3] On 20 October, however, Aziz withdrew the negative vote and expressed the hope that agreement between Afghanistan and Pakistan would be reached as a result of the discussions then taking place through diplomatic channels.[4]

In November 1947 Sardar Najibullah Khan came to Karachi as special envoy of His Majesty King Zahir Shah of Afghanistan, and held talks with Pakistani officials. On his return home Najibullah said in a broadcast that Afghanistan had made three demands on

[1] Pyarelal, *Mahatma Gandhi: The Last Phase*, II, p. 281.
[2] ibid., p. 282.
[3] *General Assembly Official Records, 92nd Plenary Meeting*, 30 Sept. 1947.
[4] ibid., 20 Oct. 1947.

Pakistan: first, the tribal areas inhabited by Pathans and Afghans must be constituted into a free, sovereign province; secondly, Pakistan must give Afghanistan access to the sea either by the creation of an Afghan corridor in West Baluchistan or by allotting a free Afghan Zone in Karachi; and thirdly, Afghanistan and Pakistan should enter into a treaty which should permit one party to remain neutral if the other was attacked.[1]

A brief description of some of the developments will illustrate the trend of Pakistani–Afghan relations during the years immediately following.

On 12 July 1949 a Pakistani Air Force plane bombed an Afghan village near the border but, a joint commission of the representatives of both countries having found that the bombing was accidental, the matter was peacefully settled upon payment of damages by Pakistan. But the amicable end of the plane incident did not cure the root of the trouble. King Zahir Shah chose the inauguration of the seventh session of the Afghan National Assembly on 30 June 1949 as the occasion for making an anti-Pakistani speech, and the Assembly itself proceeded to pass a resolution repudiating all treaties, conventions, and agreements signed between the Afghan and British Governments before the birth of Pakistan and rejecting the Durand Line as the international frontier between Afghanistan and Pakistan. The resolution also referred to the alleged repression of the 'Afghan' provinces and states from Chitral to Baluchistan and promised support to the Afghan Government in its efforts to achieve freedom for the inhabitants of those places.[2] Afghan radio and press propaganda against Pakistan continued unabated and there were also reports of Afghan raids into Pakistan.

Afghan sources asserted that, in August 1949, a number of Afridi tribesmen met at Tirah and inaugurated the 'National Assembly of Pakhtunistan'.[3] Another *jirga* was stated to have met at Razmak and elected the Faqir of Ipi as the President of southern 'Pakhtunistan'.[4] In an exclusive interview published in the *Indian News Chronicle* on 4 March 1950 Sardar Najibullah Khan, Afghan Ambassador to India, said that tribesmen were electing regional assemblies preparatory to electing a Central Assembly to set up a Central Government for 'Pakhtunistan'.

[1] I. H. Baqai, 'Relations Between Afghanistan and Pakistan', *Pakistan Horizon*, Sept. 1948.
[2] *Dawn*, 15 July 1949.
[3] Rahman Pazhwak, *Pakhtunistan*, p. 124.
[4] Arnold Fletcher, *Afghanistan: Highway of Conquest*, p. 255.

Prime Minister Liaquat Ali Khan said in the Constituent Assembly of Pakistan on 9 January 1950 that these 'national assemblies have not been formed by the people of the areas concerned but they have been set up on paper in Kabul'.[1]

As could well be expected, India did not fail to encourage Afghanistan's efforts to harass Pakistan. A number of 'Pakhtunistan' days were celebrated in Indian cities and Indian orators and editors upheld Afghan claims.[2]

On the credit side, the Government of Pakistan, in December 1947, ordered the withdrawal of troops from the frontier areas. This was a sensible move, because if the sense of freedom and belonging to Pakistan was to be brought home to the tribesmen, it was essential that there no longer be an army of occupation in their homeland to gall their sense of self-respect. The Pakistani authorities also, despite innumerable demands on their slender resources, earnestly set about improving the economic and social conditions in the tract. *The Times* noted, on 29 June 1949, that the tribesmen continued to draw from the Pakistani exchequer some 50 million rupees a year in subsidies, just as they did in British days, and pointed out that this sum exceeded the total budget of Afghanistan. The Government was also embarked on large-scale hydroelectric and irrigation schemes to bring greater prosperity to the tribesmen.

A natural result of the tension between the two countries was the virtual stoppage of trade between them and the interruption of transit facilities which landlocked Afghanistan had traditionally enjoyed through Pakistani ports and territory. To reduce her dependence on Pakistan, Afghanistan, in July 1950, signed a trade and transit agreement with the Soviet Union, who had been eagerly waiting for just such a chance to come her way. The Soviets agreed to export petroleum products, cotton cloth, sugar, and other commodities in return for Afghan wool and raw cotton. They also agreed to permit free transit of Afghan goods through Soviet territory, and to build petrol storage tanks within Afghanistan. The Soviets continued skilfully to press their advantage and by 1952 trade between the USSR and Afghanistan had doubled, and some Soviet technicians had arrived in Afghanistan. In 1954 the Soviet

---

[1] A writer who made half a dozen trips through the tribal area in 1951–4 found that 'the whole "governmental organization" of "Pakhtunistan" appears to exist in theory rather than in fact, and even the theory is often elusive'. James W. Spain, *The Pathan Borderland*, p. 237.

[2] Arnold Fletcher, *Afghanistan: Highway of Conquest*, p. 255.

Union granted a loan of approximately $18 million for the construction of more storage tanks, wheat silos, a flour mill and a bakery, and for the paving of streets in Kabul.[1]

II. An Examination of the Afghan Case

One of the more substantial statements of the Afghan case has been made in the form of a 153-page book called *Pakhtunistan* by Rahman Pazhwak,[2] an Afghan career diplomat. Without mentioning any time in history when a unit comprising the areas now claimed for 'Pakhtunistan' ever stood by itself politically, the Afghan protagonist avers that the most important districts and passes which form the 'Pakhtunistan' of 'today' are Chitral, Hazara, Kohistan, Swat, Dir, Buner, Peshawar, Tirah, Bajaur, Kohat, Bannu, Dera-Ghazi-Khan, Dera-Ismail-Khan, Waziristan, Khyber, Pezu, Gomal, Bolan, and Malakand.[3] He then gives a description of these districts and their natural resources and concludes that the existing and potential wealth of the area is such that 'the Pakhtuns have realized that once the preservation of their freedom and independence is assured, to which all their energies have inescapably been bent in the past, they can proceed to build a prosperous life for themselves in their homeland'. A factor of great importance, according to the Afghan author, is that 'Pakhtunistan' has the advantage of access to the sea in Baluchistan.[4] Then follows a list of 'clans' which inhabit 'Pakhtunistan' and it is noteworthy that the total runs to no less than twenty-three separate clans.

In a society where the social and administrative unit throughout history has been the tribe, and where the first loyalty has traditionally been given to that unit, there is obviously little chance of a feeling of national unity being born, still less of its getting firmly established. There would be resentment against outside interference and foreign domination no doubt, and the various tribes on the northwest frontier of the Indian subcontinent, after the manner of

---

[1] John N. Gatch, Jr., 'The Soviet Aid Programme', *Current Problems in Afghanistan*, p. 143.

[2] The book does not bear the publisher's name nor the year of publication. Its foreword indicates that the author was serving in the Embassy of Afghanistan in London when he wrote it and that it was probably published privately in the early nineteen-fifties.

[3] p. 10. See also p. 8. It may be pointed out that the area includes a number of non-Pakhtun territories such as Chitral, Kohistan, Hazara, Dera-Ghazi-Khan, and Baluchistan south of Quetta, i.e. the states of Kalat, Kharan, Makran, Las Bela, and the Chagai area and Bolan.

[4] p. 27.

mountainous people elsewhere, have managed to preserve their own peculiar way of life. But it hardly follows from this that collectively they have ever formed a nation. It is, therefore, not surprising that the only time in history when they are stated by Pazhwak to have converted the dream of nationhood into reality is 'today'. After mentioning the poet Khushhal Khatak's fight for independence against the Emperor Aurengzeb, he adds: 'The poet's wish has today been fulfilled by the hoisting of the flag of independent Pakhtunistan.'[1]

What the Afghans call 'Pakhtunistan' is located on the traditional invasion route to the subcontinent of India and has been the pathway of countless immigrants, conquerors, and raiders, of which the first recorded in history were the Aryans who entered India in about 1500 B.C. Consequently, the frontier tracts of India, like the Balkans which are the gateway to Europe, have had a kaleidoscopic history, and to pick out any single period in the past as a guide to the present is a futile exercise. If we take the comparatively stable eras of Indian history as our guide—and this seems the most rational thing to do—it will be found that 'Pakhtunistan', wholly or in part, has formed a portion of empires whose centre of power lay in the rich and more densely populated plains of India. None of the substantial empires—the Mauryan, the Khushan, the Moghul, and the British[2]—ever ruled India from Afghanistan. Mahmud of Ghazni, Timur, Nadir Shah, and Ahmad Shah Durrani were raiders who swooped down upon the fertile plains of northern India primarily to plunder the wealth of the prosperous cities there, and only Ahmad Shah Durrani was an Afghan. The 'Afghan' or 'Pathan' kings who ruled India adopted that country as their homeland and became Indians in the same way as the Moghuls did after them.

Even Afghanistan herself as a united and independent country is a comparative newcomer to the family of nations. 'At a time when a stream of cultures from east and west was meeting in the great centres of literature and science in Samarqand and Herat, or at a later period when India was developing the culture and art which flourished under the Mogul Empire, the Afghans were an obscure and troublesome tribe of shepherds and highwaymen. . . . The true Afghans had never been looked on as other than savage wild men of the hills by their neighbours until they suddenly emerged 200

[1] p. 49.
[2] The Gupta empire did not extend beyond the Punjab in the north-west.

years ago as sovereigns of a vast dominion.'[1] The author of this empire was one Ahmad Khan, a captain in the armed hordes of Nadir Shah of Persia and a prince of the Abdali tribe of Afghanistan. At this time the Moghul empire, in decay since the death of Aurengzeb, was still reeling under the impact of Nadir's ferocious sack of Delhi in 1739. When Nadir was murdered in 1747 Ahmad Khan got his chance to liberate Afghanistan from the yoke of Persia and to build an empire of his own. He marched to Kandahar and, upon being elected by some tribes as the first King of Afghanistan, became 'Ahmad Shah'. 'This is the year', writes Amir Abdur Rahman in his autobiography, 'in which the history of Afghanistan made a start in having an elected king and constitutional government to govern the country.'[2] Ahmad Shah assumed the title of Durr-i-Durran (Pearl of Pearls), reputedly because he liked to wear a pearl earring, and from then on the Abdalis began to be called the Durranis. Before his death in 1773, Ahmad Shah 'swept eight times across the Indus, and ravaged the Punjab as far as Delhi'.[3] It was in the course of one of these incursions that he routed the Mahrattas at Panipat in 1761. Next year he defeated the Sikhs near Lahore and with the annexation of Kashmir his empire reached its high watermark, stretching from the Atrek River to Delhi and from the borders of Tibet to the Indian Ocean.[4] It is this Afghan empire of Ahmad Shah that his successors have hankered after ever since, and which, therefore, is the real source of the problem of 'Pakhtunistan' today.

But Ahmad Shah's effort was a mere flash in the pan of history. The empire he had so suddenly acquired quickly began to decay. The task of founding an enduring dynasty 'was too great for a people who were still largely tribal . . . possessing no true national cohesion. . . . Already in Ahmad Shah's lifetime signs were apparent that it was not possible to retain hold of northern India from a base in Qandahar. In an attempt to arrange a settlement of the Panjab, Ahmad Shah recognized in 1761 the Mogul Prince Shah Alam II as Emperor at Delhi, while in 1767 he gave up the central Panjab to the Sikhs, retaining under his own control Peshawar and the northern Panjab.'[5]

Ahmad Shah was succeeded by his son Timur Shah, 'whose

[1] W. K. Fraser-Tytler, *Afghanistan*, p. 51.
[2] *The Life [Autobiography] of Abdur Rahman Amir of Afghanistan*, II, p. 215.
[3] Olaf Caroe, *The Pathans*, p. 256.
[4] W. K. Fraser-Tytler, *Afghanistan*, p. 64.
[5] ibid., pp. 64, 65.

character was marked by indolence ... [which] rendered him incapable of keeping together the tribes which had been conquered by his father, and the kingdom began to decline ... [and] upon his death in 1793, which occurred at Kabul, a struggle for the monarchy ensued between his numerous sons ... from 1793, after Timur Shah's death, the fightings, the misfortunes, and the violent deaths of the kings and chiefs were innumerable. The breakdown of the Constitutional Government ... was brought about by the kings' habits of self-indulgence and intoxication, and their partiality for one person or one clan to the exclusion of the others. These characteristics of the Suddozai kings resulted in their losing the kingdom, and turning Afghanistan into a petty state after its being a vast empire before it fell into their hands.'[1]

The state of utter anarchy following Timur Shah's death continued till 1826 when Dost Muhammad Khan finally prevailed over his rivals and imposed a semblance of stability upon the troubled kingdom. But by this time little was left of the vast empire of Ahmad Shah. Amir Dost Muhammad's writ ran for 'less than a hundred miles from Kabul in any direction. Seldom can an empire have disintegrated quite so rapidly or a dynasty shown itself less capable of unity and sustained effort.'[2]

Amongst the territories lost during the internecine strife was the Peshawar valley. It had been under the Governorship of Sultan Muhammad Khan when Ranjit Singh defeated the Afghans at Nowshera in 1823 and took it. He retained Sultan Muhammad as titular Governor for some time but later assumed direct control.

Despite wars with the Sikhs and the British, and a period of exile in India as a British prisoner, Dost Muhammad succeeded in consolidating his hold over Afghanistan before his death in 1863. His ambition to recover Peshawar, however, was never satisfied because after the Sikhs, that city was occupied by the British (1849), who retained possession of it till the transfer of power in India. The present monarch of Afghanistan, Zahir Shah, and his family are the direct descendants of Sultan Muhammad and 'the lure of Peshawar is a passion, deep in their hearts'.[3]

After Dost Muhammad another struggle for succession ensued till one of his sons, Sher Ali, came out victorious in 1868 and became Amir. In 1878 Britain declared war against Sher Ali to forestall

---

[1] The Life of Abdur Rahman Amir of Afghanistan, II, pp. 217, 218.
[2] W. K. Fraser-Tytler, Afghanistan, p. 71.
[3] Sir Olaf Caroe, The Pathans, p. 435.

suspected Russian moves to gain influence at the court of Kabul and in 1879, Sher Ali having died, dictated the treaty of Gandamak to his son Yakub Khan, compelling him to cede the districts of Kurram, Pishin, and Sibi and the control of the Khyber and Michini passes to the British. The Amir also undertook not to have any foreign relations except with Britain and agreed to the posting of a permanent British resident at Kabul, escorted by a small force. In return Britain guaranteed the defence of Afghanistan against foreign aggression. Thus, in effect, Afghanistan was no longer a sovereign state but became a dependency of Great Britain. It was not till 1919 that Britain agreed to restore full independence to Afghanistan by relinquishing control over her external affairs.

A few months after the treaty of Gandamak had been signed a fresh fracas broke out in Kabul and the newly arrived British Agent was murdered. General Roberts marched to Kabul and Afghanistan was again occupied. Amir Yakub Khan abdicated and was taken to India. Looking round for an acceptable occupant for the Afghan throne, Britain's choice fell upon Abdur Rahman, a grandson of Amir Dost Muhammad,[1] who, having been forced to flee his country by Sher Ali, had been living in Russian Turkestan as an exile for the past eleven years and, regarding the moment opportune for rehabilitating his fortune, was at this time wending his way home. He was invited by the British Resident to come to Kabul and assume charge of the kingdom.

Before finally accepting the offer, Abdur Rahman inquired what the boundaries of his dominion would be and what would be the nature of his relations with the British Government.[2] The Resident's reply on the first point was that 'the whole province of Kandahar has been placed under a separate ruler, except Pishin and Sibi, which are retained in British possession. Consequently, the Government is not able to enter into any negotiations with you on these points, nor in respect to arrangements with regard to the north-west frontier, which were concluded with the ex-Amir Mahomed Yakub Khan. With these reservations the British Government are willing that you should establish over Afghanistan (including Herat, the possession of which cannot be guaranteed to you, though Government are not disposed to hinder measures which you may take to

---

[1] Abdur Rahman was the son of Afzul Khan, the eldest surviving son of Amir Dost Muhammad. After Dost Muhammad's death, however, it was not Afzul Khan but Sher Ali who had managed to grab the throne.

[2] *The Life of Abdur Rahman, Amir of Afghanistan*, I, p. 193.

obtain possession of it) as complete and extensive authority as has hitherto been exercised by any Amir of your family.' On the second point the Resident said equally bluntly: '. . . it is plain that the Kabul ruler can have no political relations with any foreign power except the English'.[1] The Amir was, however, assured that a British Resident would not be stationed at Kabul though 'it may be advisable to station by agreement a Mahomedan agent of the British Government at Kabul'. Abdur Rahman accepted the British terms except that he did not give his consent to the separation of Kandahar from the kingdom.[2] The Resident accordingly held 'an audience' at Kabul on 22 July 1880 and proclaimed Abdur Rahman Amir.

Three things are thus clear: first, that Abdur Rahman owed his elevation to the throne to the British Government; second, that he was to have no control over external relations and was thus not a fully sovereign ruler; third, that he agreed to the stipulation that he would not be able to enter into any negotiations with the British Government 'in respect to arrangements with regard to the northwest frontier which were concluded with ex-Amir Mahomed Yakub Khan [by the treaty of Gandamak]'. Under the circumstances it can hardly be pleaded on behalf of Abdur Rahman that he was deprived of any part of what is supposed to constitute 'Pakhtunistan' under duress. He never possessed the area in the first instance and had clearly accepted the rulership of Afghanistan on the understanding that arrangements which had already been concluded with Yakub Khan were no longer negotiable.

The circumstances under which the Durand Agreement was signed by Abdur Rahman provide further help in appraising the nature of that border settlement. Though Abdur Rahman had been seated on the throne of Kabul by the British, his life, to use his own words, was 'not a bed of roses. On the contrary I was surrounded by difficulties of all kinds. Here began my first severe fight, against my own relatives, my own subjects and my own people.[3] . . . The claimants to the throne were so numerous that it is impossible to make a list of their names.'[4] There were troubles and signs of a general rebellion all over the country and he had to fight 'four civil wars', besides having to put down several smaller disturbances.[5]

After he had consolidated his position to a satisfactory extent,

[1] *The Life of Abdur Rahman, Amir of Afghanistan*, I, p. 194.

[2] ibid., p. 195.

[3] ibid., p. 210.

[4] ibid., p. 226.

[5] ibid, p. 249.

Abdur Rahman's mind turned towards reforms 'necessary for making Afghanistan a great nation in the future ... [but] it was of the first and greatest importance to mark out a boundary line all round Afghanistan, so that we should first know what provinces really belonged to Afghanistan before thinking of introducing any reforms and improvements therein.'[1]

The Amir likened his country to a poor goat on whom both the lion (Britain) and the bear (Russia) had fixed their eyes. He first moved to have his border with Russia settled with the help of Britain and, 'having settled my boundary with all my neighbours, I thought it necessary to set out the boundaries between my country and India, so that the boundary line should be definitely marked out around my dominions, as a strong wall for protection'.[2] The method suggested by him to the Viceroy was that a British Mission be sent to Kabul to negotiate the matter, and he 'requested that Sir Mortimer Durand, the Foreign Secretary, might be appointed as the head of it'.[3] The Viceroy, however, appointed Lord Roberts to lead the proposed Mission. The Amir thought Roberts was an unwise choice because of the latter's part in the recent war against Afghanistan and his known support for a 'forward policy'. Though the Viceroy insisted upon his own choice, Abdur Rahman was able to delay the matter with one pretext or another till Lord Roberts left India on retirement. Thereupon the Amir 'at once invited the Mission to visit Kabul'.[4] In a letter to the Viceroy Abdur Rahman pleaded that the frontier tribes be included in his dominions because, as a fellow Muslim, he would 'gradually make them peaceful subjects and good friends of Great Britain', but his 'advice was not appreciated'.[5] However, the Amir got his wish to have Durand as head of the Mission and the latter arrived in Kabul in September 1893.

The boundary, as decided upon by the parties, was made the subject of an agreement signed by the Amir on 12 November 1893.[6] At a public Durbar on the following day the Amir thanked the Mission 'for their wise way of settling the disputes. ... All the representatives and officials of my kingdom who were present

---

[1] *The Life of Abdur Rahman, Amir of Afghanistan*, II, p. 176.
[2] ibid., p. 154.
[3] ibid., p. 155.
[4] ibid., p. 157.
[5] ibid., p. 158.
[6] For relevant extracts from the Durand Agreement see Olaf Caroe, *The Pathans*, p. 463.

received a copy of the address of the deputation to which they had all set their seals, and in which they expressed their satisfaction and consent to the agreements and understandings. . . . The misunderstandings and disputes which were arising about these frontier matters were put to an end, and after the boundary lines had been marked out according to the above-mentioned agreements by the Commissioners of both Governments, a general peace and harmony reigned between the two Governments, which I pray God may continue for ever.'[1] Though the Amir did not get from the agreement all he wanted, he was realistic enough, in all the circumstances, to state: 'I am quite contented and satisfied that I have gained more than I have lost by British friendship.'[2]

Basically, the Amir's position was but little different from that of numerous princes in India who ruled the 'states' under British paramountcy. It was a mere accident of history that the British Government did not actually annex Afghanistan and make her a part of their Indian empire. Geographically, a much better frontier than the Durand Line would have been the line of the Hindu Kush mountains, but 'in the interests of British policy, it was desirable to keep a strip of Afghan territory between the British and Russian Empires, the idea being that frontier incidents under such conditions would have less importance than if the outposts were held by British and Russian troops respectively'.[3] Had it suited the British purpose to add the whole of Afghanistan to their Indian empire, that country today would surely have formed the north-western province of Pakistan.

In 1905 Abdur Rahman's son and successor, Habibullah, signed a pact with the British Government, reaffirming that he would abide by the 'agreements and compacts' concluded by his late father.[4] During the First World War Habibullah wisely resisted the temptation to take advantage of the temporary difficulties of Britain despite the fact that Muslim Turkey had joined the Axis Powers and a German–Turkish Mission journeyed to Kabul to press him to join their cause.

However, in 1919, when India was seething with internal discontent, Amanullah, son of Habibullah, launched an attack on the frontier in the hope of recovering 'Peshawar and areas in the Derajat

---

[1] *The Life of Abdur Rahman, Amir of Afghanistan*, II, pp. 162, 163, and 164.
[2] ibid., p. 237.
[3] Sir Percy Sykes, *Sir Mortimer Durand*, p. 213.
[4] For extracts see Olaf Caroe, *The Pathans*, p. 464.

up to the river Indus'.[1] The invasion was contained and the Afghans were obliged to sue for peace. Britain, too, exhausted by war and beset with political unrest in India, was in no mood to prolong the conflict. Two treaties followed: the interim Treaty of Rawalpindi (1919) and the permanent Anglo-Afghan Treaty (1921).[2] These, in effect, reaffirmed the Durand Agreement. Responding to the mood of the times, the British Government also declared that Afghanistan henceforth would be 'officially free and independent in its internal and external affairs'. Amanullah was addressed as His Majesty in a letter from King George V and in 1926 assumed the title of Padishah (King).

Though Amanullah had confirmed the Durand Line as the border in the treaties just mentioned, he did not at heart abandon his desire to add the frontier areas to his possessions. When he visited Russia in 1928 *Izvestia*, with the dual object of pleasing the royal guest and having a swipe at capitalist Britain, said that 'the belt of independent tribes, which the British have pacified and converted into advanced posts for their aggressive policy, must under Afghan national policy, be incorporated into Afghanistan, to which they belong by tribal relationship and economic ties. . . .'[3] In the middle of the nineteen-fifties Khrushchev gave expression to similar thoughts, to spite Pakistan for her pro-West stance and to curry favour with the ruling clique in Afghanistan.

When Nadir Shah, father of the present Afghan monarch, ascended the throne in 1930, the validity of the treaty of 1921 was reaffirmed by an exchange of letters between the British Secretary of State for Foreign Affairs and the Afghan Minister in London.[4] We have already described the constitutional arrangements under which the territories comprising 'Pakhtunistan' elected to join Pakistan. A speech in the House of Commons on 30 June 1950 by Noel-Baker, Secretary of State for Commonwealth Relations, set out the resulting legal position: 'It is His Majesty's Government's view that Pakistan is in international law the inheritor of the rights and duties of the old Government of India, and of His Majesty's Government in the United Kingdom, in these territories, and that the Durand Line is the international frontier.'[5] This view was

---

[1] G. N. Molesworth, *Afghanistan 1919*, p. 23.
[2] For extracts see Olaf Caroe, *The Pathans*, p. 464.
[3] *The Times*, 3 May 1928.
[4] For texts see Olaf Caroe, *The Pathans*, p. 465.
[5] ibid.

repeated in Parliament by Foreign Secretary Lord Home (3 November 1955), Prime Minister Anthony Eden (1 March 1956), and Prime Minister Harold Macmillan (20 May 1960).

Let us now list, and examine the validity of, the specific arguments which Afghan spokesmen adduce when campaigning for 'Pakhtunistan'.

1. **The Durand Line was established under duress**—We have pointed out that the Durand Agreement was negotiated at the request of Amir Abdur Rahman himself, by a British official of the Amir's own choice, and that the Amir and his advisers publicly accepted it and declared themselves satisfied with it. As a matter of fact Abdur Rahman had accepted the kingship in the first instance on the clear understanding that the status of the north-west frontier as decided by the treaty of Gandamak was not negotiable. The Durand Line merely gave a more precise shape to the mutual understanding already existing in principle. For half a century afterwards each and every Afghan ruler reaffirmed the validity of the Durand Line as the agreed frontier between Afghanistan and India.

2. **Even after the Durand Agreement the tribal territory remained separate and independent**—This myth is largely the result of the administrative arrangements which came into force in 1901. From the annexation of the Punjab by the British until 1901 the five frontier districts had formed a part of the Punjab and the Punjab Government also exercised a loose control over the tribal tracts. Though others before him had recognized the anomaly of a provincial government administering a frontier region of international import, it was left to Curzon to bring matters to a head. In a minute to the Government at home, he represented that the existing system 'interposes between the Foreign Minister of India and his subordinate agents not an Ambassador or a Minister or a Consul, but the elaborate mechanism of a local government and the necessarily exalted personality of a Lieutenant-Governor'.[1] Put more directly, the basic argument for a change was that the management of tribal affairs was inseparable from the conduct of foreign policy and defence of a highly sensitive international frontier.[2] Accordingly, the entire frontier area was detached from the Punjab

---

[1] Olaf Caroe, *The Pathans*, p. 416.
[2] ibid., p. 417.

in 1901 and placed under the direct charge of the Government of India. A new North-West Frontier Province consisting of the five settled districts was created and, though the tribal territory was placed under the same Chief Commissioner, its tradition of local autonomy, based on agreements between the individual tribes and the British Government, was not disturbed. The advance in local self-government brought by the Act of 1919 was not extended to the Frontier Province till 1932 when it was raised from a Chief Commissioner's to a Governor's Province. Subsequently, the province shared equally with other parts of British India in the reforms under the 1935 Act. But the position in the tribal tract remained unaltered throughout and to emphasize the uniqueness of the latter it was now officially designated the 'Tribal Areas'. Clearly, the purpose behind the 1901 separation of the frontier territories would have been lost if the Tribal Areas afterwards had been allowed the same system of government as the rest of India. The only way in which they could be kept clear of a cumbersome local administration and of representative institutions, which proved to be a source of increasing embarrassment to the ruling power elsewhere, including the settled districts of the North-West Frontier Province, was by continuing the original arrangements under which both sides got what they wanted—the tribesmen retained their own traditional form of local independence and the British Government continued its direct overall control of an area which, as pointed out by the Simon Commission, was not only the frontier of India but 'an international frontier of the first importance from the military point of view for the whole empire'.

However, the fact that it suited the purpose of the British Government not to extend to the Tribal Areas the administrative system which, either by choice or by necessity, they gradually built up in the rest of India, does not mean that internationally those Areas were any more independent than the rest of the country. 'Perhaps one of the difficulties in enabling the situation to be thoroughly understood in Britain, America and other Western countries, even to this day,' points out a shrewd observer, 'is that in the great wealth of fiction, films, and writing, the tribal areas have often been referred to as "no-man's land" or by similar vague terms. The fact is, of course, that there has not been, since 1893, any territory the responsibilty for which was in any doubt.'[1] Indeed the whole purpose

---

[1] *Asiatic Review*, July 1950.

of negotiating the Durand Line was to delimit the territories over which the Amir and the British Government respectively were entitled to exercise undisputed sovereignty.[1]

3. As the British Government in India has ceased to exist the Anglo-Afghan Treaty of 1921 is null and void—This argument does not require a lengthy discussion. It is a well-settled proposition of international law that 'according to the principle *res transit cum suo onere*, treaties of the extinct State concerning boundary lines ... remain valid, and all rights and duties arising from such treaties of the extinct State devolve on the absorbing State'.[2]

4. The inhabitants of 'Pakhtunistan' are one nation and the Durand Line arbitrarily splits the nation into two—There are several interesting aspects of this much repeated and seemingly plausible proposition. In the first place the Durand Line was not arbitrarily drawn. 'It generally follows tribal boundaries, separating those tribes which go to market in Peshawar, Kohat, Bannu, Tank, and Quetta from those with economic links with Khorasan, having Kabul, Ghazni and Kandahar as their market towns. Only in two cases—the Mohmands and the Wazirs—is a tribe divided. The Mohmands were always a two-headed Janus, many of the upper sections looking to Lalpura and Jalalabad rather than to Peshawar. These sections were left to the Amir of Afghanistan. ... As regards the Wazirs: a few Wazirs living in Birmal were left on the Afghan side of the line, though the great bulk of the tribe remained in India.'[3]

Secondly, Afghanistan's concern for the unity of Pakhtuns is less than genuine because she does not include the Pakhtuns on her side of the line in the proposed state of 'Pakhtunistan'. The 'Pakhtunistan' of her conception would consist solely of areas now within Pakistan. The Pakhtuns would, therefore, continue to be split within two sovereign states. 'During an amiable, lengthy and courteous interview with me,' interestingly recounts Griffiths, 'the Prime Minister [of Afghanistan] for just one brief instant

---

[1] Article 2 of the Agreement ran: 'The Government of India will at no time exercise interference in the territories lying beyond this line on the side of Afghanistan, and His Highness the Amir will at no time exercise interference in the territories lying beyond this line on the side of India.'

[2] *Oppenheim's International Law*, ed. Lauterpacht, I (ch. 1 s. 82b), cited by W. K. Fraser-Tytler, *Afghanistan*, p. 309.

[3] John C. Griffiths, *Afghanistan*, Appendix I, Historical Note by Sir Olaf Caroe.

4

sparked a flash of anger; it was when I asked him whether he thought any part of Afghanistan should become part of Pushtunistan. His sharp "never" and subsequent rebuke of my "irrelevant" question betrayed, not only strength of feeling, but perhaps also an awareness of the ambiguity and weakness of the arguments for an independent Pushtunistan.'[1]

When the Afghan Foreign Minister, Mohammad Naim, visited Pakistan in January 1960, the Pakistani Foreign Minister, Manzur Qadir, baffled him with an unexpected proposal. He said that the wishes of Pakhtuns on both sides of the line should be ascertained as to whether they all desired to live together in Afghanistan or Pakistan. Since the Pakhtuns of Pakistan have already declared in favour of Pakistan in a referendum, it remains to ask the Pakhtuns of Afghanistan. In all probability their verdict would be in favour of Pakistan. If not, the matter could be considered further. Naim's only answer was that he had not come to negotiate. Manzur Qadir repeated the offer publicly on 7 March.[2] As two-thirds of all Pakhtuns live in Pakistan and only one-third in Afghanistan, it would appear more rational for the minority to join the majority.

Thirdly, it is not correct that the Pushto-speaking tribes collectively form a nation. As already mentioned, they never constituted a cohesive unit of any sort by themselves throughout the long history of the ancient part of the world in which they live. The first loyalty of every tribesman has always been to his own particular tribe and, far from having any sense of unity, they are notorious for perpetual inter-tribal feuds.

Fourthly, there are innumerable instances all the world over where persons speaking the same language, or belonging to the same tribe, form a part of more than one nation. Any attempt to redraw boundaries of states according to tribal or linguistic considerations would throw innumerable countries into the melting pot and create far more problems than it would solve. It was no doubt with such a realization in mind that, despite the manifest defects in many cases of the international frontiers left behind by the departing colonial powers, the members of the Second Non-Aligned Nations Conference in their communiqué from Cairo

[1] ibid., p. 62.
[2] *Dawn*, 8 March 1960. On an earlier occasion Naim had made the interesting observation that the issue did not concern the Pushto-speaking tribesmen living in Afghanistan because their interests were well 'looked after'. *Asian Recorder*, 1955, p. 575.

on 10 October 1964 pledged themselves 'to respect frontiers as they existed when the States gained independence'.

In central Asia in particular any attempt to redraw political boundaries tribe-wise would lead to utter chaos. 'Any major un-picking on linguistic lines of South Asia's existing frontiers, were it to happen, might immediately cause the Afghan Kingdom to fall apart. The northern tract, logically, would then join with the Soviet Union's Central Asian Republics; the western with Persia; and the rest with Pakistan's present Pathan tract—where the Pakistani Pathans, having the higher standards of living and education, would doubtless take the lead, and Kabul become secondary to Peshawar, the better-developed country.'[1]

In truth, after the establishment of the Durand Line, the tribes-men allotted to Muslim Afghanistan were no less restive and desirous of freedom to pursue their own way of life than those given to infidel Britain. If Afghanistan was Muslim, British India offered cash allowances and greater opportunities of employment and trade. Many thousands of young tribesmen earned a regular living by joining the ranks of the Indian Army irregular corps and the constabulary, and large numbers of their brethren regularly flocked to the comparatively more flourishing towns of the settled districts for barter and trade. They looked upon Peshawar and not Kabul as their metropolis. 'The biggest potential factor in Afghan influence was, I suppose, that while the British ruled the tribes felt that, in the last resort, they could appeal to an Islamic champion against an alien power. But in truth history has little to support that apprehension. . . . Not only were they on the whole content to remain under British rule, but they sometimes showed the Afghan Government such antagonism that the latter had to appeal for the British Government's help.'[2]

As a part of Muslim Pakistan, the facilities for trade, employ-ment and other opportunities have multiplied for the tribesmen as well as for the inhabitants of the former Settled Districts. The Pathans 'have now learned to look unmistakably to the east for education, service and all the higher things of life; the social, economic and political ideas of Durranis have become to them an anachronism. For them Kabul irredentism is empty of meaning; political amalgamation, should it ever come, would take a very

[1] Ian Stephens, *Pakistan*, p. 50.
[2] Sir George Cunningham, 'Pakistan's North-West Frontier and the Tribes', *States-man*, 28 May 1949.

different shape. Peshawar would absorb Kabul, not Kabul Peshawar.'[1] One respected writer regards the fusion of Afghanistan, once known as India the Less, and Pakistan as inevitable because the Hindu Kush today is no less the 'great frontier barrier' of the subcontinent than it always was in the past.[2]

---

[1] Olaf Caroe, *The Pathans*, p. 437. On the eve of partition, when Mountbatten visited the north-west frontier, the mass demonstrations he encountered both in Peshawar and the tribal areas were in favour of Pakistan and not at all in favour of independence or joining Afghanistan. 'Perhaps the basic flaw in the entire Afghan position', observes an American scholar, 'has been Kabul's wrong assessment of the extent to which Pathans in the north-west area have identified themselves with the new Muslim state of Pakistan.' George L. Montagno, 'Pak-Afghan Detente', *Asian Survey*, Dec. 1963.

[2] W. K. Fraser-Tytler, *Afghanistan*, pp. 139, 186, and 300.

5 Pakistan and the Communist Powers

I. The Ideological Factor in Pakistan's Foreign Policy

Today[1] Pakistan professes to be equally friendly with the USA, Russia, and China. The proclaimed guide-posts of foreign policy are geographical compulsions and friendship with all, irrespective of differences in ideology and social systems. Until 1962, however, ideology was an important element in Pakistani foreign policy, and translated into practice it meant preference for the Western countries and dislike of Communism. Communism in the early years of that period was no less uncompromising. Unless a newly independent country underwent a Communist revolution it remained 'bourgeois', capitalist-dominated, and a tool of imperialism. Communist countries now vociferously tout the principle of co-existence with all, but it was only when the expected Communist revolutions did not materialize that they decided to employ co-operation instead of disruption as the means to win over the third world. The new policy won India's friendship readily because she professed to be neutral in the East-West cold war and had worked for good relations with the Communist countries from the outset of independence. With Pakistan it was not so easy to effect a change. Added to the ideological barrier was the difficulty that she had been palpably pro-West in her foreign policy, and in 1954 had openly subscribed to the Western system of defence alliances. It was not till Pakistan's alliance with the West had cooled off, in the wake of the latter's arms aid to India in 1962, that the requisite climate for a real improvement in Pakistan's relations with the Communist world was created.

For a proper understanding of the history of Pakistani foreign policy it is necessary to consider how Pakistan and the Communist countries viewed one another before they shed their mutual dislike. Pakistanis all along have undoubtedly regarded India as the greatest

[1] Dec. 1970.

91

and most imminent source of danger to their country and the problem of defence against India has been uppermost in their mind. At the same time, however, for several years they regarded Communism as a serious threat to Islamic ideology and genuinely believed that Russia and China would not hesitate to use physical force to achieve their objectives.

Long before the movement for Pakistan was born, the poet Iqbal had declared in a letter to the daily *Zamindar* of Lahore on 'Islam and Bolshevism' that 'To hold Bolshevist views, in my opinion, is to place oneself outside the pale of Islam.'[1] He also took a dismal view of a nation which does not believe in God:

> Denied celestial grace a nation goes
> No further than electricity or steam;
> Death to the heart, machines stand sovereign,
> Engines that crush all sense of human kindness.[2]

A survey of Pakistani opinion after independence will vividly illustrate how seriously Pakistanis viewed the threat from Communism to their spiritual and physical existence and will refute the notion that Pakistan tricked a gullible America into giving her arms aid avowedly for fighting Communism but in reality for use solely against India.

On 12 April 1950 Prime Minister Liaquat Ali Khan proposed that the United States should encourage the idea of territorial guarantees to India and Pakistan to allow them to spend more on economic improvement, 'which would keep out the potential menace of Communism'.[3]

In the discussion on the Korean War in the Constituent Assembly of Pakistan a member said that Pakistan was right in supporting the United Nations policy in Korea not only because of her loyalty to the world body but also 'because Islam is against Communism and Pakistan cannot allow Communism to capture one country after another'.[4]

Commenting on Russia's protest over American arms aid to Pakistan, *Dawn* formulated six charges against the 'Kremlin bosses', the fifth of which was that 'they have reduced the Russian people to a sub-human species because without complete freedom of thought

---

[1] Iqbal's letter (in Urdu) dated 23 June 1923 to the *Zamindar*, Lahore, reproduced in *Guftar-i-Iqbal*, p. 6.
[2] V. G. Kiernan, *Poems From Iqbal*, p. 43.
[3] *New York Times*, 13 April 1950.
[4] Nur Ahmed on 11 Oct. 1950.

man cannot remain man'. Such material advantages as had accrued to the Russian people could not be 'adequate recompense for the robbery of that divine spark called the soul which is the principal factor dividing man from beast'. The sixth indictment said that 'they do not believe in God and cannot therefore have any morals, because "religion"—whatever it may be—is the basis of all moral codes'.[1]

During a foreign policy address to students at the Salimullah Muslim Hall, Dacca, on 9 December 1956, Prime Minister Suhrawardy stated that the cold war was due to the Communists' attempt to impose their ideology on the rest of the world. Pakistan had been able to attain freedom from British control, but should she become a satellite of Russia 'we shall never be able to get out of the control of our master. . . . We have seen . . . the manner in which East Germany suffered, Poland suffered, and in which Hungary has suffered.'

In 1959 President Ayub Khan wrote the foreword to a book on *The Ideology of Pakistan and its Implementation*. Among the subjects he chalked out for special study was 'how can the offensive of Hinduism and Communism against the ideology of Islam be combated?'[2] Indeed, despite political reconcilement, the abhorrence of the doctrine of Communism persists. Even after 'normalizing' Pakistan's relations with the Communist countries, Ayub called Communism 'a panacea for an acutely diseased society'.[3]

Maulana Abul Al Maududi, founder of the Jamaat-e-Islami and a noted scholar of Islamic jurisprudence, emphatically declared that Socialism based on the ideas of Marx aims at concentration of all means of production in the hands of government, which is un-Islamic. It deprives the individual of his freedom and basic rights while Islam guarantees the fullest freedom to all individuals and allows personal ownership of necessary means of livelihood to everyone.[4]

Even Maulana Abdul Hamid Khan Bhashani, chief of the National Awami Party, well known for his strong socialist bias and for his admiration of Communist China, stated in clear terms that he would 'never accept any Godless system' because the object of the struggle for Pakistan was to set up 'an ideal state where every

[1] *Dawn*, 31 March 1954.
[2] Javid Iqbal, *The Ideology of Pakistan and its Implementation*, pp. xi, xii.
[3] M. Ayub Khan, *Friends Not Masters*, p. 166.
[4] *Morning News*, Karachi, 8 May 1967.

activity in all spheres of life was to be fashioned after the dictates of Islam'.[1]

Finally, it is not without significance that the ban placed on the Communist Party throughout Pakistan in July 1954 has never been lifted.

At this point the reader is entitled to ask: if Pakistan really looked upon Communism as such a menace, why did she regard India, and not Communism, as her enemy number one? There are two good reasons why Pakistan held India in special dread. First, Pakistan felt that, should the Communist powers commit outright aggression against her, the Western powers would promptly come to her aid. In an all-out war against India, however, Pakistan felt unprotected. The Western countries might feel unhappy if India attacked Pakistan, Pakistanis argued, but they would take no sides in the conflict, treating it as a sort of civil war.[2] Left to herself, Pakistan, as the weaker party, would be destroyed. Secondly, the age of old-style colonialism having passed, the Communist countries would probably be content to see a Communist regime friendly to themselves installed in Pakistan. Pakistan would survive and could revive. India, on the other hand, would totally efface the identity of Pakistan for all time; in Indian eyes this would simply be a natural reunion of lost territory with the 'motherland'.

In marked contrast with Pakistan's poor view of Communism, her estimate of Christianity and the Western countries was noticeably benevolent. 'The most remarkable phenomenon of modern history,' Iqbal has observed, 'is the enormous rapidity with which the world of Islam is spiritually moving towards the West. There is nothing wrong in this movement, for European culture on its intellectual side is only a further development of some of the most important phases of the culture of Islam.'[3] A few days before taking office as Prime Minister, Ambassador Muhammad Ali Bogra said in Washington, on 31 March 1952, that the atheistic doctrine of Communism was 'raising its head like a hydra-headed monster' and Islam, Judaism, and Christianity, who have a belief in God,

[1] *Dawn*, 13 Dec. 1969.

[2] This actually happened during the Indo-Pakistani war of September 1965. In a statement issued on the eve of Ayub's trip to Washington in December 1965, President Johnson likened the Indo-Pakistani war to the American Civil War. For text of statement see *Dawn*, 3 Dec. 1965.

[3] Quoted by Prime Minister Chaudhri Muhammad Ali in his address to the Foreign Press Association, London, on 25 June 1956. Government of Pakistan, *Handout E. no. 3486*, dated 29 June 1956.

were faced with a challenge. They should unite and understand each other so that they could pool all their resources to fight the Communist menace which was no longer a political creed but was taking the place of religion.[1] According to *Dawn*, Communism was a 'prowling monster' but Islam shared with the democratic West the basic concept of liberty and freedom of conscience. It pleaded for closer relations between Islam, which occupied 'a pivotal place in world affairs today', and the United States, which was 'in the forefront of the new international structure'.[2]

II. Jawaharlal Nehru's Views on Communism, Russia, and China before Independence

Independent India's policy towards Russia and China was governed by two important factors: first, Hinduism's ideology being flexible and receptive, the ruling class in India did not find Communism inherently objectionable; secondly, Jawaharlal Nehru, who made the formulation of India's foreign policy 'a private monopoly',[3] had long decided to establish cordial relations with Russia and China when India became mistress of her own affairs. If he was not successful in this in the opening years it was because those countries, believing that both India and Pakistan were still tied to the apron strings of the imperialist Western countries, did not respond to his advances.

Nehru was repelled by the violence practised by the Communists to attain their goals, and by the extra-territorial loyalty owed by them to Moscow or Peking, and he could never have been a practising Communist. But his hatred of capitalism, as the breeding ground of imperialism and fascism, drove him, during the struggle for freedom, quite close to Communist philosophy. After independence, he regarded Russia and China as a beneficial counterpoise to the continuing Western threat to dominate the newly independent countries. In China, especially, he saw a large and ancient fellow Asian country which had suffered at the hands of Western imperialism and now, in collaboration with India, could shift the balance of power from Europe and North America towards long-suffering Asia.

It was in 1927 that Nehru assumed control of the foreign policy of the Indian Congress Party, and he relinquished it only when he

[1] *Dawn*, 8 April 1952.
[2] ibid., 26 Aug. 1953.
[3] Michael Brecher, *Nehru: A Political Biography*, p. 116.

left this world in 1964. In the former year he attended the International Congress Against Imperialism at Brussels and visited
Moscow. Both experiences left lasting impressions on his sensitive
mind.

Having met the South American delegates at Brussels, he realized
'how the rising imperialism of the United States, with its tremendous
resources and its immunity from outside attack, is gradually taking
a stranglehold on Central and South America' and concluded that
'the great problem of the near future will be American imperialism'.
He formed the view, further, that close co-operation between India
and China, the principal countries of Asia, was essential for the
regeneration of Asia. A joint declaration by the Indian and Chinese
delegations stated that 'for more than three thousand years the
people of India and China were united by the most intimate cultural
ties. From the days of Buddha to the end of the Mughal period and
the beginning of British domination in India this friendly intercourse continued uninterrupted.' The declaration expressed the
hope that the leaders of India would co-ordinate their struggle
with that of China 'so that by simultaneously engaging British
imperialism on two of its most vital fronts ... victory of both
peoples may be secured'.[1] This statement clearly foreshadowed the
Sino-Indian friendship which flowered from 1954–8, and also
witnessed the birth of the romantic myth of close co-operation
between India and China for more than three thousand years, a
slogan which Pakistan was not slow to pick up after Sino-Indian
cordiality had withered.

Moscow inspired Nehru with great admiration for the Communist
system which he assiduously conveyed to his countrymen, first
by letters from Russia 'which opened the eyes of the Indian people
to the tremendous happenings in that country',[2] and then by
numerous speeches and writings at home, including a book,
Soviet Russia: Some Random Sketches and Impressions, published
in 1929. The following are some of Nehru's pronouncements
during the period:

Russia stands today as the greatest opponent of imperialism.[3]

I am convinced that the only key to the solution of the world's problems

---

[1] For text of Nehru's Report on the Brussels Congress see Bimla Praśad, *The Origins
of Indian Foreign Policy*, Appendix I.
[2] K. P. S. Menon, *India and the Cold War*, p. 9.
[3] J. S. Bright (ed.), *Jawaharlal Nehru, Before and After Independence*, p. 66.

lies in Socialism . . . some glimpse we can have of this new civilization in the territories of the USSR.[1]

Modern imperialism is an outgrowth of capitalism and cannot be separated from it.[2]

Russia is not supposed to be a democratic country after the Western pattern, and yet we find the essentials of democracy present in far greater degree amongst the masses there than anywhere else.[3]

For my part, I would like to have a socialist economy all over India, and I think that the Soviet form of Government with certain variations and adaptations suited to India may well fit in here.[4]

With the passing of years Nehru's admiration for Communism became more temperate but the 'emotional hangover' continued, and 'with it the belief that Soviet achievements can be reproduced in India without its repulsive methods'.[5] In 1956 he told Tibor Mende that the people of India 'are not opposed to Communism as an ideal in society. Or to socialism; they are all the same as an ideal. It is the Communist technique of action that one rebels against.'[6]

III. Pakistan and the Soviet Union

We have already briefly referred to the adverse Soviet estimate of Pakistan when describing the sudden intervention of the Soviet Representative in the Security Council debate in January 1952.[7] Having no direct knowledge of the complicated Hindu–Muslim question in India, the Soviet Union failed to appreciate that the demand for Pakistan represented the genuine desire of the Muslims to escape both from British rule and perpetual Hindu domination. The Soviets believed that the British decision to divide the Indian subcontinent into two was nothing but a new manifestation of the old British strategy of divide and rule. British 'calculations are based', wrote the *New Times* (4 July 1947), 'on an aggravation of national antagonisms . . . on the creation of a situation that will favour British interference in India's internal affairs.' Though

---

[1] From the Presidential Address to the Indian National Congress, Lucknow, 1936.
[2] J. Nehru, *Eighteen Months in India*, p. 80.
[3] J. Nehru, *India's Freedom*, p. 45. For a later Nehru view that the Communist regime had brought 'some advantages' but at the cost of individual liberty, see J. Nehru, *Speeches*, IV, p. 376.
[4] J. Nehru, *The Unity of India*, p. 370.
[5] Michael Brecher, *Nehru: A Political Biography*, p. 587.
[6] Tibor Mende, *Nehru: Conversations on India and World Affairs*, p. 61.
[7] ch. 2.

both Indian and Pakistani leaders were criticized for accepting the division of the country, Pakistan, being foremost in the demand for separation, was viewed as the favourite tool of imperialism.

The Course of Soviet-Pakistani Relations

Not surprisingly, Soviet–Pakistani relations got off to a cool start. Nehru, on the other hand, stretched out a friendly hand to the USSR even before India became constitutionally independent. In a broadcast, upon assuming charge of the External Affairs portfolio in the Interim Government, the Indian leader greeted the Soviet Union and said, 'Inevitably we shall have to undertake many common tasks and have much to do with each other.' To signify the great importance he attached to Moscow he nominated his own sister, Vijaya Lakshmi Pandit, as Ambassador to the USSR. Liaquat, who headed the Muslim League contingent in the Interim Government, said that he did not wish an ambassador appointed to Moscow,[1] but he was unable to block the move and Mrs. Pandit duly presented her credentials to the President of the Soviet Union on 13 August 1947. For her part Pakistan felt miffed with Russia because the latter had moved slowly in extending recognition to Pakistan and Russian leaders had sent no congratulatory messages to Jinnah when Pakistan came into existence. It also irked Pakistan that, while all the Western members of the Security Council initially strove to have the Kashmir dispute solved on fair terms, the Soviet Union remained impassively neutral. Because the *status quo* was quite acceptable to India and not at all to Pakistan, the Soviet attitude in effect favoured India.

The first move to establish diplomatic relations between Pakistan and Russia was not made till 13 April 1948, on which date Foreign Minister Zafrulla Khan in New York proposed to Deputy Foreign Minister Andrei Gromyko that their countries exchange ambassadors. It was believed that Pakistan took the initiative in improving relations with the USSR to offset the shift, then under way, of the Western countries towards India on the Kashmir question. But the Pakistani move ran out of steam because, though the Soviet agreement to establish diplomatic relations was announced within a month, it was not till another seventeen months had passed that Pakistan named her first Ambassador to the USSR. The nominee finally presented his credentials in Moscow on the last day of 1949.

[1] Alan Campbell-Johnson, *Mission With Mountbatten*, p. 114.

His counterpart from Russia took even longer to show up in Pakistan and assumed charge of his office on 22 March 1950.

Two events in the first part of 1949 caused Russia and Pakistan to sit up and take a fresh look at their relationship. The first was India's decision in April to remain within the Commonwealth. That the Commonwealth had gone to the extent of shedding its cherished monarchical character to keep republican India within its ranks, was taken by Pakistan as further confirmation of her view that India could always get her own way in the Commonwealth while Pakistan would continue to be taken for granted. Russia, already suspicious of India, thought India's agreement to maintain her ties with the Commonwealth, in contravention of India's own past declarations, was a clear sign that she was leaning towards the Western countries in their cold war with the USSR. The second development, coming close on the heels of the first, was the announcement by Prime Minister Nehru in Bombay on 7 May that he had accepted an invitation to visit the United States in October. This news caused a flutter in Karachi, because Liaquat had received no such invitation, and in Moscow, where it was read as further proof of India's proclivity towards the West.

The Pakistani–Soviet response was not long in coming. It was announced in Karachi on 8 June that Prime Minister Liaquat Ali Khan and his wife had accepted an invitation from the Soviet Government to visit Moscow. The *Daily Telegraph* noted that the Pakistani Prime Minister would be the first Commonwealth Head of Government to go to Russia and was 'expected to time his journey to coincide with the visit of Pandit Nehru, the Prime Minister of India, to the United States in October'. Liaquat complained of Britain's stepmotherly treatment of Pakistan and said meaningfully, 'Pakistan cannot afford to wait. She must take her friends where she finds them.'[1]

In the end, however, Liaquat's visit to Moscow never materialized and the result of the entire episode was a further setback to Soviet–Pakistani relations. But the manœuvre did succeed in shaking the United States out of a posture of comparative indifference towards Pakistan. On 10 December it was announced in Pakistan that the Prime Minister and his wife had received a personal invitation from President Harry S. Truman to visit the USA in May 1950. Though 'well-informed circles' in Karachi maintained that the acceptance of the American President's invitation did not in any

[1] *Pakistan News*, 11 June 1949.

way affect the position as regards the Prime Minister's visit to Moscow,[1] the correspondent of the *Daily Telegraph* opined that Pakistan's 'flirtation' with Russia appeared to have ended.[2]

In the meantime Soviet criticism of Pakistani policies picked up again, and increased in intensity after Liaquat had given expression to friendly sentiments towards his American hosts during his tour of their country in the following spring. On the eve of the International Islamic Economic Conference at Karachi, the *New Times* observed that the purpose of the conference was to prepare the ground for an anti-Soviet Muslim military and political bloc.[3] Commenting on Liaquat's visit to the USA, the same periodical wrote that the upshot of his visit might be unmistakably guessed from the 'servile zeal' with which he hastened to proclaim his solidarity with the ugly deeds of American imperialism in Korea.[4]

The Pakistani Prime Minister appeared willing to journey to Moscow after his trip to the USA, but the Soviet Union on the one hand assumed a sphinx-like silence about the visit and on the other became increasingly acrimonious about Pakistan's alleged anti-Soviet moves in partnership with 'imperialist' Britain and America. Liaquat Ali Khan's intended trip to Moscow thus simply faded away in the course of time.

That Prime Minister Liaquat Ali Khan did not go to Moscow but went instead to the USA has been rightly interpreted by most Pakistani commentators to mean that he had openly chosen friendship with the United States in preference to cordiality with the USSR. Analysing the reasons why he went to the USA and not to the Soviet Union, a Study Group of the Pakistan Institute of Internal Affairs wrote: 'There are important divergences of outlook between Pakistan, with its Islamic background, and the Soviet Union with its background of Marxism which is atheistic. . . . Pakistan had noticed the subservience which was forced upon the allies of the Soviet Union. . . . Furthermore, there was the question whether Russia could supply the aid, both material and technical, which Pakistan so urgently needed.'[5]

[1] *Dawn*, 12 Dec. 1949.
[2] *Daily Telegraph*, 12 Dec. 1949.
[3] No. 47 of 1949.
[4] *New Times*, No. 28 of 1950.
[5] *Pakistan Horizon*, March 1956. For other similar views see K. Sarwar Hasan, *The Strategic Interests of Pakistan*, p. 2; Hafeez-ur-Rahman Khan, 'Pakistan's Relations with the U.S.S.R.', *Pakistan Horizon*, 1st Quarter 1961; and Aslam Siddiqi, *Pakistan Seeks Security*, p. 97.

Another consideration that must have weighed with Pakistan policy makers in choosing Western friendship at the time was the fact that in the United Nations, where the Kashmir case was pending, the Western countries enjoyed a far greater voting strength than Russia and her satellites.

Liaquat's cold-shouldering of the Soviet Union sorely wounded the pride of the Soviet leaders who are highly sensitive to political snubs of any sort. Moscow's grievance on the subject was amply expressed to Pakistani diplomatists for years to come, and Ayub took special care in 1965 to fix the dates of his trips to China, Russia, and the US in the order in which the invitations had been received.

IV. Pakistan and China

When Pakistan started her life as an independent country the situation in China was uncertain. A bitter struggle between Mao's Red Army and Chiang Kai-shek's Nationalist forces was in progress. Though Pakistan recognized the latter as the lawful Government of China, there was no love lost between her and Chiang Kai-shek, whose partiality for Gandhi and Nehru was well known. Neither side displayed any haste in exchanging diplomatic representatives and no embassy was established by either country during Chiang's time. Panikkar, the first Indian Ambassador, on the other hand, took up his duties in China in the spring of 1948.

Nor did Pakistan take special notice when the People's Republic of China was proclaimed on 1 October 1949. India, however, reacted to the change at once. Just as she later became the 'floor leader'[1] in the campaign to seat Communist China in the United Nations, she now not only immediately decided to recognize Mao's regime herself but also assumed the mission of persuading others to do the same. Within two days of the Chinese invitation to all foreign representatives in Peking to establish diplomatic relations, a reply came from Prime Minister Nehru 'couched in very friendly terms, indicating there would be early recognition and exchange of representatives'.[2] During a stopover in London on 10 October, en route to Washington, Nehru was stated to have pressed Prime Minister Attlee for an early recognition of Communist China and to be planning to do the same when he met President Truman. 'The Indian Prime Minister was reported to feel that India and Burma

[1] Senator Knowland's description in 1956 of Indian efforts to bring Communist China into the United Nations.
[2] K. M. Panikkar, *In Two Chinas*, p. 61.

must acknowledge the new Communist regime, even if they have to take the step alone.'[1] Gordon Walker, who was a member of the Attlee Cabinet at the time, confirms that the United Kingdom recognized Communist China largely under India's influence.[2]

Pakistan was undoubtedly interested in the developments inside China, and there was no reason why she should not have recognized the new regime in the normal course of events, but she felt no special urgency to hurry the process. However, consultations between members of the Commonwealth made it clear that India would soon extend recognition to the People's Republic and Britain would follow suit. It was expected at the time that Communist China would occupy the Chinese seat in the United Nations before long[3] and would partake in the discussions on Kashmir as a permanent member of the Security Council, with the right of veto. Clearly, it was not in Pakistan's interest to be left too far behind India in the rush to recognize new China.

Another reason which weighed with Pakistan was trade. Only a few weeks before Mao's party replaced the Nationalist Government in China, Pakistan's trade with India had come to a virtual halt in the wake of the devaluation of the Indian rupee, and Pakistan was anxiously looking round for customers for her raw jute and cotton and for suppliers of coal. At a luncheon meeting of the National Press Club in Washington, D.C., on 4 May 1950, Prime Minister Liaquat Ali Khan explained that Pakistan had recognized the People's Republic of China, 'accepting an established fact and in order to ease the flow of trade'. During the Korean War Pakistan abstained from voting on the United Nations resolution imposing an embargo on the export of certain goods to Communist China and North Korea. In February 1953 Prime Minister Nazimuddin said the contemplated blockade of China 'would affect many friends of the United States who want to trade with China. In our case we want to sell our cotton.'[4]

Pakistan's exports to China in 1952 shot up to $83.8 million or 15.7 per cent of the total, and the balance of trade heavily favoured

[1] *New York Herald Tribune*, 11 Oct. 1949.

[2] Patrick Gordon Walker, *The Commonwealth*, p. 315.

[3] In a speech in the House of Commons on 14 Dec. 1950 Attlee said the United Kingdom believed that it was right that the representation in the United Nations should belong to the new rulers of China, that Britain had been working for this end, and believed that, but for the Korean War, this objective would have been achieved. J. C. Kundra, *Indian Foreign Policy, 1947-54*, p. 181.

[4] Mushtaq Ahmad, *The United Nations and Pakistan*, p. 85.

Pakistan because her imports from China that year totalled only $2.2 million or 0.4 per cent.[1] After the slump in the price of raw materials following the ceasefire in Korea, Sino-Pakistani trade registered a sharp decline, but the heavy purchases of Pakistani raw materials by China, and the supply of coal by her at a critical juncture, left behind the feeling that China had acted like a good Samaritan at a time when India was bent upon Pakistan's economic destruction, and this impression made its own invisible contribution to the relations between Pakistan and China in the years that followed.

But let us get back to the chronology of new China's recognition. Though India was willing to act in the matter without delay, the Chinese called for negotiations preparatory to the establishment of diplomatic relations, in order to satisfy themselves that the powers concerned had made a complete break with the Nationalist Government in Formosa.[2] Consequently it was not till 30 December 1949 that India could announce her recognition. Pakistan, the first Muslim country to take such a step, followed on 4 January, and the United Kingdom two days later. The Chinese Ambassador-designate arrived in Karachi on 3 September 1951 and General A. M. Raza, the first Ambassador of Pakistan to China, presented his credentials to Chairman Mao Tse-tung at Peking on 13 November 1951.[3]

Having recognized the People's Republic as the lawful government of China, Pakistan considered it logical to support that government's claim to fill the Chinese seat in the United Nations. In a plenary meeting of the General Assembly, on 25 September 1950, Foreign Minister Zafrulla Khan argued that China was not applying for admission to the United Nations. She was a permanent member of the Security Council. The sole point for determination was who was to represent China. The Nationalist Government, whose delegation was still sitting in the United Nations, had for months ceased to exercise jurisdiction over any portion of the Chinese mainland. Could it be pretended that it was the Nationalist Government that effectively represented China? Or, could it be denied that the Peking Government did in fact represent the Chinese people?

Communist China fully shared Russia's view that any Asian

---

[1] Hafeez-ur-Rahman Khan, 'Pakistan's Relations with the People's Republic of China', *Pakistan Horizon*, 3rd Quarter 1961.

[2] K. P. Karunakaran, *India in World Affairs, February 1950–December 1953*, p. 68.

[3] The Indian Ambassador had already presented his letter of credence to the new regime in China on 20 May 1950.

country which had not undergone a Communist revolution was 'bourgeois' and only nominally independent. Despite Nehru's utter goodwill towards her, China considered the Indian Prime Minister a 'running dog' of imperialism to be deposed by the Indian Communists as quickly as possible. She further agreed with the Soviet Union that the division of India into Pakistan and India was an imperialist trick. About Kashmir, too, China believed that the United States, through her manipulation of the Security Council, wished to send her own troops to turn that principality into a military base. China expressed satisfaction at the talks which Muhammad Ali Bogra and Nehru conducted in August 1953 outside the ambit of the Security Council and declared that 'this friendly approach to the settlement of disputes through consultation is indispensable to the peaceful settlement of all international issues'.[1] These views no doubt displayed a lack of understanding of the reality of Muslim nationalism, which had won Pakistan against determined Hindu opposition, and also of Pakistan's problem that direct negotiations with India on Kashmir were not likely to break India's hold over the best parts of Kashmir. But the real targets of the Chinese attack were the USA and the United Kingdom. There was little evidence of positive hostility towards Pakistan; at any rate, such verbal darts as China directed towards her were nowhere near as vitriolic as those which the Soviet Union threw at Pakistan or China herself aimed at India. What was the reason for this marked difference between the attitudes of the two Communist powers, whose policies in those days had so much else in common? Why did the Soviet Union make Pakistan the target for her bitterest attacks, while China from the outset reserved such treatment for India, in spite of Nehru's best efforts to win China's goodwill?

The reason lay in the fact that the Soviet Union was more concerned with developments in Kashmir and the Middle East, where, as already indicated, Pakistan appeared to be the bigger culprit, while China felt greater anxiety about happenings in Tibet, where she suspected India to be the chief villain.

Though Tibet had enjoyed *de facto* independence since the collapse of the Manchu dynasty in 1911, successive Chinese regimes had continued to regard it as a part of China. Communist China alleged that American and British imperialism had nefarious designs on Tibet and that India under Nehru's leadership was acting as their chief accomplice in the evil objective. A Chinese publication,

[1] *Survey of China Mainland Press*, no. 642, 29 Aug.-1 Sept. 1953, pp. 23-4.

World Culture (Shanghai), had written on 9 September 1949 that in the wake of the Second World War American imperialism had sent spies into Tibet and attempted to assume control of Tibet. 'Today,' the article continued, 'British imperialism has become a hireling of American imperialism, and India is in effect in the control of American imperialism.'[1] A week later the same paper declared Nehru to be a 'loyal slave of imperialism' who had already been made 'the substitute of Chiang Kai-shek by the imperialists'.[2] A Tibetan leader said that all Tibetans must 'rise against the plot of British and American imperialism and its lackey, Nehru, to annex Tibet'.[3]

Nehru had landed at Washington on 11 October 1949 to commence an official visit, only a few days after the People's Republic had announced its own installation at Peking. *World Culture* made the Indian Prime Minister's visit to America the occasion for an article captioned 'American Imperialism Lays Hand on a New Slave'. The author referred to Nehru as 'this slave whom American imperialism has just squeezed out of the hands of British imperialism'.[4]

China also traditionally claimed Nepal, Bhutan, Sikkim, and certain areas on the borders of India as parts of greater China. In 1949 and 1950 India had made agreements with the principalities of Bhutan and Sikkim, obtaining control of their foreign policies, and, in the case of Sikkim, also of her defence. In 1950 India had also signed a treaty with the kingdom of Nepal, stipulating that mutual consultations would be held in the face of external threat to either party, and followed it up with economic aid to Nepal as well as assistance to improve Nepalese defence. These significant moves in the border-lands, which China hoped would belong to her one day, did not fail to increase China's concern about Indian intentions.

On 7 October 1950 forty thousand Chinese troops marched into East Tibet and launched a full-scale attack to 'liberate' her. On the following day the Government of India addressed a note to China and called her action 'most surprising and regrettable'. China, replying four days later, made it clear that 'no foreign influence will be tolerated in Tibet'. She also considered that India's attitude had been 'affected by foreign influences hostile to China'.

Though India and China exchanged further notes on the subject,

[1] Girilal Jain, *Panchsheela and After*, p. 7.
[2] ibid., p. 9.
[3] *B.B.C. Monitoring Service*, Part V, no. 21, 13 Sept. 1949 (The Far East).
[4] Girilal Jain, *Panchsheela and After*, p. 12.

Nehru, in fact, had decided to sacrifice the future of Tibet in the hope of winning Chinese friendship. Panikkar says that the only area where the interests of India and China overlapped was Tibet, 'and knowing the importance that every Chinese government, including the Kuomintang, had attached to exclusive Chinese authority over that area, I had, even before I started for Peking, come to the conclusion that the British policy (which we were sup-posed to have inherited) of looking upon Tibet as an area in which we had special interests could not be maintained. The Prime Minister had also in general agreed with this view.'[1] Indeed, the Indian Ambassador afterwards strove to justify the Chinese action in Tibet in exactly the same terms as did the Chinese themselves: the 'British and American intrigues in Tibet against the interest of both Tibet and China were ripening and preparations were afoot to make Tibet a base against China and the Soviet Union. . . . It was high time for China . . . to take steps for the liberation of Tibet as it had done for the rest of the Chinese territory.'[2]

In November 1950 the Tibetan Government complained to the United Nations against Chinese aggression in Tibet, but the debate on the question in the General Assembly was suspended because the Indian representative held out the assurance that his Govern-ment 'was certain that the Tibetan question could still be settled by peaceful means'. Meanwhile the Indian Prime Minister publicly pleaded that the People's Republic in China was a coalition govern-ment embodying a majority of non-Communist elements. Their policy was devoted entirely to internal politics, especially their economic situation. 'It has been universally recognized that they are far removed from what might be called Communist policy, although the leaders are undoubtedly Communists.'[3]

Pakistan's attitude towards the turmoil in Tibet was even less critical than Nehru's, and gave China still less cause for complaint. *Dawn*, reporting 'Karachi Reactions' to the Chinese invasion of Tibet, said the news 'has not caused any stir in the Pakistani capital. Pakistan, it may be noted, has not taken any direct interest in the affairs of Tibet which has always been legally under the suzerainty of China.'[4] The same issue quoted the Pakistani Ambassador to the United States, M. A. H. Ispahani, as having said that Pakistan was

---

[1] K. M. Panikkar, *In Two Chinas*, p. 102.
[2] P. C. Chakravarti, *India's China Policy*, p. 48.
[3] *Statesman*, 17 Oct. 1950.
[4] *Dawn*, 28 Oct. 1950.

quite removed from Tibet and he did not think it would make any difference to Pakistan if the Communists controlled Tibet. When Tibet complained to the United Nations against Chinese aggression, Pakistan declared she would remain neutral in the proceedings.[1]

Both Pakistan and India, of course, overlooked certain important implications of China's occupation of Tibet. First, neither country seems to have realized that a resurgent China now stood poised at the northern gateways of the subcontinent and could henceforth directly intervene in the affairs of both countries. China's claim to Nepal, Bhutan, Sikkim, and certain areas of northern India, her 2,500-mile-long undemarcated border with India, and her 300-mile-long undefined border with Pakistan-controlled Kashmir, contained much potential for friction and strife. While it was clear to objective outside observers that 'a classic pattern for a border dispute'[2] was inherent in the situation, Indian official policy was based on the premise that 'a friendly China and a friendly Tibet are the best guarantee of the defence of our country'.[3] When, during a visit home late in 1951, Ambassador Panikkar's attention was drawn to the large influx of Chinese troops into Tibet, he shrugged off the implication that this might constitute a danger to India with the tart observation that he did not think 'there is anything wrong in the troops of Red China moving about in their own territory'.[4] Secondly, though India and Pakistan professed to stand for the liberation of all Afro-Asian countries from foreign domination, in the case of Tibet they stood aside while the clock was turned back on the freedom of that unfortunate land. They conveniently disregarded the fact that Chinese sovereignty over Tibet was the illegitimate product of Chinese imperialism. After India and China had fallen out with each other, Nehru himself voiced the reality that the Chinese State had grown to its present dimensions by imperialism. 'The State grew in that way,' he said, 'and came to Tibet.'[5] By virtue of her size and distinct geographical, linguistic, cultural, and political personality, and her tradition of autonomy, Tibet is certainly more deserving of independence than several other countries

---

[1] *Dawn*, 19 Nov. 1950.

[2] Robert Trumbull, New Delhi correspondent of the *New York Times* in a report published in the *Times of India* on 7 Dec. 1950, quoted by A. G. Noorani, *Our Credulity and Negligence*, p. 8.

[3] Deputy Minister for External Affairs, B. V. Keskar, quoted by Ton That Thien, *India and Southeast Asia*, p. 288.

[4] P. C. Chakravarti, *India's China Policy*, p. 49.

[5] J. Nehru, *Speeches*, IV, p. 210.

whose shackles of thraldom have been shattered by the twentieth-century 'explosion of independence'.

During the Korean War Pakistan did not contribute any armed forces to the United Nations command and refrained from voting on the resolution branding the People's Republic of China as an aggressor in Korea. On the whole, however, Pakistan was sympathetic to the United States policy towards Korea, and China could very well have taken exception to certain aspects of Pakistani policy, but China was remarkably patient towards Pakistan. All in all, it seems fairly clear that Communist China had coolly calculated from the very beginning that in the long run it would be with India that her national interests would clash and that forbearance with Pakistan in the meantime might ultimately pay a useful dividend.

China's presence in the Himalayas worked to Pakistan's advantage in the Indo-Pakistani war of 1965, but only the future will reveal its long-term effect on the ideological and political fortunes of the subcontinent.

6 Pakistan and the Western Powers

I. Pakistan and the Commonwealth

On the eve of independence it was generally believed that, afterwards, India would not stay in the Commonwealth, while it was taken for granted that Pakistan would. For Britain to be able to reconcile India and manage to keep both the new Dominions within the Commonwealth was a notable diplomatic achievement, to understand the extent of which it is necessary to go back some years.

The Indian National Congress had committed itself to severing the Commonwealth link at least as early as 1930. On 2 January that year the Working Committee decided that 26 January be observed as *purna swaraj* day[1] (complete independence day). A declaration drafted at that meeting was read to the people all over India on 26 January 1930 as part of the celebrations, and the recitation was repeated annually till independence became a fact. The declaration stated *inter alia*: 'The British Government in India has not only deprived the Indian people of their freedom but has based itself on the exploitation of the masses, and has ruined India economically, politically, culturally and spiritually. We believe, therefore, that India must sever the British connection and attain *purna swaraj* or complete independence.'[2] On the eve of 'independence day' Gandhi emphasized: 'Remember the 26th is the day not to declare independence but to declare that we will be satisfied with nothing less than complete independence as opposed to Dominion Status so called.'[3]

---

[1] To this day India celebrates 26 January as her independence day, not 15 August on which date she became constitutionally independent.

[2] For text of declaration see Pattabi Sitaramayya, *The History of the Indian National Congress*, I, p. 363.

[3] D. G. Tendulkar, *Mahatma*, III, p. 8. Gandhi, however, was not consistent in his attitude towards Dominion Status. In 1939 he said he would accept such a status, if offered. H. V. Hodson, *The Great Divide*, p. 318.

Nehru, who was the chief spokesman for Congress on external affairs, reiterated on numerous occasions that India would never agree to have any constitutional link with Britain after independence. To Nehru the 'idea behind Dominion Status, of a mother country closely connected with her daughter nations, all of them having a common cultural background, seemed totally inapplicable to India'.[1] In August 1940 he said the whole conception of Dominion Status for India was dead as a doornail.[2]

The Muslim League, on the other hand, had no anti-British tradition. As a matter of fact, during the difficult years of the Second World War, when the Congress party first declined co-operation in the war effort and then launched the 'Quit India' movement, the more estranged Congress became from the British Government, the more were the latter forced to rely on the Muslims. For their part the Muslims fully realized that they had little chance of winning Pakistan against the opposition of the much more powerful Congress Party unless they were backed up by the British. The Muslim League deprecated the 'Quit India' resolution and allowed the Muslims to co-operate in the war effort.

Naturally, however, this special relationship between the British Government and the Indian Muslims could endure only as long as it suited both sides. It was clearly beneficial for Britain to lean towards the Muslim minority while she intended to rule India and had to keep the Hindu majority in check. But once she had decided to relinquish power, the balance of her national interest immediately shifted in the direction of favouring the Hindus, for it seemed clear that, whether India remained united or was split into two, the Hindus of India under the banner of the Congress Party would be a far more important factor in international life than the Muslims. That the Labour Party at this time happened to be in office in the United Kingdom greatly facilitated the process of *rapprochement* between Britain and the Congress leadership. Labour traditionally had been sympathetic to Congress causes and many members of the top echelons in both parties had long been on terms of personal friendship with one another. Attlee, Cripps, Pethick-Lawrence and others in Labour ranks admired the Congress leaders as progressive intellectuals and doughty fighters for the freedom of their country. Jinnah and the League, on the other hand, were pictured by them as reactionaries and treated with scant respect. This was vividly

---

[1] J. Nehru, *The Discovery of India*, p. 428.
[2] H. V. Hodson, *The Great Divide*, p. 87.

brought out in a BBC-TV 'conversation' between Attlee and Francis Williams in 1959:

> Attlee: I never liked Jinnah. I knew him as long ago as 1927. I never liked him.
>
> Williams: Why?
>
> Attlee: I don't think he was very genuine, you know . . . I thought a great deal of his ambition was for Master Jinnah rather than anything else.[1]

Personal friendships between Labour and Congress leaders notwithstanding, the task before the British statesmen was a formidable one, because a lot of lost ground had to be recovered. Britain had to soothe the feeling of hostility between herself and the Congress Party which only recently—during the 'Quit India' movement—had stood at its highest point, and she had to demonstrate by positive actions, to the satisfaction of the Congress leaders, that the game of favouring the Muslims had definitely ended.

A beginning was made by getting rid of Wavell, who had incurred the wrath of Congress,[2] and replacing him as Viceroy by Mountbatten, who was more acceptable to that party and who was directed to work towards 'a unitary Government for British India and the Indian States, if possible within the British Commonwealth'.[3] The phrase 'if possible within the British Commonwealth' had been inserted in Attlee's directive at the special request of Mountbatten, 'who feels that he must strive for a solution which leaves such good feeling that the Indian Parties will want to remain within the Commonwealth'.[4]

By April, however, Mountbatten had lost the first round. Jinnah remained implacable and Mountbatten came to the conclusion that Pakistan was inevitable. This further concession to Muslim opinion, though wrested from the hands of an unwilling British Government, did not make Mountbatten's objective, of keeping India within the Commonwealth, any easier. Quite obviously, the only way in which he could now win over new India was to side with her on the crucial issues of the day. How he managed to succeed, and at what price to Pakistan, must now be told.

[1] *Listener*, 22 Jan. 1959. A British observer wrote in 1949, 'Too many British Labour Party members are still thinking in terms of a progressive Congress and a reactionary Moslem League.' Richard Symonds, 'Estrangement of Pakistan: Grievances Against Britain', *Manchester Guardian*, 24 Aug. 1949.

[2] See Leonard Mosley, *The Last Days of the British Raj*, ch. 2.

[3] John Connell, *Auchinleck*, p. 864.

[4] Alan Campbell-Johnson, *Mission With Mountbatten*, p. 31.

Before Mountbatten's arrival on the scene in India, the Indian Constituent Assembly, on Nehru's motion, had, on 22 January 1947, passed the Objectives Resolution, declaring 'its firm and solemn resolve to proclaim India as an independent, sovereign republic'. Since the Commonwealth had always been a strictly monarchical organization, this measure was seen as presaging the fulfilment of the long-standing Congress pledge to cut off all constitutional ties with Britain. Mountbatten was, therefore, confronted not only with the task of healing Congress ill-feeling towards Britain and of persuading Congress to disregard its past resolutions, but also of finding some way of getting the Commonwealth to accept a republic within its ranks. In Campbell-Johnson's words, the situation called for a 'face-saving formula'.[1] When Gordon Walker, at that time Under-Secretary of State for Commonwealth Relations in Attlee's Labour Government, visited Delhi towards the end of February, Mountbatten prepared for him an *aide-mémoire* which made 'certain tentative suggestions as to how the structure of the Commonwealth could perhaps be altered, particularly in nomenclature, to allow Asian countries to remain more easily associated with it'. Mountbatten thought 'there is room for a republic within the Commonwealth'.[2]

As compared with his deep concern to accommodate India within the Commonwealth, even if it meant changing the nature of the Commonwealth itself, Mountbatten was notably brusque towards Pakistan. On 12 April 1947 Campbell-Johnson noted in his diary: '[At the Staff Meeting] Mountbatten reported on his latest meeting with Jinnah, who was apparently much shaken when Mountbatten failed to react in any way to his offer, dramatically presented, to bring Pakistan into the Commonwealth.'[3] Some days later, at another Staff Meeting, Ismay pleaded 'that it would be virtually impossible, both on moral and material grounds, to eject from the Commonwealth any part of the Commonwealth that asks to remain in'. But 'Mountbatten came down heavily against the concept of allowing only a part' of British India to remain within the Commonwealth, as this would involve the 'risk of Britain being involved in the support of one Indian sovereign State against another'.[4]

Mountbatten's much greater concern for Indian than for Pakistani

[1] Alan Campbell-Johnson, *Mission With Mountbatten*, p. 66.
[2] ibid., p. 291.
[3] ibid., p. 60.
[4] ibid., p. 81.

susceptibilities in the matter of Commonwealth membership was
not the only question regarding which Pakistanis felt that the
representatives of Great Britain had favoured India against Pakistan.
They thought also that the Radcliffe Award was grossly unfair to
them, and that the date of the transfer of power had been advanced,
from June 1948 to August 1947, under Indian pressure to the detriment of Pakistan.[1]

As Pakistan's main problems related to India, her appraisal of the
British attitude towards herself after independence depended on the
British attitude on those issues. Here again Pakistan began to feel
that in a real choice between the two, Britain would always come
down on the side of India. Two cases in point, immediately after
partition, which have already been described under Pakistan's
relations with India, were the premature closure of the Supreme
Commander's headquarters upon India's insistence, enabling her
to withhold Pakistan's share of military supplies, and the deaf ear
Britain and the other Commonwealth countries turned towards
Pakistan's request for help in controlling the communal carnage,
which had led Jinnah to complain that Great Britain was shirking
her responsibility in this respect. But Pakistan's most painful experience at the hands of Britain was the complete change in the
attitude of the British delegation towards the Kashmir question
in the Security Council when that body reconvened in March 1948,
after it had adjourned in February at the insistence of India. The
interval, as we have already noted, was utilized by India for successfully pressing the British Government, through Mountbatten, to
modify its policy in respect of Kashmir.[2] Campbell-Johnson explains that Mountbatten was unhappy at the attitude of the British
delegation to the Security Council because it was endangering his
efforts to reconcile India to Dominion Status.[3]

In October 1948 the Prime Ministers of the newly independent
Asian countries, India, Pakistan, and Ceylon, for the first time
attended a conference of the Commonwealth Prime Ministers.

[1] See in this behalf M. Rafique Afzal, *Speeches and Statements of Quaid-i-Millat
Liaquat Ali Khan*, p. 209, where Liaquat reveals that the Muslim League protested that
it would be impossible to set up a new country within the space of two months after the
announcement of the 3 June plan to partition India, but its representation was disregarded.
For the Indian wish to hurry the transfer of power, see V. P. Menon, *The Transfer of
Power in India*, p. 380 (quoting Nehru) and K. L. Panjabi, *The Indomitable Sardar*, p.
155 (quoting Sardar Patel's disclosure that he had agreed to partition on the condition
that power should be transferred within two months).
[2] See pp. 30-1.
[3] Alan Campbell-Johnson, *Mission With Mountbatten*, p. 291.

Mountbatten had retired from the Governor-Generalship of India some months earlier but, 'with his immense prestige in India', was believed to have played a full part in informal discussions relating to India's future relationship with the Commonwealth.[1] Two months after the conference, the Congress Party in India, acting no doubt under the influence of the Prime Minister, passed a resolution at the Jaipur session declaring that 'Congress would welcome India's association with independent nations of the Commonwealth for their common weal and promotion of world peace'.[2]

A special meeting of the Commonwealth Prime Ministers was called in April 1949 to consider the constitutional implications of India's willingness to remain in the Commonwealth after becoming a republic. To smooth the way, Attlee 'sent out personal envoys for preliminary talks with his fellow Prime Ministers',[3] and on 2 March he discussed the question with the Leader of the Opposition, Winston Churchill, as a result of which he was able to report to the King that 'Mr. Churchill gave it as his own opinion that it was most important to keep India within the Commonwealth. While fully agreeing with the importance of not weakening the link of the allegiance to the Crown, he thought it should be possible to retain a republican India in the Commonwealth.'[4] Under the circumstances, the outcome of the conference in April was an almost foregone conclusion. A joint communiqué of all the Prime Ministers signified that republican India had been allowed to continue her membership of the Commonwealth by accepting the King as 'the symbol of the free association of its member nations and as such the Head of the Commonwealth'.[5]

Liaquat concurred in the solution and, in fact, went with all the other Commonwealth Prime Ministers to the King personally to advise him to accept India as a republic.[6] On the merits of the question Pakistan could hardly have raised any objection. If India wished to become a republic, and all the remaining members of the Commonwealth nevertheless were willing to let her stay on in the Commonwealth, it was obviously their concern. But Pakistan could

---

[1] *Round Table*, Dec. 1948.

[2] J. Nehru, *India's Foreign Policy*, p. 138.

[3] Patrick Gordon Walker, *The Commonwealth*, p. 182.

[4] *Twilight of Empire, Memoirs of Prime Minister Clement Attlee, as Set Down by Francis Williams*, p. 218.

[5] Nicholas Mansergh (ed.), *Documents and Speeches on Commonwealth Affairs, 1931–1952*, II, p. 846.

[6] *Twilight of Empire . . .* , p. 219.

not but notice some of the broader aspects of the matter, and these served to confirm the view that India would always command preferential treatment in the Commonwealth. The *Economist* had noted during the conference that the fixed point in India's policy was 'to make India an "independent sovereign republic", and on that point public opinion in India will make no concession. . . . The task of devising a means of incorporating such a republic into the Commonwealth is, in the Indian view, a matter mainly for the other members. . . . It is the latter which must make the constitutional concessions.'[1]

At popular level, resentment in Pakistan at what was taken as a new proof of Britain's deference to India was strongly manifested. The *Times* Special Correspondent reported from Lahore that anti-British feeling in Pakistan

dates back to the partition, which many Pakistanis believe was arranged in India's favour; it was strengthened by Britain's refusal of Pakistan's request for Commonwealth mediation on the Kashmir dispute and her alleged change of front on the same dispute when it came before the United Nations. The feeling is now taking the form of resentment at the Commonwealth Prime Ministers' decision to allow India to 'eat her cake and have it' by becoming a republic and remaining a member of the Commonwealth.[2]

Several observers thought that disappointment with Britain was one of the reasons why the Pakistani Prime Minister, at about this time, accepted an invitation to visit Russia. Pakistan's decision not to change the par value of her rupee when Britain devalued her currency in September 1949 was also taken, in part, as a mark of Pakistan's assertion of economic independence of Britain.

In spite of disenchantment with the Commonwealth on many issues, Pakistan never seriously thought that she would be better off by leaving it. The official attitude of the Government, as stated by Mahmud Husain, Deputy Minister for Foreign Affairs, in the Constituent Assembly on 23 March 1950, was that Pakistan would continue in the Commonwealth so long as it was 'convenient' for her to do so.

When Pakistan decided to become a republic she too expressed the wish to maintain her ties with the Commonwealth, and a communiqué of the Prime Ministers' Conference, identical to the

[1] *Economist*, 23 April 1949.
[2] *The Times*, 16 May 1949.

one issued in the case of India, was published on 5 February 1955 to affirm that Pakistan would continue to remain within the Commonwealth. The final seal of approval to Pakistan's association with the Commonwealth was affixed by the Constituent Assembly of Pakistan on 2 March 1956, by 42 votes to 2. Chaudhri Muhammad Ali, during whose premiership the Assembly decision was taken, states that 'as the true character of the Commonwealth became more apparent, there was disillusionment, but not to the point of wishing to break away from it'. He thinks the main reason why Pakistan continued her association with the Commonwealth was her affinity with Western democratic institutions, reinforced by cultural and economic ties. Also, English was still the official language of the government and the higher courts, as well as the medium of instruction for university education. Pakistan was a member of the sterling area and had fairly large balances in London, trade with the United Kingdom predominated, the Colombo Plan brought benefits of aid in economic development, and as part of a worldwide community of nations Pakistan could exercise some influence in the shaping of world policies.[1]

II. Pakistan and the United States of America

The attitude of the Americans towards India and Pakistan initially was no exception to the general rule. The land of Gandhi and Nehru, they felt, having successfully fought for her freedom against the British, in much the same way as the Americans themselves had done, was destined to play a great role on the world stage. But the creation of Jinnah's Pakistan was a sad mistake and the future of that ill-conceived State was no more than a question mark on the surface of the globe.

During the Second World War, President Roosevelt had pressed Prime Minister Churchill for a settlement with the leaders of the Indian National Congress so that their help could be enlisted in the war effort against the expected Japanese invasion of India. The Roosevelt–Churchill exchanges show that the American leader was totally ignorant of the demands and strength of the Muslim League. His 'mind was back in the American War of Independence, and he thought of the Indian problem in terms of the thirteen colonies fighting George III'.[2] Roosevelt's prescription for India, therefore, was that a temporary government in India be set up, 'headed by a

---

[1] Chaudhri Muhammad Ali, *The Emergence of Pakistan*, p. 379.
[2] Winston S. Churchill, *The Second World War*, IV, p. 190.

small representative group, covering different castes, occupations, religions and geographies[1]—this group to be recognized as a temporary Dominion Government . . . it would be charged with setting up a body to consider a more permanent Government for the whole country.'[2]

Nearer the time of independence Henry F. Grady, Ambassador-designate of the United States to India, was criticized by the Muslim League paper *Dawn* for 'harping on what he calls "national unity" '.[3] But Grady was simply giving expression to what Americans generally believed at the time. Edgar Snow described Pakistan as 'the queerest State in the world; you can't draw its map'.[4] Within the portals of the Federal Capitol in Washington, D.C., Representative Emanuel Celler of New York, speaking the day after the announcement of the Partition Plan, called Pakistan 'a mistake, yes, a rank appeasement of Jinnah'.[5] A few days later he declared: 'Pakistan is an engraved invitation to His Majesty's Government to remain in India. . . . Pakistan is a menacing and overshadowing cloud.'[6] *Time* said, 'Pakistan [is] an economic wreck.'

The same Emanuel Celler, who had spoken of Pakistan so disparagingly, offered Prime Minister Jawaharlal Nehru congratulations upon the latter's 59th birthday and spoke of his 'wisdom, courage, and sacrifice', and also felicitated the people of India 'for having the services and talents of this great man at their disposal'.[7] Gandhi's assassination in January 1948 brought forth a tremendous effusion of tributes from Congressmen. Representative Keating said Gandhi was more than a political leader, 'almost a saint to uncounted millions of our brothers in the vast subcontinent of India'. Celler introduced a resolution to erect a monument to Gandhi's memory and ended his eulogy by joining Gandhi with Moses, Buddha, St. Francis of Assisi, and Abraham Lincoln. In contrast, the assassination of Liaquat Ali Khan in October 1951

---

[1] This obviously meant that the Congress Party should be asked to form the Government because it was only that party which claimed to represent all the interests in India.

[2] Winston S. Churchill, *The Second World War*, IV, p. 185.

[3] *New York Times*, 14 April 1947.

[4] *Round Table*, Sept. 1963. It may be pointed out that with the States of Alaska and Hawaii separated from the main body of the United States, one would encounter a similar difficulty in drawing a map of the USA.

[5] *Congressional Record (vol. 93, part 5, p. 6341) 80th Congress, 1st Session*, 4 June 1947, House.

[6] *Congressional Record, Appendix (vol. 93, part 12, p. 2968) 80th Congress, 1st Session*, 19 June 1947, House.

[7] *Congressional Record, Appendix (vol. 93, part 13, p. A4279) 80th Congress, 1st Session*, 17 Nov. 1947, House.

attracted little attention, though the Pakistani leader had only the year before made an extensive personal tour of the United States and made numerous friendly speeches.

Until 1949 the United States could not take much direct interest in the affairs of the Indian subcontinent. The cold war had broken out in Europe soon after the termination of the hot war there and America, not wishing to make a gift to Communism of what she had only just rescued from Nazism, bent all her energy towards reviving the war-ravaged non-Communist countries of Europe. Winston Churchill sounded the warning at Fulton, Missouri, on 5 March 1946 in words that have become immortal: 'From Stettin on the Baltic to Trieste in the Adriatic an iron curtain has descended across the Continent.' On 12 March 1947 President Harry S. Truman asked Congress to vote emergency military and economic aid to Greece and Turkey, and on 5 June Secretary of State Marshall expounded a plan at Harvard for the recovery of Europe. In July the Russians walked out of the Marshall Plan meeting in Paris, and the cold war began in earnest. So, when India and Pakistan commenced their respective careers as independent nations, Europe was already in the grip of the cold war.

But momentous events in Asia soon claimed America's attention. It became obvious in the summer of 1949 that the Communists in China would soon prevail over the Nationalists, and there would come into being in Asia an even more populous Communist State than Russia. American eyes now turned to India as the ideal counterpoise to China by virtue of her size and estimated potential. Hubert H. Humphrey, then a freshman senator from Minnesota and in later years to prove a consistent supporter of India, pleaded that India 'should be brought into the councils of the democratic world organization we are forming around the framework of the Atlantic Pact'.[1] In his address to the India League of America, at a dinner for Madam Pandit, Ambassador of India, on 24 May 1949, a copy of which he entered in the Congressional Record, Humphrey, forgetting that the Congress Party of India had in fact opposed the war effort, referred to India as 'a nation which fought beside us in the Second World War' and perorated: 'The interests of the United States and India are interdependent. Together we can help build a world order and a world society based on freedom and democracy. Madam Pandit, in the agony of the world's crisis today, we urge you,

[1] *Congressional Record, Appendix (vol. 95, part 13, p. A2374) 81st Congress, 1st Session,* 25 April 1949, Senate.

your brother, your country, and your people, in your zeal for democracy, in your incisive cool thinking, to help give us a vision which will blaze the path toward the realization of the great ideals we share.'

Nehru's and Liaquat's visits to the United States

Before long, an invitation was extended to Prime Minister Jawaharlal Nehru to make an official visit to the United States. At first no similar invitation was extended to Liaquat Ali Khan. It was only after Russia had invited the Pakistani Prime Minister that the United States extended the same courtesy to him. As neither Prime Minister had travelled to the New World before, these trips provided the first direct opportunity for the Americans to size up the two South Asian leaders.

The Indian Prime Minister started with all the advantages on his side. He was a household name in America already, and represented the largest non-Communist country in the world, located next door to the two Communist giants. Russia had recently exploded an atom bomb, breaking the United States supremacy in that field, and the Communists had proclaimed themselves overlords of China only a few days previously. The French-backed Bao Dai was not doing too well in Indo-China and many observers were already writing him off. 'So, it is to India', telegraphed the correspondent of the *Hindu*, 'that American eyes turn for saving Asia and the whole world from Communism.'[1]

American hopes for Nehru's collaboration did not seem unreasonable if one remembers that India at that time was putting down Communists at home with a heavy hand and was helping the government of Burma to do the same, that Russia and China were continuously berating India for her alleged subservience to the United Kingdom and the USA, and that only a few months before India had decided to remain in the Commonwealth. The last-mentioned event had been greeted by the *New York Times* as 'a historic step . . . in setting a limit to Communist conquest and opening up the prospect of a wider defense system than the Atlantic Pact'.[2]

The Indian Prime Minister landed at the National Airport, Washington, on 11 October 1949 to begin his four-week tour. In his words of welcome, Truman recalled that America had been

[1] *Hindu*, 12 Oct. 1949.
[2] *New York Times*, 28 April 1949.

discovered by Columbus in search of a new route to India and expressed the hope that Nehru's 'visit, too, will be, in a sense, a discovery of America'.[1] The simile evidently pleased the guest because during his speeches afterwards he often stated that he had come to America on a voyage of discovery.

America went all out to give Nehru a hero's welcome. This was due partly to the genuine admiration the Americans felt for the Indian leader as a sort of George Washington of India, and partly because they visualized India as the counterpart of democratic America in the East. Owing to their pre-eminence in technology, Americans are inclined to look for neat breakthroughs in other spheres of human activity also. It was pleasing to visualize the USA, the greatest democracy of the West, holding Soviet Russia in check in the Western hemisphere and India, the greatest democracy of the East, similarly blocking China in the East. The *New York Times* called Nehru 'the world's most popular individual'; the *Washington Post* declared that 'he knows the art of being king'; Secretary of State Dean Acheson ranked him with Thomas Jefferson, Woodrow Wilson, and Abraham Lincoln; Mrs. Roosevelt said that, while the USA had developed certain material values, India could give some of that spiritual leadership which Nehru represented. The *New York Times* wrote plainly: 'Washington wants India to be a bulwark against Communism ... India is potentially a great counterweight to China.'

Though Nehru had accepted discovery of America as his slogan, in fact he strove to make Americans discover the inherent wisdom and superiority of the ancient land of India. In his address at Columbia University he reminded the audience that wonderful civilizations had grown up in the East when Europe and America were still unknown to history. India was a newcomer in the modern family of nations, but she had certain advantages: she had brought no prejudices or enmities but a touch of idealism, and she had been taught by Gandhi never to subordinate means to ends. In an obvious reference to the cold war, he said that the very process of marshalling the world into two hostile camps precipitates the conflict which it has sought to avoid. It produces a sense of fear which leads men into wrong courses. The problem, therefore, becomes one of lessening and ultimately putting an end to this fear.

At another place Nehru said that, after thirty years of Gandhi's

[1] The thought was specially appropriate because the following day—12 October—happened to be Columbus Day.

leadership, India was not afraid of external aggression. Urging that fear in international affairs should be removed, he declared, 'If there is an armed conflict we are weak, we have no atom bomb, and we rejoice in not having an atom bomb.'[1]

India's policy, he explained, was not a negative and neutral policy: it was a positive and vital policy. India wished to make her full contribution but in her own way. Just as the United States had been thrust into a position of extreme importance almost against her wishes, and had to assume leadership in world affairs, so was India, in a different context, being inevitably drawn into the vortex of world affairs. Indians also knew very well that America sympathized in India's struggle for freedom but they did not admire everything in America. The United States had a reputation abroad of being materialistic and of being tough in matters of money.

Nehru said India would welcome from America a large quantity of wheat; mechanical and technological aid; and financial investments.[2] But he had not come to carry out any deal, as 'no self-respecting country wants one-sided assistance'.[3] However, while not caring to explain what America would get in return for the material assistance India expected from that country, he spelled out clearly what America could not expect from India. At the National Press Club he told a packed audience that any talk of an Asian Defence Pact would be premature. What was more important than a defence pact was the development of a psychological background of co-operation. India definitely did not want leadership in Asia or anywhere else. On the following day he declared in New York, 'We have no intention to commit ourselves to anybody at any time.'[4] He expressed the hope that India would have close ties with the USA but enigmatically added, in the same breath, 'The most intimate ties are ties which are not ties.'[5] Lowell Mellet of the *Washington Evening Star* disconsolately commented: 'A wise man came out of the East the other day and rode up Broadway. New York turned out to meet him. . . . Before the day was done, the visitor . . . [had] answered the question uppermost in the mind of the Government at least: Where does India, or he as India's leader,

[1] However, after the short border war with China, Nehru said, at Rohtak, on 9 March 1963, that it was good China did not have an atom bomb. If she had it, nobody could say when she would use it. A. G. Noorani, *Our Credulity and Negligence*, p. 119.
[2] *Jawaharlal's Discovery of America*, pp. 63, 81.
[3] ibid., p. 71.
[4] *New York Times*, 16 Oct. 1949.
[5] *Jawaharlal's Discovery of America*, p. 26.

stand in the cold war between the United States and Russia? The answer, in effect, is that India wants no part of that war.'

The Indian leader's declaration, from the podium of the United States Congress, that 'where freedom is menaced, or justice threatened, or where aggression takes place, we cannot be and shall not be neutral', evoked the most enthusiastic applause and comment. Americans associated aggression with Communism, and took it for granted that Nehru's remarks were directed against that menace. 'But in India the interpretation was different and the Press contended that what Pandit Nehru meant by the threats to justice and freedom were the threats of imperial domination and discrimination.'[1] This was not surprising because Nehru believed that, while to the West the issue of the day might be Communism, 'to us it is colonialism'.[2]

Some in America bluntly expressed their disappointment as soon as it became clear that Nehru wanted no part in the East-West confrontation. 'If India insists on remaining aloof in the cold war,' wrote the *Washington Daily News* on 17 October, 'cannot we, at least, start saving wear and tear on our welcome carpets for the candid visitor.' Others controlled their inner feelings, still hoping Nehru would eventually come round to their way of thinking. But everyone was well aware that the tour, on the whole, had generated more irritation than goodwill. The remark of a State Department official summed up the result: 'We had a kind of sentimental image of Nehru and Indian independence, a feeling that nothing could create any problems between us. The more we heard the less certain we were.'[3] Nehru's audience could hardly have failed to recognize the gap between his advice to others and his policies concerning India's own interests. He said that Gandhi's principle of non-violence had not been applicable in the cases of Hyderabad and Kashmir, and nimbly quoted Gandhi as having stated that people should 'resist aggression to the point of death'.[4]

The Soviet and Chinese comments on the Nehru visit to the USA were naturally in keeping with their generally low opinion at that time of Indian leadership. The *New Times* said that 'the vacancy left behind by Chiang Kai-shek is being offered to Nehru',[5]

[1] K. P. Karunakaran, *India in World Affairs, Aug. 1947–Jan. 1950*, p. 46.
[2] Phillips Talbot and S. L. Poplai, *India and America*, p. 157.
[3] Selig S. Harrison, 'Case History of a Mistake', *New Republic*, 10 Aug. 1959.
[4] *Jawaharlal's Discovery of America*, p. 143.
[5] *New Times*, no. 42, 1949.

while *World Culture* informed its readers that 'American Imperialism Lays Hand on a New Slave'.

Liaquat's visit to the USA in May 1950 provided the first real opportunity for Pakistani leadership to explain the goals and aspirations of the new Muslim State to the leaders and people of the world's most powerful state. The Pakistani statesman personally was little known to Americans but he worked diligently to overcome the handicaps under which he started. Reversing Nehru's slogan, he said that the purpose of his visit was to assist America to discover Pakistan.

Being aware that the real reasons for the establishment of Pakistan were not sufficiently understood abroad, and that many thought of Pakistan as a backward theocratic state as compared to a forward-looking secular India, Liaquat's first effort was to enlighten his audiences on these subjects. Partition came about, he explained, because a hundred million Muslims found themselves in a minority in British India and were convinced that under Hindu majority rule their culture was in danger of effacement and their already inferior economic position was likely to sink further. Such a large discontented minority in the vast Indo-Pakistani subcontinent 'would have been the greatest single unstable element in the world'. In the Islamic ideology of Pakistan there was no room for theocracy, because Islam stands for freedom of conscience, condemns coercion, has no priesthood, and abhors the caste system.[1] Though Islam frowns upon large accumulations of unearned wealth, it fully respects the rights of private ownership and private enterprise.

In the world around them Pakistanis 'find dark forces at work threatening to extinguish the torch of civilization which liberal institutions such as yours are trying to keep alive', but 'no threat or persuasion, no material peril or ideological allurement can deflect' Pakistanis from their chosen ideology. Pakistan's Islamic ideology not only gave stability to Pakistan herself but provided religious and cultural links between her and the Middle East countries which would 'prove a stabilizing factor in Asia'.

Some utterances of the Pakistani Prime Minister and his wife were even more full of meaning. He said Pakistan attached the greatest importance to economic development through 'the good will and co-operation of free and peaceful nations'; ideologically and strategically Pakistan held a position of great responsibility and she

[1] Unless otherwise stated, the subject matter of Liaquat's addresses has been taken from Liaquat Ali Khan, *Pakistan: The Heart of Asia.*

was resolved 'to throw all her weight to help the maintenance of stability in Asia'; 'Pakistan extends her hand of friendship to the freedom-loving peoples of the world'; should America decide that construction is the best way to defy destruction, she would find 'the people of Pakistan amongst your staunchest friends'. He expressed the hope 'that the future will unfold itself in ways which will also make them [Pakistan and US] comrades, in the noble task of maintaining peace and in translating the great constructive dreams of democracy into reality'. Begum Liaquat Ali Khan declared in the course of her address at the City Hall, New York: 'We believe that a civilization or a society which concerns itself with material things alone cannot endure.'

Liaquat also tried to procure arms for the Pakistani forces, saying that such assistance would serve the interests of the entire free world. At a news conference in Washington he said that Pakistan occupied a very strategic position and that was the reason why he was interested in procuring up-to-date equipment for his armed forces. He said that because Pakistan had her own Islamic way of life, Communism was not likely to find fertile ground there; the two ways of life 'exclude each other'.[1] A few days later *Dawn* reported that the Pakistani Prime Minister had had secret talks in Washington with Defense Secretary Louis Johnson and the Joint Chiefs of Staff during which he outlined Pakistan's arms needs. He stressed his nation's strategic position and the fighting qualities of her anti-Communist Muslim warriors.[2] At a press conference in Ottawa on 30 May he complained that the people who asked him why he was buying arms did not appreciate the fact that Pakistan defended the Khyber Pass through which the subcontinent had been invaded ninety times. He added that he did not know what forces the Russians, whose territory lay a few miles north of the Khyber Pass, had, because 'they have not given me any intimation'.[3] Reviewing his visit to the USA and Canada on Radio Pakistan, he expressed himself satisfied with the talks he had had with the statesmen of both countries regarding 'the problems facing Pakistan and also the question of her integrity and safety', and the supply of 'such material which may be needed for strengthening and stabilizing Pakistan'.[4]

[1] *New York Times*, 5 May 1950.
[2] *Dawn*, 21 May 1950.
[3] ibid., 3 June 1950.
[4] M. Rafique Afzal (ed.), *Speeches and Statements of Quaid-i-Millat Liaquat Ali Khan*, p. 429.

That Liaquat had gone to America in preference to the USSR was generally taken to mean that he preferred friendship with the United States to friendship with the Soviet Union. His American hosts also put a similar construction on the meaning of his visit to their country and on his conduct and words there. His declaration before Congress that no risk of ideological allurement could deflect Pakistan from her chosen path of free democracy was taken by the *New York Times* as 'a pledge that the Pakistanis will stand and be counted among those who are devoted to freedom, regardless of the cost'.[1] President Lloyd Cobb of International House, New Orleans, introducing Liaquat Ali Khan at a dinner in the latter's honour, hailed Pakistan as a 'bulwark in the subcontinent and the Middle East against Communism as it seeks to press down from the north'.[2]

Not surprisingly, the USSR viewed Liaquat's activities in the USA with deep suspicion. In a typical comment the *Moscow Literary Gazette* said that Liaquat Ali Khan had been 'transformed into the Pakistani variety of Chiang Kai-shek or Syngman Rhee'.[3]

Though Liaquat Ali Khan's visit roused considerable interest in the United States, it did not match the popular acclaim and attention lavished on Jawaharlal Nehru. *Newsweek* reported that, when the distinguished Pakistani guest showed up at the Senate, it took this top US law-making body half an hour to round up a quorum, and then the visiting Prime Minister addressed a listless third-full chamber.[4] The fact of the matter was that India was still America's number one choice in Asia. Nehru's visit had been unfruitful, but he had not yet done anything markedly overt in the international field to make India look a hopeless case in American eyes. A *New York Times* editorial pleaded for a greater effort at mutual understanding between the United States and India because, it argued, the struggle for Asia could be won or lost in the mind of one man— Jawaharlal Nehru—who was the counterweight on the democratic side to Mao Tse-tung on the Communist side and whose support was worth many divisions.[5] It was not until 1951, after Nehru, amongst other activities, had shown his hand in the Korean War negotiations and refused to attend the Japanese Peace Conference,

---

[1] *New York Times*, 5 May 1950.
[2] *Dawn*, 25 May 1950.
[3] Quoted in *Hindu*, 28 July 1950.
[4] *Newsweek*, 15 May 1950.
[5] *New York Times*, 29 Aug. 1950.

that responsible opinion in America began openly to despair of him.

Some years later when Pakistan's alliance with the United States fell from favour among Pakistanis, many tried to heap the entire blame for the pro-American policy on those who formally signed the agreements and disregarded the fact that the last-named were logically pursuing the trend set by their first Prime Minister. Liaquat's main anxiety was to ensure the survival of a virtually unarmed Pakistan in the face of recurrent threats of war from a much stronger neighbour. He realized that if Pakistan wanted outside material and moral support she had to lean on one side or the other, and both practical and ideological considerations pointed in the direction of America. That deep concern for Pakistan's safety overshadowed Liaquat's thoughts at all times was graphically manifested when he was shot by an assassin in 1951. His last words were 'May God protect Pakistan.'

The Korean War

In concrete terms Pakistan's contribution to the United Nations effort in Korea was 5,000 tons of wheat and India's an ambulance unit. India's assistance was the more significant because, as Krishna Menon put it, Indian units were there 'and they took the risks of war'.[1] Prime Minister Attlee also approvingly said, 'We got Indian support, India didn't send troops but she sent the Red Cross.'[2] Indeed, the despatch of such a corps conformed to India's traditional method of showing solidarity with a cause. Gandhi had commanded an ambulance unit in the South African War and had also organized one to serve in the First World War. Nehru had referred to the medical mission sent by the Congress Party to China in 1939, during the Japanese aggression, as a method of 'asserting our foreign policy'.[3] In the Korean War itself, though sixteen nations sent troops, others, including some NATO members (Italy, Denmark, and Norway), sent medical detachments only. But in the United States the image of India left behind by the Korean episode was of an appeaser of China and that of Pakistan of a staunch supporter of the West. Years later President Kennedy, welcoming President Ayub to the United States, said, 'during the difficult days which faced our country at the time of the war in Korea, one

[1] Michael Brecher, *India and World Politics*, p. 36.
[2] *Twilight of Empire, Memoirs of Prime Minister Clement Attlee*, as set down by Francis Williams, p. 238.
[3] J. Nehru, *Unity of India*, p. 336.

of the first to offer us assistance was your country.'[1] The reason
America viewed the Indian role in the Korean conflict with disapproval and the Pakistani part with approbation, does not lie in
the actual contribution of the two countries to the United Nations
military campaign but in their general policy towards that war.

It was on 25 June 1950 that North Korea, a satellite of the Soviet
Union, had crossed the 38th parallel and launched an attack on
South Korea. Meeting on the same day, the Security Council
declared it a breach of the peace and demanded a cessation of
hostilities and the withdrawal of North Korean forces. It also called
upon all members to render every assistance to the United Nations
in the execution of the resolution. Two days later President Truman
ordered the United States armed forces to intervene on behalf of
South Korea. Later on the same day, the Security Council passed
another resolution, recommending that members of the United
Nations furnish to South Korea such assistance as might be necessary to repel the attack. India, then a member of the Security
Council, voted for both resolutions. The Russian delegation, not
yet having returned to the Security Council after walking out in
January, was unable to block the passage of the resolutions by veto.[2]

At the outbreak of war Liaquat Ali Khan was still in the United
States recovering from an operation. He lost no time in declaring
in a public statement that his Government 'will back the United
Nations to the fullest' in any action it may take in the Korean War.[3]
On 30 June 1950 the Permanent Representative of Pakistan to the
United Nations formally confirmed, in a letter to the Secretary-
General, that the Government of Pakistan 'will give their full
support to measures proposed in the Security Council resolution
to stop hostilities'. In New York Liaquat said that Pakistan accepted
the United Nations resolution to aid South Korea, 'knowing full
well what its implications are'.[4]

A brigade of Pakistani troops was getting ready to leave for
Korea and the Americans had offered to equip it with modern
weapons. But Liaquat's advisers were not agreed on the wisdom

---

[1] *United States Department of State Bulletin* (henceforth *USDSB*), 7 Aug. 1961, p.
239.
[2] The Soviet delegation had walked out of the Security Council on 13 January 1950
following the defeat of the Soviet resolution to exclude Nationalist China from the
Council, as a step towards seating the People's Republic of China, and did not return till
1 August 1950.
[3] *Dawn*, 28 June 1950.
[4] ibid., 2 July 1950.

of intervening in a manner which might irretrievably commit Pakistan to the Western camp without getting anything tangible in return.[1] Accordingly, the United States was asked whether she would come to Pakistan's aid if Pakistan was attacked by India.[2] As such an assurance was not forthcoming it was decided not to send any Pakistani contingent to Korea. A few days after Liaquat's assassination, his successor Prime Minister Nazimuddin told a correspondent of the *New York Herald Tribune* that 'a happy solution of the Kashmir problem would release our defence forces and put us in a position seriously to consider sending troops to Korea'.[3]

India had begun by supporting the United Nations resolutions of 25 and 27 June but, before long, assumed the role of a mediator between the contending parties. On 13 July Nehru addressed identical messages to Premier Stalin and Secretary Acheson. India's purpose, he said, was to localize the conflict and to facilitate a peaceful settlement by breaking the deadlock in the Security Council, so that the representative of China could take a seat in it and the USSR could return to it to negotiate peace and help in finding a permanent solution of the Korean problem. Stalin replied that he fully shared Nehru's point of view regarding the expediency of the peaceful settlement of the Korean question through the Security Council, 'with the obligatory participation of the representatives of the five great powers, including the People's Government of China'.[4] Acheson, however, said that the termination of the aggression from North Korea could not be made contingent upon the determination of other questions before the United Nations. He pointed out that Russia's absence from the Security Council was solely due to her own unilateral decision, and added that the question of China's seat in the United Nations must be resolved on its merits and 'should not be dictated by an unlawful aggression'.[5]

These exchanges mark a turning point in India's relations with the United States on the one hand and with Russia and China on the other. This was the first occasion on which India and America had

[1] That Liaquat's advisers were split over the question of sending troops to Korea has been related to me by more than one of the advisers themselves.

[2] M. A. H. Ispahani, 'The Foreign Policy of Pakistan, 1947–64', *Pakistan Horizon*, 3rd Quarter 1964, p. 237. Ispahani was Pakistani Ambassador to the United States at the time.

[3] Quoted by *Indian Press Digests, for the period 16 Sept. to 15 Nov. 1951*, vol. I, no. 2, p. 5.

[4] R. Palme Dutt, *India Today and Tomorrow*, p. 289.

[5] *USDSB*, 31 July 1950, pp. 170–1.

openly differed on a concrete international problem of great importance, while India and the Communist powers had fundamentally
agreed. In the Lower House of the US Congress, Representative
Mason of Illinois compared Nehru's proposal to Chamberlain's
Munich Agreement, and in the Upper House Senator Knowland
of California approvingly read into the Record an article in the
Washington News which, referring to Nehru's letters to Stalin and
Acheson, said that the Indian Prime Minister's 'proposal could not
have been more acceptable to Moscow if Stalin himself had made
it'.[1]

The United Nations forces had been initially thrown back in
Korea but towards the end of September had regained control of
South Korea and were poised to carry the fighting across the 38th
parallel into North Korea. At midnight on 2 October 1950 Premier
Chou En-lai summoned Ambassador Panikkar and told him that
China would intervene in Korea if the United Nations forces
crossed the 38th parallel. The warning was duly conveyed to the
USA and the UN but was disregarded. In a resolution passed on
7 October the General Assembly,[2] by recommending that steps be
taken to ensure conditions of stability throughout Korea and for the
establishment of a unified Korea, implicitly authorized the United
Nations command to move into North Korea. Though India
abstained in the voting on the resolution, Nehru was in fact strongly
opposed to the United Nations forces crossing the 38th parallel.
When the line had been passed, he said, 'The military mind has
taken over.'[3] This was too much even for the *New York Times*,
which hitherto had worked so hard towards Indo-US cordiality.
An editorial on 12 October addressed some 'Plain Words to Indians':
'Pandit Nehru purports to speak for Asia, but it is the voice of
abnegation; his criticism now turns out to have been obstructive,
his policy is appeasement. Worst of all one fails to find a valid
moral judgement in his attitude.'

Pakistan, on the other hand, had been one of the co-sponsors
of the 7 October resolution, and on 11 October Prime Minister
Liaquat Ali Khan said in Parliament that the 38th parallel had never
been recognized by the General Assembly as a permanent boundary

[1] *Congressional Record, Appendix (vol. 96, p. A5382), 81st Congress, 2nd Session,*
25 July 1950; *Congressional Record (vol. 96, p. 12576), 81st Congress, 2nd Session,* 25
July 1950.
[2] Russia in the meantime having returned to the Security Council, further action
through that organ was no longer feasible.
[3] Vincent Sheen, 'The Case For India', *Foreign Affairs,* Oct. 1951.

and that, in any case, North Korea had destroyed the line by crossing it first. When the United Nations forces neared the Manchurian
and Siberian borders, Chinese troops joined North Koreans (25
October 1950). The United Nations forces were once again compelled to fall below the 38th parallel and did not cross it again till
May 1951. Truce negotiations began on 10 July 1951 and an
armistice was finally signed on 27 July 1953.

The entry of Communist China into the lists seemed to many a
prelude to World War III, and President Truman's announcement
on 30 November, that the United States might use an atom bomb
in Korea, caused a flutter in the chancelleries of the world. Attlee
promptly flew to Washington to dissuade the American President
from escalating the Korean War into an all-out war between America
and China. Both Nehru and Liaquat expressed themselves against
the use of an atom bomb. The Pakistani Premier, deprecating the
assumption that Communist China did not want peace, urged a
ceasefire on the 38th parallel.[1]

Though India and Pakistan were one in their wish to avoid a
world war, their policies in other respects remained different. In
the General Assembly resolution of 1 February 1951, declaring
that by directly assisting the aggressors in Korea Communist
China had 'itself engaged in aggression in Korea', Pakistan was
content to remain neutral while India joined the Soviet bloc in
voting against the resolution. Indian spokesmen gave two main
reasons for their opposition to condemning China as an aggressor.
First, as stated by the Indian representative in the Political Committee of the General Assembly, India was not convinced that the
participation of the Chinese forces in the fighting in Korea was due
to any aggressive intention; it was more probably due to the threats
to the territorial integrity of China.[2] Secondly, as Prime Minister
Nehru declared, the condemnation of a party 'would not help in
solving the problem . . . would only increase the tension and further
inflame the passions of both the States';[3] it could not lead to
peace but only to an intensification of the conflict.[4]

After an interval of comparative inactivity, India again renewed
her mediatory efforts when the negotiations between the parties
became deadlocked over the question of the repatriation of prisoners

[1] *Dawn*, 8 Dec. 1950, quoted by Mushtaq Ahmad, *The United Nations and Pakistan*,
p. 91.
[2] K. P. Karunakaran, *India in World Affairs, Feb. 1950–Dec. 1953*, p. 106.
[3] J. Nehru, *India's Foreign Policy*, p. 418.
[4] J. Nehru, *Speeches*, II, p. 273.

of war, and ultimately a settlement was effected broadly on the lines
which India had advocated. India also served as chairman of the
Neutral Nations Repatriation Commission for Korea and exclusively supplied armed forces to assist the Commission in its task.
Indian forces won high praise for the commendable way in which
they discharged their onerous task.

Before the final curtain dropped on the Korean scene, another
controversy, in which the main actors were the USA and India,
introduced a further note of acrimony between them. This related
to the membership of the Political Conference on Korea. The
Armistice Agreement had stipulated that 'A Political Conference of
a higher level of both sides be held' to resolve the question of the
withdrawal of all foreign forces from Korea and settle the Korean
question peacefully.[1] The matter of membership came up for
consideration when the General Assembly met in special session in
August 1953. In the Political Committee the majority favoured
India's inclusion, but a two-thirds majority needed in the plenary
session was not forthcoming and India persuaded her supporters
not to press the matter further. American opposition to India's
membership was for two reasons: first, that the armistice agreement
had called for a conference of 'two sides' and India, not being
identified with either the Communists or with the forces fighting
aggression in Korea, did not fit into either side; and, secondly,
because India's conduct had incurred the profound distrust of the
Republic of Korea who was directly concerned in the matter.
Once more, Pakistan supported the United States' position by
voting against India's participation in the Conference.

Pandit Nehru spoke on the subject to Parliament on 17 September
1953. 'It is not realized by many of the Great Powers of the world,'
he said angrily, 'that the countries of Asia, however weak they might
be, do not propose to be ignored, bypassed and sat upon.' More
temperately, he argued that it would be helpful if neutral countries
were represented 'because they can sometimes help in toning down
differences and easing tensions'.

Diplomatically, Pakistan came fairly well out of the Korean
affair. The fact that she had not sent any troops to fight against the
Communists enabled the People's Republic to continue trade and
normal diplomatic relations with Pakistan. And the United States,
though sorely disappointed that Pakistan had sent no fighting men,

---

[1] K. P. Karunakaran, *India in World Affairs, Feb. 1950–Dec. 1953*, p. 122.

accepted Pakistani protestations that, but for her troubles with India, she would have supported the United Nations command militarily. Of course, the United States satisfaction with Pakistan was heightened by the former's positive displeasure with India. Apart from the running differences already noted, Nehru repeatedly asserted that, if Communist China had not been wrongfully kept out of the United Nations, there would have been no Korean War.[1] As the United States was the main obstacle to the seating of Communist China in the United Nations, the Indian Prime Minister implicitly placed the entire blame for the Korean outbreak on America. Moreover, though purporting to be impartial, Indians seemed to be comparatively more sympathetic to China. As an Indian writer explains, new China's initial victories over Mac-Arthur 'were hailed all over Asia as a fitting reply to the humiliations suffered by the Asian peoples at the hands of the Western powers'.[2] Ambassador Panikkar declared on 26 January 1951: 'Mao Tse-tung's leadership has raised the international status of the peoples of Asia.'[3] In notable contrast to Indian acerbity towards America, Menon was significantly tolerant in the face of Chinese criticism of an Indian proposal regarding the repatriation of prisoners of war. In his cable Chou En-lai had used such epithets as 'ranting, de-generate, absurd, deceitful, sly', but Krishna Menon magnanimously said, 'They appear to be very angry with us, but we must not be angry with them and we must persevere as best we can for peace.'[4] Early in 1951 Nehru gave his own interpretation of Chinese objec-tives to Volney D. Hurd of the *Christian Science Monitor:* 'Com-munist China is not imperialist. It wishes most of all to carry out its own revolution. For this it wishes to see Tibet and Formosa under Chinese control and Korea freed of foreigners, considering this necessary for its own protection in this formative period.'[5]

A side effect of Indo-US differences over the UN resolution censuring China as an aggressor in Korea was that action by the United States Congress on the Indian request for wheat, already

---

[1] For example: 'I am inclined to think that many of the subsequent dangerous developments, including the Korean development, might not have taken place' if China had entered the United Nations at an earlier stage (in Parliament on 3 Aug. 1950); 'I am convinced that there would have been no Korean War if the People's Govern-ment of China had been in the United Nations'. J. Nehru, *Speeches*, III, p. 270.

[2] K. Gupta, *Indian Foreign Policy*, p. 49.

[3] ibid.

[4] *Hindustan Times*, 17 Dec. 1952, quoted by *Indian Press Digests*, vol. II, 3, p. 29.

[5] *Christian Science Monitor*, 22 Jan. 1951.

much delayed, was further postponed,[1] with predictable further deterioration of the American image in Indian eyes.

Senator Knowland summed up American feelings concerning India's behaviour during the Korean conflict: 'When the first test came to the free world . . . the Government of India contributed not a single soldier, not a single sailor, not a single airman to aid in resisting aggression in Korea . . . when the chips were down India was not there.'[2]

Japanese Peace Treaty

The outbreak of the cold war between the erstwhile allies in the war against Japan had delayed peace-making with the latter after the Second World War but, with the emergence of a potentially strong Communist China and the outbreak of the Korean War, the United States felt impelled to take urgent steps to convert Japan into an ally against Communist inroads in the Far East. In September 1950 Truman nominated John Foster Dulles as his personal representative to negotiate a peace treaty with Japan, to be signed by nations who had been at war with her. Having issued a joint draft of the proposed treaty, the USA and Britain called a conference to meet at San Francisco in September 1951 to sign the treaty. The rule was that representatives could give their views but the conference would not be competent to modify the terms of the treaty. Communist China was not invited. Among those who were invited, but remained unreconciled to the contents of the treaty, were the USSR and India. The treaty was signed at San Francisco on 8 September 1951 by 48 of the 51 countries who had sent delegates. Those who came but did not subscribe were the USSR, Czechoslovakia, and Poland; India, Burma, and Yugoslavia had refused to attend. On the same day, as a part of the peace settlement, the United States signed a security pact with Japan, granting the former the right to station her forces in Japan.

Chou En-lai declared the treaty was aimed at resurrecting Japanese militarism and was an instrument for preparing another aggressive war.[3] The Soviet Union alleged that the territorial issues in the treaty were 'settled . . . in conformity with the aggressive strategical plans of the Pentagon'.[4] India objected to the treaty on

[1] *New York Times*, 26 Jan. 1951.

[2] *Congressional Record* (vol. *100*, p. *655*), *83rd Congress, 2nd Session*, 22 Jan. 1954, Senate.

[3] M. Markov, 'After San Francisco', *New Times*, no. 39, 1951.

[4] *New Times*, no. 37, 1951.

the grounds that it was not sufficiently magnanimous to Japan; that its terms were such that all interested parties could not sign it; that the security pact between the United States and Japan had been made a part of the peace arrangements; and that there was no provision for the return of Formosa to China.[1]

In reply, the United States quoted the Prime Minister of Japan that 'the treaty, as it stands, reflects abundantly American fairness, magnanimity and idealism'. The American note also stated that the Allied Powers had gone to great pains to ensure that the treaty would be such as to enable all the Allies to subscribe to it; that the US-Japanese security arrangements conformed to the desire of the Japanese people, who 'do not want Japan to become a defenseless nation'; and that to postpone the conclusion of the treaty till all the Allied Powers were agreed upon the future of Formosa, would delay the treaty indefinitely.

Pakistan not only signed the Japanese Peace treaty but also voiced powerful support for it from the floor of the conference. Foreign Minister Zafrulla Khan claimed it was 'a good treaty' offering justice and reconciliation, not vengeance and oppression.[2] He referred to the Chinese as a 'great people' who had suffered the most at the hands of power-drunk Japan, and deplored their absence 'because of the difference among the allied nations as to who is entitled to represent' them. In Pakistan's judgement the matter of representation no longer admitted of doubt, but Pakistan had no right to impose her view on others. He also regretted that India and Burma had not attended the conference but pointed out that their absence was voluntary and for reasons Pakistan was 'unable to appreciate'. So far as the treatment of Japan was concerned, India had found the treaty too restrictive and Burma had found it too liberal. It was well not to forget, however, 'that there are represented among us Asiatic states numbering well over a quarter of the assembled allied nations', the people of some of which had suffered at the hands of the Japanese possibly more than the people of Burma and certainly more than the people of India.

Pakistan's unequivocal support at a critical juncture left a deep impression on the minds of the Americans. Two years later, Dulles, as Secretary of State, supporting Pakistan's request for the supply

[1] For text of Indian Note and the US reply thereto see *USDSB*, 3 Sept. 1951, pp. 385-8.
[2] For full text of Zafrulla's speech see Govt. of Pakistan *Handout E. no. 3414*, 9 Sept. 1951.

of wheat, recalled that at the time of the Japanese Peace Treaty the Soviet Union tried to portray the treaty as being imposed upon Japan by a few Western Powers headed by the United States, and that 'at that juncture Pakistan furnished a leadership which brought to that conference a substantial number of Asian countries'.[1]

India's decision to boycott the San Francisco conference, on the other hand, caused deep resentment in the USA. The *Washington Daily News* observed that Nehru's country was saved from Japanese subjugation by the might of American arms, 'yet India's Prime Minister not only wants the Japanese Peace Treaty to be redrafted in accordance with his views, but also presumes to name the signatories to that document'.[2] Inside the Capitol, Senators Knowland and Bridges complained that India had sided with the Soviet Union, and the former declared, 'We had better start taking a realistic view of just who our friends are in the struggle for a free world.'[3] The *New York Times* referred to the Indian Prime Minister as the 'Lost Leader' and called his reasons for staying away from the peace conference 'specious and misguided'.[4] At the other end of the seesaw, India rose sharply in the estimation of Russia and China, and a basic change in their policy towards her soon became manifest.

Added to the divergent attitudes of India and Pakistan towards the Korean War, their diametrically opposed roles in the diplomacy relating to the Japanese Peace Treaty further accelerated the process of US estrangement from India and friendship towards Pakistan. Not long after calling Nehru the 'Lost Leader', the *New York Times* singled out Pakistan as America's 'one sure friend in South Asia'.[5]

In retrospect it seems clear that by 1951 circumstances were already pushing both Pakistan and the United States towards an alliance which they formally consummated in 1954.

---

[1] *Wheat to Pakistan: Hearings on H.R. 5659, 5660, and 5661 before the House Committee on Agriculture and Forestry*, 15 June 1953, pp. 8, 9.

[2] *Washington Daily News*, 11 Aug. 1951, quoted in Govt. of Pakistan, *Handout E. No. 3025*, 13 Aug. 1951.

[3] *Congressional Record* (vol. 97, pp. 10742–3), 82nd Congress, 1st Session, 28 Aug. 1951.

[4] *New York Times*, 28 Aug. 1951.

[5] ibid., 15 Sept. 1951.

7 Pakistan in the United Nations

Several reasons combined to enable Pakistan to play a significant role in the United Nations in the years immediately following her admission to the world organization in September 1947. The explosion of membership, which accompanied the attainment of independence by several African countries, had not yet taken place and India and Pakistan were initially the main spokesmen for Afro-Asia. Many of the issues which came up for consideration at the time related to the right of self-determination and independence of peoples who were still struggling to be free, and India and Pakistan, having been the most prominent sufferers from imperialism, were regarded as the natural spokesmen for them. Several countries whose problems came up for discussion had predominantly Muslim populations, which made Pakistan an ardent advocate of their cause. Lastly, in Sir Zafrulla Khan, her first Foreign Minister, Pakistan had the most eloquent, able and respected Afro-Asian diplomat to project her image and policies abroad.

Pakistan's general attitude towards the United Nations has naturally been conditioned by her own experience and needs. In her disputes with India, the balance of power being against her, she has needed outside support. Starting with high hopes in the United Nations, she gradually realized that it is almost powerless if an important country chooses to defy its resolutions. Pakistan, therefore, has consistently pleaded that the United Nations should have greater authority, and an international force at its disposal to enforce its decisions. Pakistan thinks there is no alternative to the United Nations, because no other forum exists where a weaker nation can appeal to the conscience of the world against the high-handedness of a stronger antagonist. As such, the United Nations is a greater necessity for the less powerful countries than for the big powers.

We have already discussed the Korean question and the Kashmir dispute. A reference to some other important questions of the day will further help towards appreciating the part played by Pakistan in the United Nations.

I. Palestine Issue

The Palestine problem was the offspring of two contradictory promises made by Britain. First, a pledge was given to the Arabs during the First World War that, in the event of an Allied victory, the Arabs would be granted independence. Secondly, and subsequently, the Balfour Declaration said that His Majesty's Government favoured the setting up of a Jewish National Home in Palestine. The question was referred to the United Nations by Britain, who held Palestine under a League of Nations Mandate.

When Pakistan became a member of the United Nations, two proposals were under consideration: (1) partition of Palestine and the creation of a Jewish state, and (2) establishment of a unitary state compromising the whole of Palestine with safeguards for the Jewish minority.

Zafrulla, for Pakistan, forcefully opposed partition.[1] He argued that the pledge given to the Arabs, being earlier in time, should have precedence over the Balfour Declaration. As it was being doubted whether Palestine was included in the pledge to the Arabs, the question could be referred to the International Court of Justice which could also be asked to decide the legality and scope of the Balfour Declaration. As to the humanitarian aspect of the question, Zafrulla suggested that the Jewish displaced persons should be repatriated to their original countries and those who could not be repatriated ought to be allotted to Member States in accordance with their capacity to receive such refugees.

The Pakistani Foreign Minister accused the Western Powers of forcibly driving 'a Western wedge into the heart of the Middle East' and said, 'Remember, nations of the West, that you may need friends tomorrow, that you may need allies in the Middle East. I beg of you not to ruin and blast your credit in those lands.' He warned also that 'if partition is accepted, the fatal step will have

---

[1] For Pakistan's role in the Palestine problem see Zafrulla's speeches in *General Assembly Official Records, 126th Plenary Meeting,* 28 Nov. 1947, pp. 1366–79, and *General Assembly Official Records, First Committee, 217th Meeting,* 30 Nov. 1948, pp. 815–16; Zafrulla's press conference in May 1948 (text issued by Govt. of Pakistan in a *Handout* without number and date). For Pakistan's role in the United Nations on the whole see Mushtaq Ahmad, *The United Nations and Pakistan,* and K. Sarwar Hasan, *Pakistan and the United Nations.*

been taken. The Arabs and the Jews will have been set by the ears and never again will there be a chance of bringing them together. Too many unfinished vendettas will then bar the way.'

Many people asked why Pakistan, herself a child of territorial division, was against the partition of Palestine. Zafrulla said the analogy was false because: (1) The population of Pakistan was 80 million, i.e. more than 100 times that of the Jewish population of Palestine, and the disproportion between the territory involved was even more striking. (2) In India, however unwilling the majority party was to agree to partition, eventually partition came about as the result of an agreement. If both Jews and Arabs came to an agreement that partition was the only solution, Pakistan would be the first to vote for such a course. (3) In India the Muslim minority was an integral part of the population; in Palestine a minority had been artificially created by settling Jews against the express will of the people. (4) Muslims in India had claimed only those regions where they were in a majority. In Palestine the Jews were in a minority everywhere except in Jaffa, one out of fourteen sub-districts.

The vote on the Palestine question was due to be taken in the plenary session of the General Assembly on the afternoon of 26 November 1947, and Zafrulla, who was lobbying actively, is positive that the proposal for partition would have failed to secure the required two-thirds majority that day. At lunch time it began to be rumoured that the President intended to adjourn the meeting in the afternoon. Zafrulla and Foreign Minister Fadhil of Iraq protested to the President but the latter said that the staff was unwilling to sit late because it was Thanksgiving Eve. 'The curious thing is,' Zafrulla states, 'that ever since then not only has the staff worked late on Thanksgiving Eve but the Assembly has sat regularly on Thanksgiving Day till 2 p.m.' When the session was resumed on 29 November some of the votes had shifted and the resolution for partition was carried through. Zafrulla feels convinced that 'it was the personal intervention of President Truman that brought about these changes'.[1]

II. Treatment of Citizens of Indian Origin in South Africa

Both India and Pakistan strongly disapproved the racial discrimination practised by the Government of South Africa against persons of Indian origin who had gone to South Africa as labourers. Gandhi had started his political career in South Africa and had conducted

[1] *Reminiscences of Sir Muhammad Zafrulla Khan*, pp. 359–62.

his first experiment in Civil Disobedience there, and Jinnah's first speech upon election to the Imperial Legislative Council had also concerned the ill-treatment of Indians in South Africa.

India had submitted the issue to the General Assembly in June 1946, and when Pakistan joined the United Nations both countries joined hands in the cause. South Africa took up the position that Indians there enjoyed better economic, social, and educational advantages than they did in India; that the question being essentially within the domestic jurisdiction of South Africa, the United Nations was not competent to deal with it; and that an advisory opinion be sought from the International Court of Justice on whether the matter was essentially within the domestic jurisdiction of South Africa.

Various Pakistani spokesmen refuted the South African contentions by arguing that a violation of human rights was a matter of international concern and ceased to be a question of domestic jurisdiction; that the labour conditions of Indians in South Africa having formed the subject of agreements between the Governments of India and Natal, and later between the governments of India and the Union of South Africa, the treatment of Indians in South Africa could not be regarded as exclusively a domestic affair; and that, even if the International Court of Justice ruled the matter to be a purely domestic question, the problem would continue and had to be solved in order to improve relations between South Africa on one side and India and Pakistan on the other.

In 1957 the Assembly passed a resolution asking South Africa to revise her policies, but without effect, and the problem continues to this day.

When South Africa decided to become a republic the question of her continuance as a member of the Commonwealth after assuming that status came up for consideration by the Commonwealth Prime Ministers in March 1961. The occasion evoked a general debate on South Africa's racial policies and it became clear that, if South Africa was allowed to remain in the Commonwealth, some other countries, notably India and Pakistan, would leave it. Yielding to the inevitable, South Africa withdrew her application and ceased to be a member of the Commonwealth.

III. Colonial Questions

Jinnah had set the tone of Pakistan's policy towards colonial questions by declaring: 'Our heart and soul go out in sympathy with those who are struggling for their freedom. . . . If subjugation and exploitation are carried on, there will be no peace and there will be no end to wars.'[1] We have already referred to Pakistan's support of Indonesia in her struggle for independence from Dutch rule. A reference to some other concrete cases will show further how indefatigably Zafrulla worked in the cause of freedom from colonial domination.

Former Italian Colonies in Africa

At the conclusion of the Second World War Britain was occupying Libya (except the Fezzan), Eritrea, and Italian Somaliland, and France was occupying the Fezzan. In the third session of the General Assembly the First Committee was of the view that Libya should become independent after ten years and that in the meantime she should be divided into three trusteeships—that of Britain in Cyrenaica, France in the Fezzan, and Italy in Tripolitania. Italy was further to hold Italian Somaliland as a trustee. Eritrea was to be divided between the Sudan and Ethiopia.

Zafrulla played a leading role in marshalling opposition to these proposals. He pleaded hard for immediate independence for a united Libya and proposed a greater Somaliland consisting of Italian, French, and British Somalilands and certain areas of Ethiopia. The General Assembly threw out the recommendation of the First Committee in respect of Libya and in November 1949 decided that the whole of Libya should become an independent state by January 1952. Pakistan's efforts thus helped towards blocking a course which would have put the question of Libya's independence into cold storage for ten years and might have perpetuated her division into three parts.

The Pakistani Foreign Minister also strongly opposed Italian trusteeship over Italian Somaliland. The General Assembly finally placed that country under United Nations trusteeship, which was to end with the independence of Italian Somaliland in 1960.

Ethiopia strove to obtain Eritrea as war compensation from Italy. Zafrulla castigated the subconscious approach that Eritrea was 'a bundle of chattels belonging to Italy' which had been taken away from Italy, 'and the question was whether it should be given as a reward or a prize to Ethiopia'. Pakistan supported independence for Eritrea but could not muster the requisite majority to carry through the proposal. Ultimately a compromise was effected that Eritrea should federate with Ethiopia as an autonomous unit.

[1] *Dawn*, 28 Dec. 1949, quoted by M. A. Chaudhri, 'Pakistan and East Asia', *Pakistan Horizon*, March 1959, p. 35.

Tunisia, Morocco, and Algeria
Pakistan played a prominent part in the campaign for the independence of these countries and for having the question considered by the United Nations, against the French objection that the matter fell exclusively within France's domestic jurisdiction. Eventually all three countries won independence by negotiations with France, but the pressure of world opinion undoubtedly affected both the timing and the result of the negotiations.

IV. General
In East-West differences regarding the scope of the provisions of the Charter, Pakistan usually followed an independent line. Three examples will illustrate the point.

1. On the question of admission of new members the Western Powers, faced with the Soviet veto against membership of countries of which the Soviet Union did not approve, propounded the view that unanimity of the five permanent members of the Security Council was not essential for a 'recommendation' of the Council favouring membership. Zafrulla Khan for Pakistan supported the Soviet contention that the admission of new members was a substantive question requiring the unanimity of the permanent members, and not a procedural matter requiring a simple majority in the Council. In an advisory opinion the International Court of Justice rejected the Western view.

2. In 1947 the General Assembly created the Interim Committee or the 'Little Assembly' for one year to deal with questions relating to peace and security. This was done to get over the problem of deadlock among the permanent members in the Security Council. The Soviet Union had opposed the proposal on the ground that it was an 'attempt to get rid of the veto by creating an organ parallel to the Council' and had refused to sit on it. In 1948 the life of the Interim Committee was extended for another year. Pakistan had supported the setting up of the Committee initially, but in 1949 was the only non-Communist country to vote against its prolongation for an indefinite period.

3. When the Soviet Union ended her boycott and returned to the Security Council[1] it was clear that the Council would no longer be able to take effective action in Korea or in any similar situation elsewhere. On 3 November 1950 the General Assembly, mainly on United States' initiative, passed the Uniting For Peace resolution

[1] See p. 127.

which authorized the Assembly to make recommendations for collective measures if the Security Council failed to exercise its primary responsibility to maintain peace and security because of lack of unanimity among the permanent members.

Though India formally abstained from voting on the resolution, she was in fact opposed to it. Nehru said, 'It seems like converting the United Nations into a larger edition of the Atlantic Pact and making it a war organization more than one devoted to peace.'[1] Consistently with her general view, that the United Nations ought to be made a more effective organization, Pakistan voted in favour of the resolution. Zafrulla conceded that under Article 11 (2) enforcement action lay within the exclusive domain of the Security Council, but he argued that recommendations could be made by the Assembly and that it could be held that, where the Council had been unable to act, the General Assembly had a responsibility to take action under Article 10.

V. Zafrulla's Brilliance
It is difficult to overestimate Zafrulla's services to Pakistan in the early years of independence. In the first years, without an organized Foreign Office to prepare adequate briefs for him, he often managed to function as a formidable one-man secretariat. He possessed an encyclopaedic memory and the gift of devastating repartee. While sponsoring Pakistan's membership of the United Nations, Hector McNeil, the British Delegate, said, 'Sir Zafrulla Khan is well known to many of us. He will be a great asset in the work of the Assembly and the Committees.'

Zafrulla's performance as the chief Pakistani spokesman abroad won unqualified praise from friend and foe alike. In the Constituent Assembly of Pakistan members frequently paid glowing tributes to their Foreign Minister. Feroze Khan Noon said, 'The whole world knows that an advocate and jurist of his calibre does not exist in any country in the world. . . . I know during my tours in Arab countries, the Arab kings had his speeches translated two or three times and read to their people to tell them what this great man has done for them.' Begum Shah Nawaz, who had worked with Zafrulla in a number of conferences, declared that he had placed the name of Pakistan on the world map.[2] Prime Minister Liaquat Ali Khan also praised the 'great part' Zafrulla had played in the halls of the United

---

[1] K. P. Karunakaran, *India in World Affairs, Feb. 1950–Dec. 1953*, p. 136.
[2] On 24 May 1948.

Nations in the cause of the freedom of Afro-Asian countries.[1] Though Pakistan's claim to Kashmir is inherently just, it could have suffered by poor presentation in the face of Indians who are noted for the gift of the gab. The former Chief Justice of India, Mehr Chand Mahajan, said Zafrulla's 'brilliant advocacy stole a march over the Indian delegation'.[2] Campbell-Johnson, too, thought Zafrulla's exceptional pleading was one of the main factors in turning the tables on India, who had gone to the United Nations as the complainant in the Kashmir case.[3]

VI. Why did not Pakistan's Independent Stand on Colonial Issues Adversely Affect her Relations with Western Powers?

Zafrulla could truthfully aver that 'Whenever there is a question of liberty and independence from imperialism or of opposing colonialism, of pushing forward a people's march towards freedom, Pakistan is always to the fore and second to none.'[4] As a result of this policy, Pakistan was often found voting on the same side as the Soviet bloc, and against the Western Powers, on colonial issues. However, this did not impair her image as fundamentally a good friend of the West. The reason for this was that Pakistan did not classify the two leaders of the Western camp as imperialist powers. Pakistani leaders frequently praised the United Kingdom for voluntarily liquidating her empire and they commended the United States for her dislike of colonialism. In a remarkable address to the General Assembly, Zafrulla castigated the remnants of colonialism and 'the arrogant assumption that certain sections of mankind are entitled, as of right, to exercise domination over other groups of their fellow-beings'. In the course of the same speech, however, he observed that 'Great Britain, which has set an example in this regard to the other colonial powers, is continuing its efforts to carry on the process in its West African colonies'. He went on to praise the statement which John Foster Dulles had made to the Assembly the previous day and quoted from it, as well as from Dulles's speech at the Japanese Peace Treaty Conference, and noted 'with particular gratification the reaffirmation on behalf of the Government of the United States of the belief expressed in the Declaration of Independence that governments derive their just powers only from the

---

[1] In the Constituent Assembly on 11 Oct. 1950.
[2] M. C. Mahajan, *Looking Back*, p. 172.
[3] Alan Campbell-Johnson, *Mission With Mountbatten*, p. 287.
[4] In the Constituent Assembly on 27 March 1952.

consent of the governed'.[1] During his American tour Prime Minister Liaquat Ali Khan had also said, 'You have no colonies and I believe no territorial ambitions. Has not your history, therefore, equipped you more than most nations to be among the leading architects of the enlightened internationalism of the future?'[2]

Pakistan's anti-imperial moves often led India and Pakistan into the same voting lobby, but this harmony was obscured by their acrimonious exchanges in the debates relating to their disputes with each other. As recent victims of foreign domination, their indignation at the continuation of the same evil elsewhere was undoubtedly sincere, but it must be added that, not having any colonial possessions of their own, it was easier for both of them to adopt a high moral attitude towards colonial issues than towards questions in which their own national interests were directly at stake.

---

[1] *General Assembly Official Records, 437th Plenary Meeting,* 18 Sept. 1953.
[2] Liaquat Ali Khan, *Pakistan, The Heart of Asia,* p. 76.

Part 2

The Aligned Years
(1954-1962)

8 Pakistan Joins the Western Defence System

I. Two Myths

Before we describe Pakistan's entry into the Western system of security alliances it would be pertinent to mention two common assertions which do not accord with facts. The first is that Pakistan was completely neutral till a 'palace revolution', by which Prime Minister Nazimuddin was replaced by Muhammad Ali Bogra, suddenly brought with it a change in Pakistan's foreign policy, turning it from an independent policy to one subservient to the USA. The second is that the 'unwise' American decision to supply arms to Pakistan resulted in the 'loss' of Indian friendship to America.

An ardent desire to cultivate brotherly relations with all Muslim states was, of course, an inherent element in Pakistan's make-up, and in that one respect she was never uncommitted. But as regards the East-West cold war, two different trends were discernible in Pakistan's foreign policy till 1950. First, there was the natural desire on the part of the Pakistani leaders to keep out of big-power conflicts. Three days after Pakistan became a sovereign state Prime Minister Liaquat Ali Khan announced that Pakistan would take no sides in the conflict of ideologies between the nations,[1] and six months later Governor-General Jinnah affirmed, 'Our foreign policy is one of friendliness and goodwill towards all the nations of the world.'[2]

At the same time, however, Pakistan did not consider neutralism an eternal prescription as Nehru did. It was realized that it was not always easy to avoid taking sides in power politics, and there were clear indications where Pakistan's preference lay. Jinnah had realistically stated in 1946, 'Naturally no nation stands by itself.

[1] *New York Times*, 18 Aug. 1947.
[2] Quaid-i-Azam Mahomed Ali Jinnah, *Speeches as Governor-General of Pakistan, 1947–1948*, p. 65.

There will be an alliance with other nations whose interests are common.'[1] Prime Minister Liaquat Ali Khan told a press conference at Cairo on 10 May 1949 that Pakistan was making a socialistic experiment which would help combat Communist penetration in South-East Asia.[2] Two days later in an interview with the Cairo correspondent of *The Times*, Liaquat said the countries of the world were divided into those who favoured and those who opposed Communism. The Muslim countries between Cairo and Karachi had an important part to play. It should be the concern of the Western powers to strengthen the Middle East countries.[3] The *Economist* assessed in August 1948 that in the event of war India would remain neutral but Pakistan would side with the free countries against Russia.[4] *Dawn* understood Pakistan's foreign policy to have been one of greater co-operation with the Anglo-American bloc.[5]

After 1950 when Liaquat, having received invitations from both the USSR and the USA, cast the die in favour of the latter, the situation was no longer ambiguous. Other manifestations of greater affinity with America, such as Pakistan's attitude towards the Korean War and the Japanese Peace Treaty, inevitably followed. The *New York Times* special correspondent from Karachi reported that 'in contrast to India's aloofness from the struggle between Communism and democracy, Pakistan has been almost aggressive in her moral commitment to the Western Powers'.[6] Prime Minister Liaquat Ali Khan complained to Marguerite Higgins of the *New York Herald Tribune* that the USA wrongly equated Pakistan's foreign policy with that of Nehru's India. Pakistan, he stressed, was opposed to isolation in any sense and was prepared to make sacrifices for the collective security system being built by the democratic world.[7]

Liaquat's immediate successor, Prime Minister Nazimuddin, held office for some eighteen months only and scarcely had time to leave a distinctive imprint on his country's foreign policy. But it is not without significance that in 1953, when Pakistan was faced with a serious famine, it was to the USA that Nazimuddin turned for free help. Citing the incident as proof that Nazimuddin con-

[1] Jamil-ud-Din Ahmad, *Some Recent Speeches and Writings of Mr. Jinnah*, II, p. 384.
[2] *Dawn*, 11 May 1949.
[3] *The Times*, 13 May 1949.
[4] *Economist*, 14 Aug. 1948.
[5] *Dawn*, 21 Feb. 1949.
[6] *New York Times*, 15 Sept. 1951.
[7] *Pakistan Times*, 3 Oct. 1951.

tinued his predecessor's policy of greater friendship with America, Finance Minister Amjad Ali reminded the Pakistani Parliament, in a foreign affairs debate on 4 September 1958, that Nazimuddin had deputed him (Amjad Ali) to the USA to ask for one million tons of wheat as a gift, and not against a cash loan as India had done, because Pakistan did not have enough foreign exchange to pay for such a large quantity of grain.

Indeed, the need for economic assistance added much urgency to the existing trend towards friendship with America. Having started her independence with virtually no military hardware, Pakistan's greatest need had always been modern weapons, which are tremendously expensive and usually released from government control only for countries who are politically friendly. Though Pakistan's first years were prosperous, the strain of the armament race with her larger neighbour had been keenly felt from the beginning. After the crisis with India in the summer of 1951, Pakistan's expenditure on defence inevitably escalated. At this critical juncture her political and economic fortunes suddenly faltered. Prime Minister Liaquat Ali Khan's assassination in October 1951 introduced a new element of uncertainty into Pakistan's internal stability, and early in 1952 prices of jute and cotton fibres, upon which her foreign trade solely rested, began to drop precipitately. While the general commodity price index dropped from 162 to 123 between June 1951 and December 1952, fibres fell from 193 to 98.[1] Pakistan's foreign exchange earnings shrank from Rs.288 crores in 1951 to Rs.192 crores during 1952, and were expected to fall to Rs.150 crores in 1953. Gold and sterling reserves, which had stood at Rs.148.7 crores on 1 January 1952, were reduced to Rs.60.61 crores by the beginning of 1953. The prospect of a severe wheat famine in 1953 thus greatly aggravated an already serious situation.

The second assertion—that the United States 'lost' India's friendship because of her decision to provide arms to Pakistan—is equally untenable. Undoubtedly, the augmentation of Pakistan's military strength was a matter of direct concern to India, and America's decision to give arms aid immediately became the biggest single problem between the USA and India, just as the arms assistance to India, following the October 1962 Sino-Indian border clash, was to become the biggest single irritant in Pakistani–US

[1] The statistical information offered here is taken from Finance Minister Chaudhri Muhammad Ali's budget speech in the Constituent Assembly (Legislative) on 14 March 1953.

relations. But the implication that, apart from the question of military supplies to Pakistan, all was well between India and the USA, is wholly misleading. Fundamental differences between India and America were apparent long before any formal ties were forged between Pakistan and the USA, and, indeed, these differences were one of the main causes which drove the USA towards Pakistan. Chester Bowles complained that it was bad arithmetic to 'alienate' 360 million Indians in order to aid 80 million Pakistanis.[1] But the way Americans who worked for a US–Pakistani alliance looked at the problem was that, if 360 million Indians were not willing to co-operate in the common cause, it was poor arithmetic to refuse also the proffered friendship of 80 million Pakistanis. In truth, India had not only spurned all US advances but in most ways had acted contrary to United States interests. Nixon's biographer states that Vice-President Nixon's recommendation of military aid to Pakistan 'was eventually carried through as a counterforce to the confirmed neutralism of Jawaharlal Nehru's India'.[2]

We have already described the important respects in which the Indian attitude towards the Korean War and the Japanese Peace Treaty was closer to the Communist than to the US point of view. These differences in policy, of course, stemmed from deep-seated differences between the Indian and the American outlook. First, the most crucial issue of the day for the Americans was Communism; to Nehru and his fellow Indians it was colonialism.[3] But this was not all. Indians alleged further that the USA assisted colonial powers by her policies and herself exercised economic imperialism, if not the outmoded territorial colonialism. On the eve of partition Krishna Menon believed that the object of United States policy was to create an economic, political, and military vacuum in India which America would fill.[4] Prime Minister Attlee confirmed that, in the eyes of Asians, the 'number one exploiter, even more imperialist than Britain', was now America.[5] Giving an 'Indian View' in a *Foreign Affairs* article, Ambassador Panikkar wrote that in India most people were inclined to consider that the United States was deliberately opposing India at every stage and was following an anti-

---

[1] Chester Bowles, 'A US Policy for Asia', *New Leader*, 22 Feb. 1954.
[2] Ralph de Toledano, *Nixon*, p. 164.
[3] Nehru, quoted by Norman D. Palmer, 'India's Position In Asia', *Journal of International Affairs*, no. 2, 1963.
[4] H. V. Hodson, *The Great Divide*, p. 243.
[5] *Twilight of Empire, Memoirs of Prime Minister Clement Attlee, as Set Down by Francis Williams*, p. 238.

Asian policy with the object of reducing the new countries of Asia to a 'condition of political dependence'.[1] In the Eighth Session of the General Assembly the Indian delegate, alleging that the United States was establishing and perpetuating a new form of colonialism in Puerto Rico, sought to have the whole Puerto Rican matter investigated.[2]

India and America also held widely differing views on capitalism and socialism. Nehru believed that modern imperialism was an outgrowth of capitalism[3] and a Congress resolution, presumably drafted by him, declared that Fascism and Nazism were forms of intensified imperialism.[4] But Communism was not imperialistic;[5] a socialist economy could be made self-sufficient and had no need for expansion.[6] Nehru thought it was not justifiable to equate private enterprise and democracy because, 'in the final analysis, real democracy and unrestrained private enterprise are incompatible'.[7] Nehru's socialist views were so anathematic to Truman that when Chester Bowles was appointed Ambassador to India in 1951 he was asked by the President to 'find out if that fellow Nehru is a Communist at heart'.[8] Supreme Court Justice William O. Douglas has also revealed that when he once quoted Nehru to Truman, Truman dismissed the Indian leader as a 'Communist'.[9]

On the supreme question of the day, how to preserve peace, Nehru's approach was that the psychology of fear should be converted to one of mutual trust and that this could best be done by creating and enlarging an area of peace, an area which 'does not want war, works for peace in a positive way and believes in cooperation'.[10] The Americans believed, on the other hand, that the only argument the Communists respected was superior force and that it was, therefore, necessary for the non-Communist countries to build up collective defence.

The author of the 'Indian View' listed three aspects of policy

[1] 'Middle Ground Between America and Russia: An Indian View', by P, *Foreign Affairs*, Jan. 1954. See M. S. Rajan, *India in World Affairs, 1954–1956*, p. 646, for the revelation that P stood for K. M. Panikkar.

[2] *Report on the Eighth Session of the General Assembly of the United Nations: House Report 1695, 83rd Congress, 2nd Session*, Washington, D.C., 1953, p. 2.

[3] J. Nehru, *Eighteen Months in India*, p. 80.

[4] N. V. Rajkumar (ed.), *The Background of India's Foreign Policy*, p. 62.

[5] J. Nehru, *An Autobiography*, p. 163.

[6] J. Nehru, *The Discovery of India*, p. 555.

[7] M. S. Rajan, *India in World Affairs, 1954–1956*, p. 622.

[8] *New York Herald Tribune*, 19 April 1953.

[9] *Parade Magazine, St. Paul Sunday Pioneer Press*, 6 Aug. 1967.

[10] J. Nehru, *Speeches*, II, p. 326.

6

where the United States and India did not see eye to eye: in their
attitude towards the menace of expansionist Communism; the
colonialism of European nations; and China. 'All these three are
basic factors in the complex international problem of today,' he
observed, 'and while a difference on any one of them is sufficient
to create misunderstanding, a difference on all three amounts to a
major conflict of opinion.'[1]

While blaming both sides for the East–West cold war, Indians
regarded the USA as the greater culprit. According to Panikkar, 'the
course of the cold war, whatever its origins, was being determined
by the opportunist policies of the US.'[2] And Radhakrishnan, on his
return to India after relinquishing his post as Ambassador to the
USSR, declared: 'We find that at present there is a group of
Western nations trying to crush Russia. If Hitler were alive today,
he would have considered the present moment a supreme triumph
of his philosophy.'[3]

Having zealously but unsuccessfully courted India, it seemed
but logical to most Americans that they should turn to the second
largest non-Communist country of mainland Asia, Pakistan. As the
US–Pakistani alliance was consummated during the Republican
regime of Eisenhower, its critics have ascribed it entirely to Secretary Dulles's susceptibility to 'pactitis'. But in fact the administrative wheels had begun to turn much earlier, and 'Dulles was
carrying to its logical conclusion a policy which had been allowed
to go very far within the Pentagon and the State Department before
he ever took office'.[4] By November 1952 matters had sufficiently
advanced for Admiral Arthur W. Radford, United States Commander-in-Chief in the Pacific, to pay a visit to Pakistan, to stay
as the guest of the Governor-General in Karachi, to visit the Khyber
Pass, and to be honoured at a reception given by the Prime Minister.[5]
Before leaving Karachi Radford declared that Pakistan enjoyed a
strategic position and had an important role to play in the world
fight against Communism.[6]

As already mentioned, both Russia and Communist China at
first shunned Nehru's regime as a bourgeois government which

[1] 'Middle Ground Between America and Russia: An Indian View', by P, *Foreign
Affairs*, Jan. 1954.
[2] K. M. Panikkar, *In Two Chinas*, p. 168.
[3] K. Gupta, *Indian Foreign Policy*, p. 93.
[4] Selig S. Harrison, 'Case History of a Mistake', *New Republic*, 10 Aug. 1959.
[5] *Dawn*, 10 Nov. 1952.
[6] *Dawn*, 13 Nov. 1952.

must be overthrown by a Communist revolution. At its Second Congress, the Communist Party of India, meeting at Calcutta in February 1948, decided that a 'revolutionary upsurge' was seething in India, and that the phase of 'armed clashes' had arrived.[1] In response to a message of greetings from the Communist Party of India upon the inauguration of the People's Republic of China at Peking in October 1949, Mao Tse-tung predicted that, 'Like free China, free India will one day emerge in the socialist and People's Democratic family; that day will end the imperialist reactionary era in the history of mankind.'[2] The Government of India, however, reacted vigorously to the Communist offensive inside India, and by 1949 at least 100,000 Communists and their sympathizers had been jailed without trial. This failure of the Communist onslaught, taken together with new manifestations of Nehru's role in international affairs, led to a reappraisal of Communist policy towards India. Sardar Patel's death in November 1950 removed from the scene the strongest voice in India against Communism, and gave Nehru an almost free hand to guide the destiny of his country in accordance with his own wishes. At the end of December 1950, R. Palme Dutt, one of Britain's leading Marxist theoreticians, said in London that Nehru's attitude towards the Korean War and Communist China were important signs of a change in Indian foreign policy which deserved to be promoted further. The call to armed rebellion was suspended soon afterwards, and Nehru was tentatively accepted as 'a potential friend of "peace"'.[3] With Nehru's refusal to attend the Japanese Peace Treaty, for reasons similar to Russian's objections to the Treaty, Communist doubts as to India's usefulness were finally resolved. Nehru had shown himself to be as anxious as the Communists themselves to remove American presence from Asia. To Nehru, the retreat of US power meant a step towards the resurgence of Asia under the joint leadership of India and China. To the Communists, the elimination of American power seemed a necessary pre-condition for successful Communist insurgency in Asian lands. The direct assault on Korea had only served to bring back Americans in greater strength; a more patient approach was required. For the realization of long-term Communist objectives it appeared wiser to work with Nehru for the time being. In the spring of 1952 Stalin declared that the peaceful coexistence of

[1] Gene D. Overstreet and Marshall Windmiller, *Communism in India*, p. 273.
[2] P. C. Chakravarti, *India's China Policy*, p. 11.
[3] Overstreet and Windmiller, *Communism in India*, pp. 304-5.

capitalism and Communism was fully possible, and in October of the same year the 19th Congress of the Communist Party of the Soviet Union, as well as the Asian and Pacific Peace Conference in Peking, officially adopted the policy of peaceful coexistence with countries having different social systems.[1] The door to friendship with Russia and China, at which Nehru had at first knocked in vain, was at last ajar.

II. Advent of Eisenhower and Dulles

Changes of regime in 1953 in Russia, America, and Pakistan all added new impulses to the moyes already under way. Eisenhower's inauguration as President, with John Foster Dulles as Secretary of State, brought a new look to politics in Washington; Muhammad Ali Bogra's shift from ambassadorship in the USA to prime ministership in Karachi brought an avowed admirer of America to the helm of affairs in Pakistan; and the death of Stalin removed that stoic hardliner from the Kremlin and brought the lively Khrushchev to the fore there.

Though Dulles's style of diplomacy made him the symbol of the American policy of collective security, military pacts were not his invention, nor did they die with him. After the Second World War America and Russia emerged as the strongest powers in the world, each standing for a way of life which the other thought incompatible with her own: rivalry for world supremacy between them was inevitable, and by 1947 the cold war had descended upon Europe with the possibility of a hot war and Communist-supported revolutions always in the offing. In a *Foreign Affairs* article George Kennan, head of the Policy Planning Staff of the State Department during the Truman Administration, spelled out the appropriate action to meet the situation: 'The main element of any United States policy towards the Soviet Union must be that of long-term, patient but firm and vigilant containment of Russian expansive tendencies. . . .'[2] Truman himself, in an address to Congress on 12 March 1947, enunciated the doctrine which was given his name: 'It must be the policy of the United States to support free peoples who are resisting attempted subjugation by armed minorities or by outside pressure.' Two often overlooked aspects of this pronouncement are that: (1) though Greece and Turkey were to be the immediate beneficiaries of the statement, the scope of policy was

---

[1] A. Doak Barnett, *Communist China and Asia*, pp. 96–7.
[2] 'The Sources of Soviet Conflict', *Foreign Affairs*, July 1947, p. 575.

not limited to any region; (2) the Doctrine would be operative not only against external aggression but also against internal insurgency by armed minorities.

When North Korea, assisted by Russia, attacked South Korea, Truman immediately ordered the United States armed forces to go to the assistance of South Korea. The direct intervention of Communist China further emphasized the fact that the Korean War was a part of the world-wide conflict between East and West. In Indo-China, too, the character of the war against France changed after the Communists assumed control in Peking in 1949 and began to train and equip Vietminh forces. To meet the situation, the United States decided in May 1950 to grant economic and military aid to France and the Associate States of Indo-China which averaged $500 million annually to the end of 1953.[1] Thus when Eisenhower assumed the Presidency in January 1953, the United States was already involved in both the trouble spots in Asia—Korea and Indo-China. The change of administration 'produced no change of policy but a more strenuous effort to make the old policy work'.[2]

Besides attending to the conflagrations in Korea and Indo-China, the Truman Administration took preventive measures to meet future emergencies. To give a bipartisan stamp to the American effort, the President, in April 1950, appointed John Sherman Cooper, Republican ex-Senator from Kentucky, and John Foster Dulles, another Republican, as consultants to the State Department. During 1951 Dulles negotiated security treaties, on behalf of Truman's Democratic Administration, with Australia and New Zealand, the Philippines, and Japan.[3]

In the late nineteen-fifties and during the Presidential campaign of John F. Kennedy it became fashionable to ridicule Dulles's proclivity for defence pacts, and it was conveniently forgotten that the foundation of the policy had been laid by the Truman Administration. However, when the Democrats under the Kennedy and Johnson Administrations were subjected to criticism for themselves escalating American participation in the South-East Asian conflict, they answered that in reality they were merely honouring a bipartisan commitment going back to the days of Harry S. Truman.

---

[1] Oliver E. Clubb, Jr., *The United States and the Sino-Soviet Bloc in Southeast Asia,* p. 54.
[2] ibid
[3] See Secretary Dulles's statement on *The Southeast Asia Collective Defense Treaty: Hearings before Senate Committee on Foreign Relations, 83rd Congress, 2nd Session,* 11 Nov. 1954, p. 205.

Secretary of State Dean Rusk, who had served as Assistant Secretary of State for Far Eastern Affairs under Truman, told the Committee on Foreign Relations that 'during the Truman Administration, there was a policy conclusion on the part of ourselves, the British and the French that the security of Southeast Asia was vital to the free world. . . . During the Truman Administration, I recall, there was a little ceremony welcoming the 200th ship carrying assistance to Indo-China.' The actual steps taken over the years in relation to what is required in South-East Asia, Rusk explained, had been conditioned by the action which the Communists took there.[1] On the eve of President Johnson's trip to the Far East in October 1966 David Lawrence pointed out that what was being said by President Johnson and Secretary Rusk about the purposes of the United States in cementing the relationship of the free countries of Asia, bore a remarkable resemblance to what Dulles said when the Manila Treaty was formulated in 1954.[2]

Whatever his other faults, Dulles left little scope for a misunderstanding of US intentions. Many competent observers think North Korea was encouraged to attack South Korea by a declaration by Secretary Acheson on 12 January 1950, impliedly placing Korea outside the American 'defensive perimeter'. He said this ran along the Aleutians to Japan and the Ryukyus and thence to the Philippines.'[3] It is also interesting to speculate to what extent John F. Kennedy's criticism of the defence pacts encouraged the Communists to step up tension both in Europe and South-East Asia soon after he assumed the Presidency. Nor was Dulles's 'brinkmanship' without its own purpose. At times this can be the only way of preventing war by miscalculation. Indeed, it was not until Kennedy resorted to 'brinkmanship' over Cuba, a more hair-raising performance than any confrontation staged by Dulles, that the Russians felt convinced that the young President meant business and adopted a softer line towards him.

It is possible to argue that what made sense to Truman and Dulles is no longer a sensible line today. A militarily weaker opponent can be deterred from disturbing the *status quo* by a threat of massive retaliation, but when both sides attain the capacity to annihilate each other the only sensible course left is to talk things

[1] *Foreign Assistance 1966: Hearings on S2859 and S2861 before the Senate Committee on Foreign Relations, 89th Congress, 2nd Session,* 18 April 1966, p. 108.

[2] *Minneapolis Tribune,* 12 Oct. 1966.

[3] Dean Acheson, *Present at the Creation,* pp. 357, 691. Dulles called Acheson's statement 'a tragic mistake'—James Shepley, 'How Dulles Averted War', *Life,* 16 Jan. 1956.

out. In a changing world no policy can be eternally sound. But the fact remains that Dulles had overwhelming bipartisan support in his day and the prestige of the United States stood much higher then than it does today.[1] The afterwards much-maligned Manila Pact which set up SEATO, for instance, was ratified by the Senate by a record margin of 84 votes to 1.

Because national interest is not a partisan matter, foreign policy cannot be either. It was Democratic Truman who went to war in Korea and it was Republican Eisenhower who negotiated peace there; again, it was Democratic Truman who promised help not only against external aggression but also against internal revolution, and it was Democratic Kennedy and Johnson who had to intervene in the war in Vietnam, while it fell to Republican Nixon to shy away from the conflict and give notice to his allies to face local insurgency unaided. The question is not whether Dulles's policy was the perfect answer to the problems of his day. There can be no perfect answer to international troubles because whatever action one side may take the opposite side is bound to react to nullify it, and this zig-zag game can go on and on, calling for ever-changing responses. If in the face of American preparedness the Communists changed their tactics, calling for a different kind of response, it was proof not of the failure of Dulles's policy but of its success. Even as late as 28 August 1968, when frustration with the war in Vietnam was running high, Secretary Rusk, speaking before the Democratic Platform Committee, said that the question of collective security was still a central one and warned his audience, before they abandoned collective security, to 'be sure that we have something better to put in its place'.

Dulles, Nehru, Zafrulla

Dulles saw the struggle against Communism as a moral crusade: if it was only power politics and did not involve a threat 'to the basic moral principles of our Judeo-Christian civilization, and indeed the civilization which is based upon other great religions', it would not be treated as a worldwide struggle. Unless the free nations met it everywhere, they would be defeated.[2] The strong

[1] I had the privilege of attending some conferences at which the American delegation was led by John Foster Dulles. He was highly respected by all other delegates for the masterful exposition of his views, his dedication to principles he thought were right, and his reliability as a good friend. Even Khrushchev confessed his admiration for Dulles. A. M. Schlesinger, Jr., *A Thousand Days*, p. 398.

[2] 'Secretary Dulles Discusses US Foreign Policy For British Television Broadcast', *USDSB*, 10 Nov. 1958.

religious trait in his character went back to his childhood in a church-going family in Watertown, N.Y., where his father was a Presbyterian minister.

This intense commitment to his own cause as a moral issue made Dulles inflexible and uncompromising as a negotiator, effective for combating Communism but not capable of arriving at a working arrangement with its adherents.[1] In this he greatly resembled India's Jawaharlal Nehru, who too passionately clung to his views as moral anchors without which the ship of state would founder. President Kennedy regarded Nehru 'as almost the John Foster Dulles of neutralism'.[2]

Both Nehru and Dulles purported to base their philosophies on the recent history of their respective countries, but this led them to diametrically opposite courses. Nehru believed Gandhi's successful leadership had demonstrated the correct psychological approach to the problems of the world; defence preparations only generated fear and increased the chances of war. Dulles thought the lesson of the two world wars, in which large coalitions had defeated the forces of evil, was that strength in the form of collective security was the right answer.[3]

On the other hand Dulles got on much better with Pakistani leaders, whose thinking was closer to his. Zafrulla and Dulles had a special regard for each other. Both had a legal background and Zafrulla, like Dulles, was devoutly religious. At the Japanese Peace Conference Dulles warmly congratulated Zafrulla on making 'the speech' of the conference,[4] and in the United Nations General Assembly Zafrulla returned the compliment by declaring that he had 'long admired the lofty views and noble concepts of Mr. Dulles'.[5]

III. Straws in the Wind

With the installation of Eisenhower as President in January 1953 the process of Pakistani–US *rapprochement* was expected to be speeded up. During the Presidential election campaign the Republican platform had promised to encourage 'the development of collective security' and to 'end neglect of the Far East which Stalin

[1] For example at the Geneva Conference of 1954, Dulles succeeded 'in never once acknowledging Mr. Chou En-lai's existence'. Anthony Eden, *Full Circle*, p. 117.

[2] Arthur M. Schlesinger, Jr., *A Thousand Days*, p. 523.

[3] Secretary Dulles's statement, *Mutual Security Act of 1958: Hearings Before Senate Committee on Foreign Relations, 85th Congress, 2nd Session*, 24 March 1958, p. 145.

[4] Related to me by a person who was present at the occasion.

[5] In the General Debate on 18 Sept. 1953.

has long identified as the road to victory over the West'.[1] The Republican majority leader, William Knowland, said Pakistan was more realistic than India about the danger from Communism and he thought Pakistan could become another Turkey.[2] President Eisenhower said in his inaugural address that the strength of all free peoples lies in unity and that destiny had laid upon America the responsibility of the free world's leadership. His Administration would help 'proven friends of freedom' to achieve their own security and well-being.

While the new administration was raising hope in Pakistan, it was exciting suspicion in India. Nehru said in Parliament that 'even war is too serious a thing to be handed over to a soldier to control, much less peace. Now, this intrusion of the military mentality in the chancelleries of the world is a dangerous development of today.'[3] This brought forth the rejoinder in Congress by Representative Bentley that when, in return for US help, the head of the Government of India 'criticizes our President for his so-called military mentality and, by inference, states that Mr. Eisenhower's thinking is a menace to the cause of world peace, I say when that happens, by heaven, it is too much'.[4]

Dulles's Trip to the Near East

Speculating on Secretary Dulles's projected trip to Asia, the *New York Times* opined that India was not likely to align herself with the free world but the Secretary 'will have made an additional contribution to the cause of peace' if he could bring about closer ties with Pakistan.[5] On the eve of the trip the State Department told a *Dawn* representative in a written reply that the US would welcome Pakistan's joining forces with other Middle East countries in a regional defence organization.[6] Dulles visited India, Pakistan, and other countries in the Near East during May and on his return reported to the nation in an address on radio and television.[7] About India, he said that he had not always agreed with Nehru but did clear up some misunderstandings. On Pakistan he struck

[1] Adopted by the Republican National Convention at Chicago, Ill., on 10 July 1952.
[2] *U.S. News and World Report*, 30 Oct. 1953.
[3] *Lok Sabha Debates*, 18 Feb. 1953, col. 454.
[4] *Congressional Record, Appendix* (vol. 99, p. A1492), 83rd Congress, 1st Session, 25 March 1953, House.
[5] *New York Times*, 13 Jan. 1953.
[6] *Dawn*, 7 April 1953.
[7] For Dulles's 'Report on Near East Trip' see *New York Times*, 2 June 1953, and *USDSB*, 15 June 1953.

a warmer note and stated that 'the strong spiritual faith and martial spirit of the people make them a dependable bulwark against Communism' and that his party had met with a feeling of warm friendship on the part of the people of Pakistan towards the United States. Regarding the prospects of a Middle East organization, he observed that many of the Arab League countries were engrossed in quarrels with Israel, Great Britain, and France, but there was more concern in the northern countries where the Soviet Union was nearer.

Wheat Assistance to Pakistan

The histories of the Indian and Pakistani Wheat Bills well illustrate the state of India's and Pakistan's relations with the USA at the time. India had at first desired one million tons of wheat from the USA in 1949, and during his trip to the USA Nehru had often referred to the Indian requirement. A satisfactory arrangement between the two countries, however, could not be evolved. Towards the end of 1950 India faced an even graver emergency, and on 16 December Ambassador Madam Pandit requested the United States Government for two million tons of food grains on easy terms. While the request was pending before the US Congress, the resolution proposing that China be censured as an aggressor in Korea came up in the United Nations, and, on 24 January 1951, Prime Minister Nehru strongly expressed himself against it. In a formal statement on the following day President Truman asserted that he believed in 'calling an aggressor an aggressor' and that his country was solidly behind him in so stigmatizing Communist China. On the same day Senator Tom Connolly, chairman of the Senate Foreign Relations Committee, side-tracked India's request for wheat by referring it to the Near East Affairs sub-committee for consideration. 'It was plain he was in no hurry to provide aid to that country ... while it so strongly opposed the United States policy in the United Nations on China.'[1] In a special message on 12 February Truman pressed Congress for prompt action, saying that India's stability was essential to the future of free institutions in Asia. There were important political differences between the US and India but that should not blind Americans to the needs of the Indian people.[2] Though the majority of the members of Congress were sympathetic to the Indian request, legislation was held

[1] *New York Times*, 26 Jan. 1951.
[2] For text of Truman's message see *USDSB*, 26 Feb. 1951.

up by the obstructionism of a group of legislators opposed to Indian policies, and it was not till 15 June that the President was able to sign the India Emergency Food Act, granting a loan of $190 million for the supply of two million tons of wheat.

In the meantime China and the USSR had fully utilized the situation to project themselves as the true friends of India and to portray the USA as a heartless opportunist seeking to make political capital out of other people's misery. Untrammelled by democratic processes of legislation, the two Communist countries had been able to promise help at once, China offering one million tons of rice and Russia a similar quantity of wheat. By 16 March a total of 22,300 tons of Chinese rice had already reached India[1] and on 2 June the first Soviet shipment had arrived in Bombay.[2] Communist supplies were given wide publicity and a warm welcome, while American tardiness was bitterly criticized.

In the case of Pakistan's request for US wheat, everything went right from the beginning. At a press conference on 9 April 1953 Prime Minister Nazimuddin declared that Pakistan must import a minimum of $1\frac{1}{2}$ million tons of wheat during the coming year if widespread famine was to be prevented, that it was beyond Pakistan's resources to purchase such a large quantity, and that it had been decided to seek aid from the US. He emphasized that supplies must start within three months.[3]

Representative Javits supported Pakistan's request because he considered the 'Dominion of Pakistan to be an element of great strength to the people of the free world in South and Southeast Asia'.[4] On 10 June President Eisenhower moved Congress to grant Pakistan's request because 'between the people of Pakistan and the people of the United States there exists a strong bond of friendship'.[5] In the hearings before the Senate Committee on Agriculture and Forestry Secretary Dulles said Pakistan and the USA were 'very friendly to each other, that the people of Pakistan were strong in their Islamic faith which is absolutely opposed, as our faith is, to the view of Soviet Communism which treats man as a mechanical thing to be dealt with on a purely materialistic basis', that the

---

[1] *New China News Agency*, 19 April 1951.

[2] V. V. Balabushevich and A. M. Dyakov (eds.), *A Contemporary History of India*, 1964, p. 515.

[3] Govt. of Pakistan, *Handout E.1605*, 9 April 1953.

[4] *Congressional Record (vol. 99, p.3487), 83rd Congress, 1st Session*, 21 April 1953, House.

[5] *USDSB*, 30 June 1953.

people of Pakistan had a splendid military tradition, that in Karachi he had been met by a guard of honour which was 'the finest' he had ever seen, and that at the time of the Japanese Peace Treaty when America needed help she 'got it in very full measure from our good friends of Pakistan', not in any way hoping at that time for favours from the United States but because 'they believed the same kind of things we believe'. Dulles pointed to Pakistan's and Turkey's positions on the map and called them 'two very strong bulwarks' in an area which was not clear about its mode of resistance to Soviet Communism.[1]

The Bill was finalized by Congress so expeditiously that Eisenhower was able to sign it on 25 June. 'We are proud to have such staunch friends as the people of Pakistan', the President declared, adding that the swift action by Congress in making possible the aid within two weeks of his message, reflected the sympathy and concern of the people of the United States for the people of Pakistan. Within twenty-four hours after the President had assented to the Act, the *Anchorage Victory*, laden with 9,860 tons of wheat as the first instalment, sailed from Baltimore.

Visit of Pakistani Officials to the USA
In October 1953 General Ayub Khan, Commander-in-Chief of the Pakistani Army, arrived in Washington, followed in November by Governor-General Ghulam Muhammad and Foreign Minister Zafrulla Khan. Their activities in the American capital gave rise to rumours that Pakistan and America were negotiating a military alliance. But it seems no final decision was taken at this stage. *Newsweek* wrote that the informal talks had involved the possibility of a sizeable military assistance programme for Pakistan, similar to the aid given to Turkey.[2]

Americans no doubt had long been agreed that their global strategy against Communism demanded a militarily stronger Pakistan, but they still hesitated to take the final plunge for fear of offending India. A State Department official admitted that informal discussions had been going on 'for the last year or two',[3] but President Eisenhower said at a press conference that the US would be

[1] Secretary Dulles's Statements: *Wheat for Pakistan: Hearings on S.2112, before the Senate Committee on Agriculture and Forestry, 83rd Congress, 1st Session,* 12 June 1953, pp. 4–5, and *Wheat for Pakistan: Hearings on H.R. 5659, 5660, 5661, before the House Committee on Agriculture and Forestry, 83rd Congress, 1st Session,* 15 June 1953, pp. 8–9.
[2] *Newsweek,* 30 Nov. 1953.
[3] *New York Times,* 13 Nov. 1953.

most cautious about doing anything that would cause hysteria in India, and his Administration's effort would be to produce friendship with the entire subcontinent, not with just one nation.[1]

Nixon's Visit
The last hurdle was crossed after Vice-President Nixon, at the behest of the President, had visited India and Pakistan, among other Asian countries.

During his three-day stay in Karachi, in the first part of December, Nixon told the Pakistanis that he was convinced the people of Pakistan had a firm determination to thwart Communist ambitions,[2] and that the USA would be proud to support Pakistan in industrial development and also in defence.[3]

On his return the Vice-President urged that the ring around the Soviet empire be closed by creating a military crescent comprising Turkey, Iran, Pakistan, Indo-China, Formosa, and Japan. He recommended military aid to Pakistan and thought the United States decision on the subject must be guided by what was best for America and should not be deflected by any fear of Indian reaction. Nixon's effective two-hour presentation at the National Security Council clinched the argument and it was finally decided to offer military assistance to Pakistan.[4]

IV. The Turco-Pakistan Pact and the US-Pakistan Mutual Defence Assistance Agreement

It was decided that US military assistance to Pakistan should be given in the context of a pact between Pakistan and Turkey. In the words of a *New York Times* despatch, 'once the nations on the Soviet Union's southern border have agreed to work together to defend themselves against Soviet aggression, then the United States will offer to become their arsenal.'[5] Accordingly, a joint communiqué released simultaneously in Karachi and Ankara, on 19 February 1954, declared that Pakistan and Turkey had agreed to study methods of closer collaboration in the political, economic, and cultural spheres, as well as ways 'of strengthening peace and security in their own interest as also in that of all peace-loving·nations'.[6]

[1] ibid., 19 Nov. 1953.
[2] *Dawn*, 9 Dec. 1953.
[3] ibid., 8 Dec. 1953.
[4] Ralph de Toledano, *Nixon*, p. 163.
[5] *New York Times*, 14 Feb. 1954.
[6] For text see *Dawn*, 20 Feb. 1954.

Prime Minister Muhammad Ali Bogra commended the announcement to his countrymen as 'the first concrete major step towards strengthening the Muslim world'.[1]

On 22 February Bogra told a press conference in Karachi that Pakistan had requested US military assistance under the Mutual Security Act. Three days later President Eisenhower announced in Washington that he had decided to respond favourably to Pakistan's request in the interests of increased stability and strength in the Middle East.

Bogra assured his own countrymen that the United States had not asked for any bases in Pakistan, nor had Pakistan offered any. He said a momentous step forward had been taken towards strengthening the Muslim world, and also that the US military aid would enable Pakistan to achieve adequate defensive strength without having to assume an increasing burden on her economy.[2] In his monthly broadcast, Bogra said that the US Government's decision to grant military aid to Pakistan was 'perhaps the most effective step ever taken to ensure the security and progress of our country'.[3]

The declaration of intent in the Turco-Pakistani communiqué of 19 February was given concrete shape in an agreement signed in Karachi on 2 April. Article IV, dealing with co-operation in defence, stated that this would cover exchange of information on technical experience and progress, endeavours to meet the requirements in production of arms and ammunition, and co-operation under Article 51 of the United Nations Charter, against unprovoked attack.[4]

Next followed the conclusion of a Mutual Defence Assistance Agreement between Pakistan and the United States, by which the United States undertook to give military equipment and training to the Pakistani armed forces. Simultaneously with the signing of the agreement, on 19 May, both governments announced that it did not establish a military alliance, nor any military bases in Pakistan for the United States.[5]

As Indians alleged during the 1965 Indo-Pakistani war that Pakistan had been furnished with American armour on the condition that it would 'never' be used against India, it is relevant to examine precisely what conditions were attached to the arms given to

[1] *Dawn*, 20 Feb. 1954.
[2] ibid., 26 Feb. 1954.
[3] ibid., 2 March 1954.
[4] For text of Agreement see *Pakistan Affairs*, 9 April 1954.
[5] *Dawn*, 20 May 1954.

Pakistan. Article I (2) of the agreement stipulated: 'The Government of Pakistan will use this assistance exclusively to maintain its internal security, its legitimate self-defence, or to permit it to participate in the defence of the area or in United Nations collective security arrangements and measures, and Pakistan will not undertake any act of aggression against any other nation.'[1] The meaning of these words is plain enough and Horace A. Hildreth, US Ambassador to Pakistan, was merely reiterating the obvious when he explained that the 'only limitation' on the use of US military aid given to Pakistan and other countries of the world was that it would not be used for the purpose of aggression but for repelling aggression, and that 'if Bharat attacked Pakistan there could be no limitation to the use of American military aid'.[2]

V. The Manila Pact

After the cease-fire in Korea in July 1953, China had been able to increase the scale of her assistance to North Vietnam, making the French position in Indo-China progressively worse. On 13 March 1954 a large Vietminh force surrounded the French garrison at Dien Bien Phu. A few days later Secretary Dulles declared that the imposition of the Communist system on South-East Asia 'should not be passively accepted but should be met by united action'.[3] Britain, however, thought direct intervention by the US would lead to a third world war. She counselled patience till the conclusion of the Geneva Conference, which was due to convene on 26 April to consider the situation in Korea as well as in Indo-China. The fall of Dien Bien Phu on 7 May, a day before the Geneva Conference was due to take up the question of Indo-China, raised fresh fears of American intervention in the war. Prime Minister Churchill and Foreign Secretary Eden flew to Washington to dissuade the United States Government from acting precipitately. An Anglo-American study group was, however, set up in Washington to work out a scheme for collective defence in South-East Asia.

A settlement, consisting of three cease-fire agreements and a Final Declaration by the Conference, was finally reached at Geneva on 21 July. As the tide of war was definitely running in favour of the Communists, a major factor persuading them to accept the *status*

---

[1] ibid.
[2] ibid, 13 March 1957; see also ibid., 1 April 1954 for an earlier statement to the same effect.
[3] Anthony Eden, *Full Circle*, p. 91.

quo was no doubt the threat of American intervention, so much criticized at the time by Britain and India. Cambodia, Laos, and Vietnam were to be fully independent but would not join any military alliance. Vietnam was to be divided at the 17th parallel, pending elections to be held in July 1956. India (Chairman), Canada, and Poland were together to provide International Armistice Commissions, one each for Cambodia, Laos, and Vietnam, to supervise the carrying out of the armistices. Neither South Vietnam nor the United States signed the armistice agreements or endorsed the Final Declaration, but the latter made a Unilateral Declaration that she 'will refrain from the threat or use of force to disturb them'.

As already arranged, the next step was to work out a collective defence arrangement for South-East Asia for which recommendations had already been prepared by the working group in Washington. A conference at Manila resulted in the South-East Asia Collective Defense Treaty[1] of 8 September 1954, creating an alliance consisting of Pakistan, Thailand, the Philippines, USA, United Kingdom, France, Australia, and New Zealand, and a proclamation of general principles entitled the Pacific Charter.[2] Following India's lead, Ceylon, Burma, and Indonesia had declined to come to Manila. Pakistan, after some hesitation, had accepted the invitation and was represented at the meeting by Foreign Minister Zafrulla Khan.

The Manila Pact made no provision for any standing armed forces. The parties agreed to develop their capacity 'to resist armed attack and to prevent and counter subversive activities directed from without' (Article II), and to co-operate to promote economic progress and social well-being (Article III). In the case of an armed attack against the territory of any of the parties in the treaty area or against any State designated by the protocol to the treaty, whose government invited or consented to such intervention, each party would 'act to meet the common danger with its constitutional processes'. If the threat was other than armed attack, the parties would 'consult immediately' to agree on measures for common defence (Article IV, 1, 2). The protocol to the treaty designated Cambodia, Laos, and South Vietnam as the States to whom Articles III and IV would be applicable.

[1] SEACDT being hard to pronounce, the organization became popularly known as SEATO, and in 1955 the latter term was officially adopted. Americans at first had been reluctant to accept the term SEATO because it sounded like NATO which maintained standing armed forces.

[2] For texts of the Manila Pact and the Pacific Charter see George Modelski, *SEATO*, p. 289.

The promises of the Manila Pact as well as its membership and area are quite impressive, but its performance has belied expectations. Subversion is inherently difficult to define and identify and it relates to the internal affairs of the threatened country. It is, therefore, difficult to plan any collective action to counter such danger. With regard to economic co-operation, it became clear at the first council meeting that donor members favoured continuation of economic co-operation mainly through existing channels—bilateral agreements, the Colombo Plan, and ECAFE.

SEATO also did not shape up as a strong shield against armed attack. As none of the major powers who belonged to it had their homelands in the SEATO area, the Manila Pact did not stipulate— as NATO did—that an attack against any member would be considered an attack against all, calling for instant action. The United States was against setting up any joint military command. Secretary Dulles said at Manila that the United States' responsibilities were so vast and so far-flung that she could 'serve best, not by earmarking forces for particular areas of the Far East, but by developing the deterrent of mobile striking power, plus strategically placed reserves'.

Pakistan had good reason to feel dissatisfied with SEATO. It was made amply clear that she would receive no protection from SEATO against an Indian attack, which was her most immediate concern. The United States wrote a reservation into the treaty that her obligation under Article IV, paragraph 1, would extend only to cases of Communist aggression.[1] Zafrulla argued valiantly that 'all aggression is evil', but he was unable to prevent the US from entering the rider. In fact the US had proposed that the treaty should refer to Communist aggression, but this was not acceptable to the other members, specially to Australia and New Zealand who feared the possibility of Japanese resurgence. Australia, moreover, had an unsettled dispute with Indonesia over New Guinea which could lead to confrontation with that non-Communist country. The deletion of the word Communist from the main text, however, brought no gain to Pakistan. Australia and New Zealand publicly declared that they did not regard themselves bound by SEATO to take military action against any fellow member of the Commonwealth.[2] Britain did not make any similar statement publicly but no one had any doubt that her position was no different. That left

---

[1] It may be pointed out that the US reservation is out of step with the UN Charter which does not make any distinction between different varieties of aggression.
[2] Ralph Braibanti, *International Implications of the Manila Pact*, pp. 21–3.

France, the Philippines, and Thailand, and it was inconceivable that
they would fight for Pakistan against India while the USA and the
three Commonwealth countries stood aside.

Pakistan's approach to SEATO had in fact been lukewarm from
the beginning. Until 1959, when the Sino-Indian border trouble
erupted openly, Pakistan was not conscious of any direct threat to
the subcontinent from China. Moreover, the countries of Indo-
China, being predominantly non-Muslim, did not rouse Pakistan's
concern as much as the countries of the Middle East. She attended
the Manila conference without commitment. The decision whether
to join SEATO was to be taken after Zafrulla had reported back to
the Cabinet at home. Consequently, when Zafrulla appended his
signature to the pact he wrote above it, 'Signed for transmission to
my Government for its consideration and action in accordance with
the Constitution of Pakistan'.[1] As the date for the first Council
Meeting approached, Anglo-American pressure on Pakistan to
declare her adherence was intensified, and it was at last announced
on 19 January 1955 that Pakistan had decided to ratify the Manila
Pact. Indeed, she could hardly have done otherwise because one
of the purposes of US military assistance under the Mutual Defence
Agreement was to 'permit' the Government of Pakistan 'to participate in the defence of the area'. If Pakistan had refused to join
SEATO, the US could have declined to give the arms which she so
desperately needed. The sharp increase in US economic aid from
1954 would also not have materialized.

However, once in SEATO, Pakistan became a zealous member of
the organization till the 'reappraisal' of foreign policy in 1962-3.
The reason for this was that alliance with the USA became the
sheet-anchor of Pakistani foreign policy and Pakistan was genuinely
anxious to contribute her full share to that relationship. In fact she
complained that the organization was not strong enough to fulfil its
promise. In October 1956 Foreign Minister Feroze Khan Noon
said Pakistan wanted the defence pacts to which she belonged to
require that, like NATO, an attack on one member would be
considered an attack on all.[2] At Wellington in 1958, where he had
gone to attend the Council meeting, the then Foreign Minister
Manzur Qadir told a press conference that Pakistan was in favour of
SEATO being developed on NATO lines, with supreme head-

---

[1] These words do not appear on the published versions of the treaty and are, therefore,
usually lost sight of.
[2] *Dawn*, 22 Oct. 1956.

quarters and with SEATO forces earmarked for SEATO tasks in each member country.[1] During the Laotian crisis in December 1960 President Ayub said more than once that Pakistan would never hesitate to carry out its responsibility as a member of SEATO.[2]

VI. The Baghdad Pact

The Baghdad Pact was designed to counter the long-standing Russian policy of expansion southwards, in the direction of the Caspian and the Black Seas, and into Central Asia, where the absorption of the ancient Muslim Khanates had already brought Russia to the borders of Afghanistan, close to the historical gateway to the Indian subcontinent. Though the leaders of the Communist revolution outwardly disavowed Czarist policies, in fact they had never taken their eyes off the warm waters of the south. During the secret negotiations for a Soviet–German–Italian–Japanese treaty, in November 1940, Soviet Foreign Minister Molotov proposed that 'the area south of Batum and Baku in the general direction of the Persian Gulf should be recognized as the centre of the aspirations of the Soviet Union'.[3]

After the Second World War, the tremendous increase in Middle East oil production made the area even more important. Geographically, the region lies astride the routes to South Asia and Africa. In wartime its control by Russia would outflank NATO, and its use by the Western countries would provide a useful springboard for an assault on the USSR over a wide front. Britain, who had traditionally barred the Russian advance towards India, was too weak after the Second World War to checkmate Russian moves single-handed. In 1951–2 there were talks first about the establishment of a Middle East Command sponsored by the US, UK, France, and Turkey, and then of a Middle East Defence Organization. Both schemes, however, failed, principally because they did not attract the Near Eastern countries of the region on whose membership these arrangements were to be based. Iran and Egypt had unsettled disputes with Britain about oil and the Suez base respectively. And the Arab States were too preoccupied with their conflict with Israel to think of participating in an alliance under Western leadership to contain the Soviet Union.

[1] ibid, 8 April 1958.
[2] ibid., 15 and 21 Dec. 1960.
[3] *Central Treaty Organization*, R.5296/64, Feb. 1964, p. 2, Reference Division, Central Office of Information, London.

During 1954 the question of Middle East defence grew in urgency because Britain abandoned the Suez base in October and the Anglo-Iraqi Treaty of 1930 was about to expire. A Mutual Defence Assistance Agreement between Iraq and the USA was signed on 21 April 1954, and later in the year the Iraqi Premier, Nuri es-Said Pasha, proposed that the moribund Arab League Collective Security Pact of 1950 be widened and strengthened. Nuri also journeyed to Cairo, London, and Istanbul. He could not persuade Nasser to co-operate with the West but found the Turks more willing. A Pact of Mutual Co-operation was accordingly signed at Baghdad by Iraq and Turkey on 24 February 1955. Britain joined the Baghdad Pact on 5 April, Pakistan on 23 September, and Iran on 3 November.[1]

The Baghdad Pact provided that 'the high contracting parties will co-operate for their security and defence', but that such measures as they agree to take 'may form the subject of special agreements with each other' (Article 1). Also, that 'this pact shall be open for accession to any member State of the Arab League or any other State actively concerned with the security and peace in this region and which is fully recognized by both the high contracting parties.'[2] Like SEATO, the Baghdad Pact left much to be desired. It set up no joint military command.

After the July 1958 revolution, Iraq ceased to participate in pact activities; in October the headquarters were shifted to Ankara; in March 1959 Iraq formally relinquished her membership; and in August the name of the organization was changed to the Central Treaty Organization.

The USA had canvassed for the Baghdad Pact and later fully participated in its work, but never officially signed the treaty. Ambassador Waldemar J. Gallman, United States observer at the Council meeting in November 1955, gave two reasons why the US thought she could contribute more by remaining out of the pact: (1) US adherence might further estrange Egypt and her Arab allies, and (2) America's alliance with Iraq, a member of the Arab League, would evoke an Israeli counter-demand for a mutual defence treaty, which could become an issue in the next presidential election. A treaty with Israel would cause the Arabs, including

---

[1] After the fall of Premier Mosaddeq in 1953, the Shah of Iran had begun to incline towards alignment with the West.

[2] As Iraq did not recognize Israel, the inclusion of the latter in the Baghdad Pact was immediately ruled out.

Iraq, to reject alliances with the US and make them receptive to Soviet overtures.[1] At a later date the reluctance of the US to join the Pact was ascribed to the State Department estimate that the Senate would refuse to approve it unless some special guarantees were given to Israel also. This would cause new trouble with the Arab states.[2] Though the US actively participated in all the important committees of the Pact, including the military committee, her refusal to become a full member cast a doubt upon the degree of her commitment to the alliance, and contrasted strangely with her conduct as the chief sponsor of the Pact.

Pakistan joined the Baghdad Pact with greater enthusiasm than SEATO because she had always stood for special ties with Muslim countries. Further, she believed at the time that the Soviet Union really posed a threat to the Middle East.

However, Pakistan was once again told by her Western friends that she would not get from the alliance what she needed most: protection against an attack by India. When the USA joined the military committee of the Baghdad Pact, she stated that her participation was 'related solely to the Communist menace and carries no connotations with respect to intra-area matters'.[3] British Defence Minister Duncan Sandys declared that both Britain and America had promised to defend the Baghdad Pact region against Communist aggression only.[4]

After joining the Pact Pakistan worked hard to make it solid and strong. On the eve of the Council meeting in January 1958, Prime Minister Feroze Khan Noon said that the Baghdad Pact should have the same rule as NATO, that aggression against one is aggression against all.[5] At about the same time it was reported that the Muslim members favoured the creation of a joint command under an American commander.[6] President Ayub Khan revealed at a press conference in October 1959 that Pakistan had been insisting upon a command structure for CENTO but that one difficulty was that America was not a full member of the organization.[7] Turkey, being a member of NATO, did not feel the need for a unified command under CENTO, but Pakistan and Iran, especially Iran who

[1] *New York Times*, 27 Nov. 1955.
[2] ibid., 31 Jan. 1958.
[3] *Asian Recorder*, 1957, p. 1395.
[4] *Dawn*, 13 Feb. 1959.
[5] ibid., 12 Jan. 1958.
[6] ibid., 29 Jan. 1958.
[7] ibid., 24 Oct. 1959.

belonged to no other alliance, continued to press for putting more substance into the partnership, and at the ninth Council meeting (April 1961) succeeded in getting a military staff commander of the rank of full General appointed with a view to 'improve the co-ordination of defence planning'.[1] But this was no more than a 'semantic victory' because the General was to command his military committee only, no troops.[2] In the following year Iran and Pakistan again proposed that CENTO should have a Central Military Command on the lines of NATO, but the USA, Britain, and Turkey showed little enthusiasm for the idea.[3]

In the early sixties all three Muslim members of CENTO cooled off towards the Western powers and moved to improve relations with the Soviet Union. Iran felt she had received insufficient military hardware from her Western allies and also not enough moral support in her cold war with the United Arab Republic; Turkey complained of Western attitudes in her quarrel with Greece over Cyprus; and Pakistan had the painful experience of watching her closest Western allies, the USA and the UK, supply arms to India. But CENTO served to increase the physical contacts, friendship, and mutual understanding between these three members, already joined together by ties of culture, common religion, and geography, and they put these assets to concrete use by founding a parallel organization under the name of Regional Co-operation for Development.

The Baghdad Pact was criticized by the Arab countries for breaking Arab solidarity by enticing Iraq into its ranks. Some critics say it also spurred the Soviet Union to increase her influence in the Middle East, instead of keeping her out. The difficulty in rebutting this criticism lies in the fact that, while it is easy enough to point to what the Soviet Union has been able to achieve, there is no sure way of measuring what she has been prevented from getting. It is doubtful whether the absence of the Pact would have inhibited that super-power from interfering in the region that adjoins her for hundreds of miles and has been the subject of her close attention at least since the days of Czar Peter the Great. Indeed, a completely clear field could very well have facilitated the successful staging of Communist-supported revolutions all over the Middle East. It is true no military command was set up, but no one doubted that any

[1] *The Times*, 29 April 1961.
[2] *New York Times*, 30 April 1961.
[3] *Dawn*, 27 April 1962.

reckless move by the Soviet Union would be countered immediately by CENTO with United States help. A defence alliance is meant to serve not only as a physical deterrent to a potential aggressor but also as a psychological deterrent.

Without a doubt, the largest single factor which opened Arab doors to the Soviet Union was the planting of the state of Israel in the midst of Arab lands and the continuing US support to her, which preceded the Baghdad Pact and continues unabated long after that pact has lost its original meaning.

9 Pakistan's Contribution to the Alliance

Pakistan's contribution as a zealous ally of the West is best illustrated by describing her role in the important international developments of the period.

I. The Colombo Conference

Towards the end of April 1954, when the international conference on Indo-China assembled at Geneva, the Prime Ministers of the five South Asian countries—India, Pakistan, Ceylon, Burma, and Indonesia—also met at Colombo to deliberate the same problem. A joint communiqué (2 May) recommended an immediate ceasefire in Indo-China, a declaration by France that she was committed to the complete independence of Indo-China, and a settlement by negotiation.

The Prime Ministers also regretted that colonialism still existed in various parts of the world and pronounced it a violation of fundamental human rights and a threat to peace. They further 'declared their unshakeable determination to resist interference in the affairs of their countries by external Communist, anti-Communist, or other agencies'. The mention of 'external Communism' alongside 'colonialism' was the result of a behind-the-scenes effort by the Pakistani Prime Minister, Muhammad Ali Bogra, supported by Sir John Kotelawala of Ceylon.

When the meeting opened, Pakistan introduced a resolution declaring that international Communism was 'the biggest potential danger to democracy in the region'.[1] But Nehru, who strongly favoured condemnation of colonialism, fought 'tooth and nail' to bar condemnation of Communism from any formal resolution.[2] It was argued by India and Indonesia that colonialism represented

[1] *International Studies, India's Relations with Pakistan*, vol. 8, no. 1–2, July–Oct. 1966, p. 169.
[2] *New York Times*, 30 April 1954.

an active threat while Communism was merely an ideology. Bogra rejoined that colonialism was a dying cult but Communism was a new and aggressive factor. 'We can rid ourselves of colonialism,' he said, 'but any country overrun by Communism would be lost forever.'[1] He indicated that if Communism also was not condemned, he could not support the resolution against colonialism.[2]

The Pakistani Premier was able not only to get external Communism condemned as the twin evil of colonialism, but he succeeded also in neutralizing another Nehru proposal. The Indian Prime Minister wished the communiqué to recommend that the USA, the USSR, the UK, and China should make an agreement on non-intervention, denying direct or indirect aid to the combatants in Indo-China. Bogra subscribed to the Western fears that this would deliver Indo-China to the Communists because, while the Western powers would feel restrained by the agreement, the Communists would not hesitate to breach it surreptitiously.[3] In the end the joint declaration simply said that the success of the 'direct negotiations will be greatly helped by an agreement on the part of all countries concerned, particularly China, the UK, the USA, and the USSR on the steps necessary to prevent a recurrence of hostilities'.

II. The Asian-African Conference at Bandung
During the Colombo Conference Prime Minister Ali Sastroamid-jojo of Indonesia proposed a larger meeting of Afro-Asian countries, and in their final communiqué his colleagues authorized him 'to explore the possibility of such a conference'.

After obtaining their agreement in principle, Sastroamidjojo invited the Colombo Prime Ministers to Bogor, Indonesia, at the end of December 1954, to plan the proposed conference. The sponsors left it to the conference to decide its own procedure and agenda but indicated that the objects of calling an Asian-African conference were to consider problems of special interest to Asian and African peoples, e.g. racialism and colonialism, and to view the position of Asians and Africans in the world and the contribution they could make to world peace and co-operation.[4]

They also decided which countries to invite. Bogra objected to Communist China being invited, but gave way when he found that

---

[1] *Dawn*, 1 May 1954.
[2] *Times of India*, 1 May 1954.
[3] Ton That Thien, *India and Southeast Asia*, pp. 194–5, 299; M. S. Rajan, *India in World Affairs, 1954–1956*, pp. 126–7; *Economist*, 1 May 1954.
[4] For text of Bogor communiqué see *Asian Recorder*, 1955, p. 9.

even Kotelawala was partly siding with Nehru and U Nu on this issue.[1] The Pakistani Premier, however, was successful in opposing India's and Burma's bid to include Israel. He said if Israel were invited the Arabs would not attend.[2]

The conference opened at Bandung, Indonesia, on 18 April 1955 and concluded with a joint communiqué on 25 April. It was attended by representatives of twenty-nine nations with an aggregate population of 1.4 billion, more than half of all mankind. As the invitees included countries of all shades of political colour— Communist, non-aligned, and those allied with the West—the final statement, which was subject to the rule of unanimity, was the product of animated debates. On paper China gained little, but in fact she benefited the most. India, the most important of the sponsoring nations and led at the conference by Nehru, seconded by Krishna Menon, was expected to dominate the proceedings but fared the worst.

Pakistan approached the conference warily. Of the sponsoring countries she was the only one formally aligned with the West, though Ceylon at the time was also pro-West in her outlook. At Colombo Pakistan and Ceylon had barely held their own against India, Indonesia, and Burma. In the event Pakistan had good reason to feel satisfied with the outcome of the Bandung assembly. Bogra was not the only pro-Western leader there: representatives of Ceylon, Turkey, Iraq, Iran, Thailand, and the Philippines all spoke the same political language as Bogra and were men of eloquence and experience. And Premier Chou En-lai of China declared at the very outset that 'the Chinese Delegation has come here to seek unity and not to quarrel'.[3]

The Western countries feared that Bandung might turn out to be a forum for venting long-pent-up anti-white and anti-colonial grievances and might start a concerted Afro-Asian movement to challenge Western supremacy. The crash, resulting from a 'timed infernal machine', of a chartered Indian airliner, 'Kashmir Princess', carrying several members of the Chinese delegation from Hong Kong to Jakarta, was interpreted by China as an effort by the 'American–Chiang Kai-shek agents' to sabotage the conference. But the gloomy Western forecasts proved groundless. The pro-

---

[1] George Modelski, *SEATO*, p. 214. Also W. F. Van Eekelen, *Indian Foreign Policy and the Border Dispute with China*, p. 51.

[2] George McT. Kahin, *The Asian-African Conference*, p. 3.

[3] ibid., p. 52.

tagonists of neutralism and Communism remained on the defensive throughout the conference, and no permanent Afro-Asian organization was set up.

The most important visible achievement of the conference was its call to all nations to base their policies on the ten principles enunciated in the last part of the conference communiqué. Two of these principles are specially notable for our purpose: 'Respect for the right of each nation to defend itself singly or collectively, in conformity with the Charter of the United Nations', and 'Settlement of all international disputes by peaceful means, such as negotiation, conciliation, arbitration or judicial settlement'. Another pronouncement which emerged after much controversy was that 'colonialism in all its manifestations is an evil which should speedily be brought to an end'.[1]

Bogra's first success related to the question whether there should be any public opening speeches by the leaders of the various delegations. On 17 April, one day before the scheduled opening of the conference, Nehru had persuaded the twenty-one delegations which had arrived by then that there would be no preliminary speeches at the open session, and only printed texts would be circulated. His plea was that this would save time and avoid controversy. When Bogra, on arrival later, learned of the decision, he protested vehemently that such an important matter had been considered in the absence of eight delegations, including Pakistan who was one of the sponsors of the conference. He said the occasion was important and the delegates should have the right to speak in person if they wanted to do so. Backed by the other late arrivals, and some delegates who had had second thoughts, Bogra succeeded in getting the earlier decision reversed. This displeased Nehru so much that he walked out of the conference in a huff. He neither delivered an opening speech nor circulated one. Chou En-lai trod the path of compromise, as he was to do later throughout the conference. He circulated his main speech and also delivered a supplementary speech personally.[2] This first wordy skirmish set the pattern for the rest of the proceedings. Bogra and Nehru would often take diametrically opposite stands and Chou En-lai would help resolve the differences by suggesting a compromise.

A heated argument erupted when India, Burma, and China pressed the conference to adopt the Five Principles of Co-existence

---

[1] For text of Bandung communiqué see *Asian Recorder*, 1955, p. 191.

[2] *Dawn*, 25 April 1955.

as a guide to international conduct and Bogra proposed 'Seven Pillars of Peace' as a more realistic alternative. The two additional principles which Bogra sought to add to Nehru's five were the right to self-defence singly or collectively and the undertaking to solve all international disputes by peaceful means such as negotiation and arbitration. Both were unpalatable to Nehru. He said Bogra had put forward the right of self-defence with the object of asking the conference, 'under cover of words', to accept the principle of the military pacts of which Pakistan was a member. The second addition was seen as a ruse to make it difficult for India to refuse arbitration of the Kashmir problem. Chou En-lai saved the situation by declaring that, as all the delegates did not agree to the five principles, 'we can add to these five principles or we can subtract from them'.[1]

The controversy on the colonialism clause originated when the Irani delegate, Djalal Abdoh, referred to Soviet colonialism. Bogra, who, among others, supported him, said it was unrealistic to ignore Soviet imperialism which had turned many countries into satellites and had brought so many people under its iron heel. But, he said, 'China is by no means an imperialist nation and she has no satellites . . . she has not brought any other country under her heel.' Bogra asked Chou En-lai not to misunderstand the criticism, which is 'not directed against an invitee, a fellow delegate who, we appreciate very much, has shown a great deal of conciliation'.[2] Nehru said the countries of Eastern Europe were not colonies because the United Nations, by admitting them to membership, had recognized them as independent. Once again it was Chou En-lai who first gave way, provided the word 'manifestation' was used instead of 'forms'. However, in the light of the debate in the conference, no one had any doubt that the expression 'colonialism in all its manifestations' in the joint declaration was meant to cover both Western and Russian colonialism.

Noting that some delegates had said that 'peaceful co-existence' was a term used by Communists, the Chinese Premier also offered to change that term.[3] Consequently, the phrase 'peaceful co-existence' does not occur anywhere in the communiqué.

Other examples of Chou En-lai's diplomatic effort were his acceptance of the United Nations' Fundamental Principles of

[1] George McT. Kahin, *The Asian-African Conference*, p. 59.
[2] ibid., pp. 19–20.
[3] ibid., p. 57.

Human Rights; his declaration that different social systems did not prevent countries from seeking common ground; his assurance that China did not wish to expand Communist activities outside her own country; his plea that China was the victim of American subversion rather than a perpetrator of subversion abroad; his denial that there was any bamboo curtain round China and his open invitation to several delegates to come and see things for themselves; his support for the Arab position on Palestine; and his offer to sit down with the United States Government 'to discuss the question of relaxing tension in the Far East and especially the question of relaxing tension in the Taiwan area'. Outside the conference, he pleased the Indonesians by concluding a treaty which ended the dual nationality of persons of Chinese descent in Indonesia. This was read as a hopeful sign by other South-East Asian countries apprehensive of the Chinese minority in their midst.

The Chinese Premier, moreover, had on the very first day said that, in order to avoid differences, he had decided not to ask the conference to support the People's Republic of China's claim to Formosa nor her right to sit in the UN. As a result, though the communiqué listed a number of countries whom the conferees considered entitled to UN membership, it was silent about China's case.

What, broadly, were the achievements of the conference? First, the tensions which were dangerously mounting up at the time around Formosa were eased. Though Chou's offer to sit down and talk with the United States did not bear fruit, his repeated professions of peace and reasonableness before the representatives of the twenty-eight Afro-Asian nations, whom China wished so much to court, precluded resort to violence at least for some time to come. Second, the sense of Afro-Asian solidarity amongst the participants increased to a degree, resulting in greater co-operation among them in the United Nations. Third, the conference increased the feeling of self-importance of the various participating Afro-Asian countries, lessening the feeling of inferiority resulting from prolonged subservience to the West.

China was the biggest beneficiary of Bandung. Chou En-lai proved to be the star of the conference and won universal acclaim for his spirit of accommodation and diplomatic skill. Both Bogra and Kotelawala, Communism's strongest critics, publicly praised the Chinese Premier for his sincerity and reasonableness. As Chou En-lai himself said, 'The Asian-African Conference furnished

a very precious opportunity for the leaders of China to make
extensive contacts with the leaders of many Asian-African countries.'[1]
China's isolation was ended. By 1957 she had established diplomatic relations with twenty-nine countries. In the brief Sino-
Indian armed confrontation of 1962, China was able dramatically
to demonstrate her superior physical power over her Asian rival,
and the growth of her stature in the Afro-Asian world was not
arrested till 1965, when circumstances compelled her to turn in-
wards to stage a 'cultural revolution'.

For Pakistan, the chief significance of Bandung lay in the fact
that the top leaders of Pakistan and China, in their very first personal
encounter, had achieved a better understanding of each other's point
of view. Chou En-lai revealed on 23 April that two days previously
he had paid a visit to the Prime Minister of Pakistan and 'he told
me that although Pakistan was a party to a military treaty, Pakistan
was not against China. Pakistan had no fear China would commit
aggression against her. ... The Prime Minister of Pakistan further
assured that if the United States should take aggressive action under
the military treaty or if the United States launched a global war,
Pakistan would not be involved in it just as it was not involved in
the Korean War ... through these explanations we achieve a
mutual understanding.'[2] For his part Bogra, when asked afterwards
to elaborate his own statement that he and Chou En-lai were beginning to understand each other's point of view, said, 'I am anti-
Communist but I do realize that China has its own problems, some
of which may have been solved by Communism.' He said his
meeting with the Chinese Premier would have no effect on the
foreign policy of Pakistan 'except that our relations with China
will be more friendly'.[3]

Bogra was also prominent among those who had successfully
pressed Chou En-lai behind the scenes to issue a conciliatory
statement on Formosa. However, the immediate response of the
State Department was that the Nationalist Government must be

---

[1] Address to Third Session of the First National People's Conference, 28 June 1956,
People's China, supplement, p. 7.

[2] George McT. Kahin, *The Asian-African Conference,* p. 57. Bogra was factually
correct. Pakistan's obligation as an ally was to prevent aggression, not to become a party
to aggression. Horace Hildreth, US Ambassador to Pakistan, had conceded that
Pakistan might adopt a neutral attitude in a third world war because there was no agreement between Pakistan and America that Pakistan would join a war against the Russian
bloc if she accepted military aid from the US. *Dawn,* 1 April 1954.

[3] *Dawn,* 29 April 1955.

represented as an equal at any such talks, and to list steps Communist China could take as evidence of her *bona fides*.[1] The Pakistani Premier was stated to have wrung a promise from Chou En-lai that, if the Americans responded favourably to his offer of negotiations, Chou En-lai would announce the release of American fliers then in Chinese custody,[2] and he was greatly disappointed at the American attitude.

Bandung opened the way to a greater exchange of visits between Pakistanis and Chinese. Chou En-lai had invited Bogra to China and advantage was taken of the offer by Prime Minister Suhrawardy in 1956. Chou En-lai returned the visit later the same year and the two countries also exchanged numerous other delegations. Though Sino-Pakistani relations inevitably came under occasional strain while Pakistan was committed to the West, the personal contacts initiated at Bandung helped smooth the transition to a more cordial relationship when both sides desired it in the following decade.

A major consequence of Bandung was the eclipse of India as the prospective leader of Asia. As an Indian writer said in retrospect, Nehru had brought China into the circle of brotherhood in Asia at Bandung 'but subsequent events showed that the Chinese preferred to use their new contact to pursue a diplomacy that would push India into the background and raise themselves to the leadership of Asia'.[3] Though the Bandung communiqué had recommended that the sponsors consider the convening of another meeting of the Conference, India was no longer keen to suffer another Afro-Asian gathering and preferred in the future to work for a conference restricted to non-aligned nations from which both China and Pakistan would be automatically excluded.

III. The Suez Crisis

The crisis in the Suez area, following the nationalization of the Suez Canal Company[4] by Egypt in July 1956, convulsed public

---

[1] *Collective Defence in South-East Asia*, A Report by a Chatham House Study Group, p. 70.

[2] George McT. Kahin, *The Asian-African Conference*, p. 29; Congressman Adam C. Powell, Jr.'s statement on the Bandung Conference, *Mutual Security Act 1955, Hearings Before the Committee on Foreign Relations, United States Senate, 84th Congress, 10 May 1955*, pp. 157-8. Powell had attended the Bandung Conference as a visitor despite State Department efforts to dissuade him.

[3] *Hindu Weekly*, 18 Oct. 1965.

[4] Though Egypt was popularly stated to have nationalized the Suez Canal, in fact she had nationalized the Suez Canal Company which had been operating under a concession granted by Egypt in 1856.

opinion in Pakistan more than any other event since independence. For the people the issue was clear: a sister Muslim country was being threatened by two Western imperial powers, Britain and France, and by the Western protégé in the Middle East, Israel. At government level the problem did not seem so simple. There was sympathy for Egypt, no doubt, but this was tempered by two other considerations. First, there was the desire not to offend Pakistan's newly acquired allies, the USA and the UK, whose material and moral assistance was so essential for facing India. Secondly, 56 per cent of Pakistan's exports and 49 per cent of her imports passed through the Suez Canal and she had a vested interest in the efficient operation of the waterway. Pakistan evidently shared the Western view that Egypt did not possess the technical and managerial capacity to run the canal without outside help. In the result, there was a gap between public opinion, which was unreservedly in favour of Egypt, and official policy, which was pulled in more than one direction. On the whole the Government attitude seems to have been one of guarded support for the Western position, especially that of the USA who favoured international management of the canal but in Secretary Dulles's words did 'not intend to shoot our way through'. With the USSR fully backing Egypt and the USA critical of Britain's and France's conduct, the two last-named countries inevitably had to climb down in the end and President Nasser not only kept the canal but made himself a hero into the bargain.

An outline of the salient facts will help in understanding Pakistan's role in the affair. It was on 16 November 1869 that the Suez Canal, which had been under construction for ten years under the direction of a Frenchman, Ferdinand de Lesseps, was declared open. Initially France owned 200,000 shares and Egypt 175,000. Britain purchased the Egyptian shares in 1875 and assumed the guardianship of the canal, which formed a vital link in communications leading to India, the Far East, Australia, and New Zealand. The canal was operated by a private company under a concession granted by Egypt, which was due to expire in 1968. A Convention signed in 1888 at Constantinople declared that the canal would 'always be free and open, in time of war as in time of peace, to every vessel of commerce or of war, without distinction of flag'. Under pressure from the revolutionary government which had ousted King Farouq in 1952, Britain, in October 1954, agreed to evacuate her military base in Suez, and left its defence to the Egyptians. In 1955 Egypt formulated a scheme to build a High Dam at Aswan on the Nile and it was believed the project would be financed by the UK, USA, and others. On 19 July 1956 the United States announced that she would not participate in the project because it had become doubtful whether Egypt could contribute her share of the cost.[1] Britain and the International Bank soon followed suit. Nasser responded a week later by nationalizing the canal company and declaring that Egypt herself would build the dam with revenues from the canal. Britain and France felt that the Egyptian move threatened the economic life of Western Europe, 50 per cent of whose oil supplies passed through the canal. Both countries, moreover, were emotionally stirred. Until recently they had between them dominated the Middle East and were sensitive to any new affronts there. A Frenchman had conceived and built the canal and Britain had long prized it as a symbol of her world stature. Nasser was getting arms from the USSR, had bitterly criticized the Baghdad Pact, and provided encouragement and assistance to anti-Western elements everywhere in the Middle East. His new bold venture, if successful, could boost his influence further to the detriment of the Western powers. In particular it would make the French position in Algeria much more difficult. Ultimately, it would make it easier for Russia to penetrate the Middle East. The USA had no comparable historical or economic ties with the Suez Canal and, moreover, genuinely believed that the use of force by Britain and France smacked of old-style colonialism which had no place in the middle of the twentieth century.

Dulles flew to London whence a three-power statement by Britain, France, and the US was issued, stating that the Egyptian action had threatened the freedom of the canal and it was necessary that 'operating arrangements, under an international system' should be restored.[2] The three powers also called a conference of twenty-four nations principally concerned with the use of the canal. Egypt and Greece did not attend but the remaining twenty-two users met in London from 16 to 23 August. A United States proposal, incorporating some amendments suggested by Pakistan, Ethiopia, Iran, and Turkey, was adopted by eighteen members of the conference, including Pakistan, as their joint declaration. While recognizing the sovereign rights of Egypt, the declaration asserted the principle

[1] Egypt had made an arms deal with Czechoslovakia, followed by another with the USSR. Egypt's Western critics said that the purchases of arms would drain Egypt's treasury.

[2] Anthony Eden, *Full Circle*, p. 439.

7

of international control and entrusted the operation of the canal to a board of which Egypt would be a member.[1] Four countries— India, Indonesia, Ceylon, and the USSR—favoured a purely advisory board, having no powers of control. A committee headed by Premier Robert Menzies of Australia tried to sell the proposals of the majority to Nasser in Cairo from 3 to 7 September, but was unsuccessful. The Egyptian leader said an international authority would mean 'the restoration of collective colonialism'.[2]

On 12 September the Western powers announced that they would create a Users' Association which would run the canal and pay Egypt appropriately for the facilities provided by her. Three days later Nasser declared that Egypt would 'resist any attempt on the part of any nation or group of nations to have an international body exercise Egypt's sovereign rights'.[3] A second conference met in London on 19 September, and the Suez Canal Users' Association (SCUA) held its inaugural meeting there on 1 October. As recourse to further direct negotiations with Egypt held no prospect of success, Britain and France took their proposals to the Security Council but their resolution was vetoed by Russia (13 October).

In the middle of feverish diplomatic activity and mounting tension, the world heard on 29 October that Israel had launched an attack on Egypt 'to eliminate the Egyptian *fedayeen* bases'. The United States immediately asked the Security Council to order the Israeli forces to withdraw and to call upon all members of the United Nations to refrain from the use of force, but the resolution was vetoed by Britain and France. At twelve hours' notice, after calling upon Israel and Egypt to stop fighting and withdraw their forces to a distance of ten miles from the canal, Britain and France commenced military action against Egypt.[4] An air attack was launched on 31 October, and on 5 November paratroops were dropped on Port Said. According to Sir Anthony Eden the purpose was 'to separate the belligerents and to guarantee freedom of transit through the canal by ships of all nations'.[5]

At the request of Yugoslavia, the Security Council decided that the situation be placed before an emergency session of the General Assembly to be summoned under the Uniting for Peace resolution. On 2 November the Assembly passed a US resolution urging an

[1] ibid.
[2] ibid., p. 470.
[3] ibid., p. 486.
[4] Israel had accepted, and Egypt had rejected, the Anglo-French terms.
[5] Anthony Eden, *Full Circle*, p. 527.

immediate cease-fire. Two days later the Assembly approved two motions, an Afro-Asian resolution asking the Secretary-General to arrange with the parties the implementation of the cease-fire, and a Canadian proposal asking him urgently to submit a plan for setting up 'an emergency international United Nations force to supervise and secure the cessation of hostilities'. On 5 November the Soviet Premier, Marshal Bulganin, wrote to Eden that the war with Egypt could grow into a third world war and threatened the use of rockets. Pressed thus by friend and foe, Britain and France ordered their forces to cease fighting at midnight on 6 November. On 7 November the Assembly passed another resolution sponsored by Afro-Asian countries, once more calling upon the parties to withdraw their forces. The Assembly having also approved the Secretary-General's plans for a UN force, the first batch of the United Nations Emergency Force (UNEF) reached Egypt on 15 November. On 24 November the Assembly again endorsed an Afro-Asian resolution demanding troop withdrawals, and by 22 December all Anglo-French forces had left Egypt. Two further resolutions had to be passed, on 19 January and 2 February 1957, insisting upon the withdrawal of the Israeli forces, before the Secretary-General could report, on 8 March, that the Israeli troops, too, had vacated Egyptian territory, marking the end of the Suez crisis.

Nasser's action in nationalizing the canal immediately evoked popular support in Pakistan, but official circles at first refrained from saying anything on its merits. In the first statement of any consequence a Foreign Office spokesman said that Pakistan would favour 'such a control of the Suez as would ensure free transit of goods and reasonable dues' but declined to make any comment on the merits of nationalization.[1] On 2 August Foreign Minister Hamidul Huq Chowdhury stated that Pakistan had not questioned Egypt's right to nationalize a 'commercial concern' within the country and the only question was how far the exercise of that right affected other countries.[2] Prime Minister Chaudhri Muhammad Ali said Egypt had the right to nationalize the canal but that Pakistan and many other nations were 'vitally concerned with the maintenance of the freedom of navigation in the canal'.[3]

At the First London Conference, Foreign Minister Hamidul Huq said that the act of nationalizing the Suez Company by Egypt 'was

[1] *Dawn*, 2 Aug. 1956.
[2] ibid., 3 Aug. 1956.
[3] Govt. of Pakistan, *Handout*, dated 14 Aug. 1956.

an exercise of her sovereignty', but added that nationalization 'at the time and under the circumstances had shaken the confidence' of a large number of interested countries and it was one of the principal objectives of the conference to restore that confidence. He proposed that 'an effective machinery be set up in active collaboration with Egypt to ensure the efficient, unfettered and continuous freedom of navigation of all nations'.[1] Anthony Eden says that Pakistan, Iran, and Turkey were in favour of reasserting international control over the canal but they 'wished to emphasize Egyptian sovereignty over the canal. . . . It was no inroad on Egyptian sovereignty to ask for international control of passage through the canal in return for a financial return. At the conference we were [therefore] able to meet the Pakistani, Iranian and Turkish point of view by accepting their amendments.'[2] This reasoning, however, was not acceptable to Egypt, who considered international control of the canal in any form inconsistent with her sovereignty over it.

Public opinion in Pakistan in the meantime was running far ahead of the Government moves. The secretary of the East Pakistan Awami League, Mujibur Rahman, called for observing a 'Suez Day'. A public meeting in Lahore, the biggest since partition, attended by over 300,000 persons, protested against 'lukewarm support from the Pakistani Government to the Egyptian cause'. Protest meetings were also held in the other principal towns of both wings of the country.[3] Dawn's London correspondent noted that the Suez conference was the first occasion on which Pakistan had lent her moral support to the West in its quarrel with a Muslim country.[4] The Muslim League Parliamentary Party declared in a resolution that the imposition of international control was a direct interference with the sovereign rights of Egypt, and pledged wholehearted support to Egypt.[5]

In September 1956 there was a change of government in Pakistan. Huseyn Shaheed Suhrawardy took over as Prime Minister and Feroze Khan Noon as Foreign Minister. Pakistan sent Noon to the Second London Conference without commitment. At the conference the Pakistani delegate pointed out that, Nasser having already rejected the concept of a Canal Users' Association, there

[1] For text of Hamidul Huq's speech at the conference on 18 Aug. 1956 see Govt. of Pakistan, Handout E. no. 4463, dated 19 Aug. 1956.
[2] Anthony Eden, Full Circle, p. 450.
[3] Dawn., 17 Aug. 1956.
[4] ibid., 9 Sept. 1956.
[5] ibid., 14 Sept. 1956.

were only two alternatives left: (1) the use of force, and (2) reference to the Security Council. As pursuance of the proposal in its existing form would mean an imposed settlement, Pakistan could not associate herself with it. Noon proposed that the users invite Egypt to negotiate a fresh settlement. If this did not bear fruit, the matter should be taken to the Security Council.[1] When the Users' Association was set up, Pakistan declined to join it.

When the tripartite invasion of Egypt took place, the issue was clearer. Both the Government and the people of Pakistan were one in condemning the aggression. But there was still a difference over how far Pakistan should go. The Government employed all the diplomatic pressure at its command to bring about a cease-fire and withdrawal of hostile forces from the soil of Egypt, but stood for a resumption of friendly relations with Britain and France after they had evacuated their forces from Egypt in obedience to the Security Council resolutions. The majority of the vocal people of Pakistan, on the other hand, demanded severance of Commonwealth ties, expulsion of the UK from the Baghdad Pact, and termination of diplomatic relations with France. *Dawn* greeted the Anglo-French invasion by writing an editorial, 'Hitler Reborn'; public demonstrations erupted all over Pakistan; in Dacca angry crowds burnt down the British Information Services Office and smashed the windows of the French Consulate; at the British High Commission in Karachi thousands of students burnt the Union Jack; and the Working Committee of the Muslim League demanded Pakistan's withdrawal from the Commonwealth and Britain's expulsion from the Baghdad Pact.

Suez was the only issue on which the official policy of Pakistan lagged behind that of India in its support to a Muslim country. India was completely against any form of international control in operating the canal and Nehru, with his deep-seated abhorrence of any manifestation of Western imperialism against any Afro–Asian country, condemned Anglo–French policy in much stronger terms. 'Asia is on the march,' he declared, 'and is emerging to take its rightful place in world affairs';[2] also, the use of military force against Egypt by the United Kingdom and France was a 'reversion to past colonial methods'.[3]

---

[1] For text of Noon's speech see Govt. of Pakistan, *Handout E. no. 4960*, dated 20 Sept. 1956.

[2] *Hindu*, 2 Aug. 1956, quoted by M. S. Rajan, *India in World Affairs 1954–56*.

[3] *Lok Sabha Debates*, 16 Nov. 1956, col. 261.

Suhrawardy sent for American, British, and French envoys and demanded the immediate withdrawal of foreign troops from Egypt. He told the British representative that, if Britain persisted in aggression, Pakistan would withdraw from the Commonwealth. He said also that the Baghdad Pact could not survive if one of the members continued such aggression.[1] The Premier declared publicly that if Britain and France refused to accept the UN directive, the rest of the world would be justified in using force against the aggressors.[2]

At the initiative of Pakistan, the Prime Ministers of the Muslim members of the Baghdad Pact met at Teheran and demanded the withdrawal of all invading forces from Egypt and the settlement of the Suez problem under UN auspices. At Iraq's motion, Britain was excluded from the meeting.

Suhrawardy, however, refused to bow before public agitation that Pakistan leave the Commonwealth or the Baghdad Pact. 'I refuse to be isolated', he said. 'We must have friends.'[3] He said the British attack on Egypt had to be condemned, but it had been an attack to see that the Suez Canal remained free. Britain did not wish to reoccupy Egypt. Owing to the closure of the canal, goods came to Pakistan via the Cape and cost 30 per cent more.[4] Nasser's action was not the right method. Britain must continue the Baghdad Pact to save four weak Muslim countries.[5] After Britain and France had withdrawn their forces from Egypt, the Pakistani Premier contrasted their conduct with that of Russia, who had refused to obey the United Nations demands in respect of Hungary, and said there was no longer any reason why the UK should not again participate in the Baghdad Pact.[6] On 27 March it was announced that Iraq now had no objection to sitting with Britain in the Baghdad Pact meetings. Accordingly, when the next Council session took place at Karachi in June 1957, Britain resumed her place in the organization.[7]

IV. The Crisis in Hungary

To the people of Pakistan generally, the crisis in Hungary was not of

[1] *Dawn*, 9 Nov. 1956.
[2] ibid., 3 Nov. 1956.
[3] *Daily Telegraph*, 15 Nov. 1956.
[4] The canal was not reopened till 24 April 1957.
[5] *The Times*, 3 Dec. 1956.
[6] Statement in National Assembly on 22 Feb. 1957.
[7] For tension between the Governments of Pakistan and Egypt during the Suez affair see ch. 10, The Cost of Alliance, and for appreciation in Pakistan of United States policy during the crisis see ch. 12, The Course of Alliance.

much direct concern. As a prominent Muslim Leaguer, Mian Mumtaz Muhammad Daultana, put it, 'We had sympathy for Hungary, but for Egypt we felt as if our very bodies were being lacerated.'[1]

The disturbances in Hungary, which started just before the Suez invasion, resulted from Khrushchev's process of de-Stalinization in Russia. There were demands for greater freedom in Poland and Hungary. In Poland the movement was partly successful but in Hungary it met a different fate. Starting in Budapest on 23 October, demonstrations erupted all over the country, and there were clashes between the Hungarian people and Soviet troops already stationed in Hungary under the Warsaw Pact. The matter was first brought to the notice of the Security Council by the United States, Britain, and France. On 2 November Premier Imre Nagy complained that large additional Soviet forces had entered the country and appealed to the Security Council for assistance towards withdrawal of those forces. A US resolution asking the USSR to desist from intervention having been vetoed by the USSR, the Council referred the question to the General Assembly under the Uniting for Peace resolution. In a number of resolutions the Assembly condemned the Soviet action, proposed free elections under UN auspices, asked the Secretary-General to investigate the situation and to depute observers to the scene. Janos Kadar, who had ousted Nagy with Soviet help, declined to accept observers, and refused admission to the Secretary-General as well as to a Special Committee appointed by the Assembly. Russian forces remained in Hungary and the popular movement was crushed. In its report the Special Committee said the revolution in Hungary had been a spontaneous national uprising and declared there was no justification for Soviet intervention.

For the Government of Pakistan, the Hungarian situation presented none of the complications of the Suez question. The Russian action seemed a clear violation of the principles of democracy and freedom. As an ally of the West, on poor terms with Russia in those days, Pakistan had no compunction in wholeheartedly joining the Western countries in condemning Russian action and in supporting proposals for UN intervention. With Kashmir in mind, Pakistan was specially interested in the Assembly's call for free elections in Hungary and the stationing there of UN observers. 'We feel', said Begum Ikramullah, 'that this organization, by allowing its decisions

[1] Mumtaz Muhammad Daultana, 'Reflections on Pakistan's Foreign Policy', *Dawn*, 10 Dec. 1956.

to be flouted or ignored with equanimity in the past, has reached a stage when its own effective existence is in jeopardy. Its efficacy in the future depends on the manner in which it can handle the questions that are now engaging our attention.'[1] During Prime Minister Chou En-lai's visit to Pakistan he and Suhrawardy sharply differed on the Hungarian question. Chou En-lai defended the Soviet Union while Suhrawardy asserted that the USSR had interfered in the internal affairs of Hungary.[2]

Nehru was slow in criticizing the Soviet invasion of Hungary. At first he said the situation was not clear. At a later date he played down Soviet guilt by saying that the invasion had resulted from the instinct of self-preservation. The Russians may have thought that the Anglo-French invasion of Egypt was a prelude to a third world war and acted in Hungary to protect their flank.[3] In Parliament Nehru conceded, on 19 November, that the majority of the people of Hungary rose in insurrection to achieve a change but were suppressed. However, in the United Nations Krishna Menon abstained on the resolution condemning the USSR on the ground that such action would not assist in a solution.[4] India also abstained in the condemnatory resolution of the Assembly based on the report of the Special Committee.

India, moreover, was the only non-Communist country to vote against the recommendation to hold free elections in Hungary under UN auspices. Nehru explained that 'the most objectionable part' of the resolution was that which demanded that elections should be held under the supervision of the United Nations. 'Any acceptance of intervention of this type, namely foreign supervised elections,' he said, 'seemed to us to set a bad precedent which might be utilized in the future for intervention in other countries.'[5] The Indian Prime Minister here undoubtedly was thinking of India's own earlier promise of elections in Kashmir under UN auspices, which he now wished the world to forget and which, by a twist of history, had become Pakistan's most persistent demand.

V. The Middle East Crisis
The Suez crisis had boosted Nasser's prestige as a stout-hearted

[1] *General Assembly Official Records, 606th Plenary Meeting,* 4 Dec. 1956, quoted by K. Sarwar Hasan, *Pakistan and the United Nations,* p. 271.
[2] *Dawn,* 24 Dec. 1956.
[3] J. Nehru, *Speeches,* IV, p. 383; K. P. S. Menon, *India and the Cold War,* p. 50.
[4] Ross N. Berkes and Mohinder S. Bedi, *The Diplomacy of India,* p. 54.
[5] J. Nehru, *India's Foreign Policy,* p. 556.

anti-imperialist. It had also enhanced Soviet popularity among the Arabs who believed that the invasion of Egypt had been halted mainly because of Soviet threats to intervene with 'volunteers' and rockets. Nasserite and leftist elements everywhere in the Middle East were much emboldened and Iraq, the only Arab country whose rulers had dared to join the Baghdad Pact, and the pro-Western regimes in Jordan and Lebanon, came under increased pressure. British influence, already on the wane since the end of the Second World War, having received a grievous blow from the Suez misadventure, the task of countering Russian designs in the Middle East inevitably fell on American shoulders. The Middle East continued to rumble till it exploded in July 1958, with a savage revolution in Iraq and near-revolutions in Lebanon and Jordan. During this difficult period the Government of Pakistan continued to give unqualified support to US policies.

The first overt sign that the 'northern tier' states were now under the direct protection of America was a US declaration, on 29 November 1956, that 'a threat to the territorial integrity or political independence of the members [of the Baghdad Pact] would be viewed by the United States with the utmost gravity'.[1] Officials in Washington said the statement had been timed to make clear American concern for the welfare of those four countries at a time when the Baghdad alliance was being sharply assailed by other Arab leaders and Russia for allegedly playing an upsetting role in the Middle East.[2]

To obtain national backing for the policy, the President approached Congress on 5 January 1957 for authorization: (1) to assist the Middle East to develop its economic strength; (2) to undertake programmes of military assistance; and (3) 'to include the employment of the armed forces of the US to secure and protect the territorial integrity and political independence of such nations requesting such aid against overt armed aggression from any nation controlled by international Communism'.[3] The Eisenhower 'Doctrine' was welcomed in Pakistan. It was taken to mean that America, though not formally a member of the Baghdad Pact, was now, to all intents and purposes, in the pact. After meeting in Ankara, the four Muslim members of the Baghdad Pact, in their communiqué of 21 January, supported Eisenhower's plan 'as best

[1] USDSB, 10 Dec. 1956, p. 918.
[2] Dawn, 1 Dec. 1956.
[3] George Lenczowski, The Middle East in World Affairs, p. 676.

designed to maintain peace in this area and advance the economic well-being of the people'.[1]

One criticism levelled in the Senate Foreign Relations Committee against the proposals of the President was 'that the limitation to Communist aggression overlooked the real danger arising from conflicts that arose in other ways, as recent events had shown', but Dulles rejected the suggestion of extending the commitment to cover non-Communist aggression 'on the ground that such a problem would be suitably handled by the United Nations'.[2]

A Joint Resolution of Congress, signed by Eisenhower on 9 March, authorized the President

to undertake, in the general area of the Middle East, military assistance programs with any nation or group of nations of that area desiring such assistance. Furthermore, the United States regards as vital to the national interest and world peace the preservation of the independence and integrity of the nations of the Middle East. To this end, if the President determines the necessity thereof, the United States is prepared to use armed forces to assist any such nation or group of such nations requesting assistance against armed aggression from any country controlled by international communism. . . .[3]

In the meantime pressures were developing in Jordan, Syria, and Lebanon. King Hussein's firmness in dismissing his pro-Nasser Prime Minister, and a demonstration by the American Sixth Fleet in the eastern Mediterranean, saved him from disaster. In Syria the drift towards Nasser culminated in Egypt and Syria joining together (1 February 1958) to form the United Arab Republic. In reply, the pro-Western Hashemite kingdoms of Jordan and Iraq formed the 'Arab Union'. The rising tide of Arab nationalism also made the position of Camille Chamoun, the Christian President of Lebanon, increasingly difficult, and in May 1958 the country found itself in the throes of a civil war.

Since joining the Baghdad Pact, Iraq, a rival of Egypt for primacy in the Arab world, had been Cairo's special target. In the end Nuri's conservative regime proved no match for the revolutionary forces for whom Nasser had become the symbol of Arab solidarity. On 14 July 1958 a startled world heard that General Abdul Karim Kassem had seized power in Baghdad and that the entire royal

---

[1] For text of communiqué see *Dawn*, 22 Jan. 1957.
[2] John C. Campbell, *Defense of the Middle East*, p. 123.
[3] *USDSB*, 25 March 1957.

family had been slaughtered. Premier Nuri evaded capture for a while, but was caught a few days later and killed.

For the moment it seemed as if the entire Western position in the Middle East would collapse. Many observers thought the revolution in Iraq would mean the end of the Baghdad Pact, the collapse of King Hussein's regime in Jordan and Chamoun's in Lebanon, and fresh perils for the King of Saudi Arabia, who had displayed affinity with his fellow kings of Iraq and Jordan.

A meeting of the Muslim members of the Baghdad Pact had been scheduled in Istanbul on 14 July, to prepare a joint protest at the forthcoming regular meeting of the pact Council in London. Their complaints were: refusal of the US to join the pact as a full member, softness towards Nasser, and fear that the US would not assist Chamoun whose position was worsening.[1] On hearing of the developments in Iraq, it was decided to move the meeting to the quieter atmosphere of Ankara. In the meantime, in response to appeals from the Governments of Lebanon and Jordan, American marines had landed in Lebanon (15 July) and British paratroops in Jordan (16 July). This demonstration of firm and quick action so impressed the leaders who had foregathered in Ankara that, instead of formulating a list of grievances, the Presidents of Pakistan and Turkey and the Shah of Iran telegraphed to Eisenhower their 'appreciation and gratitude for this momentous decision in which we have deep satisfaction and relief'.[2] In a joint declaration they also pledged their 'whole-hearted support by every possible means to any measures which might be taken to halt international gangsterism in the Middle East'.[3]

As the Eisenhower Doctrine was meant to cover only cases of 'armed aggression from any country controlled by international Communism', the President claimed to have acted under the broader purview of the United Nations Charter which 'recognizes [that it] is the inherent right of all nations to work together and to seek help when necessary to preserve their independence'.[4] He explained that the rebels in Lebanon were backed by 'official Cairo, Damascus, and Soviet radios' and supported by arms and money across the Syrian border. 'There are in Lebanon about 2,500 Americans,' the President said, 'and we cannot ... stand idly by when Lebanon

[1] *Dawn*, 15 July 1958; *New York Times*, 17 July 1958.
[2] *USDSB*, 4 Aug. 1958.
[3] *Dawn*, 18 July 1958.
[4] *USDSB*, 4 Aug. 1958.

appeals for evidence of our concern and when Lebanon may not be able to preserve internal order and to defend itself against indirect aggression.'

In contrast with the unqualified support of the Pakistani authorities to the dispatch of American and British troops to the Middle East, Prime Minister Nehru bitterly criticized the Anglo-US action. 'If outside powers intervene in the internal affairs of Iraq and Lebanon,' he declared, 'there is a danger of total annihilation of humanity.'[1]

With Iraq out of the Baghdad Pact, the remaining members met in London to mend their fences. Iraq's participation in the pact had originally been regarded as a step towards broader Arab membership, but in fact it had served to intensify Arab opposition to the pact and to isolate Iraq in the Arab fraternity. It was now hoped that Iraq's exit might prove to be a blessing in disguise. Secretary Dulles personally attended the London meeting as an observer to rally the pact members, and he told them to have no fear that, if they faced situations similar to Lebanon and Jordan, the US would fail to act, even at 'great risk', to maintain their independence and integrity. Pointing out that for the US to join the pact as a full member would mean the writing of a new treaty and its ratification by two-thirds of the Senate, he adopted the simple expedient of signing the Declaration of the conference along with the full members. The first paragraph of the Declaration stated: 'The members declared their determination to maintain their collective security and to resist aggression, direct or indirect.'[2] Dulles also orally promised increased military aid to the three Asian members. These steps were represented by 'American sources' as being just as good as signing a treaty.[3]

The London Declaration promised further that the US would 'promptly' enter into agreements with the other declarants to co-operate in their security and defence. Accordingly, identical bilateral Defence Agreements were signed by the US with Pakistan, Iran, and Turkey on 5 March 1959. Article II assured the continuation of US military and economic aid to Pakistan and Article I, which roused some speculation as to its scope, said:

[1] *Hindu*, 17 July 1958. The American and British troops left Lebanon and Jordan early in November in response to a resolution of the General Assembly which established a 'United Nations Presence' in the person of a Special Representative of the Secretary-General with Headquarters at Amman.

[2] For text of the 28 July 1958 London Declaration see *Dawn*, 6 March 1959.

[3] *New York Times*, 29 July 1958.

In case of aggression against Pakistan, the Government of the USA in accordance with the Constitution of the USA will take such appropriate action, including the use of armed forces, as may be mutually agreed upon and as is envisaged in the Joint Resolution to promote peace and stability in the ‘Middle East, in order to assist the Government of Pakistan at its request.[1]

As the text did not contain the word Communist, some Pakistani spokesmen[2] interpreted Article I to mean that the US had undertaken to defend Pakistan against aggression from any source, thereby implying that Pakistan could now count upon direct US assistance against Indian aggression also. But they had overlooked the import of the phrase ‘as is envisaged in the Joint Resolution [of Congress dated 9 March 1957]’, which had referred to ‘armed aggression from any country controlled by international Communism’. In view of the wider interpretation on the part of Pakistani spokesmen, the Government of India approached the American authorities for clarification and were ‘specifically assured’ that the agreement could not be used against India.[3]

VI. The U-2 Incident
On 1 May 1960 a high-flying U-2 spy plane, equipped with advanced photographic equipment, was shot down in the interior of Russia. The incident was first revealed by Premier Khrushchev on 5 May. At first the United States Defense Department stated that the plane had been engaged on weather reconnaissance but, as the pilot had been captured alive, the truth could no longer be suppressed. It transpired that the plane had taken off from Peshawar in Pakistan for espionage over the Soviet Union. Its destination was Bodo in Norway. Both Pakistani and Norwegian authorities denied having any knowledge that the plane was on a spying mission, and Khrushchev, in his report to the Supreme Soviet, conceded the possibility that countries where American aircraft were based did not know what was being done by the Americans. ‘But’, warned the Soviet Premier, ‘they ought to know for their own good, because they might be the sufferers of the Americans’ playing with fire.’

The Pakistani authorities denied that America had any military

---

[1] *Dawn*, 6 March 1959.
[2] For instance, see comments of a Foreign Office spokesman in *Dawn*, 7 March 1959.
[3] J. Nehru, *India's Foreign Policy*, p. 475.

bases in Pakistan. They admitted there was an American communications base[1] but said it had no airstrip of its own. It appears
that the ill-fated U-2 had taken off from the Peshawar airport but
Pakistanis were not privy to its purpose or route. The disclosure,
therefore, that the plane had been engaged on an intelligence mission
over the USSR came as a shock to them. It was felt that no country,
however friendly, should be allowed to use Pakistani territory as a
base for hostile activities against another country. A protest was
lodged with the US Government and an assurance was obtained
that there would be no repetition of the incident.

At the same time, however, Pakistan did not waver in her friendship with America and presented a bold front to the USSR. At
the Czechoslovak National Day party in Moscow on 9 May,
Khrushchev publicly threatened the Pakistani chargé d'affaires
that if any other spy plane flew from Peshawar into the Soviet Union,
that city would be struck with rockets.[2] President Ayub Khan, who
was in London at the time, said, 'After all, Russian threats are not
new things for us. We are not afraid of such threats.'[3] Dawn's
editorial, 'So what?', ran:

After all, if war does come, none of us will escape its ravage, and whether
we punctiliously keep our own bases inviolate or not, the Russians are
not going to spare us on that account. They are not that sort of gentle
people ... there is something refreshing about Washington's disclosure
that in order to safeguard the Free World against surprise attacks by
Russia and her allies the appropriate agencies of the American defence
system have been systematically collecting as much data as possible of
Russian offensive and defensive installations.

Noting that Russia had repeatedly refused the US proposal
for 'open skies',[4] the article concluded that it was 'the Soviet Union

---

[1] This base at Badaber, near Peshawar, had been leased out to the US in 1959. Selig
S. Harrison, in 'America, India and Pakistan' (Harper's Magazine, July 1966), says the
name of the base was 'Headquarters, 5235th Communications Group, USAF', and that
Americans could 'listen in' from there on the Soviet military communications system,
and monitor key defence testing-sites in Central Asia. Tyura Tam, the Soviet Cape
Kennedy, was only 675 miles away, and the rest of the major Russian military re-
search centres were all concentrated in the desert fastnesses of Tadzhikistan and
Kazakhistan.

[2] New York Times, 10 May 1960.

[3] Dawn, 11 May 1960; Morning News, 11 May 1960.

[4] It was at a summit meeting in July 1955 that Eisenhower had first suggested that
the Americans and the Russians should provide facilities for aerial photography over
each other's territory as an assurance against a surprise attack.

and her flashy and boisterous leader Nikita Khrushchev at whose door the blame squarely rests'.[1]

The State Department spokesman, Lincoln White, said it was 'typical that the Soviet Union singles out as the objective of its threats, those smaller countries of the free world who bear no responsibility for the recent incident'. There should be no doubt, he declared, that the US would honour her commitments for common defence to countries which the USSR was threatening.[2]

Ayub, still in London, explained that the Americans were Pakistan's friends. Their planes visited Pakistan. Pakistanis did not know where they went after leaving Pakistan.[3] He alleged that Russian planes had been flying over Pakistan for some time.[4] About Russian threats, the Pakistani President said, 'These harsh things of life have to be faced.' If Russia attacked Pakistan, the latter would not be alone. It would mean world war. The source of attack would not remain unscathed. The retaliation might not come from Pakistan but it would come from somewhere else.[5]

The American communications base was permitted to continue its surveillance. Its value had become even greater after the U-2 flights were terminated.

VII. Other Questions

The Question of Tibet

As an ally of the US Pakistan also modified her attitude towards certain questions in which China had a direct interest. As mentioned earlier, Pakistan had remained neutral when the Chinese forcibly occupied Tibet in 1950. She modified her posture, however, when world interest in Tibet was revived in 1959, as a consequence of an anti-Chinese rising in Lhasa. To escape Chinese reprisals the Dalai Lama was compelled to flee to India. At a press conference at Mussoorie on 20 June he declared that the Chinese Communists had exterminated more than 65,000 Tibetans, demolished 1,000 monasteries, and done their best to stamp out the Buddhist faith. On 9 September he cabled an appeal to the Secretary-General of the United Nations. Malaya and Ireland took up Tibet's cause and submitted a resolution to the General Assembly calling for 'respect for the fundamental human rights of the Tibetan people and for

[1] *Dawn*, 11 May 1960.
[2] *New York Times*, 11 May 1960.
[3] ibid., 14 May 1960.
[4] *Dawn*, 17 May 1960.
[5] ibid., 18 May 1960..

their distinctive cultural and religious life'.[1] The resolution was carried on 21 October by 45 votes to 9, with 26 abstentions. Those voting for the resolution included the US and Pakistan. Britain and India figured amongst the abstainers. Nehru had advised the Dalai Lama not to approach the UN because no good would come of it. Prince Aly Khan, speaking for Pakistan, rejected the 'cynical opinion that there is very little the United Nations can do about the situation in Tibet'. The Assembly had an effective means at its disposal, namely, world opinion.[2]

The Laotian Crisis

A fresh crisis in Laos was set off in August 1960 when Captain Kong Lae, a parachute battalion commander, occupied Vientiane and ousted the anti-Communist government headed by Prince Somsanith as Premier and General Phoumi as Defence Minister, and installed the neutralist former Premier, Prince Souvanna Phouma, as head of a new Ministry. On 9 December General Phoumi recaptured Vientiane and his nominee, Prince Boun Oum, assumed the premiership. Boun Oum's government received military supplies from the US while the neutralist and leftist[3] factions, who had joined hands, were backed by the Soviet Union. On 24 March 1961 President Kennedy accepted the proposal that Laos should have a neutral government. The 1954 Geneva Conference was thereupon revived and adjourned on 23 July 1962, after the Laotian princes had agreed among themselves to entrust the premiership to Souvanna Phouma, and after Phouma had held out the assurance that he would adhere to a policy of strict neutrality and Laos would not accept the protection of any military alliance, thus repudiating SEATO's cover. The powers participating in the Geneva Conference affirmed that they would respect Laos's neutrality and refrain from meddling in her internal affairs.

We have already noted that Pakistan was a zealous member both of SEATO and CENTO and that it was the USA, and some other members, who hesitated to give teeth to the pacts by setting up military commands under them. During the crisis in Laos, Pakistan, in line with her general policy at the time, favoured strong SEATO intervention in favour of the anti-Communist elements. President Ayub indicated that Pakistan was prepared to send an armed con-

---

[1] For text of resolution see H. E. Richardson, *Tibet and Its History*, p. 286.
[2] *General Assembly Official Records, 832nd Plenary Meeting*, 20 Oct. 1959.
[3] The left-wing Pathet Lao was led by Prince Souphannouvong.

tingent to Laos if SEATO decided to intervene there. Pakistan would never hesitate to shoulder her responsibility as a SEATO member, he declared.[1] He repeated the offer a few days later.[2]

Representation of China in the United Nations

When the question of Chinese representation in the UN was first debated in that organization in 1950, Pakistan had supported the claim of the Communist regime to the seat reserved for China. During the ten years that followed, the question was not substantively considered in the United Nations. The United States was able to find sufficient support in the General Assembly to have it postponed. There was no roll-call vote in 1951, and the voting pattern for that year is, therefore, not known. During the remaining years Pakistan, in deference to US wishes, voted for the deferment resolution seven times and abstained from voting twice (in 1952 and 1957).[3]

The Question of 'Two Chinas'

Communist China regards the island of Formosa as an integral part of China and her bitterest complaint against the US is that, by protecting Chiang Kai-shek and recognizing him as the lawful head of the Government of China, the US is not only depriving China of Formosa now but intends to perpetuate the wrong by setting up Formosa as an independent state, thus creating two Chinas.

After forming an alliance with the US, Pakistan also began occasionally to speak in terms of 'two Chinas'. During the 1955 Far Eastern crisis, Prime Minister Bogra said the Formosan question should be settled in the UN and that 'Pakistan might recognize the Nationalist Government if it styles itself as the Government of Formosa [only, and not of mainland China]'.[4] A few days later he said the future of Formosa should be decided on the basis that the Western powers should recognize the Communist regime on mainland China and the claim of the Nationalists should be limited to Formosa.[5] President Ayub thought the Formosan question could be resolved on the basis of a formula to accommodate both the People's Republic and the Nationalists in the United Nations.[6]

[1] Dawn, 15 Dec. 1960.
[2] ibid., 21 Dec. 1960.
[3] In 1957 Pakistan subsequently changed her vote in favour of the US move for the postponement of the question.
[4] Dawn, 26 Jan. 1955.
[5] The Times, 17 Feb. 1955.
[6] M. Ayub Khan, Speeches, IV, p. 52.

From 29 June to 5 July 1959 a Muslim Haj Mission from Taiwan visited Karachi on its way to Mecca. On 21 July the Foreign Office of the People's Republic handed over a strong protest note to the Pakistani Ambassador in Peking complaining that the Haj mission, with the connivance of the Government of Pakistan, had carried out 'a series of activities openly slandering China'; despite a protest by the Chinese embassy, the mission had been received personally by the Pakistani Foreign Minister; and in the preceding few months Pakistan had stepped up her support for the US plot to create 'two Chinas'.[1]

---

[1] For text of Chinese protest note see *Survey of China Mainland Press*, no. 2063, 27 July 1959, p. 39.

10 The Cost of Alliance

I. Relations with Muslim States

Tension with Egypt

Prime Minister Muhammad Ali Bogra had commended to his countrymen the security agreement with Turkey and the agreement for military assistance with the USA as major steps towards strengthening the Muslim world. After Iraq had joined the Baghdad Pact it was hoped her example would be followed by other Arab countries, making the organization a commonwealth of Muslim nations. However, instead of bringing the Muslim countries closer to each other, these developments served to alienate the Arab countries further from those who had signed the pact. In the van of the forces of opposition to the pact was Egypt, the most important Arab country, followed by Saudi Arabia, the cradle of Islam.

Tension between Pakistan and Afghanistan also reached new heights during the years of Pakistan's close association with the Western powers. There was no doubt that there had always been trouble between them, but Pakistan's new policy of commitment to the West, and Afghanistan's increasing reliance, for transit facilities and military and economic assistance, on the Soviet Union, could not but intensify the discord. Pakistan's over-dependence on America and continued political disruption at home, in fact, lowered her prestige among all her Afro-Asian peers. But the most painful price for alliance with the West was the bitterness it provoked with sister Muslim countries, the very reverse of Pakistan's fondest dream.

When the proposals for establishing a Middle East Command, or a Middle East Defence Organization, were in the air, Egyptian spokesmen had said that the evacuation of the Suez base by Britain, and a satisfactory settlement of the Sudanese question, were necessary conditions for Egypt's participation in any Middle Eastern defence alliance. In October 1951 Britain offered to hand over the Suez base to Egypt, on the condition that Egypt would join the

USA, Britain, France, and Turkey in the Middle East Defence Organization, and that the British military base in the Suez zone would become the allied base. In Egyptian eyes, 'what was offered was that several foreign devils should take the place vacated by one foreign devil'.[1] The proposal was, therefore, immediately rejected by Egypt. Towards the end of October the Egyptian Government unilaterally repudiated the Anglo-Egyptian Treaty, ending the authorization accorded to Britain to maintain troops in the Suez area. Egypt was also anxious that, until Anglo-Egyptian differences were settled to Egypt's satisfaction, Pakistan and the other countries of the Middle East should not join the Western powers in any plan for the defence of the Middle East. It was feared that, if the Western countries were able to make progress in defence arrangements without Egypt, there would be less need and urgency for Britain to come to terms with Egypt.

Egypt was, therefore, most indignant when Pakistan and Turkey announced their intention to go ahead with their plans for collaboration in defence (19 February 1954), while Britain was still holding the Suez base and Anglo-Egyptian parleys were at a critical stage.[2] Cairo radio said the Turco-Pakistani Agreement would be 'a catastrophe for Islam ... the first stab in our back. The next one will probably occur when Iraq joins the plot.'[3] The Government-owned paper *Al-Gamhouria* stated editorially that the military alliance between Pakistan, Turkey, and the West would be a sword severing the ties between Pakistan and the Arab world.[4]

When Nuri Pasha announced at Baghdad (on 13 January 1955) that Iraq would soon sign a mutual assistance pact with Turkey, Nasser was furious and immediately summoned a conference of Arab Prime Ministers at Cairo to dissuade Iraq. Nuri failed to turn up at the meeting, whereupon a delegation was dispatched to Iraq to discuss the question, but without result. Nasser was, however, successful in making Jordan reverse her announced decision to accede to the pact.

Egyptian objections to the Baghdad Pact were that it was 'imperialist', because it had been imposed from outside and had not sprung from the heart of the Arab world; that, by luring Iraq into

[1] Hugh J. Schonfield, *Suez Canal in World Affairs*, p. 141, quoted by K. P. Karunakaran, *India in World Affairs, Feb. 1950–Dec. 1953*, p. 36.
[2] It was in October 1954 that Egypt and Britain finally signed an agreement that British forces would leave the Suez base in twenty months.
[3] *Dawn*, 22 Feb. 1954.
[4] Quoted by *Jin Min Jih Pao*, 23 March 1954—*Survey of China Mainland Press*, no. 773, 24 March 1954, pp. 17–18.

the fold, the pact had split Arab solidarity; that, having evacuated the Suez base, Britain had re-entered the Middle East by conjuring up the Baghdad Pact; and that, by focusing on the danger from the north, the pact diverted Arab attention from the real danger which came from Israel.

During and following the Suez crisis, Pakistani-Egyptian relations reached their lowest. Nasser complained that Foreign Minister Hamidul Huq, who had seen him at Cairo on 14 August on his way to the First London Conference, had gone back on his promise to give full support to the Egyptian position. In a well-publicized interview with Frank Moraes of the *Times of India*, in the first week of September, the Egyptian President said, 'Do you know that before the London conference the Pakistani Foreign Minister, who came to see me, spoke for three hours and he vowed support for Egypt's cause? You know what he did?'[1]

There was a brief relaxation when Pakistan refused to join the Users' Association, but a new pitch of acrimony was quickly reached when it was reported that Nasser had rejected the Pakistani offer of a contingent for the United Nations Emergency Force. That he had accepted Indian troops doubled the anguish in Pakistan. It was believed that the Egyptian Premier had decided to keep out Pakistani forces because he had been pressed to do so by Russia and India; because Pakistan was allied with Britain in the Baghdad Pact and with both Britain and France in SEATO; and because the Pakistani force, and troops from other countries with ties with the West, might not get out of Egypt when Egypt wanted them to do so.

A further blow to Pakistani pride was administered a few days later, when Suhrawardy was about to leave for Cairo. The Egyptian Ambassador to Pakistan hurried to the Pakistani Premier and warned him that President Nasser did not consider it a suitable time for a visit to Cairo. Suhrawardy had no option but to give up the idea. *Dawn* angrily denounced Nasser as 'Cairo's modern little Pharaoh'[2] and 'this turbulent egoist' in whose veins 'not the blood of Islam should seem to flow but the turbid waters of the Nile'.[3]

---

[1] *The Times*, 3 Sept. 1956. According to Egyptians, this was the second occasion on which Pakistan had let them down. They used to chide Pakistani diplomats that Governor-General Ghulam Muhammad had assured Egyptian leaders that Pakistan would not conclude any agreement with the West which could be used as pressure on Egypt. However, Pakistan signed her first agreement with the West while Anglo-Egyptian negotiations about the evacuation of Suez were at a crucial stage.

[2] *Dawn*, 25 Nov. 1956.

[3] ibid., 1 Dec. 1956.

By reportedly declaring that 'Suez is as dear to Egypt as Kashmir is to India',[1] Nasser pricked Pakistan's tenderest spot. A campaign against Pakistan was sustained by Egyptian information media for months to come. Suhrawardy was called 'the tail of colonialism', 'a greater lover of Britain and America than the English and Americans themselves', and Pakistan was painted as Egypt's enemy number one, who must be cowed before Egypt could handle the West effectively.[2]

Suhrawardy stood his ground and asked:

When Egypt, which claims to be a champion of the Arab cause and the anti-Israel cause, chooses to recognize and make friends with India and to have the armies of India on its soil, the India which recognizes Israel, and has trade relations with it, and amicable relations with it, and refuses to allow Pakistani troops as a part of the United Nations Force, am I to consider that Israel is the pivot of Arab policy?[3]

He alleged that Egypt regarded the division of India as a mistake and favoured Pakistan's reunion with India, and also treated Kashmir as a part of India. Pointing out that Egypt claimed to be a secular and not a Muslim state, he said Pakistan would have to delete Islam from her constitution if she desired to form a 'Muslim combination' with 'Arab nationalism'.[4]

Tension with Saudi Arabia

When Pakistan joined the Baghdad Pact, the Saudi Arabian Embassy in Pakistan took the unusual step of issuing a press handout containing the text of a Radio Mecca broadcast, urging Pakistan to drop her membership of the pact and 'return to the right path'. The broadcast called Pakistan's act 'a stab in the heart of the Arab and Muslim states' and said it had caused surprise and astonishment that Pakistan, who had always felt proud of her Islamic faith and declared her respect for all Arabs and Muslims, should have joined Turkey, who 'feels honoured by co-operating with the Jewish state'.[5]

Pakistanis, perennially critical of the discriminatory policy of the Government of India towards the Muslim minority, were further dismayed when King Saud, speaking as the guardian of the

[1] *Round Table*, March 1957.
[2] *Dawn*, 11 Aug. 1957.
[3] *National Assembly of Pakistan Debates*, 25 Feb. 1957, p. 1099.
[4] ibid., 4 Sept. 1958, pp. 373–5.
[5] *Dawn*, 26 Sept. 1955.

Muslim holy places, publicly thanked Prime Minister Nehru and his Government for their policy towards the Muslims. 'I desire to say', he proclaimed, 'to my Muslim brethren all over the world with satisfaction that the fate of Indian Muslims is in safe hands.'[1] But worse was to follow.

When Nehru arrived in the Saudi Arabian capital on a visit in September 1956, he was warmly greeted with the slogan '*marhaba rasool al salam*'. This immediately aroused widespread resentment amongst Pakistanis. The Saudi Arabian Embassy in Karachi hastily issued a press release explaining that the phrase meant 'Welcome Messenger of Peace' and not 'Welcome Prophet of Peace', as interpreted by Pakistanis. Pakistani feelings, however, were not assuaged. *Dawn* wrote: 'Most Muslims in this country know what the literal meaning of the word *rasool* is, but they also know that it has acquired a sacred connotation since the advent of the Holy Prophet whom the *Kalima* specifically describes as "Mohammad-ur-Rasool Allah—Mohammad, the Messenger of God".'

Reviewing King Saud's and President Nasser's unfriendly attitude towards Pakistan, the article advised fellow-Pakistanis to 'calmly and dispassionately take all these bitter truths into consideration and restrain to some extent their vain expectations from the so-called Muslim world' and to recognize that 'for the present' Pakistanis were the lone upholders of the ideology of Islam.[2]

Tension with Afghanistan

When it was rumoured that the United States might supply military aid to Pakistan, the Afghan Embassy in Delhi issued a statement that such assistance would strengthen Pakistan as a 'colonial' power over the 'freedom-seeking people of Pakhtunistan'.[3]

Afghanistan reacted sharply to the Pakistani announcement, in March 1955, that the various parts of the western wing of Pakistan would be amalgamated into one administrative unit under the name of West Pakistan. It was alleged that this would further erase the separate identity of the Pakhtuns in Pakistan.

Besides spewing out vile propaganda against Pakistan by all possible means, the Afghan authorities connived at a mob attack on the Pakistani Embassy and Chancery at Kabul on 30 March

[1] *Hindu*, 11 Dec. 1955, quoted by M. S. Rajan, *India in World Affairs, 1954–56*, p. 478. See also *Asian Recorder*, 1955, p. 535, for a similar pronouncement.
[2] *Dawn*, 27 Sept. 1956.
[3] *New York Times*, 23 Dec. 1953.

1955. Both buildings were ransacked. The Pakistani flag at the Chancery was pulled down and torn and in its place the 'Pakhtunistan flag' was hoisted. The Pakistani Consulates at Jalalabad and Kandahar were similarly attacked. Diplomatic relations were broken off and the Afghan-Pakistani border remained closed for five months.

A reconciliation was temporarily effected by the good offices of some Muslim countries and diplomatic ties were resumed, but the situation again deteriorated in October when West Pakistan was officially inaugurated. Afghanistan's Grand National Assembly, the *Loi Jirga*, traditionally convened at times of national emergency, met at Kabul in the middle of November and passed a resolution declaring that Afghanistan did not recognize the 'Pakhtunistan' territories as a part of Pakistan and demanding that Afghanistan's defences be strengthened by all possible means.[1]

At this delicate juncture Russia, having a score of her own to settle with Pakistan for her openly pro-Western policy, took a hand in the game. In December 1955 Premier Nikolai Bulganin visited Kabul, accompanied by Nikita Khrushchev, First Secretary of the Soviet Communist Party, and declared, 'We sympathize with Afghanistan's policy on the Pushtunistan issue.'[2]

The Soviet Union also exploited the situation to increase Afghanistan's dependence on Soviet assistance. During their visit Bulganin and Khrushchev offered a credit of $100 million for economic development. In 1957 an additional credit of $15 million was provided for oil exploration. In 1959 the Soviet Union agreed to build the Kushk-Kandahar road and the Shindand military airfield at a total cost of $85 million. By the end of 1960 the total of Soviet assistance, including military aid, was estimated to be $300 million, and about 1,600 Soviet civil and military technicians were believed to be in Afghanistan.

Some improvement in Pakistani-Afghan relations resulted from an exchange of visits, starting with President Iskander Mirza's visit to Kabul in August 1956, followed by visits to each other's country, in the course of the next two years, by Premiers Daud and Suhrawardy and King Zahir Shah. During this period an Air Agreement and a Transit Trade Agreement were made, and a direct radio-telephone link was established.

[1] *Asian Recorder*, 1955, p. 521.
[2] N. A. Bulganin and N. S. Khrushchev, *Visit of Friendship to India, Burma, and Afghanistan*, p. 202.

In October 1958 Ayub Khan assumed power in Pakistan. He desired good relations with Afghanistan but, himself a Pakhtun and heading a Pakhtun-dominated administration,[1] he could not understand the Afghan grievance that Pakhtuns in Pakistan were an oppressed people. A few weeks after a visit to Rawalpindi, in January 1960, Foreign Minister Naim said at Kabul that Pakistan had refused to discuss the 'Pakhtunistan' issue and complained that Ayub Khan's regime was even more adamant against the 'Pakhtunistan' demand than President Mirza, who desired 'to find some sort of solution'.[2] Not long afterwards Khrushchev, now Premier of the USSR, again travelled through Kabul. A joint communiqué, marking his talks with the Afghan leaders, asserted that a solution of the 'Pakhtunistan' problem should be reached by implementing the United Nations Charter 'principle of self-determination'.[3]

In the meantime, besides a vilifying propaganda offensive against Pakistan,[4] posters and handbills were distributed in the tribal area inciting the tribesmen to rise against the Government of Pakistan.[5] Towards the end of September 1960, a *lashkar* estimated to be 15,000 strong penetrated into Pakistani territory near Bajaur but was repulsed with heavy losses.

On account of harassment by Afghan Intelligence officials, shopkeepers, landlords of houses, and others, it became virtually impossible for Pakistani personnel attached to the Consulates in Afghanistan to discharge their duties. Accordingly, Pakistan informed Afghanistan on 22 August 1961 that the Pakistani Consulates at Jalalabad and Kandahar would be closed down, and demanded that the Afghan Consulates and Trade Agencies in Peshawar and Quetta be also closed. Afghanistan retaliated by severing diplomatic relations with Pakistan and closing the border.

This phase of Pakistani-Afghan relations, the most unfortunate of all, ended in March 1963 with the resignation of Premier Daud, a cousin of King Zahir Shah, who had ruled Afghanistan with an

---

[1] Two of Ayub's Cabinet Ministers (General Azam and F. M. Khan) and the Commander-in-Chief of the Pakistani Army (General Musa) were Pakhtuns.

[2] *Dawn*, 29 Feb. 1960.

[3] ibid., 6 March 1960.

[4] For example, Radio Kabul said on 21 Nov. 1959: 'The dictatorial military regime in Pakistan is turning Pakhtunistan into hell and rubble.' *The Bajaur Incident*, an undated Government of Pakistan booklet, p. 8.

[5] One of the posters in Pushtu, distributed by the Afghans in Sept. 1960, read: 'O all Pakhtunistani brethren! . . . Your sacred land . . . today is being trampled under the dirty feet of Pakistani imperialism . . . Pakhtun warriors! rise up . . . and oust the aggressive Pakistani authorities from your land.' ibid., p. 14.

iron hand for nearly ten years and made the demand for 'Pakhtunistan' one of the main planks of his policy. With him also went his
brother, Foreign Minister Naim.

II. Relations with the Soviet Union

Even before Pakistan signed up with the West, the Soviet Union
had suspected that she would let her territory be used as a springboard for attacks on the USSR. After Pakistan had subscribed to
the Western security system, this suspicion became almost a conviction. Protest notes, warning Pakistan of the dire consequences of
allowing military bases to be constructed in Pakistan, were regularly
addressed to the Pakistani Government, and were as regularly
rejected as being without foundation. Pakistan's participation in
SEATO and CENTO was also criticized as collaboration in the
intended Western aggression against Russia and China. As retribution for Pakistan's unfriendly acts, the Soviet leadership openly
supported India's claim to Kashmir and Afghanistan's demand for
'Pakhtunistan'.

At the same time, however, the door was never shut to reconciliation. It was clearly stated that, if Pakistan mended her ways, the
Soviet Union would be prepared to beam on her as beneficently
as she did on neutral India.

According to *New Times* the immediate purpose of the Turco-
Pakistani alliance was to convert Pakistan into an American military
base.[1] A Soviet note, protesting against US military aid to Pakistan,
accused her of placing military bases at the disposal of the United
States and of placing the Pakistani Army under a foreign command
by accepting foreign advisers.[2] A Soviet Foreign Office statement
published in *Pravda* on 15 September said SEATO was 'directed
against the security interests of Asia and the Far East and, at the
same time, against the freedom and national independence of the
Asian peoples'. An article in *New Times* alleged that the Baghdad
Pact constituted a threat not only to the Soviet Union 'but to all the
peace-loving countries of Asia and Africa, and especially to those
defending their national independence and opposing colonialism'.[3]

In the meantime the Soviet Union had been going all out to
win India's favour. By 1954 Russia had sufficiently recovered from
the ravages of the Second World War to embark upon a programme

---

[1] *New Times*, no. 9, 1954, p. 18.
[2] *Dawn*, 5 May 1954.
[3] *New Times*, no. 50, 1955, p. 19.

of economic assistance to less developed countries. Among the earliest beneficiaries of the new policy were Afghanistan and India. In February 1955 the Soviet Union undertook to build for India a modern iron and steel mill at Bhilai. In June Nehru was invited to Russia on a two-week visit and accorded an unprecedented welcome. He said he had found 'a passion for peace' everywhere he had gone and was so deeply moved that when taking leave of his hosts he told them that he was leaving a part of his heart behind.

Of even greater significance was the three-week return visit in November-December of the same year of Premier Bulganin and First Secretary Khrushchev. Huge crowds greeted them wherever they went with chants of '*Hindi-Russi Bhai Bhai*' (Indians and Russians are brothers), and '*Hindi-Russi Ek Hai*' (Indians and Russians are one). Besides calling India and the Soviet Union 'allies' in the struggle for world peace,[1] and promising all the help India needed to make her industrially strong,[2] the Soviet leaders gave emphatic support to the political questions nearest India's heart. The Russians 'were grieved that the imperialist forces succeeded in dividing India into two parts'.[3] Portugal in Goa was like a tick which fastens itself to a healthy body.[4] At Srinagar Khrushchev noted that Kashmir was 'nearest of all to the Central Asian republics of the Soviet Union' and said it was a pleasure to visit the State 'because it is the birthplace of your esteemed Premier Mr. Nehru'. He also declared that the fact that Kashmir was one of the states of the Republic of India had been decided by the people of Kashmir.[5]

In their Joint Declaration the Soviet visitors and Prime Minister Nehru condemned the formation of military alliances, alleging that they had extended the area of the cold war and increased tension.[6] At the airport parting Nehru said, 'It appears that on this occasion a part of our heart has been separated from us.' Khrushchev, not to be outdone, replied, 'I am also leaving a small part of my heart behind to the people of India.'[7] Later he told the Supreme Soviet, 'As a beloved brother is welcomed in a loving family, so we

---

[1] N. A. Bulganin and N. S. Khrushchev, *Visit of Friendship to India, Burma, and Afghanistan*, p. 13.

[2] ibid., p. 52.

[3] ibid., p. 111.

[4] ibid., p. 96.

[5] ibid., pp. 107, 112. Though Nehru's ancestors came from Kashmir, he had not been born there. He was born at Allahabad in India.

[6] ibid., p. 304.

[7] M. S. Rajan, *India in World Affairs, 1954-56*, p. 324.

were welcomed in the great family of the peoples of India.' On the
way home Bulganin and Khrushchev stayed at Kabul for four days
and there belaboured Pakistan further by siding with Afghanistan
on the 'Pakhtunistan' issue.

Other moments of tension between Pakistan and the USSR
followed when the Soviet Union accused Pakistan of supporting the
'colonizing proposals' of the Western powers for the future of the
Suez Canal; when Pakistan strongly criticized the Russian invasion
of Hungary; when, in February 1957, Russia cast her first veto in
the Security Council proceedings on Kashmir to bar a resolution
stating that the use of a temporary United Nations Force to facilitate
demilitarization deserved consideration; when Pakistan signed the
bilateral Defence Agreement with the US in March 1959; when, in
the autumn of 1959, President Ayub Khan referred to the possibility of a concerted Russian-Chinese drive towards the Indian
Ocean in five years as part of their plan for Communist world
domination; and when the American U-2 spy plane, having taken
off from Peshawar, was brought down in Russia in May 1960.

However, running parallel all the time to these manifestations
of strain, were declarations from the Soviet leadership that Pakistan
could win their friendship at any time by abandoning her imprudent
foreign policy. The nightmare of possible atomic launching sites
so close to Soviet territory was too frightening to be ignored.

In his address to the Supreme Soviet in August 1953, Premier
Malenkov said Russia placed great value on good relations with both
India and Pakistan.[1] Khrushchev, in his speech at Srinagar on
10 December 1956, while condemning partition as the old trick of
'divide and rule', was careful to add, 'But the establishment of two
separate states—India and Pakistan—is a decided issue, and I have
not stated my opinion on this score so frankly in order that the
question might be re-examined in any quarter.' He castigated
Pakistani foreign policy, but stated at the same time that the Soviet
Union 'should very much like' to have friendly relations with
Pakistan, 'and it is not our fault that such relations have so far not
developed. But we shall persistently strive to improve these relations in the interest of peace.'[2] When reporting on the South Asian
tour to the Supreme Soviet, Bulganin declared that the Soviet
Union would like to have no less friendly relations with Pakistan

[1] *New York Times*, 9 Aug. 1953.
[2] N. A. Bulganin and N. S. Khrushchev, *Visit of Friendship to India, Burma, and
Afghanistan*, pp. 111, 114.

than she had with India, Burma, and Afghanistan, and also that the Soviet Union would continue to endeavour to improve her relations with Pakistan.[1]

These gestures were followed by Bulganin's written replies to a Pakistani editor's questions, in the course of which the former said the Soviet Union could share her knowledge of the peaceful applications of atomic energy with Pakistan and that there were real possibilities for an expansion of trade based on an exchange of Soviet industrial and agricultural machinery for Pakistani agricultural and livestock products.[2] While attending the National Day reception at the Pakistani Embassy in Kabul on 23 March 1956, Foreign Minister Molotov told the Pakistani Chargé d'Affaires that the Soviet Union was ready to build a steel mill for Pakistan like the one she was constructing in India.[3]

First Deputy Soviet Premier Anastas Mikoyan led a formidable forty-man delegation to Karachi in March 1956 to participate in the ceremonies inaugurating Pakistan as a republic under her newly framed constitution, and made a strong bid for Pakistani goodwill. He offered aid without strings, and stated that Premier Bulganin and Khrushchev were always ready to come to Pakistan and were waiting only for an invitation.[4] In a somewhat involved statement on Kashmir he conceded that the issue was a 'very important question' for Pakistan. He said that Bulganin and Khrushchev had expressed their views in India after assessing public opinion but significantly observed, in the same breath, 'It is not for us to decide finally the question of Kashmir. It should be decided by the people of Kashmir.'[5] Mikoyan also invited the Pakistani Parliament to send a delegation to visit the Soviet Union.

A trade pact was signed in Karachi between Pakistan and a visiting Soviet delegation in June 1956, resulting in transactions worth Rs.20 million during 1957.[6] The leader of the delegation said that his side would have been glad to discuss the question of assistance in oil-boring, drilling, or refining but that Pakistan had not raised such a question.[7]

Mikoyan's offer of aid had been immediately turned down. A

[1] ibid., p. 249.
[2] New York Times, 7 Feb. 1956.
[3] ibid, 24 March 1956.
[4] ibid., 25, 27 March 1956.
[5] Dawn, 26 March 1956.
[6] ibid., 28 June 1956 and 7 Nov. 1958.
[7] ibid., 29 June 1958.

Pakistani Government official had declared publicly, 'Nobody wants aid from them and that is our policy.'[1] His invitation to a parliamentary delegation to visit Russia, however, was accepted in August 1956. M. A. Khuro, leader of the delegation, revealed to *Dawn*'s London correspondent after the tour that the delegation had been assured by Bulganin and Khrushchev, in a two-hour discussion on Soviet-Pakistani relations, that the USSR was anxious to cultivate close relations with Pakistan. Khuro gained the impression that the Russians had not yet said their last word on Kashmir, and thought it would be wrong to infer from Khrushchev's statement in Srinagar that the USSR had, on this issue, finally ranged herself on the side of India.[2]

By 1958, the Pakistani-US alliance having come under strain,[3] there was a noticeable softening of the Pakistani attitude towards the Soviet Union. The hurling into space of Sputnik I by the Russians on 4 October 1957, moreover, had been read as a clear sign everywhere that the USSR was on the threshold of an impressive technical and economic breakthrough. The *New York Times* noted that the speeches of the head of the visiting Russian parliamentary delegation, offering aid 'without strings', were prominently displayed on the front page of Pakistani newspapers and were winning the acclaim of the man in the street.[4] *Dawn* reported that Pakistan's foreign policy was under re-examination and that one of the suggestions was to improve relations with the Soviet Union in the cultural and economic fields.[5] The newspaper also observed editorially that it was 'a far-fetched idea' that the Soviet Union or China posed any physical threat to Pakistan, but that if war came Pakistan was sure to be attacked, perhaps with nuclear weapons, 'not because we are a prize in ourselves but because we appear to Soviet eyes as having taken sides militarily with the enemies of the Soviet Union'.[6]

The growing uncertainty in foreign policy, however, was halted in October 1958 when Ayub Khan took up the reins of power. As one of the chief architects of friendship with America, he tried to mend that deteriorating alliance. There was no move for some time towards an easier relationship with the Soviet Union. But after Pakistani-US relations resumed their uneven course, the Soviet

[1] *New York Times*, 27 March 1956.
[2] *Dawn*, 10 Aug. 1956.
[3] See ch. 12.
[4] *New York Times*, 31 Jan. 1958.
[5] *Dawn*, 30 March 1958.
[6] ibid., 31 March 1958.

Embassy in Pakistan again broached the subject of petroleum exploration. This time the U-2 incident killed the negotiations before any noticeable progress could be registered. When excitement had subsided, Ayub gave the signal for a fresh start by saying, in June 1960, that he saw no reason why Pakistan could not 'do business' with the Soviet Union.[1] Talks were thereafter resumed and ultimately resulted in the Pakistani-Soviet Agreement of 4 March 1961. Pakistan was granted a loan of $30 million and promised technical assistance and equipment for exploration for oil. Though the negotiations were accompanied by numerous Pakistani official statements that the proposed arrangement did not signify any change in her foreign policy, the successful conclusion of such an important agreement was not without significance. The ice was broken.

III. Relations with China

Chinese rhetoric tends to confuse the real tenor of her foreign policy but the rationale of China's endeavour, and its consistency, become clear if it is remembered that her central objective is to gain acceptance as the world's third super power, along with the USA and the USSR, and as the only one of those three who really cares for the welfare and independence of the Afro-Asian victims of colonialism and neo-colonialism. China deliberately presents a bold and defiant front to America and Russia, who do not yet accept her as an equal, and displays a comparatively benign attitude towards the Afro-Asian countries, who are weaker than herself. The former posture serves to impress the Afro-Asians, and the latter to lure them. To this general rule of leniency towards Afro-Asians, there is one exception, India, because she is too large to accept China's hegemony and is, in fact, China's potential rival for pre eminence in the very family of nations which China wishes to rally, just as China herself in the Communist world is too big to be a mere satellite of the Soviet Union. China's policy towards Pakistan, in particular, is an object-lesson in how to attain long-term national goals by calm calculation, forbearance, and diplomatic skill. In her durable Prime Minister, Chou En-lai, China enjoys the leadership of a past master of diplomatic finesse. After Bulganin and Khrushchev had pleased India, and angered Pakistan, by their visit to India in 1955, Chou En-lai went one better and made equally successful visits to both India and Pakistan in 1956. More than

[1] *New York Times*, 27 June 1960.

anyone else he is responsible for making compatible the two societies which, ordinarily, should constitute opposing international poles— China, the unabashed promoter of extreme Marxism, and Pakistan, the most zealous upholder of Islam.

We have already mentioned how China restrained herself in the early years in the face of Pakistan's openly expressed dislike of Communism and her pro-West policies. When Pakistan formally joined the Western defence arrangements, China could very well have lost patience with Pakistan, but she continued to display exemplary foresight. It must be remembered that, from April 1954, when India signed a treaty with China recognizing Tibet as a 'region of China', till the escape into India of the Dalai Lama at the end of March 1959, Sino-Indian friendship was at its highest point. Indians and Chinese in those days were '*bhai bhai*'. For China to have been able to enjoy India's close friendship during that period without unduly straining her relations with India's enemy, Pakistan, was diplomatic tightrope-walking of the most skilful variety.

Though Pakistan's Western allies regarded both Russia and China as equally dangerous to world peace, China was able to convince Pakistanis that she was different from Russia. When Pakistan decided to accept American military assistance, William Clark of the *Observer* reported from Karachi that it was 'most noticeable that Communist China is not regarded as a grave menace, but rather a fellow Asian country dealing with common Asian problems of population, growth, food resources and land reform'.[1] China also gave Pakistanis the comforting feeling that she appreciated the peculiar nature of Indo-Pakistani relations.

Addressing the First National People's Congress of the People's Republic of China, on 23 September 1954, Chou En-lai criticized the newly formed SEATO but insisted that the principles of co-existence should apply to China's relations with all Asian countries including Pakistan.[2] Even more significant was Chou En-lai's parting message to Ambassador Raza when the latter left for Teheran on transfer. The Chinese Premier said he had felt personally hurt at the time Pakistan joined SEATO because he regarded Pakistan as a friend, but added that he fully understood her peculiar circumstances and hoped she would continue to play a decisive part in bringing peace to the world.[3]

[1] *Observer*, 14 March 1954.
[2] *People's China*, 16 Oct. 1954.
[3] *Hindu*, 27 Nov. 1954.

At Bandung Chou En-lai had invited Bogra to visit China. China chose the time of Bulganin's and Khrushchev's Indian visit to repeat the invitation in more concrete form. The *Manchester Guardian* perceptively commented on China's move: 'If Moscow is trying to tighten its links with India, it is natural that China should examine the possibilities of a link with Pakistan.'[1]

Prime Minister Suhrawardy made a ten-day· visit to China in October 1956 and was cordially received by Chairman Mao Tse-tung and others. Chou En-lai told Pakistani newsmen that, although Pakistan was a member of SEATO, there was no reason why China could not be friendly with her. China and Pakistan had many points in common and, though they differed in some ways, the two countries had no conflict of interests.[2] *Dawn* said Chou En-lai's statement had made 'new history in international relations by giving so broad-minded a lead'.[3]

During Chou En-lai's own visit to Pakistan in December, his views were embodied in a joint communiqué: 'The two Prime Ministers are of the view that the difference between the political systems of Pakistan and China and the divergence of views on many problems should not prevent the strengthening of friendship between their two countries. . . . They are happy to place on record that there is no real conflict of interests between the two countries.'[4] At Dacca the Chinese Premier was given a 'spectacular ovation' by 100,000 citizens. The East Pakistan Chief Minister, Ataur Rahman, who presided over the meeting, paid tribute to Chou En-lai's statesmanship and hoped he would assume the leadership of Asia.[5]

Suhrawardy was so impressed by his exchanges with Chou En-lai that he wrote to Eisenhower supporting the claim of the People's Republic to represent China in the United Nations, and also urging recognition of the People's Republic by the United States, but Eisenhower expressed his inability to accept Pakistan's point of view.[6] The Pakistani Premier also made a prediction in Parliament that was little noticed at the time but which in hindsight seems extremely shrewd: 'I feel perfectly certain that when the crucial time comes China will come to our assistance.'[7]

[1] *Manchester Guardian*, 28 Dec. 1955.
[2] *Dawn*, 24 Oct. 1956.
[3] ibid., 25 Oct. 1956.
[4] ibid., 25 Dec. 1956.
[5] ibid., 30 Dec. 1956.
[6] ibid., 31 Dec. 1956.
[7] *National Assembly of Pakistan Debates*, 25 Feb. 1957, p. 1097.

With Suhrawardy's visit to the USA in July 1957, however, Sino-Pakistani relations entered a difficult phase. Despite all the display of mutual cordiality between the two Premiers, Suhrawardy had lost no time in making it clear that Chou En-lai's visit had not in any way affected the charted course of Pakistan's foreign policy: 'both knew very well how far they could go.'[1] In the USA Suhrawardy made several strongly pro-American speeches. At San Francisco he spoke critically of conditions in China but said he felt proud of Pakistan's alliance with the US, and added: 'We intend to place our resources at the disposal of the ideal which both of us are pursuing.'[2] Considering how derisive and biting Chinese comments can be, the criticism in *Jin Min Jih Pao* of Suhrawardy's San Francisco remarks was comparatively mild. The paper said that, while it was quite understandable that Suhrawardy had to say something pleasant to Washington in asking for American aid, he 'had overreached himself by joining in Secretary Dulles' slanders against the Chinese People's Republic'. The article stressed, however, that friendship between the people of China and Pakistan would not be affected by Suhrawardy's utterances.[3]

During the early part of the Ayub era Pakistan's relations with China touched their nadir. In March 1959 the Dalai Lama took refuge in India to escape the consequences of the Tibetan rebellion against China, and later that year there were armed clashes on the Sino-Indian border. Pakistan, who had hitherto viewed Russia as the chief danger to the peace of South Asia, now began to see China in that light. Foreign Minister Manzur Qadir said in a television programme in Washington that 'expansionist tendencies were more noticeable in China than in Russia'.[4] Ayub repeatedly invited India to join Pakistan in defending the subcontinent. Pakistan also caused offence to Peking in a number of other ways.

China's press called Pakistan's action in voting for the US resolution designed to postpone the question of China's seat in the United Nations, despite herself recognizing the Communist regime, 'double-dealing tactics' and 'an unfriendly act'.[5] It said that, in criticizing the happenings in Tibet, the Pakistani papers had been 'playing imperialist propaganda tunes'.[6] Ayub's efforts to build up

[1] *Dawn*, 30 Dec. 1956.
[2] ibid., 21 July 1957.
[3] *Survey of China Mainland Press*, no. 1579, 29 July 1957, pp. 29-30.
[4] Government of Pakistan, *Handout E. no. 2741*, 31 May 1960.
[5] *Peking Review*, 30 Sept. 1958.
[6] *Survey of China Mainland Press*, no. 2005, 4 May 1959, p. 34.

a Pakistani-Indian system of joint defence were described as a 'vicious role' and the Pakistani Government was advised to 'pull up the horse before the precipice'.[1]

Perhaps the most remarkable achievement of Chinese diplomacy concerned China's attitude on Kashmir during the heyday of her friendship with India. The Indians thought China fully supported their claim to Kashmir, but when the time came for China to please Pakistan, she was able to come out in full support of the Pakistani position without having to go through the painful process of eating her own words. Khrushchev's handling of the same sizzling subject made the subsequent shift of his successors look much clumsier.

During his press conference in Calcutta in December 1956, just before he visited Pakistan, Chou En-lai was asked whether his offer to India to co-operate in defending her territorial integrity included Kashmir. He replied: 'The Kashmir question is an outstanding question between India and Pakistan. We hope that this question will be settled satisfactorily. India and Pakistan are sister countries. The peoples of these two countries are of the same race. There is no dispute between these two countries which cannot be settled.'[2] In Pakistan, a few days later, the Chinese Premier admitted that he had discussed the Kashmir problem with both Nehru and Suhrawardy but refused to make any comments on the merits of the case because he was 'still studying the question'. He expressed the hope, however, that Pakistan and India would settle this question directly between themselves.[3]

Later, at Colombo, Chou En-lai and his Ceylonese counterpart referred to Kashmir in their joint statement: 'We are deeply distressed by the unfortunate situation that has arisen in the dispute between Pakistan and India in regard to Kashmir. We appeal to both parties concerned, in their own as well as the wider interests of Asian-African solidarity, to strive further for a peaceful settlement of this problem.'[4] Pakistanis, having already experienced the futility of direct talks with India, were annoyed at Chou En-lai's view that the problem should be settled bilaterally by India and Pakistan. Suhrawardy called it 'the Communist and neutralist line'.[5]

But China's recommendation that the question be decided by direct negotiations between the two disputants was, in fact, not

---

[1] *Peking Review*, 28 July 1959. For Ayub's offers of joint defence to India see ch. 11.
[2] *Hindu*, 11 Dec. 1956.
[3] *Dawn*, 25 Dec. 1956.
[4] *Hindu*, 6 Feb. 1957.
[5] *Dawn*, 16 Feb. 1957.

meant to favour India but to prevent the United States from exploiting the dispute to her advantage. 'To have this question referred to the United Nations, which, in the circumstances of today, is under the control of the United States,' explained Chou En-lai, 'can only give rise to the danger of foreign interference.'[1] In reality the Chinese position was more favourable to Pakistan than to India. China's suggestion, that the dispute be resolved by bilateral discussions, related to procedure, but her recognition that the final disposition of Kashmir was still a matter of legitimate dispute struck at the very root of India's basic position that Kashmir was already a part of India.

During the discussion of the Sino-Indian boundary by Indian and Chinese officials in 1960, China refused to discuss 'the boundary west of Karakoram Pass between China's Sinkiang and Kashmir'[2] because of 'the present actual situation in Kashmir'. It was at this juncture that India, for the first time, woke up to the reality that China had 'declined to recognize the accession of Kashmir to India'.[3] In her note, protesting against the Sino-Pakistani boundary agreement, India wrote that she had 'so far believed' that China had accepted Indian sovereignty over Kashmir 'without reservation'. Peking called the 'allegation' totally untenable and pointed out that: 'The Indian Government could not cite any official Chinese document to prove this arbitrary contention but, basing itself solely on the guesswork and impression of Indian diplomatic officials who have been to China, insisted that Chinese Government authorities had made statements to that effect.'[4]

[1] *People's China*, 1 April 1957.
[2] *Report of the Officials of the Governments of India and the People's Republic of China on the Boundary Question*, p. 11.
[3] *Summary of the Report of the Officials of the Government of India and People's Republic of China on the Boundary Question*, p. 1.
[4] *Notes, Memoranda, and Letters Exchanged Between the Governments of India and China, White Paper No. VI*, p. 99.

11 Relations with India

I. Indian Reaction to US Military Aid to Pakistan

Much of India's criticism of the receipt of US military assistance by Pakistan and of Pakistan's subscription to SEATO and the Baghdad Pact was couched in general moralistic terms. However, it was not difficult to see that India regarded Pakistan's case in a special light because it was against India's national interest to see Pakistan becoming militarily stronger.

Two pronouncements of the Indian Prime Minister, one before Pakistan joined the Western defence system and the other after it, well illustrate how the change in Pakistani policy affected Nehru's view. On 8 March 1948 he said:

I can understand ... some of the smaller countries of Asia being forced by circumstances to bow down before some of the greater powers and becoming practically satellites of those powers, because they cannot help it. The power opposed to them is so great and they have nowhere to turn.[1]

But on 25 February 1955 he turned round and declared:

I can understand ... military alliances between great powers. That would have some meaning. But I do not understand military pacts and alliances between a huge giant of a power and a little pigmy of a country.[2]

Nehru first took cognizance of the question of US military assistance to Pakistan when the American press began to speculate that Governor-General Ghulam Muhammad had gone to the USA to negotiate a military alliance. He wrote a 'personal letter' to Bogra on 10 November 1953, and five days later publicly said 'we are deeply concerned'.[3] On 9 December the Indian Premier formally wrote to Bogra and opened an argument which lasted till Bogra's letter of 21

[1] J. Nehru, *India's Foreign Policy*, p. 32.
[2] ibid., p. 66.
[3] *Dawn*, 16 Nov. 1953.

September 1954. As India herself was destined to ask for United States military assistance in 1962, it is pertinent to tabulate here her main objections to such aid to Pakistan.

Nehru–Bogra Correspondence[1]

NEHRU:

An expansion of Pakistan's war resources can only be looked upon as an unfriendly act in India and one that is fraught with danger.[2]

Such a step is not compatible with true independence.[3]

It imperils the freedom of Asian countries and brings in the intervention of a foreign power in Asia.[4]

No person to my knowledge imagines that Pakistan can be in danger of invasion from the north.[5]

BOGRA:

India's military and economic potential is far greater than Pakistan's. There can be no reason why any attempt on the part of Pakistan to strengthen her defences should be looked upon as an unfriendly act in India. I am sure it is not your view that friendship between India and Pakistan can be established only on the basis of the present great disparity in their military potential.[6]

Rightly or wrongly we do believe that a threat to our security exists. That being so, we must take appropriate steps to strengthen our defences.[7]

Since weakness inevitably invites aggression, it seems to me extraordinary that steps taken by a country to strengthen its defences should be considered steps in the direction of war.[8]

Other Statements

Addressing the *Lok Sabha* on 23 December, Nehru said that, if a Western country gives military aid to an Eastern country, the past history of Asia comes up before him, 'the history of colonial domination creeping in here and establishing itself'; US military aid to Pakistan would upset the existing 'equilibrium'; and the

---

[1] *Negotiations Between the Prime Ministers of Pakistan and India Regarding the Kashmir Dispute, June 1953–September 1954*, Govt. of Pakistan, 1954.

[2] ibid., p. 55.

[3] ibid., p. 64.

[4] ibid., p. 74.

[5] ibid., p. 78. This is interesting because India later asked for US military aid precisely because she felt threatened by China from the north.

[6] ibid., p. 58.

[7] ibid., p. 82.

[8] ibid.

whole of Pakistan becomes a military base. He also regarded United States military aid to Pakistan as a form of intervention in Indo-Pakistani problems.[1] On 2 January 1954 the Indian leader described American aid to Pakistan 'as a step toward war, even world war'.[2]

Bogra asked, 'Should we remain weak just to suit another country?' In his view the real threat to peace in Asia arose not from Pakistan's wish to strengthen her defences but from the continuance of the Kashmir dispute, which was poisoning Indo-Pakistani relations. He thought it strange that Nehru should think arms aid to Pakistan would mean a return to colonial subjugation because India herself received millions of American dollars as grants and loans, enabling her to spend tremendous amounts on armed forces.

Some statements of the Indian Prime Minister and his Defence Minister and chief foreign policy adviser, Krishna Menon, not long before the outbreak of the Sino-Indian border war of 1962, during which India requested military help from other countries, are specially noteworthy. During the Kashmir debate in the Security Council Menon claimed on 3 May 1962 that India's relations with China 'were happy, and we hope they will continue to be happy in the time to come'. Some days later the *Times of India*'s Washington correspondent reported that the United States Administration was willing to assist India's military build-up as India faced a fight with China, but Menon said arrogantly that he would not 'drop a post card to the Pentagon'. He expressed annoyance that Indian public opinion appeared more concerned about the border dispute with China than with the 'more immediate threats from Pakistan'.[3] When some members of parliament pressed Nehru on 14 August 1962 to accept foreign aid for the defence of India against the looming Chinese threat, he told them, 'I do not think we shall maintain our independence for long if we go about seeking military aid from others to defend ourselves.' India should defend herself and 'die if necessary in the attempt'.[4] Eight days later Nehru asserted from the same floor that military help from other countries was 'basically and fundamentally opposed to a non-alignment policy'. It meant 'practically becoming aligned' to the country from which help is taken.[5]

[1] *Lok Sabha Debates*, 1 March 1954, col. 971.
[2] R. P. Stebbins, *The United States in World Affairs*, 1954, p. 324.
[3] *Times of India*, 24 May 1962, quoted by A. G. Noorani, *Our Credulity and Negligence*, pp. 76, 77.
[4] *Lok Sabha Debates*, 14 Aug. 1962, cols. 1754, 1772.
[5] ibid. 22 Aug. 1962, col. 2990.

Eisenhower's Assurances to India

The day before the public announcement that the US would give military assistance to Pakistan, the American Ambassador to India, George V. Allen, delivered to Prime Minister Nehru a courteous letter from President Eisenhower, assuring him that the step did not in any way affect America's friendship for India, and that if American aid was misused and directed against another country 'in aggression' he would 'undertake immediately, in accordance with my constitutional authority, appropriate action both within and without the UN to thwart such aggression'. Eisenhower added that the US believed it to be in the interest of the free world that India should have a strong military defence capability and that if India should require military aid under the mutual security legislation, her request would receive his 'most sympathetic consideration'.[1]

In his formal reply Nehru blandly told Eisenhower that India would continue to pursue her existing policy, but in Parliament he said pungently: 'If we object to military aid being given to Pakistan, we would be hypocrites and unprincipled opportunists to accept such aid ourselves.'[2] It was reported that the members of the *Lok Sabha* laughed when Nehru said, 'the President of the United States has been good enough to suggest that he would consider sympathetically any request from us for military aid'.[3] Nehru also declared bravely that in future India would rely less on foreign aid.[4]

Public Agitation in India

In order to put pressure on the United States, Nehru also whipped up public demonstrations in India. On 16 December 1953 he directed the Congress Party to organize country-wide protests against the projected Pakistani-US alliance. New Delhi was plastered with posters saying, 'Yanks, quit Asia.'[5]

Bogra warned that if a US-Pakistan military aid agreement was not consummated Asians would think that America had been frightened by protests from Bharat and Russia.[6] In the event the

---

[1] *USDSB*, 15 March 1954, p. 400.
[2] *Lok Sabha Debates*, 1 March 1954, col. 970.
[3] *Washington Post*, 2 March 1954, cited by Senator Fulbright, Congressional Record, 2 March 1954, p. 2481.
[4] J. W. Spain, 'Military Assistance for Pakistan', *American Political Science Review*, Sept. 1954.
[5] *New York Times*, 23 Dec. 1953.
[6] *Dawn*, 12 Jan. 1954.

Indian tactics made both Pakistan and the USA more determined to go through with the contemplated arrangements. The state of Indo-Pakistani relations being what it was, the louder the Indian denunciation, the more convinced Pakistanis felt that the proposal must be good for Pakistan; and a world power like the USA could hardly afford to give the appearance of being pushed around by Indian agitation.

The *New York Times* revealed that, at the very time Indians were so bitterly criticizing the proposal for US military assistance to Pakistan, a team of American military technicians was actually in India training Indian Air Force personnel to operate the USC-119 'Flying Boxcar', of which India was purchasing twenty-six with US Government aid.[1] Moreover, India herself had been giving military assistance to independent Nepal since 1950, and in 1952-3 there was an Indian military contingent of almost battalion strength in Nepal to train Nepalese personnel.[2]

Indian Criticism of SEATO and the Baghdad Pact
Nehru's criticism of SEATO and the Baghdad Pact followed predictable lines: SEATO reversed the trend of conciliation released by the Geneva settlement; it converted the area into a potential area of war; it might extend its scope to Goa as had NATO; its concern with subversion meant that the members would concern themselves with internal developments in the area; and it was dominated by big powers who would dictate to the three weak Asian members.

About the Baghdad Pact he said that it had weakened and broken up the Arab League, and, instead of keeping out the Soviet Union, it had made her take greater interest in the Middle East. Both pacts, he complained, 'tend to encircle us'.[3]

India's Counter-Offensive
Less than two months after Eisenhower had announced the grant · of military assistance to Pakistan, India signed the well-known agreement with China which purported to regulate 'Trade and Intercourse' between India and the 'Tibet Region of China'[4] but

---

[1] *New York Times*, 5 March 1954, quoted by J. W. Spain, 'Military Assistance for Pakistan', *American Political Science Review*, Sept. 1954, p. 750.

[2] *Asian Recorder*, 1969, p. 9057.

[3] In *Lok Sabha* on 29 March 1956.

[4] For text of the Sino-Indian Agreement of 29 April 1954 see H. E. Richardson, *Tibet and Its History*, p. 278.

the real importance of which lay in the fact that India officially conceded that Tibet was an integral part of China. According to Nehru, however, the 'major thing' about the agreement was its preamble, which embodied the five principles, known as *panchsheel*, as the basis for Sino-Indian relations: respect for each other's territorial integrity and sovereignty; non-aggression; non-interference in each other's internal affairs; equality and mutual benefit; and peaceful co-existence. He wished the area of peace created by the agreement could be extended to cover the rest of the world.[1]

To many observers the mere recitation of five principles seemed a flimsy shield for world peace. The *panchsheel*, commented the *Economist*, is 'an admirably pious doctrine' but not a policy; for the basis of a policy must be the power to carry it out.[2] Acharya Kripalani, a former President of the Indian National Congress, caustically calling *panchsheel* 'the great doctrine we have given to the world', said that it 'was born in sin, because it was enunciated to put the seal of our approval upon the destruction of an ancient nation [Tibet] which was associated with us spiritually and culturally'.[3]

After Nehru's death an official Indian Committee on the re-organization of the Foreign Service frankly conceded that the Chinese attack on the Indian frontiers in 1962 had destroyed 'the illusion that unilateral demonstration of peace and goodwill can be a substitute for strength and ability to defend ourselves',[4] but during the years that immediately followed the Sino-Indian agreement, Prime Minister Nehru sedulously held out *panchsheel* to the whole world as the practical alternative to the Western chain of military pacts. At the Avadi session, in January 1955, the Congress Party stated in its foreign policy resolution that these five principles represented the policy of India in international affairs, and 'put forward the alternative of collective peace to the preparation for collective war'.

Dulles and Nehru roamed different parts of the world like two prophets seeking followers for their respective paths to peace. Dulles condemned neutralism as immoral and favoured military preparedness as a shield against war; Nehru offered *panchsheel* as the panacea for peace and denounced military pacts as instru-

---

[1] J. Nehru, *India's Foreign Policy*, p. 303.
[2] *Economist*, 12 May 1956, p. 586.
[3] *Lok Sabha Debates*, 19 Aug. 1958, col. 1676.
[4] *Asian Recorder*, 1966, p. 7444.

ments of war. Nehru said *panchsheel* 'are a challenge to the world and we want the answer of every country as to what they think about them ... every country ... if it is honest in its desire for peace, must accept them; there is no way out.'[1] During the years 1954–6 Nehru visited twenty-six countries. The *Statesman* compared his reception in Europe to President Wilson's arrival in 1918, and another Indian newspaper claimed that no man evoked such love in any people.[2]

A Nehru–Chou En-lai joint communiqué issued in New Delhi on 28 June 1954 asserted that if *panchsheel* were applied 'in international relations generally, they would form a solid foundation for peace and security'. Similarly, a Nehru–Bulganin joint declaration published in Moscow a year later stated that 'the wider acceptance' of *panchsheel* 'will enlarge the area of peace'. A Russian writer proclaimed, 'Now, shoulder to shoulder, Moscow, Peking, and Delhi are fighting the great battle for world peace.'[3]

Sino-Indian relations, in particular, catapulted to a high level of cordiality. To Nehru such a development appeared to be a part of the welcome process of the liquidation of Western dominance and the resurgence of Asia. In his July 1954 letter to the Presidents of the State Congress Committees he explained that his and Chou En-lai's joint statement of the previous month had given expression to 'something that is giving Asia a place of her own in world affairs'.[4] By August 1955 there were 135 primary branches and 14 provincial branches of the India–China Friendship Association in India. A Chinese scholar ecstatically wrote, 'When a Chinese delegate receives a garland from the Indian people or when an Indian delegate holds a Chinese child in his arms, the souls of two great peoples are welded together.'[5]

However, it was not any inherent magic in *panchsheel* that sustained its apparent glamour till the Sino-Indian border war ended it in 1962. What made the India–China–Russia chorus harmonious for a time was that each of them, for different reasons, wished to impair Western efforts towards setting up a system of joint defence against Communist expansion. There was nothing to prevent any of the parties from ceasing to pay lip-service to *panchsheel* at any moment, and the verbal structure of the formula

[1] *Lok Sabha Debates*, 31 March 1955, col. 3901.
[2] *The Times*, 14 July 1955.
[3] *New Times*, no. 45, 1955, p. 18.
[4] *Round Table*, Sept. 1954.
[5] *Hindu*, 14 Nov. 1954.

immediately crumbled when China decided to humble India on the battlefield.

Nevertheless, while the slogan of *panchsheel* flourished, it was a source of great discomfiture for the Western countries, especially the United States. It was not surprising that the Communists and the Western countries should each have called the other war-mongers and themselves peace-loving, but when non-aligned India certified that Western policies were leading towards war, and Russia and China stood for peace, the balance of credibility in the eyes of many Afro-Asian countries was tilted in favour of the Communists. Prime Minister Nehru professed to be neutral but in fact he had definitely thrown his weight against the Western countries in the most crucial issue of the day—how to preserve peace.

II. The Kashmir Dispute

In his very first letter to Bogra, protesting against the proposal for US military assistance to Pakistan, Nehru said that such aid would affect Indo-Pakistani questions, especially Kashmir.[1] In subsequent communications he stated that such assistance 'produces a qualitative change in the existing situation' and that India could 'take no risks now, as we were prepared to take previously, and we must retain full liberty to keep such forces and military equipment in Kashmir State as we may consider necessary in view of this new threat to us'. Bogra replied that the overall military strength of Pakistan or India outside the state could have no bearing on the question of demilitarization in the state, and that he could not help feeling that a wholly extraneous issue had been put forward as yet another reason for declining to hold a plebiscite in Kashmir.

The Expert Committee, envisaged in the Bogra–Nehru communiqué of 20 August 1953, met once in December and then became a casualty of the deadlock between the two Prime Ministers, and the Plebiscite Administrator, who was to be appointed by the end of April 1954, was never nominated.

Some hope for better relations between India and Pakistan was generated in January 1955 when Governor-General Ghulam Muhammad accepted the invitation of his Indian counterpart to attend the Republic Day celebrations in New Delhi, and called for

[1] As already mentioned, Nehru first formally protested to Bogra against the proposal for US military assistance in his letter of 9 Dec. 1953. The Bogra–Nehru exchanges here described are summarized from *Negotiations Between the Prime Ministers of Pakistan and India Regarding the Kashmir Dispute, June 1953–September 1954*, Govt. of Pakistan, 1954.

an end to Indo-Pakistani disputes. It was arranged that the two
Prime Ministers should meet again. Consequently Bogra and Nehru
discussed Kashmir once more in Delhi in May. Though some 'new
ideas' on Kashmir were reportedly examined, nothing tangible
resulted from the discussions and, in his broadcast to the nation on
1 June, Bogra said there was no question of giving up the Pakistani
demand for a plebiscite in Kashmir. In a speech to Parliament on
29 March 1956, and at a public meeting on 13 April, Nehru revealed
the nature of the 'new ideas' he had presented to Bogra. On the
former occasion he stated that he had told Bogra that the 'facts had
to be recognized as they were. It was no good proceeding on the
basis of old things.' He was more concrete at the public meeting and
said he had told the Pakistanis that India would consider partition
of Kashmir on the basis of the cease-fire line with minor adjustments.[1]

In the meantime the process of amalgamation of Kashmir with
the Union of India continued. On 6 February 1954 the Constituent
Assembly of Kashmir accepted the recommendation of the Basic
Principles Committee that Kashmir should remain acceded to India.
Premier Bakshi Ghulam Muhammad said that the Assembly was
only giving 'final shape' to the decision which had been taken more
than six years previously. He also said that no power on earth, not
even the Security Council, could challenge the decision. A provision
of the Constitution of Kashmir, as finalized by the Constituent
Assembly on 17 November 1956, enunciated that the 'State is and
shall be an integral part of the Union of India'. The Constitution
was to come into force on 26 January 1957. With the opening of the
Banihal tunnel, in December 1956, India also obtained direct all-
year-round access to Kashmir, and was now in a stronger position
militarily to put down any interference with her possession.

At the same time Indian leaders openly began to shy away from
their commitment to let the future of Kashmir be determined by a
free vote of the people. Home Minister Govind Ballabh Pant said at
Srinagar on 8 July 1955 that the Constitutent Assembly had been
convened primarily for the purpose of determining the question of
accession and that the tide could not be turned.[2] Karachi was
further shocked when Nehru declared, in the Lok Sabha on 29
March 1956, that 'Pakistan is out of court until it performs its
primary duty by getting out of that part of Kashmir on which it has

---

[1] New York Times, 14 April 1956.
[2] Hindu, 9 July 1955, quoted by Sisir Gupta, Kashmir, p. 293.

committed aggression',[1] and that India wanted to avoid any step 'which would upset things that have settled down and which might lead to migration of people this way or that way'.[2] Asked at a press conference whether his speech in Parliament implied that he was no longer in favour of holding a plebiscite in Kashmir, Nehru replied, 'It is largely so.'[3]

These developments impelled Pakistan to request the Security Council on 2 January 1957 to take up the Kashmir question again. That the Security Council had come to life in the Suez and Hungarian crises encouraged Pakistanis to hope that the Council might bestir itself on the Kashmir issue also. Thus, after a lapse of more than four years,[4] Kashmir was debated once more during several sessions of the Council in January and February 1957.

The Security Council, on 24 January 1957, by a vote of ten to none, with the Soviet Union abstaining, reaffirmed the previous resolutions of the Council and the UNCIP, that the final disposition of Kashmir would be made by a plebiscite under UN auspices, and also the Council resolution of 30 March 1951, that any action taken by the Constituent Assembly of Kashmir would not constitute a disposition of the State in accordance with the above principle. Another resolution, introduced on 14 February, however, was barred by a Soviet veto, the first such action on Kashmir. The resolution had requested the current President of the Security Council, Gunnar Jarring of Sweden, to explore with the two governments proposals for settling the Kashmir dispute and to consider the use of a UN force as suggested by Pakistan. During the discussion, Krishna Menon for India had peremptorily declared, 'The Security Council dare not ask us to accept the introduction of foreign troops on our sacred soil.' Apparently he saw no contradiction between the Indian refusal to permit UN forces in Kashmir and India's own recent contribution of troops to serve in the United Nations Middle East Emergency Force. A milder resolution, asking Jarring to strive for a settlement but omitting the mention of a UN force, was thereupon approved on 21 February, with the Soviet Union abstaining.

Jarring submitted his report to the Security Council on 27 April 1957.[5] Both Governments, he said, had declared before him that

---

[1] J. Nehru, *Speeches*, III, p. 222.
[2] ibid., p. 223.
[3] *New York Times*, 3 April 1956.
[4] It had last been considered by the Security Council on 23 Dec. 1952.
[5] For text of Jarring Report see *S/3821*, 29 April 1957.

they felt bound by the UNCIP resolutions of 13 August 1948 and
5 January 1949. He had, therefore, proceeded to explore what was
impeding the implementation of these resolutions. The Government of India stated that two factors had prevented their implementation. One was that Pakistan had not implemented Part I of the
resolution of 13 August 1948, and the other that the Security Council had not acceded to the Indian demand to declare Pakistan an
aggressor nor had Pakistan yet given up the aggression. Jarring
pointed out that 'regardless of the merits of the present position
taken by . . . [the Indian] Government, it could not be overlooked
that they had accepted the two UNCIP resolutions'. Pakistan represented that Part I of the first resolution had been obeyed and the
time had come for Part II to be enforced.

Jarring thereupon asked both Governments if they would be
prepared to submit the question, whether or not Part I had been
implemented, to arbitration. If the arbitrator found that the
implementation had been incomplete, he would be empowered to
indicate what measures should be taken to complete it. Pakistan
fell in with the suggestion but the Government of India declined to
accept Jarring's proposal.

Though Jarring had been impartial in his concrete efforts to
resolve the deadlock, he interjected an *obiter dictum* in his report
which favoured the Indian contention, that the passage of time had
made the implementation of the original resolutions progressively
more difficult:[1] 'the implementation of international agreements of
an *ad hoc* character, which has not been achieved fairly speedily,
may become progressively more difficult because the situation with
which they were to cope has tended to change.' These observations,
in fact, seemed to release India from her own affirmation before
Jarring that she was still bound by the original resolutions on
Kashmir. Not surprisingly, India soon reverted, even more
vehemently than before, to the position that she was no longer
bound by her promise of a plebiscite in Kashmir.

After debating the Jarring report, the Security Council passed
another resolution, on 2 December 1958, asking the United Nations
Representative for India and Pakistan, Frank P. Graham, to visit
the subcontinent for a further attempt at settling the dispute on the
basis of the resolutions of 13 August 1948 and 5 January 1949. On

[1] In a speech in *Lok Sabha* on 9 April 1958, Nehru approvingly said that in the Jarring
report there 'was the first glimmering . . . of what the problem was today'. J. Nehru,
India's Foreign Policy, p. 489.

28 March 1958 Graham reported that he had again failed in his mission because his proposals regarding demilitarization had been turned down by India with the standing excuse that Pakistan had not discharged her initial obligations under the United Nations resolutions. India had even rejected Graham's proposal that the two Prime Ministers should meet under his auspices, saying that this would 'place the aggressor and the aggressed [against] on the same footing'.[1]

In the meantime Sheikh Abdullah, having been released from jail on 8 January 1958, had immediately proceeded to criticize the decision of the Constituent Assembly to accede to India on the ground that the Assembly had become an unrepresentative body after he, its founder, had been arrested in August 1953. He also stated that Kashmir's original accession to India had been provisional, that the only solution of the problem was a plebiscite, and that the invasion by Pakistan had taken place after the oppression of the Muslims in Jammu.[2] He was clapped into prison on 29 April 1958 and silenced once more.

III. The Noon-Nehru Border Agreement

Though the Kashmir problem had proved intractable, Noon (now Prime Minister) and Nehru were able to solve some border disputes by mutual adjustment. At Nehru's invitation, his Pakistani counterpart visited Delhi from 9 to 11 September 1958, and a joint communiqué, issued on the latter date, said that they had arrived at 'a good settlement' in regard to all the border disputes in the Eastern region, except two. They could not resolve any of the disputes in the Western region but asked their Foreign Secretaries to submit proposals for the settlement of the unresolved disputes in both regions.[3]

Nehru explained the result of the settlement in Parliament in two speeches, on 12 September and 9 December. One matter that had been agreed upon was that pockets of Pakistani territory in India, and Indian territory in Pakistan, should be exchanged. Another was that the Berubari Union, which had been in Indian possession since partition, should be divided between Pakistan and India equally.

[1] For text of Graham's Report, see S/3984, 31 March 1958.
[2] Sisir Gupta, Kashmir, p. 385; Dawn, 18 Jan., 2 Feb. 1958.
[3] For text of communiqué see Pakistan Affairs, Washington, D. C., 1 Oct. 1958.

In the 12 September speech the Indian Prime Minister revealed an unusual situation. Normally it was Pakistan who wished to submit Indo-Pakistani disputes to arbitration and India who stood for bilateral negotiations only. But on this occasion the Pakistani Premier had not been agreeable 'for the present' to refer one of the border disputes to a third party, while India, evidently, wished to do so. Nehru used the opportunity for making an extraordinary statement: 'We have thought, and we still think, that the best course to decide any outstanding matter, that cannot be decided by mutual talks, is to refer it to an independent party or tribunal. Either we come to an agreement ourselves or ask somebody else to advise us and accept whatever decision is arrived at, whether it is in our favour or against us. There is no other way.'

IV. Revolution in Pakistan

Less than a month after the Noon–Nehru border settlement, a revolution in Pakistan resulted in the abrogation of the Constitution and the installation of the Commander-in-Chief of the army, General Muhammad Ayub Khan, as President. The immediate effect of this change on Indo-Pakistani relations was not favourable. At a press conference on 22 October Ayub said that he would try 'desperately' to settle Kashmir and the canal waters dispute with India amicably, but 'if we are forced to adopt means other than peaceful, the blame will surely lie at the doorstep of Bharat'.[1] Nehru commented angrily that nowhere in the wide world was there such a naked military dictatorship as in Pakistan and that 'inherent in such a system are always certain risks and dangers'.[2] The Indian leader warned on another occasion that aggression by Pakistan against Kashmir would be regarded as aggression against India and would be met everywhere and not only in Kashmir.[3]

On 27 March 1959 Ayub said more realistically that neither Pakistan nor India could get away with an attack on the other. He ruled out the possibility of armed conflict 'unless it is forced upon us', and added that, once Indo-Pakistani basic differences had been justly settled, Pakistan would be only too glad to enter into a relationship of mutual co-operation with India.[4]

[1] *Dawn*, 23 Oct. 1958.
[2] J. Nehru, *India's Foreign Policy*, p. 494.
[3] *Hindu*, 16 Dec. 1958.
[4] *Dawn*, 28 March 1959.

V. Developments in Tibet and Pakistan's Offer of Joint Defence

Four days later the Dalai Lama escaped into India from Tibet and was courteously received and granted political asylum. Several thousand Tibetan refugees, who followed, were similarly treated. The Chinese were enraged at the manifestations of sympathy in India for the Dalai Lama and his country and alleged that India was holding the God-King under duress, that the Dalai Lama's statements criticizing China had been drafted by Indians, that India was towing the line of the imperialist powers, and that the centre of the anti-Communist rebellion in Tibet was on Indian soil. Nehru commented sadly, 'They have used the language of the cold war regardless of truth and propriety.' India's friendship with China, which hitherto had been the main plank of Indian foreign policy, was now at an end and Sino-Indian relations from this point progressively deteriorated, creating an entirely new situation.

Developments in Tibet resulted in some quick rethinking in Pakistan also. Pakistanis, who had so far regarded Russia as the greatest danger to peace, now began to feel that it was China who posed the more immediate threat. To Ayub's practical mind it seemed only logical that Pakistan and India should join hands to meet the common danger from outside. On 24 April 1959 he publicly proclaimed at Rawalpindi that, in the event of an external threat, Pakistan and India should defend the subcontinent in co-operation with each other.[1]

On 26 August 1959 the first publicized Sino-Indian border incident took place at Longju in NEFA (North-East Frontier Area). From the time when *panchsheel* had been proclaimed, the Chinese had allegedly made no less than twelve incursions into territory which India claimed to be hers, but the Government of India had suppressed news about them, believing that public excitement would reduce the chances of a peaceful settlement. However, tempers having already risen over recent events in Tibet, the looming danger could no longer be hidden from the Indian public after the exchange of fire at Longju, and Nehru described the tense border situation to Parliament on 28 August. Public anxiety and excitement now began to grow apace.

Ayub lost no time in arranging to meet Nehru at Delhi airport,

[1] *Dawn*, 25 April 1959.

during a diplomatic fuel stop, on his way by air from Karachi to Dacca, on 1 September 1959. After the meeting the Pakistani president disclosed his thoughts to reporters:

My submission is that whatever happened in the past, the time has now come when we should be thinking of having a rational and neighbourly relationship with each other. . . . I, as a military man, can foresee one danger, and that is that if we go on squabbling in this way and do not resolve our problems, we shall be defeated in detail. History tells us that is how invasions had always come to this subcontinent.[1]

Ayub's appreciation of the happenings in Tibet, and of the roads being built in Afghanistan, was that the subcontinent would become militarily vulnerable to a concerted Sino-Soviet invasion in five years' time and could be defended only if India and Pakistan stood together.[2] He expressed similar views in an article he contributed to *Foreign Affairs*.[3] Knowing India's aversion to military pacts and her penchant for non-alignment, Ayub explained that India and Pakistan could continue to have separate foreign policies and safeguard their own respective frontiers in case of common danger to both countries.[4] A mere understanding would be sufficient; it need not be a 'covenanted pact'.[5] The Pakistani offer of joint defence, however, was subject to the condition that big problems like Kashmir and the canal waters must be settled.[6]

Not surprisingly, Communist China sent Pakistan a note inquiring against whom the Pakistanis were proposing joint defence.[7] But, ironically enough, Nehru also vehemently asked, 'when people say we [should] have a common defence policy—against whom?'[8] Nehru argued that defence was closely allied to foreign policy and that India's outlook on foreign policy was different from that of Pakistan. Referring to Ayub's statement, that the offer of joint defence was subject to the settlement of the Kashmir question, Nehru remarked that this showed that 'common defence was not the real issue at all but something else—the Kashmir issue'.[9] All the Indian Premier offered in concrete terms was a reiteration of his

[1] *Hindu Weekly Review*, 7 Sept. 1959.
[2] *Dawn*, 24 Oct. 1959.
[3] 'Pakistan Perspective', *Foreign Affairs*, July 1960, p. 556.
[4] *Dawn*, 9 Nov. 1959.
[5] *Hindu*, 22 Jan. 1960.
[6] *Dawn*, 11 May 1959, 27 Jan. 1960, 14 May 1960.
[7] *New York Times*, 13 Oct. 1959.
[8] *Rajya Sabha Debates*, 4 May 1959, cols. 1674, 1676.
[9] *Dawn*, 14 Feb. 1960.

longstanding proposal that India and Pakistan should make a no-war pact.[1]

VI. Border Agreements and Indus Waters Treaty
Though Ayub was unsuccessful in securing India's co-operation in defence, the improved climate in both countries, generated by his friendly initiative, did not remain entirely unproductive. Commendable progress was made in the settlement of border disputes, both in the East and the West, and the Indus Waters Treaty was also finalized.

The border issues were discussed at two ministerial conferences. A joint communiqué, released on 24 October after the first conference, disclosed that the various questions were discussed 'in a positive and constructive spirit' and that disputes relating to India's Eastern border with Pakistan had been resolved. It was affirmed, further, that 'all' outstanding boundary disputes, if not settled by negotiation, would be referred to an impartial tribunal.[2]

The second conference met during January 1960 and managed to decide four out of five West Pakistan–India border questions. Only the Kutch–Sindh boundary dispute remained outstanding. Both sides agreed to collect further data concerning it and to discuss it later.[3]

Ayub and Nehru also appended their signatures to the Indus Waters Treaty in Karachi, on 19 September 1960, and ended that chronic problem.

VII. Deadlock over Kashmir
After completing the Indus Treaty at Karachi, Nehru stayed on in Pakistan until 23 September, and discussed the Kashmir dispute with Ayub at length. But all their joint statement could report was that 'this was a difficult question which required careful consideration of all aspects. The President and Prime Minister agreed to give further thought to this question with a view to finding a solution.'[4]

By August 1961 Ayub had begun to despair of success: 'I have pleaded with all humility with the Prime Minister of India, but I

---

[1] *Hindu*, 19 Jan. 1960.
[2] For text of communiqué see *Asian Recorder*, 1959, p. 3000.
[3] For text of communiqué see *Asian Recorder*, 1960, p. 3120.
[4] For text of joint communiqué of 23 Sept. 1960, see *Pakistan Horizon*, 4th Quarter 1960.

have not been able to get him to agree to a proper solution of this [Kashmir] problem. . . . We have come up against a blank wall.' He explained why Pakistan could not accept the cease-fire line as a permanent boundary: 'If you look at the map of Kashmir, you will see the location of the three rivers on which the life of the whole of West Pakistan, of some 45 million people, depends. As our population increases, every drop of that water has got to be husbanded, stored and utilized. Then there is the added problem of our physical security. The present cease-fire line is just like a grip around our neck.'[1]

With the approach of the third general elections in India, scheduled to take place in the first part of 1962, the election campaign there registered a progressively high tempo. At midnight on 17–18 December 1961 Indian troops invaded, and forcibly occupied, the Portuguese colony of Goa, contrary to numerous official statements in the past that force would never be used to solve the Goa issue.[2]

After this incident, Nehru pleaded that India's use of military force in Goa had not violated Gandhi's principles of non-violence and reminded his fellow countrymen that Gandhi had approved India's action in Kashmir, which was not non-violent.[3] Defence Minister Krishna Menon declared that India had not abjured violence in regard to any country which violated India's interests.[4] He also alleged that Pakistan had invaded 'our territory'. The entire State of Kashmir, he claimed, 'is part of the Indian Union', and added, 'Those who have no right to be on union territory must vacate this territory.'[5] On 4 January 1962, at the 67th Session of Congress at Patna, the President of the Indian National Congress,

---

[1] *Pakistan Horizon*, 4th Quarter 1961.

[2] e.g., NEHRU: 'The fact that war [against Portuguese possessions] is a little war does not make it less than a war. You may call it by any name you like. If a little war is justifiable under [certain] circumstances, a big war is also justifiable under certain other circumstances. There is no ground or principle left then in saying that war should be avoided and solutions sought on peaceful lines.' *Rajya Sabha Debates*, 6 Sept. 1955, col. 2098; and MENON: 'In this problem of Goa the test is not so much for Portugal as for us. It is one of those things where there is a sort of challenge that we have thrown out to the world that every problem is capable of being resolved by negotiations, that it is possible to bring about the liquidation of an authoritarian and imperial regime in any country by the use of non-violent and peaceful methods. Other methods are foreign to us and inapplicable to the situation. There is also no way of our proving it to the world except by example.' *Rajya Sabha Debates*, 27 Aug. 1954, col. 578.

[3] *Hindu Weekly Review*, 1 Jan. 1962.

[4] *Hindustan Times*, 26 Dec. 1961.

[5] *New York Times*, 7 Jan. 1962.

N. S. Reddy, threatened that India might move to take some 42,000 square miles of Kashmir occupied by Pakistan and China.[1]

'The net result of this pre-election posturing and prancing,' commented an India editor, 'has been to consolidate the image of India in foreign eyes as a wolf of aggression masquerading in a non-violent sheep's clothing.'[2]

Alarmed by these belligerent utterances, Pakistan approached the Security Council, on 11 January 1962, to take up the Kashmir case again. The Council heard the case intermittently from 1 February till 22 June. Pakistan was represented by Sir Zafrulla Khan[3] and India, from 2 May, by Krishna Menon.

Zafrulla quoted extensively from recent speeches of responsible Indians, threatening to eradicate Pakistan's 'aggression' from Kashmir, and said any such Indian move was likely to touch off a bigger war. He urged the council to act in time to save the situation. In response to the Indian claim that the people's welfare was far better looked after on the Indian side of the cease-fire line, Zafrulla said, 'Then why not hold a plebiscite? Let it take in Azad Kashmir also, and, if they want to go into this paradise on the other side, the whole dispute will come to an end.'[4] As to the contention that the passage of time had made the original resolutions unsuitable, the Pakistani spokesman pointed out that the acceptance of such a doctrine would enable any party who finds an international agreement awkward to thwart its fulfilment and then turn round and say that nothing need be done because a long time had elapsed.[5] Once again the Pakistani representative stated that Pakistan was agreeable 'to any method that may be suggested', including a reference to the International Court of Justice, for determining the obligations of the parties and other matters which were holding up progress.[6]

Menon reiterated that accession to India 'is full, it is complete, it is final',[7] and said, 'This is the 104th meeting on this subject, I believe. You can hold 200 meetings. We will come here every time you ask us, but on no condition shall we trade our sovereignty.'[8]

[1] Christian Science Monitor, 8 Jan. 1962, quoted in S/5058.
[2] Frank Moraes quoted in Dawn, 9 Jan. 1962.
[3] Zafrulla had returned to Pakistani service in 1961, as Permanent Representative of Pakistan to the United Nations, on completion of his first term as a judge of the International Court of Justice.
[4] Security Council Official Records, 1011th Meeting, 4 May 1962.
[5] 1008th Meeting, 2 May 1962.
[6] 1008th Meeting, 2 May 1962, and 1016th Meeting, 22 June 1962.
[7] 1009th Meeting, 3 May 1962.
[8] 1009th Meeting, 3 May 1962.

He said further that the Kashmir question 'is not a dispute but a situation. . . . How can there be a dispute between us and Pakistan in a matter in which Pakistan has no *locus standi*?'[1] Menon rejected the proposal to refer the matter to 'what is called mediation or arbitration' or to take it to the International Court, because it was a political issue.[2]

In the end the entire exercise proved fruitless. Even a comparatively innocuous resolution, introduced by Ireland on 22 June, asking the parties to enter into fresh negotiations, was vetoed by the USSR.

Kennedy Suggests Eugene Black as Kashmir Mediator

On 24 January 1962, after Pakistan had requested a meeting of the Security Council but before the Council had met to discuss the question, President Kennedy revealed at a press conference that he had recommended to India and Pakistan that they accept the good offices of Eugene Black, President of the World Bank, to find a solution of the Kashmir problem. Black had already shown his diplomatic prowess by successfully persuading the parties to agree to a settlement of the Indus Waters problem on the lines proposed by the Bank. As usual, Pakistan accepted the suggestion but India rejected it because, in the words of Prime Minister Nehru, 'mediation meant acceptance of a third nation sitting in judgment over the issue of sovereignty'.[3]

VIII. The Sino-Indian Border Clash

In the meantime India and China were inexorably moving towards an armed clash on the Himalayan frontier. After the incidents of 1959, India had embarked upon a 'forward defensive policy' which meant building numerous new outposts on the frontier. As an Indian General has stated, 'there was no reason why we should not play a game of chess and battle of wits with them, so far as the question of establishing posts was concerned. If they advance in one place, we should advance in another. . . . By the end of the year [1961] we had established over fifty such posts in Ladakh and NEFA and hence our occupational rights in some 2000 square miles of Indian territory.'[4]

---

[1] *1011th Meeting*, 4 May 1962.
[2] *1011th Meeting*, 4 May 1962, and *1016th Meeting*, 22 June 1962.
[3] *Asian Recorder*, 1962, p. 4452.
[4] Lt.-Gen. B. M. Kaul, *The Untold Story*, p. 280.

Nehru told the *Lok Sabha*, on 28 November 1961, that in the past two years the situation on the Sino-Indian frontier had been changing 'progressively in our favour' and that India would continue to strengthen her position so that 'ultimately we may be in a position to take action to recover such territory as is in their possession'.[1] On 20 June 1962 he again informed the same House that India's advantage over China on the frontier was growing and the position was 'getting better and better'.[2]

The phase which saw the brief Sino-Indian border war opened on 8 September 1962, when the Chinese crossed Thagla Ridge, which India claimed as the boundary, and threatened the Indian post of Dhola,[3] but matters did not get out of hand till Nehru ignited the smouldering embers on 12 October with a public declaration that the Indian Army had been ordered to clear the Chinese out of Indian territory. 'It was', remarked the *Economist*, 'as if Chamberlain had given way to Churchill.' The Indian move evoked a massive Chinese counter-attack on 20 October on both the eastern and western fronts, putting the units of the Indian Army to ignominious flight everywhere.[4] So one-sided was the clash that, while the Chinese rounded up some 4,000 Indians as prisoners of war, the Indians could not capture even one Chinese soldier.[5] The fighting stopped on 21 November with a unilateral declaration by the Chinese that they would cease fire and withdraw to positions twenty kilometres behind the line of actual control, as it had existed on 7 November 1959.[6]

[1] *Lok Sabha Debates*, cols. 1857-8.

[2] ibid., col. 11935.

[3] Neville Maxwell points out that Thagla Ridge, in fact, was three to four miles north of the McMahon Line, and the Dhola post, which the Indians had established in June 1962, was also on the Chinese side of the line. *India's China War*, p. 295.

[4] When President Ayub visited China in 1965 he was told by 'the highest authority in the country' that the conflict was the direct outcome of Indian provocations. A stage had been reached when the Premier and the Chief of Staff could bear it no longer (*Friends Not Masters*, p. 135).

The expression 'counter-attack', to describe the Chinese reaction to the Indian Army's attempt to dislodge the Chinese forces, has been taken from the text of the speech made by Ambassador B. K. Nehru of India to the National Press Club, Washington, on 21 Nov. 1962.

[5] Lt.-Gen. B. M. Kaul, *The Untold Story*, p. 439; *Asian Recorder*, 1963, p. 5340.

[6] The Chinese assault, evidently, had been launched with the limited objective of consolidating the Chinese position in the Ladakh sector where China had converted an old caravan route across the disputed Aksai Chin plateau into a strategic road connecting Sinkiang with Tibet. The eastern sector was pressed because that area is more vital to India, and the Chinese hoped India might accede to their wishes in the west to relieve the east. See S. M. Burke, 'The Sino-Indian Conflict', *Journal of International Affairs*, vol. XVII, no. 2, 1963.

This armed encounter between China and India, the world's most populous countries and Pakistan's immediate neighbours, violently shook the South Asian kaleidoscope, and heralded the emergence of an entirely new pattern.

12 The Course of Alliance

There was an imbalance in Pakistan's alliance with the Western countries[1] from the very beginning. Pakistan was quite prepared to pay the Western price for the partnership. She regarded international Communism a menace to the Islamic way of life, and had no compunction in combating any aggressive moves by it. Pakistan's allies, however, could offer only a part of the price demanded by Pakistan. They were willing to provide protection against Communism, but never came round to doing so against India. In fact they seldom made a secret of their decided preference for India. As soon as China fell into Communist hands, the Americans calculated that India was the only country who could save the rest of Asia from Communism because of her impressive bulk and potential resources. In the hope eventually of winning over India to her side, the US patiently tolerated innumerable slights from India, in much the same way as China put up with Pakistani provocations of various kinds. At first the Western countries pampered India in the hope that she would join hands with them in containing Communism. When India made it quite plain that she was not willing to participate in any such plan, they invited Pakistan to join the system. But India continued to be the main centre of their attention. The reasons now advanced for befriending India were, first, that she could save Asia by her example, if not by her direct effort. If India could outdo China in economic development and social progress, the less developed countries, it was argued, would follow India's method of advancement through free institutions, in preference to China's by totalitarian means. Secondly, it was stated that, without Western aid and comfort, India could collapse economically and politically and herself turn Communist, and this would irretrievably shift the balance of world power against the free world.

[1] As the USA is the dominant member of the Western world, the story of Pakistan's alliance with the West is largely a narrative of Pakistani-US relations.

The shadow of India thus hovered ominously over the Western–Pakistani alliance all the time. It powerfully affected its entire course, and ultimately succeeded in breaking it down.

The only way in which this situation could have been remedied was to persuade India and Pakistan to compose their differences and present a united front to outside danger. Pakistan was not only willing to follow such a course but actually proposed it repeatedly. The real problem was that India had the upper hand in Kashmir by reason of her superior physical power and actual possession of the most coveted part, and she was not at all willing to budge from this position of vantage. The US and Britain did wish India and Pakistan to come to terms, and employed considerable diplomatic pressure to that end. But they never cut off aid to India, which alone could have put any real teeth into their efforts. The Indians, having correctly diagnosed that they could get all the assistance they needed and also hold on to Kashmir, never felt any real necessity to conciliate Pakistan. After the 1957–8 financial crisis India became the largest recipient of aid both from the USA and the USSR, causing Pakistanis to question the value of alignment more than ever. Four circumstances prevented Pakistan from breaking away from the West at that time. First, she had become so dependent on the US that she could not face the prospect of losing American help. Secondly, though US economic aid to India was stepped up, Pakistan, as an ally, still enjoyed one advantage over India: Pakistan was getting military assistance but India was not. Thirdly, Ayub Khan, himself one of the principal architects of the Pakistani-US alliance, assumed power in October 1958 and his first impulse was to improve the deteriorating Pakistani-American relationship. Fourthly, there was at that time no big power to whom Pakistan could turn for protection against India, if she left the Western fold.

It was the Sino-Indian border war of 1962 that threw everything into the melting pot and created fresh options. It offered the Western countries a unique opportunity for influencing India to settle the Kashmir dispute, and reach an understanding with Pakistan. They tried to do so but not to the extent of declining India's request for arms if she refused to respond to reasonable suggestions. The extension of US military assistance to India meant that the last vestige of distinction between an ally and a neutral had disappeared. In fact it meant the strengthening of Pakistan's most determined foe by Pakistan's closest ally. The circumstances which created this new problem for Pakistan, however, brought with them also a possible way out. Because of her own open hostility to India, China was now willing to help Pakistan against India. By choice Pakistan would have preferred to remain allied with the USA, but the terms of alliance were no longer endurable and Pakistan moved to balance the loss by forging a positive relationship with China.

Pakistan's break with the USA was unfortunate because it had not resulted from any inherent incompatibility between the two countries. Americans and Pakistanis got on remarkably well at personal level, and their views on world affairs, and on ideological and economic matters, were basically similar. It was ironical that American friendship with Pakistan should have ended because of a third country—India—whose neutrality and socialistic bias differed materially from the American outlook. Not surprisingly, the net result was that the USA lost a potentially staunch ally in Pakistan, without gaining a real friend in India.

I. Pakistani and American Reaction to the Grant of US Military Assistance to Pakistan

Pakistanis were not unaware that they had been chosen as allies only after the Indians had turned down the American overtures. They hoped, however, that time and experience would bring Pakistan and the USA closer. At any rate, the need for arms and allies was so desperate at that time that the news that American arms were on the way brought a tremendous sense of relief to most Pakistanis. There were dissident voices too, no doubt, but they were a comparatively small minority. In the USA, on the other hand, a number of powerful political figures adversely criticized the new development. Their criticism was not that Pakistan was an undesirable friend but that the alliance would upset larger India. Together these persons, chiefly Democrats, formed an effective pro-Indian lobby which never slackened its efforts.

During Vice-President Nixon's visit to Pakistan, *Dawn*, the most influential Pakistani newspaper at that time, referred to the prospect of a military pact between Pakistan and the USA as 'heart-uplifting news' and said that 'the people of Pakistan will be found overwhelmingly in favour of such an alliance' because there had been increasing realization that Pakistan was gradually becoming friendless and isolated.[1] Commenting later on the Turco-

---

[1] *Dawn*, 9 Dec. 1953.

Pakistani communiqué of 19 February 1954, *Dawn* observed that it heralded 'the biggest event of Muslim and even world significance since the birth of Pakistan'.[1] *Dawn* also enthusiastically greeted the grant of US military supplies to Pakistan as 'a glorious chapter in our history'.[2]

Amongst those who proclaimed their approval of the new moves were Miss Jinnah, the sister of the Quaid-i-Azam; Nurul Amin, Chief Minister of East Pakistan; Maulana Abdul Hamid Badayuni, President of the Jamiat-ul-Ulema-i-Islam; and Dr. Khan Sahib, the veteran leader of the Frontier Province. When the question of US military aid was raised in the Constituent Assembly in March 1954, most speakers fully supported the proposal. The main dissidents were the Hindu members from East Pakistan and the leftist member, Iftikharuddin.

The most vocal critics of ties with the West were Maulana Abdul Hamid Bhashani, the pro–Peking East Pakistani leader, and other leftists, who were especially active in East Pakistan. The burden of criticism was that acceptance of military assistance would mean loss of freedom and the return of imperialism. Though the hard critics represented a small minority, certain circumstances served to exaggerate their strength. Iftikharuddin controlled the newspapers *Pakistan Times* and *Imroz*, and they naturally reflected his views. Also, it so happened that the first elections ever held in East Pakistan took place in March 1954 in the middle of the debate over the question of American arms. The Eastern wing was seething with discontent at the Western wing's 'imperialist' domination and the Communistic as well as the other opposition elements exploited that feeling to the full. The ruling Muslim League Party was ignominiously trounced by the opposition United Front, winning only 9 seats in a house of 309.

A close look at the election, however, shows that foreign policy was not directly an issue though opposition speakers did not hesitate to use it during the campaign as one more stick with which to beat the Government party. The United Front's 21-point election manifesto[3] was entirely silent on foreign policy. It concentrated upon popular local demands, the chief of which were that Bengali must be one of the State languages of Pakistan; that East Bengal must have control over all subjects except defence, foreign affairs, and

[1] ibid., 20 Feb. 1954.
[2] ibid., 26 Feb. 1954.
[3] ibid., 20 Dec. 1953.

currency, and 'shall be fully autonomous and sovereign, as envisaged
in the historical Lahore Resolution'; and that East Bengal must be
made militarily self-sufficient by moving the Naval Headquarters
there and by establishing an ordnance factory in the province. The
main components of the United Front, which was a union con-
tracted for election purposes that fell apart soon afterwards, were
Fazlul Huq's Krishak Sramik (Peasants and Workers) Party and the
Awami League led by Bhashani and Suhrawardy. Fazlul Huq was a
popular mass leader but foreign policy was not his *forte*. The
Awami League manifesto did call for 'an independent foreign
policy', but Bhashani and Suhrawardy did not speak on the subject
with one voice. While Bhashani unequivocally condemned the .
alliance with America, Suhrawardy seemed favourably inclined
towards it, though he did not come out too strongly in favour of the
pact at first. During Vice-President Nixon's visit to Pakistan in
December 1953, Suhrawardy was at first reported to have said that a
military treaty with the USA would be a blow to Pakistan's independence and initiative[1] but he quickly issued a correction that 'it all
depends on what is actually proposed', whether Pakistan was asked
to surrender her independence or given military aid on honourable
terms, just as US economic aid was being given. He affirmed,
however, that Pakistan's ideological affinities were more akin to
those of Western democracies than to those of the Communist
states.[2] As time passed, Suhrawardy became less inhibited in giving
expression to his pro-Western views, and ended up by being the
most outspoken proponent of Pakistan's ties with the Western
countries.

It would thus be a mistake to read the Muslim League defeat
in the East Pakistani elections as a verdict against the central govern-
ment's foreign policy. It was more truly a revolt against East
Pakistan's stepmotherly treatment by the government at Karachi.
A landslide of votes in favour of the United Front was assured by
the fact that it was led by East Pakistan's most magnetic leaders,
Fazlul Huq and Suhrawardy, both former Chief Ministers of un-
divided Bengal. The third former Premier of united Bengal,
Nazimuddin, had been abruptly dismissed from the office of
Prime Minister of Pakistan by Ghulam Muhammad, the Punjabi
Governor-General, adding to the already numerous painful

---

[1] *Pakistan Times*, 9 Dec. 1953.

[2] *Dawn*, 9 Dec. 1953. According to the *Economist* (30 Jan. 1954), Suhrawardy executed
this *volte-face* after having a talk with Nixon.

examples of the Western wing's supremacy in national affairs.[1]
A statement issued by 162 members of the new East Pakistan
Assembly, calling upon the people of Pakistan to protest against the
military pact with the United States, was a corollary to the election
result and its real import was the same as that of the election.

That public opinion in Pakistan was in fact overwhelmingly in
favour of accepting military aid from America did not escape the
notice of experienced outside observers. The *Economist* called
acceptance of the new policy 'surprisingly unanimous'[2] and an
American writer observed that public opinion was 'in almost complete agreement' with government policy.[3]

In the USA hardly anyone thought Pakistan was a more important
country than India, and India, undoubtedly, would have been
everybody's first choice as an ally. Indeed, it was after considerable
heart-searching and hesitation that the Administration had decided
to go ahead with the proposal to strengthen Pakistan militarily. The
plunge had been taken but it soon became apparent that America's
alliance with Pakistan was going to be a delicate balancing act. The
US objective apparently was, at one and the same time, to win
Pakistan's friendship and India's goodwill. Before publicly announcing the decision to furnish military supplies to Pakistan, President
Eisenhower wrote an almost apologetic personal letter to Nehru,
saying: 'I want you to know directly from me that this step does not
in any way affect the friendship we feel for India. Quite the contrary. We will continually strive to strengthen the warm and enduring friendship between our two countries.' He also assured the
Indian Prime Minister that, should India require military help,
her request would receive his 'most sympathetic consideration'.[4]
On 4 May 1954 the American Ambassador to India, George V.
Allen, pleaded before the House Committee on Foreign Affairs
for a strong economic aid programme to India because of the US
decision to give military assistance to Pakistan.[5]

Several notable Americans openly declared that it was a mistake
for the USA to have embarked upon a programme of defence

[1] Ghulam Muhammad had appointed Muhammad Ali Bogra, another Bengali, as
Prime Minister to succeed Nazimuddin, but the dictatorial manner in which the change
had been effected was greatly resented in East Pakistan.

[2] *Economist*, 30 Jan. 1954.

[3] James W. Spain, 'Military Assistance for Pakistan', *American Political Science
Review*, Sept. 1954.

[4] *USDSB*, 15 March 1954.

[5] *Mutual Security Act of 1954, Hearings Before the House Committee on Foreig
Affairs*, 4 May 1954, p. 509.

assistance to Pakistan. Senator Fulbright put forward a typical view:
'I disapprove of this move [to supply arms to Pakistan] and I wish
the record to show very clearly my disapproval.'[1] Chester Bowles,
while critical of the decision to aid Pakistan militarily, did not
question the need for a defence system in Asia to prevent the spread
of Communism, but he stood for 'an independent multilateral
defense programme supported by all countries of South Asia'.[2]
However, he did not spell out how India, an avowed neutral,
could be persuaded to join such an effort.

Others who immediately voiced opposition to arms aid to
Pakistan were Mrs. Eleanor Roosevelt, Representative Emanuel
Celler of New York, and Dr. E. Stanley Jones, a noted missionary
connected with India. Military pacts with Asians were also assailed,
at one time or another, by such formidable figures as Dean Acheson
and John F. Kennedy. Even John Sherman Cooper, while Ambassador to India, instead of upholding the policy of the government he
represented, 'made it clear to Nehru' that his position on the
Pakistan arms build-up was not the same as that of Dulles and he
was urging a change.[3]

With so many unpredictable factors already in the air, the future
course of Pakistan's relations with the Western countries was by
no means clear.

II. Bulganin and Khrushchev's Visit to India and Afghanistan

When Bulganin and Khrushchev boldly proclaimed their unqualified support for India on Kashmir and for Afghanistan on
'Pakhtunistan', even though India and Afghanistan were neutrals
and in no way allied with the USSR, the people of Pakistan naturally
wondered how the Western countries, with whom Pakistan had cast
in her lot, would react.

The farthest Pakistan's allies went was to mention her differences
with her neighbours in the joint communiqués of the next SEATO
and Baghdad Pact Council meetings. The SEATO statement,
issued from Karachi on 8 March 1956, 'deplored statements and

---

[1] *Congressional Record, (vol. 102, part 2, p. 2481), 83rd Congress, 2nd Session,* 2 March
1954, Senate.

[2] Chester Bowles, 'A US Policy for Asia', *New Leader,* 22 Feb. 1954; see also his
Ambassador's Report, p. 258: 'Will India, together with Pakistan, Egypt, Burma and
Indonesia, move in the direction of some kind of multilateral Monroe Doctrine for the
whole region?'

[3] J. K. Galbraith, *Ambassador's Journal,* p. 42.

interventions by Soviet leaders' and 'recognized that the sovereignty of Pakistan extends up to the Durand Line'. It also noted 'that the United Nations resolutions remain in force [and] affirmed the need for an early settlement of the Kashmir question through the United Nations or by direct negotiations'.[1] In the following month the Baghdad Pact Council declared that 'specific problems which were causing tension in this area were also discussed. . . . In particular the Council emphasized the need for an early settlement of the Palestine and Kashmir disputes.'[2]

It is true that the SEATO joint statement in effect rejected Afghanistan's claim to 'Pakhtunistan',[3] but the reference to Kashmir in both communiqués amounted simply to a pious wish for a settlement. The Soviet leaders had clearly stated that Kashmir now belonged to India; there was no balancing assertion by the Western powers that it should rightfully form a part of Pakistan.

What irked Pakistanis even more was that her allies hurried to placate India, both before and after the SEATO meeting, by further watering-down their already colourless support of Pakistan. The first to arrive in Delhi, on his way to Karachi, was Selwyn Lloyd, the British Foreign Secretary. He agreed with the Indians that Kashmir was not a suitable topic for discussion at the forthcoming SEATO meeting and reiterated that view on arrival in Karachi. After Kashmir had figured in the SEATO communiqué, Lloyd, in answer to a parliamentary question, explained that the merits of the Kashmir dispute had not been discussed. All that happened was that the members had noted that the United Nations resolutions remained in force and affirmed the need for an early settlement.[4]

After the meeting, Secretary Dulles made Delhi his first stop and there held a lengthy press conference (10 March 1956).[5] About Kashmir he said: 'We did not express ourselves on the merits of the controversy, but we expressed our hope that there will be a peaceful solution by such means as are indicated by the UN which includes means of direct negotiations.' He also assured the Indians that the supply of American arms did not in any way represent a threat to India because Pakistan knew that, if she used these weapons against India in any aggressive way, 'there will be a quick ending of

[1] Text in USDSB, 19 March 1956, p. 448.
[2] Text in Asian Recorder, 1956, p. 799.
[3] This was the first occasion on which the US Government had officially recognized the Durand Line as the international border between Pakistan and Afghanistan.
[4] The Times, 20 March 1956.
[5] For details of Dulles's Delhi press conference see Asian Recorder, 1956, p. 718.

9

its good relations with the USA and that, on the contrary, under
the principles of the UN charter, the USA would be supporting
India, if it became the victim of any armed aggression'.[1]

Dulles was closely followed to India by the French Foreign
Minister, Christian Pineau, and the Australian Foreign Minister,
Richard Casey. The former said that the SEATO reference to
Kashmir simply meant that SEATO was not the competent body
to decide that issue and that the question should be sent back to the
UN.[2] Casey also affirmed that SEATO had not discussed the merits
of the Kashmir dispute.[3]

During the discussion of the budget for the Pakistani Foreign
Office in March 1956, several members of the National Assembly
severely criticized the foreign policy of the Government. Foreign
Minister Hamidul Huq tried to placate the House by declaring that
'as far as Pakistan is concerned the most notable achievement of the
SEATO is the joint reaffirmation by the members of our stand on
Kashmir and the Durand Line'.[4] But his colleagues reminded him
that Lloyd had gone to Delhi before the SEATO meeting to appease
Indians, and Dulles had done the same afterwards. They asked why
the USA and Britain had not categorically declared that Kashmir
was a part of Pakistan when the Russian leaders had emphatically
stated that Kashmir belonged to India. When the demand for the
Foreign Ministry budget was voted upon, there were 22 ayes and
16 noes. This was the largest number of votes ever cast against the
Government's foreign policy.

III. The Suez and Hungarian Crises

The echoes of Bulganin and Khrushchev's pronouncements were
still fresh when the Suez and Hungarian crises raised important
new questions.

Pakistanis had been told that one of the chief merits of their country's alliance with the West was that it was a step towards strengthening the Muslim world. When two principal Western countries,
Britain and France, joined Israel in an attack upon Egypt, an impor-

---

[1] It may be mentioned, as an interesting sidelight, that Dulles began his visit by
placing the customary wreath on the grave of Gandhi. The biggest wreath ever de-
posited till then had been that of 'those unlikely apostles of non-violence', Khrushchev
and Bulganin. But Dulles 'outgrieved them' by laying a wreath the diameter of which
exceeded that of the Russian offering by a good six inches. *Minneapolis Tribune*, 14
Sept. 1969.

[2] *Asian Recorder*, 1956, p. 720.

[3] *Hindu*, 13 March 1956.

[4] *National Assembly of Pakistan Debates*, 26 March 1956, p. 96.

tant Muslim country, Pakistanis were bewildered. But for the fact that Pakistan's principal Western ally, the USA, acquitted herself honourably in the Suez affair, and the USSR behaved even worse in Hungary than Britain and France did in Suez, Pakistan's friendship with the Western countries would have crumbled from the sheer weight of public opinion.

President Eisenhower called the Anglo-French action in Suez an 'act of aggression'[1] and supported vigorous efforts in the UN and outside to cool the crisis. Secretary Dulles stated that the USA had taken one of her most difficult decisions when she chose to be loyal to her commitments to the UN rather than to her historical ties with Britain and France.[2]

Dawn editorials, during the concurrent Russian onslaught on Hungary and the Anglo-French invasion of Egypt, correctly gauged the public mood in Pakistan at the time. While castigating the Anglo-French assault on Egypt and referring to Eden as 'Hitler Reborn', in its leader of 1 November 1956, *Dawn* called American disapproval of the Anglo-French action 'the happiest part' of the news. Another article read:

Britain's Eden and Selwyn Lloyd, France's Mollet and Pineau, and Russia's Bulganin and Khrushchev are all of the same hue and all of them have dyed deep their hands with the blood of innocents. It is unutterably ludicrous for one set to accuse the other for their crimes in Hungary or Egypt ... it is America whom destiny seems to be calling to play an increasingly decisive and helpful role. ... Our alliance with that great Democracy thus stands justified.[3]

Mumtaz Daultana, a prominent Muslim Leaguer, demanded that Pakistan leave the Commonwealth, expel the UK from the Baghdad Pact, and have no further truck with Britain and France; but he praised the stand taken by the USA against Anglo-French aggression in Egypt and stated that, if she agreed to promote the cause of strength and unity in the Islamic world, he would not oppose alliance with the USA.[4]

IV. Acheson and Bowles Recommend a Shift in American Foreign Policy

Not long after the Pakistani parliamentarians had debated the

---

[1] Quoted by Phillips Talbot and S. L. Poplai in *India and America*, p. 67.
[2] *USDSB*, 25 Feb. 1957, quoted by M. S. Venkataramani in *Undercurrents in American Foreign Relations*, p. 96.
[3] *Dawn*, 20 Nov. 1956.
[4] ibid., 16 Nov. 1956.

question of Bulganin's and Khrushchev's whole-hearted support of Indian and Afghan causes, and the pale support which Pakistan's Western allies gave to her cause, two leading Democrats contributed articles to the *New York Times Magazine*, criticizing the policy of defence pacts.

Dean Acheson's article, 'To Meet the Shifting Soviet Offensive' (15 April 1956), approved of the 'programmes' of the Democratic regime of Truman, in which Acheson himself was the Secretary of State, and in fact claimed that it was the very success of these programmes—'the Greek-Turkish operation, the Marshall Plan, NATO, Western rearmament, the re-alignment of Germany and Japan, Point Four and the meeting of force with force in Korea'— that had compelled the Soviet Union to abandon a policy of military pressure and to adopt that of political and economic blandishments. At the same time, the article said, Moscow had shifted 'the principal arena of the contest away from Europe and the Far East to uncommitted and under-developed countries of the Middle Zone'. To meet the new challenge, it was necessary that, while maintaining the margin of power to deter the Soviet Union from reverting to military pressure, the United States should add another dimension to her policy, namely, to render economic and technical assistance to the countries of the Middle Zone without 'political entanglements'. The 'policies of military pacts and political commitments' were condemned because they brought out strong resentments and counter-measures.

Chester Bowles called 'For a New Realism in Foreign Policy' (20 May 1956). He, too, asserted that the American 'position throughout the world is certainly less strong than it was three years ago', i.e. when the changeover from the Democratic to the Republican administration took place. Like Acheson, he said that the primary objective of the new Soviet tactics was to win the confidence of the uncommitted Asians, Africans, and South Americans and 'to draw them into an ever closer economic and political relationship'. American policy, based on the 'Maginot Line concept of power', had failed. Among the examples chosen to illustrate this was the arming of Pakistan, which had 'upset the balance of power in South Asia, thereby opening the door into Afghanistan for the Russians and further antagonizing India'. The correct policy was to seek 'a balance between ideas and defense: on the one hand, the bringing together under the banner of a militant new freedom of those people of the earth—and today they are by far the majority—who seek the goals that we seek, self-determination, human dignity, and expanding opportunities; and, on the other hand, the power of a massive, competent defense to provide a screen behind which those goals can be vigorously pursued.'

Though these articles condemned military alliances, both of them gave the highest priority to continued military preparedness: 'Our relative military position is one of the largest factors in our power and in our security today' (Acheson); and 'Military defense is the first essential component in our foreign policy program' (Bowles).

However, some important questions were left unanswered. It was not made clear what would happen if the Communists again resorted to armed aggression in the countries of the Middle Zone. Would the United States remain an idle spectator or would she intervene physically to check the onslaught? In the latter case, was she to fight alone or did she expect some like-minded countries of the area to stand beside her in a crisis and fight? If she desired others to join her, how were these potential allies to be cultivated if the policy of the United States in the meantime was to be one of disparagement of military alliances and of dispensation of economic and technical assistance freely to all, without distinction between friends and neutrals?

To Pakistan these articles were a clear notice that her alliance with the USA was by no means securely rooted and was likely to be shaken when the Democratic party returned to power in Washington.

V. Suhrawardy's Remarkable Performance
In September 1956, when the Suez crisis was brewing, Huseyn Shaheed Suhrawardy became Prime Minister of Pakistan and held office till October 1957. This was a difficult period because it covered the Suez and Hungarian outbreaks. Suhrawardy's handling of foreign policy at this time, when Pakistani emotions over Suez had been deeply stirred, was remarkably bold. Even more note-worthy was the fact that he was able to carry public opinion with him to an extraordinary degree in his unabashedly pro-Western stand. It is true he was helped by some special factors: he was a highly skilful parliamentarian and also knew how to stand up to a crowd; he was a popular East Pakistani and was able to win over several East Pakistanis who had previously criticized their country's close ties with the West. Nevertheless, all in all, his was a notable

achievement which showed that, given clear leadership and acceptable American policies,[1] the people of Pakistan could have remained good allies of the West.

Suhrawardy frequently defended his foreign policy in public with a frankness unheard of in Pakistan till then. In one such extempore performance he faced a large gathering of East Pakistani students in the Salimullah Muslim Hall at Dacca[2] and decried the fact 'that if we say anything in favour of America or the UK we are called "stooges of imperialism" and if we say anything in favour of Russia we are called "independent".' He would try to compose the differences between various Muslim countries but it must be remembered that all the existing Muslim governments were weak. 'The question is asked: Why don't we get together rather than be tied to a big Power like the UK or America? My answer to that is that zero plus zero plus zero plus zero is after all equal to zero.[3] We have, therefore, to go farther afield rather than get all the zeros together.'

In an article in *Foreign Affairs*, Suhrawardy had averred that Pakistani foreign policy was looked upon with suspicion by the people because it had been formulated secretly by a 'few Ministers'. He expressed his resolve 'to open the whole foreign policy of Pakistan to debate in the National Assembly and to test the issue in a vote of confidence'.[4]

During previous administrations in Pakistan, foreign policy had been debated in parliament during the budget discussion when the item relating to the Foreign Ministry was taken up. On 22 February 1957, for the first time in Pakistani history, Suhrawardy directly invited a vote on foreign policy by moving 'That the Assembly do approve the Foreign Policy of the Government'. When the tally was taken on 25 February the motion was carried by 40 votes to 2. *Dawn* commented: 'The National Assembly's approval of the Government's foreign policy is another convincing

---

[1] In the Suez crisis Britain and France had gravely offended Pakistanis by their invasion of Muslim Egypt but America, the most important member of the Western coalition, had opposed the Anglo-French incursion. It was chiefly by the trend of American policy that Pakistanis judged the state of their alliance with the West.

[2] This speech was made on 9 Dec. 1956 and its text was published by the Government of Pakistan in the form of a booklet, *Prime Minister's Statement on Foreign Policy*.

[3] Suhrawardy explained in the National Assembly that in calling Muslim countries zeros he was referring to their military potential and not to their position in the international world (see *National Assembly of Pakistan Debates*, 25 Feb. 1957, p. 1088).

[4] Though published in April 1957, the contents show the article was written before the foreign policy debate in the National Assembly in February 1957.

demonstration of the fact that never since the Quaid-i-Millat [Liaquat Ali Khan] has there been such an overwhelming measure of agreement on how this country should go about the business of living in a troubled world beset with deadly perils, shams and subterfuges.'[1]

The Awami League Party, of which Suhrawardy and Bhashani had been the co-founders, had originally declared itself in favour of 'an independent foreign policy', but in June 1957 Suhrawardy won the endorsement of the Council of the Awami League to his pro-West policy. Maulana Bhashani thereupon parted company with Suhrawardy and founded the National Awami Party.

VI. Financial Crisis in India and a Sharp Rise in US Economic Aid

Up to 1956 American as well as Indian experts believed that India was making much faster progress towards economic development than China. Two Stanford University economists wrote in May 1955 that China was lagging behind India in the production of goods as well as in the industrial sector; also that 'the peaceful land reform in India' had led to 'impressive gains in agricultural process'.[2] At the 12th session of ECAFE, the chairman of the US delegation claimed that India's rate of increase in industrial production over the previous year had been nearly 50 per cent greater than that of China.[3] Writing in *Foreign Affairs* in July 1956, the editor of the *Eastern Economist*, New Delhi, forecast that 'between 50 and 100 years from now the Indian Union will possess an economy as massive in terms of productive capacity and of welfare as that of the United States today'.[4]

In 1957 suddenly the picture changed. In June the *Economist* reported that shortage of foreign exchange threatened to retard, if not halt, India's five-year plan.[5] In mid-1958 it was apparent that India was faced with a serious foreign-exchange crisis. Sterling reserves declined from $1,567 million in March 1956 to $457 million by the end of June 1958. Food scarcity also reared its head. It was realized

[1] *Dawn*, 27 Feb. 1957.
[2] *New York Times*, 23 May 1955.
[3] *USDSB*, 5 March 1956.
[4] E. P. W. da Costa, 'India's New Five-Year Plan', *Foreign Affairs*, July 1956, p. 672.
[5] *Economist*, 15 June 1957. India's second five-year plan, which began in 1956, aimed at a rapid expansion of heavy industry, specially the steel industry. This necessitated the import of heavy machinery and equipment which had to be paid for in foreign exchange.

that China's gross national output had expanded about three times faster than that of India in the nineteen-fifties.[1] In 1958 China's rate of economic growth had been at least three times as high as India's.[2]

Soon after the foreign-exchange crisis became known, the USA expressed her readiness to come to India's rescue. At a news conference on 10 September 1957, Secretary Dulles declared that India's request for assistance would receive sympathetic consideration. In a press release on 16 January 1958 the Department of State announced that the US Government desired to assist India in meeting her economic problems.[3] In March the Development Loan Fund announced a $75 million loan and the Export-Import Bank a $150 million credit to India.[4] Five months later, representatives of the United Kingdom, Germany, Canada, Japan, and the USA met under the auspices of the International Bank for Reconstruction and Development and pledged to provide $350 million as assistance to India, towards which the USA promised $75 million. This *ad hoc* international gathering became a regular event and later came to be known as the India Consortium. A Pakistan Consortium was established in 1960.

Apart from the emergency aid described above, the United States Congress accepted the responsibility for long-term assistance to India. This resulted from a resolution introduced in the Senate on 25 March 1958, jointly by Senators John F. Kennedy and John Sherman Cooper, a former Ambassador to India. The resolution declared that the US Congress recognized 'the importance of the economic development of the Republic of India to its people, to democratic values and institutions, and to peace and stability in the world'. The policy statement singling out India, however, was struck from the bill in conference because the House conferees felt strongly that individual countries should not be named. The preamble now referred to South Asia as the area of America's special concern, but everyone knew full well that India was meant to be the main beneficiary of the increased effort. In a supplementary resolution, which was also passed by Congress, Kennedy and Cooper asked for the establishment of an international mission which could consult with India on the nature of her economic

[1] Senator John F. Kennedy in *India and the United States* (ed. Selig S. Harrison), p. 63.
[2] ibid., p. 64.
[3] *USDSB*, 3 March 1958.
[4] *USDSB*, 24 March 1958.

requirements. The State Department accordingly requested the World Bank to send a mission, and in due course a three-man 'Banker's Mission' visited both India and Pakistan. To create public support for massive aid to India, a high-powered conference on 'India and the United States' was held in Washington, D.C., in May 1959, and the participants were welcomed by Vice-President Richard Nixon.[1]

As a result of all these efforts, the volume of US aid to India from 1957 onwards registered a sharp increase, and the ratio of US aid to India and Pakistan was greatly altered to the advantage of India. The following table explains the position:

US foreign assistance—obligations and loan authorizations—to India and Pakistan (economic aid total) in millions of dollars[2]

	1953	1954	1955	1956	1957	1958	1959	1960	1961	1962
India	45.1	88.9	113.6	92.8	364.8	305.1	366.7	758.4	667.8	775.1
Pakistan	109.8	23.3	100.9	162.5	170.7	163.3	235.0	301.5	172.0	403.9

During the period 1 July 1955 to 1 February 1958 India had also received $219 million of aid from the Sino-Soviet bloc, while Pakistan had shunned all offers of assistance from that source.[3]

VII. US Rationalization for Special Treatment to India

Even when Indian-US relations were under special strain, because of the US decision to supply arms to Pakistan, Secretary Dulles had pleaded for a continuance of aid to India because, if she lost the economic competition to China, it would mean the loss of another 350 million people to Communism, bringing up the number of its adherents from 800 million to 1,200 million, which would be almost half the people of the world.[4] At the Conference on India in May 1959 Vice-President Nixon said that what happened to India could be even more important in the long run than what happened in the negotiations with regard to Berlin.[5] Senator

[1] The proceedings of the conference later appeared in the form of a book, Selig S. Harrison (ed.), *India and the United States*.

[2] *Foreign Operations Appropriations for 1964: Hearings Before a Subcommittee of the House Committee on Appropriations*, Washington, pp. 1234, 1243.

[3] *USDSB*, 24 March 1958, p. 473.

[4] *Mutual Security Act of 1954, Hearings Before the Senate Committee on Foreign Relations*, 4 June 1954, pp. 14–15.

[5] Selig S. Harrison (ed.), *India and the United States*, p. 144.

Kennedy called India 'the hinge of fate in Asia'. He also said that the dominant issue of the day was not the relative rate of growth of the United States and the Soviet Union but whether China or India would achieve a more impressive record of economic progress.[1]

Americans did not deny that there were some deep differences of foreign policy between the USA and India, but they contended that the basic values they shared far outweighed the differences which divided the two peoples. These basic values were stated to be the practice of democracy and respect for the fundamental rights of human beings.

Significantly, however, Indians did not always share the American view of themselves. An Indian scholar of world affairs observed that, while a large section of Indian opinion would not agree with the general American view that there was some conscious economic competition between India and China, Indians 'did not mind American spokesmen using that self-justification for their own satisfaction'. He noted that the Indian reaction to the American justification of 'saving India for democracy' by American aid was the same.[2] The *Times of India* (24 April 1954) commented: 'The manner in which the Eisenhower Administration is attempting to "save India for Democracy" against an opposition which regards dollars as rewards for good behaviour, is not calculated to inspire either gratitude or respect.'[3] Another Indian scholar maintained that the USA was interested 'in our experiment in democracy . . . because a change in the form of government in this country could very conceivably lead to a change in our foreign policy, gravely affecting the security of the United States'.[4]

Americans also placed India in a special category in the matter of aid from the Soviet Union. It was alleged that Soviet aid usually was a dangerous bait, the ultimate objective of which was to subvert the receiving country by exploiting the various opportunities which an aid programme created.[5] However, India was considered too big a country to get too closely tied to the Soviet Union as a result of

---

[1] John F. Kennedy, *The Strategy of Peace*, p. 222.

[2] M. S. Rajan, *India in World Affairs, 1954–56*, p. 285.

[3] ibid.

[4] A. P. Rana, 'The Nature of India's Foreign Policy', *India Quarterly*, April–June 1966.

[5] The *New York Times* (30 March 1956) complimented Pakistan for her 'political sagacity in refusing to be trapped by Moscow's offer of a trade pact' and cited Dulles's view that the Soviet trade bait had a hook inside it and a line that led to Moscow.

Soviet aid.[1] As a matter of fact it was 'very much' in the American interest that the Soviet Union continued to give economic assistance to India because that could offset the obligation which would otherwise rest upon the US and her European associates. Furthermore, it was pleasant to see Khrushchev on the horns of a dilemma 'between his friend India and his eternal brother China'.[2] Senator Humphrey recommended aid to India because there was 'no way of persuading India to dispense with Soviet help except by demonstrating the superiority and disinterestedness of free world assistance'.[3]

Because of their predisposition towards India, Americans managed to discern some advantage in whichever direction India leaned, whether towards China or towards Russia. In the early days when India was courting China, the *New York Times* Delhi correspondent divinèd: 'What Nehru is doing . . . is to offer China an alternative to intimate relations with the Soviets.'[4] Later, when India and China fell out and India cultivated better relations with the USSR, Harriman thought that India was offering Russia an alternative to close relations with China because 'if India would break with the Soviet Union, it would tend to bring the two countries [Russia and China] together'.[5]

VIII. Pakistanis as well as Americans Question the Value of Alliance

As soon as Pakistan became an ally of the United States the amount of American aid to Pakistan registered a sharp increase, but this privileged position lasted only till 1956. From 1957 the picture drastically changed: US aid to India suddenly climbed from $92·8 million in 1956 to $364·8 million in 1957, while that to Pakistan increased from $162·5 million to $170·7 million only.

That Pakistan received military aid from the US while India got only economic assistance seemed to Pakistanis a distinction without any real difference. Indeed, Western spokesmen themselves conceded that economic aid, in a sense, is 'defense support', as it made possible a larger defence budget appropriation from domestic

[1] Under-Secretary of State for Economic Affairs, Douglas Dillon, reported in *Dawn*, 12 March 1959.
[2] Harriman before the American Society of Newspaper Editors, *USDSB*, 6 May 1963.
[3] *Congressional Record* (vol. 108, p. 9965), 87th Congress, 2nd Session, 7 June 1962, Senate.
[4] *New York Times*, 5 Oct. 1952.
[5] *USDSB*, 25 Feb. 1963.

funds.[1] The Under-Secretary of State for Economic Affairs, Douglas Dillon, said India was a classic example of a country using US economic aid to buy military equipment.[2] As a matter of fact India was better off than Pakistan in an important respect: while the grant of US arms to Pakistan was subject to defined conditions as to the use of those arms and carried certain obligations, the military hardware which India purchased commercially could be used by her for any purpose she deemed fit and placed her under no obligation to assist the Western countries.

The two main beneficial results which Bogra had led his countrymen to expect from Pakistan's alliance with the West had also failed to materialize. He had forecast that the new alignment would be a step towards strengthening the Muslim world, but in fact the Baghdad Pact had further shaken its unity. He had claimed, further, that US military aid would strengthen Pakistan without placing an additional burden on her economy, but the defence budget had shot up from Rs.6,532 lakhs in 1953-4 to Rs.10,435 lakhs in 1959-60.

In the National Assembly debates, in March and September 1958, most speakers expressed dissatisfaction with the state of the US-Pakistani alliance. Even the usually pro-West Prime Minister, Feroze Khan Noon, warned that, if Pakistanis found their freedom threatened by India, they 'will break all pacts and shake hands with people whom we made enemies because of others'.[3] There was a strong demand, first, that Pakistan should cautiously move to a position of neutrality in the East-West struggle and, secondly, that fresh efforts must be made to win the close friendship of all Muslim countries.

The growing dissatisfaction with the alliance, of course, was not a one-sided affair. Several influential Americans, too, sharpened their criticism of US-Pakistani relations. Senator Wayne Morse, for instance, cited Pakistan as 'perhaps the worst example' of the effect of US military aid because it had inspired an arms race between Pakistan and India, both of whom urgently needed their resources to raise the living standards of their people.[4] Senator

[1] Phillips Talbot and S. L. Poplai, *India and America, A Study of Their Relations*, p. 92.

[2] *Dawn*, 22 Feb. 1959.

[3] This sentence is missing from the Official Report for 8 March 1958 but undoubtedly formed part of Noon's speech because it was widely quoted and never denied (see *Dawn* and *New York Times*, both of 9 March 1958, and also *National Assembly of Pakistan Debates*, 4 Sept. 1958, p. 367.

[4] *Congressional Record* (*vol. 104, p. 1942), 85th Congress, 2nd Session*, 10 Feb. 1958, Senate.

Fulbright reiterated that furnishing military aid to Pakistan had been a very shortsighted policy and asserted that events had proved it had been wrong.[1] Secretary Dulles thought the military establishment of America's allies, in some cases, was too big and disclosed that the US Government was 'working very hard in a number of quarters' to bring about some reductions. He visualized a diminution of US defence assistance spending.[2]

Even Pakistan's staunchest friends could hardly overlook her ailing economy and continued political instability. Finance Minister Amjad Ali painted a dismal picture of the state of the economy in the National Assembly on 9 September 1958. He pointed out that, except during the Korean War, the economy of Pakistan had never been strong as far as foreign exchange was concerned. In the preceding two years the position had deteriorated considerably. The foreign-exchange reserve, which included gold, stood at Rs.126·29 crores in December 1956; by June 1958 it had come down to Rs.88·04 crores, and during the last three months it had probably gone down by a further Rs.15 crores. The terms of trade had also been running against Pakistan. Taking the base of 1948 as 100, the figure had fallen to 61. Expenditure, on the other hand, had gone up from Rs.145 crores in 1954 to Rs.228 crores in 1957. The largest drain had been caused by food imports. Owing to multifarious urgent demands, Pakistan had been able to spend only $186 million on constructive works out of a total of $838 million received in foreign aid over the years.

As to political uncertainty, there had been no less than six Prime Ministers between the assassination of Liaquat Ali Khan in October 1951 and Ayub's revolution of 1958. At the provincial level, East Pakistan had witnessed a procession of eight governors and seven ministries in the four years before the revolution.

' By the summer of 1958 conditions in Pakistan had reached a crisis. Abdul Qayyum Khan, President of the Muslim League, threatened that, if the attempt to delay the promised general elections continued, 'the Baghdad tragedy [in which the royal family and the Prime Minister had been butchered] may be enacted in this country also'. He announced, further, that war was the 'only' solution of the Kashmir problem.[3] In a pandemoniac session, on

[1] *Review of Foreign Policy, 1958, Hearings Before Senate Committee on Foreign Relations,* 26 Feb. 1958, p. 241.

[2] *Mutual Security Act of 1958, Hearings on S.3318 Before Senate Committee on Foreign Relations,* 24 March 1958, pp. 180-1.

[3] *Dawn,* 20 July 1958.

20 September, the East Pakistan Assembly voted its Speaker 'insane'. Three days later some of the members assaulted the Deputy Speaker while he was occupying the Chair, and he died in hospital later. In a perceptive article entitled 'Dark Warning', the *Manchester Guardian* observed that Pakistan was exhibiting 'symptoms of parliamentary government in degeneration... Pakistan has no obvious de Gaulle; whether it has a Col. Nasser or a Brig. Kassem [of Iraq] may yet be revealed.'[1]

Less than two weeks later, on 7 October, President Iskander Mirza abrogated the constitution, declared martial law throughout Pakistan, and appointed the army chief, Muhammad Ayub Khan, as Chief Martial Law Administrator and Supreme Commander of all armed forces. On 27 October Ayub ousted Mirza and assumed undisputed control of the affairs of Pakistan.

IX. Improvement in Indo-US Relations

Just as Indian policy had originally driven the US to join hands with Pakistan, Indian policy for some time after the US-Pakistani link-up served to keep the US and Pakistan close together. The more vehemently Nehru promoted *panchsheel*, in partnership with Russia and China, as an alternative to the Western defence schemes, the greater need the Americans felt for holding on to Pakistan. Such clearly was the state of affairs until December 1956. In the first part of 1954 the correspondents of both the *Christian Science Monitor*[2] and the *Washington Post*[3] reported that in New Delhi there was a wide feeling that the United States rather than the Soviet Union might set off a third world war. Commenting on Nehru's remark on leaving Moscow in June 1955, that he was leaving behind a part of his heart, the *New York Times* wrote: 'We might be forgiven for thinking that he also left a part of his common sense behind.'[4] In September 1956 the New Delhi correspondent of the same newspaper summed up:

Unhappily the total effects of Indian foreign policy must be more pleasing to Moscow and Peiping than to Washington and London. ... India, by equating East with West, by underplaying totalitarian ruthlessness, by glossing over past records of aggression and by failing

[1] Quoted by *Dawn*, 27 Sept. 1958.
[2] 28 April 1954.
[3] 2 May 1954. Read into the Congressional Record by Senator Malone, *Congressional Record* (*vol. 100, part 7, p. 8829), 83rd Congress, 2nd Session*, 24 June 1954, Senate.
[4] 24 June 1955.

to alert Asia to Communist colonialism, has presented Asia with a distorted picture of the world. India, which fights the Communists at home, has helped to make them respectable abroad.[1]

The first tangible sign of a change for the better in Indo-US relations appeared during Nehru's visit to Washington in December 1956, in the wake of the Suez crisis. Two reasons appear to have brought a change of heart in Nehru. First, the second Indian Five-Year Plan, which had been launched earlier that year, called for a much higher expenditure in foreign exchange and therefore for increased foreign aid, because of its emphasis upon industrialization. Though India's foreign-exchange crisis did not become apparent to the outside world till 1957, Nehru, as the insider, had no doubt sensed the problem earlier. He had himself declared upon an earlier occasion that 'ultimately, foreign policy is the outcome of economic policy'.[2] Clearly, the time had come for India to take a softer line towards the US if she hoped for increased assistance from that source. That such thoughts were not far from his mind was apparent from what he said in the course of a TV and radio broadcast in Washington on 18 December 1956: 'We wish to learn from you and we plead for your friendship and your co-operation and sympathy in the great task that we have undertaken in our own country.'[3] This appealing statement was quite different in tone from the earlier arrogant utterances of the Indian Premier. Secondly, the US had come rather well out of the Suez and Hungarian crises, while the image of the Soviet Union was somewhat tarnished in Afro-Asian eyes because of her brutal suppression of the freedom movement in Hungary. 'During this period of anxiety and distress,' said Nehru, 'the United States has added greatly to its prestige by upholding the principles of the Charter of the United Nations.'[4] Contrary to his strongly expressed view at the Bandung Conference —that the Soviet Union was not an imperialist power—he now conceded, at a Washington press conference, that, if the term colonialism was used in the sense of exercising a dominating influence, the Soviet Union could be considered a colonial power, and gave the example of Hungary.[5]

By 1958 the sharp increase in US assistance to India had begun

[1] *New York Times*, 23 Sept. 1956.
[2] J. Nehru, *India's Foreign Policy*, p. 24.
[3] J. Nehru, *Speeches*, III, p. 50.
[4] ibid.
[5] *Hindu*, 20 Dec. 1956, quoted by M. S. Rajan, *India in World Affairs, 1954-56*, p. 44, footnote 4.

to produce a still more perceptible increase in Indian goodwill towards America. George V. Allen, Director of the US Information Agency and formerly Ambassador to India, giving evidence before the Senate Committee on Foreign Relations on 26 February 1958, stated that the Indian attitude was swinging back more favourably to the US.[1] During an Indian tour Averell Harriman reported that Indian leaders were finally aware of the menace of Communist China and that the expressions of friendliness which he had heard everywhere were 'a welcome contrast to the criticism and even suspicion that an American could expect to encounter a few years ago'.[2]

In marked contrast to his earlier bitter criticism of US-Pakistani treaties, Nehru readily accepted the American assurance that the US-Pakistan bilateral agreement of March 1959 was not directed against India and assured his Parliament that 'the people of the United States have nothing but goodwill for us and that they will not be parties to any agreements . . . which may threaten the security of India'.[3]

In November the *New York Times* correspondent from New Delhi reported that not since the time when Roosevelt had pleaded with Britain for Indian freedom had Indians felt as friendly towards the United States as they did 'today'. Referring to President Eisenhower's forthcoming visit to India, the dispatch observed that Eisenhower 'appears to be filling the seat that Premier Chou En-lai of Communist China vacated'.[4]

Eisenhower assured the Indian Parliament that US armed forces served not only America but also 'those of our friends and allies who, like us, have perceived the danger [of an alien philosophy backed by great military strength]'.[5] At a civic reception of unprecedented size, Nehru profusely complimented Eisenhower for raising the banner of peace in the world and told him that 'India has given you her most valuable thing—a part of her heart'.[6] He called Eisenhower's visit 'a blessing for India and the world'.[7] Not long afterwards, when Khrushchev came to Delhi, 'there was none

---

[1] *Review of Foreign Policy, 1958, Hearings Before Senate Committee on Foreign Relations*, 26 Feb. 1958, p. 236.
[2] *New York Times*, 26 Feb. 1959.
[3] J. Nehru, *Speeches*, IV, p. 290.
[4] *New York Times*, 8 Nov. 1959.
[5] Address to Indian Parliament on 10 Dec. 1959; *USDSB*, 11 Jan. 1960.
[6] J. Nehru, *India's Foreign Policy*, p. 601.
[7] *Economist*, 19 Dec. 1959.

of the near hysterical cheering and the surging through police lines that greeted President Eisenhower'.[1]

With the installation of John F. Kennedy as President of the United States in January 1961, the climate for an Indo-US *rapprochement* became more favourable than ever. India placed an army brigade at the disposal of the UN for services in the Congo. Many Africans considered this an act of 'neo-colonialism' and the *Hindu* observed that 'India is becoming the rallying banner for the moderates among Afro-Asians in the UN'.[2]

Contrary to his oft-expressed earlier view, that the critical issue of the day in Asia was colonialism, Nehru, at the Belgrade conference of non-aligned nations in September 1961, chided his colleagues for their obsession with imperialism, which he thought was on the way out, and exhorted them to concern themselves with the larger issue of world peace. In the same speech he said that the danger of war had been enhanced by the decision of the Soviet Government to start nuclear tests,[3] and blamed the Berlin wall for the current tension.[4] After the Belgrade conference, Walt Rostow was able to assure President John F. Kennedy that unaligned countries, in their position on international issues, did take into account where the aid came from.[5]

India's invasion of Goa in December 1961 shocked Americans, but they considered India too important a country to be alienated. During a Congress Committee hearing the question was raised whether India's takeover of Goa had represented an act of aggression and, thus, a violation of the Mutual Security Treaty under which certain war material had been made over to India. The official finding was that: 'India's use of armed force in the Portuguese territories of Goa, Damao, and Diu beginning on December 18, 1961, is considered by the United States to be a violation of that assurance even though the Indian Government has stated that its use of force in Goa did not constitute aggression.'[6] But it was added lightly that 'the best hope for responding to this improper use of force lay in American initiatives at the United Nations'.[7]

---

[1] *New York Times*, 20 Feb. 1960.
[2] *Hindu*, 5 March 1961, quoted by Ajoy Ghosh, *Articles and Speeches*, p. 187.
[3] J. Nehru, *Speeches*, IV, p. 363.
[4] ibid.
[5] Arthur M. Schlesinger, Jr., *A Thousand Days*, p. 521.
[6] *Foreign Assistance Act of 1962, Hearings Before Committee On Foreign Affairs, House of Representatives, 87th Congress, 2nd Session, Part IV*, 5 Apr. 1962. p. 769.
[7] ibid.

X. Ayub Tries to Revitalize the US-Pakistani Alliance

There were two reasons why Ayub exerted himself to save Pakistan's fading alliance with the USA. First, having been one of the originators of that special relationship, he was naturally reluctant to see it fail. Secondly, as the person directly responsible for the safety of Pakistan from external danger, he could not disregard the connection between her security and the receipt of military assistance from America. Both because he was temperamentally not given to mincing words, and because he was a proven friend of the USA, he could be bluntly critical of Americans, but his voice was not that of a destructive critic but of a friend anxious to improve the deteriorating partnership. Alongside his expressions of unhappiness, therefore, we also find professions of friendship for the USA and assurances that, in the hour of need, Pakistan would not be found waiting. Circumstances over which he had no control, however, were working against Ayub. The preference in the receipt of US economic aid which India had begun to enjoy before Ayub took over was never reversed, and in October 1962 the USA also initiated a programme of military assistance to India, disregarding Pakistan's protestations that such aid be made conditional upon a settlement of the Kashmir dispute. Having failed in her efforts to persuade the United States to differentiate between a neutral and an ally, it was now only a question of time for Pakistan herself to assume, in all but name, the same uncommitted position in world affairs which seemed to have served India so well over the years.

Before getting arms from the USA, Pakistan militarily was practically at the mercy of India, but early in January 1957 Ayub could declare: 'We are no more short of men and material. . . . If we are to hit a target today, it will not be the same tomorrow.'[1] While, therefore, there was a growing discontentment in Pakistan at public level with American policy, Ayub, as Commander-in-Chief of the army, felt that alliance with America was definitely to Pakistan's advantage. After a four-week official tour of the USA, in May 1958, Ayub stated that several important problems regarding military aid to Pakistan had been solved during his 'heart to heart' discussions with United States officials in Washington and he felt 'fully satisfied' with the results of his discussions there.[2] On 13 September 1958 he said, 'The Pakistani Army today is the sharpest instrument

---

[1] *Dawn*, 31 Jan. 1957, quoted by Aslam Siddiqi, *Pakistan Seeks Security*, p. 118.
[2] *Dawn*, 24 May 1958.

of peace or war and the greatest deterrent against aggression.'[1]

When the army, under Ayub, first assumed power, many Americans expressed concern that democracy had been set back in Pakistan. It was believed that Pakistan was maintaining a military establishment beyond her capacity and that her economy generally was in poor shape. During the Mutual Security Act Committee hearings in April, May, and June 1959, several legislators and witnesses questioned the wisdom of the US military programme in Pakistan. Prominent among them were Bowles, Morse, Gore, Church, Harriman, and Fulbright.

By this time Ayub had consolidated his position and had begun to earn praise both at home and abroad for his wide-ranging programme of reforms. Americans had also not failed to notice that he had perceived the Chinese threat from the north and had realistically suggested that India and Pakistan should forget their mutual differences and join hands in the defence of the subcontinent. On 22 June 1959 he issued a public rejoinder to the criticism that Pakistan was maintaining forces in excess of her requirements. He argued that, besides having to defend East Pakistan, Pakistani forces had to defend 1,400 miles of a 'very sensitive frontier on the north-west', which was also India's frontier. True, it was causing a lot of expense but Pakistan was a victim of circumstances. She had repeatedly offered to settle her differences with India and to defend the subcontinent jointly with India, but India had not appreciated the wisdom of such a gesture. He declared further: 'I would like our friends to understand very clearly that they shall find us dependable and trustworthy but, at the same time, if they think that they can lead us to confused thinking against the hard facts of life, then we just cannot oblige.'[2]

President Eisenhower's visit to Pakistan in December 1959 brought to the surface the wealth of basic goodwill towards the USA that still existed in Pakistan. The *New York Times* called the massive and emotional welcome Karachi extended to the American President 'extraordinary'. As an almost direct reply to those who criticized the size of Pakistan's defence forces, the communiqué of the two Presidents 'recognized the heavy financial burden placed upon Pakistan in its efforts to undertake substantial development projects and at the same time to maintain armed forces consonant with its national security'.[3]

[1] ibid., 19 Sept. 1958.   [2] M. Ayub Khan, *Speeches*, I, pp. 119-20.
[3] *Pakistan Horizon*, 1st Quarter 1960.

From Pakistan Eisenhower flew to India, and Pakistanis hoped he would press India to settle the issue of Kashmir. Recalling his visit to India some years later, Eisenhower said that he had found Ayub ready to negotiate but the Indians would not yield an inch. 'I found this distressing,' he commented, 'but I did get a promise from both to go slowly and not start a war.'[1]

Many Pakistanis felt disappointed that Eisenhower had not been able to influence India to agree to a resolution of the Kashmir dispute,[2] but Pakistani policy remained that of a faithful ally of the USA. In an article he contributed to *Foreign Affairs*[3] Ayub wrote: 'Pakistan has openly and unequivocally cast its lot with the West, and unlike several other countries around us, we have shut ourselves off almost completely from the possibility of any major assistance from the Communist bloc. We do not believe in hunting with the hound and running with the hare.'

Consequently, when the U-2 affair boiled up, Pakistan, as related elsewhere, stood up to Soviet threats. But alongside the wish that the Pakistani-US alliance should endure, there remained the corroding realization that India continued to be America's favourite land. American aid to India was not affected despite her refusal to heed Eisenhower's advice for a Kashmir settlement. As a matter of fact, on his return from India, Eisenhower, in his State of the Union message, expressed special concern for the progress of un-committed nations. *Time Magazine* observed that 'the year 1960 may come to be known as the year neutralism became respectable'.[4] Secretary Dulles, who consistently upheld the American alliance system, had died in May 1959, and it appeared that the era which bore his stamp was rapidly coming to a close after his disappearance from the world stage.

The U-2 incident thus occurred at a time when US-Pakistani relations were on a see-saw and Pakistanis had begun to visualize the day when it would be to their greater advantage to be friendly not only with America but also with Russia and China. The U-2 incident forced them to think even more intensely whether alliance with America was worth the physical risk it entailed in the form of Russian rockets. Originally, Pakistanis had held that ideologically as well as geographically America was a more natural friend of

---

[1] *Dawn*, 15 Oct. 1965.
[2] See, for example, editorial in *Dawn*, 23 Dec. 1959.
[3] July 1960.
[4] 24 Oct. 1960.

Pakistan than the Soviet Union or China. We have already explained the ideological aspect and it need not be recapitulated here. Geographically, the preference for America stemmed from the belief that Russia and China, as Pakistan's immediate neighbours, were likely to expand southwards, while distant America would be interested only in preventing an augmentation in Soviet and Chinese strength and would, therefore, come to the aid of the victims of the Communist assault. As a result of the jolt from the U-2 episode, 'Pakistanis suddenly seemed to become aware of three factors: that such incidents as the U-2 flight could touch off a war, that Pakistan could be a prime target and that the Soviet Union nearly touches Pakistan's northern border while the United States, her ally, is 9,000 miles away.'[1]

Continuing criticism in the United States of military aid to Pakistan now brought a sharp rejoinder from Ayub. He declared in June that Pakistanis had begun to doubt that the governmental machinery of the United States was attuned to the requirements of the nuclear age. This machinery 'appears cumbersome, sluggish, and a clumsy juggernaut'. He observed further that he saw no reason why Pakistan could not 'do business' with the Soviet Union.[2]

Meanwhile, Ayub's efforts at home for the first time brought Pakistan greater praise than India from an authoritative American source. A special study mission to Asia reported that Pakistan was undergoing 'dramatic transformation' in her political, economic, and social strata under 'dynamic leadership' while in India 'tremendous problems remain'.[3]

Though professions of solidarity with the United States continued, and in the Laotian crisis of December 1960 Ayub declared that, as a SEATO member, Pakistan was willing to contribute troops, Pakistani leadership moved also to 'do business' with Russia and China. Foreign Minister Qadir disclosed in January 1961 that talks with China to demarcate the border had been going on smoothly and added that 'Pakistan had very cordial relations with China'. About the talks on oil exploration with Russia he said that, as the Western companies had not succeeded in striking oil in Pakistan, there was no harm in allowing Russians to try their hand.[4] *Dawn* commented:

---

[1] *New York Times*, 4 July 1960.
[2] ibid., 27 June 1960.
[3] *Report of Special Study Mission to Asia: House Report 1386, 86th Congress, 2nd Session*, Washington, 1960, pp. 9–10.
[4] *Dawn*, 16 Jan. 1961.

'We are happy to find that the wind of change has begun to blow, though ever so gently, in the wake of the sighs of disenchantment.'[1]

Another event which had added to Pakistani apprehensions about the future of their ties with the USA was the success, at the Presidential polls, of Senator John F. Kennedy, an ardent supporter of India. What specially roused Pakistani anxiety was that he not only wanted 'India to win that race with China' but he also wanted 'India to be a free and thriving leader of Asia'.[2] He had also stated that American friendship should not be equated with military alliances or 'voting the Western ticket'.[3] Not realizing that he was destined to increase American intervention in Vietnam,[4] he said further that 'the Middle East and Asia were not the areas that Mr. Dulles was most successful in'; also that the concept of the Baghdad Pact was one of the unhappy monuments to Mr. Dulles in the Middle East.[5] Pakistan, the Senator considered, was already 'more nearly' receiving the amount of aid she could effectively absorb.[6] In his inaugural address Kennedy specifically pledged 'the loyalty of faithful friends' to 'those old allies whose cultural and spiritual origins we share'. This led *Dawn* to protest: 'We do not know what other countries who belong to the omitted category may have to say, but the people of Pakistan will not fail to notice the omission.'[7] The appointments of Chester Bowles as Under-Secretary of State and John Kenneth Galbraith, an adviser to President Kennedy, as Ambassador to India were read in Pakistan as visible signs of the new Administration's special concern for India.

[1] ibid., 19 Jan. 1961.

[2] John F. Kennedy, *The Strategy of Peace*, p. 143.

[3] ibid., p. 157.

[4] When Kennedy became President, there were about 600 American advisers in South Vietnam, but by the time of his death there were over 20,000 American troops in that country and Diem had just been killed in a coup. Schlesinger says Kennedy 'realized that Vietnam was his great failure in foreign policy'. Pierre Salinger, *With Kennedy*, pp. 319–20; Arthur M. Schlesinger, Jr., *A Thousand Days*, p. 997. In his State of the Union message on 11 January 1962, Kennedy declared: 'The systematic aggression now bleeding that country is not a "war of liberation", for Vietnam is already free. It is a war of attempted subjugation—and it will be resisted.'

[5] J. F. Kennedy, *The Strategy of Peace*, p. 219.

[6] ibid., p. 154.

[7] *Dawn*, 22 Jan. 1961. Kennedy's statement brings to mind Henry A. Kissinger's observation that 'in neither SEATO nor the Baghdad Pact are we associated with partners with whom we share the degree of common purpose conferred by the cultural heritage which unites us with our European allies'. Henry A. Kissinger, *Nuclear Weapons and Foreign Policy*, p. 239. Kissinger's remark is factually unimpeachable but if the United States, having become the world's foremost power, has developed world-wide interests, how is she to avoid dealing with friends and foes of diverse cultures?

On 7 March 1961 the White House announced that President Ayub had accepted President Kennedy's invitation to visit the United States in November. In the meantime a storm of protest arose in Pakistan when Vice-President Lyndon B. Johnson, after a visit to India and Pakistan, revealed at a press conference in Washington on 26 May that, at President Kennedy's request, he had asked Nehru 'to extend his leadership to other areas in Southeast Asia'.[1] As a Pakistani leader said, to tell Pakistanis that India would be their leader was the unkindest cut of all.

Americans had also irritated Ayub by questioning him about the use of American weapons in the skirmishes on the Pakistani-Afghan border. 'United States should be mindful of the fact', he responded, 'that, if our territory was violated, we would spend our time dealing with the enemy rather than in putting American weapons in cotton wool.'[2] What had specially irked the Pakistani President was the fact that no one had criticized the Afghans who had freely used Soviet-supplied arms in the same fighting.

A report from Washington that the US was contemplating the grant of military aid to neutrals increased Pakistani chagrin. At this stage Washington concluded that a personal meeting between Presidents Ayub and Kennedy was essential if the progressive deterioration of US-Pakistani relations was to be arrested. On 19 June it was announced that Ayub's visit to Washington had been advanced from November to 11 July. On his way to Washington Ayub warned, in a TV interview in London, that if India became too powerful her smaller Asian neighbours would have to seek China's protection and that China would respond favourably to such a move.[3]

By the time Ayub arrived in Washington, the youthful American President had had some educative brushes with the hard realities of world politics. The Cuban missile crisis, in which he was to win his international spurs, was still more than a year off. But he had experienced the Bay of Pigs disaster in April, and a 'somber' two-day meeting with Khrushchev in Vienna in the first week of June. The Berlin crisis and the civil war in Laos were continuing. With regard to Laos, he had already declared in Dullesian terms that 'the security of all Southeast Asia will be endangered if Laos loses its neutral independence. . . . I know that every American will want his

[1] *Dawn*, 29 May 1961.
[2] *New York Times*, 30 May 1961.
[3] M. Ayub Khan, *Speeches*, IV, p. 7.

country to honour its obligations to the point that freedom and the security of the free world and ourselves may be achieved.'[1] The American military advisers had been renamed Military Assistance and Advisory Group, authorized 'to put on uniforms and accompany the Laotian troops'.[2]

Not surprisingly, therefore, in his welcome speech Kennedy assured Ayub that Americans appreciated the value of the constancy of friends and appreciatively recalled that Pakistan had been one of the first to offer assistance in the Korean War.[3] At a dinner hosted by Ayub, Kennedy said that Ayub had come to the USA at a time of hazards and that the people of the United States valued friendship in hard times.[4] In a forthright address to a joint session of Congress Ayub declared that, in case of real trouble, the only people in Asia who would stand beside America were the people of Pakistan, 'provided you are also prepared to stand by them'.[5]

The Ayub–Kennedy joint communiqué stated that President Kennedy had affirmed the desire of the United States to see a satisfactory solution of the Kashmir issue and that United States military assistance to Pakistan was being 'extended' to assist that nation to maintain forces for the preservation of her security.[6] During a Meet The Press programme, Ayub disclosed that Kennedy had agreed to raise the question of Kashmir with Nehru and to impress upon him the necessity of its solution.[7]

One of Pakistan's complaints against the USA, when the latter rendered military aid to India in October 1962, was that she had resiled from her undertaking to consult Pakistan before initiating such assistance. That such an assurance was given during Ayub's visit to Washington is clear from the record. *Dawn's* representative reported from Washington that, in his very first meeting with Kennedy, Ayub was believed to have left Kennedy and his advisers in no doubt as to how Pakistan felt about the proposal to amend the existing legislation in order to supply American armaments to India.[8] Answering a question on the subject at the National Press Club in Washington, Ayub said that US arms aid to India

[1] Arthur M. Schlesinger, Jr., *A Thousand Days,* p. 333.
[2] ibid., p. 336.
[3] *USDSB,* 7 Aug. 1961.
[4] *Dawn,* 15 July 1961.
[5] M. Ayub Khan, *Speeches,* IV, p. 30.
[6] *Pakistan Horizon,* 3rd Quarter 1961.
[7] Ayub Khan, *Speeches,* IV, p. 53.
[8] *Dawn,* 13 July 1961.

would put a tremendous strain on Pakistan's friendship with America.[1] On his return to Pakistan, Ayub told the press that the Kennedy Administration had assured Pakistan that military aid 'in the region' would not be given unless there was a very good reason and, further, that Pakistan would be consulted if any such aid was given.[2]

Though Ayub's trip to America had been an unqualified success at personal level, the Pakistan–US–India political equation had basically remained unaltered. A special study mission of the House Committee on Foreign Affairs, after a 27,000-mile trip to Asia and the Middle East between 24 October and 12 December 1961, noted 'a growing uncertainty about the vigor and direction of US leadership. Some even detected a latent neutralism among the Pakistanis.'[3] That India remained the top favourite of the USA brought forth the witticism from a 'highly placed' Pakistani that the United States used the same method in choosing friends as a Pakistani housewife: she thinks the bigger the fish the bigger the bargain.[4]

When the Kashmir case was revived by Pakistan in the Security Council in 1962, Pakistanis felt that Washington had not given them wholehearted support. Ayub said: 'Many people feel that the United States is very closely identified with India and, therefore, with aggressive Indian designs. If this goes on, I have no doubt, the smaller countries in this area will be forced to look for protection elsewhere.'[5] After a two-week tour of both wings of Pakistan, the *New York Times*' correspondent found that the United States position in Pakistan was becoming increasingly shaky.[6]

At about this time, the defeat of the right-wing forces in Laos aroused anxiety in neighbouring Thailand, and the USA promptly sent marines and ground forces to Thailand to bolster morale there. The eroded state of the Pakistani-US alliance was gleefully noted in Moscow by *International Affairs* which wrote: 'The Pakistan Government responded more than coldly to the [American] invitation to send troops to Thailand. The American request, the Karachi

[1] Ayub Khan, *Speeches*, IV, p. 36.
[2] *Dawn*, 20 July 1961; see also M. Ayub Khan, *Friends Not Masters*, p. 138.
[3] *Report of the Special Study Mission to the Far East, South Asia and the Middle East of the Committee on Foreign Affairs, House Report No. 1946, 87th Congress, 2nd Session*, Washington, D.C., 1962, p. 18.
[4] *Washington Evening Star*, 16 Jan. 1962, column by Constantine Brown, inserted by Senator Tower in *Congressional Record (vol. 108, pp. 345–6), 87th Congress, 2nd Session*, 17 Jan. 1962, Senate.
[5] *New York Times*, 11 May 1962.
[6] ibid., 13 May 1962.

correspondent of the British *Guardian* reported, has been met in Pakistan "with what looks like calculated indifference".[1]

In June 1962 martial law in Pakistan was lifted simultaneously with the inauguration of the National Assembly elected under the new Constitution. During his 'statement on foreign policy', Muhammad Ali Bogra, the newly appointed Foreign Minister, told Parliament that it did not follow from Pakistan's membership of military pacts 'that we would allow ourselves to be taken for granted'.[2]

[1] *International Affairs*, no. 6, 1962.
[2] *National Assembly of Pakistan Debates*, 27 June 1962, p. 591.

Part 3

Reappraisal of Foreign Policy
(1963 - July 1972)

13 The Aftermath of the Sino-Indian Border War

I. Indian Military Build-up with Anglo-American Assistance

As already stated, the immediate cause of the brief Sino-Indian Himalayan war was Prime Minister Nehru's command to the Indian Army to throw the Chinese out of NEFA. Nehru's injunction to the army was followed by Defence Minister Krishna Menon's brave declaration, on 14 October, that India was determined to push the Chinese out 'whether it takes one day, a hundred days, or a thousand days' and would fight 'to the last man, to the last gun' if attacked.[1]

Americans had already viewed the Indian 'forward defence policy' with favour. The Acting Chairman of the Senate Foreign Relations Committee, Sparkman, had stated in Washington in June 1962: 'We know right now that India is pressing very hard against Communist China ... I feel that we ought not to be discouraging India [by reducing US aid] at the very time that she is moving in the direction that we have been wanting her to move for a long time.'[2] When China routed the Indian forces in the Himalayas, the United States at last got the opportunity to further her long-cherished wish that India should stand up to China, and immediately initiated a programme of military assistance to India.

Though matters did not visibly move till after the heavier Chinese attacks in the latter part of October, President Ayub Khan has revealed that the US decision to furnish arms to India was arrived at early in October. On 2 October the Pakistani Ambassador to the US learned from a State Department official that Nehru had seen Ambassador Galbraith in New Delhi that morning and asked for US military assistance against China, and that Galbraith, on the authority of the US Government, had told Nehru that the United

---

[1] Quoted by A. G. Noorani, *Our Credulity and Negligence*, p. 90; *Asian Recorder*, 1962, p. 4910.
[2] *India News*, 2 July 1962.

States would supply arms to India and it was for Nehru to indicate the requirements. 'Obviously, the United States government had ignored two very important points, that their decision to give arms aid to India was arrived at without prior consultation with Pakistan; and it was communicated to India before it was communicated to Pakistan.' On the following day the Pakistani Ambassador was informed that a specific request for arms had been received from Nehru. He was asked to take the United States' word that US arms would not be used against Pakistan and was advised that Pakistan should make a gesture of goodwill towards India as this might lead to a satisfactory solution of the Kashmir problem.[1]

Six days after the Chinese had launched their 20 October offensive, Nehru addressed a general appeal for 'support and sympathy' to all Heads of Government in the world (except Portugal and South Africa), and averred that the real issue involved in the Sino-Indian conflict was 'whether the world will allow the principle of might is right to prevail in international relations'. He also claimed that India's struggle was directed 'to the elimination of deceit, dissimulation and force in international relations'.[2]

The first consignment of British military supplies arrived in India on 29 October in two Royal Air Force Britannias,[3] and on 3 November the first US arms shipment arrived in four planes which landed at Calcutta.[4] By 16 November the Indians were not only requesting the Americans for transport planes but, 'in further modification of the non-alignment policy', were also asking for pilots and crews to fly the aircraft.[5] Shortly afterwards the Indians began to plead for 'military association' with the US: they wanted the US Air Force to back them up so that their own could fly tactically without leaving the cities unprotected.[6] A squadron of United States C-130 transport planes, having arrived during November, threw a 'crucial air bridge' across the Himalayas from central India to Leh and flew fifteen to seventeen runs a day to the front, moving 150 to 180 tons of desperately needed supplies, ammunition, and equipment daily.[7]

---

[1] M. Ayub Khan, *Friends Not Masters*, p. 144–6.
[2] A. G. Noorani, *Our Credulity and Negligence*, p. 111.
[3] L. J. Kavic, *India's Quest for Security*, p. 182.
[4] J. K. Galbraith, *Ambassador's Journal*, p. 456.
[5] ibid., p. 481.
[6] ibid., p. 486. Galbraith also says that the Indians, at that time, yearned for the sight of American uniforms (p. 489).
[7] *New York Times*, 21 April and 5 July 1963.

In order to assess India's needs a high-powered American team headed by Averell Harriman arrived in India on 22 November. A similar British team led by Duncan Sandys, Secretary of State for Commonwealth Relations, reached Delhi two days later.

Though the fighting had by now ceased, the Western efforts to bolster up India militarily continued. President Kennedy and Prime Minister Harold Macmillan conferred at Nassau in December and decided that military assistance to India worth $120 million would be furnished on an 'emergency' basis by the US and the Commonwealth, in equal shares. The question of long-range assistance was kept under study, and meeting again at the end of June 1963, at Birch Grove House (Macmillan's home in Sussex), the two leaders declared that they 'were agreed on their policy of continuing to help India by providing further military aid to strengthen her defences against the threat of renewed Chinese Communist attack'.[1]

. American road engineers, and a United States Air Force airlift carrying road-building materials and equipment, helped Indians to build an all-weather highway from Srinagar to Leh, the capital of Ladakh, and to improve the airstrip at Leh. A joint defence training exercise, held in India by the Indian Air Force and the United States and British fighter squadrons, prepared 'the United States Air Force to come to India's aid if asked to do so'. Chester Bowles, Ambassador-Designate to India, said in a radio interview that the US was 'very anxious to help India' and the only question was 'the amount of military aid the Indians can absorb'.[2] On 8 April 1963 Indian Defence Minister Y. B. Chavan announced that it was proposed to double the strength of the army,[3] and early in 1964 a five-year defence plan was drawn up. The plan was expected to cost Rs.5,000 crores including foreign exchange worth Rs.680 crores.[4]

According to the *Economist* the Indian Government had secured, in May 1964, an offer of military aid from the US totalling £200 million over the coming five years. It also gave details of assistance from the USSR and the UK and commented that the build-up put India in a position to become, by Asian standards, a major military power. It would 'surely confirm the Chinese in their suspicion that Russia, India, and the Anglo-Americans have ganged up against

[1] For text of Birch Grove communiqué see *Pakistan Horizon*, 3rd Quarter, 1963.
[2] *Christian Science Monitor*, 28 May 1963.
[3] *Asian Recorder*, 1963, p. 5207.
[4] L. J. Kavic, *India's Quest for Security*, p. 193.

them. Pakistan's view must be even gloomier.' Besides other assistance, Russia had decided to bring India's supersonic MIG fighter strength to three squadrons and to speed up assistance for the manufacture of MIG fighters in India. Russia was also helping India to develop defensive missiles.[1]

By September 1965 United States economic aid to India exceeded $6 billion and to Pakistan amounted to about $3 billion. Military assistance to Pakistan came to $1.5 billion while India, out of the commitment for $200 million, had received military supplies worth $84.5 million.[2] Thus, while Pakistan had received more arms from the US, India, having received far more economic aid, had been able to shop for military hardware internationally to a much larger extent than her own resources would have permitted.

II. Pakistani Reaction to Arms Aid to India

Pakistani spokesmen attacked the grant of American arms to India on all the grounds Indians themselves had put forward when the US had decided to furnish military assistance to Pakistan, and, for good measure, added some more. It was complained, first, that Pakistan was given defence assistance in return for the obligations she had assumed as an ally of the United States, but India was getting it while she was still a professed neutral. Recalling Khrushchev's threat at the time of the U-2 incident, Foreign Minister Bhutto said, 'Khrushchev did not say that India will be annihilated. He said Peshawar would be annihilated.' Secondly, India was four times larger than Pakistan but had nonetheless pleaded that American arms to Pakistan were threatening her safety. How much more reason was there for Pakistan's concern, when India was being strengthened with American weapons? Thirdly, India's increased strength would encourage those elements in India who stood for a merger of Pakistan with India. Fourthly, the disparity of strength between the two countries would ultimately become so great that India would be in a position to achieve her objectives by simply overawing Pakistan with a show of force.

Pakistanis, however, were realistic enough not to urge an ab-

---

[1] *Economist*, 26 Sept. 1964. See also *Asian Recorder*, 1964, p. 6099, for Defence Minister Chavan's statement of 21 Sept. 1964, describing the results of his visits to the USA (May) and the USSR (Aug.–Sept.) to obtain assistance for India's five-year defence plan. For 'Arms: Who Supplied What?' see *Newsweek*, 20 Sept. 1965.

[2] Norman D. Palmer, 'India and Pakistan: The Major Recipients', *Current History*, Nov. 1965; Selig S. Harrison, 'America, India, and Pakistan', *Harper's Magazine*, July 1966.

solute ban on Western military aid to India. What they desired was
that the US and the UK should use the unique opportunity provided by the Sino-Indian confrontation to press India to accept a
reasonable solution of the Kashmir problem. Ayub wrote to Kennedy
on 2 January 1963: 'Only a speedy and just Kashmir settlement can
give us any assurance that the contemplated increase of India's
military power is not likely to be deployed against Pakistan in
future.'[1]

At the same time Ayub, initially, adopted a conciliatory attitude
towards India. Replying to Nehru's letter of 26 October, he assured
the Indian Premier that Pakistan was wedded to a policy of peace
with all neighbouring countries, 'especially India', and further
that Pakistanis were 'fully conscious of the great responsibility that
lies on your shoulders for the maintenance of peace especially
around this subcontinent'. He endorsed Nehru's plea that deceit
and force should be eliminated from international relations and
pointed out that Indo-Pakistani disputes could also be 'resolved
amicably should the Government of India decide to apply those
principles with sincerity and conviction'.[2] Ayub, further, conveyed
indications through the US and the UK that Pakistan would not do
anything to worsen India's military problems,[3] making it possible
for the Indians to switch troops from the Pakistani frontier to the
Chinese one.[4]

III. Indo-Pakistani Talks

Harriman and Sandys pointed out to Nehru that when it came to
longer-term military aid, 'the British and American peoples would
be unhappy to see that an appreciable part of the Indian army was
being deployed not for defence against China but for defence
against Pakistan.'[5]

Under concerted pressure from Harriman and Sandys, Nehru
agreed to make a new effort to settle the Kashmir dispute. An Ayub–
Nehru communiqué announced on 29 November 1962 that Indo-
Pakistani discussions would start soon 'with the object of reaching
an honourable and equitable settlement' of Kashmir and other

[1] M. Ayub Khan, *Friends Not Masters*, p. 150.
[2] The text of Ayub's reply to Nehru was published in *Pakistan Affairs*, 15 Nov.
1962, Embassy of Pakistan, Washington, D.C.
[3] *New York Times*, 10 Nov. 1962; J. K. Galbraith, *Ambassador's Journal*, p. 463.
[4] *Economist*, 4 Sept. 1965
[5] Sandys's report to the House of Commons on 3 Dec. 1962.

related matters.[1] Averell Harriman said in a radio and television programme that Kashmir 'is the most important single question before us, before the free world'.[2]

Altogether six rounds of talks were held at Minister's level. Pakistan was represented by Bhutto and India by Swaran Singh. The first session opened at Rawalpindi on 27 December and the last closed at New Delhi on 16 May 1963. At the end of the last meeting 'the two Ministers recorded with regret that no agreement could be reached on the settlement of the Kashmir dispute'.[3]

The most important rounds were the third, at which India put forward her proposal for resolving the Kashmir issue, and the last, at which Pakistan spelled out her stand. India's suggestion was simply a reiteration of the offer she had made on numerous previous occasions: that the existing cease-fire line should be recognized as the international frontier with some adjustments. This was summarily rejected by Pakistan. Pakistan offered to limit the plebiscite to the Valley and proposed that an impartial international agency hold control of the Valley for a period not exceeding fifteen months and conduct the plebiscite at the end of that period.[4] India, however, rejected this, and offered a simple no-war pact, which Pakistan had already stated many times could serve no useful purpose unless it laid down also a concrete method of settling disputes.

While the talks were in progress Indians made much of Sino-Pakistani negotiations for the settlement of the 300-mile-long undefined border between China's Sinkiang Province and that part of Kashmir which is under the control of Pakistan. They said the announcement, on the eve of the first round of the Kashmir talks, that China and Pakistan had reached agreement in principle on the location and alignment of the boundary, was 'most maladroit'.[5] When the border agreement was signed on 2 March 1963, Nehru alleged in Parliament that Sino-Pakistani moves had been 'timed to prejudice the joint talks on Kashmir'.[6] That Pakistan should have

[1] For text see *National Assembly of Pakistan Debates*, 1 Dec. 1962, p. 268.

[2] *Dawn*, 10 Dec. 1962.

[3] *Pakistan Horizon*, 2nd Quarter 1963.

[4] For a progress report on the six talks see Foreign Minister Bhutto's speech in the National Assembly of Pakistan on 17 July 1963. The *New York Times* (3 May 1963) reported that informally Ayub had indicated to Sandys that Pakistan would accept 'internationalization' of the Valley as an 'interim solution' for five to ten years. See also G. W. Choudhury, *Pakistan's Relations with India*, pp. 134-9.

[5] *Christian Science Monitor*, 29 Dec. 1962.

[6] J. Nehru, *Speeches*, IV, p. 307.

deliberately done anything that would adversely affect the Indo-Pakistani negotiations over Kashmir was an extraordinary statement on the face of it, for it was well known that it was India who favoured the *status quo* in Kashmir and Pakistan who was eager for a change: if the talks were to fail India, not Pakistan, would get her wish. The Sino-Pakistani border talks, in fact, had been planned long before the outbreak of the Sino-Indian border war.[1] Foreign Minister Bhutto explained that Pakistan could not very well freeze all other matters concerning her foreign policy because of the talks with India about Kashmir.[2] The *Manchester Guardian Weekly* incisively observed:

The Pakistanis may be excused for thinking that a bird in the hand is worth two in the bush. They have got very little from talks with India over the past decade or so. . . . There is still no evidence that India is ready to concede their minimum demand. Certainly the agreement with China may be used by India as a justification if the negotiations fail. But the Indian Government has never been at a loss for such justifications in the past.[3]

In fact, Ayub was notably flexible in his approach. Before the Kashmir talks began he stated publicly that Pakistan would be prepared to consider a solution other than plebiscite if Nehru had one in mind.[4] He also wrote to Harold Macmillan that Pakistan's attitude would not be rigid and that the Pakistani delegation would be guided by whether a solution was likely to be acceptable to the people of Kashmir, whether it safeguarded the vital interests of Pakistan, and whether it met the legitimate claims of India.[5] It was Nehru's implacability that had doomed the Indo-Pakistani negotiations on Kashmir to failure from the very beginning. The ink was barely dry on his joint statement with Ayub, that India and Pakistan would shortly make fresh efforts to settle the Kashmir dispute, when he publicly declared that 'anything which involved an upset of the present arrangement would be very harmful to the people of Kashmir as well as to the future relations of India and Pakistan'.[6] At Sandys's insistence he issued a statement on 1 December that there had 'never been any question of pre-conditions or of

[1] For details see A New Relationship with China in this chapter.
[2] *Dawn*, 23 Feb. 1963.
[3] 7 March 1963.
[4] *Asian Recorder*, 1963, p. 5022.
[5] M. Ayub Khan, *Friends Not Masters*, p. 151.
[6] In Lok Sabha on 30 Nov. 1962, J. Nehru, *Speeches*, IV, p. 302.

any restrictions' on the scope of the impending talks.[1] But he firmly continued to hold the position that the only permanent solution acceptable to India would be the recognition of the cease-fire line as the border between Pakistan and India. In a revealing interview with Selig S. Harrison of the *Washington Post*,[2] more than a week before the first round of talks opened, he said that, while India was prepared for 'adjustments in the present cease-fire line, which is not a very sensible one, we are persuaded that any major change would be the ruin of the Vale'. He also indicated that he did not attach much importance to statements of Western spokesmen linking military aid against China with a Kashmir settlement, and expressed the belief that even if a Kashmir settlement was not reached it would not 'broadly' affect the Western military aid programme. In the same interview he once more revealed what he really believed to be the final solution of all Indo-Pakistani differences: 'Confederation remains our ultimate goal though if we say it, they are alarmed and say we want to swallow them up.'

On 31 December Nehru reverted to his favourite theme, that the basic issue involved in the Kashmir dispute was that 'Pakistan should vacate aggression',[3] and in an article in *Foreign Affairs* he made the amazing assertion that the Indo-Pakistani discussions on Kashmir had 'no direct bearing on the problems we face with regard to China'.[4] He also began to exploit a new argument for holding on to the Kashmir Valley: 'Srinagar offers the only way to reach Ladakh and all of our campaigns against China depend on the Kashmir Valley.'[5] The Washington correspondent of the *Times of India*, H. R. Vohra, propagated his Prime Minister's view in a letter to the *Washington Post*: 'If India gives up the valley, we could not be interested in the defense of Ladakh which, in any case, is approachable only through the valley. Pakistan by herself could not defend Ladakh. It would, therefore, become a US responsibility under her alliances with Pakistan.' Edward G. Harris answered: 'Kashmir should be left to India, in Mr. Vohra's view, since Pakistan could not defend it against China. In the light of the past few months, neither

---

[1] *Asian Recorder*, 1962, p. 4958. See also Sandys's report to the House of Commons, on 3 Dec. 1962.

[2] *Washington Post*, 19 Dec. 1962.

[3] *Asian Recorder*, 1963, p. 5016.

[4] J. Nehru, 'Changing India', *Foreign Affairs*, April 1963.

[5] *Washington Post*, 19 Dec. 1962.

can India. In either case, the United States will be left holding the bag.'[1]

Pakistanis felt quite despondent after the fifth round of the Kashmir talks but agreed to a sixth round, hoping that the American and British delegates, who were due in Karachi at the beginning of May to attend a CENTO meeting, might be able to use their influence with India to save the situation. After the CENTO meeting, Secretaries Rusk and Sandys went over to Delhi. They were joined there by Lord Mountbatten, now Chief of the UK General Staff, whose friendship with Nehru was well known. Together they worked hard on Nehru, and on 6 May it was announced in Delhi that the Indian Government had agreed to 'low key mediation' or 'good offices' by an American or a Briton in the Kashmir dispute. The *New York Times* correspondent in his dispatch from New Delhi pointed out, however, that the acceptance of mediation by India 'in no way implies a fundamental change in the Indian claim to the disputed State of Jammu and Kashmir. . . . But it has given Mr. Rusk something to take home from his trip. . . . Perhaps most important, it will give the Kennedy Administration a better position in its efforts to get an arms aid appropriation for India from Congress this summer, because India has made a concession.'[2]

The proposal for mediation dragged on for some time after the final session of the Kashmir discussions had ended inconclusively. Ultimately it came to naught because Pakistan was unable to obtain any assurance that the effort would be purposeful and not just one more exercise in futility. While India desired the mediator to survey the entire gamut of Indo-Pakistani differences, Pakistan thought he should concentrate his efforts upon the crucial problem of Kashmir. Pakistan also required that the terms of reference for the mediator should mention the United Nations resolutions on Kashmir, that the mediator must report his recommendations to the parties within a specified time, that the parties must undertake to abide by the mediator's proposals, and that the Western long-term military aid to India be frozen while the mediation was in progress;[3] but none of these stipulations was acceptable to India.

On 15 June Nehru said, at a press conference, that mediation

[1] *Washington Post*, 8 and 17 Jan. 1963.
[2] *New York Times*, 7 May 1963.
[3] *New York Times* and *Christian Science Monitor*, 17 May 1963; *Statesman*, 10 July 1963; *Hindustan Times*, 8 Aug. 1963; *The Times*, 12 Aug. 1963; J. K. Galbraith, *Ambassador's Journal*, p. 574.

was not a suitable course.[1] In his statement in the Lok Sabha on 13 August he alleged that Pakistan had made 'impossible demands' in regard to mediation and, referring to India's offer of a settlement by making adjustments in the cease-fire line, declared that the 'concessions' which India had offered to Pakistan 'must be treated as withdrawn'.[2]

Though Nehru had blamed Pakistan for the failure of all the efforts to obtain a Kashmir settlement, it was not difficult to see who was really responsible for the breakdown. The *Economist* had noted quite early that India had agreed to talk to Pakistan 'only as a gesture to the United States and Britain' from whom she was getting vital supplies.[3] Ambassador Galbraith says, 'Carefully I persuaded everybody [in India] on the idea of a concession in the Valley. Then I saw Nehru and he turned me down flat. Then I saw him a second time and he turned me down even flatter.'[4] Obviously it was Nehru, with his deep-seated emotional attachment to Kashmir as his ancestral home, who, as usual, had proved to be the main obstacle to any reasonable accommodation. The *Daily Telegraph* observed that the talks had failed 'because India, the party in possession of everything that matters, has felt strong enough to resist the concession that any solution would require'.[5]

IV. American and British Assurances to Pakistan

Besides striving for a settlement of the Kashmir issue, the US and the UK tried to reassure Pakistan in two other ways. In the first place they extracted a definite undertaking from India that the arms supplied by them would be used only against China. Secondly, US spokesmen stated that their country was giving only such weapons to India as would be useful for fighting the Chinese in the mountains and would not affect the balance of power between India and Pakistan in the plains.

India's undertaking in respect of US arms was, in fact, twofold. First, having received assistance under the Mutual Security Act, she was under the usual obligation not to use the arms in aggression against another country. Consequently the US assured Pakistan, in precisely the same terms in which she had earlier assured India,

---

[1] *New York Times,* 16 June 1963.
[2] *Asian Recorder,* 1963, p. 5405.
[3] *Economist,* 8 Dec. 1962.
[4] *Ambassador's Journal,* p. 564; also p. 512.
[5] *Daily Telegraph,* 16 May 1963, quoted by Sharif al-Mujahid, 'India–Pakistan Relations', *Foreign Policy of Pakistan* by L. A. Sherwani and others, p. 41, footnote 1.

that 'if our assistance to India should be misused and directed against another country in aggression, the United States would undertake immediately, in accordance with constitutional authority, appropriate action both within and without the United Nations to thwart such aggression'.[1] But this was not all. Secondly—and here the US went one step further than she had gone with Pakistan—she obtained a clear undertaking from India that American arms would be employed only against China. This was done by an exchange of notes between the State Department and the Indian Ambassador to the United States. The American note stated that US assistance would be furnished to India 'for the purpose of defense against the outright Chinese aggression', on the understanding that India would offer facilities to representatives of the US Government to observe the use of the articles supplied and return those which were no longer needed for the purpose for which they had been made available. The Indian Ambassador confirmed that the understandings in the American note were correct.[2] An almost identical agreement was made between the UK and India.[3]

At his news conference on 20 November 1962, President Kennedy confirmed that 'all' American aid to India was for the purpose of defeating Chinese Communist subversion.[4] The Deputy Assistant Secretary of Defense, William P. Bundy, explained at a Committee hearing that the US–India agreement 'specified [that] the assistance was solely to resist Chinese Communist aggression' and that the purpose was more specifically worded than in the agreement with Pakistan and other countries.[5]

Pakistan was not impressed by the United States' assurance that, if India committed aggression against Pakistan, the US would act to halt the attack. Foreign Minister Bhutto said it was not easy to determine whether the first shot was fired in aggression or self-defence. Moreover, what was the good of determining the aggressor 'after there is a complete destruction of our homes and cities and villages'?[6] During a Committee hearing, Representative William S. Broomfield asked what would happen if India or Pakistan did not live up to the terms of the arms agreement with the US. General

[1] USDSB, 3 Dec. 1962.
[2] For texts see USDSB, 3 Dec. 1962.
[3] Asian Recorder, 1962, p. 4944.
[4] USDSB, 10 Dec. 1962.
[5] Foreign Assistance Act of 1963, Hearings on H.R. 5490 before the House Committee on Foreign Affairs, 88th Congress, 1st Session, 9 May 1963, p. 693.
[6] National Assembly of Pakistan Debates, 17 July 1963, pp. 1663-4.

Stephen O. Fuqua, Jr., a Director in the Office of the Assistant Secretary of Defense for International Security Affairs, replied, 'We reserve the right to pull the material out.' But, when asked whether this had ever been done, he had to reply in the negative. Realistically anticipating what really happened later, William P. Bundy thought that the sanction which was most likely to be invoked against India and Pakistan if they used the material improperly was 'ceasing of all future assistance'.[1]

On the question of type of weapons being supplied by the US to India, a typical statement was that of Assistant Secretary Phillips Talbot, at one of the Committee hearings. He said America had been 'very much concerned' with how to work out a programme which would strengthen India's defence capacity against China without being a concern to Pakistan. Six mountain divisions of the Indian Army would be equipped with items which were portable. There were no heavy tanks, for example, and no assistance which would strengthen India in any move across the plains to West Pakistan. However, when it was pointed out that the weapons being given to India included artillery, mortars, and all types of equipment which 'could be pointed to the west just as easily as they could be to the north', Talbot could do no more than state in general terms that such an act on the part of India 'would be a total violation of the commitments that India has given to us and the reactions to that that we would have both within the UN and outside I think would be rapidly effective'.[2]

It had become evident quite early in the game that the USA and UK would not play their strongest card against India, which was to serve definite notice that military assistance would be conditional on a settlement of the Kashmir dispute. On 28 December 1962 Ambassador Galbraith told a press conference in New Delhi that American assistance was 'in no way contingent on an India–Pakistan agreement on the Kashmir problem. . . . When our friends are in trouble, we are not doing business that way.'[3] Asked at his news conference on 8 March 1963 whether further military aid to India would be conditional on the success of the Indo-Pakistani negotiations on Kashmir, Secretary Rusk said, 'I would not in any sense

[1] *Foreign Assistance Act of 1963, Hearings on H.R. 5490 before the House Committee on Foreign Affairs, 88th Congress, 1st Session,* 13 May 1963, p. 716.

[2] *Foreign Operations Appropriations for 1964, Hearings Before a Sub-Committee of the House Committee on Appropriations, 88th Congress, 1st Session,* 17 July 1963, pp. 1172, 1174.

[3] Russell Brines, *The Indo-Pakistani Conflict*, p. 210.

qualify our aid purposes by this word "condition".[1] Prime Minister Macmillan similarly stated on 7 May that the provision of military equipment to India was not linked to a settlement of the Kashmir dispute.[2]

America and Britain evidently considered it sufficient that India was at last treating China as an enemy instead of a close friend and had generally made her foreign policy more favourable to them.

During the Chinese assault on India's frontier Nehru declared that European imperialism had abated but 'the People's Government of China are now following the course of aggression and imperialist expansion'.[3] He also said a few days later: 'There is no non-alignment vis-à-vis China. There is no panchsheel viv-à-vis China.'[4] In April 1963 he wrote in his article in Foreign Affairs that Indo-American relations had seldom been 'as close and cordial as they are now'. Chester Bowles, on the eve of his departure for India to serve there as Ambassador once more, said in New York: 'The Chinese attack on India and the Sino-Soviet dispute mark a sea-change in history that may well offer the United States a new possibility to use our power and influence on behalf of free societies in Asia.'[5] During his visit to the US, President Radhakrishnan affirmed, jointly with Kennedy, that their 'two countries share a mutual defensive concern to thwart the designs of Chinese aggression against the subcontinent'.[6]

However, the Pakistani view, that Western arms assistance to India be conditional on a Kashmir agreement, was not without support in the US. Ambassador Galbraith suggested that Indians be forced 'to make a generous Kashmir offer by conditioning a large aid offer upon it', but President Kennedy thought the idea would not work.[7] A Republican Party task force on Far Eastern Policy commented that, when China attacked the Indian border in October 1962, the US hastily rushed military aid to India instead of utilizing the occasion 'to exert maximum influence' on India to come to an agreement with America's ally, Pakistan.[8] But the

---

[1] USDSB, 25 March 1963.
[2] Asian Recorder, 1963, p. 5317.
[3] J. Nehru, Speeches, IV, p. 231.
[4] A. G. Noorani, Our Credulity and Negligence, p. 104.
[5] N. D. Palmer, South Asia and United States Policy, p. 315.
[6] USDSB, 24 June 1963.
[7] T. C. Sorenson, Kennedy, p. 664; see also J. K. Galbraith, Ambassador's Journal, p. 471.
[8] Critical Issues, Paper No. 10, 'The US Position in the Far East', Critical Issues Council, 1964.

Kennedy Administration went no further with India than making verbal representations to her. Instead of applying sanctions, to make the pressure for a Kashmir settlement really meaningful, they took the easier course of asking Pakistan to assure Nehru that she would take no action on the frontiers to alarm India.[1]

V. The End of an Era

On the home front President Ayub Khan summoned the National Assembly to meet in an emergency session on 21 November 1962 and was reported to have told the House in a secret session that Pakistan was faced with two dangers, Hindu imperialism and international Communism, of which the former was more pressing. He ruled out extreme action and stated that Pakistan needed friends, however imperfect they might be. The Kashmir problem could be solved either by war or by negotiation, and he indicated that he preferred a peaceful course.[2]

Foreign Minister Bogra, who spoke in the open session on 22 November, said there could be no eternal friends nor could there be eternal enemies. The only thing eternal was national interest. During the debate the general mood of the members was one of anger towards Pakistan's Western allies and of frustration that Pakistan was friendless and isolated. Also, almost everyone, including the official spokesmen, had a good word for China.

When a member suggested that, even if Pakistan was able to get Kashmir, she should not be a party to any aggression by India on China, Bhutto, who was deputizing for Foreign Minister Bogra, intervened and affirmed: 'We have declared that our friendship with China is unconditional.'[3] On the following day Bhutto gave the reason why Pakistan should hold China in special esteem: 'We admire and salute the People's Republic of China for not having taken a hostile stand on Kashmir in spite of the fact that, in the past, our relations with that great Asian neighbour were not as cordial as they are today.'[4] The Soviet Union, on the other hand, had been unsympathetic towards Pakistan on the Kashmir problem and Pakistan could not achieve 'the full extent of normalization' with her until the USSR adopted a more objective attitude towards the merits of that dispute.[5]

[1] M. Ayub Khan, *Friends Not Masters*, p. 141.
[2] *The Times* and *New York Times*, 22 Nov. 1962.
[3] *National Assembly of Pakistan Debates*, 26 Nov. 1962, p. 93.
[4] ibid., 27 Nov. 1962, p. 138.
[5] ibid.

Ayub's own pronouncements continued to be comparatively moderate for some time more. In an interview, broadcast on 6 January 1963 over ABC's TV and radio network, he denied that there was any chance of Pakistan joining the ranks of non-aligned countries and stated: 'All we want to make certain is that our safety and security are not in danger, and, if our friends do see to that, there should be no necessity of changing, or forcing us to change, our stand.'[1]

It was the Kennedy–Macmillan Birch Grove statement of 30 June 1963 which finally extinguished all hope in Pakistan that the US and the UK would refrain from giving long-term military aid to India unless she came to terms with Pakistan on Kashmir. The Indo-Pakistani talks had already terminated fruitlessly in May and now the US and the UK had openly proclaimed that the programme of military aid to India would nevertheless continue on a long-term basis. Foreign Minister Bhutto said in a press statement that because of the Birch Grove decision, 'the shadow of war that has been looming over the horizon of the subcontinent over the last decade will grow darker'.[2]

At a political meeting in the first part of July Ayub said the Western countries were helping Communism by arming India because the smaller countries of the region will be compelled to look towards China for the preservation of their freedom.[3] On 17 July 1963 Bhutto told the National Assembly that Pakistan's foreign policy was being reshaped, and apprised them of a 'new' and 'important' factor in the situation: 'If India in her frustration turned her guns against Pakistan, the international situation is such today that Pakistan would not be alone. An attack from India on Pakistan is no longer confined to the security and territorial integrity of Pakistan. An attack by India on Pakistan involves the territorial integrity and security of the largest State in Asia.'[4]

The Birch Grove communiqué, clearly, ended the era of any meaningful alliance between Pakistan and the Western countries. Confronted with the dilemma of either pleasing Pakistan or India, the United States, in conformity with her basic policy all along, had preferred to please India.

---

[1] Quoted by N. D. Palmer, *South Asia and United States Policy*, p. 180, footnote 32.
[2] Govt. of Pakistan, *Handout E. No. 2708*, dated 11 July 1963.
[3] *Dawn*, 9 July 1963.
[4] *National Assembly of Pakistan Debates*, 17 July 1963, p. 1666.

VI. A New Relationship with China

Pakistan's relations with China improved almost in direct proportion to the deterioration in Sino-Indian and US-Pakistani relations.

We have already noted that the Ayub regime, to start with, was zealously pro-Western and outspokenly anti-Communist. In 1959, when the Sino-Indian border dispute became acute, Pakistanis revised their earlier view that the Soviet Union posed the main threat to the security of the subcontinent. They surmised that both the Soviet Union and China had dangerous designs but the threat from China was now greater. But they wished, as far as possible, to keep their border free from the kind of trouble India was having with China. On 23 October 1959 Ayub disclosed at a press conference that, the Pakistani Foreign Office having received a map showing certain areas of Pakistan as part of China, Pakistan intended to approach China for a peaceful settlement of the border. He warned, however, that if the Chinese penetrated Pakistani territory, Pakistan would defend herself 'with every means at her disposal'.[1]

The trend of events for some time was not clear. Chinese patrols had been coming up to Shamshal village on the Pakistani side of the Shamshal Pass. There had been no shooting incidents but the Chinese had driven away some cattle.[2] Pakistan tightened up security measures on the Sino-Pakistani border and the border between Gilgit and Sinkiang was completely sealed.[3] From time to time Pakistani authorities also complained that their air space was being violated by planes from the north which came either from Russia or Sinkiang, 'where a big Chinese airbase existed'.[4]

As their talks with India had not yet broken down, the Chinese at first dragged their feet in respect of the Pakistani overtures for a border settlement. Nehru and Chou En-lai personally talked about the border in April 1960, and decided to have the problem examined in detail at official level. The officials of both sides discussed the matter at length but finally admitted failure and submitted separate reports on 12 December 1960. Realizing that the growing tension on the Sino-Indian border was bound ultimately to lead to a military confrontation, China now moved towards Pakistan to avoid trouble at least from that quarter, and, on 15 January 1961, Foreign Minister Manzur Qadir announced that China had agreed to the

---

[1] *Dawn*, 24 October 1959.
[2] M. Ayub Khan, *Friends Not Masters*, p. 161.
[3] *Dawn*, 24 Nov. 1959.
[4] *Dawn*, 24 Nov. 1959 and 15 May 1960.

demarcation of her border with Pakistan and that Pakistan had 'very cordial' relations with China.[1] Pakistan wrote to China on 28 March, formally proposing negotiations for a border settlement. The Chinese, still moving with caution, did not reply till 27 February 1962, when they proposed a provisional agreement pending the settlement of the Kashmir dispute. Pakistan accepted the Chinese suggestion on 19 March, and a joint communiqué announced on 3 May that the parties had decided to start negotiations. Shortly thereafter, General Raza, who had already served as Pakistan's first Ambassador in Peking and had later successfully negotiated a boundary agreement between Pakistan and Iran, was again appointed Ambassador to China with full powers to negotiate a border settlement. On 12 October, about a week before the large-scale attack on India, Sino-Pakistani border talks began in Peking, and, after the escalation in the fighting between India and China, moved quickly towards a successful conclusion. A joint communiqué, issued on 26 December 1962, stated that complete agreement in principle had been reached on the location and alignment of the boundary and, on 22 February 1963, it was declared that the parties had agreed upon a text describing the boundary alignment in detail. The final agreement was signed in Peking on 2 March. It purported to be provisional in nature and stipulated that, after the settlement of the Kashmir dispute between India and Pakistan, the sovereign authority concerned would reopen negotiations with China.

Although these facts refute the aspersion that the idea of a border accord was collusively conceived by Pakistan and China after the Sino-Indian military clash of October 1962, it is clear that 'the negotiations received an impetus after the Sino-Indian conflict and that was quite understandable because China like any other state could not afford to keep all her borders open to dangers'.[2] But there was little justification in India's complaint that Pakistan had surrendered 'not less than 2,000 square miles' of Kashmiri territory to China. The Indians themselves had contended that the border in the mountains followed the main watershed.[3] The Sino-Pakistani settlement delineated just such a boundary, deviating only to give

[1] *Dawn*, 16 Jan. 1961.

[2] Foreign Minister Zulfikar Ali Bhutto, in the Pakistan National Assembly on 17 July 1963.

[3] 'The Indian side also demonstrated that the boundary shown by them lay along the main watershed in the region and was the natural dividing line between the two countries.' *Report of the Officials of the Government of India and the People's Republic of China on the Boundary Question*, p. 2.

Pakistan 750 square miles of territory containing grazing grounds and salt mines on the other side of the Shamshal Pass which had been in the actual possession of the Chinese and where the Chinese had built roads and army barracks and outposts. Pakistan, on the other hand, was not called upon to surrender any territory under her control.[1] In any case India's criticism of the alignment agreed to by Pakistan and China was purely academic because even according to India's own terms for a Kashmir settlement with Pakistan— partition along the present cease-fire line—the areas in question would fall to Pakistan.

Though the Sino-Pakistani border accord was the first major agreement between the two countries, their cordiality had begun to grow while the negotiations were still in progress. The reason, of course, was that both needed new friends. China's alliance with the Soviet Union had begun to deteriorate even earlier than her friendship with India,[2] and prudence dictated that China should avail herself of every chance to win over Pakistan, her third largest neighbour. Pakistan, too, was looking around for a new protector in place of the United States.

During his July 1961 visit to the USA, President Ayub Khan had declared that Pakistan would vote for the seating of Communist China in the United Nations, and the Pakistani delegation duly did so in the autumn session of the General Assembly, after a lapse of ten years. A trade agreement, the first such between the two countries, providing for reciprocal most-favoured-nation treatment in matters of commerce and trade, including shipping, was signed by Pakistan and China in Karachi on 5 January 1963.

Not long after the Indo-Pakistani Kashmir talks had finally

---

[1] *The Times* special correspondent, reporting from Delhi, stated that both sides had made concessions in respect of their claims. However, he indicated the general result by heading his dispatch 'Concessions by China in Pakistan Treaty' and observed, 'In order to accommodate Pakistan in her desire for that pocket, China has diverged from the principle of watershed on which she has based her claim in this area. . . . Indian criticism today of Pakistan's "surrender" of territory ironically and even tragically underlines the fact that just such a settlement as this would have been fully acceptable in India before the news of China's furtive and deceitful occupation of territory, which Peking knows that India claimed, aroused a cry of "aggression" here.' *The Times*, 4 March 1963.

According to Alastair Lamb, Pakistan had been able to obtain from China a slightly improved version of the alignment which the British Indian government seems to have resolved to adopt in 1927. Alastair Lamb, *The China-Indian Border*, p. 175. See also S. M. Burke, 'Sino-Pakistani Relations', *Orbis*, Summer 1964.

[2] The origins of the Sino-Soviet split can be traced back to Khrushchev's denunciation of Stalin at the Twentieth Party Congress in Moscow in Feb. 1956.

collapsed, and Pakistanis were feeling frustrated, Premier Chou En-lai was reported as having said that China 'would defend Pakistan throughout the world'.[1] This was followed by Foreign Minister Bhutto's well-known statement, in the Pakistani parliament on 17 July 1963, that, in case of an Indian attack, Pakistan now would not be alone because an attack on Pakistan by India would involve 'the territorial integrity and security of the largest State in Asia'. When Bhutto visited Washington in October he denied the existence of any definite understanding between Pakistan and China, but observed that 'in case of a conflict the area's geopolitics might come into play'.[2] On the same subject Ayub had said: 'If we are attacked by India, then that means India is on the move and wants to expand. We assume that other Asiatic powers, specially China, would take notice of that.'[3]

An air transport agreement, signed in Karachi on 29 August, provided for Pakistani and Chinese airlines to operate in each other's territory. It made the Pakistan International Airlines the first international carrier to operate through Canton and Shanghai and greatly facilitated intercourse between Pakistan and China. Sino-Pakistani trade received a further boost by a barter agreement concluded in September, and, by December, China had become the biggest buyer of Pakistani cotton during the year.

In the meantime tension between India and Pakistan had reached grave proportions. The Kashmiris, already resentful of recent Indian moves to integrate Kashmir more closely with the Indian Union, rose in open revolt against the Indian occupation authorities when the sacred hair of the Holy Prophet Muhammad was stolen from the Hazratbal shrine near Srinagar on 26 December 1963. Before long, communal riots broke out in the eastern parts of India and Pakistan, resulting in a large exodus of refugees from both countries. On 20 January 1964 Pakistan requested the President of the Security Council to reopen the Kashmir case. The debate in the Council opened on 10 February but was adjourned a week later, at the request of Foreign Minister Bhutto who wished to fly home to be present during the official visit of Premier Chou En-lai, commencing on 19 February.

Having arrived in Pakistan at a time of acute national distress and anxiety, Chou En-lai won the gratitude of all Pakistanis by

[1] *Dawn*, 18 June 1963.
[2] *Dawn*, 9 Oct. 1963.
[3] *Washington Post*, 12 Sept. 1963.

fulfilling what must have been their highest wish at the time. Abandoning China's hitherto noncommittal posture on the Kashmir issue, he moved entirely to Pakistan's side. The Ayub–Chou En-lai joint communiqué 'expressed the hope that the Kashmir dispute would be resolved in accordance with the wishes of the people of Kashmir as pledged to them by India and Pakistan'. 'This is something', commented *Dawn*, 'of which some countries sharing with us the common ties of Islam, and some countries allied to us through pacts and treaties should be a little ashamed.'[1] China's new stand on Kashmir was the more remarkable because it could be cited against China by those who advocate a plebiscite solution of the Taiwan issue.

The Ayub–Chou En-lai statement also declared that the United Nations could not be considered to be fully representative of 'mankind' until the People's Republic of China was restored to its rightful place in the Organization; that, more than thirty new Afro-Asian nations having emerged since the Bandung Conference, it was time for convening a second conference of Asian and African countries; and that it was important for safeguarding world peace to achieve general disarmament, including the total prohibition and destruction of nuclear weapons.[2] But all these declarations merely reiterated positions which Pakistan had already adopted and did not, therefore, represent any new concessions on her part in return for China's support on Kashmir. Pakistan was sincerely appreciative of China's benevolence but evidently wary of again placing her reliance entirely on any one country. Therefore, while welcoming China's friendship, Pakistan strove not to damage her ties with the United States irretrievably.

Unlike communiqués issued during the visits of Chinese dignitaries to many other Afro-Asian countries, the Ayub–Chou En-lai communiqué was silent on the subject of Taiwan. On the differences between the US and China, Ayub said at a press conference that Chou En-lai had listed his grievances but 'I told him that the US also has her grievances.' About Taiwan, in particular, Ayub's view was that it was a very difficult situation: 'After all, they [Americans] are committed to supporting Chiang Kai-shek, committed to defending Taiwan ... it is an honourable commitment.' Asked whether closer relations with China would conflict with

---

[1] 26 Feb. 1964.
[2] For text of Ayub–Chou En-lai joint statement see *Pakistan Horizon*, 1st Quarter 1964.

Pakistan's obligations under SEATO and CENTO, the Pakistani President replied: 'The object of SEATO and CENTO is that war should be prevented from coming to these regions. . . . Well, if this freedom from trouble for this area can be obtained through good relations between neighbours, the object of SEATO and CENTO is being achieved.'[1]

At the Commonwealth Prime Minister's Conference Ayub opposed the demand of the Malaysian Premier that the Commonwealth should declare its joint opposition to the 'Chinese threat', and criticized Britain and America for their 'double standard' in wooing Russia and trying to isolate China.[2] Party Chairman Mao personally expressed appreciation of Ayub's stand at the Commonwealth meeting to visiting Pakistani Commerce Minister Wahiduzzaman.[3]

In marked contrast with his attitude during the Laotian crisis in December 1960, Ayub now declared that, if there were a confrontation between China and the US over North Vietnam, Pakistan would not get involved. He stated that previously Pakistan had a margin of military power, 'and then we were prepared to provide more than our share. But now, with the enlargement of Indian forces and so on, India has 3 to 1 and very soon she will have 5 to 1 lead over us . . . our capacity has been rendered ineffective by the action of our friends.'[4]

On his return from China Commerce Minister Wahiduzzaman disclosed that China had offered Pakistan a $60 million interest-free, long-term loan repayable in primary commodities and manufactured goods. The loan could be used for importing Chinese heavy machinery and complete plants for sugar and cement production.[5] During the 1964 season China again topped the list of buyers of Pakistani cotton.

President Ayub Khan timed his arrival in Peking, on an eight-day State visit, to coincide with the second anniversary of the Sino-Pakistani border agreement. He was given 'the most moving' welcome ever extended to an Asian Head of State. Though their feelings at the time were particularly inflamed, on account of the recently started American air strikes against North Vietnam, the

[1] *Pakistan Affairs*, 5 March 1964.

[2] *Dawn*, 10 July 1964; *Observer*, 12 July 1964.

[3] ibid., 17 July 1964.

[4] *Morning News*, 17 July 1964, quoted by K. B. Sayeed, 'Southeast Asia in Pakistan's Foreign Policy', *Pacific Affairs*, Summer 1968.

[5] *Dawn*, 1 Aug. 1964.

Chinese, as a remarkable gesture towards their guest, suspended public demonstrations against the American action.

Perhaps the most significant gathering during Ayub's entire visit was a mass rally in Peking. Ayub told the Chinese people that Pakistan and China were united by their common determination to eradicate the last vestiges of imperialism and colonialism 'in all their forms', and that Pakistan attached special value to the $60 million Chinese loan 'because it involves sacrifices on the part of China to promote self-reliance in a fellow Asian country'. However, he did not hesitate openly to differ from his hosts on the important subject of Vietnam. Contrary to the Chinese view, that the US had no legitimate interests in Asia and must pull out from that continent unconditionally, Ayub declared at the rally: 'Given the present scales of power, and the realities of international life, China and the United States, the two great Pacific Powers, must arrive at an understanding on the basis of equality and mutual recognition of legitimate interests.'[1] Though the other parts of Ayub's speech were loudly cheered, his statement regarding Vietnam was received by the huge audience in pin-drop silence.[2]

The communiqué stated that a cultural agreement between the two countries should be signed as soon as possible, expressed opposition to [Anglo-American] schemes to introduce nuclear weapons into the Indian Ocean,[3] repeated Pakistan's support for the right of the People's Republic of China to sit in the United Nations, 'reiterated' Pakistan's opposition to the schemes for creating 'two Chinas', 'reaffirmed' the view of both countries that the Kashmir dispute should be resolved in accordance with the wishes of the people of Kashmir, and expressed the readiness of the two countries to work for the success of the proposed Second Afro-Asian Conference.[4]

The noteworthy features of the communiqué were that Pakistan, for the first time, joined China in directly criticizing the US policy of 'two Chinas' and in opposing the introduction of nuclear weapons into the Indian Ocean, which raised the question whether she would henceforth bar United States warships carrying nuclear weapons from visiting Pakistani ports. On the other side of the ledger, the

[1] *Dawn*, 5, 6, and 9 March 1965; *New York Times*, 4 March 1965.
[2] Related to me by a person who had attended the rally.
[3] *The Times* (9 Dec. 1964) called the proposal a form of 'nuclear umbrella' to protect South and South-East Asia against the nascent nuclear power of China.
[4] *Pakistan Horizon*, 2nd Quarter 1965.

communiqué was utterly silent on the question of Vietnam, indicating that Pakistan was not willing to uphold the Chinese view on that question. On Kashmir, the Chinese support for Pakistan made some verbal advance from the Ayub–Chou En-lai communiqué in which China had joined Pakistan in merely expressing the hope that the dispute would be resolved according to the wishes of the people of Kashmir; in the new statement both countries positively affirmed that the Kashmir dispute should be resolved in accordance with the wishes of the Kashmiris.

Foreign Minister Chen Yi assured Pakistani newsmen accompanying Ayub that 'China would fight against aggressors' because 'if our friends are wiped out, how can we exist?'

Though the immediately tangible results of Ayub's visit to China were necessarily limited, the emotional impact on the minds of Pakistanis was considerable. Ayub himself had hitherto been almost wholly oriented towards the West because of his education, military training in England, service in the army, and travels exclusively in Western countries. That he was perceptibly affected by his first direct contact with China was evidenced in several ways. After going round the Museum of Chinese Revolution in Peking he recorded in the visitor's book: 'Such people with such spirit cannot help making history.' When Liu Shao-chi thanked him for these complimentary remarks, Ayub replied, 'Whatever I have written has come out of my soul.'[1] The predominant impression he had received during the visit was that 'We Orientals are basically similar.'[2]

Reviewing Ayub's visit to China, *The Times* wrote that, on reading the speeches made during the week with their emphasis on Bandung, on co-existence, and on Afro-Asian solidarity, one was reminded of Nehru's travels in the past. Noting that Ayub soon afterwards was scheduled to visit Moscow and Washington, the article pointed out: 'Ten years ago the only important Asian leader who could look for a welcome in all three of those capitals was Mr. Nehru.'[3]

VII. Towards a New Relationship with the Soviet Union
The Sino-Indian border war of 1962, for a variety of reasons, furthered the process of Soviet-Pakistani *rapprochement*, which had begun with the conclusion of the oil exploration agreement between the two countries in March 1961.

---

[1] *Dawn*, 4 March 1965.   [2] ibid., 8 March 1965.
[3] *The Times*, 8 March 1965.

First, the rush of Western arms to India caused Pakistan to move out of the Western orbit, making her virtually a non-aligned country and, therefore, more acceptable to the Soviet Union as a good neighbour. A Pakistan disaffected with the West, moreover, could influence her fellow Muslim members of CENTO, Turkey and Iran, also to adopt a more independent foreign policy.

Secondly, the Soviet Union's existing anxiety that India might be drawn into the American camp because of massive economic aid from that country, was greatly increased when the US also began to help India militarily. As explained elsewhere, the degree of Western influence had always been a matter of great concern to the USSR. During the years immediately following Indian independence, the Soviet Union was convinced that India was still a stooge of imperialism. In the middle nineteen-fifties, when India joined Russia and China in propagating *panchsheel* as the alternative to the Western-inspired defence alliances, Indo-Soviet ties reached the highest point of their cordiality. But from 1958 onwards, with the sharp increase in Western economic aid to India, Russian doubts about the direction of Indian domestic and foreign policies revived. Rightist forces in India gathered perceptible strength when India's relations with China worsened in 1959 and Nehru, who was mainly responsible for having kept India left of centre, began to lose some of his magic. Eisenhower and Khrushchev both visited India in the winter of 1959-60, but it was Eisenhower who received by far the greater acclaim.

The passage of arms between India and China offered the Right a further opportunity to strengthen its position. As Nehru himself wrote: 'The Right in India has become more clamorous, basing itself on an extreme form of nationalism; the Left, though also nationalistic, is to some extent weakened.'[1] India had not only received military supplies from the West but had also called in Western military teams to help in various ways. These activities familiarized Western experts with the Indian military machine and with important frontier areas. This was something the Russian military experts had never been able to achieve.

The *New Times* apprehensively wrote that Washington's plan was to force India into SEATO and CENTO. Almost echoing the Pakistani view, the article also alleged that the USA was trying to 'inflate the border conflict' in order to encourage the pro-Western

---

[1] J. Nehru, *Speeches*, IV, p. 414.

elements in India.[1] On 19 September 1963 *Pravda* similarly observed: 'The reactionary forces in India are using the conflict . . . for pushing India off her neutral course and drawing her into the military-political blocs of the West.'[2] It looked to the Soviet Union, at the time, as if India and Pakistan were changing places. India seemed to be coming under American domination while Pakistan was slipping out of it. To this day Soviet thinking is haunted by the question what the Right in India might do in the days to come.[3]

The third reason for Soviet overtures to Pakistan was that the Soviet Union did not wish that, having freed herself of Western control, Pakistan should now become a satellite of China, with whom the Soviet Union's relations were becoming increasingly tense.

Fourthly, India's military débâcle brought home to the Soviet Union that India was in no position to stand up to China unless she first got rid of the dead-weight of enmity with Pakistan. This realization caused the USSR gradually to assume the role of mediator between India and Pakistan. During the Indo-Pakistani war of September 1965 Washington, having burnt her fingers many times before, retreated to the sidelines, content to use her influence indirectly through the United Nations. But the Soviet Union donned the mantle discarded by the US and tried her hand at mediation by inviting Indian and Pakistani leaders to Tashkent, and she persisted in the role with varying zeal for some time afterwards. It would, no doubt, serve the interests of the Soviet Union if India and Pakistan could live together on friendly terms, co-operating in various matters, especially in defence, to offset the predominance of Chinese power on the Asian mainland. In this respect the Soviet policy, for the time being, became parallel to that of the United States.

The Soviet Union's wish to cultivate better relations with Pakistan suited Pakistan's new line of independence in foreign policy, but, owing to a greater backlog of suspicion, Soviet-Pakistani relations improved at a slower pace than Sino-Pakistani

---

[1] *New Times*, no. 50, 1962.

[2] The article from *Pravda* was reproduced as an Appendix in *The Truth About How the Leaders of the CPSU Have Allied Themselves With India Against China*, p. 67. At the time of the Sino-Indian armed clash, the Soviet Union tried to dissuade India from taking military assistance from the West by saying that, if India accepted such help, the Chinese might call upon the Soviet Union to honour the 1950 Sino-Soviet Treaty of Friendship, Alliance, and Mutual Assistance. This information was given to me at the time by a senior Indian diplomat who had direct knowledge of it.

[3] See, for example, B. Kalyagin, 'India's Ultras', *New Times*, no. 28, 1970.

relations. Also, the Soviet Union never achieved the same pitch of
cordiality with Pakistan as China, because it was China alone who
proclaimed support for Pakistan on the Kashmir dispute and promised her protection against a possible Indian attack.

Pakistan began to receive Russian signals for a friendlier relationship just as the former was losing all hope of being able to prevent
the US from extending long-term military aid to India and had
begun to warm up towards China. In June 1963 Sir Zafrulla Khan,
Pakistani Ambassador to the UN, who had visited Russia in his
capacity as the incumbent President of the UN General Assembly,
told *Dawn*'s London correspondent that, from his talks with Premier
Khrushchev and Foreign Minister Gromyko, he had gained the
impression that the Soviet Union would be 'very responsive' to any
move by Pakistan to establish closer relations in the economic and
other spheres.[1]

A visible result of the Russian desire for a new relationship with
Pakistan followed in August 1963 in the form of an £11 million
sterling Soviet loan to Pakistan, and a barter agreement.[2] An air
agreement between the two countries was signed on 7 October and
it was emphasized in the official announcement that 'the USSR has,
for the first time, granted rights to an airline to operate services
through Moscow to points beyond'.

Nor was it lost on the Soviet Union that the Pakistani touchstone for judging Soviet professions of goodwill towards Pakistan
would be the Soviet attitude towards the Kashmir dispute. Accordingly, when the question was debated again in the Security Council,
between 3 February and 18 May 1964, there was a perceptible
Soviet shift from the earlier position of unqualified support for
India. During the 1962 debate the Soviet delegate had wholly
sided with India and referred to Pakistan's original intervention in
Kashmir as 'armed aggression'. The 'principal basic fact' in the
Kashmir question, according to him, was 'the continuing occupation
of one-third of the territory of Kashmir by Pakistani troops'.[3]
The Soviet Union had also vetoed the resolution asking India and
Pakistan to enter into negotiations. In his statement on 13 May
1964, however, the Soviet representative, while going through

---

[1] *Dawn*, 26 June 1963. Sir Zafrulla told me the same thing when he was good enough
to give me an account of his talks with the Russian leaders.

[2] To diversify her trade and reduce her economic dependence on the Western
countries, Pakistan also made similar agreements with Poland, Albania, Yugoslavia,
Hungary, and Czechoslovakia.

[3] *Security Council Official Records, 1010th Meeting*, 4 May 1962.

the formality of reaffirming the earlier Soviet position—that the question of to which country Kashmir belonged had already been settled by the people of Kashmir—added in the same breath that the 'dispute' between India and Pakistan should be settled by 'the two interested parties' by peaceful means.[1]

Indians received a clear indication that the Soviet Union was formulating a new policy towards Pakistan when Vice-Premier Mikoyan visited Delhi, less than a month after Prime Minister Nehru's death. It will be recalled that it was Mikoyan who had said in Karachi in 1956 that the question of Kashmir should be finally decided by the people of Kashmir themselves. He now asked Premier Lal Bahadur Shastri whether it was not time for India and Pakistan to take stock of their relations. Could two developing countries afford to remain at odds? 'We were aware', said Shastri later, 'that they were changing their policy, and that there was nothing we could do about it.'[2]

India, however, still enjoyed preferential treatment from the Soviet Union in one important respect. She continued to receive large quantities of military aid from the USSR. A fresh pledge of $140 million was made in September 1964. Pakistan at that time was receiving no military supplies at all from Moscow. In his broadcast on 1 October 1964 Ayub said that the event of the 'gravest import' to Pakistan during the preceding month had been the announcement of further large-scale arms aid by Russia to India. Having normalized relations with her 'great neighbour', China, Pakistan wished to normalize relations with her other 'great neighbour', Russia. This, however, declared Ayub, would depend 'on whether Russia will continue to arm India against us or not'.[3]

Though Pakistan had joined the family of independent nations in 1947, her topmost leaders had never personally met their counterparts in neighbouring Russia. Both sides now felt the time had come to establish a line of direct communication at the highest level. It was announced on 14 September 1964 that President Ayub Khan had accepted the invitation of the Soviet Government to visit Russia.

A month later Khrushchev was ousted from the dual position of Premier and Communist Party Chief, and was succeeded by Leonid Brezhnev as Party Chief and Alexei Kosygin as Prime

Minister. As the outgoing Premier had been the chief architect of a policy of close friendship with India, his exit augured well for the future of Soviet-Pakistani relations. Sheikh Abdullah promptly appealed to the new Soviet leadership to revise Russia's policy on Kashmir and make it more realistic so that the people of Kashmir could determine their future through plebiscite.[1]

A few days after Khrushchev's ouster, the invitation to Ayub was renewed by the new government and the Pakistani President made an eight-day State visit to the USSR in early April 1965. On his return to Pakistan he said that it was unrealistic to expect 'radical results'[2] from the first Pakistani-Soviet summit parleys. The main immediate gain had been that a 'good many misunderstandings of the past' had been removed, making the way 'clear for friendship and co-operation between the two countries'.[3]

But Ayub's visit to Russia was not entirely without concrete result. On 7 April Pakistan and the USSR signed three agreements in Moscow: (1) an agreement under which the Soviet Government made a further loan of $50 million to assist oil exploration and the purchase of industrial machinery, and extended the existing oil exploration agreement for another five years; (2) a trade agreement, aimed at doubling Pakistani-Soviet trade by 1967; and (3) a cultural exchange agreement.

The joint communiqué also contained one positive diplomatic gain for Pakistan. Both sides declared 'resolute support for the peoples who are waging a struggle for their national liberation and independence and for the peoples who are fighting for the right to determine their future in accordance with their own will. . . . They further stated that in order to promote universal peace and harmony international agreements should be implemented.'[4] Hinting that this was a reference to Kashmir, Ayub said the principles enunciated in this part of the communiqué 'have a direct relevance to many problems of this area'.[5] Pakistan no doubt intended also that Ayub's visit to the Soviet Union should be taken as a sign by all other countries, specially by the super-powers, that Pakistan had not been pulled into the Chinese orbit.

On the question of Vietnam Ayub differed from his Russian hosts, just as he had earlier differed from the Chinese. The Moscow

[1] *Dawn*, 18 Oct. 1964.
[2] *Dawn*, 12 April 1965.
[3] *Dawn*, 21 April 1965.
[4] *Pakistan Horizon*, 2nd Quarter 1965.
[5] *Dawn*, 12 April 1965.

communiqué declared merely that both sides had 'exchanged their viewpoints' on the events in Vietnam, indicating that Russian and Pakistani views on the subject were not identical. This was meant to be a message to the US that Pakistan was not scoring gains in China and Russia at the cost of sacrificing American interests.

That Ayub's personal contact with the Soviet leadership had, in fact, opened a new era in Pakistani-Soviet relations soon became evident from the Russian attitude in the Indo–Pakistani Kutch and September wars.

VIII. A New Effort to Create a Special Relationship with Muslim Countries

When the Pakistani-US alliance began to cool off in 1958, Pakistanis emotionally reverted to the wish that had always been closest to their hearts, namely, a desire for brotherly relations with other Muslim countries. However, experience had taught them that the current guiding force in other Muslim countries was not Islamic nationalism but Arab nationalism and territorial nationalism. They therefore realistically accepted local nationalism as a fact of life, hoping it would prove to be a milestone on the way to universal Muslim nationalism. At the National Union Rally in Cairo Ayub said that, though it was 'a hard thing to say', religion in fact was no longer the 'motive power' it used to be; territorial nationalism was now the motive power.[1]

Pakistan's experience with Muslim states underscores Iqbal's exhortation that 'For the present every Muslim nation must sink into her own deeper self, temporarily focus her vision on herself alone, until all are strong and powerful to form a living family of republics.'[2]

Besides greater willingness on the part of Pakistanis to accept territorial nationalism, there was another good reason for Pakistan's greater success during the Ayub period in improving relations with Muslim countries. Under Ayub, Pakistan enjoyed a decade of political stability and economic advance and gained considerable prestige internationally. On the other hand India, who also had always paid special court to the Muslim states with a view to off-setting Pakistani influence among them, had begun to lose respect because of her economic problems and military humiliation at the hands of the Chinese.

[1] M. Ayub Khan, *Speeches*, III, p. 49.
[2] Muhammad Iqbal, *The Reconstruction of Religious Thought in Islam*, p. 159.

Pakistan and the UAR

The first Muslim state with whom Ayub endeavoured to improve Pakistani ties was the United Arab Republic. With Iraq's withdrawal from the Baghdad Pact, following the 1958 revolution, a major cause of the UAR's disapproval of Pakistan had been removed and it was hoped the UAR would now respond to friendly gestures from Pakistan. In April 1960 Nasser was invited to Pakistan and Ayub returned the visit in the following November. Both occasions were marked by a display of mutual cordiality, but the fundamentals of UAR policies remained unaffected. In Pakistan Nasser declared point-blank that he was opposed to the formation of a Muslim bloc because 'I do not wish to use Islam in interntional politics'.[1]

During the 1962 Security Council debate on Kashmir, the UAR representative, not wishing to do anything which did not have India's approval, stated that his Government did 'not favour any action which is not acceptable to the two parties'.[2] Accordingly, he abstained from voting on the Irish resolution asking India and Pakistan to enter into negotiations for the settlement of the Kashmir dispute. It was believed that the attitude of the UAR had influenced Ghana also to abstain from supporting the resolution.[3] In the National Assembly of Pakistan, Foreign Minister Bogra said 'our hearts cry out in anguish at the agonizing thought' that the UAR, who had contributed so much to the splendour of Islam and was linked with Pakistan by brotherly ties of religion, should have withheld her support in an issue of such vital importance not only to Pakistan but to the millions of Muslims of Kashmir held in colonial subjugation by India.[4]

Despite a momentary thaw in the summer of 1965, when both Ayub and Nasser were striving to make the proposed Afro-Asian Conference a success, Pakistan's relations with the UAR never reached the closeness desired by Pakistan. Together with Nehru and Tito, Nasser formed an impressive trio of leading neutrals, one each from the continents of Asia, Europe, and Africa, and they developed special ties with one another over the years. Obviously,

[1] *Dawn*, 15 April 1960.
[2] *Security Council Official Records, 1013th meeting*, 19 June 1962.
[3] Seven countries had voted in favour of the resolution: Chile, China, France, Ireland, UK, USA, and Venezuela. The UAR and Ghana abstained and the USSR and Romania voted against the resolution. The negative vote of the USSR constituted a veto.
[4] On 25 June 1962.

Nasser did not wish to do anything which might annoy India and disturb that relationship.

Regional Co-operation for Development

Perhaps the most satisfying, and potentially the most fruitful, partnership which Pakistan has so far forged with Muslim countries is the Regional Co-operation for Development (RCD), set up largely as a result of the initiative taken by President Ayub Khan in the summer of 1964. Its other members are Turkey and Iran with whom Pakistan has always enjoyed a cordial friendship. As fellow members of CENTO, the three countries had already built up a tradition of mutual consultation and co-operation. Together they form three links of a highly strategic chain.

As stated in our discussion of the Baghdad Pact, the RCD was a by-product of the growing disenchantment of Pakistan, Iran, and Turkey with their ties with the Western countries. The RCD partners, moreover, could see that the USA and the USSR were edging towards a relaxation of tension, reducing the value of military pacts. If the USA desired a more co-operative relationship with the USSR why should not Pakistan, Iran, and Turkey move in the same direction, specially when Moscow seemed so eager to play the role of a beneficent neighbour?

The idea that the three Muslim members of CENTO should meet outside CENTO auspices, to forge a new partnership, was first discussed by their representatives in Washington in April 1964, when they went there to attend the CENTO Council meeting. It was furthered in the first week of July, when the Foreign Ministers of Pakistan, Iran, and Turkey conferred at Ankara, with President Ayub Khan also in town. On 4 July Ayub told a press conference that he had proposed a new 'united front between Turkey, Pakistan and Iran'.[1]

From Ankara Ayub proceeded to London, to attend the Commonwealth Prime Ministers' Conference. On the way back he stopped at Istanbul where the Shah of Iran and President Cemal Gursel of Turkey joined him. A joint statement by the three Heads of State, issued on 22 July 1964, named the new organization 'Regional Co-operation for Development' and resolved that appropriate means should be adopted to step up co-operation 'in all fields' in a spirit of 'regional co-operation'. It was decided to create a Ministerial Council composed of Foreign Ministers and a Regional

[1] *Dawn*, 5 July 1964.

Planning Committee composed of heads of the three national planning organizations.[1] A permanent Secretariat was later established at Tehran and has been functioning effectively.

It was no doubt hoped by the founders that their new organization would attract a wider regional membership than CENTO because it contained no non-regional Western power and had no cold-war overtones. Ayub had passed through Afghanistan on the way to Ankara and sounded King Zahir Shah, but had been unable to persuade that monarch to take his country into RCD. Arab reaction to the new system was openly unfavourable. The agreement was suspected to be a disguised extension of CENTO under imperialist instigation and yet another attempt to organize a confederacy against the rising forces of Arab unity.

Though no formal alliance for mutual defence has been created, the relations of the RCD partners, who meet regularly at various levels, are growing more intimate with the passage of time. The Shah of Iran told Pakistanis that Iran had decided to share her destiny with Pakistan and 'to stand by you in good and bad days',[2] and a few months later President Cevdet Sunay said that Turco-Pakistani relations had 'reached a level far above that of alliances'.[3]

In concrete terms, the most commendable progress has been registered in the field of 'Joint Purpose Enterprises'. By January 1970 the following projects had gone into production:

Location	Description	Participants
Pakistan	Bank Note and Security Paper Project	Iran, Pakistan, and Turkey
Pakistan	Machine Tools (Turret and Capstan Lathes)	Pakistan and Turkey
Pakistan	Gear Boxes and Differential Systems	Pakistan and Turkey
Turkey	Borax and Boric Acid	Iran, Pakistan, and Turkey
Turkey	Machinery for Tea Industry	Pakistan and Turkey
Turkey	Tungsten Carbide	Pakistan and Turkey
Turkey	Locomotive Diesel Engine Project	Iran, Pakistan, and Turkey

[1] *Pakistan Horizon*, 3rd Quarter 1964.
[2] *Morning News*, 7 March 1967.
[3] *Dawn*, 29 Oct. 1967.

Location	Description	Participants
Turkey	Centrifugal and Special Filters for Chemical Industry	Pakistan and Turkey
Pakistan	Methanol Industry	Iran and Pakistan
Pakistan	Urea Formaldehyde Project	Iran and Pakistan
Iran	Glycerine	Turkey and Iran
Pakistan	Glycerine	Pakistan and Turkey
Turkey	Polystyrene Project	Pakistan and Turkey

Seven more projects were expected to go into production before the close of 1970 and thirty-one others had been approved.[1] There has been useful co-operation in some other directions also, but the important sector of trade between the RCD partners has been stubbornly stagnant.

The RCD is an attractive conception which, given internal stability and progress within the territories of its individual members, could develop impressively and serve as a model for other developing regions.

Located, as she is, right in the middle of the RCD region, Afghanistan would be the most natural fourth member of the organization. Her addition to the group would dissolve much of the unjustifiable suspicion that RCD is just a reincarnation of the Western-inspired CENTO.

Improvement in Relations with Indonesia

The improvement in Pakistan's relations with Indonesia resulted from Indonesia's tension with India and Pakistan's increasing friendship with China, which put Indonesian and Pakistani policies on the same track.

The parting of the ways between India and Indonesia can be traced back to 1959. From that year Nehru began to have second thoughts about his earlier view that China was a peace-loving country. Soekarno, on the other hand, began increasingly to admire China as a truly anti-imperialist, progressive power. Nehru annoyed Soekarno by pushing for a conference of non-aligned countries instead of working for a larger Afro-Asian conference, after the pattern of the Bandung meeting, which Soekarno favoured, remembering the prestige and satisfaction it had brought him as head of the host state. At the non-aligned conference itself, in

[1] For a complete list see *Pakistan Affairs*, 31 Jan. 1970.

Belgrade in 1961, there was noticeable tension between Nehru and
Soekarno. The former played down the issue of Western colonialism,
while the latter desired it to be the main theme of the meeting.

When the Asian Games were held at Djakarta in August-
September 1962, Indonesia barred the entry of teams from Israel
and Nationalist China by refusing visas to their personnel. G. D.
Sondhi, Vice-President of the Asian Games Federation, who was an
Indian national, criticized the Indonesians for letting political
considerations mar the success of the Games. This led to Indonesian
demonstrations against India, during which the Indian Embassy
was stoned.

A few days later, when the Sino-Indian border fighting began,
Indonesia showed no sympathy for the plight of her fellow non-
aligned country and began to forge a closer relationship with China.
In Indonesian eyes China had proved to be a virile revolutionary
nation while India had been shown up as a decadent bourgeois
country, increasingly dependent on the imperialist West.

In February 1963 the International Olympic Committee suspended Indonesia from the Olympic Games for having allowed
politics to enter the realm of sport. Soekarno thereupon announced
that Indonesia would organize the Games of the New Emerging
Forces (GANEFO), and in November 1963 GANEFO were duly
held at Djakarta. Fifty-one countries, including Pakistan, the USSR,
and China, participated. The Chinese contingent, 200 strong, was
lustily cheered by the Indonesians. Soekarno himself singled out
China's Vice-Premier Ho Lung for a unique honour: during the
march-past of the Chinese team, the Indonesian chief rose and
shook hands with Ho Lung who was also on the receiving stand.

Meanwhile, a major difference between India and Indonesia had
cropped up on the question of the formation of the Malaysian
Federation, which came into existence in September 1963. India
established cordial relations with Malaysia, whose Premier, Tunku
Abdul Rahman, had been one of the few Afro-Asian leaders immediately to declare outright support for India at the time of the Sino-
Indian border war. Indonesia, on the other hand, viewed Malaysia
as a manifestation of 'neo-colonialism' and a base which Britain
would use against the revolutionary forces of the region. Soekarno,
accordingly, inaugurated a 'crush Malaysia' campaign. China
openly promised full support to Indonesia and called the two
countries 'comrades in arms'. Soekarno said that by supporting
Malaysia, which was 'an evil thing created by imperialists', Indian

leaders were being disloyal to the teachings of Gandhi who had stood for nonco-operation with evil things.[1]

The first sign that Indonesia had begun to view Pakistan in a favourable light came in the summer of 1962, when Indonesia agreed to accept a battalion of Pakistani troops to safeguard the security of West Irian for a few months, during the interim United Nations administration, preparatory to the transfer of that territory from the Netherlands to Indonesia.

In June 1963, when Soekarno visited Pakistan, a further note of cordiality was noticeable in the Ayub–Soekarno communiqué which stated that the two Presidents 'expressed their resolve to intensify their efforts to liberate the Afro-Asian peoples and to secure the right of self-determination of peoples still held in bondage. They hoped that in view of the need for strengthening the Afro-Asian solidarity, an honourable and equitable settlement of the problem of Kashmir would be reached in the near future.' The two leaders also called for the holding of a Second Afro-Asian Conference for strengthening solidarity among Asian and African countries who have to play a major role in 'a new world order'.[2]

By April 1964 China, Indonesia, and Pakistan were working closely together to make the Second Afro-Asian Conference a success. In that month Foreign Minister Bhutto went to Djakarta to participate in the preparatory meeting of the proposed conference. Besides subscribing to the final communiqué issued by the twenty-two members of the Preparatory Committee, Bhutto and the Indonesian Foreign Minister, Subandrio, published a bilateral statement which clearly indicated the degree of cordiality which had by then developed between their two countries. Indonesia now fully agreed with Pakistan that the Kashmir dispute involved the question of the fundamental rights of the people of Kashmir, and joined Pakistan in calling for 'an early solution of this dispute in accordance with the wishes of the people of the State'.[3]

Soekarno, during his visit to Pakistan in September, reiterated the same view in his joint statement with Ayub. The two Presidents further decided to establish co-operation 'along the pattern set by' RCD.[4] In March 1965 an agreement between Pakistan and Indonesia was signed, stating that 'concrete decisions' had been taken to

---

[1] *New York Times*, 23 June 1965.
[2] *Pakistan Horizon*, 3rd Quarter 1963.
[3] ibid., 2nd Quarter 1964.
[4] ibid., 4th Quarter 1964.

promote economic and cultural co-operation between the two countries, but what these decisions were was not spelled out.[1]

A second Pakistani-Indonesian conference on bilateral economic and cultural co-operation, held at Djakarta in August 1965, resulted in the 'Indonesia–Pakistan Economic and Cultural Co-operation' agreement which set up an organization (IPECC) on the lines of the RCD, but the visible results of this venture have not been nearly as impressive as those of its Middle Eastern prototype. The communiqué of the third session of the Ministerial Council, held at Djakarta on 31 July 1970, merely noted that 'the specific projects for joint ventures had been identified and steps were being taken to implement them'.[2]

IX. Pakistan and the Proposed Second Afro-Asian Conference

During the years of her enthusiastic alliance with the West, Pakistan had regarded moves for holding an Afro-Asian[3] conference as Communist–neutralist manœuvres to loosen the ties of the smaller African and Asian countries with the West, making the Afro-Asians an easier prey to the ambitions of the larger non-Western states. According to Ayub, speaking in August 1961: 'The slogan of Asia for Asians can be deadly poison for the smaller countries of Asia, meaning that these countries should not have friends who can help them to safeguard themselves.'[4]

The Bandung communiqué had visualized the convening of another Asian-African conference, and such a meeting had in fact been scheduled at Cairo in June 1956 but had to be postponed because of the unsettled conditions in the Middle East at that time. Indonesia revived the proposal in 1960 but with little success till Pakistan and China joined hands with her after the Sino-Indian border war. Pakistan, having cooled towards her alliance with the West, now felt freer to play a new role in the Afro-Asian world of which she was an important part. China, whose relations with India and the USSR had worsened, wished to line up the Afro-Asian world behind herself and weaken the influence of her principal competitors there. India, never enthusiastic about a second gather-

[1] ibid., 2nd Quarter 1965, p. 182.

[2] *Pakistan Document Series*, Aug. 1970, vol. II, no. 9.

[3] In official documents the first conference at Bandung was designated Asian–African Conference and the second scheduled to take place in Algeria was called the Second African–Asian Conference.

[4] *Pakistan Horizon*, 4th Quarter 1961.

ing of Asian and African countries after her poor experience of the first, worked actively against the proposal for a second conference, fearing a combined onslaught from China, Pakistan, and Indonesia. As a counter-offensive to the proposal for an Afro-Asian meeting, India began to work for another non-aligned conference from which both Pakistan and China would be excluded, but which would include New Delhi's long-standing friend, Yugoslavia.

In January 1964 a Preparatory Committee met at Djakarta and drew up arrangements for the Afro-Asian Conference. In the end, however, China, Indonesia, and Pakistan, who had worked as a 'troika' to make the Second Afro-Asian Conference a success, lost the battle of Bandung v. Belgrade, principally because ten days before the date of the conference the host country, Algeria, was convulsed by a revolution and, on 25 June 1965, a bomb exploded at the very site where the conference was due to open on 29 June. The conference was postponed till 5 November, but in the meantime Pakistan became involved in a war with India, and Soekarno was reduced to a figurehead by a military junta, following the failure of a Communist-inspired coup, which seriously damaged Sino-Indonesian relations. China now declared she would not attend the meeting, whereupon the conference was administered a *coup de grâce* by the announcement that it had been postponed *sine die*. In the summer of 1966 China got involved in her own 'cultural revolution' and nothing more was heard about the Afro-Asian conference.

X. Further Deterioration of Pakistani-US Relations

Washington did not express much concern at Pakistan's efforts to 'normalize' her relations with the USSR because the US herself was no longer averse to cultivating a better understanding with that country. But Pakistan's growing ties with China was another matter. US spokesmen criticized almost every step towards greater Sino-Pakistani co-operation. By the time the Indo-Pakistani war of September 1965 broke out, Pakistani and American leaders had almost ceased to have any meaningful communication with each other. A step-by-step review of events will assist towards understanding the cumulative effect of the various incidents, which singly may not seem important enough to have cast such a deep shadow over Pakistani-US relations.

With regard to the Sino-Pakistani border agreement of March 1963, the State Department had said that 'on the basis of available information it would appear that the agreement serves the interest of Pakistan'.[1] However, the news that Pakistan would conclude a civil aviation agreement with China in August caused a State Department official to complain: 'We look upon this as an unfortunate breach of free world solidarity and take a dim view of it.'[2]

Further heat was generated when, the day after Pakistan signed the air agreement with China, the State Department announced the suspension of a promised $4.3 million loan to Pakistan for the construction of a new airport at Dacca. It was threatened that further action might be taken if US spare parts were used by Pakistan International Airlines for maintenance purposes at Chinese airports.[3] 'Competent sources' in Rawalpindi reported that Pakistan would not 'beg' assistance from America, and experts had been directed to study the consequences of aid cessation.[4] The air-pact crisis, however, subsided when the US made it known that she would not object to PIA using Boeing aircraft on the route to China because US authorities were 'satisfied that the spare parts would remain under the control of a friendly Government'.[5]

Both sides seemed reluctant to let matters get out of hand. At a committee hearing on 12 December, Assistant Secretary Phillips Talbot said that the US had made clear her concern that, even if marginal benefits accrued to Pakistan from trade, boundary, and air agreements with China, 'the political effect is to give advantage to an enemy against which we are formally allied'. Nevertheless, the US continued to believe that her national interests and those of Pakistan coincided and that this was recognized by Pakistan as well.[6] For his part, Ayub assured Americans, in a television broadcast on 4 November 1963, that Pakistanis basically were still friends of the West and that 'if there seems to be any deviation from that, it is because of certain steps taken by the West which have jeopardized our security'.[7] But other irritating incidents followed and sorely tried the patience of both sides.

[1] *Washington Post*, 3 March 1963.

[2] 'Red China–Pakistan Flight Pact Stirs United States', *Washington Post*, 30 June 1963, inserted by Senator Morse into *Congressional Record (vol. 109, p. 12269) 88th Congress, 1st Session*, 9 July 1963, Senate.

[3] *The Times*, 31 Aug. 1963.

[4] *Dawn*, 13 Sept. 1963.

[5] ibid., 19 Dec. 1963.

[6] *Foreign Assistance & Related Agencies Appropriations for 1964, Hearings on H.R. 9499 before the Senate Committee on Appropriations, 88th Congress, 1st Session*, 12 Dec. 1963, p. 467.

[7] *Channel 13, WNDT—New York and the N.E.T. Network, in conversation with Arnold Michaelis.*

The announcement in Karachi, in December 1963, that Premier Chou En-lai had been invited to Pakistan for a one-week visit, led the State Department Press Officer to comment: 'We consider it unfortunate that the leaders of the Chinese Communist regime should be accorded an opportunity to pay a friendly visit to Pakistan, a country allied with us.'[1]

After Pakistanis had gained Chou En-lai's endorsement of their own view of the Kashmir problem, United States officials visibly downgraded the importance of that problem. In December 1962 Assistant Secretary of State Harriman had called Kashmir the 'most important question' before the free world,[2] but on 8 April 1964 Talbot said, if Kashmir were the most important thing in the world for the United States, it would be her duty to tell India and Pakistan that they would get no more aid until Kashmir was settled, but it was more important for the US to limit the opportunities of Communist powers to move in.[3] When Kashmir was debated in the Security Council in February and May 1964, the American representative formally maintained the earlier US position, that the people of the State had the right to determine their future, but he did not call for any positive initiative by the United Nations for resolving the deadlock. His suggestion was that India and Pakistan should enter into bilateral negotiations and 'consider the possibility' of recourse to the good offices of a country or a person of their choice to assist them.[4] *Dawn*'s special correspondent reported from the United Nations that, for the first time, Russia and America 'appeared to be working together closely to avoid a showdown on Kashmir' and that the 'unfriendly and unco-operative American attitude in UN lobbies has been greatly responsible for the inconclusive nature of the Kashmir debate'. The Bolivian delegate and 'one African member of the Council' confessed privately that they had adopted a less helpful attitude because of US pressure.[5] With the Russians now not wishing to offend Pakistan by casting a veto to protect India's position, and the US not wishing to displease India by calling for a positive resolution, the debate in the

---

[1] *Evening Star*, Washington, D.C., 12 Dec. 1963, quoted in *Foreign Assistance and Related Agencies Appropriations for 1964, Hearings on H.R. 9499 before the Senate Committee on Appropriations, 88th Congress, 1st Session*, 12 Dec. 1963, p. 440.

[2] *Dawn*, 10 Dec. 1962.

[3] *Foreign Assistance Act of 1964, Hearings Before the House Committee on Foreign Affairs, 88th Congress, 2nd Session*, 8 April 1964, p. 238.

[4] *Security Council Official Records, 1091st Meeting*, 14 Feb. 1964.

[5] *Dawn*, 17, 19 Feb. 1964.

Security Council fizzled out with a summation by the President of the various views expressed by the members.

The next notable episode in the series of US-Pakistani collisions occurred in April 1965 when President Johnson suddenly post-poned Ayub's scheduled visit to Washington. At the same time he deferred a visit by Premier Shastri and, in the words of the *Economist*, thereby 'achieved the unusual diplomatic feat of giving equal offence to both [India and Pakistan] simultaneously'.

Ayub's visit to the American capital had been announced on 17 February, and had been fixed to take place on 25 April. Shastri had been invited on 23 March to come to Washington on 2 June. On 16 April Johnson sent messages to both leaders 'suggesting' that the visit in each case be put back until the autumn. A White House spokesman said the visits had been postponed because of the Congressional workload and the situation in Vietnam. At a news conference Johnson himself said he had postponed the two visits because he could talk to Ayub and Shastri more meaningfully after Congress had legislated on the requests of Pakistan and India for foreign aid. If they had come on the dates originally fixed, 'I would not know what the Congress would do'.[1]

However, the official explanations satisfied no one. It was generally believed that Ayub's visit had been postponed because Pakistan was becoming too intimate with China, and Shastri's because of annoyance over India's opposition to the bombing of Vietnam and also because of Johnson's wish not to differentiate between India and Pakistan.[2]

Though Ayub's visit had been cancelled rather more abruptly—only nine days before he was due to arrive in Washington—Indians felt much more incensed at the rebuff than Pakistanis. Persons close to Shastri told the Delhi correspondent of the *New York Times* that the Premier had been 'deeply hurt' by the sudden postponement of his visit to America and that it would be 'a long time' before the damage to United States-Indian relations could be repaired. What Indians found 'intolerably galling' was that Shastri was being equated with Ayub.[3] This was an interesting twist be-cause not long ago Pakistanis, as allies of the US, used to object to Pakistan being treated on the same footing as India who was neutral. Evidently Indians now felt that their stand against China virtually

[1] *New York Times,* 28 April 1965.
[2] ibid., 21 April 1965.
[3] ibid., 20, 21 April 1965.

made them allies of the US, while Pakistan's friendship with Peking had turned Pakistan into a neutral country, if not an ally of China. In an angry letter to the *New York Times*, H. R. Vohra, Washington correspondent of the *Times of India*, complained that the postponement of Shastri's visit came at a moment when Indo-United States relations had achieved 'an unaccustomed harmony' of which the 'greatest source' was 'the mutual understanding on Chinese Communism and India's sworn determination to serve as a bulwark against its machinations across a 2,000-mile-long border'.[1]

American officials, at this juncture, began to refer to the developing US-Pakistani differences in stronger terms. At a Committee hearing on 6 May 1965 Phillips Talbot said that when Ayub came to Washington, US differences with Pakistan 'on Communist China and on other issues' would be discussed by the heads of the two governments 'in the frankest fashion'. At the same time William B. Macomber, Jr., Assistant Administrator, Bureau for Near East and South Asia Aid, stated that during his last visit to Pakistan he had met with 'very senior people' and had made it 'very clear' that the US was increasingly concerned about Pakistan's growing intimacy with China, and 'predicted that if the trend continued it would have an adverse effect' on the US level of aid to Pakistan.[2]

Johnson now evidently decided that the time had come to hold a dialogue with Pakistan on the entire gamut of US-Pakistani relations. Bhutto disclosed, in the National Assembly on 13 July, that the American Ambassador had seen Ayub on 3 July and conveyed the message from his President that the Consortium meeting, which was due to meet on 27 July to discuss aid for Pakistan, was being postponed till 27 September. The United States had suggested that 'in this period of time, if the Government of Pakistan so wishes', the two governments could discuss 'certain other problems'.[3]

Since in the pre-Consortium meeting in June the delegates, including the US representative, had praised Pakistan's economic performance, approved the Third Plan, and recommended the grant of the full amount of $500 million requested by Pakistan, the Pakistanis had regarded formal approval by the Consortium as a mere formality. They saw the US move to postpone the Consortium

[1] ibid., 28 April 1965, quoted in *Congressional Record* (vol. III, part 7, p. 8885) 89th Congress, 1st Session, 29 April 1962, House.
[2] *Foreign Assistance and Related Agencies Appropriations for 1966, Hearings Before a Subcommittee of the Committee on Appropriations, 89th Congress, 1st Session*, 6 May 1965, pp. 991–2.
[3] *National Assembly of Pakistan Debates*, 13 July 1965, p. 1326.

meeting as pure political pressure to change the direction of Pakistan's foreign policy.

Speaking at a Muslim League meeting on the day following Bhutto's disclosure of Johnson's message, Ayub angrily declared that his recent foreign travels had been undertaken to find new friends, not new masters.[1] Pakistan had explained her policy to the United States several times but the latter did not listen. This might be because 'power drunk' countries often do not pay heed to smaller countries. Anti-US rallies erupted in all the main cities of Pakistan, and in Dacca one of them had to be tear-gassed by the police to protect the United States Information Center from the crowd.

Instead of opening a new dialogue with Pakistan, Johnson's move thus suspended even the existing dialogue between the two countries. It was reported in early August that Ayub had refused to see the American Ambassador for two weeks and had asked him to get in touch with the Foreign Office, unless there was a message from President Johnson. At the other end, after the Pakistani Ambassador had had three rounds of talks with Secretary Rusk, the effort was abandoned because it was felt that the discussions were becoming pointless with neither side willing to concede anything. President Johnson also had not received the Ambassador for a month.[2]

A dispatch dated 29 August in the *New York Times* said that the friendly air between Pakistan and the US had gone and the stage had been set for 'a major adjustment or a bitter and costly quarrel'. Washington had halted further aid commitments until it obtained assurances of 'at least friendly and respectful' dealings. Officials wanted to know what benefits the US would get from further aid to Pakistan.[3]

While the barometer of Pakistani-US friendship continued rapidly to fall, that of Indo-US cordiality registered a quick recovery from the low point in April when Shastri's visit to the US had been called off. It was reported that Ambassador Chester Bowles and John P. Lewis, Director of the Agency for International Development Operations in India, had proposed a doubling of United States aid to India from $435 million to $900 million a year.[4] The

[1] Subsequently Ayub chose *Friends Not Masters* as the title of his political autobiography.
[2] *Dawn*, 11 Aug. 1965; *Hindu Weekly*, 16 Aug. 1965.
[3] *New York Times*, 30 Aug. 1965.
[4] ibid., 21 July 1965.

Washington correspondent of the *Hindu* also wrote that 'respect and sympathy' for India in the US had considerably increased because of the modification in her foreign policy during the past two years.[1]

Thus, when India and Pakistan were nearing the brink of the September war, India once again ranked comparatively high in Washington's esteem, while Pakistan was scarcely on speaking terms with the United States.

The main reason why Ayub thought he could defy the US, and even face the total loss of American aid, was no doubt that his own house was in better shape than it had ever been before. Pakistan had maintained the lead she had taken over India in 1960 in the race for economic development. In January 1965 the *New York Times* observed that 'Pakistan may be on its way toward an economic milestones that so far has been reached by only one other populous country, the United States.'[2] Further, Pakistan had already opened aid channels with the USSR and China and hoped that these countries would come to her rescue if America cut off all assistance. Politically, too, Ayub seemed to be firmly in the saddle. Early in 1965 he had won the Presidential election against Miss Fatima Jinnah, sister of the Quaid-i-Azam, who had the support of the Combined Opposition Parties, and he had interpreted the result as 'a clear mandate to pursue my internal and external policies'.[3]

[1] *Hindu Weekly*, 23 Aug. 1965.
[2] *New York Times*, 18 Jan. 1965.
[3] *Dawn*, 3 Jan. 1965.

14 The Indo-Pakistani Wars of 1965

I. The Drift Towards War

In some respects the Indo-Pakistani war of September 1965 was not unlike the Indo-Pakistani Kashmir war of 1948. On the earlier occasion India tried to heap the entire blame upon Pakistan by accusing her of first assisting the tribesmen who invaded Kashmir and then directly intervening with the regular Pakistani forces. In 1965 India again blamed Pakistan for starting the war by sending guerrillas across the cease-fire line in Kashmir and following this up with intervention by the Pakistani army. However, it was not lost on perceptive observers that it was a series of India's own actions in both cases which ultimately made the Indo-Pakistani armed clash inevitable. To comprehend the real causes of the September war we must untangle the skein of events from the summer of 1963, when the six rounds of Indo-Pakistani talks on Kashmir ended without result and Nehru withdrew the 'concession' of settling the Kashmir problem by turning the cease-fire line into a permanent boundary.

A smaller war, in the Rann of Kutch, flared up almost accidentally, in the spring of 1965. It was a long-standing border dispute which suddenly escalated into fighting because ruffled tempers on both sides needed only an excuse to start shooting.

Communal Tension in India and Pakistan and Upheaval in Kashmir
An Indian action, which began systematically in the middle of 1962 and gathered momentum in 1963-4, was the eviction of Indian Muslims from Tripura and Assam into East Pakistan. The expulsion began under the cover of security measures which India was then taking because of rising tension on the Sino-Indian border. Referring to the Indian 'pretext' that these people had entered India unlawfully and were simply being sent back, *The Times* correspondent wrote from East Pakistan that 'the evidence available

from them shows that most were long settled in Tripura, even for generations'.[1]

During the same period events inside Kashmir were also moving towards a climax. On 3 October 1963 Bakshi Ghulam Muhammad, the outgoing Prime Minister of Kashmir,[2] announced moves to amalgamate Kashmir more fully into the Indian Union. Six members of the Indian Lok Sabha would be chosen from the State, and the Sadar-i-Riyasat and the Prime Minister would henceforth be called Governor and Chief Minister respectively, as in the provinces of India. Nehru confirmed in a speech in the Lok Sabha on 27 November that a 'gradual erosion' of Article 370 of the Indian Constitution, which allowed Kashmir a special status, was in progress. Inside Kashmir the seething anger of the people at Indian designs openly exploded when a sacred hair of the Holy Prophet was stolen on 27 December from the Hazratbal mosque near Srinagar.[3] Richard Critchfield of the *Sunday Star* wrote this eye-witness account of 'the defiant struggle of Kashmir's four million Moslems to be free': 'After two weeks it is impossible for an outsider, even one deeply sympathetic toward India, to believe India can continue to hold onto Kashmir . . . India's 15-year attempt to win over Kashmiris is ending in tragic failure.'[4] Ayub called the upheaval in Kashmir 'a spontaneous referendum' against the Indian hold there.[5]

The Kashmir disturbances sparked off rioting and killings in East Pakistan and West Bengal, where communal passions were already running high. In his letter to the Indian President on 13 January 1964, Ayub stated that 20,000 Muslim refugees had crossed from West Bengal into East Pakistan within the previous two days.[6] Indian sources similarly alleged that a large stream of Hindus from East Pakistan was flooding West Bengal.[7] In March Khanna, the Indian Minister for Works, declared, 'Pakistan is India's enemy number one and its challenge has to be met.' Defence Minister

[1] *The Times,* 6 Dec. 1963.

[2] Bakshi Ghulam Muhammad resigned on 4 Oct. 1963 under the 'Kamraj Plan' and was briefly succeeded by Shamsuddin. In Feb. 1964 Ghulam Muhammad Sadiq became Prime Minister of Kashmir.

[3] It was surreptitiously returned on 3 Jan. 1964.

[4] *Sunday Star,* 19 Jan. 1964.

[5] M. Ayub Khan, *Speeches,* VI, p. 133.

[6] *Pakistan Horizon,* 1st Quarter 1964.

[7] On 19 March Nehru put the figure of Hindu refugees in West Bengal at 'over 125,000'; the Pakistani High Commissioner in India at about the same time said the Muslim refugees in East Pakistan numbered 173,000. *Asian Recorder,* 1964, p. 5774; *New York Times,* 22 March 1964.

Chavan threatened on the same day, 'We shall see that India becomes the graveyard of Pakistan.'[1]

The Home Ministers of India and Pakistan conferred at New Delhi from 7 to 11 April but could not reach any agreement. Neither side made any secret of the fact that the talks had failed because India rejected Pakistan's proposal that an international tribunal, consisting of one judge each from India and Pakistan and a third from an agreed country, be set up to decide whether the Muslims evicted from India were of Indian or Pakistani nationality. According to India there could be no question of introducing an international authority to decide a purely internal issue.[2]

The Security Council again Discusses the Kashmir Question
In the meantime the Kashmir question had been taken up by the Security Council, at Pakistan's request. Foreign Minister Bhutto, in a letter to the President of the Council on 16 January, had requested an immediate meeting to consider the grave situation in Kashmir and the resulting dangerous tension in the eastern part of the subcontinent. The debate in the Council opened on 3 February and dragged on till 18 May.

As stated in the last chapter, both the super-powers, the USA and the USSR, wished to avoid a showdown on Kashmir. In substance they deferred to the Indian wish that the Security Council should not pass any new resolution on Kashmir, but at the same time they did not wish to go too far in India's direction lest Pakistan be irretrievably driven into China's embrace. On the last day the President of the Council simply reviewed what the members had said at the various sessions, dividing his presentation into two parts. The first set forth the unanimous view of the members, that India and Pakistan should resume their contacts 'to resolve by negotiations their differences', especially those relating to Kashmir. The second described the view of the majority, that the Secretary-General of the United Nations might usefully assist the parties in their negotiations, as well as that of the minority (the Soviet Union and Czechoslovakia), that 'the intervention of any outside elements' might complicate the negotiations instead of facilitating them. M. C. Chagla, the Indian representative, made it clear that the Secretary-General should not come to India 'in the context of the Kashmir dispute'.[3]

---

[1] G. W. Choudhury, *Pakistan's Relations with India*, p. 178.
[2] *Hindu Weekly*, 13 April 1964.
[3] *1117th Meeting*, 18 May 1964.

Nehru Releases Abdullah

On 8 April 1964, more than a month before the Security Council concluded its debate on Kashmir, Sheikh Abdullah was released from prison. He had been in prison since his arrest on 8 August 1953, except for about a hundred days in the early part of 1958. The charge, that he and the other defendants had conspired to bring about Kashmir's accession to Pakistan, was withdrawn, resulting in the acquittal of all.

It was believed that the violent agitation in Kashmir, plus the communal violence in eastern India and East Pakistan, had driven Nehru to the conclusion that the passage of time had not cooled the Kashmir problem and he must make a fresh effort to solve it. He thought a visit to Pakistan by Abdullah was a good method of opening a dialogue on the subject.

Reportedly with the blessing of Rajagopalachari, Abdullah declared himself in favour of an Indo-Pakistani condominium as a solution for the Kashmir problem. India and Pakistan would share sovereignty over Kashmir which apparently would require a joint defence agreement to share responsibility for the integrity of Kashmir.[1]

The Sheikh arrived in Rawalpindi on 24 May and was given a hero's welcome. After conferring with Ayub, Abdullah announced, on 26 May, that Ayub and Nehru would meet in New Delhi in June to end the Kashmir dispute. But his mission ended abruptly because of Nehru's death on the following day, and he hurried back to New Delhi.

Some writers have wondered whether there was anything more at the back of Nehru's mind during his last mortal days than has so far been disclosed. But the available record is reasonably clear. It appears that, though Nehru had decided to make a new effort to establish peace between India and Pakistan, on the crucial question of the terms for a settlement he was still clinging to his favourite idea of a confederation between India and Pakistan. This is evident from what has already been stated above, as well as from some other pieces of information from Pakistani and Indian sources. Ayub has written in his autobiography, *Friends Not Masters*, that Abdullah had brought the 'absurd proposal' of confederation between India, Pakistan, and Kashmir, and has expressed surprise that Abdullah should have made a suggestion which would end Pakistan's independence.[2] More importantly, Nehru's own speech in Parliament, his

[1] *New York Times*, 10 May 1964.   [2] p. 128.

last major pronouncement before his death, revealed that his tenacious mind was still holding on to the idea that the final solution of
all Indo-Pakistani problems was for India and Pakistan to forge
constitutional links with each other: 'I would have hoped that India
and Pakistan would be able to come together much closer, even
constitutionally closer. I do not say so because this annoys Pakistan.'[1]

Nehru's Death

Nehru's death temporarily relaxed the tension in Indo-Pakistani
relations, but in the end his successor proved incapable of making
even the gestures and utterances of peace by which Nehru had
managed at least to stave off open war between the two neighbours.
Lal Bahadur Shastri, possessing less political skill and stature than
his more illustrious predecessor, could ill afford to incur the criticism
of the extremist elements among his countrymen by saying or doing
anything which might smack of a concession to Pakistan.

In his broadcast to the nation on 1 June, Ayub appealed for a
'fresh outlook' on Indo-Pakistani relations and extended 'a warm
hand of friendship' to the people of India. Two days later Shastri
told a press conference in his own capital that he was impressed by
Ayub's broadcast. The two leaders also exchanged cordial messages.
Nothing tangible, however, was done to ease the situation.

Ayub and Shastri met face to face for the first time on 12 October,
when Shastri stopped over for a few hours at Karachi, on his way
home from the Cairo conference of non-aligned countries. They
affirmed, in their joint communiqué, that it was necessary to settle
outstanding disputes on an equitable basis, and agreed that discussions be held 'at the earliest possible moment'. They undertook
to 'remain in touch' to determine how these objectives could be
best realized.[2]

However, instead of making any attempt to find an amicable
solution of Indo-Pakistani differences, the Shastri Government began
to add more fuel to the fire by taking steps to absorb Kashmir
further into the body politic of India. On 3 December Shastri said
the Kashmir problem occupied a 'secondary place' to peaceful
relations between India and Pakistan,[3] and on the following day
Home Minister G. L. Nanda announced his Government's decision
to apply to the state Articles 356 and 357 of the Indian Constitution,

[1] *Lok Sabha Debates*, 13 April 1964, col. 10717.
[2] *Pakistan Horizon*, 4th Quarter 1964, p. 397.
[3] *Dawn*, 4 Dec. 1964.

which would enable the President of India to proclaim Presidential rule in Kashmir and legislate there. With regard to Article 370, which allowed Kashmir a special status under the Indian Constitution, Nanda said, 'It is not a wall. It is a tunnel. A good deal of traffic has passed already, more will pass now.'[1]

On 9 January 1965 the Indian National Congress decided to establish its own branch in Kashmir, and Premier Sadiq said the local National Conference, which had hitherto formed the Governments in Kashmir, would be dissolved and its members would enrol in the New Congress organization in the state. This, he said, would bring Kashmir into the 'political mainstream of India'. On the same day, the Plebiscite Front of Sheikh Abdullah appealed to Kashmiris to observe 15 January as a day of protest against the Indian decision to bring Kashmir further within the purview of the Indian Constitution. Huge crowds turned out on the prescribed day and the police had to open fire to disperse the processions. 'If one thing is absolutely plain about Kashmir,' wrote the correspondent of the *Economist* from Kashmir, 'it is that after 17 years with India, the Kashmir valley—bar its few Hindus—wants to join Pakistan.'[2]

In the midst of growing tension, Indian troops occupied the East Pakistani enclave of Dahagram on 17 March and exchanged fire with Pakistani troops for a fortnight before withdrawing. The *Economist* noted that India's relations with Pakistan were now as bad as they had ever been and commented that 'for this, Indian actions tending to integrate Kashmir are directly to blame'.[3]

In an atmosphere so heavily charged with frustration and anger, it needed but an accidental spark to touch off a conflagration. The ignition was provided by the exchange of fire on 9 April across the disputed border in the Rann of Kutch, and India and Pakistan found themselves drawn into the first of their two undeclared wars of 1965.

II. The Rann of Kutch War

The roots of the Indo-Pakistani dispute concerning the Rann of Kutch go back to the days of British rule in India. At that time the Rann was the bone of contention between the princely state of

[1] *Asian Recorder*, 1964, p. 6212.
[2] *Economist*, 16 Jan. 1965.
[3] ibid., 3 April 1965.

Kutch and the British Indian province of Sindh. When the sub-continent was partitioned, the issue was inherited by India, to whom Kutch acceded, and Pakistan, whom Sindh joined.

Pakistan's stand was that the border between India and Pakistan ran through the middle of the Rann. India claimed that the boundary ran along the northern edge of the Rann. The dispute thus involved some 3,500 square miles of territory. Each side contended that the boundary claimed by it was the traditional, well-established, and well-recognized boundary.[1]

Diplomatic notes concerning the dispute were first exchanged between Pakistan and India in 1948. On 23 December 1955 Anil K. Chanda, the Indian Deputy Minister for External Affairs, stated that 'for some time' the Pakistani Government had been advancing a claim to the northern portion of the Rann and Pakistan nationals had been trespassing across the border. He asserted that Pakistan's claim was baseless and had been rebutted by India in correspondence with Pakistan.[2] A few months later Prime Minister Chaudhri Muhammad Ali complained in the Constituent Assembly of Pakistan that Indian armed forces had attacked Pakistani border police posts at Chhad Bet on 17, 19, and 25 February and 2 March.[3]

The problem was first discussed at diplomatic level in January 1960. As already stated in an earlier chapter,[4] it was decided on that occasion that both sides would collect further data and discuss the question later. No further effort, however, was made to solve the dispute.

Border incidents began to take place with increasing frequency from January 1965 onwards, reflecting the deteriorating condition of Indo-Pakistani relations in general. Large-scale fighting flared up on 9 April, with each side blaming the other for provoking the clash. By all accounts the Indian forces were badly mauled in the Kutch area by the Pakistani army, which led Shastri to say on 29 April that, if the fighting continued, 'the Army will decide its own strategy and deploy its manpower and equipment in the way it deems best'.[5] This was taken by everyone to mean that the Indian

---

[1] These were the positions taken up by Pakistan and India before the international tribunal which ultimately determined the dispute. *Pakistan Horizon*, 3rd Quarter 1968.

[2] *Hindu*, 24 Dec. 1955.

[3] On 19 March 1956.

[4] See p. 234.

[5] *Hindu Weekly*, 3 May 1965.

army would launch an attack on Lahore, the principal city in West Pakistan nearest to India.

Johnson having only recently given offence to both India and Pakistan by unilaterally cancelling Shastri's and Ayub's scheduled visits to Washington, the USA was in no position to press the parties to stop fighting in the Rann. Russia was still regarded by Pakistan as biased in favour of India. So it was left to Britain to persuade the parties to accept an informal lull from 30 April till a formal cease-fire could be negotiated. The lull was briefly interrupted twice but, when Ayub and Shastri went to London to attend the Commonwealth Prime Ministers' Conference, Prime Minister Harold Wilson successfully persuaded them to sign an agreement on 30 June to resolve the dispute peacefully.

Besides making the cease-fire permanent, the agreement laid down a self-executing procedure for the settlement of the dispute. It was stipulated that an effort would first be made to settle the question by bilateral discussion at Minister's level. If no agreement was reached 'within two months of the cease-fire' the two Governments would have recourse to a tribunal as contemplated by the joint communiqué of 24 October 1959.[1] Such a tribunal, to be constituted 'within four months of the cease-fire', would consist of three persons, one each to be nominated by India and Pakistan and the third, who would be the chairman, to be jointly selected by the two parties. Should the parties be unable to agree on the selection of the chairman 'within three months of the cease-fire', they would request the Secretary-General of the United Nations to nominate the chairman. It was agreed further that the decision of the tribunal 'shall be binding' on both Governments and that the tribunal 'shall remain in being until its findings have been implemented in full'.[2]

It is to the credit of both India and Pakistan that, though their relations worsened and they fought a bigger war in September, both faithfully observed the terms of the agreement of 30 June 1965. Owing to tension between the two countries a Foreign Minister's meeting fixed at Delhi for 20 August had to be cancelled and the matter was automatically referred to a tribunal. Pakistan nominated Nasrolla Entezam, an Irani diplomat, and India, Ales Bebler, a Yugoslav judge. The Secretary-General selected Judge Gunnar Lagergren of Sweden as chairman.

[1] See p. 234.
[2] Text in *Pakistan Horizon*, 3rd Quarter 1965.

The tribunal announced its verdict on 19 February 1969, award-
ing about 350 square miles in the northern part of the disputed
Rann of Kutch to Pakistan and the rest to India. India's share was
much larger but it was mostly sea-marsh, often under water, while
Pakistan's included some crucial elevation points. Though neither
side had got all it wanted, there was much more criticism of the
tribunal's decision in India than in Pakistan. But Mrs. Indira
Gandhi, who had succeeded Shastri as Premier in January 1966,
successfully resisted all suggestions to nullify the award or to delay
its implementation. The curtain on this episode was rung down at
Islamabad on 4 July 1969, when Indian and Pakistani plenipoten-
tiaries signed the last documents and maps, in token of finally
ending the dispute.

J. P. Narain asked his countrymen to treat the Kutch agreement
'as an object lesson in peace-making' and endorsed the Pakistani
view that India and Pakistan thereafter apply this method to all
disputes, 'including that of Kashmir'. If the Indian offer of a no-war
declaration were not to be reduced to a mere slogan, he argued, 'we
must state as a corollary that we are prepared to agree to commonly
evolved procedures for the settlement of all disputes'.[1]

Before picking up the thread of our story, it would be pertinent
to allude to one more aspect of the Kutch War, the question of the
use of American arms by India and Pakistan, a matter which later
in the same year, during the September war, was to be debated even
more loudly. Though the Indians were far more vocal in their
complaint than Pakistanis, the New Delhi correspondent of the
New York Times pointed out that 'both sides appear to be using
American-supplied war material against each other in contravention
of conditions under which it was received'.[2]

III. The September War

The Kutch war was but a symptom of the deep-seated canker of
Kashmir which continued to fester and poison Indo-Pakistani
relations.

Realizing that India was determined to absorb Kashmir into the
Indian Union, in disregard of the wishes of the Kashmiris, Abdullah
had left India on 22 February 1965 to enlist the support of the international community in his cause. He went to the UAR, Britain,
France, and Algeria. At Algiers Abdullah met Premier Chou En-lai,

---

[1] *Hindu Weekly*, 26 July 1965.
[2] *New York Times*, 30 April 1965.

who invited him to China. India thereupon declared all the endorse-
ments on Abdullah's passport invalid, save those necessary for a
pilgrimage to Mecca and return to India. After visiting Saudi
Arabia, Abdullah, therefore, was compelled to return to India and
was promptly taken into custody as soon as he landed on Indian
soil on 8 May.

While Abdullah was abroad the Kashmir Legislative Assembly
had adopted the Constitution Amendment Bill (30 March) providing that: (1) the Sadar-i-Riyasat would henceforth be known as
Governor and would be appointed by the President of India,
instead of being elected by the local Assembly; and (2) the Prime
Minister would be styled Chief Minister, as in the states of the Indian
Union. The enactment had added to the existing feeling of anger
amongst the Kashmiris, and Abdullah's arrest acted as the signal
for a new burst of protests in Kashmir. Four persons were killed
by police fire on the very first day.

On 5 June an Action Committee, combining nine Kashmiri opposition groups, launched a Gandhi-type non-violent civil disobedience
movement, demanding the release of Abdullah and the fulfilment
of India's pledge to let the Kashmiris choose between India and
Pakistan.[1] Despite the best efforts of the pro-Indian Sadiq Government, the agitation continued with increasing tempo.

On 8 August a clandestine radio station, describing itself as the
Sada-e-Kashmir (Voice of Kashmir), announced that a Revolutionary Council, to conduct an all-out war of liberation against
Indian imperialism, was being set up on 9 August to mark the 12th
anniversary of Sheikh Abdullah's arrest on 9 August 1953.[2] Two
days later posters, splashed across the walls of Srinagar and other
towns in Indian-held Kashmir, claimed the establishment of a
National Government of the people of Jammu and Kashmir.[3]

The Indians alleged that the *Sada-e-Kashmir* broadcasting station
was located in Pakistan, and denied that the people of Kashmir were
in revolt. But, as the *Daily Telegraph* (26 August) pointed out,
'what is unquestionable is that India is confronted with serious
discontent and a strong Kashmiri nationalist movement which cannot be blamed on Pakistan though she may exploit it.'[4]

The happenings inside Indian-held Kashmir could not but have

[1] *New York Times*, 9, 11 June 1965.
[2] *Dawn*, 9 Aug. 1965.
[3] ibid., 11 Aug. 1965.
[4] Quoted in *Pakistan Horizon*, 3rd Quarter 1965.

repercussions on the other side of the cease-fire line. Azad Kash-miris became increasingly restive, itching to go to the assistance of their kinsmen. Tension along the cease-fire line mounted. There had been more incidents on the cease-fire line in May than in any month in the previous eighteen years.

On 17 May Indian troops in battalion strength had crossed the cease-fire line and occupied three Pakistani posts in the Kargil area, allegedly to protect the Srinagar–Leh highway from being cut by Pakistanis. This was the first time since 1949 that either country had violated the cease-fire line in strength and occupied territory on the other side. Under United Nations and United States pressure the Indians had withdrawn from the posts on 30 June, on which date the agreement to terminate hostilities in the Rann of Kutch was signed.

With the continuing agitation against Indian rule in Kashmir, and its brutal suppression by the Sadiq Government, backed by a 150,000-strong Indian army, it was merely a question of time for the Azad Kashmiris to reach the end of their patience and go to the assistance of their hapless countrymen. For some days, starting on 5 August, armed Azad Kashmiris crossed the cease-fire line into Indian-held Kashmir to join fellow Kashmiris in their struggle for self-determination. Indians alleged they were personnel of the Pakistani army in disguise.

India now made a series of new moves across the cease-fire line with her regular armed forces. On 16 August Indian troops once more crossed the line and reoccupied the three posts they had vacated in June.[1] Defence Minister Chavan declared: 'Whenever it was found necessary to cross the cease-fire line in order to defend the cease-fire line and other areas, we have done so. If it is found necessary, I have no doubt that we will not fail to do it again.'[2] A few days later India claimed she had seized a wide stretch of Pakistani-controlled territory and her troops had dug in just fourteen miles from the Azad Kashmir capital of Muzzaffarabad.[3] Soon after-wards the Indian forces launched 'the third large-scale Indian assault across the United Nations cease-fire line in 13 days' in a drive south from Uri to link up with Indian units near Poonch.[4]

The Indian forces were also the first to commit an act of hostility

---

[1] *Hindu Weekly*, 23 Aug. 1965.
[2] *Asian Recorder*, 1965, p. 6654.
[3] *Minneapolis Tribune*, 27 Aug. 1965.
[4] *New York Times*, 29 Aug. 1965.

outside Kashmir. On 23 August they shelled the village of Awan Sharif in West Pakistan with guns on the Indian side of Kashmir, killing twenty men, women, and children and wounding thirteen. After a personal visit to the village the *New York Times* correspondent reported: 'There were fresh pockmarks on the walls and the door frames of the simple village mosque, and several houses were badly damaged. Darkening patches of blood showed where people had been standing when the shells landed. . . . Although Awan Sharif is near the border, any military importance it might have was not apparent.'[1]

On 30 August the Indians claimed that they had captured at least nine important Pakistani positions in a major offensive into Azad Kashmir. These included the strategic 8,600-feet-high Haji Pir Pass. Thus Indian troops were now 'at least twenty-five miles within Pakistani-held Kashmir'.[2] On the following day India said her troops held a 'dominating position' in a 200-square-mile chunk of Azad Kashmir in the Uri–Poonch sector. All-India Radio referred to India's newly acquired positions as the 'liberated areas' of Kashmir and it was reported that civil administration was being extended to these territories. These reports were taken to mean that 'India was no longer merely trying to cut off further infiltration into Indian Kashmir but was openly embarking on a "war of liberation" in Pakistani-held Kashmir'.[3]

It was at this juncture that, on 1 September, an official statement from Rawalpindi announced that, to forestall further aggression by Indian troops, Azad Kashmiri forces, supported by the Pakistani army, had crossed the cease-fire line and occupied two Indian posts in the Chhamb area of the Jammu-Bhimber sector. This was the first time, since the establishment of the cease-fire line, that the Pakistani army had advanced beyond that limit.

India now threw her air force into the battle—another first to her credit—and Pakistan followed suit. By 5 September the Pakistani forces had occupied Jaurian near Akhnoor, the road junction linking Jammu with Srinagar and Poonch, and the Indian land route to the Valley was seriously threatened.

At 3 a.m. on 6 September, without a formal declaration of war, Indians crossed the international border of West Pakistan and launched a three-pronged offensive against Lahore. Two days later

[1] ibid., 28 Aug. 1965.
[2] ibid., 31 Aug. 1965.
[3] ibid., 1 Sept. 1965.

another attack was mounted in the Sialkot sector and a third front was opened in Rajasthan.

The main diplomatic effort to stop the fighting was conducted under United Nations auspices and a cease-fire came into effect on 23 September. Before describing the role of the United Nations and the attitude of the various countries, it would be pertinent to comment on certain other aspects of the war.

Who was more to blame for the war?

The Indians placed their entire stress on the guerrillas who began to infiltrate into Indian-held Kashmir from the Azad Kashmir side of the cease-fire line early in August, conveniently forgetting that the cease-fire line had first been breached in strength by their own regular units in May. In his broadcast to the nation, on 13 August, Shastri called the guerrilla infiltration 'a thinly disguised armed attack on our country organized by Pakistan' which had to be met 'as such'.[1] But, as *The Times* had observed a day earlier, 'To ask why it happened, one has to go back to last December when the Indians, by bringing Kashmir into the legislative orbit of the Indian Parliament, seemed to be marking the case as closed.' Sheikh Abdullah also held India responsible for the war, saying that 'because India shut the doors for negotiations, Pakistan being a party, had sent the infiltrators'.[2] Russell Brines, similarly, points out that the Indian measures to equalize Kashmir with other Indian states meant, in effect, that New Delhi had no further intention of seriously negotiating a new status for Kashmir. 'By adding the new policy over Kashmir to the accumulated concern over rearmament,' he sums up, 'New Delhi made military action almost inevitable.'[3]

Pakistan did not deny that armed infiltrators had crossed the cease-fire line from Azad Kashmir, but refuted the Indian allegation that they belonged to a special unit of the Pakistani army named 'Gibraltar Forces'. Pakistani spokesmen said the infiltrators were Azad Kashmiri war veterans who had persuaded their government to give them arms to go to the assistance of their kinsmen on the other side of the cease-fire line.[4] As Foreign Minister Bhutto put it: 'Infiltrators can only come from outside. The cease-fire line is an arbitrary line [that] divides the same people and these people are

[1] K. C. Saxena, *Pakistan: Her Relations with India (1947–1966)*, p. 79.
[2] *Hindu Weekly*, 22 April 1968.
[3] R. Brines, *The Indo-Pakistani Conflict*, pp. 284–6.
[4] *Security Council Official Records, 1240th meeting*, 18 Sept. 1965; *President Ayub on the Crisis Over Kashmir*, p. 22.

Kashmiris who have the same blood, same culture, same language, same stock and you cannot infiltrate in your own home. . . . How can you commit aggression against your own people? You can only liberate your own people.'[1]

No independent observer supported the Indian assertion that the armed personnel in question were members of the Pakistani army. In a report to the Security Council the Secretary-General said that 'in most cases' their identity 'could not be verified'.[2] The *New York Times* special correspondent reported from Srinagar on 13 August that 'the infiltrators appear to have been recruited mainly from among the people of Azad Kashmir'.[3] In his study of the Kashmir problem Alastair Lamb has also concluded that it is not clear whether, in August 1965, Pakistani troops had joined Azad Kashmiris in infiltrating across the cease-fire line, as claimed by India.[4]

On the other hand, there is positive indication that Azad Kashmiris had been spoiling to join their brethren across the cease-fire line in their unequal struggle against the Indian army. Louis Dupree, who personally visited Azad Kashmir in the spring of 1965, was told by President Abdul Hamid Khan: 'For almost 20 years the Pakistanis have held back our people, but we have been waiting for an opportunity to strike to wage a war of independence. We look to Algeria as a guide . . . we are waiting and watching, but not for long.'[5]

Patrick Seale of the *Observer* found that the Azad Kashmiri army was a 'fine fighting force some 20,000 strong'. Azad Kashmiris told him persistently that they did not recognize the cease-fire line because it was fixed bilaterally by India and Pakistan, without consulting the Kashmiris. 'This argument', he wrote, 'is sometimes pushed to the point of saying that if only Pakistan would loose her hold over Azad Kashmir her people would proceed Algerian-style to liberate their countrymen across the border. Indeed by early summer impatience and frustration had reached the stage when men were openly saying that Pakistan was not interested in a solution and that President Ayub had failed them.'[6]

Indian assertions to the contrary notwithstanding, the rest of the world treats Kashmir as disputed territory, and the Kashmir

---

[1] Z. A. Bhutto, *Important Press Conferences Held in 1965*, p. 38.
[2] *S/6651*, 3 Sept. 1965, para. 6.
[3] *New York Times*, 14 Aug. 1965.
[4] Alastair Lamb, *The Kashmir Problem*, p. 120.
[5] Louis Dupree, *First Reflections on the Second Kashmir War*, p. 14.
[6] *Observer*, 10 Oct. 1965.

question is still pending on the agenda of the Security Council as an unsolved problem. While, therefore, Indo-Pakistani fighting was confined to Kashmiri territory, the world community did not treat it as a full-scale international war. Not surprisingly, India's invasion of West Pakistan brought forth condemnation from several sources. Prime Minister Wilson called India's act a 'distressing response' to the resolution of the Security Council calling for a cease-fire.[1] The correspondent of the *New York Times* reported from Delhi: 'India has ruefully discovered that her invasion of the Pakistani Punjab last Monday had little support in the rest of the world and in fact dissipated most of the sympathy built by charges of infiltration of Kashmir by Pakistanis.'[2]

Even Premier Kosygin of the USSR, who was friendlier to India than to Pakistan, and President Nasser of the UAR, who had always maintained special ties with New Delhi, criticized India for having crossed the international line. Kosygin 'took exception to India's crossing the international border' and wrote to Shastri requesting 'New Delhi to immediately order cease-fire and withdraw its forces behind the cease-fire line in Jammu and Kashmir and the international border elsewhere'.[3] Nasser made it plain to Krishna Menon that the attack on Lahore was a gross violation of international frontiers.[4] In line with their usual custom in comparable situations, to admonish the West more than others, the Indians severely criticized Wilson but quietly swallowed Kosygin's and Nasser's remonstrations.

John Kenneth Galbraith, former Ambassador to India, said at a Committee hearing afterwards that, if the USA had not supplied arms, Pakistan would not have sought 'a military solution' of the Kashmir dispute in 1965.[5] Another distinguished American, Secretary of Defense Robert S. McNamara, however, reminded the Committee[6] that there had been 'centuries and centuries' of conflict between Hindus and Muslims and that at the time of partition,

[1] *The Times*, 7 Sept. 1965.
[2] *New York Times*, 11 Sept 1965.
[3] *Hindu Weekly*, 20 Sept. 1965.
[4] Z. A. Bhutto, *The Myth of Independence*, p. 75. See also Bhutto's statement to the same effect in the National Assembly on 15 March 1966, at page 492 of the *Official Report*.
[5] *Foreign Assistance 1966, Hearings Before the Committee on Foreign Relations, United States Senate, 89th Congress, 2nd Session on S.2859 and S.2861*, 25 April 1966, p. 234.
[6] ibid., 11 May 1966, p. 671.

'without any aid from us, several hundred thousand people were killed'. He could have added that the first Kashmir war between India and Pakistan had also been fought before any American arms had been shipped to the subcontinent and that the stoppage of American military assistance in 1965 neither prevented the parties from continuing to arm themselves nor did it eliminate the possibility of further conflict.

Pakistanis believe that it was Russian and American military equipment and their friendly attitude that emboldened India to foreclose the Kashmir issue and embark upon the 'liberation' of Azad Kashmir. As the *Sunday Times* observed, the humiliation of the Indian army at the hands of the Chinese in 1962 'sat on Indian flesh like a boil that had to burst'.[1] That India had subsequently come out second best in the Kutch fighting only increased the impatience of her armed forces to show what they could do. It was reported in a respected Indian newspaper that the 'joy of the members [of the Indian Parliament on 24 September] over the success of the Indian forces over the American Patton tanks and Sabre Jets was overwhelming and one could say has been carried to the extent of hurting American feelings'.[2] President Radhakrishnan in a broadcast on 25 September declared, 'We have today retrieved our prestige.'[3] On the following day Shastri said: 'There was perhaps a feeling of demoralization, a feeling that we were a weak nation unable to defend ourselves. That feeling had to go and I am glad that it has now gone.'[4] As a part of the celebrations on his 61st birthday, on 2 October 1965, Shastri cut a giant-sized cake, the replica of a Patton tank, and gleefully exclaimed, 'I have also destroyed a tank.'[5]

Who won the war?
Each side said its war aims were limited and that these were attained. Both, therefore, claimed victory.

General Muhammad Musa, Commander-in-Chief of the Pakistani army, believed that India's aim was (1) to capture the entire territory of Azad Kashmir, and (2) to defeat the Pakistani army and dictate humiliating terms to Pakistan. 'Not only was the enemy

[1] *Sunday Times*, 12 Sept. 1965, quoted in *Pakistan Horizon*, 4th Quarter 1965.
[2] *Hindu Weekly*, 4 Oct. 1965.
[3] ibid.
[4] ibid.
[5] ibid., 11 Oct. 1965.

powerfully contained,' he commented, 'but he was put to heavy losses. For every *shaheed*, ten Indians fell.'[1]

General J. N. Chaudhuri, Chief of the Indian Army Staff, stated that the fronts across the international border had to be opened to relieve the pressure of the Pakistani armoured thrust into Kashmir. It was not his idea to capture Lahore or any other city, as it would have tied up troops and the object of 'causing attrition to Pakistan's armour' would have been lost. Though Pakistan had received 'a good knock', he concluded, it would not be correct to say that she had been 'knocked out'.[2]

The estimates of territorial and military losses, as published by the Defence Ministries of Pakistan and India, greatly differed from each other:[3]

I. Territory	Pakistani Govt.'s Estimates	Indian Govt.'s Estimates
A. Indian territory captured by Pakistan (sq. miles.)	1617*	210†
B. Pakistani territory captured by India (sq. miles)	446*	740†

*Source: Pakistani Govt.'s estimates of 24 Sept. 1965—*Dawn*, Karachi, 6 Oct. 1965.

†Source: Indian Govt.'s statement of 7 Oct. 1965—*Keesing's Contemporary Archives*, p. 21108.

II. Men and Material	Pakistani Govt.'s Estimates‡		Indian Govt.'s Estimates§	
	Pakistan	India	Pakistan	India
A. Men killed	1033	9500	4802	1333
B. Tanks lost	165	475	475	128
C. Aircraft destroyed	14	110	73	35

‡Source: Statement of the Defence Ministry of Pakistan of 4 Dec. 1965—*Dawn*, Karachi, 5 Dec. 1965.

§Source: Statement of the Defence Ministry of India of 25 Sept. 1965—*Keesing's Contemporary Archives*, p. 21108.

As Alastair Lamb has written, 'India failed to break through to Lahore. Pakistan failed both to cut the Indian line of communica-

---

[1] *Pakistan Horizon*, 4th Quarter 1965.

[2] *Hindu Weekly*, 4 Oct. 1965.

[3] For fuller details see *Pakistan Horizon*, 4th Quarter 1965, whence this information has been gathered. Contrary to Indian official figures, an Indian columnist wrote: 'A justifiable assumption may be that the casualties on the Pakistani side are less than India's.' *Hindu Weekly*, 22 Nov. 1965.

tion in Kashmir and to start the long-expected tank promenade down the Grand Trunk Road to Delhi.'[1] But certain aspects of the unfinished war were fairly evident.

Despite its fourfold numerical advantage, the Indian army was quickly stalled in its offensive and suffered severe punishment. There was nothing to suggest that India did not wish to take Lahore. In fact 'the Indian authorities allowed their own people, as well as the outside world, to believe that the push towards or around Lahore was a serious one'.[2] Indian sources jubilantly announced that the Indian army had reached 'the outskirts of Lahore before sunset [of 6 September] after smashing through the Pakistani defences'.[3] According to Western experts, if the Indian advance could have been carried to its 'logical conclusion' it would have certainly split West Pakistan militarily into three isolated zones with their main lateral lines of road and rail communications cut at Lahore and Hyderabad.[4]

The Pakistani navy and air force did markedly well. Units of the Pakistani navy, disregarding Indian superiority in warships, audaciously sailed to Dwarka, some two hundred miles south of Karachi, and destroyed powerful radar installations which were being used to direct air raids against Karachi and West Pakistan. Further, the Pakistani navy kept the Indian navy away from the shores of Pakistan and claimed to have sunk an Indian frigate.

Pakistani claims of complete mastery in the air and overwhelming victories over the Indian air force were endorsed by a professional American publication, *Aviation Week and Space Technology*.[5] It was pointed out that at the start of the conflict Indian air power had an approximately 5:1 numerical superiority. Though both sides claimed air victory, the Pakistani air force fully documented its case (also confirmed by the US Military Assistance Advisory Group) by publicly detailing its nineteen losses. It also flew virtually its entire air strength over a victory parade to refute Indian claims to have destroyed more than a hundred Pakistani aircraft. India eventually admitted the loss of seventy-five aircraft.

Some Consequences of the War

When war broke out the Pakistani economy, including the crucial agricultural sector, was in a better state of health than the Indian

[1] Alastair Lamb, *The Kashmir Problem*, p. 123.
[2] *Economist*, 18 Sept. 1965.
[3] *Asian Recorder*, 1965, p. 6688.
[4] ibid., p. 6691.
[5] 2 Dec. 1968; a McGraw-Hill publication.

economy. Consequently, the shock of war and suspension of American aid was felt by India to a much greater degree. As *The Times* put it, 'The difference is that of the same blow to a man walking upstairs and to another whose foot has already slipped on the way down—Pakistan in the past couple of years had been doing well economically while India had already begun to slip.'[1] Two successive drought years, 1965–6 and 1966–7, further aggravated India's distress. Her Gross National Product decreased by 5.2 per cent in 1965–6 and rose by only 1.1 per cent in the following year.[2] In June 1966 India was compelled to devalue her rupee by 36.5 per cent. It was not till 1967–8 that, following a good monsoon, Indian agricultural production improved, and not for another year that the industrial recession ended.

Pakistan too had to modify her development programme in the light of new conditions. Because of the favourable momentum already built up, she managed to increase her Gross National Product in 1965–6 by 4.6 per cent and did even better in the succeeding two years. But, in the long run, the rate of growth was affected by the suspension of US economic assistance, the reduced volume of foreign aid, and the cessation of American military supplies on a grant basis, which placed a tremendous additional burden on Pakistan's foreign-exchange resources.

Internationally, Indian prestige, which had been slipping for some years past, fell still lower. If after the Sino–Indian border war of 1962 anyone had still entertained any hope that India might be able to stand up to China, he could no longer justifiably do so.

Both countries displayed a certain degree of communal maturity. In neither were the minorities molested. India had repeatedly asserted in the past that any change in the status of Kashmir would result in the victimization of Muslims all over India. Now the world had seen that there had been a war over Kashmir but there had been no communal rioting anywhere.

In a way, the absence of total victory by either side had a sobering effect on both countries. An ignominious defeat, besides raising grave political questions, would have created heady arrogance in the victor and rankling humiliation in the vanquished. Now Pakistan was no longer so afraid of losing her independence at the hands of her big neighbour as she used to be, and India could no

---

[1] *The Times,* 29 Oct. 1965.

[2] *Current Notes,* Department of External Affairs, Canberra, Australia, April 1970, p. 173.

longer take a victory over her smaller neighbour for granted. India, moreover, was put on notice that in any future conflict with Pakistan she would have to consider the possibility of Chinese intervention in support of Pakistan and the escalation of war to global dimensions.

The war visibly ended Pakistan's special ties with the USA and weakened India's special relationship with the USSR. No longer dependent on any one country, Pakistan felt free to give real meaning to her already expressed wish to have equally good relations with all countries on a reciprocal basis.

Pakistan also had the satisfaction of getting more sympathy from the Afro-Asian community than India. Among her supporters there were conservative nations such as Saudi Arabia, Turkey, and Iran as well as revolutionary regimes such as those of China and Indonesia. Of special value to Pakistan emotionally was the positive support extended to her by most Muslim countries.[1]

At home, however, Shastri, having passed away at Tashkent,[2] escaped personal criticism of his policy, but Ayub was taken to task by his countrymen in both wings of Pakistan. As strong-man rule is sustained by visible success and prestige, the criticism of Ayub's war policy paved the way for the series of events which eventually brought his regime down.

The Times special correspondent in the subcontinent had foreseen that sooner or later the question would be raised in Pakistan: 'What about Kashmir, if we had such a great victory why is that unattainable? Why don't we clinch our victory?'[3] After the Tashkent Declaration, which its critics said had frozen the Kashmir problem, this question rose to the surface in West Pakistan, which had been the direct target of the Indian attack. Protest processions were organized in several cities. Two lives, including that of a student, were lost at Lahore in the police firing, and West Pakistani schools and universities had to close down.

In East Pakistan the discontent with the war took a different form. Nurul Amin, leader of the Combined Opposition Parties in the National Assembly, accepted the Tashkent Declaration as a 'hard fact of life' but called the Indo-Pakistani war 'futile and senseless'.[4] Another East Pakistani spokesman complained in the National Assembly that the war had endangered the lives of seven

[1] See p. 353.
[2] The Tashkent Declaration to which Shastri and Ayub subscribed on 10 Jan. 1966 will be described under the section '*The USSR and the Indo-Pakistani War*'.
[3] *The Times*, 29 Oct. 1965.
[4] *Dawn*, 5 Feb. 1966.

crores of Muslims of India and ten crores of Muslims of Pakistan for only forty lakhs of Muslims of Kashmir.[1] East Pakistanis said they had been completely cut off from the Western wing during the war and were defenceless if India had attacked them. Their feelings were not assuaged by Foreign Minister Bhutto's revelation that India had not attacked East Pakistan because China had told the USA, in their bilateral discussions at Warsaw, that she would intervene in the war if India attacked East Pakistan.[2] 'If we really owe the salvation of East Pakistan during the war not to the military strength West Pakistan always boasted about, but only to the fortuitous circumstance of Chinese hostility to India,' a prominent Bangalee is reported to have asked, 'what need have we of West Pakistan?'[3] It was during this period that the long-standing East Pakistani demand for self-sufficiency in defence gathered new strength, and Sheikh Mujibur Rahman formally formulated his six points, demanding almost complete autonomy for East Pakistan. The war thus gave a fillip to the forces working towards the estrangement of the two wings of Pakistan.

IV. The World and the September War

The United Nations and the Indo-Pakistani War
Secretary-General U Thant said in a public statement on 24 August that the situation in Kashmir posed 'a very serious and dangerous threat to peace'. On 1 September, immediately after the Pakistani army had crossed the cease-fire line and joined battle with the Indian forces in the Chhamb area, he sent identical telegrams to Shastri and Ayub, pleading for a cease-fire and withdrawal of forces to their own respective sides of the cease-fire line.[4] U Thant also submitted a report to the Security Council on 3 September. In this he dated the 'current serious trouble' from 5 August when, as indicated to him by General Nimmo, armed men began to cross the cease-fire line from the Pakistani side, 'even though in most cases the actual identity of those engaging in the armed attacks on the Indian side of the line and their actual crossing of it could not be verified by direct observation or evidence'.[5]

[1] Moulana Abul Hafez Mohsenuddin Ahmad, *National Assembly of Pakistan Debates*, 15 March 1966, p. 477.
[2] *National Assembly of Pakistan Debates*, 15 March 1966, p. 499.
[3] *New York Times*, 22 April 1966.
[4] K. Sarwar Hasan (ed.), *Documents on the Foreign Relations of Pakistan, The Kashmir Question*, p. 437.
[5] S/6651.

On the following day the Security Council passed a resolution, the first of a string of five concerning the Indo-Pakistani war.[1] It called for a cease-fire and withdrawal of all armed personnel to the positions held by them before 5 August. By another resolution, on 6 September, the Security Council noted the extension of fighting 'with deep concern', and repeated the exhortation contained in the previous resolution. Pakistanis were disappointed that neither of these resolutions contained any promise that an effort would be made to solve the Kashmir problem in terms of the past resolutions of the United Nations.

With a view to implementing the cease-fire resolutions, the Secretary-General personally visited Pakistan and India from 9 to 15 September, and conferred with the leaders of both countries. On 12 September he wrote to Ayub and Shastri asking them to 'order a cease-fire without conditions'. Ayub represented that a 'purposeful cease-fire' must provide for a self-executing arrangement for the final settlement of the Kashmir dispute which was the 'root cause' of the Indo-Pakistani conflict. Shastri answered that India 'shall not agree to any disposition which will leave the door open for further infiltrations'.[2] In their talks with the Secretary-General, Indians were also reported to have stated that, as a guarantee against further trouble, they would hold on to some strategic points they had recently captured on the Pakistan side of the cease-fire line.[3] On receipt of a further message from the Secretary-General, however, Shastri wrote back on 15 September expressing his willingness 'to order a simple cease-fire', if Pakistan would agree to do the same. The Secretary-General left for New York, after addressing an appeal to Shastri and Ayub to make a new effort to settle their differences by bilateral discussions.

On 16 September the Chinese Government handed over an ultimatum to the Indian Embassy in Peking demanding that India dismantle all its 'military works' on the Chinese side of the China–Sikkim boundary, or on the boundary itself, within three days, and return the kidnapped Chinese border inhabitants and seized livestock, or else 'bear full responsibility for all the grave consequences arising therefrom'.[4]

---

[1] For texts of all these five resolutions see *Pakistan Horizon*, 4th Quarter 1965.
[2] For texts of Secretary-General's letter of 12 Sept. and Ayub's and Shastri's replies see Sarwar Hasan (ed.), *Documents on the Foreign Relations of Pakistan, The Kashmir Question*, pp. 451–5.
[3] *New York Times*, 14 Sept. 1965.
[4] *Notes, Memoranda and Letters Exchanged Between the Governments of India and China, White Paper No. XII*, p. 42.

It was now feared that, if the Indo-Pakistani war continued much longer, China might intervene on behalf of Pakistan. This would bring in the USA on India's side, resulting in a major war of unpredictable dimensions. The members of the Security Council, therefore, hastened to pass a more meaningful resolution on 20 September which not only called for a cease-fire but demanded that it take effect on 22 September at 0700 GMT, promising also that, as soon as the cease-fire and withdrawal of forces had taken place, they would consider 'what steps could be taken to assist towards a settlement of the political problems underlying the present conflict'. The time limit for enforcing the cease-fire having been extended by a few hours, the parties stopped fighting at 3 a.m. West Pakistan time on 23 September. It was the first time in the course of the long Indo-Pakistani dispute that the Security Council had 'demanded' that the parties should do anything definite. The 20 September resolution also called on 'all states to refrain from any action which might aggravate the situation in the area'. This was read as a joint US–USSR warning to China not to widen the war by joining Pakistan.

As the cease-fire was not holding too well, the Council, by another resolution passed on 27 September, called upon the parties to honour the terms of the resolution of 20 September. The fifth resolution of the series, dated 5 November, reaffirmed the resolution of 20 September, insisted that there be an end to cease-fire violations, and demanded that the representatives of the parties meet with a representative of the Secretary-General for the purpose of formulating an agreed plan for the withdrawals by both parties.

During a meeting of the Security Council on 22 September Foreign Minister Bhutto declared that Pakistan was giving 'this last chance' to the Security Council to discharge its responsibility. If the Council failed to act 'within a certain period of time Pakistan will have to withdraw from the United Nations'. To pressmen Bhutto said Pakistan would allow the Security Council till 1 January 1966 to take meaningful steps to resolve the Kashmir deadlock.[1] This notice, however, was withdrawn on 7 November, when Law Minister S. M. Zafar issued a statement that there was no question of Pakistan leaving the United Nations.[2]

[1] *Dawn*, 25 Sept. 1965.
[2] See statement of S. A. Rahman in the *National Assembly of Pakistan Debates*, 17 Nov. 1965, p. 92.

The USA and the Indo-Pakistani War

The Indo-Pakistani war was a depressing experience for the United States because she saw in it a complete failure of her diplomacy and an utter waste of American treasure. Having furnished massive economic aid and arms to both countries for opposing Communism, the USA saw the two neighbours wasting their resources by fighting each other. It was an even more disappointing experience for Pakistan because her closest ally, while professing neutrality, which would have been bad enough, appeared to be more sympathetic towards India.

The Washington correspondent of the *New York Times* reported on 3 September that, although officials had long sympathized with many of Pakistan's grievances on the Kashmir issue, they had 'bitterly blamed' Pakistan in recent weeks for 'provoking the current crisis'.[1] On 8 September the US suspended arms deliveries both to India and to Pakistan, stating that this was being done to add weight to the Security Council's call for a cease-fire. A day later the State Department issued a statement declaring US neutrality in the Indo-Pakistani conflict.[2]

At a press conference on 15 September Ayub appealed to the United States to play a positive role because she had 'a lot of influence' both in India and Pakistan.[3] A White House spokesman, however, ruled out any direct diplomatic intervention and reiterated US policy that the route to peace was through the United Nations.[4]

It was only when it appeared that China might intervene in the war that the US really bestirred herself and used her influence to get the key resolution of 20 September passed. During the emergency Ambassador Arthur Goldberg called the Kashmir dispute 'the most serious problem' at the United Nations and in the world.[5] He also referred to the cease-fire as 'only the first step', the next being the task of finding a solution to the underlying sources of the conflict.[6] But once the flames of war had subsided, all the members of the Security Council, including the United States, lost their sense of urgency. Gone were the days when the USA championed the right of the Kashmiris to decide their own future.

[1] *New York Times*, 4 Sept. 1965.
[2] *Pakistan Horizon*, 4th Quarter 1965.
[3] *President Ayub on the Crisis Over Kashmir*, p. 23.
[4] *Hindu Weekly*, 20 Sept. 1965.
[5] *USDSB*, 4 Oct. 1965, p. 545.
[6] ibid., 11 Oct. 1965, p. 579.

Did Pakistanis and Indians use American weapons?

Pakistan had obtained almost all her military supplies from the USA while India had procured hers from other countries as well. Quantitatively, therefore, Pakistan undoubtedly used more American military hardware than India. India, however, had received considerably more economic assistance from the US than Pakistan. This massive addition to her own resources had enabled India to shop for the implements of war in the international market. In other words, if more American weapons were fighting on the side of Pakistan, more American money was fighting for India.

That India, no less than Pakistan, used American military supplies, admits of no doubt. We have already shown that India had no compunction in using American arms in Goa, Kutch, and Kashmir. Robert McCloskey, the State Department press spokesman, unequivocally stated on 7 September that American military supplies were 'being used freely by both sides'[1] in the Indo-Pakistani war.

Who was more to blame for the use of American weapons?

Both India and Pakistan were under an equal obligation under the terms of the Mutual Security Act not to use American weapons in aggression against another country. Since no impartial international authority gave a finding as to which one of the two was the aggressor, both claimed that they had used the US war material in self-defence. But India had further accepted the restriction that she would use the American military supplies only against China; and this condition she clearly contravened. The USA, however, not wishing to offend either party, adopted a non-committal attitude towards the whole affair. An authoritative exposition of the American position was given by the Assistant Secretary of State for Defense, Douglas MacArthur II, in reply to a letter from Senator Wayne Morse:

> We do have evidence of the use of American-supplied equipment by Pakistan during the India–Pakistan hostilities. Under our military assistance agreements, Pakistan is of course free to use United States military equipment for legitimate self-defense.
>
> Equipment furnished to India under the 1962 agreement between India and the United States was furnished for the purpose of defense against outright Chinese aggression directed from Peking. We have been informed that India made some use of American-supplied equipment in the hostilities with Pakistan. But India has alleged Chinese–Pakistani collusion in the recent conflict.

[1] *Minneapolis Tribune*, 8 Sept. 1965.

As you know, the circumstances under which the hostilities developed were such that the blame could not be assessed.[1]

Was the US bound to assist Pakistan?

The terms of the US-Pakistani bilateral Agreement of March 1959 covered Communist aggression only. The US had also made a reservation in respect of paragraph 1 of Article IV of the Manila Pact, which dealt with action to meet an armed attack, that this provision would apply only to Communist aggression. But the reservation affirmed that 'in the event of other aggression or armed attack it [the US] will consult' with other members as enjoined by paragraph 2 of Article IV. Pakistanis were, therefore, entitled to complain that SEATO members did not even consult together during the Indo-Pakistani war. About CENTO the US took up the technical position that she was not a member of that pact.

When the US decided to give arms aid to Pakistan she had held out assurances to India that, if Pakistan used American weapons against India in aggression, the US would act to thwart such aggression. Identical assurances were given to Pakistan when the US rendered similar aid to India. In the words of James M. Langley, US Ambassador to Pakistan, 'The United States would come to the aid of either Pakistan or India, depending on which was aggressed against.'[2] The undertaking given to both sides remained a dead letter because the US did not consider it politic to brand either party an aggressor.

However, there remains another category of assurance offered by the US to Pakistan more than once. Taking exception to a headline in the Pakistani press, 'US not to help Pakistan if attacked by a non-Red Power', Ambassador Horace A. Hildreth wrote to Prime Minister Suhrawardy and drew his attention to the statement of the State Department issued on 19 November 1956 to the effect that 'A threat to the territorial integrity or political independence of the [Baghdad Pact] members would be viewed by the United States with utmost gravity.'[3] Again, the preamble of the US-Pakistan bilateral Defense Agreement of 5 March 1959 said: 'The US regards as vital to its national interest and to world

[1] For text of MacArthur's letter see R. A. Jafri, *Ayub, Soldier and Statesman*, p. 519.
[2] *Dawn*, 22 April 1959. Secretary Dulles had also assured Foreign Minister Noon at Washington on 23 November 1959 that 'the US promptly and effectively would come to the assistance of Pakistan if it were subjected to armed aggression'. *Dawn*, 24 Nov. 1957.
[3] ibid., 27 Feb. 1957.

12

peace the preservation of the independence and integrity of Pakistan.'[1] This was reiterated in the Ayub–Kennedy joint communiqué of 13 July 1961 in these words: 'The two Presidents reaffirmed the solemn purpose of the bilateral agreement signed by the two Governments on March 5, 1959, which declares among other things that the Government of the United States of America regards as vital to its national interest and to world peace the preservation of the independence and integrity of Pakistan.'[2] Not without justification did Pakistanis allege that, by remaining neutral when India threatened the territorial integrity and independence of Pakistan by her invasion of West Pakistan, the United States had gone back on her assurances.

Pakistanis were not unaware of the great importance Washington had always attached to New Delhi's goodwill. As realists they knew that the US would never send G.I.s to shoot down Indians to protect Pakistan. Ayub said on 20 July 1962 that Pakistan's allies would come to her help in case of a world war but in case of local wars she had to depend upon her own resources.[3] A *Dawn* editorial also complained that the US and UK had never 'committed themselves in clear terms to come militarily to the aid of Pakistan and help Pakistan ward off an Indian attack'.[4] What Pakistanis did expect, however, was that the US would use her great influence to stop the Indian invasion across the international line which threatened Pakistani independence. Not only did the US belie this expectation but she did something which was tantamount to intervention on behalf of India. The stoppage of arms supplies to the belligerents hurt Pakistan immeasurably more, because she was totally dependent on America for such supplies; India continued to receive war material from Russia, France, and other sources, and had a far more developed war industry of her own. As *The Times* explained, Pakistan's stamina in war was limited not by her own capacities but by the Pentagon. She had been allowed to accumulate only some thirty days' supplies for her weapons.[5] The decision to suspend the delivery of military supplies, observed the *New York Times*, 'was reinforced by diplomatic moves that stripped away more and more of the veneer of United States neutrality. The Johnson Administration gave short shrift to

[1] ibid., 6 March 1959.
[2] *Pakistan Horizon*, 3rd Quarter 1961.
[3] *Dawn*, 21 July 1962.
[4] ibid., 1 Aug. 1963.
[5] 28 Oct. 1965.

Pakistan's effort to enlist the help of the Central Treaty Organization against an "aggressor". Moreover, officials indicated that the United States favours a cease-fire on terms that India has said she would accept but at which Pakistan has balked thus far.'[1]

China alleged that India could not have attacked Pakistan without the consent and help of the USA,[2] and a member of the Pakistani National Assembly also asserted that India had invaded Pakistani territory with the knowledge and consent of the US.[3] But the Leader of the House, on behalf of the Government, said it was not correct to say that America was directly responsible for the armed conflict between India and Pakistan.[4]

Though Pakistanis felt let down by America during the September war, they were not oblivious to the fact that their alliance with the USA, on the whole, had been of inestimable value. After Liaquat's death Pakistan entered a period of economic distress and political turmoil, and many doubted her capacity to survive. United States economic and military assistance during those crucial years might very well have been the reason for Pakistan's continuation as an independent nation. Reliance on another country for survival can never be a perfect arrangement but thoughtful Pakistanis have acknowledged the much-needed strength US arms brought to Pakistan.

Mushtaq Ahmad wrote in 1955 that 'the only guarantee of [Pakistan's] survival [after 1952] was military aid from the United States'.[5] More recently others have said: 'While it is true that military assistance was not made available for use against India, nevertheless its possession did act as a deterrent against India.'[6] 'It was with the help of arms received as aid from the United States that Pakistan was able to hold its own against India in the war of September 1965.'[7]

The UK and the Indo-Pakistani War
Knowing how shrilly Indians react to any criticism of their conduct from the Western countries, Wilson displayed commendable

---

[1] *New York Times*, 8 Sept. 1965.
[2] *Minneapolis Tribune*, 10 Sept. 1965.
[3] Mashiur Rahman, on 17 Nov. 1965, *National Assembly of Pakistan Debates*, p. 97.
[4] *National Assembly of Pakistan Debates*, 20 Nov. 1965, p. 302.
[5] Mushtaq Ahmad, *The United Nations and Pakistan*, p. 140.
[6] Z. A. Bhutto, *The Myth of Independence*, p. 111.
[7] Sarwar Hasan, 'The Background of American Arms Aid to Pakistan', *Pakistan Horizon*, 2nd Quarter 1967.

moral courage in speaking out against India's invasion of Pakistan across the international border. Wilson's statement gave rise to the usual spate of demonstrations in India and demands that India should leave the Commonwealth. One bright commentator suggested that the Labour Party in Britain was jealous of the Congress Party in India because the latter had made a greater success of 'democratic socialism'.[1]

Indians also alleged that the UK had cut off war supplies which had been paid for, but it was explained by a Whitehall spokesman that the shipments suspended to India and Pakistan on 9 September were arms aid and supplies from government stocks. No export licences for commercial orders for military stores were revoked. But shipowners had been reluctant to load consignments of military stores for either country because of the measures both had taken to seize contraband.[2]

About her responsibility under CENTO, Britain took up the position that she had always made it plain that CENTO and similar defence alliances would never be employed against a Commonwealth partner.[3]

China and the Indo-Pakistani War

China had fully supported Pakistan in the Kutch dispute, saying that 'the Indian-provoked armed conflict was an attempt by the Indian Government to occupy this disputed territory by force'.[4]

When the Consortium meeting was postponed, at the United States' behest, Foreign Minister Bhutto conferred with the Chinese and Russian Ambassadors. The Chinese Ambassador thereafter left for Peking for consultations.[5] On his return he publicly declared at Islamabad that China would give Pakistan whatever aid she could within her capacity.[6]

Foreign Minister Chen Yi, during a well-timed stopover in Karachi on 4 September, on his way to Mali, blamed India for being the first to violate the cease-fire line and declared, 'We support the just action taken by Pakistan to repel the Indian armed aggression.'[7] Immediately after India had launched an attack on West Pakistan,

[1] *Hindu Weekly*, 25 Oct. 1965.

[2] *Guardian*, 2 Oct. 1965.

[3] Commonwealth Secretary Arthur Bottomley quoted by the *Hindu Weekly*, 13 Sept. 1965.

[4] *Peking Review*, 14 May 1965.

[5] *Dawn*, 3 Aug. 1965.

[6] ibid., 4 Aug. 1965.

[7] ibid, 5 Sept. 1965; *New York Times*, 5 Sept. 1965.

the Chinese Government issued a statement that India's aggression concerned all her neighbours and that China was strengthening her defences and heightening her alertness along the borders.[1] In a note to India, China protested against successive serious violations of China's territory by Indian troops and asked India to dismantle all the 'aggressive military structures' she had illegally built beyond or on the China–Sikkim border, or else 'bear responsibility for all consequences arising therefrom'.[2]

Referring, no doubt, to the position adopted by the USA and the USSR in the controversy between India and Pakistan and the Security Council resolutions of 4 and 6 September, which had simply asked for a cease-fire, Chou En-lai said on 9 September that 'to appeal for peace without distinguishing between right and wrong will only encourage the aggressor'. He called India the outright aggressor in the Indo-Pakistani conflict and castigated the policies of 'US imperialism' and the 'modern revisionists [the USSR]'.

On 16 September China gave India the ultimatum we have already described and this immediately caused everyone to sit up and take notice. Secretary-General U Thant said 'a real danger to world peace' was now imminent. The British Ambassador to the USA flew to London for consultations and the British Foreign Secretary, Michael Stewart, called the Chinese ultimatum a 'serious, indeed dangerous, development'. In Washington, B. K. Nehru, the Indian Ambassador, declared, 'It certainly is our impression that they [the Chinese] are serious about this, that they will attack.'[3]

It was under these circumstances that the Security Council, which hitherto had only 'called' for a cease-fire without fixing a time limit, now 'demanded' a cease-fire by a specified hour and, for the first time during the crisis, promised to assist in resolving the cause of the strife. Foreign Minister Bhutto called the resolutions of 4 and 6 September 'Indian Resolutions', because, he said, they called for the restoration of the *status quo*, which India desired. He labelled the resolution of 20 September a 'China Resolution' because it was motivated by China's ultimatum to India which 'shook the foundations of the United Nations and caused the Great Powers great concern'.[4]

[1] *Dawn*, 8 Sept. 1965.
[2] ibid., 9 Sept. 1965.
[3] *Daily Telegraph*, 18 Sept. 1965.
[4] Z. A. Bhutto, *Important Press Conferences*, pp. 11, 12.

To see what the Security Council would do, the Chinese had extended their ultimatum to India by another three days. Two days after the resolution of 20 September Peking Radio announced that Indian troops had withdrawn from the Chinese side of the border, after destroying the military installations there.

Besides causing the Security Council to pass a resolution which Pakistanis considered more satisfactory than the earlier ones, China had also saved poorly defended and isolated East Pakistan from an Indian invasion. The *New York Times* correspondent had reported from New Delhi on 10 September that there were hints that India might attack East Pakistan.[1] The Indians evidently stayed their hand because of the warning Peking sent them through the US Ambassador in Warsaw. As an East Pakistani member of the National Assembly put it, China in this way had 'shared the defence of Pakistan'.[2]

Though deeply grateful for China's invaluable assistance during the most crucial crisis Pakistan had ever faced, Pakistanis were aware of the danger of becoming totally dependent on China. Ayub exchanged courteous letters with Kosygin and ultimately accepted his invitation to meet Shastri at Tashkent. The Pakistani President also publicly invited the USA to play a more positive role in the Indo-Pakistani conflict. Pakistanis were not unmindful of the fact that, if China invaded India, 'then Pakistan and Kashmir will be forgotten'.[3] Law Minister S. M. Zafar vehemently declared, in the Security Council on 18 September: 'The last thing that we wish . . . is that the Kashmir dispute should become embroiled in the conflicts and rivalries between the great powers.'

A special kind of relationship between Pakistan and China had, nevertheless, been forged, providing yet one more illustration of the plain truth that community· of interests creates a far stronger bond between nations than scraps of paper called treaties. Many responsible Pakistanis sincerely believed that, whereas the US had not been averse to Pakistan being taught a bitter lesson by India, China would have come to Pakistan's aid physically, if she had really desired it.[4]

China also supplied war material to Pakistan, including T-59

---

[1] *New York Times*, 11 Sept. 1965.

[2] Mashiur Rahman, on 17 Nov. 1965, *National Assembly of Pakistan Debates*, p. 98.

[3] *Daily Telegraph* correspondent's report from Rawalpindi published on 21 Sept. 1965.

[4] Impression gathered by me in Pakistan during a visit in the first part of 1966.

tanks and MIG-19 fighter planes. These were displayed in the National Day military parade at Rawalpindi on 23 March 1966, but had evidently arrived too late for use in the September war.

The USSR and the Indo-Pakistani War

The gradual shift in Soviet policy from one of complete support of India to one of neutrality in Indo-Pakistani disputes, which had been perceptible to insiders for some time, became manifest to all during the Kutch war. Reflecting the view of 'Soviet official circles', *Tass*, in a statement circulated on 8 May, expressed the hope that India and Pakistan would settle the Kutch dispute by peaceful means 'with consideration for the interests of both sides'.[1]

When the Consortium meeting was postponed, the Soviet Ambassador to Pakistan declared that 'some concrete proposals' were being discussed between Moscow and Rawalpindi for economic and other assistance to Pakistan.[2] On 20 August the Soviet Union made a Rs.1.5 crore loan to Pakistan for the purchase of machinery for airport construction.

In the meantime the situation in Kashmir was becoming increasingly dangerous because of the escalating Indian military offensive across the cease-fire line. *Pravda* wrote: 'We would like that Soviet-Pakistani relations like our traditional friendship with India, be a stabilizing factor in Asia and facilitate a normalization of the relations between Pakistan and India.'[3]

On 4 September Kosygin wrote to Shastri and Ayub, expressing concern at the military conflict 'in an area directly adjacent to the borders of the Soviet Union', and offered the good offices of the Soviet Union towards a peaceful settlement of Indo-Pakistani differences.[4] When India crossed the international frontier, Kosygin, for the first time, was more critical of one party than the other. He took exception to India's action and asked New Delhi to order cease-fire and withdraw Indian forces behind the cease-fire line in Kashmir and the international frontier elsewhere.[5] The Soviet Union no doubt believed that, if China entered the war on the side of Pakistan, the USA would join India. Apart from the unpredictable consequences of a major war on Soviet borders, such a development would have brought Pakistan under the complete domination

[1] *Asian Recorder*, 1965, p. 6464.
[2] *Dawn*, 30 July 1965.
[3] ibid., 25 Aug. 1965.
[4] *Pakistan Horizon*, 4th Quarter 1965.
[5] *Hindu Weekly*, 20 Sept. 1965.

of China and India under that of the USA, undermining Soviet influence in both the major South Asian countries.

On 17 September Kosygin renewed his offer to mediate between India and Pakistan in more specific terms. He invited the two Governments to confer on Soviet territory, at Tashkent 'for instance', and added that he too could 'take part in this meeting', if desired by both sides.[1] Ayub replied that, for such a meeting to be successful, the ground would first have to be prepared, and suggested that this be done in the Security Council in which the Soviet Union was a 'most influential and important member'.[2] Shastri said the Soviet proposal could be considered only after the cessation of military activities and the creation of a calmer atmosphere.[3] To convince Pakistanis of Russia's impartiality, the Soviet Embassy in Karachi issued a press commentary on 12 November which stated: 'Attempts are made at times to claim that the Soviet Union is allegedly not objective and is inclined to support one side at the expense of the other. Such opinions are far from the reality.'[4]

In the meantime it was becoming increasingly clear that, with the acceptance of the cease-fire by the parties and the withdrawal of the Chinese ultimatum, the Security Council had lost its sense of urgency to strive for a solution of the Kashmir dispute. The Russians, however, were still pressing India and Pakistan to confer at Tashkent. Dmitry Polyansky, a member of the Presidium of the CPSV Central Committee, said in Moscow, 'It is the sincere desire of the Soviet Union that the dangerous conflict between India and Pakistan should be completely extinguished.'[5]

Seeing the Soviet offer of mediation as the only possible chance for a Kashmir settlement, Pakistan now showed greater eagerness to avail herself of the Soviet invitation than India, who wished the *status quo* to remain undisturbed. Foreign Minister Bhutto announced Pakistan's affirmative response on 11 November.[6] Shastri dragged his feet for some time and consented to meet Ayub only after the latter had agreed to discuss the 'total relationship' between India and Pakistan.[7] A Soviet Government communiqué formally

---

[1] *Pakistan Horizon*, 4th Quarter 1965.
[2] *Dawn*, 26 Sept. 1965.
[3] *Observer*, 26 Sept. 1965.
[4] *Dawn*, 14 Nov. 1965, quoted in *Pakistan Horizon*, 4th Quarter 1965.
[5] *Soviet News*, 9 Nov. 1965.
[6] *Hindu Weekly*, 15 Nov. 1965.
[7] ibid., 29 Nov. 1965.

announced on 8 December that Shastri and Ayub would meet at
Tashkent on 4 January 1966.

The Tashkent conference lasted from 4 to 10 January. Premier
Kosygin earned the praise of both sides for his untiring efforts to
get Ayub and Shastri to subscribe to a joint 'Declaration'.[1] As
neither party wished to resume hostilities, the Declaration was in
the nature of a face-saving compromise, capable of being interpreted in different ways. In concrete terms its main achievement
was the agreement between the parties to withdraw, not later than
25 February 1966, 'all armed personnel' to the positions held before
5 August 1964. A date in early August had to be chosen as the fixed
point if Indian forces were to be evicted from all the territory they
had seized in their offensive into Azad Kashmir during that month.
August 5 was a convenient date because the parties were agreed
that infiltration from Azad Kashmir into Indian-held Kashmir had
begun on that day. In accepting it as the guidepost for withdrawal
of forces, neither side gave up its basic contentions. Each held
to its own position on the question of who the infiltrators were and
why they had crossed the cease-fire line.

Neither party at Tashkent obtained what it had earlier declared
to be its essential conditions for withdrawal behind the original
boundaries. The Pakistanis did not get a self-executing machinery
for the settlement of the Kashmir dispute. They had to be content
with the pale assurances that both sides 'will continue meetings
both at the highest and at other levels on matters of direct concern
to both countries', and that both sides had 'recognized the need to
set up joint Pakistani-Indian bodies which will report to their
Governments in order to decide what further steps should be
taken'. The Indians had to vacate all the territory in Azad Kashmir
without obtaining any clear guarantee that there would be no repetition of armed infiltration from Azad Kashmir. 'The issue of the
infiltrators to which Mr. Shastri and India attached great importance,' commented an Indian columnist, 'practically faded out of the
Tashkent discussions.'[2] Other Indian demands that were also rejected by Pakistan were: (a) that the Declaration should contain a
clause to dissuade Pakistan from having relations with third countries
of a nature that might injure the vital interests of India: this was

[1] For text of the Tashkent Declaration see *Asian Recorder*, 1966, p. 6896.
[2] K. Rangaswami in *Hindu Weekly*, 24 Jan. 1966. Shastri had said that India would
not withdraw from Haji Pir even if the whole world went against her. K. C. Saxena,
Pakistan, Her Relations with India, 1947–1966, p. 265.

obviously meant to circumscribe Pakistan's friendly relations with China;[1] (b) the freezing of the cease-fire line as the permanent border; (c) a no-war pact, without a definite arrangement for the settlement of disputes.[2]

The Indians claimed that the parties' reaffirmation, in the Declaration, of 'their obligation under the [UN] Charter, not to have recourse to force', amounted to a no-war declaration. Bhutto quoted Article 51 of the Charter that 'Nothing in the present Charter shall impair the inherent right of individual or collective self-defence' and argued that nothing in the Charter precluded Pakistan's right to assist Kashmiris, who are victims of Indian aggression.[3] According to the Indians, the agreement in the Declaration not to interfere in the 'internal affairs of each other' barred Pakistan from interference with India's possession of Kashmir. Pakistanis replied that a disputed territory cannot be regarded as the internal affair of one of the claimants.

Of the three participants in the discussions at Tashkent, the Soviet Union was the only one to emerge with unqualified satisfaction. Emphasizing the difficult nature of the task facing Kosygin at the conference, *The Times* had observed that the Soviet Union was trying 'to open a lock that has no key'.[4] Soviet success in getting Pakistan and India to talk on neutral ground, and agree to a statement, was a feat no other country had performed before. It greatly raised the prestige of the Soviet Union in the Afro-Asian arena where she was competing for influence with China. Soviet diplomacy, long successfully excluded from the subcontinent by the British presence there, had made a dramatic breakthrough and proved itself a major factor in the power politics of South Asia. Finally, Russia, hitherto often labelled a potential aggressor by the West, was able dramatically to project herself as a peacemaker at a time when the US was escalating the war in Vietnam.

Perhaps Pakistan's most substantial gain was a further erosion of India's special relationship with the USSR. Soviet economic assistance to Pakistan progressively increased, and in due course Russia offered military aid to Pakistan, on the same terms as to India. The Soviet Union also quietly dropped her support of Afghanistan on the issue of 'Pakhtunistan'. Tashkent, thus, enabled

---

[1] *Dawn*, 21 Jan. 1966.
[2] ibid., 30 Jan. 1966; see also *Hindu Weekly*, 24 Jan. 1966.
[3] *National Assembly of Pakistan Debates*, 15 March, p. 504.
[4] *The Times*, 3 Jan. 1966.

Pakistan to practise her policy of friendly relations with all the three foremost world powers, the USA, the USSR, and China, on a 'bilateral' basis.

China did not relish the sight of the Soviet Union playing such an influential role in South Asian affairs. She must have felt, also, that the Soviet Union was trying to wean Pakistan away from the close relationship China had so assiduously built up with her. The *Ren Min Ribao* alleged that the Declaration was 'a product of joint US–Soviet plotting' and that the objective of the Soviet Union had been 'to weaken the united struggle against imperialism in Asia and Africa'.[1] A resolution of the Afro-Asian Writers' Conference at Peking, in June 1966, stated that the 'notorious' Tashkent Conference had been 'designed, under the fraudulent screen of "peaceful" settlement of Indo-Pakistani disputes, to get Pakistan to join with India for "joint defence against China" '.[2]

The Muslim Countries and the Indo-Pakistani War

Undoubtedly the most satisfying aspect of the Indo-Pakistani war for Pakistanis was the sympathy and support they received from sister Muslim countries, for whom they had always cherished special feelings. The entire Muslim world, with the exception of Yemen and the UAR, expressed sympathy for Pakistan's cause, and even the Yemen and the UAR did not side with India but professed neutrality.

In fact there were indications that the UAR was more sympathetic to Pakistan than to India, but she did not wish to demonstrate this openly lest her tradition of co-operation with India as a fellow non-aligned nation be damaged. The semi-official UAR daily *Al-Gamhouria* wrote that it was the duty of all Asian-African leaders to strive for a settlement of the Indo-Pakistani conflict by allowing Kashmiris to decide their future through a plebiscite.[3] At the Casablanca Arab Summit Conference the UAR subscribed to the communiqué which called upon India and Pakistan to put an end to their conflict 'in accordance with the principles and resolutions of the United Nations'.[4] When Krishna Menon travelled to Cairo to win UAR support for India, he was told that India had committed

---

[1] Quoted in *Dawn*, 16 Feb. 1966.
[2] *Peking Review*, 1 April 1966, quoted by B. S. Gupta in 'A Maoist Line for India', *The China Quarterly*, Jan.–March 1966, p. 9.
[3] Quoted in *Dawn*, 20 Sept. 1965.
[4] *Dawn*, 20 Sept. 1965.

aggression by crossing the international frontier and that Cairo
could not support her in spite of Indo-UAR friendship.[1]

Immediately after the invasion of West Pakistan, Pakistan invoked CENTO. Though Britain and the USA disclaimed responsibility under the pact, the two Muslim members, Iran and Turkey,
responded favourably to Pakistan's appeal for help. An Irani
Government statement referred to the Indian attack on Pakistan as
'aggression' and declared that the people of Iran 'shall not fail to
extend every possible assistance to their Pakistani brothers and
sisters'.[2] The Prime Minister of Turkey, similarly, issued a statement that India's action in extending hostilities 'outside the area of
dispute in Kashmir itself' had caused deep concern in Turkey,
Pakistan's ally in CENTO.[3] On 10 September the Prime Ministers
of Iran and Turkey jointly expressed disapproval of the Indian
attack on Pakistan.[4]

Though Iran and Turkey could not respond favourably to
Pakistan's appeal for jet aircraft, presumably because the US would
have objected to the transfer of material which she had given, both
countries decided to 'use all national possibilities' to aid Pakistan,
including jet fuel and gasoline from Iran and guns and ammunition
from Turkey.[5] Large numbers of Iranis and Turks volunteered to
fight against India and a number of nurses from both countries
actually flew to Pakistan and served there.

A Saudi Arabian Embassy statement, issued in Karachi, declared India was 'committing aggression against our Pakistani and
Kashmiri brethren'.[6] Amir Mishaal, brother of King Feisal of
Saudi Arabia and Governor of Mecca, along with members of other
leading families of Jedda, volunteered to fight for Pakistan in the
jihad against India. The Amir also arranged for daily prayers in
Kaaba Sharif for the success of Pakistan.[7] Students and schoolboys
collected funds and the entire population acted as if Pakistan's
cause was their own.[8] The Saudi Arabian Embassy in Pakistan
refrained from celebrating the National Day of their country

---

[1] *National Assembly of Pakistan Debates*, 15 March 1966, p. 492.
[2] *Pakistan Horizon*, 4th Quarter 1965.
[3] ibid.
[4] ibid.
[5] *New York Times*, 11 Sept. 1965.
[6] *Dawn*, 11 Sept. 1965.
[7] ibid., 18 Sept. 1965.
[8] Khwaja Shahabuddin, 'King Feisal As I Knew Him', *Dawn* (Supplement), 19 April
1966.

and, instead, donated £1,000 to the Pakistan National Defence Fund.[1]

Jordan, too, treated Pakistan's war as her own. King Hussein said Jordan would stand by the side of Pakistan 'till right is restored, justice is done'. A fund was opened to collect money for Pakistan's defence needs.[2]

An Algerian Government statement declared that, having struggled for almost eight years to achieve the recognition of its right of self-determination, Algeria could not but support the application of that principle for the settlement of the problem of Kashmir.[3] In an official statement, Syria also expressed her belief 'in the sacred right of its [Kashmir's] people to decide its own future'.[4]

Indonesia's support of Pakistan was vociferous as well as generous. From 1 September onwards there were several demonstrations of solidarity in Djakarta, in one of which the Indian Embassy was ransacked, three cars burnt, the Indian flag snatched away, and the office of the Indian information service occupied.[5] Soekarno assured 'an emissary from Pakistan' that Indonesia's army, navy, and air force were available for Pakistan.[1] *The Times* correspondent from Karachi reported:

A small flotilla of Russian craft from the Indonesian Navy, lying in Karachi harbour, is the most conspicuous contribution made by Pakistan's various friends to her rearmament. There are six vessels, two submarines, two missile-carrying boats in size between a frigate and a large motor torpedo boat, and two similar vessels without missiles. They came on a 'good will visit' several weeks ago, but it is believed here that they have either been lent to the Pakistan Navy or even made over to it. . . . It is understood that MiGs have been offered by both Indonesia and China.[7]

The Government of Afghanistan adopted a neutral attitude towards the Indo-Pakistani war but public sympathy was manifestly with Pakistan. 'Quite a few people here', wrote the representative of *The Times* from Kabul, 'speak of Pakistanis as fighting to hold

[1] *Dawn*, 24 Sept. 1965.
[2] *Pakistan Times*, 20 Sept. 1967.
[3] *Pakistan Horizon*, 4th Quarter 1965.
[4] ibid.
[5] *International Studies, India's Relations with Pakistan*, July–Oct., 1966, pp. 173–4.
[6] Foreign Minister Bhutto at the Convocation of the Sindh University at Hyderabad on 4 May 1966, *Dawn*, 5 May 1966.
[7] *The Times*, 18 Dec. 1965.

back a wave of Indian expansionism that, unhindered, might try to roll to the Hindu Kush.'[1]

There was, however, one predominantly Muslim country, Malaysia, which favoured India during the fateful crisis of 1965. Malaya had previously been one of the few Afro-Asian countries which had unhesitatingly sided with India against China. Tunku Abdul Rahman, who later became Malaysia's first Prime Minister, had condemned China's invasion of Tibet as well as China's 'aggression' against India in 1962. He had also launched a public campaign, the 'Save Democracy Fund', which raised more than $1 million to help India against China.[2] During the Security Council debate on 18 September 1965, the Malaysian representative, R. Ramani, who had been born and educated in South India, not only blamed Pakistan for starting the current conflict but suggested that the very creation of Pakistan was a mistake. The Kashmir problem 'began simmering', he asserted, 'on that fateful day in August 1947 when one ancient country and one ancient people were cut into two unequal parts'.[3] He also lightly dismissed the past resolutions of the United Nations calling for a plebiscite in Kashmir as 'ancient resolutions from the musty records of the past'. These utterances shocked Pakistanis because Pakistan had never given Malaysia any legitimate cause for grievance Despite Pakistan's close friendship with Indonesia at the time, she gave no support to Indonesia in her 'confrontation' with Malaysia. Ayub had declared that Pakistan regarded both Indonesia and Malaysia as 'common friends'.[4] In fact Pakistan had gone against Indonesia's wish by favouring Malaysian participation in the proposed second Afro-Asian conference. Pakistan's protest having brought forth an affirmation from the Government of Malaysia that Ramani was only reflecting the official policy of his Government, Pakistan severed diplomatic relations with Malaysia. The Shah of Iran, who had previously persuaded Pakistan and Afghanistan to resume diplomatic ties, performed a similar service by mediating between Pakistan and Malaysia. In September 1966 Pakistan and Malaysia announced that they would again exchange High Commissioners.

In addition to Malaysia, the only countries in the world who

---

[1] ibid., 5 Oct. 1965. My own impression formed during a visit to Kabul in early 1966 tallies with this observation.

[2] Tunku Abdul Rahman, 'Malaysia: Key Area in Southeast Asia', *Foreign Affairs*, July 1965. Malyasia came into existence on 16 Sept. 1963.

[3] *Security Council Official Records, 1241st Meeting*, 18 Sept. 1965.

[4] *Dawn*, 16 Jan. 1965.

favoured India were Yugoslavia and Singapore. Commenting on the state of India's 'Foreign Relations', a *Hindu* editorial noted her isolation in the wars against China and Pakistan and ruefully observed that all India 'had achieved since independence was to maintain fairly easy relations superficially with most of the world', without establishing a firm friendship with any country on a give-and-take basis.[1]

[1] *Hindu Weekly*, 18 April 1966.

15 Consolidation of 'Bilateralism' (1966-1970)

When the Indo-Pakistani war ended there was a certain imbalance in Pakistan's new policy of 'bilateralism'. Owing to their respective attitudes during the war, the Chinese ranked much higher in Pakistan's esteem than the United States and the Soviet Union. The USSR had played the honest broker between India and Pakistan at Tashkent, but she was still giving military assistance to India only. Pakistan desired equal friendship with the USA and the USSR, but had not yet closed down the American intelligence base near Peshawar, which had been the source of so much anxiety to the USSR. The USA was under severe criticism for not caring if her ally Pakistan was overrun by neutral India, and for having hurt her at a crucial moment by cutting off military supplies. These imbalances were gradually smoothed out after the war, and in 1970 President Yahya Khan was able to achieve what Ayub had failed to do in 1965, namely, to make friendly visits in succession to all the three greatest powers in the world, the USSR, the USA, and China. Pakistan has not yet relinquished her membership of SEATO and CENTO, but she remains a member of these defence pacts in name only. Foreign Minister Arshad Husain explained in the National Assembly, on 28 June 1968, that Pakistan no longer takes any part in the military side of these pacts and attends the Ministerial Council meetings as an observer only. Pakistan's interest in the organizations is confined to their cultural and economic activities. Out of deference to the wishes of the other members, Pakistan has not denounced her connection formally and prefers to let the pacts 'wither on the vine'.[1]

Pakistan's prescription of 'bilateralism' of course is primarily meant to save herself from getting scorched by the friction between the big powers. She has never been uncommitted in respect of Muslim countries and, as far as can be foreseen, never will be.

[1] *National Assembly of Pakistan Debates*, 28 June 1968, p. 3192.

During recent years she has further enhanced her standing in the Muslim world. The Arab-Israeli war of 1967 gave Pakistan an opportunity to return the sympathy and support the Muslim countries had extended to her in 1965, and the RCD has been progressing smoothly. At Rabat in September 1969 Pakistan successfully thwarted India's bid to force her way into the summit conference of Muslim countries. India took her revenge a year later by keeping Pakistan out of the Luska non-aligned summit meeting (September 1970), but Pakistan wisely did not get excited about the affair, and her setback, therefore, passed comparatively unnoticed.

Having cast off the shackles of involvement in East-West rivalry, Pakistan felt free once more to play a more vigorous role in the affairs of the United Nations. She was elected to the Security Council (by a record vote)[1] as well as to the Economic and Social Council, was nominated to the Conference of the Committee on Disarmament, presided over the Non-nuclear Powers Conference, and her Ambassador to the United Nations, Agha Shahi, was voted to the Chair of the First Committee of the General Assembly.

Though the war with India had tarnished Ayub's image as the magic man of Pakistan, it was not the direct cause of his fall. It was the accumulating discontent with his domestic policies, which following his loss of prestige could be more boldly aired by his opponents, that really toppled him in March 1969.[2] His policy of 'bilateralism' towards the big powers had been successful, and was continued by Yahya.

I. What is 'Bilateralism'?

A considered and authoritative exposition of Pakistan's policy of 'bilateralism' is contained in Ayub's book *Friends Not Masters*,[3] and in his successor President General Agha Muhammad Yahya Khan's address to the Iranian Parliament on 30 October 1969.[4]

Ayub explains that it was the force of circumstances which had compelled Pakistan to reappraise her policy of 'complete' identification with the West. He starts the argument by taking Pakistan's

---

[1] Securing all the 118 votes cast: *Dawn*, 8 Nov. 1967.

[2] Ayub's early years were highly promising but his system of 'basic democracies', though theoretically not without merit, in practice created an unpopular corps of low-level politicians whose main concern was to keep Ayub in power and fill their own coffers with ill-gotten gains. The economic advance under him also benefited only the thin upper layer of big business. And an illness, early in 1968, left behind an impaired heart.

[3] pp. 114–21.

[4] Text distributed as a supplement to *Pakistan Affairs* (undated).

geographical location, which is that she has the 'dubious distinction' of having three big neighbours, the USSR, China, and India. The prospects of establishing normal relations with India being dim, the best thing is to have an understanding with the remaining two. In addition it is necessary to have satisfactory relations with the United States, who has global interests and is in a position to render large-scale economic assistance which Pakistan so urgently requires to attain her development goals. To avoid antagonizing anyone, the strategy evolved was to set up a 'bilateral' relationship with every one of the three big powers.

As 'it would be like walking on a triangular tightrope', it was vital to determine the 'limits of tolerance' within which 'bilateral equations might be constructed'. The big powers might have their differences but Pakistan need not get involved in that: '[we should neither] philosophize about their problems nor ... act as busy-bodies.' This approach is dictated by a sense of Pakistan's limitations: 'We have neither the desire nor the capacity to get mixed up in their wranglings. We are not in a position either to influence their decisions or to solve their problems. The basis of our foreign policy thus is that we stay within our own means, political as well as economic.'

Yahya enunciated the same principles in a slightly different fashion:

Experience tells us that over-commitment to any one power is not in our interest. The interests of great powers keep on changing. Small powers can only react to those changes and the process of adjustment becomes rather difficult for over-committed small powers. We therefore try to hold a balance in our relations with the major powers around us and with the USA. We do not solicit the friendship of one at the expense of the interests of another. We feel that this policy of non-involvement has to be genuine and not a thinly disguised bargaining device. We do not try to play off one power against another and most decidedly we do not play on both sides of the street.

In Yahya's view small and middling powers can 'best satisfy their legitimate and laudable urge' for making a contribution to the world order by cultivating their small neighbours and by extending co-operation with like-minded nations so as to lessen their dependence on outside powers. He did not say so in so many words but he was, in fact, commending the RCD type of regional self-help.

II. Pakistan and the Great Powers

Relations with China
China reached the pinnacle of her popularity in Pakistan during the
Indo-Pakistani war of September 1965 and the months immediately
following. The most cheered weapons in the Independence Day
parade, on 23 March 1966, were the MIGs and tanks which China
had recently given to Pakistan. Three days later the Chinese
President, Liu Shao-chi, arrived in Rawalpindi on a State visit.[1]
He and his party, which included Foreign Minister Chen Yi,
were received in both wings of Pakistan with unprecedented enthusiasm. Chen Yi touched the hearts of all Pakistanis at a reception
in the famous Shalimar Gardens in Lahore, when he used the Urdu
expression *mujahidana dosti*[2] to describe the nature of Sino-
Pakistani friendship.

Despite her genuine sense of gratitude to China, Pakistan took
care not to offend the USSR and the USA in any way. In the
middle of the Liu visit, Foreign Minister Bhutto told pressmen
that Pakistan's friendship with China was not going to be at the
cost of her relations with the USA.[3] The *Hindu Weekly* commented
that Liu's visit had been a failure because the Ayub–Liu statement
had avoided Liu's favourite topic, Vietnam.[4] This line of argument
overlooked the fact that the Ayub–Johnson communiqué of December 1965 also had not said anything about Vietnam which might
have comforted the American President.

However, a high pitch of emotion can hardly be sustained for
long and it was only natural that, after a full expression of Pakistan's
gratitude for China's help during the Indo-Pakistani conflict, the
tempo of friendship between the two countries should descend to a
more rational level, especially if Pakistan was to practise her professed policy of equally friendly relations with China, the USSR,
and the United States.

Twice during the period under review there was speculation

[1] My wife and I happened to be in Pakistan during the Chinese President's visit.
President Ayub Khan as well as President Liu Shao-chi honoured us by inviting us to
the State banquets they gave for each other. This enabled me to talk to some of the
Chinese guests personally.
[2] The bond of friendship between those who wage a holy war (*jihad*) in a common
cause.
[3] *Hindu Weekly*, 18 April 1966.
[4] ibid., 14 April 1966.

that Pakistan was reverting to a pro-Western policy. The first occasion was during June 1966 when, two days after the US had announced that she was resuming economic aid to India and Pakistan, Ayub disclosed that Foreign Minister Bhutto, who was regarded as a strong protagonist of special ties with China, would proceed on leave for 'medical treatment'. Ayub declared that there would be no change in foreign policy, but the suspicion lingered that Bhutto's departure presaged a less enthusiastic China policy. The appointment of Sharifuddin Pirzada as Foreign Minister on 20 July made it clear that Bhutto would not return to his post.

To acquaint himself with the situation at firsthand, Premier Chou En-lai, who was to make a brief stopover at Karachi on his way home from Albania, extended his stay and went to Rawalpindi to discuss with Ayub the rumoured shift in Pakistani policy. At a dinner in honour of the visiting premier, Ayub openly assured his guest that Sino-Pakistani friendship was 'not based on expediency but on principles and will continue to flourish over the years'.[1]

On 12 July it was announced that Finance Minister M. Shoaib, believed to be pro-American, would also soon relinquish his cabinet post to take up a position in the World Bank. This was generally interpreted as a balancing act meant to restore the equilibrium disturbed by the departure of the pro-Chinese Bhutto.

The second time there were surmises that the tide of Sino-Pakistani friendship had begun to recede was in the middle period of the Chinese 'cultural revolution', when the future direction of Chinese policy was unclear. Evidently to scotch these rumours, Foreign Minister Arshad Husain went to China in August on a week's goodwill visit. On his return Husain declared that the rumours of strain in Sino-Pakistani relations had been 'put to eternal sleep' as a result of his visit.[2]

The truth of the matter is that some swaying alternately to right and left is unavoidable in pursuing a foreign policy which admittedly is like 'walking on a triangular tightrope'. But this manoeuvring, as in the case of the acrobat, is meant to regain and retain the balance, not to lose it.

In his address to the General Assembly on 22 October 1970, Yahya said friendly relations with China were 'the cornerstone' of Pakistani policy, and pleaded that the USA, the USSR, and China should harmonize their relations in the interests of world peace.

[1] M. Ayub Khan, *Speeches*, VIII, p. 192.
[2] *Dawn*, 20 Aug. 1968.

Upon arrival at Peking on 10 November for a five-day visit, Yahya, in the words of the joint communiqué, was accorded a 'magnificent and enthusiastic reception'. The Pakistani leader said the right of self-determination must be allowed to the people everywhere, 'be it in Kashmir, in Indo-China, and African territories under colonial domination'.[1] In the joint communiqué China reiterated her support for Pakistan 'against all forms of outside aggression', and for the Kashmiris in their struggle for the right of self-determination. Pakistan affirmed that 'Taiwan was an inalienable part' of China, and agreed with China that 'the struggle of the three peoples of Indo-China for national liberation was just'.[2] The positive declaration that Taiwan was a part of China, and the equation of the strife in Indo-China with the struggle for freedom in Kashmir against the occupation forces, represented new concessions by Pakistan to Chinese sensitivity on these issues.

At the economic level, Sino-Pakistani relations have pursued a uniformly smooth course. In addition to the loan of $60 million given to Pakistan in 1965, and another loan of $40.50 million advanced in 1969, China gave $6.90 million to Pakistan for the purchase of food. During President Yahya Khan's visit to Peking, China pledged a further 500 million yuans (over $200 million) for Pakistan's Fourth Five-Year Plan, thus doubling the amount of assistance given towards the previous Plan.

Notable among Chinese-assisted projects are a heavy mechanical complex at Taxila and an ordnance factory in East Pakistan. The Chinese have also offered assistance in solving the perennial flood problem in East Pakistan, and a Chinese team has surveyed the feasibility of a bridge over the river Brahmaputra which would integrate two regions of East Pakistan. A much appreciated gift to Pakistan from the 'Muslims of the People's Republic of China' has been a magnificent 65-foot glass chandelier for the mausoleum of Quaid-i-Azam Muhammad Ali Jinnah.

Sino-Pakistani trade increased fourfold between 1962/3 and 1968/9, from a two-way turnover of Rs.60 million to Rs.240 million, and the balance of trade has remained constantly in Pakistan's favour.[3] Lin Hai-yun, Acting Foreign Trade Minister, told Pakistanis that, in trading with their country, China never took into account the 'profit motive' but wished 'just to help Pakistan as a

[1] ibid., 12 Nov. 1970.
[2] ibid., 16 Nov. 1970.
[3] ibid., 12 May, 25 March 1970.

real friend'.[1] The 'silk route' from Sinkiang to Gilgit, which had been closed in 1949, was reopened with the arrival of the first Chinese caravan in Gilgit in August 1969. Overland trade is expected to receive a further boost when the proposed 'jeepable' road linking Sinkiang with Gilgit is completed. Presumably, China has also been furnishing war supplies to Pakistan, but the nature and extent of these have not been publicized.

In the geopolitics of today neither Pakistan nor China can afford to lose the other's goodwill. Pakistanis are fully conscious that China is the only big power which supports Pakistan on the crucial Kashmir issue and seems likely to continue to uphold them in other confrontations with India. China, too, can hardly disregard the fact that Pakistan is not only a highly strategic neighbour but currently also the largest country in the world friendly to her.

Relations with the Soviet Union
In the years following the Tashkent conference, Russian economic assistance to Pakistan, and trade between the two countries, escalated smoothly, but on the sensitive question of the supply of Soviet military equipment matters moved at a slower pace. The Russians evidently were reluctant to do anything that would impair their relations with India. Pakistan, however, kept up the pressure. Before Tashkent, Pakistanis used to deplore the transfer of Soviet arms to India, but did not openly press that such arms be supplied to themselves. After Tashkent, they began to take the Russian profession of equal concern with the welfare of India and Pakistan as a reason for demanding the same facilities as India for acquiring Soviet arms. A mere cessation of the flow of weaponry to India was no longer deemed sufficient. Having armed India 'to the teeth', declared Ayub, if Russia were now to close off supplies to the subcontinent it could affect only Pakistan. It would be unfair to Pakistan.[2]

Of course the Russians, too, had a complaint of their own against Pakistan: the US still enjoyed the use of the American surveillance base at Badaber near Peshawar, and it was not till Pakistan decided to close down this base that the Russians agreed to supply her with arms.

President Ayub Khan journeyed to Moscow in September 1967, and Premier Kosygin returned the visit in April 1968, the

[1] ibid., 1 June 1969.
[2] *The Times*, 18 April 1967.

first ever paid to Pakistan by a Soviet Head of Government. Promises of increased technical and economic aid were made on both occasions but Pakistanis were unable to obtain any Soviet commitment regarding the supply of arms. However, by serving notice on the US on 7 April, a few days before Kosygin's arrival in Pakistan, that the lease of the American communications base would not be renewed beyond the existing limit of 1 July 1968, Pakistan had removed the last cause of Soviet grievance, and the grant of Soviet military assistance was now only a question of time.

Following a trip to the USSR by a Pakistani military delegation headed by the Commander-in-Chief of the Pakistani Army, General Yahya Khan, it was announced on 9 July that the Soviet Union had agreed to sell arms to Pakistan.[1] The Washington correspondent of the *Hindu* enviously noted that Pakistan had become the first country in the world to get such supplies from all three major powers.[2] Prime Minister Indira Gandhi called the Soviet decision 'unexpected' and 'fraught with danger' as it might incite Pakistan to launch 'fresh offensives' against India.[3]

During President Yahya Khan's visit to the Soviet Union in June 1970, Russia agreed to provide assistance for the Fourth Five-Year Plan as well as for the construction of a steel mill in Karachi with an annual production capacity of one million tons. It was decided, further, to conclude a long-term trade agreement covering the period 1971–5. As Pakistanis had long desired a steel mill, they found the Soviet promise to help in building the mill especially gratifying.

But on political matters neither side got all it wanted. Pakistan would have liked the Soviet Union to use her influence for the settlement of Indo-Pakistani disputes, but the Soviet side expressed the belief that those disputes should be settled 'through bilateral negotiations'. The Soviet Union would have liked the communiqué directly to condemn US involvement in Indo-China, but the statement simply expressed 'concern' over the expansion of foreign interference in Cambodia and called for the 'withdrawal of [all] foreign troops from Indo-China'.[4]

On the economic front the volume of two-way trade, which had amounted to only Rs.42.8 million in 1962, rose to Rs.326 million

[1] *New York Times*, 10 July 1968.
[2] *Hindu Weekly*, 15 July 1968.
[3] ibid., 15, 22 July 1968.
[4] Text in *Pakistan Horizon*, 3rd Quarter 1970.

in 1966, and Soviet aid by the latter year amounted to $91 million, including $30 million for oil exploration and $11 million for the purchase of agricultural machinery.[1] A fresh loan agreement involving Rs.40 crores was signed in Moscow on 9 September 1966. Another credit amounting to 60 million roubles was granted in August 1968. The credit for the steel mill, promised during Yahya's visit in June 1970, was expected to come to a further $200 million.

Soviet-assisted industrial projects in Pakistan include two plants for manufacturing electrical equipment, a 200-megawatt thermal power station on the Indus at Giddu, twenty radio stations, and a high-voltage grid more than 1,000 km long.[2] The Soviet Government has also assisted in improving the port at Gwadur and has signed a ten-year agreement for co-operation in the peaceful uses of atomic energy.

Though the Soviet Union doubtless wanted to wean Pakistan away from the Western embrace and also make it possible for her to avoid over-dependence on China, these were not the only reasons she wished to cultivate good relations with Pakistan. India's rout in the brief Sino-Indian war of 1962 had dramatically demonstrated that she could not possibly stand against China alone. Accordingly, the Russians gradually came round to the view, so long held by the Americans, that India and Pakistan should compose their differences and face China jointly. Party leader Leonid Brezhnev said, at the International Meeting of Communist and Workers Parties in Moscow on 7 June 1969, 'We are of the opinion that the course of events is also putting on the agenda the task of creating a system of collective security in Asia.'[3] A month later Izvestia stated that the proposed Asian collective security system would be open to all Asian countries, including the Soviet Union, who, being 'simultaneously a European and an Asian power, is vitally interested in having all the peoples in Asia live in peace'.[4] But this idea appealed neither to India, who professes non-alignment, nor to Pakistan, who is anxious to avoid anything which would have the appearance of ganging-up against China.

The Soviet Union also suggested 'constructive co-operation' between Pakistan, Afghanistan, India, Iran, and the Soviet Union. As this proposal was in tune with India's policy, calling for Indo-Pakistani collaboration in secondary matters so that the main issue

---

[1] By June 1970, 5,000 Soviet tractors and 2,000 bulldozers were in use in Pakistan.
[2] Dawn, 28 June 1970.
[3] International Affairs, no. 7, 1969.
[4] Quoted in New York Times, 24 July 1969.

of Kashmir might be pushed into the background, Indian reaction to it was favourable. But Pakistan turned it down for two reasons: first, because it was unrealistic to talk about regional co-operation which included India and Pakistan while their relations remained bedevilled by major disputes, and secondly, because the proposal had the appearance of a step towards the creation of a system of collective security directed against China.[1]

The Soviet Union was not unaware that unsolved disputes were the basic cause of the strain in Indo-Pakistani relations, and in his joint statement with Ayub, on 21 April 1968, Kosygin affirmed that a resolution of Indo-Pakistani disputes would 'meet the vital interests of the peoples of these countries as well as of universal peace'. After Pakistan, Kosygin went to India and there urged Indira Gandhi 'to enter into a dialogue with Pakistan on the Kashmir issue'.[2] The details of the Indian Premier's reaction on that occasion did not become known, but a formal letter from Kosygin on 6 July 1968, pressing Mrs. Gandhi to settle the Farakka Barrage dispute with Pakistan on the lines of the Indus Waters Treaty of 1960,[3] brought forth sharp public reproof from Indian sources, reminiscent of the fate of American initiatives in the past to compose Indo-Pakistani differences. As the World Bank had acted as mediator in the Indus Waters dispute, the Indians suspected that Kosygin was suggesting mediation in the case of Farakka also. An Indian Foreign Office spokesman stated that it was not necessary to agree with the Soviet Premier 'all along the line'. The latter would be told that his way of thinking on the Farakka dispute 'is not right'.[4]

All in all, however, there is not the same degree of community of interests between the Soviet Union and Pakistan as there is between China and Pakistan. Owing to her larger size and her confrontation with China, India serves Soviet interests better than smaller Pakistan who is friendly towards China. The USSR has invested much armour and treasure in India and, if compelled to make a clear-cut choice, would probably side with her in preference to Pakistan. On 9 November 1970, Foreign Minister Swaran Singh told the Lok Sabha that the Soviet Union had assured India that she would not supply any more military hardware to Pakistan.[5]

---

[1] *Dawn*, 11 July 1969.
[2] *Hindu Weekly*, 15 July 1968.
[3] *Asian Recorder*, 1968, p. 8468. For details of the Farakka dispute see section IV of this chapter.
[4] *Hindu Weekly*, 22 July 1968.
[5] *Statesman Weekly*, 14 Nov. 1970.

Relations with the USA

A few days after India and Pakistan had accepted the cease-fire in their September war, the White House renewed invitations to President Ayub Khan and Prime Minister Shastri to re-schedule their respective visits to the US, which had been 'postponed' by President Johnson in April. Ayub flew to Washington for two days towards the middle of December.[1]

It had been given out at Rawalpindi that the Pakistani President intended to present himself at the White House as a complainant and not as a petitioner. He sought nothing from Johnson except understanding.[2] Though Ayub assured Johnson that there was no secret alliance between Pakistan and China,[3] Johnson failed to get anything worthwhile out of the visitor on Vietnam. The communiqué simply expressed the hope that the conflict in Vietnam would be peacefully resolved. Evidently both sides accepted Ayub's plea that the two countries, having different obligations, should understand each other's difficulties and be content with a relationship in which neither party does anything against the interests of the other.[4] A White House spokesman affirmed that Johnson had 'expressed his sympathetic understanding of the special position of Pakistan'. President Ayub had asked for 'nothing save understanding and he is carrying that back with him'.[5] This was a far cry from the once lavish affirmations of faithful alliance, but it accorded with the changed climate of the day.

The flow of US economic aid to Pakistan and India was resumed in February 1966, when Vice-President Hubert Humphrey, during a visit to the subcontinent, announced a loan of $50 million for Pakistan in Karachi and a loan of double that amount for India in New Delhi. On 15 June 1966 the State Department announced that the US was resuming full-scale economic aid to India and Pakistan because the two countries were once again 'concentrating on the urgent tasks of national development'.[6] Two days later, as we have already mentioned, Ayub announced that Foreign Minister Bhutto,

[1] Shastri having died at Tashkent in Jan. 1966, Prime Minister Indira Gandhi went to the US in March 1966.

[2] *The Times*, 10 Dec. 1965.

[3] I learned this from a person in a position to know what transpired between the two Presidents.

[4] *USDSB*, 3 Jan. 1966.

[5] *Dawn*, 17 Dec. 1965.

[6] *USDSB*, 4 July 1966.

regarded by most observers as zealously pro-Chinese, would proceed on leave for 'medical treatment'.

At a Congressional Committee hearing in April 1966, Defense Secretary McNamara disclosed that, though military aid to India and Pakistan had not been reinstituted, the US had been selling to both 'certain items of a nonlethal character that are associated with military equipment', for example, bulldozers and spare parts for trucks.[1] He said a military aid programme to either India or Pakistan would 'depend in the future upon a further reconciliation of the conflicts between those two nations'. If Pakistan's conflict with India could be resolved, 'there will be no reason for Pakistan to remain close to Red China'.[2]

Another year having passed without any sign of 'further reconciliation' between India and Pakistan, the Department of State, on 12 April 1967, issued a statement that the US had decided not to resume 'grant military assistance' to India and Pakistan but had 'decided to remove present US Government restrictions on the kinds of spare parts which may be sold to Pakistan and India for previously supplied equipment'.[3]

Both India and Pakistan criticized the new policy. India alleged that the supply of 'spare parts for lethal weapons' to Pakistan would reactivate her military machine, and Pakistan complained that the American decision would affect her more adversely because, while India had been acquiring military equipment from diverse sources, and had been increasing her own production, Pakistan's main source of military supplies was the US. Officials in Washington conceded that the long-term effects of the curb might be more serious for Pakistan than for India.[4]

Tying the supply of weapons to a *rapprochement* between Pakistan and India was not the only lever which the US employed for pressing the two countries to co-operate with each other. From time to time she also proposed that India and Pakistan undertake joint ventures. This was not dissimilar to the Soviet proposal for regional co-operation which we have already described, and it evoked the same reaction. Indians welcomed it; Pakistanis rejected it.

As Richard Nixon had been one of the original architects of the

[1] The sale of US non-lethal military supplies to India and Pakistan had commenced in February 1966, at about the same time as the resumption of economic aid.

[2] *Foreign Assistance 1966: Hearings on S.2859 and S.2861 before the Committee on Foreign Relations, 89th Congress, 2nd Session,* 20 April 1966, pp. 175–6.

[3] *Pakistan Horizon,* 2nd Quarter 1967, p. 200.

[4] *New York Times,* 13 April 1967.

US-Pakistani alliance, his installation as President early in 1969 raised Pakistani hopes for greater warmth in her relations with America. In the May 1969 Aid Consortium meeting in Paris, the US delegation gave strong support to Pakistani requests for assistance,[1] and Nixon was given an enthusiastic reception on arrival in Pakistan on 1 August. He reminded Pakistanis that he had played 'some role' in cementing friendship between the US and Pakistan, and assured them that now as President, 'with somewhat more influence', he was going to work for the cause of the same friendship.[2]

On 8 October 1970, a few days before Yahya was due in the US to address the General Assembly during the 25th Anniversary celebrations of the UN and to confer with Nixon, it was announced in Washington that as 'an exception to the general policy', the US had decided to sell Pakistan 'several items of military equipment to replace equipment previously supplied'.[3] It was believed that the arms would include twin-jet B-57 Canberra bombers, F-104 jet fighters, and armoured personnel carriers, but not tanks.[4]

In India the usual storm of protest immediately broke out, but at a news conference in Washington on 29 October the US Assistant Secretary of State, J. Sisco, expressed indignation at the contrast between India's 'muted' reaction to the large-scale sale of Russian weapons and the exaggerated allegations against the US for the sale to Pakistan of a 'small packet' of old military equipment. The US supplies, he asserted, would in no way affect the balance of power in the subcontinent. He emphasized that the US action was not discriminatory against India, whose request would be considered on a par with Pakistan's. The fact remained that there was no pending request from India, while Pakistan had persistently pursued her requests. It was not in the interests of India or the US that Pakistan should be left to the mercy of Russia or China.[5] That India had not asked for US arms, a Pakistani spokesman said, showed that she was fully equipped and the purpose of her protests was to keep Pakistan weak.[6]

Just as the USSR's doubts about the trend of India's policies indirectly furthered Soviet-Pakistani relations, so the United States misgivings about India assisted the cause of US-Pakistani relations.

[1] *Dawn*, 22, 23, 24 May 1969.
[2] *New York Times* and *Dawn*, 2 Aug. 1967.
[3] *Dept. of State DPC 191 Transcript of Press, Radio and TV News Briefing*, 8 Oct. 1970.
[4] *New York Times*, 11 Oct. 1970.
[5] *Asian Recorder*, 1970, p. 9876.
[6] *Dawn*, 16 Oct. 1970.

The US constantly urged India to liberalize controls over her economy and to permit greater scope to private enterprise,[1] but she had no assurance that India would not move further along the road to socialism. Pakistani methods of economic development, on the other hand, won praise from US spokesmen, and in the seven years between 1961 and 1968, when private foreign investment in Pakistan registered a growth of 95.7 per cent, the biggest contribution to the increase was made by American investors.[2] India was also always in the forefront of critics of American involvement in the war in Indo-China, and her view of how to terminate the conflict would have given the Communists essentially all they wanted: American troops should be the first foreign force to leave the scene of battle, and a government comprising 'all elements of South Vietnam' should be installed.[3]

III. Pakistan and the Muslim World

The Arab-Israeli War of 1967
The six-day Arab-Israeli war provided Pakistan with another opportunity to display her solidarity with Muslim causes. During the hostilities, involving Israel on one side and the UAR, Syria, and Jordan on the other, Israeli forces occupied all of Sinai, the Gaza Strip, the Syrian heights overlooking the Sea of Galilee, Jerusalem, and all of Jordan west of the Jordan river. A cease-fire was brought about after repeated calls for one by the Security Council, and on 22 November 1967 the Council accepted a British draft which became the basic resolution for the political settlement of the Middle East crisis. It called for the 'withdrawal of Israeli armed forces from territories occupied in the recent conflict', the termination of 'all claims on states of belligerency', and the acknowledgement of the right of 'every state in the area . . . to live in peace within secure and recognized boundaries'.

When the war broke out, the Foreign Minister of Pakistan promptly condemned Israel for 'naked aggression' and Ayub wrote to the Arab Heads of State that Pakistan would do her utmost to render them whatever 'material help' they required.[4] In the National Assembly the Foreign Minister said that, 'perhaps with the exception of Kashmir', no other issue had stirred the people of Pakistan

[1] See *Hindu Weekly*, 5 Sept. and 21 Nov. 1966, for example.
[2] *Dawn*, 30 Jan. 1968.
[3] See *India News*, 26 June, 6 Nov., and 13 Nov. 1970, for example.
[4] *National Assembly of Pakistan Debates*, 6 June 1967, p. 997.

as had the Arab-Israeli war.[1] In the United Nations Pakistani
representatives ardently pleaded the Arab cause and submitted the
resolution by which the General Assembly declared invalid the
measures taken by Israel to change the status of the city of Jerusalem.

Officially India, too, gave strong support to the Arabs, but Prime
Minister Indira Gandhi did not dominate Indian politics to the
same extent as her father at the time of the Suez crisis of 1956. Several
influential personalities criticized Government policy as too pro-
Arab and contrary to the spirit of non-alignment. Mrs. Pandit, aunt
of Prime Minister Indira Gandhi, called India's attitude towards
Israel 'illogical'[2] and Acharya Kripalani said India's policy was
'based on cowardice' because she had failed to accord full diplomatic
status to Israel for fear of the Arabs.[3]

*The First Islamic Summit Conference and the First and Second
Islamic Conferences of Foreign Ministers*
On 21 August 1969 the Muslim world was shocked to learn that
extensive damage by arson had been caused to the holy *Al-Aqsa*
Mosque in Jerusalem, which was under the military occupation of
Israel.

President Yahya Khan issued a statement deploring the desecration of the mosque which was the first *Qibla* of the Muslims[4] and one
of their holiest shrines. He said Muslim unity was a paramount
necessity at that juncture and Pakistan would concert her course of
action with other Muslim countries.[5]

President Nasser urged King Feisal, in the latter's capacity as the
custodian of the Muslim shrines at Mecca and Medina, to take the
initiative in convening a summit conference of Muslim States to
consider the situation arising out of the vandalism in Jerusalem.
This suggestion was endorsed by an urgently summoned ministerial
meeting of the fourteen members of the Arab League, which
authorized King Feisal and King Hassan II of Morocco to organize a
Muslim summit meeting.

Hassan having offered to play host to the conference, leaders
representing twenty-five countries met at Rabat on 22 September.
The Palestine Liberation Organization was invited to attend as an

[1] ibid., p. 995.
[2] *Hindu Weekly*, 24 June 1967.
[3] ibid.
[4] The Muslims said their prayers facing Jerusalem until they adopted the practice of
facing Mecca.
[5] *Dawn*, 24 Aug. 1969.

observer, despite opposition by Turkey and Iran. Earlier in September a seven-nation preparatory meeting, of which Pakistan was a member, had met in the same capital and adopted the principle that only those countries should be invited to the summit who had a majority of Muslim population or had Islam as the state religion.[1]

At its termination, on 25 September, the Rabat Conference issued a Declaration of which the preamble stated that the participants were convinced that their common creed constituted a powerful factor for fostering understanding between them. The Declaration said that the Governments represented at the summit 'shall consult together' to promote collaboration between them. A Permanent Secretariat would be established at Jedda 'pending the liberation of Jerusalem'. It appealed to the international community to secure the withdrawal of Israel from all Arab territories occupied during the war of 1967. Finally, the authors of the joint Declaration affirmed their full support to the 'Palestine people for the restitution of its usurped rights and in its struggle for national liberation'.[2]

India, who had not been invited to Rabat, expressed great indignation at being ignored and pressed for admission on the ground that she had a population of fifty-five million Muslims. On the morning of 23 September the conference accepted King Feisal's proposal to invite a delegation from India. A statement issued by the Pakistani delegation said: 'In recognition of the historic and abiding concern of the great Muslim community in the Indian-Pakistani subcontinent, the Islamic summit adopted a proposal by His Majesty King Feisal of Saudi Arabia to accord representation to the Muslims of India.'[3] When the parley resumed in the afternoon Yahya noticed that India was represented by her Ambassador to Morocco, Sardar Gurbachan Singh, a Sikh. The Pakistani President thereupon decided to stay away from the hall until India was excluded.

Pakistan gave two grounds for her stand. First, she took the view that the conference had decided to allow the participation of the Indian Muslims, not of the Indian Government. Any Indian delegation would, therefore, have to be mandated by the Indian Muslim community and not by the Government. Secondly, Pakistan argued that, if the criterion for participation was to be changed by including India, then other countries with large Muslim populations, such

---

[1] ibid., 23 Sept. 1969.
[2] Text in *Pakistan Horizon*, 4th Quarter 1969.
[3] *Dawn*, 24 Sept. 1969.

as China, Russia, and Ghana, ought also be asked to send representatives.[1] Turkey, Iran, and Jordan stood firmly beside Pakistan
and threatened to boycott the proceedings. Ultimately it was decided
to exclude the Indian delegation from future sessions of the conference.

In his closing prayer King Hassan, the conference President,
said, 'May God help Muslims in Palestine, in India, and wherever
they are being persecuted.'[2]

Mrs. Gandhi's Government was severely criticized at home for
the rebuff at Rabat. An editorial in the *Statesman* summed up the
general feeling: 'New Delhi has only itself to blame for the humiliation
to which India has been subjected at the Islamic summit at Rabat
in being asked to withdraw from a conference to which it had secured
a belated invitation only after persistent and, at times, pathetic
importuning. . . . The very idea of secular India wanting to go to a
conference of Islamic States was open to serious objection.'[3]

The Muslim Foreign Ministers' Conferences at Jedda (24 to
26 March 1970) and at Karachi (26 to 28 December 1970) gave
further shape to the decisions taken at Rabat. A budget of US
$450,000 was approved for the Secretariat for 1971; Tunku Abdul
Rahman, Prime Minister of Malaysia, resigned his office to become
the first Secretary-General of the Secretariat; and proposals for
setting up an Islamic Bank and an Islamic International News
Agency, for the 'creation and reinforcement' of Islamic Cultural
Centres, and for drafting a charter for the Islamic Conference were
referred to various experts.

The 'revolutionary' regimes of Iraq and Syria declined to attend
the Rabat, Jedda, and Karachi conferences, and the UAR was a
lukewarm participant.

Muslim solidarity could be a great force in world politics but it
remains to be seen whether Islam in the twentieth century is a
strong enough force to weld together such a large number of
heterogeneous peoples into a meaningful partnership. The Rabat
Declaration called for Israel's withdrawal from all Arab lands
occupied by her in the 1967 war and also affirmed support to the
people of Palestine for the restitution of their rights, but did not
prescribe any sanctions against Israel, such as severance of diplomatic relations or economic boycott. Pakistan, for one, would do

[1] ibid., 25 Sept. 1969.
[2] ibid., 27 Sept. 1969.
[3] *Statesman Weekly*, 27 Sept. 1969.

well first to demonstrate that the people of her own two geographical units can form one brotherhood under the flag of Islam.

Other Developments

The Foreign Minister of the UAR repeated his country's view, during his visit to Pakistan in September 1967, that there would be no 'Muslim brotherhood' because brotherhood, in his view, should embrace all men of good purpose.[1] However, President Nasser died in September 1969 and it remains to be seen how rigidly his successor will adhere to all his policies. After meeting 'my brother' Sadat at Cairo on his way to the USA in October 1970, Yahya said he found the new UAR President 'sympathetic to Pakistan's viewpoint on important present-day issues'.[2] Though Mrs. Gandhi also went to the USA in the autumn of 1970, Sadat asked Yahya, not the Indian Premier, to convey the Arab point of view to Nixon.[3] Hasan El Tohamy, Minister of State and Political Adviser to the President, who led the UAR delegation to the Karachi Islamic Foreign Ministers' Conference, called the meeting 'a landmark for forging Islamic co-operation' and wished Pakistan to be 'the real cornerstone' in that process.[4]

Indonesia improved her relations with India after Soekarno fell from power, in the wake of the unsuccessful Communist-supported *coup d'état* in the autumn of 1965, and also ended her confrontation with Malaysia, but her relations with Pakistan remained cordial. Foreign Minister Adam Malik affirmed in Karachi in November 1966 that ties between Pakistan and Indonesia were not based on transient considerations but were deeply rooted in the 'common faith' of the two countries.[5] In the joint communiqué, Malik reiterated his Government's stand that the Kashmir dispute should be settled 'in accordance with the wishes of the people of the State'.[6] Not long afterwards when the Indian Foreign Minister, M. C. Chagla, claimed that Indonesia would no longer support Pakistan on the Kashmir question,[7] the Indonesian Ambassador to Pakistan promptly refuted the assertion and declared that his country's position remained unaltered.[8]

[1] *Pakistan Times*, 21 Sept. 1967.
[2] *Dawn*, 19, 20 Oct. 1970.
[3] ibid., 27 Oct. 1970.
[4] ibid., 31 Oct. 1970.
[5] ibid., 4 Nov. 1966.
[6] Text in *Pakistan Horizon*, 4th Quarter 1966.
[7] *Morning News*, 24 Jan. 1967.
[8] ibid. 7 Feb. 1967.

Forgetting Indonesia's rap on his knuckles, Chagla declared on 27 April 1967 that, if another conflict broke out between India and Pakistan, Iran would no longer assist Pakistan militarily.[1] Before the night had passed, an Iranian Foreign Ministry statement asserted that Chagla had been clearly told that, in the event of war between India and Pakistan, Iran would unhesitatingly help Pakistan in every possible way.[2]

As stated elsewhere, the Malaysian representative had not only supported India in the Security Council during the September 1965 debate concerning the Kashmir war, but he had also criticized the very creation of Pakistan on the basis of Islamic ideology. However, after the Malaysian-Pakistani rift had been mended, the High Commissioner-designate of Malaysia to Pakistan declared that it was the 'cornerstone' of the policy of his country strongly to support the Security Council resolutions for resolving the Kashmir dispute.[3] Tunku Abdul Rahman, whose administration had supported the observations of its representative in the Security Council in 1965, after confirmation as Secretary-General of the Islamic Secretariat drew the attention of the assembled delegates in Karachi to the words of the Prophet enjoining Muslims to regard one another as brothers, and cited Pakistan as a country who drew her strength from the Islamic faith.[4]

It had grieved Pakistan in the past that, though she had always treated Arab causes as her own, her solicitude had not been reciprocated. It was difficult for her to understand why the Arabs treated India with such consideration, in spite of the fact that India had recognized the State of Israel and had quietly collaborated with Israel in different ways. In a special article from Jerusalem Terence Smith of the *New York Times* revealed that Israel 'supplied India with a substantial quantity of Israeli-manufactured 120-mm. mortars during the Indian-Chinese confrontation in 1962' and that Israel also 'conducts an agricultural programme in India that is unofficial, if not actually covert'.[5]

Premier Daud having resigned on 9 March 1963, diplomatic relations between Pakistan and Afghanistan, which had been

[1] *Hindu Weekly*, 1 May 1967.
[2] *Morning News*, 3 May 1967.
[3] ibid., 15 Nov. 1967.
[4] For text of speech see *Dawn*, 27 Dec. 1970.
[5] *New York Times*, 28 Aug. 1968. See also Neville Maxwell, *India's China War*, p. 385, where he, too, confirms that India received 'heavy mortars' from Israel during the 1962 Sino-Indian crisis.

broken off in August 1961, were re-established on 28 May 1963, through the good offices of the Shah of Iran. Further internal changes in Afghanistan since then, by and large, have also been favourable for an improved relationship with Pakistan. One important development was the adoption by Afghanistan of a comparatively more liberal constitution in 1964, and the elections under it in the following year further weakened the political power of the royal family and the Daud faction. Ayub's resignation from office in Pakistan similarly assisted the process of *rapprochement* between the two countries. Yahya has pursued a more conciliatory line towards Afghanistan.

The post-Daud Governments, however, did not feel secure enough entirely to abandon the 'Pakhtunistan' agitation. Kabul Radio toned down, but did not stop, anti-Pakistani broadcasts. It was believed that the Afghan Government needed to keep up these broadcasts to placate the anti-Pakistani supporters of Daud.[1] Kabul also continued to celebrate 'Pakhtunistan Day'[2] and the Afghan representatives referred to the question of 'Pakhtunistan' in their speeches in the General Assembly of the United Nations, in 1965, 1968, and 1969, though they did not request the United Nations formally to take cognizance of the dispute.

What really eased the situation was the order promulgated, on 1 April 1970, that the one unit of West Pakistan would be broken up into its original locally autonomous parts, including the old North-West Frontier Province. Though Afghanistan had kept up the façade of the demand for 'Pakhtunistan', she had long realized the unreality of that idea and had been willing to settle for a locally self-governing north-west frontier province within Pakistan;[3] and the people of the area themselves, of course, had never seriously demanded anything beyond that. On 23 October 1970 Ghaffar Khan said that all his political objectives had been achieved. He had wanted the British to go and they had gone. Then there came one unit in West Pakistan and that was a 'cancer' but that also had gone.[4]

Another factor which must have brought home to the protagonists of 'Pakhtunistan' the hopelessness of their demand was that the

[1] *Christian Science Monitor*, 30 March 1964.

[2] For example, see *Kabul Times*, 2 Sept. 1965, for an Afghan account of the celebrations, and *Dawn*, 13 Oct. 1968, for description by a Pakistani eye-witness.

[3] I verified this impression by talking to responsible Afghans in Kabul in the spring of 1966 and the autumn of 1967.

[4] *Dawn*, 24 Oct. 1970.

USSR, who had been the only major power to encourage the agitation, quietly dropped that support when her relations with Pakistan eased. Ghaffar Khan told an Indian journalist in April 1968 that both the US and the USSR were urging the Afghan Government not to provoke any controversy with Pakistan over the 'Pakhtunistan' issue.[1] He also revealed, in October 1970, that the Soviet Union had asked for 'specific permission' from Pakistan before he could be allowed to enter the USSR.[2]

A visit by Pakistani Finance Minister Mozzafar Ali Qizilbash to Kabul in May 1970 resulted in an agreement to exploit the possibilities of increased economic co-operation between the two countries. This co-operation was expected to cover a variety of fields, ranging from utilization of Afghanistan's iron ore deposits to investment of Pakistani capital in industrial ventures in Afghanistan. Afghanistan also accepted the Pakistani offer of technical assistance in the form of training facilities in medicine, engineering, irrigation, and fertilizers.[3]

In the competition between India and Pakistan to woo the Muslim States, the tide at last seems to have definitely turned in favour of Pakistan. Muslims of other lands have begun to realize that the Hindu-dominated Government of India courts them mainly to prevent them from siding with Pakistan, and not because of any natural sympathy for Muslim causes. Noting the new trend in the Islamic countries, Indian Foreign Minister Dinesh Singh told the Indian Parliament, in April 1970, that India was 'deeply concerned' with the concept of Pan-Islamism being promoted by 'some Arab countries'.[4]

IV. Stalemate with India

The promise contained in the Tashkent Declaration, that India and Pakistan 'would continue meetings' at the highest level, was redeemed by the two countries only once: an Indo-Pakistani conference, at Foreign Ministers' level, was held at Rawalpindi on 1 and 2 March 1966.

Before the meeting convened, India and Pakistan debated the usual question, whether or not the Kashmir dispute should be specifically put on the agenda. The difficulty was resolved by

---

[1] *Hindu Weekly*, 29 April 1968.
[2] *Peshawar Times*, quoted in *Dawn*, 24 Oct. 1970.
[3] *Pakistan Affairs*, 31 May 1970.
[4] *Statesman Weekly*, 11 April 1970.

adopting the Indian suggestion that the agenda should simply be 'implementation of the Tashkent Declaration'. However, both sides conceded afterwards that, in fact, the discussion had mainly centred round Kashmir. The joint communiqué stated: 'The Pakistan side pointed out the special importance of reaching a settlement of the Jammu and Kashmir dispute. Both sides agreed that all disputes between India and Pakistan should be resolved to promote and strengthen peace between the two countries.'[1]

Bhutto interpreted the words of the joint statement to imply that India had accepted that Kashmir was disputed territory and was willing to hold further discussions with Pakistan for its settlement. However, Swaran Singh said Kashmir had been discussed simply because India had agreed not to refuse to discuss 'any issue that Pakistan might raise'.[2] The Indian Government view, he declared, remained that India's sovereignty over Kashmir was not negotiable.[3] A number of letters were exchanged between the two governments afterwards to arrange another high-level meeting, but none could be held because no assurance was forthcoming from India that the Kashmir question would be meaningfully discussed.

Their latest exchange, in the General Assembly on 1 October 1970, showed that neither side had budged from its position. Swaran Singh asserted that India was 'always willing' to enter into bilateral negotiations with Pakistan 'on this [Kashmir] and on all other Indo-Pakistani differences without any preconditions', but immediately added that the position that Kashmir is an integral part of India 'cannot be changed'. Agha Shahi wearily commented, 'they say that Kashmir is an integral part of India and simultaneously offer to open negotiations on Kashmir. We do not understand this.'[4]

From time to time Indian spokesmen also repeated their proposal that India and Pakistan make a joint no-war declaration. Here again both sides continued to stick to the positions they had first adopted in the days of Nehru and Liaquat.

Developments inside Kashmir

After the cease-fire between India and Pakistan in September 1965, Indian and Kashmiri state officials issued 'statement after statement . . . stressing the finality of Kashmir's accession to India and

[1] *Pakistan Horizon*, 2nd Quarter 1966, p. 193.
[2] *Asian Recorder*, 1966, p. 7020.
[3] *Pakistan Times*, 5 March 1966.
[4] *A/PV 1857*.

categorically ruling out the possibility of a plebiscite'.[1] From Srinagar Rawle Knox reported the response of the Kashmiri people to these pronouncements: 'When Indians say that Mr. Nehru's promise of a plebiscite in Kashmir is nullified by Pakistan's indisputable aggression they seem to forget that this promise was not made to Pakistan but to the Kashmiris. The Kashmiris have not forgotten.'[2]

In February 1967 elections took place in Kashmir, as part of the Indian General Election, but, as the *Economist* pointed out, elections in Kashmir were quite different from those in the rest of India:

Important sections of opinion are barred from participation by constraints, legal or otherwise. Indian election law requires every candidate to swear allegiance to a constitution which those unreconciled to Kashmir's accession to India cannot bring themselves to recognise. Even if they were willing to overlook this procedural problem it is hardly worthwhile for them to participate while their leaders from Sheikh Abdullah downwards are in detention, their newspapers muzzled, and their headquarters under government custody. Not surprisingly, the Plebiscite Front, which provides a common platform to all those unwilling to accept Kashmir's present status, is boycotting the election.[3]

Early in January 1968 the Government of India lifted the State of Emergency, which had been imposed in November 1962 at the time of the skirmishes with China, and freed a number of prisoners who were being held without trial. Among those thus set at liberty was the veteran Kashmiri leader, Sheikh Muhammad Abdullah, who immediately picked up the thread of his political activity from where he had been compelled to drop it upon his incarceration in May 1965. The refrain of Abdullah's speeches everywhere was that the people of Kashmir had still to decide whether the State should remain in India, or join Pakistan, or become independent. In a speech at Srinagar he declared that the people of the Valley were so resentful of Indian rule that they would vote overwhelmingly for Pakistan, if offered a choice between the two countries.[4]

At a convention called by himself at Srinagar from 10 to 17 October 1968, to find a solution to the Kashmir problem, the Sheikh repeated the suggestion he had made in his article in

[1] David E. Lockwood, 'Sheikh Abdullah and the Politics of Kashmir', *Asian Survey*, May 1969.
[2] *Daily Telegraph*, 12 Oct. 1965.
[3] *Economist*, 18 Feb. 1967.
[4] *New York Times*, 12 Aug. 1968.

Foreign Affairs (April 1965) that the representatives of India, Pakistan, and Kashmir should meet at a round-table conference to find a solution to the Kashmir question.[1] At a public meeting held outside the Convention, Abdullah produced the slogan, 'We do or die to achieve the freedom of Kashmir.'[2] When the second session of the Kashmir Convention was held, in the summer of 1970, only a few feeble voices were raised in favour of India. Most delegates favoured either accession to Pakistan or independence.[3]

In January 1971 the police arrested 'hundreds of workers' of the Plebiscite Front and barred Abdullah from entering his home state for three months because Mrs. Indira Gandhi, Prime Minister of India, and Ghulam Sadiq, the Chief Minister of Kashmir, 'are aware that their party would be defeated if the Plebiscite Front contested the [forthcoming mid-term] elections'.[4] The people of Srinagar retaliated by openly celebrating Pakistan's hockey victory over India in the Asian Games, and the highjacking of an Indian plane to Lahore by two members of the Kashmir Liberation Front.[5]

The Farakka Barrage Dispute

Another dispute, which first appeared as a small cloud on the horizon in 1951, progressively assumed major proportions in the nineteen-sixties, as the Indian barrage on the Ganges neared completion.

In 1951 Pakistan came to know from Indian press reports that India intended to construct a barrage across the Ganges at Farakka, eleven miles upstream from the point where the river enters East Pakistan, to draw off the water from its traditional course through Pakistan. India's stated objective was to divert the flow into the Bhagirathi-Hoogly river for the purpose of improving navigation into the port of Calcutta by flushing out the growing accumulation of silt, but the project was designed also to improve communication facilities, drainage and sanitation, and the water supply to the city of Calcutta. Indeed, it was claimed the project was of 'strategic and international importance'.[6]

Pakistan contends that 'it has been confirmed by independent

---

[1] *Asian Recorder*, 1968, p. 8602.
[2] *The Times*, 14 Oct. 1968.
[3] *Hindustan Times*, quoted in *Dawn*, 30 June 1970.
[4] *The Times*, 11 Jan. 1971.
[5] *Hindustan Times*, 4 Feb. 1971.
[6] Statement of the Minister of Industries and Natural Resources, *National Assembly of Pakistan Debates*, p. 1382.

expert assessment'[1] that some of the consequences of the dam for the livelihood of 65 million East Pakistanis would be:

First, because of the diversion of waters at the dam, almost the entire flow of the River Ganges into East Pakistan could be stopped in the dry season, turning hundreds of thousands of acres of cultivated land into wasteland.

Second, as a result, the channel of the river in East Pakistan will become silted, and in the flood season almost half of the area of East Pakistan will be flooded every year.

Third, the coastal areas of East Pakistan will become uncultivable in consequence of the greater penetration of seawater into the delta owing to the lack of drainage of fresh water into the sea.

Fourth, as a result of the drastic reduction in water supply, a number of agricultural projects, including those being planned, will be seriously affected.[2]

In Pakistan's view there is no reason why an equitable sharing of the waters of the Ganges cannot be worked out through the good offices of the World Bank, whose assistance had resulted in the Indo–Pakistani agreement of 1960 concerning the Indus waters. Pakistan avers that India's stand, that the lower riparian has no say in the disposal of the water resources of an international river, is untenable in international law.[3]

According to India, the Ganges is not an international river but 'is overwhelmingly an Indian river'. India claims to have approached the matter of the utilization of the waters 'in the Eastern Rivers complex in a spirit of co-operative approach with Pakistan'. The delay in settlement was due to the fact that Pakistan had 'refused to furnish the required data' at the meetings which had been going on for several years at official level. India intended to go ahead with the project and was not prepared to 'internationalize' the issue which was 'purely bilateral'. Pakistan's stand amounted to a 'negation of international law, and specially of riparian law as it exists today'.[4]

If India was sure of international law on the subject, why, asks Pakistan, should India 'fear to have recourse to arbitration to

[1] ibid., p. 1383.
[2] Foreign Minister Arshad Husain's statement in the General Assembly, *A/PV 1692*, 11 Oct. 1968.
[3] *A/PV 1681*, 4 Oct. 1968.
[4] *A/PV 1682*, 4 Oct. 1968.

settle the matter, or to judicial settlement by the International Court of Justice, which Pakistan is prepared to accept?"[1]

Though Pakistan raised the question with India as soon as she came to know of the project, and India held out assurances, in 1953 and again in 1957, that she would abide by the principle of co-operative development of the Ganges waters, the experts who were to exchange technical data, as a first step in the negotiations, did not meet till 1960. By January 1962 they had met on four occasions without achieving any concrete result. To move the matter forward Pakistan proposed, in November 1962 and again in May 1963, that the talks be raised to Minister's level, but India did not agree.[2] It was agreed in August 1965 that another meeting of experts should be held soon, but this decision was nullified by the outbreak of the Indo-Pakistani war that September. In January 1968 the parties agreed to hold a final meeting of experts, and this took place on 13 May 1968. Pakistan renewed her pressure for a Minister's meeting but India agreed to upgrade the talks to Secretary's level only.

Then followed a series of five Secretary-level conferences, in the period December 1968 to July 1970. Some progress was eventually made at the last of these meetings: both sides agreed that 'the point of delivery of supplies to Pakistan of such quantum of water, as may be agreed upon, will be at Farakka'.[3] This meant that India had accepted, at least in principle, that Pakistan was entitled to a share of the Ganges waters below the Indian barrage. But the important question of the quantity of water still remained to be determined. Though the joint communiqué had promised another meeting 'in 3 to 6 months, at a level to be agreed to by the two Governments, to consider the quantum of water to be supplied to Pakistan at Farakka and other unresolved issues relating thereto and to eastern rivers', no meeting was in sight when the year 1970 closed. If left unresolved for any length of time, the Ganges waters question could pose as great a danger to Indo-Pakistani relations as did the Indus waters dispute.

Need for Indo-Pakistani Conciliation
About the Farakka Barrage India is at least willing to talk to

---

[1] A/PV 1692, 11 Oct. 1968.

[2] Speech of the leader of the Pakistani delegation at the opening of the Indo-Pakistani talks on 24 Feb. 1970, *Pakistan Horizon*, 1st Quarter 1970.

[3] Text of joint communiqué in *Pakistan Horizon*, 3rd Quarter 1970.

Pakistan and this leaves hope that that problem may yet be amicably resolved. However, India treats the Kashmir question as closed and no longer open to modification by negotiation.

This frustrating habit of refusing to negotiate international disputes on a reasonable basis leaves an opponent with only two equally desperate alternatives: either to let India settle all questions according to her own sweet will or to go to war with India. This attitude has already caused two wars between India and Pakistan over Kashmir and one war between India and China[1] over the Himalayan frontier. Secretary-General U Thant warned the world community that one clear lesson of the Indo-Pakistani war of September 1965 had been that it was dangerous to leave 'without a solution grave problems affecting relations between States, in the hope that the mere passage of time may solve them'.[2] Sheikh Abdullah has also warned that, if India persists in her old policies, another war with Pakistan will erupt.[3] 'I wish Indians could understand', said Kingsley Martin, 'that only Indians think the Kashmir problem finally settled.'[4]

In his day Nehru used to defend the Indian presence in Kashmir on 'moral' grounds, but his right-hand man Krishna Menon has frankly admitted that 'political morality was pretty much a "text book approach" to public affairs' and that the real reason why India does not permit a plebiscite in Kashmir is that 'we would lose it'.[5]

A favourite theme of Indian leaders is that Kashmir is a symbol

---

[1] Neville Maxwell in his article 'China and India', in *China Quarterly*, July-Sept. 1970, and in his book *India's China War*, has shown that the Sino-Indian boundary differences could not be fruitfully negotiated because India had decided at an early stage that, while she would 'talk' to China about the dispute she would not 'negotiate' it. Nehru's view was that, 'There is a difference between negotiations and talks ... talking must always be encouraged ... talking may not yield any result' (p. 141 of the book). In his footnote on the same page, Maxwell cites India's attitude towards Pakistan on the question of Kashmir as another example of the same Indian method of conducting foreign policy. He points out that 'the Indian Government, even after the 1965 war with Pakistan, frequently reiterated its willingness to talk with Pakistan over Kashmir, while at the same time reassuring domestic opinion that Kashmir was and would remain "not negotiable".' For Maxwell's overall conclusion why the Sino-Indian dispute could not be subjected to fruitful negotiations, see the last paragraph of the article.

[2] *Introduction to the Annual Report of the Secretary-General on the Work of the Organization*, New York, 1965, p. 12.

[3] *Asian Recorder*, 1968, p. 8294.

[4] Khalida Qureshi, 'Diplomacy of the India-Pakistan War', *Pakistan Horizon*, 4th Quarter 1965.

[5] A. B. Tourtellot, 'Kashmir: Dilemma of a People Adrift', *Saturday Review*, 6 March 1965.

of Indian secularism and that Hindu–Muslim tension would be revived if Kashmir were to be disposed of on the basis of the theory that Hindus and Muslims constitute two separate nations. The fallacy of this line of argument has been exposed by another prominent Indian Hindu, Jayaprakash Narain, by a counter-question: 'Suppose we had to keep the Muslims of Kashmir within India by force; would that also be an example of our secularism?'[1]

Moreover, the real touchstone, whether Kashmir is a symbol of India's success in practising secularism or is in fact the main cause of its continued failure, is the actual state of affairs for the last twenty-odd years, not what Hindu leaders have been claiming verbally. The Muslims of Kashmir themselves have certainly not left the world in any doubt about what they think of the matter. Abdullah has called India's image of secularism 'horrifying and repelling' and has emphatically proclaimed that the Muslims of Kashmir, in particular, 'hated that image'.[2] As to conditions inside India, Narain, in the article just cited, has pointed out that 'the same Kashmir, that is supposed to be an example of Indian secularism, has occasioned a nasty upsurge of Hindu communalism', though, India being a Hindu-majority country, this communalism is able deceptively to appear in the garb of Indian nationalism.

It is not easy to catch the meaning of Indian statements, such as Nehru's that 'we did not accept it [the partition of India] at any time on the basis of a two-nation theory but on the basis of some kind of territorial determination'.[3] Nehru himself has recorded Attlee's response when the former, during the informal discussion of Kashmir by the Commonwealth Prime Ministers' Conference in January 1951, claimed, as usual, that India had never accepted the two-nation theory: 'Attlee pointed out rather warmly that past history did not quite fit . . . what I had said. The division of India had largely been based on a religious basis. He did not like this religious basis at all, and he had tried to avoid it but facts were too strong.'[4] 'The "one-nation" theory', points out Lamb, 'did not prevent Pakistan from coming into being; it did, however, guarantee

---

[1] Jayaprakash Narain, 'The Need to Re-Think', *Hindustan Times*, 15 May 1964, reproduced as Appendix V in A. G. Noorani, *The Kashmir Question.*

[2] *Asian Recorder*, 1968, p. 8294.

[3] J. Nehru, *India's Foreign Policy*, p. 456.

[4] P. L. Lakhanpal, *Essential Documents and Notes on Kashmir Dispute*, p. 227. Attlee, of course, knew the situation well because, as Prime Minister, he had been primarily responsible for the British decision to partition India.

that the relations between Pakistan and India would be subjected to constant stress and strain.'[1]

Indian leaders say that, if Kashmir leaves the Indian Union, it would strengthen the other separatist forces in India. This assertion overlooks the plain fact that there is no overwhelmingly Muslim area in India and none could, therefore, present the same problem as Kashmir. By settling this debilitating issue India, on the contrary, would be able to concentrate more effectively on countering secessionist pressures elsewhere.

The need for Indo-Pakistani amity is urgent and necessary from every conceivable point of view. The boundaries of the two neighbours do not follow any natural barrier. The subcontinent they jointly inhabit, therefore, forms a single unit for purposes of defence, protected by the Himalayas on the north and by the sea on the south. Quite obviously, it can be effectively defended only if the two countries act in concert.

A factor making their co-operation specially essential is that the most vulnerable parts of both Pakistan and India lie in the eastern part of the subcontinent. East Pakistan is militarily accessible from all sides and the thinnest part of India's waistline also lies in the same area. By one swift stroke China can isolate Assam and NEFA from the rest of India and, at the same time, threaten Indian as well as Pakistani Bengal. That these very parts happen to be the ones most disaffected with their respective central governments increases their vulnerability to slow penetration as well. In the colourful words of the Indian Home Minister, Y. B. Chavan, 'local Maoism was raising its ugly head' in Naxalbari while China, 'with Red Book in one hand and a sword in the other', was 'dancing outside'.[2]

One big reason why Asia has been the most disturbed continent in the world after the Second World War, and remains potentially the most inflammable region, is the disparity between the power of China and that of the remaining countries of Asia. Europe plus North America can counter any threat the Soviet Union can pose to the Western world. But China's neighbours cannot block the inroads of that giant without supplicating the assistance of one, or both, of the super-powers, who are white, western, and alien to the region. This kind of co-operation, whatever the partners themselves might say, is bound to be regarded by others as a new form of 'imperialism'. To be acceptable, in the latter part of the

[1] Alastair Lamb, *The Kashmir Problem*, p. 14.
[2] *Hindu Weekly*, 10 July 1967.

twentieth century, a balance of power in any region must result from the interplay of its own indigenous forces. Only India and Pakistan acting together can produce such a healthy equilibrium in Asia.[1]

The idea, of course, is not that they should together confront China. That would be no way to build lasting peace. On the contrary, such a confrontation would probably lead to a third world war. The objective should be to generate a feeling of security by the existence of a natural counterpoise to the colossus of Asia. The need for American and Russian interference in South and South-East Asian lands, where they have no territorial interests of their own, would be lessened, freeing them both of much useless burden and concern. In turn, this would relieve China of the anxiety she endures at the sight of the two super-powers trying to control events in her own backyard, thereby threatening her security and rightful position as a great power. China would then have less cause to make belligerent noises, and more freedom to attend to the arts of peace.

Though it is equally incumbent upon both India and Pakistan to strive for a *rapprochement*, circumstances have placed a higher responsibility in this behalf upon Indian shoulders. First, what Nehru called the 'emotional upset' on account of the creation of Pakistan has been greater in India than in Pakistan. It is apparent to the rest of the world that by far the greatest threat to India, ideologically as well as physically, is posed by China, but an Indian of Krishna Menon's expertise in foreign affairs maintains that 'even today . . . our main enemy is Pakistan'.[2] A greater effort on the part of Indians is needed to forget the past. Secondly, possession favours India in both the major disputes between herself and Pakistan. In Kashmir she holds the predominantly Muslim Valley against the wish of its inhabitants, and she is the upper riparian in the Ganges dispute. She must bring herself to allow Pakistan's rightful claims in both these cases. Thirdly: 'It is in the nature of things that India as the larger of the two powers would have to be the first to display political maturity and large-heartedness for a process of accommodation to get under way.'[3]

India and Pakistan are heirs to an ancient civilization. Their

---

[1] It is not easy to visualize Japan's future role. Geographically she is Asian; technologically she is Western; but emotionally she is not accepted as one of themselves either by Asian or by Western countries.

[2] Michael Brecher, *India and World Politics*, p. 154.

[3] Selig S. Harrison, 'Troubled India and her Neighbours', *Foreign Affairs*, Jan. 1965.

peoples individually are bright and intelligent. What they seem to lack is mutual trust, collective wisdom, and the capacity for joint effort. Neither country so far has been able to evolve a real consensus on matters of national concern, and they have moved but little on the road to social justice. Externally, whatever the appearance, the reality today is that Pakistan principally depends upon China to save her independence in the face of another Indian attack, and India upon the USSR to protect her against China. Both of them also need the prop of outside economic assistance to further their development plans. Can this be called true independence?

How to Resolve Indo-Pakistani Disputes?

Of the two main disputes which at present plague Indo-Pakistani relations, that relating to the Farakka barrage is less involved, and less charged with emotion, than the one concerning Kashmir. Should the already much protracted direct negotiations fail to bear fruit in the reasonably near future, the parties should invite the World Bank to mediate or arbitrate the Farakka issue. As mentioned elsewhere, Premier Kosygin, who, if anything, is more friendly to India than to Pakistan, has already recommended this obviously fair and sensible course.

In the matter of the Kashmir dispute, Pakistan has been comparatively more flexible than India. Though India keeps harping on the theme that Pakistan has no concern with Kashmir, Pakistan recognizes India as a party whose legitimate interests must be satisfied. Ayub wrote to Kennedy on 2 January 1963: 'Despite the discouraging and provocative utterances of Mr. Nehru on the subject, we are pursuing our sincere efforts to negotiate with India a solution which would meet three requirements: respect of the wishes of the people of Jammu and Kashmir; protection of the vital interests of Pakistan; and due regard for such claims of India as can be considered legitimate.'[1]

India, on the other hand, keeps repeating that Pakistan is the 'aggressor' in Kashmir, that the United Nations resolutions could not be implemented because Pakistan refused to move her troops out of Azad Kashmir, and that Kashmir's accession to India is complete and irrevocable; but she does not agree to have the validity of these pleas examined by the World Court or an impartial arbitrator. In fact, she does not at all suggest any rational course for breaking the impasse.

[1] M. Ayub Khan, *Friends Not Masters*, p. 150.

Of course the persons most directly concerned with the future of Kashmir are the people of Kashmir. As the word independence has a magic pull, the people of the Valley, if given the choice between joining India, or Pakistan, or becoming independent, could very well elect the last of these alternatives. Most outsiders, and several Indians,[1] believe that Abdullah would certainly opt for independence if he could, and Bakhshi Ghulam Muhammad is also known to have indicated his preference for independence.[2]

Pakistan's chief emphasis being upon the right of the Kashmiris to determine their own future, she would undoubtedly accept the verdict of the people of Kashmir if they opted for complete independence. Ayub was asked at the National Press Club in Washington, on 13 July 1961, about the possibility of Kashmir's independence. His reply was that Kashmir belonged to the Kashmiris and they certainly had every right to say what they felt. All Pakistan was interested in was to see that they were 'free to vote in a United Nations' plebiscite'.[3]

If an impartial plebiscite were to be conducted India would certainly lose and feel humiliated. She is, therefore, not likely to let a plebiscite be held. But, as India herself originally selected plebiscite as the best method of deciding Kashmir's future affiliation and, jointly with Pakistan, committed herself to that course before the United Nations, plebiscite as the means of solving the problem must hold the stage till the parties can agree to some other alternative.

The best way out would seem to be the one suggested by Abdullah: that the parties concerned should meet round a table and hammer out a mutually acceptable solution. There could be partition of the state on a more rational basis than the present cease-fire line, or independence for the Valley and division of the remaining territory between India and Pakistan, or independence for the entire state.

However, the Indian-Pakistani-Kashmiri summit meeting should not be allowed to become yet another wasted effort. As an earnest of their determination to end the problem of Kashmir, the parties

---

[1] See the views of Kingsley Martin in *New Statesman*, 19 March 1965; of Rangaswami in *Hindu Weekly*, 12 April 1965; of Taya Zinkin in *Hindu Weekly*, 23 Jan. 1967; of the *New York Times* in its editorial of 22 Jan. 1968; of John Ridley in the *Daily Telegraph*, 21 Oct. 1965; of W. R. Crocker in *Nehru*, p. 95; and of General B. M. Kaul in *The Untold Story*, pp. 137, 141.

[2] *Hindu Weekly*, 5 Oct. 1964.

[3] M. Ayub Khan, *Speeches*, IV, p. 37; for a similar statement by Foreign Minister Bhutto, see *Dawn*, 27 March 1964.

must undertake beforehand that, if no amicable solution is forthcoming within six months of the opening day of the joint conference,
the question would be determined in the following manner:

(1) A high-powered arbitration board, for instance one consisting
of the Secretary-General of the United Nations, the President
of the International Bank for Reconstruction and Development,
and the President of the International Court of Justice (or any
other mutually acceptable judge of that court, since the current
President, Sir Zafrulla Khan, is a Pakistani), be constituted and
authorized to make a binding award. Or,

(2) The entire State of Jammu and Kashmir should be made independent, and jointly sponsored by India and Pakistan for membership of the United Nations. The United Nations should be
requested to guarantee Kashmir's neutrality and inviolability.
Incidentally, the assumption of a positive role of this nature
would give a much needed fillip to the wilting world organization.
It could serve as a precedent for the United Nations to carry
similar responsibilities in other sensitive areas of the world, such
as the Middle East and South-East Asia.

The choice between the two alternatives sketched above should be
made, and announced, as a part of the agreed overall plan.

*Will the Settlement of the Kashmir Problem End Indo-Pakistani
Tension?*
Nehru asserted in Parliament, in August 1961, that Indo-Pakistani
relations were 'not dependent on Kashmir'. Even if the Kashmir
question was solved, Pakistani leaders would 'fiercely attack' India
because the concept of Pakistan was based on hatred of India.[1]
But back in March 1955 he had conceded that 'it [Kashmir] is the
most difficult of all the problems between India and Pakistan'.[2]
And away from the public gallery, he frankly admitted, before
Ambassador Galbraith, that a settlement of the Kashmir dispute
'would help quiet communal troubles [i.e. Hindu–Moslem friction]
in India'.[3]

    Pakistan has no unsatisfied territorial demands other than Kash-
mir. With Kashmir under Indian occupation, Pakistanis feel that

---

[1] J. Nehru, *Speeches*, IV, p. 294.
[2] J. Nehru, *Speeches*, III, p. 215.
[3] J. K. Galbraith, *Ambassador's Journal*, p. 278.

the fight to keep the Muslim majority areas of the subcontinent free
of Hindu domination is still unfinished. In essence, therefore, the
war of succession between Hindus and Muslims, which broke out
on the eve of the departure of the British from the subcontinent, still
has not reached its logical termination. 'The value of an early
settlement of this [Kashmir] dispute', Frank P. Graham, the United
Nations Representative, told the Security Council, 'would in my
view, be tremendous for (1) the four million people of the State,
(2) the four hundred million people of the two nations involved
[India and Pakistan], and (3) the people of the world.'[1]

The Indian view that 'what Pakistan needs is not only the solution
of Kashmir and other problems to her satisfaction, but a rough
measure of equality in military capabilities',[2] does less than justice
to the actual record. Like everyone·else, the Pakistani leaders would
no doubt like to make their country as strong as possible, but they
are realistic, practical men, whatever their other limitations might
be. On the question of the respective military strengths acceptable
to Pakistan, General Yahya Khan publicly stated, as Commander-
in-Chief of the Pakistani Army: 'What we are anxious to do is to
maintain a 4 to 1 ratio with India. For we feel that if that is the
ratio between the two armed forces, we shall be able to hold India
[defensively].'[3]

At the outbreak of Sino-Indian hostilities in 1962, Ayub acknowledged India's special importance in South Asia by writing
in his letter to Nehru: 'We are fully conscious of the great responsibility that lies on your shoulders for the maintenance of peace,
especially around this subcontinent.'[4] Again, in the middle of the
Indo–Pakistani war of 1965, Ayub acknowledged that 'Pakistan had
all along been aware that, being a smaller country, she could not
take the place of India or assume the role India is capable of playing',
but realistically cautioned that 'Indian leadership should also realize
that they could not play their due role unless India secured the help
of Pakistan for it'.[5] The *Round Table* perceptively commented:
'There is general acceptance [in Pakistan] of the facts that India is a
larger, wealthier, and more important country than Pakistan ...
the complaints ... against India are directed, not against her

[1] *Reports on Kashmir by United Nations Representatives*, Govt. of Pakistan, 1958, p. 198.
[2] Sisir Gupta, 'The Need for a Strong India', *Round Table*, Jan. 1967, p. 64.
[3] In a special interview with Z. A. Suleri, *Pakistan Times*, 27 Oct. 1967.
[4] *Pakistan Affairs*, 15 Nov. 1962.
[5] *President Ayub on the Crisis Over Kashmir*, p. 26.

superior wealth and power, but against her behaviour towards Pakistan over particular issues.'[1]

Owing to their common background, the relationship between India and Pakistan, in fact, is not one of pure hatred but of mixed feelings of love and hate, and it is up to the leaders to nourish one strand or the other. Nehru had rightly assessed that they 'can either be more than friends or become more than enemies'.[2] That the common man on both sides would like nothing better than that this burden of tension be lifted from his shoulders, is amply demonstrated by the genuine cordiality with which Pakistanis and Indians greet each other when they happen to meet privately, and by the genuine public welcome each side extends to the leaders of the other when the latter arrive in pursuit of peace and goodwill. A single bold and imaginative gesture on the part of India, the bigger and stronger of the two sister nations, would immediately bring into the open the presently suppressed feelings of goodwill which Indians and Pakistanis have for each other.

V. Has Pakistan's Foreign Policy Been Successful?

To make a proper assessment of Pakistan's foreign policy it is necessary to bear in mind her national objectives in relation to the outside world. First and foremost, Pakistan was faced with the necessity of preserving her security and independence against the designs and pressures of much stronger India, who made no secret of her feeling that Pakistan was a natural part of mother India and must revert to her. Secondly, Pakistan had a great urge to forge brotherly ties with the other Muslim countries of the world.

The reader will have seen that Pakistan has been measurably successful in both directions, despite the crushing problems plaguing her at birth, and the internal instability which has shaken her from time to time. Though the larger and more powerful India had all the apparent advantages on her side, especially during the first seventeen years when Jawaharlal Nehru sat in the seat of power, Pakistan stood up to India with remarkable fortitude. She also exhibited great resourcefulness in times of national peril. Her setbacks so far have been almost wholly on the home front, not in external relations.

Pakistan's natural inclination at first was to remain uncommitted in the East-West rivalry but, after the 1950 and 1951 scares of war

---

[1] *Round Table*, March 1960.
[2] J. Nehru, *Speeches*, II, p. 447.

with India, it became apparent that she needed a powerful friend to balance India's great advantages. She then moved to forge an alliance with the USA, at that time the obvious, indeed the only, choice: first, because America was ideologically more attractive than the USSR; secondly, because she was the most powerful country in the world; and thirdly, because, having escaped direct war damage, she was the only great power then in a position effectively to help others. This alliance had its disappointments but it served its most essential purpose. By strengthening Pakistan militarily, and saving her from collapsing under the weight of crippling food shortages and economic problems, America probably saved Pakistan's existence as an independent country during her tender infancy.

Another frightening test came in the summer of 1963, after the Indo-Pakistani talks on Kashmir had ended in failure and the Anglo-US Birch Grove communiqué of 30 June made it clear that Pakistan's Western allies would continue to augment India's war potential, without insisting upon an Indo-Pakistani *rapprochement*. As the USSR was already supplying war material to India, Pakistan was now faced with the sight of her enemy being strengthened by both great powers. With remarkable resilience, Foreign Minister Bhutto, in less than three weeks, was able to revive the sagging morale of the members of the National Assembly by assuring them that, if India turned her guns against Pakistan, Pakistan would not be alone, because a new factor had been brought into the situation: an attack by India on Pakistan would involve the security of 'the largest State in Asia'. And China did, in fact, make threatening gestures on the frontiers of India during the Indo-Pakistani war of 1965, causing India, the US, and the USSR to take notice, and extinguish the flames of war.

Towards her second goal—a special relationship with the Muslim world—Pakistan's progress at first was slow and, at times, painful, but she persevered and in the last decade has achieved visible success. At the crucial time of war with India, Pakistan had the great satisfaction of receiving sympathy and support from almost all the Muslim countries, except Malaysia. King Hassan's concluding prayer at the Rabat summit showed that other Muslim countries are becoming increasingly aware of the plight of fellow Muslims in India and Kashmir.

Some Pakistanis have alleged that Pakistan followed an independent course as long as her destiny was controlled by popular leaders but that she adopted a servile policy after Prime Minister Nazimuddin was dismissed from office, as the result of a 'palace revolution', and power passed into the hands of 'service men'. This line of reasoning ignores certain obvious facts. First, it was Liaquat Ali Khan who, realizing that Pakistan was in dire need of outside help, gave the first visible twist to Pakistan's foreign policy in the direction of greater friendship with America by choosing to go to that country, though an earlier invitation from Moscow was still pending. His successor, Nazimuddin, too, dispatched a special envoy to Washington, not to Moscow, to solicit wheat when Pakistan was threatened by famine. Secondly, it is wrong to think that patriotism has been the monopoly of either officials or politicians in Pakistan. The truth of the matter is that every single policy maker, whatever his label, tried to serve the interests of Pakistan as best he could under the prevailing circumstances. Suhrawardy, perhaps the greatest politician after Liaquat, was also the most zealous advocate of friendship with the West, and he carried public opinion with him, both inside and outside Parliament, to an unprecedented degree. Mian Mumtaz Daultana, a leading politician, affirmed in the National Assembly on 8 March 1958: 'Although the Governments have been changing, every Government has followed the same [foreign] policy.'[1] Ayub, the most prominent official, spans two periods. As Commander-in-Chief he took a leading part in formulating the alliance with America, but it was also he, as President, who ultimately transformed the policy into an independent one. Another former service chief, Yahya Khan, is presently upholding the virtually non-aligned status.

Those Indians who call Pakistan's policy of friendship with China opportunist, should realize that, as compared to their own country's complete somersault, involving a shift from closest friendship with China to bitter enmity with her, the modification in Pakistan's policy, involving a shift from alliance with the West to friendship with all powers, is a mere adjustment. In fact, a great many Indians frankly envy Pakistan's diplomatic skill in simultaneously maintaining good relations with the United States, the Soviet Union, and China, and in obtaining economic and military aid from them all, just as Pakistanis once used to admire India's dexterity in being able to obtain assistance from both East and West.

Pakistan, decidedly, has committed no blunder comparable to India's in so readily putting the seal of approval on China's forcible

[1] *National Assembly of Pakistan Debates*, p. 1013.

possession of Tibet and enabling China to influence the destiny of the subcontinent from a place of vantage. As a distinguished Indian, Acharya Kripalani, has written, the Indian policy towards Tibet "had the appearance of weakness and opportunism, of purchasing Chinese friendship at the cost of Tibet'.[1] The cost in military terms is incalculable. A study, prepared for the Institute of Defence Studies and Analyses in New Delhi, points out that India's population centres have become 'far more vulnerable to a missile or even air-borne nuclear attack from bases in Tibet than China's population centres from India'.[2] The study, in fact, could have gone further and said that in time China will be able to deploy Inter-Continental Ballistic Missiles in the impregnable, uncharted vastness of the Roof of the World and from there threaten all the main population centres of the world. In conventional warfare, too, the Chinese armed forces can pour down the Himalayan incline and threaten the densely populated industrial areas of India, as they did in 1962, while the Indians, even after scaling the high mountains, will reach only the bleak spaces of Tibet. The importance which India has hitherto enjoyed in world politics has been due more to her impressive size than to the wisdom and actual achievements of her policies.

Except that a stalemate since 1965 has kept Pakistan's relations with India frozen, the success of Pakistan's foreign policy today is obvious, but Pakistanis should beware that this remarkable state of affairs can endure only if it is continuously backed up by stability and progress at home. A great deal will also depend upon the attitude of the big powers. The delicate balance can be upset if Pakistani policy exceeds the limit of toleration of any one of them.

The greatest success of Pakistan's foreign policy—and this is equally true of Indian foreign policy of course, will come on the day when the twin countries of India and Pakistan bury the hatchet and settle down to a co-operative neighbourly relationship. The question whether there is any hope that they will ever be able to settle their differences amicably was put to Quaid-i-Azam Mohammad Ali Jinnah on 11 March 1948, and what he said then seems to hold true today. 'Yes,' he replied emphatically, 'provided the Indian Government will shed its superiority complex and will deal with Pakistan on an equal footing and fully appreciate the realities.'[3]

---

[1] Acharya J. B. Kripalani, 'For Principled Neutrality', *Foreign Affairs*, Oct. 1959.
[2] Asian Recorder, 1968, p. 8281.
[3] M. Rafique Afzal (ed.), *Selected Speeches and Statements of the Quaid-i-Azam Mohammad Ali Jinnah*, p. 459.

Should India and Pakistan continue along their present mutually destructive courses the existing edifice of South Asia will certainly begin to crumble before long. India might be tempted to take the short-sighted view that, if Pakistan's eastern wing collapses, it would prove the fallacy of the two-nation theory according to which Pakistan was created. However, any satisfaction which India might derive from such an event would be illusory because the next move in that kind of a game would be a revival of the movement for a united and independent Bengal, comprising what is now East Pakistan, Indian Bengal, Assam, and the North-East Frontier Agency. The resulting turmoil would create just the conditions Communism is waiting for. With a major foothold in the eastern part of the subcontinent, Communism would be in a position to penetrate the remaining areas. The South of India would probably fall next, and West Pakistan last. After that the medieval, feudal Middle East would be in no position to turn back the leaping flames of the revolution.

And that would not be all. In a maelstrom of these proportions Russia and the United States would surely be drawn in, with un-predictable consequences for the peace of the world.

16 The Emergence of Bangladesh

I. The Emergence of Bangladesh

The problem of East Pakistan, now the independent state of Bangladesh, suddenly burst upon the consciousness of the world on 25 March 1971, when Yahya Khan ordered the Pakistani army 'to do their duty and fully restore the authority of the Government' and a flood of refugees from East Pakistan began to pour into the adjoining districts of India. This explosion, however, was the logical culmination of pressures which had been building up continuously, though with varying intensity, from the early days of Pakistan. The pages of the *National Assembly of Pakistan Debates* over the years are replete with speeches of East Pakistani members demanding a greater share in their country's resources and in its civil and military administration.

In fact the roots of the problem stretch even further: the area which subsequently became East Pakistan had long been a backward tract, and the chances for the reduction of the existing disparity between the two wings of the new state of Pakistan were not improved when most migrating Muslim capitalists and industrialists from Bombay and other parts of India chose Karachi in West Pakistan as their new home, and put their money and skills to work there.

Several circumstances demanded that the province and people of East Pakistan be imaginatively and considerately treated by those who were called upon to guide the destiny of Pakistan. While East Pakistanis suffered from an acute sense of inferiority, West Pakistanis were intoxicated with an arrogant feeling of superiority.

In addition to this tremendous psychological chasm, the two wings
were physically parted by one thousand miles of forbidden Indian
territory, and emotionally alienated from each other by differences
of race, language, and culture. The feeling of Islamic solidarity, and
the common fear of Hindu domination, had brought the two distant
peoples together for the time being, but to make the union binding
it was essential that both of them should have sincerely practised the
principles of Islamic brotherhood which they professed.

The writing on the wall first appeared in March 1948, when
Quaid-i-Azam Muhammad Ali Jinnah made his only post-inde-
pendence visit to Dacca. A section of the crowd immediately walked
out of a public meeting at the Racecourse when he announced that
Urdu would be the only State language of Pakistan. Later, when he
repeated the proposal in his convocation address at the local university, there was such a commotion that he had to leave without
finishing the speech. Prime Minister Nazimuddin's renewed insistence in 1952 that Urdu would be the sole State language caused
serious rioting in the East Pakistani capital during which, on 21
February, two students were killed by police firing and immediately
became national heroes.

An even more portentous signal flashed in March 1954 when a
United Front of purely East Pakistani parties, fighting for a 21-point
programme, overwhelmed the ruling Muslim League Party in the
East Pakistani elections. Their platform clearly foreshadowed
Mujibur Rahman's six points[1] which ultimately sundered the union

---

[1] Mujib's six points were: (1) Pakistan shall be a Federation on the basis of the
Lahore Resolution; (2) the Federal Government shall deal only with Defence and
Foreign Affairs; (3) there shall either be two separate but freely convertible currencies
or one currency with constitutional provisions to prevent the flight of capital from East
Pakistan; (4) the power of taxation shall vest in the federating units which shall contribute towards the expenditure of the Federal Government; (5) each wing shall control
its own foreign exchange earnings and both shall contribute towards the foreign exchange
requirements of the Federal Government; (6) a militia or a para-military force shall be
set up for East Pakistan.

These points were elaborated by their author in a pamphlet, *6-Point Formula: Our
Right to Live*, published on 23 March 1966. Mujib explained that the object of the
sixth point was that East Pakistan be made self-sufficient in defence and more specifically that an ordnance factory, a military academy, and the headquarters of the
Pakistani navy must be set up in East Pakistan.

The 21-point manifesto had demanded, among other things, that Bengali be made
one of the State languages of Pakistan and that the martyrdom of those who lost their
lives in the language disturbances of 1952 be commemorated by erecting memorials and
observing 21 February as an annual public holiday. But it was the nineteenth of these
points which mainly inspired Mujib's six points. It ran as follows: 'Secure all subjects,
including residuary powers, except Defence, Foreign Affairs and Currency, for East

between East and West Pakistan. Thus, the bipolarity of Pakistani politics, which many observers first noted after Mujib's sweeping election victory on the basis of his six points in December 1970, in fact dates back to 1954.

Several factors at that time, and during the ensuing years, favoured the Establishment in West Pakistan and progressively increased the chagrin of East Pakistanis:

1. The grant of US military assistance which strengthened the position of the predominantly West Pakistani army.

2. The amalgamation of the various political units of West Pakistan into One Unit which East Pakistanis believed was designed to enable the people of West Pakistan to talk to the people of East Pakistan 'with one voice' and prevent the latter from using their numerical superiority.[1]

3. The acceptance of parity between the two parts of Pakistan in the membership of the National Assembly under the 1956 and

[1] This view was expressed in the Constituent Assembly of Pakistan on 30 Sept. 1955 by Abul Mansur Ahmad, an East Pakistani member.

Earlier (24 Aug. 1955) Fazlur Rahman, a former minister in the Central Government, had stated from the same floor: 'Sir, it has been stated that the greatest merit of this Bill is to do away with the distinction between Punjabis and Sindhis and Pathans and this and that but you do not realize that by dividing Pakistan into two, you are manifoldly magnifying that provincialism, by making it a local patriotism for the two regions. Then no longer the cry will be Punjabis and Sindhis but the cry will be Bengalis and non-Bengalis.'

Mujibur Rahman thought the creation of One Unit in West Pakistan had strengthened the case for granting full regional autonomy to each of the two parts of Pakistan, leaving only Foreign Affairs, Defence, and Currency in the hands of the Centre. *Constituent Assembly of Pakistan Debates*, 30 Sept. 1955, p. 1409.

Bengal which shall be fully autonomous and sovereign, as envisaged in the historic Lahore Resolution, and establish naval headquarters, and an ordnance factory so as to make it militarily self-sufficient. The present *Ansar* force shall be converted into a regular militia and equipped with arms.' *Dawn*, 20 Dec. 1953.

West Pakistanis long having conceded that Bengali would be one of the State languages of Pakistan, Mujib had no need to repeat this demand in his programme.

During the 1954 election Mujib had campaigned for the 21 points as a zealous lieutenant of Suhrawardy, leader of the Awami League, which was one of the two main components of the United Front.

The famous Muslim League Resolution of 23 March 1940, popularly known as the Pakistan Resolution or the Lahore Resolution, cited in the 21 points as well as in the six points, demanded that the Muslim majority areas of north-western and eastern India 'be grouped to constitute independent states in which the constituent units shall be autonomous and sovereign'.

A later resolution (9 April 1946) of the Muslim League Legislators' Convention asked that the two Muslim majority zones of India be constituted into 'a' sovereign independent state, but its critics say that the Legislators were not competent to amend the 1940 resolution which had been passed by a full session of the League.

1962 constitutions which further neutralized the leverage of the eastern part's numerical ascendancy.

4. The assumption of power by the military under Ayub Khan in 1958 which concentrated power almost entirely in West Pakistani hands.

Mujib got his chance to speak up in February 1966 in the wake of the Indo-Pakistani war during which East Pakistan had been isolated from its central government and stood defenceless against a possible Indian thrust. He reiterated the standing East Pakistani demands for autonomy and self-sufficiency in defence under the new label of six points.

Interestingly, Ayub's response was a blueprint of the policies which Yahya was actually to practise later. At a meeting of the Convention Muslim League in Dacca he threatened that he would accept the challenge of civil war and use the 'language of weapons' if the nation faced 'disruption'.[1]

From April 1966 onwards Mujib was arrested, released, and rearrested a number of times and finally, in January 1968, he was implicated in the Agarthala Conspiracy Case. He was released in February the next year to partake in the parleys Ayub Khan was then holding with political leaders of various shades.

The East Pakistani leader's final chance arrived with the elections of December 1970. His Awami League captured all but two of the East Pakistani seats in the National Assembly, a total of 160, thus gaining an absolute majority in the 300-member central legislature. Had that body, therefore, proceeded to perform its allotted task of framing a new constitution for Pakistan, there was nothing to stop Mujib from basing the enactment on his six points.

The deadlock resulted from the fact that Yahya Khan as well as Bhutto, whose People's Party had swept the polls in West Pakistan, believed that the enforcement of the six-point scheme would mean the virtual disintegration of Pakistan. Their contention was not without force but the passing of the years had loaded the dice against the West Pakistani leaders. East Pakistanis no longer were in a mood to continue meaningful ties with West Pakistan which had always worked to their detriment in the past. And once most of them had decided to go their own way it was almost impossible to hold their land by force for any length of time from a base hundreds of miles away across hostile India, and utterly impossible to do so after

[1] *Dawn*, 21 March 1966.

India had directly intervened in the fighting in November 1971.[1]
Yahya's decision to use military force in East Pakistan, therefore,
was not only a fatal political error but also a grave military blunder
for which Pakistan had to pay dearly. In truth, if West Pakistanis
really wished their union with East Pakistan to endure, they should
have woken up to realities much earlier and pursued utterly different political and economic policies from the very inception of
Pakistan.

I. Has the Two-Nation Theory Been Proved False?

Indians say the emergence of Bangladesh has falsified the two-
nation theory on the basis of which Pakistan was created. From this
they wish the world to infer that their own stand, that all the
peoples of the subcontinent constitute but one nation, has been
vindicated. But had the recent upheaval been a proof of the sound-
ness of such a notion, not three nations would have emerged from it
but only one. Bangladesh would have offered to become a part of
India and the people of West Pakistan would have risen against their
defeated and discredited military overlords and compelled them to
follow the same path. Indeed, the setting up of two Muslim majority
states, one in the north-west and the other in the north-east, would
seem to have vindicated the argument implied in the original
Pakistan Resolution that two separate and sovereign Muslim states
in the subcontinent would be more viable than a unitary Muslim
state comprising two distant parts. Both Pakistan and Bangladesh
seem equally determined to maintain their independent identities.
Geographic and political compulsions are making Mujib talk of
secularism and eternal friendship with India, but what distinguishes
Bangladesh from that half of Bengal which forms a part of India
other than that it is a predominantly Muslim area?

It is not so much the concept of Islamic solidarity which has been
proved wanting as the un-Islamic conduct of those who purport to
follow that ideal. If West Pakistanis had behaved like true Muslims
they would have displayed greater brotherly love towards their

[1] An Indian Government spokesman admitted that Indian forces crossed the East
Pakistani border on 21 November 1971. Of course he speciously excused the offensive
by alleging that this was done when the Indians saw 'Pakistani tanks advancing menac-
ingly towards Indian territory'. *Statesman Weekly*, 27 Nov. 1971. As if the hands of the
Pakistani army were not already filled with millions of rebellious East Pakistanis and
swarms of guerrillas trained and equipped by India! The Pakistani army in East
Pakistan having surrendered on 16 December 1971, the war ended on the following
day when Yahya accepted India's unilaterally declared cease-fire.

eastern brothers during the last quarter of a century, and a greater willingness to share their wealth with them.

Nor should two special circumstances be overlooked. First, the two wings of Pakistan were separated by one thousand miles of India and the latter was able continuously to exert tremendous pressure to snap the ties holding the two parts together. Secondly, East Pakistan contained a large Hindu minority which regarded India as its natural motherland and considered it its patriotic duty to undermine the State of Pakistan. Not only was this disruptive element of 25 per cent strong but its members, being businessmen, bankers, teachers, doctors, and lawyers, wielded an influence far beyond their numbers.

Clearly, it was only the link of Islam which managed to hold together East and West Pakistan for so many years despite the constant strain to which it was subjected by Pakistanis themselves and by formidable extraneous forces.

No one can foretell the future but it can scarcely be argued on the basis of the existing evidence that the two-nation theory has lost its relevance.

II. The Role of Outside Powers in the East Pakistani Crises.

Ever since the 1962 Sino-Indian war the Indians had been sensitive to the threat of a joint Sino-Pakistani drive against themselves, and the experience of the 1965 war with Pakistan had only heightened that fear. When it was announced in July 1971 that, as a result of Henry Kissinger's secret visit to China via Pakistan, President Nixon would visit China, many Indians thought a US–China– Pakistan axis was being formed and felt depressingly isolated. Whatever its long-term consequences might turn out to be, the Nixon visit to China certainly signified a palpable shift in American policy, from one of strengthening India as a counterpoise to China to one of trying to cultivate better relations with China, despite India's obvious discomfiture. The Soviet Union, obviously, was the only power in the world strong enough to furnish India with the necessary re-assurance. Not surprisingly, Mrs. Gandhi lost no time in accepting the proposal which the Russians had been pressing with little success since 1969,[1] and within a month signed with them a Treaty of

---

[1] As the chances of Sino–Soviet reconciliation faded, the Soviet Union became increasingly preoccupied with the idea of containing China by a 'system of collective security in Asia'. It is not without significance that Brezhnev first came out with this proposal not long after the spring 1969 Ussuri River hostilities between the Chinese and Russian

Peace, Friendship and Co-operation. Clause IX of the covenant, which India admittedly invoked on the eve of her military offensive in East Pakistan,[1] stipulated that 'In the event of either Party being subjected to an attack or a threat thereof, the High Contracting Parties shall immediately enter into mutual consultations in order to remove such threat and to take appropriate effective measures to ensure peace and the security of their countries.'[2]

Noting that, despite the claim in the Swaran Singh–Gromyko joint statement marking the treaty—that the accord was 'an outstanding historic event'—Indian Government spokesmen continued to assert that non-alignment had remained unscathed, the *Statesman* caustically observed that official comment would have been 'all the better for clearly declaring that foreign policy has taken a new direction. . . . There is no visible harm in acknowledging that, in the context of the Nixon–Chou dialogue, Bangladesh, and Pakistan's hostile attitude, New Delhi deemed it fit to seek an assurance from a sympathetic quarter. This is, however, quite a different thing from suggesting that all is as it was before and that non-alignment has emerged with a new shine.' The article also ridiculed the fiction that the treaty was not directed against any country when it was evident that Pakistan was 'the target' and the pact had been 'welcomed for precisely this reason'.[3] On 28 October the Indian Foreign Minister assured his countrymen that India could count upon the Soviet Union for 'total support' in the event of a conflict with Pakistan.[4]

During the Indo-Pakistani war Indians got alarmed when the

[1] M. S. Rajan, 'Indo-Soviet Treaty and Nonalignment', *India News*, 10 March 1972; also *Statesman Weekly*, 11 Dec. 1971.
[2] *Asian Recorder*, 1971, p. 10330.
[3] *Statesman Weekly*, 14 Aug. 1971.
[4] *Asian Recorder*, 1971, p. 10501.

---

forces. See pp. 366–7 for some further details concerning the Soviet efforts. By eagerly concluding treaties with military overtones not only with India but also with Egypt (27 May 1971) and Iraq (9 April 1972), the Soviet leaders seem to be following Dulles's policy of defence pacts which they used to decry so much. To this growing chain, Bangladesh is linked by her treaty of Friendship, Co-operation and Peace with India (19 March 1972).

Just as American commentators made no secret of the fact that their defence chain was an anti-Communist front, the Russians are now frankly saying that their alliances are designed to serve 'the purposes of uniting progressive Arab states on an anti-imperialist basis'. *International Affairs*, 6 June 1972, p. 65. The Soviet Union has also eclipsed the United States as the main source of arms for the countries of the Third World. Walter Sullivan, 'Survey Says Soviet Leads in Sending Arms to Third World Nations', *New York Times*, 14 June 1972. Sullivan's article is based on a report by the Stockholm International Peace Research Institute.

REAPPRAISAL (1963 - July 1972)

Chinese began ostensibly to collect 'weather data for locations in Tibet' and President Nixon ordered a task force of the Seventh Fleet to patrol the Indian Ocean, but the Soviet Ambassador to India assured his hosts that the Soviet Union would open a diversionary action against the Chinese and would not allow the Seventh Fleet to intervene.[1] The Soviet Union also blocked any effective action by the United Nations by using her veto in the Security Council till East Pakistan had been conquered by India.

China gave Pakistan strong verbal support throughout the period of tension but did not give India any ultimatum comparable to the one she had delivered during the 1965 war. The main reason, of course, was that this time she definitely would have had to reckon with the Soviet Union, who in 1965 had taken a neutral stance in the Indo-Pakistani dispute. Obviously China did not wish to give that super power a pretext for a pre-emptive strike against the nascent Chinese atomic capability which the Soviet military commanders are said to desire so much.[2] At any rate the struggle in East Pakistan, being essentially a civil war, was not the kind of confrontation in which outside powers would normally wish to take a direct hand. It was a different question when, after conquering East Pakistan, India wished to turn her attention towards Azad Kashmir and West Pakistan. Whether China would have physically intervened on the western front will never be known because India unilaterally declared a cease-fire there before things had gone very far.[3] Bhutto's[4] overall view is that 'within the limitations China did what she could ... a series of successive blunders were committed by the Yahya regime ... you have to take all these factors into consideration ... but whatever China's participation, we have not lost confidence in China's friendship or China's words.'[5]

During the Pakistani President's visit to Peking in February 1972,

[1] *New York Times*, 11 Jan. 1972. In his Foreign Policy *Report to the Congress* on 9 Feb. 1971, President Nixon disclosed that the Soviet Union was 'willing ... to make military moves to deter China, on India's behalf' (p. 150).

[2] As put by a Western diplomat, the Soviet-Indian Treaty 'scared the hell out of the Chinese'. *New York Times*, 15 Feb. 1972.

[3] It must be pointed out, however, that, their pungent verbal sallies notwithstanding, the Communist Chinese have been singularly cautious in action. The two wars they have so far fought, the Korean war and the Himalayan war, were both defensive actions in which they joined the battle only when they felt that their own borders had begun to be directly threatened.

[4] Yahya having resigned on 20 Dec. 1971, following the débâcle in East Pakistan, Bhutto had been immediately sworn in as the new President.

[5] Bhutto's interview with Ian McIntyre for the B.B.C. Text in *Dawn*, 20 Feb. 1972.

China decided to change into grants the loans already being utilized, and deferred by twenty years the repayment of the loan provided in 1970.[1] Reportedly, China has also delivered to Pakistan substantial quantities of new military equipment, including jet fighters and tanks.[2]

As China is more likely to advance her interests in the subcontinent by encouraging and assisting the revolutionary pro-Peking elements than by direct conquest, it is a moot question whether or not the new conditions will make it easier for China to pursue her long-term objectives. Of the three South Asian nations, India under Indira Gandhi, at present, seems to be in the best shape but a country of 550 million people whose fortunes are propped up by the charisma of a single human being must be deemed to be living on the brink of uncertainty.

The United States' efforts were directed towards preventing a war between India and Pakistan and, after war had broken out, towards bringing about a cease-fire. On the one hand she made clear to Pakistan that in her view 'a lasting political solution could be found only on the basis of some form of autonomy for East Pakistan',[3] and on the other she warned India that she could only regard an Indian resort to arms as 'a tragic mistake'. In addition, Secretary of State Rogers gave notice to the Indian Ambassador on 11 August 1971 that the Administration could not continue economic assistance to a nation that started a war.[4] Nixon also obtained an assurance from Yahya that Mujib would not be executed.[5]

Upon the outbreak of war in the western sector the United States requested an urgent session of the Security Council, but a resolution calling for a cease-fire and withdrawal of forces was vetoed by the Soviet Union. Ambassador Bush pleaded before the Council that the very purpose of the United Nations would 'be thwarted if a situation is accepted in which a government intervenes across its borders in the affairs of another with military forces, in violation of the United Nations Charter'.[6] On 12 December the United States called for another urgent session of the Council to press for an end

---

[1] For text of Bhutto–Chou En-lai communiqué see *Morning News*, 3 Feb. 1972.

[2] *New York Times*, 3 June 1972.

[3] Richard Nixon, *A Report to the Congress, Feb. 9, 1972*, p. 145.

[4] ibid., p. 146. The US development loans to Pakistan had been cut off in April 1971 after Yahya Khan had ordered the army to restore order in East Pakistan, but aid to Pakistan was fully resumed on 19 June 1972.

[5] Richard Nixon, *A Report to the Congress, Feb. 9, 1972*, p. 145.

[6] ibid., p. 148.

to the hostilities but once more the move was frustrated by a Soviet veto.

At the height of the fighting in East Pakistan, President Nixon ordered a US task force of the Seventh Fleet to patrol the Indian Ocean, ostensibly to evacuate American citizens if it became necessary, but, in fact, to relieve the pressure on the beleaguered Pakistani forces.[1]

During the week of 6 December the United States received 'convincing evidence' that India was contemplating the seizure of Azad Kashmir and the destruction of Pakistan's military forces in the west. She repeatedly asked India for assurances to the contrary but did not receive them.[2]

However, though the United States was not able to restrain India directly, she was successful in her efforts to influence India through the Soviet Union, who 'is indispensable to India'.[3] 'The Soviets deserve credit for restraint, after East Pakistan went down, to get the cease-fire.'[4]

Apart from his own reading of the situation in South Asia, Nixon may have favoured Pakistan because any serious differences between the US and China over the situation in South Asia might have jeopardized the opening of a constructive dialogue with the Chinese leaders during his projected trip to China.[5]

In the Nixon–Chou joint communiqué the two sides stated their positions on South Asia separately but both called for a withdrawal of Indian and Pakistani forces to their own respective territories and to their own sides of the cease-fire line in Kashmir. China, in addition, reiterated her support to the people of Kashmir 'in their struggle for the right of self-determination'.[6]

Most Afro-Asian countries, having recalcitrant minorities within their own borders, were sympathetic to Pakistan. Taking up the question, after the Soviet Union had barred action in the

---

[1] See Jack Anderson's report, based on secret White House Papers, in *St. Paul Dispatch*, 31 Dec. 1971.

[2] Richard Nixon, *A Report to the Congress, Feb. 9, 1972*, p. 147. Indian occupation of Azad Kashmir would have deprived Pakistan not only of control of that territory but also of her sole common frontier with China.

[3] 'An Interview with the President: "The Jury Is Out" ', *Time*, 3 Jan. 1972.

[4] ibid.

[5] For this surmise see James Reston's dispatch 'Politics and Strategy' in *New York Times*, 12, Jan. 1972, and Robert N. Magill's letter in the 22 Dec. 1971 issue of the same newspaper. Magill is a former member of the Policy Planning Council, Department of State.

[6] For text of communiqué see *New York Times*, 28 Feb. 1972.

Security Council by casting a veto on 6 December, the General Assembly by 104 votes to 11 called upon India and Pakistan to stop fighting and withdraw their forces from each other's territory.[1]

The Muslim states of the Middle East felt specially concerned at the danger Pakistan faced at the hands of India. Saudi Arabia lent Pakistan seventy-five war planes in October 1971[2] and Jordan sent ten during the war.[3] Consequently, President Bhutto's first visit abroad after the war was paid to Afghanistan and the next to the Middle East and North Africa, and he called these travels 'a journey among brothers'.

III. Prospect

Under the new realities of the loss of East Pakistan, and a relatively much stronger India, Pakistanis will have to take a fresh look at the direction of their external policy. Previously they considered themselves both a South-East Asian and a Middle Eastern power. With West Pakistan standing alone, they are likely to turn towards the adjoining Muslim Middle East even more whole-heartedly than before.

Pakistanis are also bound to think again whether defence pacts are really as useless as they had come to believe. They are already asking themselves whether India's pact with the Soviet Union did not substantially contribute to her success in the Bangladesh emergency. Bhutto previously had argued that Pakistan should relinquish her membership of SEATO and CENTO because her allies had failed to rally to the support of Pakistan in the 1965 war against India. However, with the Indo-Soviet Treaty evidently in mind, he has pragmatically come round to the view that Pakistan should not renounce her alliance with the United States but make it more meaningful than before. Reportedly, he also broached the subject of a treaty with China but the Chinese seem to prefer to base their relations with other countries on community of interests rather than on formal ties.[4] After all, the thirty-year pact they made with the Russians in 1950 did not prevent Sino-Soviet relations from deteriorating when the objectives of the two countries began to diverge.

China's stock in Pakistan continues to stand high and that of America, which had begun to rise again after Nixon had taken over

---

[1] *General Assembly, A/RES/2793 (XXVI)*, 9 Dec. 1971.
[2] *Asian Recorder*, 1971, p. 10473.
[3] *New York Times*, 3 June 1972.
[4] *Asian Recorder*, 1972, p. 10673.

as President, has risen further. All the same, Pakistan cannot overlook the proximity and power of the Soviet Union. Of the great
powers, the Soviet Union alone at present seems capable of exercising a restraining influence over India. She is also a profitable trading
partner for Pakistan and a good source of technical and economic
assistance. After his trips to the Muslim states and China, President
Bhutto journeyed to Moscow and arranged for the restoration of
'Soviet-Pakistan trade, economic, scientific, technological and other
ties which came to be disrupted as a result of the events of 1971'.[1]

Bhutto has affirmed that Pakistan's policy towards the three
Great Powers, the USA, the USSR, and the People's Republic of
China, would remain one of 'bilateral' relations which he defined
once more as the pursuit of national interest 'without taking a
partisan approach to the Great Power differences'.[2]

At the same time Pakistan remains geographically locked in the
same subcontinent as India and recent events have underlined the
necessity for seeking a new relationship with her.

India, who in the past had uniformly insisted that the smaller
issues must be settled first so that a friendlier climate could be
created for tackling the thorny question of Kashmir, is now saying
that it will not be enough to solve the peripheral issues. She is
insisting that all the issues be solved simultaneously, 'to end the
threat of another conflict for all time',[3] and is pressing for the
acceptance of her longstanding demand that the existing cease-fire
line in Kashmir be declared the international border between India
and Pakistan so that she can retain possession of the Valley.

She has the upper hand because of her recent victory, occupation
of territory in Azad Kashmir and elsewhere, and the possession of
some 90,000 Pakistani prisoners (including 20,000 civil servants and
women and children), who according to the Geneva Convention
should have been released at the time of the cease-fire[4] but are being
retained by their captors as a valuable bargaining counter.

But the Kashmir dispute is not likely to lend itself to an offhand
bilateral resolution by India and Pakistan. Bhutto has said that the

[1] For text of Bhutto-Kosygin communiqué of 18 March 1972 see *Dawn,* 19 March
1972.
[2] President Bhutto's inaugural address to the National Assembly of Pakistan. Text in
Dawn, 15 and 16 April 1972.
[3] Foreign Minister Swaran Singh, quoted in *India News,* 5 May 1972.
[4] 'Prisoners of War shall be released and repatriated without delay after the cessation
of active hostilities.' Article 118 of the Third Geneva Convention of 1949. Indian actions
also defy Security Council Resolution 307 of 21 Dec. 1971, calling for a withdrawal of
forces and observance of the Geneva Convention of 1949.

right of self-determination of the Kashmiris 'has not been bestowed on them either by India or Pakistan. It is their inherent right which no one can take away from them.'[1]

Prem Nath Bazaz also rightly points out that 'the Kashmir problem does not arise, as is commonly believed, because Pakistan wants to have the state by hook or by crook, but because India has failed to convince the large majority of Kashmiri Muslims during the last twenty-two years that they can live happily and fearlessly in India.'[2]

In fact, Maulvi Farooq, chairman of the Kashmiri Awami Action Committee, thinks the creation of Bangladesh has strengthened his party's hands because 'like the people of Bangladesh we are also struggling to keep our identity as a nation'.[3]

The news that the order forbidding Sheikh Abdullah from entering Kashmir had been rescinded, immediately led to public jubilation in his homeland. Eye-witness Robert Trumbull of the *New York Times* wrote from Srinagar on 7 June 1972 that this 'public outpouring of loyalty' to Abdullah 'indicated that the defiant Muslims of Kashmir remain unreconciled after nearly 25 years of Indian rule'.[4]

On the question of Pakistani prisoners the Indian position is that the Pakistanis surrendered to the joint India-Bangladesh command and that Bangladesh, therefore, is a necessary party to any discussions relating to the disposition of the captives. The matter is further complicated by the facts that Mujib refuses to meet Bhutto till Pakistan recognizes Bangladesh, and continues to insist that some 1,500 Pakistanis be tried as war criminals.[5] Pakistan will probably be compelled to recognize Bangladesh before any substantive talks on the prisoners of war issue can get under way.

In their first summit meeting after the 1971 war, President Bhutto and Prime Minister Indira Gandhi, conferring at Simla from 28 June till 3 July 1972, recorded some progress towards normalizing Indo-Pakistani relations. They decided to initiate steps to resume communications, travel facilities, and trade between the two countries. They also agreed to withdraw their forces to their own respective sides of the international border.

---

[1] *Dawn*, 16 April 1972.
[2] Prem Nath Bazaz, *Whither India After Independence?*, p. 187.
[3] *New York Times*, 10 June 1972.
[4] ibid.
[5] Of course even this does not explain why the remaining 88,500 prisoners, including 20,000 civilians, are being detained indefinitely.

The two sides, further, promised to refrain from the use of force 'in accordance with the Charter of the United Nations'. This was a compromise between India's renewed demand for a formal no-war declaration and Pakistan's continuing position that verbal assurances by themselves are of little value.[1] Bhutto thinks that it all finally boils down to a question of trust: 'There will have to be mutual trust and confidence. For our part we are prepared to give trust.'[2] The formula adopted gives something to both sides. India can aver that the parties have, in effect, made a no-war pact, and Pakistan can plead that they have not accepted any obligations beyond those which they already owe each other as fellow-members of the United Nations.

On Kashmir the parties consented only to freeze the present line of control 'without prejudice to the recognized position of either side'.

Evidently wishing to bulldoze a final settlement while Pakistan is still licking her wounds, India desired 'a package deal', but Pakistan favoured 'a step by step' approach. It was clearly unrealistic to imagine that the numerous complicated matters which are at issue between the two neighbours could all be resolved in one sitting and, not surprisingly, the joint communiqué recorded that they had agreed to tackle the various problems 'step by step'. There will be further summit negotiations and 'in the meanwhile the representatives of the two sides will meet to discuss further the modalities and arrangements for the establishment of durable peace and normalization of relations, including the questions of repatriation of prisoners of war and civilian internees, a final settlement of Jammu and Kashmir and the resumption of diplomatic relations.'[3]

Indo-Pakistani relations for years to come are bound to be greatly influenced by the amount of wisdom and generosity with which India treats her fallen neighbour at this critical juncture. The cultivation of a belief in India's benevolence in the minds of her smaller neighbours would be the surest method of realizing Indira Gandhi's oft-proclaimed wish to keep the subcontinent free from the baneful effects of big-power rivalry.

Be that as it may, all is not lost. What remains of Pakistan is a compact geographical unit, inhabited by sixty million virile people. Self-sufficiency in food, and its existing state of general develop-

[1] See pp. 48–53.
[2] *Dawn*, 4 May 1972.
[3] For text of Indo-Pakistani summit communiqué see *New York Times*, 4 July 1972.

ment, make the area one of the most viable parts of the subcontinent. It is not the fact of separation that is so sad as the tragic manner in which it has taken place.

The greatest danger to Pakistan's well-being still lies in the chronic disease of political bickering and in the traditional regional rivalries which have received new encouragement from the unfortunate East Pakistani episode. If Pakistanis can learn from their past mistakes, and unitedly direct their energy into constructive channels, they still might be able to count themselves among the more fortunate peoples of the world.

Part 4

Change and Continutity
(1972-1989)

17 The Foreign Policy of Zulfiqar Ali Bhutto

Zulfiqar Ali Bhutto envisaged a foreign policy that liberated Pakistan from its American dependence. He perceived the Muslim nation in a different role than that cast by his predecessors; a role more in keeping with the country's projected stature in the Islamic world, a stature that could also provide him with the necessary credentials to be its spokesman. The United States did not prevent India from intervening in Pakistan's civil war, nor could it secure the country's territorial integrity, or deny the Bengali claim to Bangladesh. Pakistan may have been Washington's most allied ally but the Americans were powerless in restoring the *status quo ante*. Thus a rump Pakistan found itself in a new environment and given the disarray within as well as the prevailing national despair, the time seemed opportune not only for a new national beginning, but for a new framework to support the nation's foreign policy.

I. Personality and Foreign Policy

Bhutto was the man of the hour. He was a gifted and educated leader as well as a person with considerable public experience. By background, upbringing, and service he among all the other Pakistani luminaries appeared destined for the task that now lay upon him. Steeled by the affection of the masses, armed with a significant coalition, counselled by bright advisors, Bhutto was called to administer to a nation that had suffered the trauma of humiliating defeat, that had been forced to submit to dismemberment, that seemed to have lost direction and was on the verge of rejecting its ethos. In such dire circumstances it was all the more remarkable that Zulfiqar Ali Bhutto dreamed of placing Pakistan in the forefront of the Muslim nations, or that he aspired to be the recognized spokesman for Third World causes. But Bhutto was no ordinary politician. He was at his best when challenged by great issues, and while others fretted the past, Bhutto pressed forward with his preconceived plans. He took up difficult assignments and blunted assaults on his performance. He was not sidetracked by criticism and even appeared to gain strength from controversy. Bhutto insisted on being his own foreign minister and although his critics questioned his multi-dimensional activities, he did not hesitate to describe his diplomatic *bona fides*, his abiding interest in foreign policy matters, and his broad experience in international relations.[1]

Only a supremely confident personality could have taken the Pakistani nation along the course that Bhutto pursued in the years following the civil war. Only months after the debacle in East Pakistan, Bhutto turned the nation's foreign policy in new and virtually uncharted directions. He met Prime Minister Indira Gandhi and accepted the Simla Accords. In his meeting with Mrs. Gandhi, he all but abandoned the Kashmiris, while the Bengalis were quickly forgotten as the sons of Pakistan. He gave up the notion of protracted war with India and urged a normalization of relations between Islamabad and New Delhi. This was the same Zulfiqar Ali who had counselled Ayub Khan to engage India in open combat, the same outspoken personality who called upon Pakistan to liberate Kashmir in 1965. Indeed, this was the same Bhutto who declared he would never abandon East Pakistan to the Indian army of occupation. This was the same spellbinding orator who on 15 December 1971, in a dramatic speech before the Security Council of the United Nations, insisted he could never remain silent when aggression was being legalized. 'I will not be a party to it. We will fight, we will go back and fight. My country beckons me. Why should I waste my time here in the Security Council? I will not be a party to the ignominious surrender of part of my country. You can take your Security Council. Here you are. I am going.'[2] Bhutto's abrupt exist from the United Nations was a dramatic moment in the history of the Organization. The event also revealed much more about the man who destiny had called to lead Pakistan towards a new and uncertain future.

Bhutto labelled his foreign policy 'bilateralism.'[3] The use of the term implied Pakistan would cease taking sides in the Cold War, would deal equally with the superpowers, would strenghten its ties with China, and begin a process of expanding relations with communist countries in Eastern Europe as well as with North Korea. Standing arrangements with the United States were to be honoured

[1] Pakistan's Foreign Relations, *Mr. Zulfiqar Ali Bhutto, Prime Minister of Pakistan, Address to the Parliament*, 21 December 1973, Islamabad: Government of Pakistan, 1973, p. 19.

[2] Zulfiqar Ali Bhutto, *Speeches Before the United Nations Security Council*, Karachi: Government of Pakistan, December 1971, p. 41.

[3] See Lawrence Ziring, 'Bhutto's Foreign Policy; 1972-73,' Henry Korson, ed., *Contemporary Problems of Pakistan*, Leiden: E. J. Brill, 1974, pp. 56-80.

but Bhutto was keen to point out that the United States had suspended military assistance to Pakistan during the 1965 war with India and that its arms embargo was still largely in place.

Although the United States had gestured support to Pakistan after the Indian army invaded East Pakistan in 1971, and Washington had ordered the nuclear carrier *Enterprise* into the Bay of Bengal in an effort to intimidate New Delhi, Bhutto did not believe the Americans deserved special consideration or had proved to be a loyal and faithful ally. More significant, with the civil war over and Bangladesh a *fait accompli*, Bhutto's efforts at distancing Islamabad from Washington marked him as a genuinely independent, if not freewheeling leader of the Third World.

Bhutto announced Pakistan's withdrawal from the Southeast Asia Treaty Organization (SEATO) following the loss of the eastern province. He also terminated Pakistan's membership in the Commonwealth of Nations. External commitments to the West were judged needlessly burdensome, and although he reluctantly sustained the country's role in the Central Treaty Organization (CENTO), he was seen groping for the opportunity to cut his ties with that association too. Clearly, Pakistan's continuing presence in CENTO was an expression of friendship towards Iran and Turkey rather than a commitment to the American anti-Soviet policy. For Bhutto, international communism appeared a lesser problem when compared with alliances that increased tensions between neighbouring states. But there was more to Bhutto's thinking than his conviction that Moscow did not threaten Pakistan.

What was left of Pakistan, he reasoned, was solidly Islamic. Moreover, Pakistan formed the eastern frontier of the Muslim heartland and looked westward towards Iran and Turkey, into the Arab Middle East to Egypt and the states of North Africa. Pakistan, Bhutto declared, was a Middle East country, a nation which drew its purpose and identity from the dry sands of the Arabian peninsula, not from the steamy jungles of the subcontinent. Bhutto hosted the Islamic Summit of heads of states in Lahore in February 1974 to demonstrate his intimacy with the Muslim nations. The Summit also underlined his quest for stature among those of shared culture. No other event did more to enhance Bhutto's *bona fides* as a leader of the less developed states. Moreover, the experience reinforced Bhutto's belief that he could manage Pakistan's security without significant input from Washington.

Encouraged by the success of the Islamic Conference which also became the catalyst for Islamabad's recognition of Bangladesh's sovereignty, Bhutto had plans to call a Third World Summit, which he said would be aimed at bridging differences between the continents, between the aligned and non-aligned, and between the ideologically and/or culturally disparate members of the developing world. Bhutto pointed to a new stage of national liberation where 'equality of opportunity does not depend on charity through larger foreign assistance or piecemeal reform. It will signal the turning away from the threat of a simmering and potentially disastrous confrontation to the promise of a global partnership.' The 'summit of the poor,' as he identified the projected meeting, would take direct action to relieve tensions among Third World nations and direct their resources and energies at the complementary goals of modernization and progressive change.[1]

Bhutto was especially impressed with developments in the People's Republic of China. Mao Zedong's policies, which focused on agrarian reform and culminated in the establishment of the rural communes, were seized upon by Bhutto and efforts were launched to replicate their kind in Pakistan. Bhutto was heralded as the *Quaid-e-Awam*, the Leader of the People, and he even adopted a modified Mao uniform for his public forays into the country's hinterland. But for all his success in reaching out towards the masses, Bhutto had difficulty in sustaining his mystique among the urbanized elites. The latter were quick to describe the Prime Minister's performance as demagogic and self-serving. Opposition to his rule had emerged from within the student community, had reached explosive proportions in the Balochistan insurgency, and finally, had penetrated the armed forces. Hardly simple critics, Bhutto could not ward off, let alone repress his tormentors and his strenuous, often violent attempts to neutralize them, only escalated the conflict and provided his political foes with the leverage to unseat him.

Bhutto was not only an astute and knowledgeable observer of international events, he was also a complex personality driven to lead. He did not trust his more intimate colleagues and he was reluctant to delegate even mundane matters to others in the ruling apparatus. Overly protective of his prerogatives, Bhutto insisted on surrounding himself with those who would not question his decisions, but he also could not avoid losing those who had assisted his rise. Moreover, the fissures which opened in his inner circle could not be contained there and soon his whole governmental edifice began to crumble. Although a new Constitution had been put into force in 1973, Bhutto side-

---

[1] Lawrence Ziring, 'American Foreign Policy and Pakistan,' *Panorama 28*, 18, 1977, p.35.

stepped limitations on his authority and employed questionable tactics to ward off perceived threats from his real or imaginary adversaries. As a consequence, Bhutto's international successes were not mirrored in his political manoeuvres at home. In foreign policy, he received high marks as an innovator and perspicacious Third World leader. In Pakistan, however, he refused to adapt, to display flexibility or communion with those whose support he could not do without. Blinded by personal arrogance, Bhutto did not see where he was tending. Firm in the belief he could master any situation, he failed utterly in gauging the impact of his personal behavior on his policies and programmes.

When Bhutto was swept aside in still another military *coup* in July 1977, many of his ideas went with him. The connection between domestic conditions and foreign policy was never more pronounced. Bhutto's foreign policy did not die with him but the departure of the *Quaid-e-Awam* meant Pakistani diplomacy would return to a more conventional and predictable track.

II. The Simla Accords

Pakistan viewed India as its number one enemy from the first moments following the transfer of power in 1947. The two countries celebrated their independence while locked in internecine struggle, a scenario which was to be repeated again in 1965, and still again, but far more violently in 1971. Bhutto had always postured himself as anti-Indian and some of his more passionate speeches were reserved for attacks on his larger neighbour. Words, however, are seldom similar to deeds, and Bhutto's actions in regard to New Delhi were seldom in balance with his oratory.

Bhutto's speeches were almost always emotionally charged, ideas were expressed with poetic fervour and keyed to provoke and nourish the sentiments of his audience. Bhutto's actual performance followed another track; although exceptions might be cited, it was carefully modulated with an eye to positive goals. Bhutto's willingness, even eagerness to meet Prime Minister Gandhi in the Indian hill station of Simla hardly six months after the surrender of the Pakistan army in East Pakistan is a case in point. After frequent public assertions about not yielding to Indian machinations or duplicity, Bhutto was most eager to come to terms with Indira and India. Moreover, the agreement arrived at in Simla could not have been anticipated from the rhetoric that preceded the summit. Nor was Bhutto concerned that his decision to co-operate with Indian authorities could be exploited by his enemies in Pakistan.

The irony in this situation was the advantage he had personally gained by condemning Ayub Khan's handling of the deliberations in Tashkent in 1965. The unpopularity of that agreement gave Bhutto the chance to exploit mass sentiment. He was also able to represent himself as a staunch resistance fighter in a protracted campaign against superior but immoral forces. Compromise was not a viable scenario. Once responsible for official policy, however, Bhutto assumed a totally different posture. At Simla he not only showed willingness to negotiate, he was also prepared to yield to the demands of the stronger party. But perhaps more interesting than Bhutto's change of heart was the general lack of popular disfavour with his actions. Pakistanis believed they were winning the 1965 war; they were well aware they had lost the 1971 encounter. In 1972, the people of Pakistan were prepared to acknowledge India's greater prowess in the subcontinent. Therefore, unlike 1965 when Ayub faced strong public reaction to his peace moves, after Bangladesh, Bhutto was largely insulated from such assaults.

The surrender of the Pakistani garrison in East Pakistan, the incarceration of 93,000 soldiers and dependents, the threat to try 195 of this number for war crimes was uppermost in the minds of the Pakistani people and Bhutto seized the opportunity to ease the emotional strain of his countrymen by getting Indira to agree to the repatriation of those being held, in return for Pakistani concessions. On 2 July 1972, Bhutto agreed to put an end to the long period of conflict and confrontation and to acknowledge the greater military power of New Delhi. Bhutto pledged his country to an era of 'peaceful coexistence' with India, and expressed his willingness to avoid unilateral actions that might threaten the neighbouring country. He also accepted the inviolability of the ceasefire line in Jammu-Kashmir, thus seeming to support India's claim to two-thirds of Kashmir. The Simla Agreement seemed to say the line of control separating Indian Kashmir from Azad Kashmir was now a legal international frontier.

Simla had demonstrated India's preponderant power in the subcontinent. After this act, Pakistan could no longer claim to be the equal of its neighbour. Moreover, the event confirmed New Delhi's intention to expand its military prowess, and its armed forces are now recognized as the fourth largest in the world. The accords also drew an official end to the 'two nation' argument that the Muslim League had used in establishing independent Pakistan. Islamabad could no longer justify its position in South Asia as a consequence of two distinct religious communities. Bangladesh had shown and the accords seemed to confirm that Muslim identities were not nearly as important as regional, ethnic and secular forces.

Simla specified respect for the national unity, territorial integrity, political independence and sovereign equality of the signatory states. Each was to refrain from the use of force against the other and to seek peaceful means to redress their differences. They also agreed to lower the bombast hurled at each other by their respective propaganda machines, and to avoid arousing popular passions that threatened their new found harmony of interest. The issue of the prisoners of war was not completely resolved but the accords addressed on-going negotiations aimed at resolving that outstanding problem.[1]

At the subsequent meeting in New Delhi which followed Pakistan's submission of the prisoner issue to the International Court of Justice, a partial agreement was hammered out. India had held up the matter of the prisoners thereby hoping to pressure Pakistan into recognizing the independence of Bangladesh. Thus, when Bhutto signalled New Delhi that recognition was in the offing, the Indians agreed to return the bulk of the soldiers. On 28 August 1973, more than a year after Simla, the Delhi Agreement was signed between India and Pakistan and the prisoners of war began their return to Pakistan. The 195 that were held for war crimes were not included in this arrangement but New Delhi agreed to retain them rather than transfer them to Bangladeshi control as had been first indicated. The Delhi Agreement also made the case before the International Court *functus officio* and Islamabad withdrew it. The issue of the 195 prisoners continued to cause alarm in Pakistan but this problem was finally rectified to everyone's satisfaction in February 1974 when Pakistan officially recognized Bangladesh and the remaining incarcerated soldiers were permitted to return to Pakistan.

The Simla Accords and the developments flowing from them did not please everyone in Pakistan, but the prevailing consensus held that Bhutto had done as well as could be expected. Moreover, the more sophisticated Pakistanis wanted better relations with India. They acknowledged India's greater strength and few among them wished to provoke another conflict. Bhutto therefore emerged from the negotiations stronger in resolve as well as more assured about the content of his new foreign policy.

---

[1] D.C. Jha, 'The Basic Foundation and Determinants of Pakistan's Foreign Policy,' Surendra Chopra, ed., *Perspectives on Pakistan's Foreign Policy,* Amritsar: Guru Nanak Dev University Press, 1983, pp. 23-4.

III. The Islamic States

The loss of East Pakistan necessitated a course correction in Pakistan's foreign policy. For strategic as well as sentimental reasons, Pakistan focused its attention on the Islamic states of the Middle East. Although Afghanistan had been a troublesome neighbour since the independence of the subcontinental state, Pakistan maintained good relations with the other Muslim nations and it was to them that Bhutto turned in seeking a new mooring for Pakistani identity and purpose. Islamabad's reorientation came at a propitious moment. Bhutto's emergence as the ruler of Pakistan coincided with both a renaissance in the world of Islam and the strengthened reputation of the Persian Gulf-dominated Organization of Petroleum Exporting Countries (OPEC). Muslim nations were alive with activity and the oil producers among them enjoyed unprecedented leverage in international economic and financial circles. The Islamic states could neither be taken for granted nor forced into submissiveness. Moreover, Pakistan had long championed Muslim solidarity. Its work on behalf of the Muslim community *(ummah)* may have been more verbal than practical but it was now prepared to make a larger commitment of resources and services.

Only three weeks after assuming the presidency, Bhutto visited Kabul where he began a dialogue with Afghan leaders on the status of relations between their two countries. In January 1972 he embarked on a 'Journey of Renaissance' a 10,000 mile odyssey of goodwill to Iran, Turkey, Morocco, Tunisia, Algeria, Libya, Egypt and Syria. In May and June he sought to complete the circuit, visiting Saudi Arabia, Kuwait, the United Arab Emirates, Iraq, Lebanon, Jordan, Somalia, Ethiopia, Sudan, Nigeria, Guinea, and Mauritania. The tour was aimed at establishing direct, personal, and intimate contact between Bhutto and the leaders of the Muslim countries. Its most immediate purpose, however, was psychological. It was keyed to impact on the Pakistani nation, to boost national morale in the wake of the dismemberment and humiliating loss to India. Bhutto's well-publicized tour demonstrated to Pakistanis they were not alone. But it also inaugurated a creative phase in Pakistani diplomacy and focused the government's attention on the advantages it might reap in a familiar, but also receptive environment. The Pakistan Foreign Office established the following guidelines for its upgraded policy towards the Muslim nations:

1. Pakistan considered Arab nationalism, Iranian nationalism, and Turkish nationalism no more antithetical to Islamic solidarity than Pakistani nationalism.

2. Pakistan remained scrupulously impartial in all inter-Arab disputes.
3. Pakistan followed the principle of 'bilateralism' in its relations with all nations, including the Islamic states. The government emphasized its intention to maintain friendly relations with one state or group of states without antagonizing others.
4. Pakistan intended to maintain relations with fraternal Islamic states irrespective of variations in political systems, international alliances or ideology.
5. Pakistan's relations with Muslim states would be expressed through the establishment of permanent international institutions.
6. Pakistan would promote the Arab cause at every opportunity and raise the issue of Palestine from a regional to a universal plane.
7. Pakistan would avoid becoming embroiled in conflicts between rival Muslim states but it would urge bilateral settlement of disputes, or provide good offices or mediation if called upon.
8. Pakistan would aid Muslim minorities residing in non-Muslim states and would request the Islamic nations to join in the effort.[1]

Bhutto publicly renounced H.S. Suhrawardy's statement in 1956 that the Muslim countries of the Middle East were nothing more than zero plus zero. He likewise repudiated Ayub Khan's reaction to the Arab-Israeli War of 1967, calling it 'lukewarm and lackadaisical.' Pakistan, he declared, was committed to a diplomatic initiative that focused on a united approach to the Middle East problem. In the aftermath of the 1973 Ramadan War, therefore, the Prime Minister called for the convening of the Second Islamic Summit Conference, and with assistance from Saudi Arabia's King Faisal, it was held in Lahore on 22-24 February 1974.

The Islamic Summit brought together the rulers of thirty-five member states and the leaders of the Palestine Liberation Organization. Twenty-six states were represented by their monarchs, or heads of state or government. Prime Minister Bhutto, as host of the summit, presided over its deliberations. As Chairman for the summit Bhutto had centre stage and the opportunity to address a variety of questions, not the least of which was the problem of Palestine and the Muslim desire to reclaim Jerusalem. The summit's objective, he reiterated,

[1] *Pakistan's Relations with the Islamic States: A Review,* Islamabad: Ministry of Foreign Affairs, Government of Pakistan, 21 February 1977, pp. 20-1.

was peace not war, and a balanced world order for all peoples. On world issues, and geographically, the Islamic people formed what Bhutto described as the 'mid-most nation.' He added that this position imposed a special responsibility on the Muslim states, that they should strive toward the realization of worldwide equity and justice.

The Muslim leaders envisaged the building of a framework of political and economic co-operation to promote true Muslim unity. More prosperous Muslim nations were urged to assist those less fortunate and especially burdened by world inflationary conditions. Bhutto proposed, and before the summit adjourned, the leaders agreed to form a Committee of Representatives and Experts and an Islamic Solidarity Fund. The purpose of these new institutions was the provision of material and cultural assistance by and for the Muslim states.

Summit resolutions were pressed at the Fifth Islamic Conference of Foreign Ministers which convened in Kuala Lumpur, Malaysia, in June 1974. Pakistan advanced proposals slated to enhance economic co-operation between the Muslim states and specific recommendations of trade, finance and technical co-operation were adopted. With Pakistani prompting, the Finance Ministers of the Islamic countries approved the Articles of Agreement of the Islamic Development Bank in August 1974. The Islamic Development Bank took shape from this meeting and it began operations with a subscribed capital of two billion dollars, largely drawn from the oil-producing states. At the Sixth Islamic Conference of Foreign Ministers convened in Jeddah, Saudia Arabia, in July 1975, Pakistan was elected to serve on the Jerusalem Committee and plans were moved forward to develop strategies for the 'liberation' of 'occupied Palestine' and the 'Holy City.' Also at this meeting, Pakistan proposed that the Islamic Conference seek observer status at the United Nations, a position conferred by the UN at the Seventh Islamic Conference of Foreign Ministers which met in Istanbul, Turkey, in May 1976. Islamabad pressed and won the Conference's support for a programme to provide material assistance to liberation movements in southern Africa and newly independent states. Islamabad also convinced the Muslim states of the value to be gained in transforming the Committee of Eight Representatives and Experts into a more representative Islamic Commission for Economic, Cultural and Social Affairs. The Seventh Islamic Conference also adopted Pakistan's call to assist the Turkish Cypriot community as well as Bangladesh's struggle with India over the distribution of Ganges water.

Pakistan hosted the first session of the new Islamic Commission for Economic, Cultural, and Social Affairs in Karachi in January 1977. The member states of the Commission used the occasion to laud Prime Minister Bhutto for his sincerity of purpose and his devotion to Islamic unity and Muslim development. The Commission proceeded to adopt a broad programme of cooperation that spanned trade, the transfer of resources, money and finance, food and agriculture, and industrialization and technology. Throughout these activities, Pakistan's central theme was the intertwining of Muslim interests and the pooling of Muslim resources. Bhutto's promotion of Joint Ministerial Commissions among the Islamic states also enhanced his policy of bilateralism, and programmes were begun or planned between Islamabad and Tehran, Riyadh, Tripoli, Kuwait, Baghdad and the United Arab Emirates. These latter arrangements also facilitated the movement of Pakistani labour to the oil-producing states of the Middle East. More than two million Pakistanis would ultimately take up temporary residence in the Gulf states and their remittances to Pakistan became an important source of Pakistani foreign exchange.

At the level of military co-operation Pakistan was also a major actor in other Islamic states. From 1972 to 1977 Pakistan concluded military protocols with Kuwait, Iraq, Oman, the United Arab Emirates, Libya, and Saudi Arabia, and provided access to military installations and services to Bahrain, Egypt, Indonesia, Iran, Jordan, Malaysia, Qatar, Syria, Sudan, and Turkey. The Palestine Liberation Organization also entered into separate agreements with Islamabad. Under the terms of these protocols and agreements Islamabad provided training facilities in Pakistani defence institutions for members of the armed forces of the contracting states. Islamabad also posted special contingents from Pakistan's several services in these same countries. The mission of the 'overseas' contingents was declared to be training and technical assistance, but some also assumed duties of a tactical nature. Saudi Arabia received the greater attention in that well in excess of ten thousand men from the regular Pakistan army were deployed there. Riyadh paid for such assistance, in part by agreeing to assist Pakistan in the purchase of sophisticated weapons systems from the United States and Europe. Oman was another country receiving special military attention from Islamabad. The Sultan of Oman compensated for the loss of British army personnel by both permitting the stationing of Pakistani forces in the territory and by recruiting Balochis from Pakistan to serve in his royal armed forces.

During the Bhutto years, Pakistan drew close to Libya's Muammar Qaddafi. Islamabad was rumoured to have arranged with Qaddafi for the acquisition of uranium ore for Pakistan's nuclear programme. Another rumour spoke of Pakistan and Libya engaged in a joint programme to build an atomic weapon. Although these rumours were rejected most vehemently by the Pakistani Foreign Office, Bhutto was on record, following the 1974 detonation of an Indian nuclear device, to establish Pakistan as a nuclear power. In one of his more memorable speeches, Bhutto decried the international efforts aimed at preventing a Muslim country from acquiring such capability. Bhutto spoke emotionally about the need for an 'Islamic bomb,' and particularly Pakistan's quest for security which was now even more threatened by India's demonstration of atomic power.[1]

Muammar Qaddafi was one of the heads of state attending the 1974 Islamic Summit in Lahore and his appearance greatly angered the Shah of Iran. Despite Tehran's protests, however, and true to his principle of bilateralism, Bhutto refused to rescind his invitation to the Libyan leader. In the end, it was the Shah who absented himself from the gathering of Muslim leaders. It remains unclear if Bhutto's decision to press ahead with Pakistan's nuclear programme had any bearing on the Qaddafi-Shah controversy. But it can be noted that in the five years between 1972 and 1977 the Shah of Iran and Bhutto met fifteen times, a record unequalled by any other exchange. It is also important to note that Qaddafi-Bhutto relations soured in 1975. It is not clear what caused the strain in their relations but it has been hinted the Shah's pressure on Bhutto was not an insignificant factor in Bhutto's decision to put distance between himself and the Libyan leader.

On this matter of the frequency of contacts with Muslim heads of state and government, Bhutto visited Saudi Arabia four times and received King Khaled in Pakistan in 1976. Khaled had succeeded to the throne following the assassination of King Faisal in 1975. Bhutto visited Turkey five times and received the Turkish President in Pakistan in 1975. He visited the United Arab Emirates and Kuwait on two occassions. And given Pakistan's intimacy with the sheikhdoms of the Persian Gulf, the rulers of Abu Dhabi and Dubai built estates in Pakistan and established their 'second homes' there.

Bhutto's Middle East policy not only cemented cultural ties, it also made Pakistan the recipient of much needed economic and financial

---

[1] G.S. Bhargava, *South Asian Security After Afghanistan*, Boston: Lexington Books, 1983, pp. 134-6.

assistance. This assistance can be divided into three categories. In the
matter of general purpose programmes, Pakistan received funds
from the following countries:[1]

Iran	$730.00 million
UAE	$100.00 million
Libya	$80.00 million
Qatar	$10.00 million
OPEC Special Fund	$21.45 million

In the second category, project assistance, Pakistan received from:

Saudi Arabia	$130.00 million
UAE	$92.00 million
Iran	$75.00 million
Libya	$53.00 million
Kuwait	$45.00 million

In the final category, Relief Grants, Pakistan received from:

Libya	$16.00 million
Saudi Arabia	$10.00 million
UAE	$8.00 million
Kuwait	$5.00 million
Qatar	$1.00 million
Iran and others	$2.70 million

During this period, the Muslim countries became Pakistan's
largest market for its exports, moving up from a twenty per cent share
to more than one-third. Pakistani colleges and universities also began
drawing significant numbers of students from the Muslim nations.
Cultural co-operation agreements were entered into with Libya,
Algeria, Sudan, Kuwait, Mauritania and Iraq. Similar arrangements
were being completed with Saudi Arabia, Malaysia, and the People's
Democratic Republic of Yemen when Bhutto was ousted. Bhutto
also promoted the teaching and use of Arabic and Persian in Pakistan.
He completed arrangements with Saudi Arabia for the construction
of the King Faisal Mosque in Islamabad and co-sponsored with
Riyadh the establishment of an Islamic Center on the same location.

Having resolved the Bangladesh question, Pakistan's rivalry with
Afghanistan represented the only important conflict with a Muslim

[1] All figures are derived from *Relations with Islamic States,* op. cit., pp. 28-9.

country. Bhutto aggressively pursued improved relations with Kabul, and Afghanistan was the first country he visited after coming to power. Later, observing the 1973 *coup* in Kabul that ousted the monarchy, Bhutto moved quickly to recognize the new government of Mohammad Daud. Daud had never been a friend of Pakistan and indeed was seen as the lifeforce behind the 'Pakhtunistan' movement that sought an independent homeland for the Pathans of the northwest frontier. Bhutto hoped to defuse the situation by offering friendship to the new government, while at the same time crushing an insurgency allegedly engineered from Kabul in Pakistan's Balochistan province.[1]

As a gesture of goodwill, he permitted the overflight of Pakistani territory by Afghan cargo-bearing aircraft. He sanctioned the right of Afghan traders to ply their trucks through Pakistan to India. He gave drought relief to Kabul in an effort to counter the worst effects of the 1972-3 famine in Afghanistan. Relief supplies were again sent to Afghanistan in 1976 when an earthquake levelled homes and caused a heavy loss of life. Pakistan also unilaterally suspended propaganda attacks on Kabul. Invited back to Kabul in 1976, Bhutto found President Mohammad Daud receptive to his entreaties for peace and cooperation. Two months later Daud visited Islamabad amid much public celebration. After thirty years of considerable unpleasantness, Pakistan-Afghanistan relations never appeared more promising than in 1977.

Bhutto was determined to weld the Muslim states into a solid association of like-minded actors. As he envisaged it, the benefits to be derived from such a grouping would be enough to satisfy the individual as well as collective needs of the members. The success of the effort certainly would meet many of Pakistan's objectives, and of importance to Bhutto, it would go a long way in separating Islamabad from its traditional dependence on the United States. Needless to note, the success of the programme also added immeasurably to Bhutto's reputation as a bright, capable, and strong Muslim leader.

IV. China, the Soviet Union and the Communist World
Bhutto had established his position in the first rank of Pakistani leaders by his high profile in foreign affairs. Educated at the University of California, Berkeley, in the United States, Oxford University's Christ Church College and Lincoln's Inn in Britain, Zulfiqar Ali concentrated his studies in political science and international relations. He was the first Asian to be appointed a lecturer in

[1] See Government of Pakistan, *White Paper on Baluchistan,* Islamabad: 19 October 1974.

international law at the University of Southampton in England. Shortly thereafter he served on the Pakistan delegation to the 12th Session of the United Nations General Assembly. Before accepting a portfolio in Ayub Khan's first cabinet in 1958, he led the Pakistan delegation at the UN Conference on the Law of the Sea.[1] Bhutto thus had ample opportunity to trace the development of Pakistan's foreign policy, to weigh its successes and to identify its weaknesses. Given his knowledge of the United States and Great Britain, their pursuits and interests, Bhutto was mindful of the need to reframe Pakistan's foreign relations, to bring them into greater harmony with the region in which it found itself, and with the Asian world of which it was an inextricable part. Bhutto was brought into Ayub's cabinet as Minister in charge of National Reconstruction, Broadcasting, and Minorities, but his real interest lay in foreign affairs, and he was not content until the Field Marshal allowed him to take up the foreign ministry portfolio after the retirement of Manzur Qadir and the death of Mohammad Ali. Given that opportunity in 1963, Bhutto moved swiftly to reshape Pakistan's foreign policy with a special gesture of friendship and cooperation towards the People's Republic of China.

Pakistan had recognized Beijing in 1950 but the two countries avoided developing their relationship because of ideological and strategic differences. As late as 1959, Ayub had offered his hand to India and had sought to promote a joint defence of the subcontinent against a perceived Chinese threat. The Indian Prime Minister, Jawaharlal Nehru, rejected Ayub's offer and nothing came of the matter. Nevertheless, the incident revealed how the Pakistan government, and especially the Pakistan army, viewed the defence situation at that time. Manzur Qadir had opened the approach to China in 1961, but Pakistan did not begin to press the Chinese on the matter of improved relations until after the Sino-Indian border war of 1962. The Pakistani shift toward China was also accelerated by Washington's decision to rush sophisticated weapons systems to India. Whereas Washington perceived China aggressively pushing its interests beyond the Himalayas, the Pakistanis insisted the heavy shipments of United States arms to New Delhi would upset the delicate balance of power in the subcontinent. Pakistan accused Washington of betraying a trust, and after Pakistan received Beijing's support in its claim to Kashmir, conditions were ripe for a modification in Pakistani foreign policy towards at least a segment of the communist world.

[1] *Who's Who in Pakistan*, 1962-63, Lahore: Barque and Company, 1963, pp. 7-8.

The Indo-Pakistani War of 1965 brought Pakistan and China into more intimate embrace. Washington's decision suspending arms supplies to the belligerents fell hardest on Pakistan which was almost totally dependent on American weapons and spare parts.

Bhutto condemned the American action and in so doing questioned Pakistan's continuing membership in SEATO and CENTO. On the other hand, China loomed as Pakistan's most important security shield. Beijing did what Washington could not: it threatened New Delhi with still another invasion if it did not cease and desist in its attack on Pakistan. Although China did not play so dramatic a role in the Indo-Pakistani war of 1971 it had a reservoir of goodwill in Pakistan and it was this source that Bhutto drew from in pressing Pakistan's more even-handed foreign policy in the 1970s.[1]

Bhutto visited China in 1971 and was received warmly by Mao Zedong. His visit, however, was more than ceremonial. The Pakistani leader anticipated receiving military stores to compensate for the cut-off in American arms. And Chou En-lai's statement that the Chinese were not 'ammunition merchants' but would extend military assistance to Pakistan on a *gratis* basis and would assist in securing the country against a future Indian threat was welcome news to Bhutto and Pakistanis in general. China also announced it had cancelled a $110 million debt Pakistan had accrued during its 1965 war with India. It also deferred payment for twenty years on a $200 million loan Pakistan received from Beijing in 1970. Sino-Pakistani relations maintained their amicability throughout the Bhutto years, although by 1977 Pakistani military authorities began to realize that the Chinese could not supply the sophisticated weapons systems they wished to obtain.

Bhutto sought to find in the Soviet Union what he could not obtain in China. He also wanted to supplement his China policy by a more friendly approach towards Moscow. The success of such a venture could pay added dividends in a diminished Indian threat, and possibly in more positive relations with Afghanistan. Bhutto visited the Soviet Union in 1972. Although little material benefit was derived from the opening to Moscow, Bhutto signalled the Kremlin leaders that Islamabad's policies did not threaten Soviet interests. Moreover, Pakistan's continuing association, but modified relationship with Washington, in no way disturbed the balance in the region, let alone the country's independent foreign policy.

[1] See Anwar H. Syed, *China and Pakistan: Diplomacy of an Entente Cordiale,* Amherst: Massachusetts University Press, 1974.

Bhutto showed considerable interest in Leonid Brezhnev's call for an Asian Collective Security Pact, but he refrained from either condemning or encouraging it. While questioning the future intentions of the Soviet state toward Pakistan, Bhutto nevertheless reiterated his belief that 'the Soviet Union is not going to interfere in Pakistan's internal affairs or carve out another Bangladesh or some other country.'[1] It was Bhutto's intention to instil trust in Pakistan's relations with Moscow, and from these efforts new technical and cultural exchange agreements were signed. The Soviets also played an important role in Pakistan's industrialization plans. The country's first steel mill was built in Karachi with Soviet financial aid and technical assistance, although it was not inaugurated until 1983. Bhutto also initiated a barter-trade protocol with Moscow which was officially entered into some time after his death.

In addition to the envisaged expanded relations with China and the Soviet Union, Bhutto developed greater intimacy with the Democratic People's Republic of Korea (North Korea). Cultural and technical exchange missions criss-crossed one another, but North Korea provided Pakistan with more tangible assistance than the latter could make available to the northeast Asian state. Bhutto obviously admired Kim II Sung, the fountain-head of power in North Korea. Moreover, he was deeply moved by the discipline displayed by Kim's communist subjects. Bhutto attempted to transplant some of that discipline in Pakistan, but it was a clear misreading of his own people. When Bhutto arranged for the North Koreans to train Pakistani children for public gymnastic programmes, such as the performance at the Islamabad stadium during the celebration of Quaid-i-Azam Mohammad Ali Jinnah's 100th birth anniversary in 1976, the Pakistanis in attendance were noticeably distressed and uncomfortable. Bhutto, it was whispered, 'had gone too far.'

Pakistan's ties to Eastern Europe were also expanded during the Bhutto years. Technical and economic as well as trade agreements were entered into with Czechoslovakia, Poland, Bulgaria and Romania, and wherever possible, arrangements were made on the basis of barter. Although these barter arrangements were dubious in the development of the Pakistani economy, the technical assistance provided by East European countries in establishing small industries and in building Pakistani infrastructure was welcome. The ties to these communist states also provided Pakistan with an added sense of security in the aftermath of the civil war.

[1]*Address to the Parliament,* ibid., p. 29.

V. The United States

Sensing strategic isolation, and denied its share of the military stores of British India, Pakistan sought to cultivate the United States following the transfer of power. M.A.H. Ispahani, an intimate confidant of Mohammad Ali Jinnah, was sent to Washington as the country's first ambassador and a programme was inaugurated to enlist American assistance. The decision to have Prime Minister Liaquat Ali Khan make his first visit to the United States rather than the Soviet Union in 1950 is still debated in Pakistan. Critics of US policy have long held that Pakistan's destiny would have been different had the foreign office chosen Moscow.[1] But Washington was the choice and in the mid-fifties Pakistan was successful in influencing the United States to agree to a bilateral Mutual Defence Pact. That agreement was certified again in 1959 and it remains the single most important act between the two countries.[2] But much has transpired in the interim, and Pakistan has learned to question the reliability, albeit the dependability of its superpower ally. Nevertheless, it seems never to have seriously considered abandoning the connection.

Pakistan's relations with the United States were mixed at best and during the Bhutto years they were made even more ambiguous. Henry Byroade, the American ambassador, was perhaps the only American official that Bhutto allowed to enter his inner circle. After a distinguished diplomatic career that began during World War II, Byroade was serving in his last post. A military man by training, Byroade was committed to the idea of Pakistan as a vital link in the American-forged containment of the Soviet Union. He therefore laboured to have the arms embargo lifted, noting it had been imposed many years before by Lyndon Johnson and had been sustained without real cause. Byroade's persistence paid off when the embargo was officially lifted in 1975. But several more years were to pass before significant weapons transfers would be made to Islamabad.

Jimmy Carter became President during Bhutto's last year in office and he had virtually no interest in modernizing Pakistan's now antiquated military establishment. Carter had in fact set his sights on wooing India, especially after the electoral success of the *Janata* Party, and he did not want to do anything that might antagonize New

[1] Note the views of J.A. Rahim, Secretary General of the Pakistan People's Party. *Address to the Parliament*, op. cit., pp. 7-8.

[2] William J. Barnds, *India, Pakistan, and the Great Powers,* New York: Praeger, 1972, pp. 104-6.

Delhi. The transfer of more sophisticated weapons to Islamabad, he concluded, merely churned up the mutual enmity of the two South Asian neighbours. As time would tell, only the Soviet invasion of Afghanistan in December 1979 aroused Carter's concern for a militarily secure Pakistan.

Bhutto's bilateral foreign policy was not well received in United States diplomatic circles. Some American officials considered it a smokescreen to cover Bhutto's desire to improve Pakistan's relations with the communist world. Bhutto's reference to Islamic Socialism, his strengthened ties with China, his attempted rapprochement with Moscow, his championing of Muslim causes, especially the matter of Palestine and Jerusalem, the alacrity with which he adopted any emotional Third World demand, and no doubt most important, his insistence on the production of an 'Islamic bomb' as well as the criticism his government levelled against the United States, was all the evidence needed to prove Bhutto was no friend of the United States. Given the opportunity, Washington concluded Bhutto could reverse Pakistan's foreign policy and seek more intimate association with the socialist bloc.

Bhutto made the most of the strain in Pakistani-American relations. Anti-Americanism had surfaced in Pakistan as early as 1958 and it had continued to spread and intensify through the 1965 war with India, and the civil war in East Pakistan. After the dismemberment, Pakistanis were energized to reidentify their situation and purpose. Bhutto had pointed the country in the direction of Muslim Middle East causes and the nation's underlying Islamic sentiment generated movements away from western associations. Moreover, Bhutto's programme also made the Pakistani left more respectable, and opportunities for public service were seized upon by heretofore suppressed or harrassed elements of society. Initially, Bhutto articulated the desires of Pakistani youth. He also represented the position of those who wished to discard the American dependency. In a way, Bhutto re-energized Pakistani nationalism which had been seared in the events of 1971.

With the passage of time, Bhutto's rule may have become too dependent on sustained hostility towards the United States. Never certain about the strength of his domestic constituency, Bhutto made enemies of the several components that had formed his winning coalition. Ultimately, he polarized the country into warring groups, classes and regions. 'The increasing socialist rhetoric of Bhutto and the secularization of politics through Bhutto's brand of socialism. . .

accentuated class conflict. . . although refreshing to radicals. . . it struck at the very roots of Pakistan.'[1]

Bhutto's negative attitude toward matters American was picked up by elements within Pakistani society and that policy fared better than his experiments in domestic reform. Indeed, he used the former to drive home the latter. To a degree such tactics can be useful, but in the long term they cease to have utility. Nevertheless, the assault on the American presence was pressed to a conclusion.

Clearly, the United States had long been an active player inside Pakistan. Most Pakistanis instinctively believed Washington influenced and shaped Pakistani political and economic life. Bhutto's attack on the American connection, therefore, was facilitated by the fertile ground that sustained the attack. Toward the end of his life, Bhutto was convinced the Pakistan National Alliance, the movement that had been assembled to challenge his rule in the 1977 elections, was a manifestation and instrument of the Americans. The subsequent *coup* of July 1977, he believed, had been provoked by the United States.[2] Washington, he concluded, stood to gain from his demise. Indeed, during his long and debilitating tenure in an Islamabad prison, he indirectly accused the United States of engineering the military *coup* that drove him from power. In his last testament printed after his death under the title *If I am Assassinated...*, Bhutto devotes an entire chapter to what he calls the 'foreign hand' that was determined to destroy him. There is little question that the term 'foreign hand' refers to the behind-the-scenes activities of the Americans in Pakistan, as well as their collaborators among the Pakistani opposition.

VI. In Conclusion

From his jail cell Bhutto explains how he learned the politics of power from Napoleon and the politics of poverty from Karl Marx. Although he imbibed their lessons well, they could not instruct him on the peculiar politics of Pakistan. Bhutto failed only in the latter. The man from Sindh, the son of a wealthy aristocrat, himself one of the nation's supreme landholders, dreamed of great deeds, of a destiny not made for simple mortals. Bhutto counted himself among the stars in the heavens. A certain mysticism propelled him. He was called to greatness; he was also called to sacrifice and to martyrdom. In his final

[1] Ataur Rahman, *Pakistan and America: Dependency Relations*, New Delhi: Young Asia Publications, 1982, pp. 95-6.

[2] Zulfiqar Ali Bhutto, *If I am Assassinated. . .* , New Delhi: Vikas Publishing, 1979, pp. 168-71.

statement he speaks about his role in life, how misunderstood he was, how under-appreciated his moment upon the stage of history:

'As I sit in the four walls of this tiny death cell, my mind reflects on the canvas of my life spent with dedication in the service of my people.... In my solitary confinement I sometimes think I have lived the past twice over. ... I recall many momentous occasions: the partition, the rebellious mood of youth, the epic struggles, the Indo-Pakistan wars, the Security Council, the matching of wits with giants. If, out of the whole mosaic of the past, I had to select one piece from my most crucial and momentous achievements, I would not refer to my contributions in the 1965 war, nor the creative bilateral foreign policy I embarked upon for the glory of the nation. I would not refer to that period when I picked up the broken pieces of an asundered land in 1971, nor the Simla Agreement. I would perhaps not refer to the blood, sweat and tears I shed in seeking to create a society marked with equity and justice, my tireless efforts to bring a smile on the face and contentment in the souls of the people who had shed bitter tears...my single most important achievement which I believe will dominate the portrait of my public life is an agreement which I arrived at after an assiduous and tenacious endeavour spanning over eleven years of negotiations... the agreement of mine, concluded in June 1976, will perhaps be my greatest achievement and contribution to the survival of our people and our nation.'[1]

Bhutto leaves the issue at this point, allowing the reader to deal with its cryptic conclusion. Bhutto, of course, was referring to the agreement entered into with New Delhi for the renewal of diplomatic relations between Pakistan and India, the exchange of ambassadors and the opening of sustained dialogue. Bhutto believed the normalization of relations with India would lead to increased understanding of the other's position, and in the new ambience of conversation and negotiation a way would yet be found to improve and strengthen positive relationships. That Bhutto would point to this agreement as his crowning achievement in light of all the other, more dramatic and more memorable events with which his name is associated, reveals something about the man that was not apparent earlier.

Bhutto was a solid statesman but a poor politician. He was comfortable in the realm of international affairs, but hesitant and uncertain in domestic matters. In foreign relations he was open and thoughtful, imaginative and optimistic; in national situations he was

[1] Ibid., p. 223.

guarded, overbearing, defensive and foreboding. In the world arena
he was magnanimous and generous; at home he was deceitful, impul-
sive, and power-hungry. This is not to suggest that Bhutto was
schizoid. It is simply to suggest that Zulfiqar Ali Bhutto, for all his
outward appearances of strength and will, was frightened by the
power that had been conferred upon him, and even more fearful that
it would be wrested from him by forces more familiar with its uses.
Bhutto read the situation correctly; he failed in dealing with it
because he could not transcend his inner self; he could not apply the
appropriate tactics. Bhutto came to power with an unassailable combination of supporters. He possessed more than the usual talent and
had already compiled a unique public record. Moreover, Pakistani
society was with him. But he lost it all even faster than he had won it.
If Bhutto could only have learned more about himself and his nation!
Bhutto did not apply at home what he practiced abroad. He among
all others should have known that domestic conditions determine
foreign policy; even good foreign policy does not make for successful
national politics.

18 Zia's Legacy—Balanced Consistency
The Calm in the Storm

Mohammad Zia ul-Haq never basked in the popularity enjoyed by the man he forced from power. He is remembered in the outside world as the hangman of Zulfiqar Ali Bhutto, and even in Pakistan the controversy surrounding his name prevents rational appraisal of his tenure as President of Pakistan. His violent death in August 1988 only deepened the Zia enigma. A balanced picture of Zia's rule may never be possible, but the record shows the soldier-president served Pakistan at a time of renewed crisis. A less disciplined, more politically-inspired leader might have reacted differently to events, but it is doubtful he or she would have been more effective in the office. Nor had Zia been groomed for the role he was to play in the last eleven years of his life. Neither training nor ambition marked him for political ascendancy. Lust for power and privilege seemed to escape him. From the beginning to the end of his reign Zia was guided by the military code that dominated and directed his life. He led Pakistan in accordance with strict doctrine, and both his domestic and foreign policies conformed to a pre-set agenda that emphasized the preservation and survival of the nation. Zia was not a risk-taker. He was not given to gambling with the country's future, and nowhere is this more evident than in his management of Pakistan's foreign policy.

I. Continuity in Pakistan's Foreign Policy
Zia took the reins from Zulfiqar Ali Bhutto while the latter was in full stride. Without a foreign policy programme of his own, Zia picked up Bhutto's cadence and generally held to the course of his discredited predecessor. In his first few months in office Zia visited Saudi Arabia, Iran, the UAE, Afghanistan, Kuwait, Turkey, Libya, Jordan, and China. The purpose of the visits was familiarization and the maintenance of contacts at the highest level with Islamic and other friendly or neighbouring states. With the exception of Afghanistan, these were the countries that Pakistan had especially

cultivated, and on whom it had come to depend for moral as well as material support. Moreover, many of the Islamic states on Zia's itinerary were home to hundreds of thousands of Pakistanis who worked there and the government was ever mindful of the need to ensure their continued domicile. Bhutto's sudden removal had not been anticipated, hence Zia was constrained to explain the reasons for the *coup* and to emphasize the Martial Law administration's intention to hold to commitments made during the tenure of the previous regime.

Toward the end of 1977, Zia hosted the visit to Pakistan of his Bangladeshi counterpart, President General Ziaur Rahman. The two generals shared common experiences, and the fact that Zia was serving in Jordan and had not participated in the 1971 civil war, made it easier for the two men to embrace one another. Ziaur Rahman told Zia that the days of Bangladesh-Pakistan hostility were behind them and that the interests of their two countries called for greater co-operation. The Bangladesh President expressed the need to free his country from its Indian dependence, and he used the occasion to brief Zia about his plan for a South Asian cultural and economic association. As former brothers-in-arms the two men were said to have talked openly about their mutual concerns and interests.[1] Ziaur Rahman is reported to have registered satisfaction that Bhutto had been removed. As a principal in the events leading up to the civil war, Bhutto was a grey eminence to most Bangladeshis. And although Zia had not yet indicated a desire to protract his rule, Ziaur Rahman's behaviour left little doubt he was more comfortable with his army counterpart in Islamabad. Pressing issues prevented their forming a more intimate relationship in the years that followed, but the establishment of the South Asian Association for Regional Cooperation (SAARC) in 1981 was a notable product of their deliberations. Ziaur Rahman's death at the hands of assassins in that same year prevented the maturation of their relationship.

The British Prime Minister also made a brief visit to Pakistan in January 1978, but the arrival of President Mohammad Daud in March had far more significance. The Afghan leader had been Pakistan's most ardent Muslim nemesis. Daud was the architect of Afghan hostility towards Pakistan. He was the leading exponent of the 'Pakhtunistan Movement' which had plagued Pakistani governments since independence. And he was a persistent critic of

[1] 'Joint Communique issued at the conclusion of the visit to Pakistan of Bangladesh's President Ziaur Rahman, 23 December 1977,' *Foreign Affairs Pakistan*, 4, 12, Islamabad: Government of Pakistan, December 1977, pp. 36-8.

Islamabad's ties to the United States, and especially to Washington's alliance systems. Daud had marched to the tune of a different drummer. He had sided with India in its disputes with Pakistan, had provided some of Pakistan's more disgruntled opposition leaders with asylum and assistance, was alleged to have supported and armed Pakistani dissidents and terrorists, and seemed to have placed his lot in the hands of Moscow. Moreover, the Kremlin had championed his policies and nurtured his military establishment for almost three decades.[1]

After Daud's *coup d'etat* against his cousin, Zahir Shah, in 1973, the act which terminated the Afghan monarchy, Daud began to transform Afghanistan into a republic. Bhutto saw the possibility of a new relationship with Kabul and he signalled Daud of his desire to commence new talks for the purpose of reconciling their differences. A breakthrough apparently was made in 1976 during a meeting between the two principals. Although these conversations were interrupted by the *coup* that forced Bhutto from power in July 1977, Zia picked up the thread and flew to Kabul that October. During their meeting the two men agreed that the dialogue initiated by Bhutto should continue. Daud's visit to Pakistan in March 1978, therefore, was the culmination of several years of persistent endeavour. It was also facilitated by the Shah of Iran who used his good offices with both parties to engender an atmosphere of collegiality for their deliberations. The Shah had caught Daud's attention with an offer of money that was to help Afghanistan wean itself from its dependence on Moscow. Coupled with Pakistan's demonstration of concern and willingness to help the Kabul government manage Afghanistan's unique problem, the Shah's intervention apparently caused Daud to reappraise his long-standing hostility towards Pakistan.

Daud's welcome in Islamabad was unprecedented. Crowds of spectators were mobilized for the official reception and the generally unemotional Afghan President was literally overwhelmed by the magnitude and character of the greeting. Symbolically at least, the Pakistani nation indicated its desire to resolve their outstanding differences. Daud appeared receptive to the idea of peace with his eastern neighbour and in a speech at the Shalimar Gardens in Lahore he voiced the thought that 'we are waiting for the day when God Almighty will give us the wisdom and foresight to find a just and

---

[1] See Lawrence Ziring, *Iran, Turkey, and Afghanistan: A Political Chronology,* New York: Praeger, 1981.

honourable solution to our political problems and become allies.'[1] In his public reply, General Zia reaffirmed Pakistan's determination to find a mutually acceptable solution. Zia ceremonially toasted the health and happiness of the Afghan leader and wished him a long life in the pursuit of progress and prosperity for his country. As he uttered those words, he could not have known that in a little more than a month Daud would himself be the target of an army *coup*, and would die in the halls of his palace.

Pakistan entered into a volley of international agreements during the first year of the new administration and there was no indication of a change in direction or objective in the country's foreign policy. Just as efforts were made to improve relations with Afghanistan, energies were also turned in the direction of India. A telecommunication agreement was signed with New Delhi in October 1977, and the Salal Hydroelectric Plant on the Chenab river was approved in April 1978. Agreements were also entered into with the socialist governments of Romania, Hungary, Mozambique, and Yugoslavia, and General Zia personally hosted the visit of the North Korean Vice-President Pak Sung Chul, and Libya's Vice President, Abdus Salam Ahmad Jalloud. One highlight of Zia's first year in office was the inaugural ceremony of the Karakorum Highway at Thakot on 18 June 1978. Built largely with Chinese labour and resources, the highway brought Pakistan and China into even closer embrace and solidified their common association.

By contrast, relations with the United States remained in a state of relative tension. American aid to Pakistan had been largely suspended in April 1977, before Bhutto's fall. The running controversy between the two governments centred on the country's nuclear programme, and, more specifically, on the reprocessing plant being constructed in Pakistan by France. Islamabad had insisted that the plant met all the guidelines for international safeguards and that neither Paris nor the Vienna-based International Atomic Energy Agency had shown concern that the plant might be used for the manufacture of weapons-grade plutonium. In an interview with a correspondent of the *Washington Post* on 11 March 1978, General Zia argued that Pakistan had the sovereign right to acquire nuclear-processing technology as a means to boosting its energy production. Zia complained that the Carter administration had unfairly accused Pakistan of promoting nuclear proliferation. Scoffing at the attack,

[1] 'Speech by President Mohammad Daud of Afghanistan at the civic reception given in his honour at the Shalimar Gardens, Lahore', *Foreign Affairs Pakistan*, 5, 3, Islamabad: Government of Pakistan, 1973, p. 2.

he cited countries like Brazil and Israel, who he said, possessed more advanced nuclear programmes. Unlike Pakistan, they were neither pressured nor criticized.[1]

Generally speaking, Zia did not receive a good press in the United States. The manner in which he had achieved power, his defiant attitude, his orthodox Islamic practices, were not slated to win him many friends in or outside the American government. United States newspapers focused their attention on Zia's austere values, and particularly, his insistence on the use of Islamic prescription for alleged crimes against society. During this formative period American journals were full of articles describing crime and punishment in Pakistan, and especially the matter of public floggings that were said to be carried out in strict accordance with Islamic law. Photographs of these public punishments appeared in US and west European newspapers, and American thinking about Pakistan was fixed on what was judged medieval behaviour unbefitting a contemporary society. Moreover, the Carter administration's tilt towards New Delhi and the comparatively more balanced Press coverage given to Indian affairs added to the strain in American-Pakistani relations.

For its part Pakistan continued to pursue reconciliation with India. Zia attended the funeral in Nairobi of Kenyan President Jomo Kenyatta in September 1978 and, while there, met Prime Minister Morarji Desai whose *Janata* Party had defeated Indira Gandhi's Congress Party in the 1977 parliamentary elections. Desai brought fresh ideas to India's foreign policy and high priority was given to strengthening communication and understanding with Islamabad. Zia talked of their meeting as the beginning of a new dialogue and said the exchange was 'exploratory, good, friendly and profitable.'[2] Looking ahead to continuing discussions, the two leaders entertained reciprocal visits. Zia did not hesitate to reveal that he believed Desai was a man Pakistan could do business with.

On his return from Nairobi, Zia paid a call on the Shah in Tehran and then visited Noor Mohammad Taraki, the new leader of Afghanistan, and the ceremonial head of the People's Democratic Party of Afghanistan *(Khalq)*. The *Khalq,* a Marxist organization, engineered the April *coup* against Daud and was seeking to consolidate its revolution. Supported by the Soviet Union, the Afghan Marxists

[1] 'Interview by General Mohammad Zia-ul-Haq to the correspondent of the *Washington Post', Foreign Affairs Pakistan,* 5, 3, Islamabad: Government of Pakistan, March 1978, pp. 16-17.

[2] 'Meeting between the CMLA and the Indian Prime Minister in Nairobi, 2 September, 1978,' *Foreign Affairs Pakistan,* 5, 9-10, Islamabad: Government of Pakistan, 1978, pp. 1-2.

raised new questions about Pakistan's security and Zia walked a fine line during his brief stay in Kabul. He left Afghanistan with the public view that he was 'optimistic' about the future of Pakistani-Afghan relations; privately, however, he could not conceal his foreboding.

II. Zia at the Crossroads

The Camp David Accords between Israel and Egypt were signed in 1978. The next stage in their deliberations produced a peace treaty. But instead of praise, Anwar el-Sadat was made a target of scorn in the Arab world. A majority of Arab states severed diplomatic ties with Egypt and the country was suspended from membership in the Arab League. Although Pakistan shared the sentiments of the unreconciled Arab states, it did not emulate their actions. Nor did Islamabad support the isolation of Egypt. The new circumstances created by the treaty necessitated a change in tactics, but Zia carefully treaded a course between the parties.

Change was also in the offing in Iran where street demonstrations against the Shah had mounted in intensity in 1978. Tens of thousands of Iranians flooded Tehran's centre demanding the abdication of the Shah and the expulsion of his American advisors.[1] The authorities were powerless to control them. In the deteriorating circumstances, Pakistan's long and sustained support of the Shah proved an embarassment to the Zia administration, and Islamabad was forced to question the continuing, long term value of such a policy. As in Egypt, where Anwar el-Sadat, another friend of Pakistan had been made the target of popular abuse, Zia was hardpressed to both sustain his affection for the Shah and, at the same time, communicate to the monarch's emotional critics that Islamabad understood and sympathized with their complaint.

In India, the Morarji Desai government faced its severest test and it eventually succumbed to weaknesses within the coalition, yielding power to another, even more fragmented *Janata* faction. Zia could not prevent the closing of Pakistan's new opening to India, nor could tensions between the two countries be controlled.

The crises of 1978 became the tragedies of 1979. In Pakistan where Zia had promised national elections, attention was riveted on the fate of Zulfiqar Ali Bhutto. Bhutto had been accused by a private citizen of having ordered the murder of a political rival. He was subsequently tried for the crime, found guilty, and sentenced to death. His appeal had worked its way through the court system until it reached Zia's desk. Zia alone had the power to spare his life, but the Chief Martial

---

[1] Michael Ladeen and William Lewis, *Debacle: The American Failure in Iran*, New York: Vintage, 1982, pp. 165-94.

Law Administrator, addressing the need for uniform standards of justice and citing Islamic law, decided not to rescind the death sentence. Governments from every part of the world, from the United States, the Soviet Union, China, and the Arab states, asked Zia to forego the death penalty. Saudi Arabia called upon Zia to exile Bhutto, and Riyadh even offered to house him and to guarantee that he would never return to Pakistan. Zia acknowledged all these pleas but in the end rejected them. Bhutto was hanged in Rawalpindi prison on 4 April 1979.[1] The execution of Zulfiqar Ali Bhutto was a decisive act and Zia's future was forever sealed. Later in the year he would withdraw the election notice, announce the indefinite suspension of electoral activity, extend martial law, and abandon the notion of retiring from the political scene. Zia was no longer a stand-in for Pakistan's highest office, he was there by his own actions and his own choice. Some observers believe Zia decided to remain at the helm of the Pakistani government under pressure from his colleagues in the army high command. But Zia also had expressed the opinion that it was not time to reintroduce civilian government. With one eye on the domestic situation, Zia hoped to take advantage of the dramatic changes on the other side of Pakistan's borders.

III. The Necessity for Change

Faced with national rebellion, and with his troops unwilling to save his throne, the Shah fled Iran on 16 January 1979. On 1 February, Ayatollah Khomeini returned from exile to head a revolutionary government. Iran broke its ties with the United States and launched a vitriolic campaign aimed at purging anything and anyone that reminded Iranians of the fallen monarch or his American associates. Iran was consumed in an orgy of blood and from Pakistan's near vantage point the situation was totally unpredictable.

Conditions in Afghanistan were little better. The Marxist *Khalq* organization had been encouraged by their Soviet mentors to accept a partnership with the *Parcham* faction of the People's Democratic Party of Afghanistan. In so doing they were also obliged to include the *Parcham* leader, Babrak Karmal, as a member of their revolutionary government. But Hafizullah Amin, Karmal's *Khalqi* rival, had gained control of the government and he was determined to prevent Karmal from assuming influence over the movement. Insisting on the rapid transformation of the Afghan society, Amin implemented a host of unpopular reforms that even the Soviets found excessive.[1]

---

[1] Victoria Schofield, *Bhutto: Trial and Execution,* London: Cassell, 1979, pp. 210-37.

Resistance, therefore, became more widespread and the Soviets found themselves the central target of Afghan anger.

Moscow urged Taraki to join Karmal in opposing Amin. The Kremlin also registered concern that Amin was consorting with the Americans through Washington's ambassador to Afghanistan, Adolph Dubs. Dubs, however, was kidnapped in 1979 and later killed when the hotel room in which he was being held was attacked by Afghan troops, allegedly directed by Soviet advisors. In the confusion that is Afghanistan, the murder of Dubs was initially attributed to Amin and the tragedy brought a halt to American programmes in Afghanistan. This decision may have exposed Amin to greater attack from his enemies and his instincts called for preventive measures. Perceiving Taraki to be his mortal enemy, Amin killed his colleague, and when a broader purge of his government and party were contemplated, Moscow decided to intervene and eliminate their nemesis.

On 27 December 1979, Moscow ordered an initial force of 80,000 men into Afghanistan. The invasion surprised governments around the world. The troops, the Kremlin spokesman, announced had been requested by the Kabul government, and would stay only as long as it took to restore stability to the country. The first target of the intervention, however, revealed another purpose of the Soviet forces. Red Army units surrounded Hafizullah Amin in his headquarters and killed him. The Soviets then recognized Babrak Karmal as the Afghan Head of State and Government, and he was rushed to Kabul from his refuge in Moscow.

Pakistan was affected by each event in the neighbouring state. It had become a haven for Afghans fleeing their country, which after the Soviet invasion, had grown from a trickle to a torrent. More than three million Afghans ultimately found refuge in Pakistan. No less important, Pakistan's perennially sensitive frontier area was transformed into a rear staging area as well as central headquarters for the *mujahideen* or resistance forces that were now even more determined to carry their fight to the Marxists, and particularly their principal supporters, the Russians.

Zia could not ignore these developments or how they impacted on Pakistan's national security. In examining the options, the ruling junta concluded that the United States was their best source of military supply and protection. Washington, however, still had to be prodded into action. Jimmy Carter was not as eager as his national

---

[1] See: Anthony Arnold, *Afghanistan: The Soviet Invasion in Perspective,* Stanford: The Hoover Institution, 1981.

security advisor, Zbigniew Brzezinski, to challenge the Soviets in Afghanistan by way of Pakistan. Carter's indecision was not due to fear of the Soviet response, but to sharp differences with Islamabad.

Only a month before the Soviet invasion of Afganistan, the US embassy in Islamabad was attacked by Muslim zealots. This episode began hundreds of miles distant from Pakistan, in Saudi Arabia, with the seizure of the *Haram Sharif* in Mecca, by a group of Muslim fanatics. The Pakistani media had reported the incident, and accounts aired by them appeared to lay responsibility for the desecration of Islam's holiest shrine on the US and Zionist agents, who it was said, were interested in putting Islam up to ridicule in the non-Muslim world. The Zia government did not immediately challenge the rumours and on 24 November, a procession of Pakistani youth and religious zealots was permitted to surround the US Embassy compound in Islamabad. In the absence of adequate police defences, the emotional crowd forced its way inside the compound and attacked the embassy building. Gaining access to the structure, the demonstrators proceeded to sack and burn it.

The Pakistan government was slow to react. Zia had advance warning of the demonstration, but decided to ignore it. Stern action, it was later reported, might have caused bloodshed and a heavy loss of life. As a champion of the Islamic state, Zia could not give the appearance of favouring those believed responsible for the desecration of Islam's holiest site. But two Americans died in the seige and razing of the building. Others were injured. And Zia did not order anti-riot forces into the area until several hours after the initial assault; and by that time, all the damage had been done.

Zia issued a statement calling the incident 'regrettable.'[1] Washington, however, was incensed by the tragedy and it ordered the dependents of American officials in Islamabad to return home immediately. US -Pakistan relations reached a breaking point; nevertheless, the American mission in the country remained in place, albeit with many programmes in suspension. Zia's bad Press in the United States only got worse with this incident. The negative reports emanating from Pakistan seemed to justify earlier American criticism of Zia, his administration, and programmes. They caused the US government to reassess its commitment to the Muslim nation, and provided a new perspective from which to view Carter's

---

[1] 'President's Press Statement on the tragic incident at the American Embassy, 24 November, 1979,' *Foreign Affairs Pakistan* 6, 11, Islamabad: Government of Pakistan, 1979, p. 33.

preference for New Delhi. US-Pakistan relations might have taken another course had the Soviet army not invaded Afghanistan.

Reluctantly, Carter was drawn back to the alliance with Pakistan. The Carter Doctrine of 23 January 1980 was made to signal the Soviet Union about American intentions to defend the Persian Gulf. According to that doctrine, any attempt by Moscow to exploit the fluid conditions prevailing in the Gulf would be answered by the United States. A Soviet move in the direction of 'warm waters' was to be considered an attack on the vital interests of the United States. Some American observers believed the invasion of Afghanistan was timed by the Kremlin to exploit American problems in both Tehran and Islamabad. Without a US defence of Iran and Pakistan, both countries were perceived vulnerable to Moscow's aggressive posturing. With Soviet troops fanning out over Afghanistan, with the construction of advanced bases in easy striking distance of the Gulf, the Soviets were judged to be in a key position to intimidate the two Muslim states.

Carter could not allow Pakistan to became another Iran. Thus, it was agreed to put the burning of the embassy on a backburner, to demand compensation for the loss of life and property, but to renew assistance, including military parenphenalia, to Islamabad. When Zia registered his willingness to assume responsibility for the incident, Carter ordered the release of military stores and notified Islamabad it would make available an additional aid package of modest proportions. For this assistance, however, Washington expected Islamabad to make a commitment to the defence of Afghanistan that would facilitate *mujahideen* operations against the Russians from bases in Pakistan. Washington's plan meant Pakistan would be a 'frontline state' and the chief bulwark against the Soviet threat to the larger area.[1] Zia pondered the Carter offer, and found it short in sophisticated weapons systems. Zia made it known he wanted weapons that would dramatically raise the capabilities of the Pakistan armed forces. American assistance, he insisted, had to go far beyond the needs of the guerrillas in Afghanistan, When the Carter administration balked at this proposal, Zia had no option but to reject the entire American offer.

Islamabad refused to tangle with the Soviet Union in the absence of greater assurances from Washington. Furthermore, negotiations on a common commitment were not possible with the then current principals. Given this impasse, US-Pakistan relations were

[1] See Agha Shahi, *Pakistan's Security and Foreign Policy,* Lahore: Progressive Publishers, 1988.

frozen in reverse gear, and support for the Afghan resistance was noticeably delayed.

Carter's defeat by Ronald Reagan in the 1980 election campaign brought an end to this disquieting sequence in US-Pakistan relations. Reagan did not have any of the encumbrances of his predecessor. Moreover, the new American President was eager to challenge Soviet policy, especially in Afghanistan where he saw a determined and courageous people willing to risk everything in defence of their homeland. The Reagan administration also had a positive view of Zia's role in Pakistan affairs. Reagan was comfortable with soldiers turned politicians and his administration was largely in agreement with the programme the junta conceived for the nation's defense and progress. The Reagan administration put a high priority on weapons of war and it quickly recognized that Pakistan's armed forces, after an initial boost from the Gerald Ford presidency, had been allowed to ossify during the Carter years. Reagan, therefore, enthusiastically supported the restoration of Pakistan's military prowess, despite cries of protest from more liberal circles in the United States.

Moreover, Reagan did not share Carter's view on India. Indira Gandhi's party had won the January 1980 parliamentary elections, and she had once again become the country's Prime Minister. Mrs Gandhi's performance following her victory was watched with considerable interest in both Islamabad and Washington. And when she failed to condemn the Soviets for their invasion of Afghanistan, both capitals drew the same conclusion, that is, she sympathized with the action. Indira, it was concluded, had chosen sides, and it was not with the *mujahideen*. This situation made it easier for Reagan to consider granting Zia his request for some of the more advanced weapons systems in the US arsenal. In fact, when the administration was seemingly blocked by the Symington amendment from supplying Pakistan with new weapons, Reagan asked for and received a Congressional waiver. The Symington amendment prevented the sale or transfer of American weapons to countries known to be engaged in the production of weapons-grade nuclear material. Thus, Reagan quickly bridged the gulf between the two countries. Pakistan was offered the most substantial military assistance programme in the history of its relations with the United States, and Zia in turn agreed to place his country in the middle of the Afghan struggle.

This agreement proved to be the turning point in US-Pakistan relations. It also redirected Zia's foreign policy. Although the General would continue to nurture Pakistan's intimacy with the Islamic nations, to reinforce its diplomacy with China, to assure the larger communist world that its intentions were peaceful, Reagan's willingness to expand and modernize the Pakistani armed forces was more than Zia could resist. Zia and the junta committed themselves to a policy that was not only professionally appealing, it was also one they believed protected the short and long term security of Pakistan. In a period of considerable uncertainty, the officers who ruled Pakistan sought to capitalize on an opportunity that was no doubt fraught with major questions, but which also promised a more secure future for them and the nation.

IV. The Islamic World and Afghanistan

Zia led the diplomatic struggle against the Soviet invasion of Afghanistan. In January 1980, he presided over an extraordinary session of the Islamic Conference. The Pakistani leader condemned the Soviet action and called upon Conference representatives to join together in defence of the Islamic *millat* (nation). Zia's strategy was to 'galvanize into action' the Muslim peoples. He reminded his guests that the Islamic Conference had been organized a decade before as a response to the desecration of the *Masjid-i-Aqsa* in Jerusalem, and that the purpose of the organization from that time had been the defense of the Muslim faithful. Zia questioned why Muslim lives were in jeopardy in so many areas of the world, and now in Afghanistan too. In rhetorical reply to his query, he ventured the opinion that Muslims portray weakness to the rest of the world, a weakness that 'stems from our lack of conviction and Faith.'[1]

Examining the Afghanistan situation, Zia noted that this was the first instance since World War II that a superpower had 'made a sovereign, independent Muslim country the target of its attack.' If this precedent were allowed to succeed, he cautioned the Muslim leaders, 'what is happening in Afghanistan today will happen in another country tomorrow.' Zia called for more than 'resounding statements.' He urged the Conference to speak with one voice, to direct their efforts at Moscow, and to insist that Soviet forces be withdrawn. Zia acknowledged the action in the UN General Assembly wherein another Pakistani initiative had produced 104 votes in support of a resolution deploring the foreign intervention in Afghanistan. But he reiterated his belief that even that vote was insufficient; the Islamic Conference, he said, was duty-bound to pick up that call and to press it to a successful conclusion.

[1] 'Extraordinary session of the Islamic Conference, 26 January, 1980', *Foreign Affairs Pakistan*, 7, 1, Islamabad: Government of Pakistan, 1980, p. 2.

Zia also used the occasion to appeal for assistance in meeting the needs of the Afghan refugees who were passing into Pakistan in increasing numbers. This humanitarian problem, he asserted, was not Pakistan's alone, but must be shouldered by the whole of the Islamic *ummah* (community).

Finally, Zia called for study and deliberations on the establishment of a collective defence alliance for the Muslim *ummah* Separate national defences, he argued, were not enough to ward off aggressive intentions. 'History bears witness that only by collective and concerted action can nations withstand the challenges that are posed to them.' The activation of the Muslim *ummah* was Zia's foremost goal and the Afghan situation seemed to provide the best opportunity for its attainment. For Zia it was an act of faith. 'The establishment of Islamic *Ummah* is ordained by God and negating this would be to go against the word of God. Going against the word of God brings retribution.'[1] Zia's piety was genuine, and his plea could not be minimized. Nevertheless, the assembled Muslim leaders had little knowledge of the Afghans, and sympathy for their cause was less than that required to mount a combined effort. Moreover, each state had its own problems. Muslims were hardly of one mind and their rivalries also prevented serious consideration of Zia's proposal. Syria, Libya, South Yemen, were too dependent on the Soviet Union to take a position in opposition to the Red Army manoeuvre. Zia soon realized that he would get little more than verbal support from a majority of the Muslim states, and with the exception of Saudi Arabia and Egypt, little material assistance was forwarded to Pakistan from Muslim nations with an interest in the Afghan struggle.

The war between Iraq and Iran which erupted in the fall of 1980 provided still another opportunity for Zia to plead for co-operation among the Muslim states, but it also drew Muslim attention away from Afghanistan. Again Zia stressed the need for a unified *ummah* capable of reconciling the belligerents. Zia gave freely of himself in the pursuit of a formula that could begin the healing process. But this effort too was without a satisfactory result.[2] Zia could not 'galvanize' his brethren into a concerted and unified movement, and the several schisms in the Muslim world were more than a match for his pious sincerity.

Zia, nevertheless, persisted in his endeavour. He played an instrumental role in the formation of the Ummah Peace Committee,

---

[1] Ibid., p. 5.

[2] Lawrence Ziring, 'Government and Politics,' R.F. Nyrop, ed., *Pakistan: A Country Study*, Washington, D.C.: US Government Printing Office, 1984, p. 250.

and that body was a constant source of peaceful endeavour in the initial years of the Iran-Iraq war. Zia travelled back and forth between the belligerents, always citing the futility of their conflict, and how it was being exploited by their enemies. According to Zia, Palestinian claims were obscured by the war in the Gulf, while Afghan needs were neglected. Only Israel on the one side, and Moscow on the other, stood to gain from the Iran-Iraq war. Zia was pained that Tehran, more so than Baghdad, refused to listen to his argument.

Failing to achieve the larger goals of his diplomatic mission, but nevertheless a recipient of financial assistance from Saudi Arabia, Zia established a course for Pakistan that enabled the government to manage a complex foreign policy. Differences of interpretation as to what constituted an Islamic state did not prevent Pakistan from offering words of encouragement for the Iranian revolution. Nor did the Gulf war prevent the expansion of trade between Tehran and Islamabad or Islamabad and Baghdad. Pakistani citizens continued their trek to the Persian Gulf states in search of wealth and fortune.The remittances returned to Pakistan from this workforce amounted to $2.128 billion in 1981 and rose to still higher levels in the next two years. Pakistan's reputation as a policeman in the Gulf states was also enhanced during the period with the despatch of 20,000 Pakistani soldiers to Saudi Arabia and another 10,000 to the area sheikhdoms where they supplemented indigenous defences.[1]

Zia did not have to be reminded that three of the world's more deadly contemporary encounters were occurring within the Muslim world, and these did not even include the Arab-Israeli conflict. The war in Afghanistan, the Iran-Iraq clash, the unyielding Lebanese civil war, were among the more prominent contests during Zia's reign. The Pakistani President confronted each of them with the same determination, and although frustrated by the inflexible character of the belligerents, he had nonetheless placed Pakistan in the forefront of leadership among the Muslim states. Moreover, with the selection of Sahabzada Yaqub Khan to succeed Agha Shahi as Foreign Minister, Zia chose a close associate and former army confidant to assist him in his international manoeuvres.

Zia's task was always a delicate one. On the one side, he pursued an active policy of rearmament for the Pakistani armed forces and made it possible for arms and other supplies to reach

---

[1] The Military Balance 1983-1984, London: The Institute for Strategic Studies, 1983, p. 97.

Afghan resistance fighters. On the other, he encouraged diplomatic initiatives with all countries, and especially with Pakistan's immediate and potential enemies. Thus, while accusing Moscow of criminal actions in Afghanistan, he also promoted better relations between their two states. In 1981, for example, the Pakistan government and their Soviet counterparts inaugurated a new steel mill in Karachi that had been built with Soviet personnel and resources. Although wary of Indian machinations, and especially New Delhi's support for Soviet actions in Afghanistan, Zia sought direct contacts with Indira Gandhi and new trade and cultural agreements from her government. Zia was undaunted by the magnitude of the foreign policy dilemma. Confident he could control any situation, and over the strong objections of the *mujahideen*, he also agreed to accept the UN Secretary General's good offices in seeking a negotiated settlement for the Afghan tragedy.

V. National Security

Zia's confidence was born of an innate skill in matters of foreign policy. The 1981 revival of the 'American card' was an important, perhaps the critical aspect of his strategy. Zia's agreement with the Reagan administration on 15 June 1981 was approved by a hesitant American Congress on 9 December, and it meant Pakistan would receive from the United States $1.625 billion in economic assistance, a continuation of PL-480 Title I/III food supplies and low interest developmental loans, as well as funds for energy expansion and water management. Another component of the five-year programme was the sale of weapons on commercial terms for hard currency, reportedly supplied by Saudi Arabia. The list of weapons included reconditioned Patton tanks, self-propelled howitzers, armoured personnel carriers, and attack helicopters worth $1.5 billion. Neither arrangement raised much excitement in the Congress. The third part of the agreement, however, was another matter, and it was not approved without a struggle.

The Reagan administration sanctioned the sale of 40 F-16A aircraft to Islamabad with their spare parts. Zia and his associates proved to be hard bargainers, insisting that the aircraft delivery dates be advanced so that the first six planes would be in Pakistani hands by the end of 1982, and the others within another year and a half. Zia rejected a substitute offer by the United States which would have given Pakistan the opportunity to co-manufacture the American F-5G, a shorter range aircraft than the F-16. Pakistan also balked and threatened to kill the deal when the United States refused to outfit the F-16 warplanes with advanced electronics. Washington subsequently yielded to most of the Pakistani demands.

American critics of the F-16 sale focused their attention on the greater threat the F-16 posed to New Delhi. Indian officials echoed this concern. Their argument centred on the possibility that the new weapon system would heighten the chances of war between India and Pakistan. But when Zia offered to sign a 'no-war' pledge with New Delhi, the Reagan administration pressed ahead with the original programme. Moreover, Reagan would not be sidetracked on the matter. He spoke of the symbolic importance of the F-16 sale, how the revitalized US -Pakistan relationship hinged on the success of the total package, and especially the F-16s. With his peculiar brand of determination, Reagan not only won out, he also received Congressional approval despite persistent rumours that Pakistan was constructing an atomic bomb. Congress had to satisfy itself with a clause authorizing annual scrutiny of Pakistan's nuclear activities.[1]

The dual strategy of preparing for war while skillfully seeking accommodations with the country's primary adversaries allowed Zia to intervene more directly in the Afghan campaign. On the one side Islamabad agreed to enter into proximity talks in Geneva with a Kabul regime that it steadfastly refused to recognize. Indeed, in the absence of official ties between the two governments, the UN mediator, Diego Cordevez, was required to meet the two parties separately, carrying the messages, proposals and replies to the principals who sat in different locations. Islamabad's overriding need was to avoid major war, and while it avoided any appearance of timidity, it also refrained from actions that could be deemed aggressive. Zia based his carefully balanced foreign policy on principle and conviction, tempered by realism. He did not hide his affinities with the *mujahideen,* nor did he interrupt the rising flow of sophisticated weapons to the resistance, but he also stoically controlled a desire for retaliation when the war across the border spilled over into Pakistan.

On the other side, Zia made the most of his ties with the Islamic world, with China, and especially with the United States. The carefully structured arrangements addressed multi-dimensional questions, and even Pakistan's 'peaceful' nuclear programme was organized so as to provide the country with a nuclear weapons option if circumstances required it.[2]

---

[1] Stephen Cohen and Marvin Weinbaum, 'Pakistan in 1981: Staying On,' *Asian Survey*, 23, 3 March 1982, pp. 144-5.

[2] Marvin Weinbaum and Stephen Cohen, 'Pakistan in 1982: Holding On,' *Asian Survey*, 23, 2 February 1983, p. 130.

Zia made a state visit to the United States in December 1982 and sought to overcome the poor Press he received there. An American cartoon of the period depicts a fumbling Reagan who cannot even recall Zia's country, shaking the blood-stained hands of the General, dressed in the uniform of the Nazi SS, with a hangman's noose gracing his left shoulder. Zia made a serious effort to correct that picture, to show himself as a responsible Asian leader burdened with enormous responsibilities. To some extent, American journalists signalled a willingness to change their reading of the Pakistani head of state, but they still displayed discomfort with the relationship. Zia, however, was not to be deterred. He had arrived in Washington following visits to the Persian Gulf states, Turkey, Iran, Southeast Asia, China, and the Soviet Union. In the latter visit he met Brezhnev's successor, Yuri Andropov, and all these contacts enhanced his credentials and marked him as an important world statesman. Clearly, neither the American Congress nor the American Press could ignore the General or allow their pre-formed perceptions to obfuscate the realities of his international stature.

Zia's middle course foreign policy, described by Yaqub Khan as 'manoeuvre with flexibility on multiple fronts'[1] was aimed at providing Pakistan with measurable security in an unstable climate. His acceptance of the UN Secretary General's mediation efforts despite the opposition from *mujahideen* factions, his stated desire that Afghanistan should be a non-aligned, free, Islamic state, 'friendly to the Soviet Union,' was not the vision of the resistance groups. Nevertheless, he stressed the necessity for compromise and even in the emotion-charged atmosphere of the Afghan conflict he was prepared to settle for an accommodation with Moscow, to allow the Kremlin to make an honourable withdrawal, and to speed the hostilities to a conclusion. Zia clung to this position for the duration of the war. He sent Yaqub Khan back to Geneva year after year with the hope that a via media could be found. Patiently, but consistently, and without modification, he pressed his view that the Soviet forces must be withdrawn, that the Soviet-installed puppet government must be dissolved, that the Afghans should be allowed to form a government of their choice, and that the refugees should be encouraged to return to their homes in peace. If these terms were met, he declared, Pakistan would do its part to influence the *mujahideen* to lay down their arms. Anything less could only perpetuate the conflict.

[1] Khalid B. Sayeed, 'Pakistan in 1983,' *Asian Survey* 24, 2, February 1984, p. 227.

In still another attempt to overcome Pakistan's disability as a frontline state, Zia directed his attention towards India. Repeated gestures of non-belligerence were meant to calm Indian fears about Pakistan's arms build up. Zia made a surprise visit to New Delhi in 1982 and from that meeting with Indira Gandhi an Indian-Pakistani Joint Commission was created to monitor activities between the two countries. Zia sought to explain the latest military assistance agreement with the United States, while Indira assured the Pakistani leader that her country would co-operate in moderating the tensions felt by both governments. Despite these assurances, however, it was Islamabad's view that India's policy in the Afghanistan conflict too closely resembled Moscow's. Zia, therefore, had visions of a geopolitical pincer movement in which Pakistan could be pressured and ultimately squeezed from two sides. His remedy against such a possibility was a forward policy capable of warding off potential disaster. He believed Pakistan had only one secure option: it had to step up its assistance to the *mujahideen* and to develop the needed leverage to control them. Moreover, Washington was now willing to provide the necessary weapons to fight a successful guerrilla war.

American arms shipments destined for *mujahideen* commanders, many of whom operated independently from one another, gave the Pakistani army the means to design something akin to a battle plan. A special inter-services intelligence unit had chief responsibility for distributing the supplies and thus for plotting tactics and directing operations. Without a formal declaration of involvement in the hostilities, Pakistani forces became an integral feature of the resistance. Zia was able to have it both ways. He supplied and often directed *mujahideen* units, and he engaged his adversaries, over the opposition of the resistance, in the ongoing exchange of proposals concerned with terminating the struggle. By its involvement at both levels, Pakistan was able to gauge the threat to itself, and in so doing to deflect it.

The immediate security problem for Pakistan during this period was not the threat posed by the Red Army on the one side, or the Indian forces on the other, but from the Afghan refugees, and particularly those who moved among them, but who were actually Afghan secret police or paramilitary.[1] Pakistan was subjected to repeated acts of terror which became more deadly and costly as the conflict progressed. Zia was called to note these assaults on Pakistani

---

[1] Pervaiz Iqbal Cheema, 'The Afghanistan Crisis and Pakistan's Security Dilemma,' *Asian Survey*, 23, 3 March 1983, pp. 234-7.

society, and to describe them as deliberate acts of intimidation. Pakistan's enemies were reluctant to commit themselves to a formal struggle but they were not reluctant to use other violent means to pressure the Zia government to cease its support of the *mujahideen*. Zia was hardpressed to deal with the law and order situation but he refused to waver from his chosen course. Despite the chorus of complaints from his political opposition about Pakistan fighting America's war, or engaging in a conflict that Pakistanis could not win, Zia defiantly held his ground.

VI. Internationalizing Ethnicity

India took advantage of Pakistan's problems in East Bengal in 1971 and thus was able to pry the eastern province away from the Pakistan federation. The Bengali issue was a constant reminder how internal questions can degenerate into international conflict. The Indo-Pakistani war of 1971 was a direct result of India's meddling in Pakistan's domestic affairs, and given that precedent, the likelihood of a repeat performance was never too far from the thinking of Islamabad's strategists.[1] Indira Gandhi ignored the internal character of the East Pakistan conflict, justifying its intervention on humanitarian grounds. But such an intrusion in the affairs of one state might well be replicated by another in the territory of the original perpetrator. Indeed, soon after the successful Indian intervention in the Pakistani civil war, India was faced with its own internal crisis in the Sikh Punjab. Moreover, now it was Islamabad which was seen intruding into matters solely the concern of New Delhi. Suspicions are not easily suppressed and in the zero-sum contest between the two rivals, India's perceived weakness was viewed as Pakistan's new strength. In spite of Pakistani denials, New Delhi accused Islamabad of supplying, training and providing sanctuary for Sikh extremists engaged in organized terror inside India.

These protestations aside, New Delhi still proved to be the more aggressive of the two states. Faced with something akin to an insurrection in Sindh Province in 1983, Islamabad also had to face a new threat from India. Prime Minister Gandhi felt compelled to comment on Sindhi unrest in a meeting of the Indian Parliament. Morever, she indicated her country's support for those inciting the disturbance. Claiming she was responding to still another democratic struggle, Mrs Gandhi ignored both Zia's bridge-building efforts as well as his criticism and belaboured the Islamabad government for failing to

[1] Hasan Askari Rizvi, *The Military and Politics in Pakistan, 1947-86*, Lahore: Progressive Publishers, 1986, p. 203.

answer the Sindhi call for ethnic freedom. Zia was noticeably disturbed by this latest intrusion by the Indian Prime Minister into Pakistani affairs. He condemned the action and warned India that Pakistan would not suffer another assault on its sovereignty. Nor was Mrs Gandhi's reply to Zia aimed at easing the situation. She described Zia's Government in terms that questioned its legitimacy and seemed more intent on pinning blame for her own Sikh problem on the Zia administration. Arguing that the Sikhs were loyal to India, she pointed to the few extremists among them who she demurred were encouraged to commit mayhem by their Pakistani mentors. Although New Delhi never provided proof of Pakistani complicity in the Sikh movement for Khalistan, prevailing Indian opinion shared her reading of the dilemma. Pakistan, it was believed, sought revenge for India's role in the creation of Bangladesh and in effect had created the Sikh problem.

When Sikh militants occupied the Golden Temple in Amritsar in 1984, Indian intelligence again insisted they were in league with Pakistani special forces and that their plan was to force New Delhi to yield to their demands for a separate Sikh state. Mrs Gandhi's decision ordering an attack on the Golden Temple in June 1984 supposedly was made with a view towards breaking the militants' connection with Islamabad. Like Zia who used his armed forces to crush the Sindhi protestors, Indira's decision led to the deaths of hundreds of Sikhs. The army assault also caused serious damage to the Sikhs' holiest shrine. Thus, in July, Sikh militants hijacked an Indian Airways jet on a domestic flight and forced its pilot to fly the aircraft to Lahore in Pakistan. The hijackers demanded the release of Sikhs imprisoned in India and the payment of $25 million in reparations by the Indian government as compensation for the damage caused to the Golden Temple. Islamabad appeared to side with the hijackers, whom they had disarmed and arrested, by refusing an Indian request that they be extradited to India.

Neither Pakistan's Sindh or India's Punjab was pacified by the counterforce measures. Conditions were in fact more tense and far more disturbed in the aftermath of the bloodletting. Both President Zia and Prime Minister Gandhi believed their violent response was justified, but both also had to acknowledge the futility of their efforts. Moreover, in October 1984, Indira was herself victimized by her decision to use force against the Sikhs. She was shot and killed in her compound in New Delhi by her Sikh bodyguards.

Zia flew to New Delhi for Indira's funeral and there met her successor, Rajiv Gandhi. Their differences, however, were not resolved by this gesture or a subsequent one wherein Zia ordered a three day period of national mourning for the slain Indian leader.

Zia's violent death in 1988 remains something of an enigma but some opinion in Pakistan hold to the view that his killing was also related to the nationalities question. Moreover, people on both sides of the border continue to believe foreign hands were involved in the deaths of these once powerful figures.

VII. Recurring Themes

Pakistan permitted the Regional Cooperation for Development (RCD), an organization that included Pakistan, Iran and Turkey, to lapse in 1979. Established in 1964 from an idea expressed by Ayub Khan, RCD never lived up to expectations; nevertheless, it did bring the three northern tier countries together and it did encourage them to promote their common heritage. More important, RCD was an association not an alliance. It made no special demands on the member-states, and it stemmed from their own initiatives, not from that of an alien power. With the secretariat housed in Tehran, RCD could not function in the wake of the Iranian revolution and its activities were put in limbo. By the mid-1980s, however, the organization regained its *bona fides* and was resurrected. President Zia announced that RCD would examine possibilities for cooperation in the fields of agriculture, industry, and trade, but that it would not assume responsibility for major projects so long as Iran was locked in its struggle with Iraq.

General Zia paid still another visit to Moscow in February 1984, this time to attend the funeral of Yuri Andropov, but unlike his previous visit he did not meet his successor. Explanations for this absence of contact was not offered, but it was clearly a Soviet decision and was more than likely related to Zia's perceived obstinacy on the Afghanistan question. Pakistan's deepening commitment to the *mujahideen* was, from Moscow's view point, prolonging the war. The Kremlin did not want Zia to believe the Soviet Union was prepared to let up in its efforts to strengthen the Babrak Karmal regime. In fact, both Islamabad and Moscow turned up the heat on the other. Pakistan bolstered the Afghan resistance at every opportunity, and Soviet and Soviet-directed Afghan units escalated their attacks on targets within Pakistan. A series of air bombings in September 1984 over the Pakistani frontier town of Parachinar, for example, cost more than 100 lives.

The Soviets were also at odds with Islamabad on the nuclear question. New Delhi publicized a story about Pakistan's 'Islamic bomb' and Moscow had picked up the theme. Both countries sought to influence Washington to reconsider its military support for Islamabad, but except for a few Democratic Senators and Congressmen, the Reagan administration refused to budge from its stated position. Reports that New Delhi was contemplating a preemptive attack on Pakistan's nuclear facilities supposedly had tacit Soviet support, but this only brought a biting reply from Islamabad. Zia served notice that any attack on Pakistani nuclear facilities would be countered by an attack on Indian installations. Washington's ambassador to Islamabad, Dean Hinton, seemed to reinforce Zia's position. He reassured Islamabad that the United States would not remain silent if Pakistan was subject to an overt attack. Shortly thereafter, Vice President George Bush visited Pakistan and he used the opportunity to reaffirm that commitment. Officially, Washington remained opposed to Pakistan's nuclear programme, but given Soviet aggression in Afghanistan, it was pledged to the preservation of Pakistan's territorial integrity. To defuse this tense situation, Zia met Rajiv in December 1985 and the two men agreed to publicly renounce attacks on their respective nuclear installations. They never formalized that intention, however.

Nevertheless, Rajiv Gandhi's emergence as India's Prime Minister seemed to offer new opportunities for dialogue and Zia found it necessary to separate the war in Afghanistan from his entreaties to New Delhi. Thus with the Geneva negotiations bogged down over the timing of the Soviet withdrawal and the future of the Karmal regime, Zia accelerated his efforts in the direction of India.

The two leaders had met in New York City for the 40th anniversary of the United Nations, while their foreign secretaries pursued a variety of avenues, including high level meetings of the Indo-Pakistani Joint Commission. The newly formed South Asian Association for Regional Cooperation also began to expand its activities during this period and a host of Pakistani and Indian representatives were able to pursue substantive contacts under its aegis, including border security issues and Sikh terrorism. On the other side of these positive activities, however, was the protraction of hostilities in Kashmir. Skirmishes between Pakistani and Indian border forces on the Siachin Glacier caused losses on both sides, and subsequent negotiations on the border dispute were without significant result. Peace between the parties was not only an elusive goal, the threat of another Indo-Pakistani war surfaced in late December 1986 and spilled over into 1987.

Massive Indian army manoeuvres in the Rajasthan desert provoked Zia to call a state of emergency and a special session of the Pakistani Parliament. With the marshalling of combat forces on both sides of the frontier, Zia made a sudden and hurried flight to India, ostensibly to attend a 'cricket match' between Indian and Pakistani teams, but in fact to meet Prime Minister Gandhi over the troop mobilization issue. What was lightly called 'cricket diplomacy,' could not obscure the most serious exchanges ever entered into by the two leaders. In the end, Zia's dramatic move paid off. India and Pakistan agreed to reduce the size of their opposed forces, and to eventually pull back all except a token number from the frontier area. War had been averted but the two neighbours were far from reconciling their outstanding differences.

Islamabad had better luck with its long term friends. In 1986 it signed a peaceful nuclear co-operation treaty with China, and a new six year $4.02 billion military and economic aid package with the United States, which included providing Pakistan with an additional 60 F-16s. When this latter agreement was approved by the US Congress in December 1987, Pakistan became the third highest recipient of American assistance, eclipsed only by Israel and Egypt. Pakistan also sustained its close relationship with the Persian Gulf states. Remittances from overseas Pakistanis fell somewhat but the feared mass return of workers from the Gulf did not materialize. Pakistan needed its friends, given the stepped up fighting in Afghanistan. By 1986, the Government recorded 700 violations of Pakistani airspace, and 150 separate shellings of Pakistani territory. Hundreds of Pakistani civilians were reported to have died as a consequence of these attacks. Acts of terror, believed to be the work of Afghan agents, also multiplied during the period, and they had caused hundreds of additional deaths. Zia, however, was not to be deterred from his oft-stated goal of a free, independent and neutral Afghanistan. Thus, he held fast to his two-track policy: he remained firm in support of the Afghan resistance fighters, but used all available channels in the search for a diplomatic settlement.

The UN mediator, Diego Cordovez, made two trips to South Asia in 1986 in the belief that a breakthrough in the long negotiations was finally possible. Still another Soviet leader had died, and still another succession had followed. In 1985, Mikhail Gorbachev took centre stage in the Kremlin, and during a later visit to New Delhi he signalled his desire to terminate the Soviet role in Afghanistan.

VIII. The Geneva Accords

After approximately six years of indirect talks in Geneva the UN mediation effort aimed at finding a way out of the Afghanistan conflict met with a partial, though nevertheless significant success.[1] On 14 April 1988 Afghanistan and Pakistan signed agreements which they hoped would produce a final overall settlement. Neither Moscow nor the *mujahideen* were parties to the negotiations although the former approved of the process whereas the latter did not. In the end, the agreements were less than Zia had bargained for. He held up the signing in the expectation he could get agreement on the formation of an interim government that would replace the Kremlin-backed regime. Babrak Karmal had been dropped in favour of Afghanistan's police chief, Najibullah, but the Pakistanis and the several factions that made up the resistance were no less opposed to the Kabul government.

Zia finally accepted the terms that left the Kabul government in place because Washington saw the opportunity to rid Afghanistan of its Soviet occupiers. Thus, the accords were prepared for signatures without the one item that Zia had judged the key to a true settlement.

Zia recognized the accords as only a first step, not the anticipated solution to the Afghan problem. With Najibullah holding fort in Kabul, with Soviet material assistance to his regime undiminished, the war was expected to enter a new phase. This meant the Afghan refugees would remain in Pakistan, as would the several resistance headquarters. Pakistan would still be a conduit for the flow of supplies to the *mujahideen,* and the Pakistani rear would still be subjected to terrorist attacks. In some respects Pakistan's security was more at risk after, than before, the accords.

Zia did not know how long he could count on the Americans to supply the *mujahideen.* Nor could Zia accurately predict how the *mujahideen* would fare in the absence of the Soviet enemy. Afghans would now be fighting Afghans exclusively and that turn of events raised still unanswerable questions about the character of the traditionally divided resistance forces. The likelihood of more serious division within *mujahideen* ranks could not be ruled out. Nor could the Soviets be discounted, given their capacity to purchase the services of one resistance faction and to use it against another.[2] Bribe-taking as well as factional and tribal conflict was ingrained in the

[1] Key Sections of the Accords on Afghanistan,' *Journal of South Asian and Middle Eastern Studies,* 9, 4, Summer 1988, pp. 105-15.

[2] See James Spain, *People of the Khyber,* New York: Praeger, 1963

Afghans, and nothing had happened in the course of the long struggle to change that condition. Clearly, there was greater opportunity to sow division now that the accords had been arrived at.

Zia's immediate answer to the problem necessitated violating that section of the accords that called for the observance of the principle of non-intervention. Pakistan could not abandon the *mujahideen* so long as the Soviet Union believed it had the continuing right to assist the Afghan government it had created. And the Soviets had declared they had every intention of sustaining the Najibullah government. For Zia, such asymmetric activity meant leaving the Afghans to fend for themselves, an impossible arrangement given their domicile in Pakistan. Moreover, Zia had managed assistance to the resistance with a mind toward needs inside Pakistan. In seeking to transform Pakistan into a chaste Islamic state, he was also thinking about Afghanistan's future. Afghanistan, he concluded, should share the same dream and represent the same values and virtues. His dream of an Islamic *ummah* might begin with the interplay between Pakistan and Afghanistan.

Peace between Pakistan and Afghanistan could only be envisioned on a foundation of genuine Muslim solidarity. Zia saw no other way to control the divisive Afghans, to regulate their combative nature, or moderate their tribalism. Hence, he saw to it that the more austere fundamentalist Afghan organizations received the lion's share of the supplies made available by the United States. But this unbalanced treatment was programmed to rebound once the Soviets completed their withdrawl and the factions began jockeying for advantageous positions *vis-a-vis* one another. Moreover, once the accords were made official, the United States indicated it could no longer support a policy which directed the heaviest portion of the supplies to Afghan fundamentalists. Zia had a tiger by the tail and the matter was unresolved at the time of his death.

On 17 August 1988, General Mohammad Zia ul-Haq, the longest serving head of the Pakistani state, was killed in a still unexplained explosion that brought down the military aircraft taking him from Bahawalpur to Islamabad. Zia's death ended an eleven year reign which was notable for its Islamization programme, but even more so for its foreign policy. Zia fooled all the pundits. He was a gifted balancer, and an astute reader of contemporary events. While never overcoming his unpopularity, he managed to steer Pakistan through a difficult decade without loss of direction or purpose. But Zia left behind all the problems that burdened his administration in the years of his rule. It remained for those who followed him to pick up the threads of his programme, or ignore them for another vision, possibly another view of Pakistan's destiny.

Epilogue

I. Perennial Issues in Pakistan's Foreign Policy

Zia's death in August 1988 made political change inside Pakistan a certainty. It had less immediate effect on the country's foreign policy. Pakistanis had been anticipating a new round of elections and an expansion of the political process. They were less certain about the course of the country's foreign policy. Although domestic questions were subject to new interpretation, Pakistan's external needs pointed to a continuation of relationships and programmes already in train. Pakistan's foreign policy may not have been cut into granite, but the foundation upon which it rested remained a predictable element in an uncertain environment.

The Chairman of the Pakistani Senate, Ghulam Ishaq Khan, in accordance with Pakistan's constitution, was sworn in as acting President when word reached Islamabad about the crash of Zia's aircraft. Marking the end of still another military phase in Pakistan's political history, Ghulam Ishaq established a date for national elections, and in October, Pakistan's High Court permitted the political parties to contest the polls. Subsequently, Benazir Bhutto's Pakistan People's Party won 92 of the 205 seats in the National Assembly and with help from several smaller parties Benazir emerged with the needed majority to form a new government. In December she was declared the country's new Prime Minister. Her party, however, did not fare as well in the provincial legislatures. Only in Sind was the PPP a clear winner. In the Punjab, the largest and most prosperous of Pakistan's four provinces, the opposition Islamic Democratic Alliance (IDA) led by Nawaz Sharif, won the electoral contest.

Benazir was a popular favorite but she did not dominate the political scene. Shortly after she became Prime Minister, Ghulam Ishaq Khan won the presidential elections, Benazir having withdrawn her candidate before the polling. Ghulam Ishaq was a durable civil servant, closely identified with Zia. So too was Sahabzada Yaqub Khan, who Benazir retained as her Foreign Minister. The coming of still another Bhutto heralded a dramatic shift in national political activity, but it was also clear that foreign policy, for the foreseeable future, would not be Benazir's exclusive preserve.

II. The Parameters

Pakistan's foreign policy is an extension of its national security requirements. Threats to the country's existence are real and significant and its foreign relations have been fashioned to maximize the chances of survival. The American connection is an obvious case in point. At the time of independence, Pakistan appeared to have only two options in countering a perceived Indian threat. It could seek assistance from Moscow, or it could strive to establish rapport with Washington. It chose Washington because the Americans had more to offer in the way of material support, but also because of shared values. The men who guided Pakistan in its early years were educated in the western tradition. Their experience was also in that cast. The Soviet Union was not an appealing, let alone a familiar alternative. But in choosing the United States, Pakistan also picked sides in the Cold War.

Pakistan was also a Third World country, and as such it looked for affinities with other Third World states. Here too, but only after 1949, there were two 'Third World superpowers' and again Pakistan was forced to choose between them. In so far as Pakistan's primary need was to avoid the grasp of its Indian neighbour, it could not embrace that power without succumbing to its influence. So Pakistan selected China, and the Asian behemoth became the non-western anchor of its foreign policy.

The third leg of Pakistan's foreign policy triad was its association with the states of the Muslim Middle East. This association was hammered into shape not from security needs, but from filial identities born of common religious experience. The need for community is very strong in Pakistan, and the country found communion as well as material opportunity among states with shared tradition. As a larger Muslim nation, it also found a leadership role waiting to be filled. By assuming that role Pakistan provided itself with a sense of purpose and strength that it could not find in isolation, or in its relations with other states. Moreover, it reinforced the notion that Pakistan's ethos was intertwined with a larger destiny that was yet to unfold.

This pattern of relationships, fashioned from both real and imaginary needs by successive Pakistani governments, is what the new government of Benazir Bhutto inherited in December 1988. And Benazir placed her stamp of approval on the matter soon after taking office. In the first six months of her administration she visited the

United States, China, and several states in the Middle East, notable among them, Saudi Arabia. In each of these visits she reiterated her government's determination to sustain agreements and commitments made by her predecessors. In assuming this posture Benazir was compelled to face down critics within her own party who called for a change in policy towards the United States. Although irritated by the character of this assault, at no point did she indicate willingness to comply with their demands. The United States, she publicly gestured, remained the linchpin of Pakistan's security and development, and she held to the course charted by those who went before her, including the one followed by Mohammad Zia ul-Haq.

III. The American Connection

Benazir's state visit to the United States in June 1989 was long on ceremony but thin in substance. US-Pakistan relations had undergone refurbishing shortly before Zia's death and the decision had already been taken to perpetuate the programmes developed at that time. Prime Minister Bhutto had earlier indicated her support for a continuation of the American connection and she repeated that intention after assuming her high office. Ms Bhutto was not given to the drama that motivated her father. Her public statements were all measured presentations, bereft of emotion and calculated to explain the points of argument.

Pakistan's shaky economy was too dependent on American aid ($3.6 billion between 1982 and 1987). The United States government had provided Pakistan with $576 million in economic and military assistance in 1988 and the Bush administration had asked for another $621 million for 1990. Moreover, the Washington-based World Bank had committed another $3.2 billion in assistance for 1989-90 through the Pakistan Aid Consortium.[1] Benazir's June visit also provided the occasion for announcing Congressional approval for the 60 additional F-16s Pakistan had requested in the new six-year $4.02 billion aid agreement entered into in 1987. The new Prime Minister could not ignore any of these vital statistics.

Given the honour of addressing a joint session of the U.S. Congress, Benazir zeroed in on the key issue threatening Pakistan's future relations with the United States, i.e., American concern that Islamabad had or was on the verge of developing a nuclear weapons capability. Benazir reiterated her government's long-stated policy not to engage in a nuclear arms race. Her government's sole objec-

---

[1] Thomas P. Thornton, *Pakistan and the United States,* New York: The Asia Society, 1989, p. 7.

tive, she endeavoured to assure the American legislators, lay in promoting the peaceful uses of atomic energy. Pakistan she noted, continues to support a policy calling for the creation of a nuclear-free South Asia and it stands by its offer to enter into an agreement with New Delhi that would give substance to that desire. Pakistan, she said, 'will not provoke a nuclear arms race' in the subcontinent.[1]

Benazir's description of her country's nuclear programme contradicted the report issued by William Webster, the American director of the Central Intelligence Agency. Just before Ms Bhutto's arrival in Washington, Webster told the US Congress that 'Pakistan was engaged in developing a nuclear capability.' He went on to note: 'what creates problems for the United States is whether that capability has reached a point that it implicates the various amendments that apply to other assistance and relief for Pakistan.' Reacting to this latest CIA report, John Glenn spoke for a number of Senators and Congressmen when he insisted the Congress already had sufficient cause to cease its aid programme to Pakistan. If not for the continuing situation in Afghanistan, he asserted, the law would be duly observed.[2] Congressional scrutiny of Pakistan's nuclear programme has always been a sore point in Islamabad where the matter is considered solely in the context of national jurisdiction. Moreover, Pakistani public opinion looks with favour on Pakistan's admission to the nuclear club and American interference is not only abrasive, it is also seen as pro-Indian and an affront to Pakistani sovereignty.

Benazir may have come along at precisely the right moment. Perhaps no other Pakistani leader can bridge this difficulty with the United States. With the war in Afghanistan in a transitional stage and US-Soviet relations at a turning point, American military assistance to Pakistan will be subject to reappraisal. Pakistan's nuclear programme, in the foreseeable future, may cause the Congress to invoke the Symington amendment. But before doing so, American legislators will have to gauge the impact of a cut-off in arms and other deliveries on Benazir's administration. Bhutto's emergence as Prime Minister of Pakistan has been acclaimed by American officials and well- wishers as a victory for democracy. As the first woman leader of a Muslim state, the young Ms Bhutto has captured the fascination and affection of a broad section of the American public. Her declarations with reference to a democratic Pakistan is not lost on American officialdom. She is a lady that few American Congressmen are

---

[1] *The New York Times,* 8 June 1989.
[2] *The New York Times,* 19 May 1989.

prepared to challenge, nor would they knowingly embarrass or destabilize her government. Ms Bhutto's assurance that her country is not producing atomic weapons, although less than convincing in the light of reports to the contrary, is nonetheless politely received in Washington, and the American arms agreement, in the short term, remains intact.

If the Pakistani military establishment continues to hold important cards in the Pakistan political contest, no one at the present time serves military interests more or relates to the United States Congress and Government better than Benazir Bhutto. Another Pakistani leader would not receive the reception prepared for Benazir in Washington. Nor would another leader come away with the same results.

United States and Pakistan foreign policies will continue to diverge, to follow independent channels of opportunity. Harmony of interest has never been essential for their relationship. The United States is a global superpower, while Pakistan will remain a regional middlepower. Pakistan's region of involvement extends into central and southwest Asia, given its concern with developments in Afghanistan, Iran, and the Arab Gulf states. The United States has less real interest in south or central Asia, but plays an even larger role than Pakistan in southwest Asia. Moreover, in the latter, Pakistan's objectives diverge sharply from that of the United States. Whereas Washington is committed to the defense of Israel, Islamabad will not recognize the Zionist state and stands with the Arab nations in pressing the objectives of the Palestinians. American policy in the Persian Gulf, and with particular reference to revolutionary Iran, is also different from that expressed in Pakistan. Pakistan is a near neighbour who often finds kind words for Tehran, speaks reverently about Iran's revolution, and engages in lucrative trade with the Shiite nation. It cannot share Washington's view that Iran is a source of major mayhem in the contemporary world. Nor will it join the United States in its effort to contain the excesses of the Iranian revolution.

By the same token, but in reverse order, the United States refuses to encourage Pakistan's hatred for India. Washington continues to look on New Delhi as a positive influence in the Third World. It ignores India's aggressive display in Sri Lanka or its bullying tactics with Nepal and Bangladesh. It has never come to grips with India's role in the dismemberment of Pakistan, or the protracted rivalry between Islamabad and New Delhi that has already spanned three wars. Washington's military aid to Islamabad is only incidentally visualized as balancing the power equation in the subcontinent. More significantly the United States would rather see that assistance deflecting Pakistan's nuclear weapons programme and not adding to Islamabad's deep strike capability. The knowledge that American-supplied weapons were used by Pakistani forces in their 1965 and 1971 wars with India, and that they would be used again in any future contest, has not been seriously weighed since the Carter administration. Washington would prefer to believe that Pakistan and India have fought their last war with one another. Few Pakistanis, or Indians, for that matter, would share that conclusion.

Pakistan's policy with China also differs from Washington's. Islamabad has strong ties with China, and Washington's complaint with Beijing following the crushing of the 'democracy movement' in June 1989, is not echoed in Islamabad. Pakistan will not cooperate with United States efforts aimed at sanctioning China. It will not hold Beijing to the same 'democratic' test that Ms Bhutto applies to Pakistan. Pakistan will not seek to influence China's domestic experience and it finds the United States attempt to do so counterproductive and strategically inopportune.

Irrespective of such differences, Pakistani ties with the United States are secure. Although the relationship has been tedious and strained, it has also been long and durable. Washington will not forget the 1979 razing of the American embassy, or the destructive attacks on American installations in Pakistan during the Suez crisis of 1956, in the aftermath of the 1965 Indo-Pakistani war, or the February 1989 assault on the American Center in Islamabad. The latter was caused by the publication in Britain and the United States of Salman Rushdie's novel *The Satanic Verses*, and in the ensuing riot six demonstrators were killed. In a public statement following the incident, Benazir, with an eye to her upcoming trip to the United States, acknowledged the sensitivities of the religious community but she also stressed her concern for the right of free speech. In a delicate situation at home, Benazir signalled Washington that such untoward events will happen but that they were not a measure of US-Pakistan relations. Washington has generally followed that same principle in its relations with Pakistan and the two countries appear destined to sustain their curious intimacy that now spans more than three decades.

IV. The Indian Problem

Although Pakistan is the recipient of advanced weapons from the United States, it cannot expect Washington to come to its assistance in a future conflict with India. Nor does Washington like to contemplate American-supplied weapons being used against India. But Washington aside, Pakistan is its own agent in Indian affairs and since the Simla Accords of 1972, Islamabad has given serious attention to moderating differences with New Delhi. That effort will continue but there is little expectation in Islamabad that improved relations will dispel the threat of war that hangs like a stationary cloud over the subcontinent. Both countries have internal problems that they cannot successfully address and which are likely to intensify with the passage of time. The question challenging their respective capitals therefore is whether they will continue to exploit each other's weakness, and hence give credence to their self-fulfilling prophecies about the inevitability of war between them.

Soon after becoming Pakistan's Prime Minister, Benazir hosted the fourth annual meeting of the South Asian Association for Regional Cooperation. The SAARC conference provided the new Prime Minister with the opportunity to exchange views with the head of state of each of the member nations, including Rajiv Gandhi. The event marked the first time since 1960 that an Indian Prime Minister had come to Pakistan on an official visit. The two Prime Ministers, by their own account, struck a cordial note, and their deliberations were crowned with some noticeable success. The leaders signed a cultural exchange agreement to facilitate movement of students, journalists, scholars, artists, and musicians between their two countries. They also agreed to a uniform arrangement on cross-border taxation. Most significant, however, was the formalizing of an agreement not to attack each other's nuclear installations, an issue that had been awaiting final signature for several years.

The latter agreement in no way dispelled India's concern that Pakistan was on the threshold of joining the nuclear club and that this development posed new strategic problems for India. Nor did it deflect Indian intention to expand its own nuclear programmes. Although New Delhi had also publicized its decision not to construct atomic weapons, it had successfully tested a missile delivery system in spring 1989, and reports had been leaked about the production of thermonuclear weapons, i.e. hydrogen bombs. All indications reinforced the conclusion that both India and Pakistan had accelerated their atomic weapons programmes.[1]

With a view to Pakistan's denial that it is engaged in a nuclear weapons programme, it can only be speculated as to why Islamabad believes it necessary to have such weaponry. First and foremost is Pakistan's perceived need for balance in its dealings with India.

[1] Ibid.

Pakistan cannot pass over the one and possibly only opportunity to demonstrate to India its resolve. Nuclear club membership will provide Pakistan with status it cannot otherwise hope to achieve. Moreover, as a nuclear power Pakistan will have the deterrent it believes essential to ward off an aggressive Indian manoeuvre. Pakistan cannot match India in conventional forces, nor does it have the industrial capacity that India enjoys in producing sophisticated weapons systems. Pakistan does not share with the United States the same arrangements New Delhi enjoys in its relations with Moscow. The Soviet Union supports and assists India's nuclear programme whereas the United States will never consent to Pakistan following such a course.

Pakistan, therefore, has operated in relative isolation to establish itself as an atomic power, and hence a major actor on the international stage. This posture has given Pakistan the second reason for its nuclear programme. Pakistan's quest for leadership in the Islamic world will be enhanced by its membership in the exclusive club. What Zulfiqar Ali Bhutto described as an 'Islamic bomb' has enormous implications, and no more so than for the other Muslim nations.

The third or final reason for Pakistan's nuclear programme is something of an extension of the latter. Benazir is committed to the legacy of her father, and her father's association with the programme is a matter she continues to nurture. She has stated on more than one occasion that Pakistan has the sovereign power to judge its own needs and that it will neither be pressured by the United States, nor intimidated by India.

This issue was high on the agenda in the July 1989 meeting between Rajiv and Benazir when the two Prime Ministers again met in Islamabad. Benazir once more publicly declared her country's interest in 'any arrangement' that would guarantee a nuclear-free subcontinent, but in their private conversations they apparently were unable to find that certain formula. Arms control and nuclear proliferation were the principal topics of discussion, but they were also the subjects most difficult to resolve to the satisfaction of the parties. Neither personality, for all their apparent friendliness, was prepared to yield to the other and their talks ended on a negative note. In their final public presentation, Benazir sparred with Rajiv over their respective arms programmes and the lighthearted atmosphere gave way to the realities of an unyielding, but for the time being, latent hostility.

At best the Bhutto-Gandhi summit of 1989 provided more urgency for those engaged in finding a formula for the five-year border war in the Himalayas. Rajiv referred to the Siachen Glacier dispute at an official banquet in his honour. 'We seek an end to clashes and conflicts that have led to the loss of so many lives in the forbidding icebound terrain of the north,' he said.[1] In reply, Benazir spoke of the Siachen Glacier as a 'flashpoint' for an expanded conflict between their two states. She noted the futility of such renewed hostility and called for a quick, statesmanlike settlement of the problem. Siachen, the world's highest battleground, was a significant test of the future relations between India and Pakistan. A breakthrough there, to the satisfaction of both parties, would be an incremental step toward the resolution of more substantial issues in the future. Failure to resolve the dilemma, however, would convince both sides that their only recourse was the military option. Both countries lamented the heavy expenditure on their armed forces when their development programmes were in such desperate straits, but neither was prepared to commence a serious diversion of resources to the public sector.

Although the United States was helpless to mediate the Pakistan-India problem, Benazir's announcement on 10 July 1989 that her country would rejoin the Commonwealth of Nations held out the hope that perhaps that body might some day address the matter. The 48 Commonwealth nations, including India, were to meet in Malaysia in October 1989, and Islamabad was expected to seek readmission prior to that date. Benazir did not have to be reminded that it was her father who had withdrawn Pakistan's membership and that his action had proven to be counter-productive. For Benazir, however, reinstatement not only meant an opportunity to join with other nations in common endeavour, it also cast Pakistan as something more than a Muslim nation, with broader interests and goals. Pakistan's acceptance by the organization was also seen as recognition of Pakistan's new democratic experiment under the leadership of Benazir Bhutto. India's sponsorship of Pakistan's membership would also stand as a positive marker in the attempt to elevate understanding between Islamabad and New Delhi.

V. The Afghanistan Opening
Benazir had been a sharp critic of Zia's policy in Afghanistan. Her party consistently called for direct negotiations with the Soviet Union as well as recognition of the Marxist Kabul government. The PPP was opposed to the American connection that made Pakistan the primary supply base and staging area for the *mujahideen*. Thus the party leaned heavily on Benazir to come to terms with Soviet power in the region, to cease assisting the resistance, and to find the most direct

[1] *The New York Times*, 17 July 1989.

way to move the refugees back across the Pakistani frontier. While in the opposition, the PPP decried Pakistani policy that permitted the United States to fight a proxy war, that made Pakistan a vulnerable frontline state, that exposed the country to a sustained reign of terror. Moreover, they attributed the perpetuation of the Afghan conflict to Washington, who, it was often repeated, wished to 'bleed the Russians,' and to Zia and the junta, who were perceived strengthening their grip on a nation ever fearful of being invaded by enemy forces.

Benazir could not reverse the policy of intervention developed by her predecessor. Foreign affairs were not her exclusive domain. As much as she probed for a political opening that would permit her to introduce a new theme in Pakistan's policy towards Afghanistan, she was mindful of the power of the army and the executive office dominated by Ghulam Ishaq. International matters were as much their concern as the Prime Minister's, and they had more influence over the civil-military apparatus. Benazir therefore was required to go along with the decision to support and direct a *mujahideen* assault on Jalalabad in January 1989. In expectation of a quick victory that would dramatically shorten the life of the Kabul government, the *mujahideen* abandoned their guerrilla tactics and launched a full-scale assault on the provincial capital. Despite all their efforts, however, the defenders of Jalalabad could not be dislodged, nor did they defect to the *mujahideen* side. After several months of costly combat, the siege was lifted, the *mujahideen* were forced to retreat, and the Pakistan government began an agonizing reassessment of its approach to the Afghan problem.

Instead of Afghans returning to their homes, more of them entered Pakistan in the course of the Jalalabad fiasco.[1] Condemnation of government policy could not be avoided and Benazir was forced to take some action aimed at disarming her critics. On 31 May she was credited with the removal of Lieutenant General Hamid Gul, the head of Inter-Services Intelligence (ISI), and the reputed mastermind behind the Jalalabad strategy.[2] Gul's ISI was responsible for channelling American military aid to the *mujahideen*, and under Zia's orders the General had seen to it that the more fundamentalist Islamic factions among the Afghan resistance organizations received the larger portion of available supplies. That strategy too, especially after American prodding, was now given greater scrutiny by Islamabad.

With the war in a new phase, the *mujahideen* factions resumed their traditional feuding, and violent confrontations were inevitable

[1] The Pakistan Times, 22 June 1989.
[2] The New York Times, 1 June 1989.

in the aftermath of the Jalalabad debacle. The 'brutal murder' of 30 commanders of one group by another was attributed to followers of Gulbuddin Hekmatyar, a longtime favourite of the late Zia ul-Haq.[1] Moreover, word of the killings came just as the United States was in the process of mounting new arms shipments to the resistance. Washington had indicated a desire to see the Ahmed Shah Massoud forces in Afghanistan's Panjshir Valley, bolstered by the resupply. It was Massoud's men who were gunned down in the tribal ambush. In estimating the staying power of the Afghan resistance, Washington apparently concluded Massoud was the best person to rally the resistance forces. More pragmatic than most of the other resistance leaders, Massoud was a member of Burhanuddin Rabbani's *Jamaat-i-Islami,* long at odds with Hekmatyar's *Hizb-i-Islami.* He was also a field commander with direct knowledge of the war and familiar to the men fighting at his side. But Massoud's problems had dramatically multiplied since the Soviet withdrawal. The enemy was no longer clearly drawn and the order of combat was not easily arrived at. More important, the factions seemed more opposed to one another than to the Kabul regime. Nor could the United States, with Zia gone, balance and control the bitterly competitive units or effectively direct the guerrilla campaign.

The United States' dilemma was written large in Pakistan. On the one side, the war continued and Pakistan's commitment to the struggle, for the immediate future at least, was undiminished. On the other, the Najibullah government seemed strengthened by the Jalalabad episode, its forces held the major metropolitan centres and showed no signs of caving in despite frequent terror bombings and indiscriminate rocket attacks on the capital. The Soviet Foreign Minister's visit to Kabul in August 1989 was viewed as a gesture of confidence in the Najibullah government, as well as a signal of defiance to Pakistan and the United States. Soviet supplies were getting through in increasing quantities and although Moscow acknowledged the heavy cost of feeding the Afghan society, in addition to providing the necessary arms for the Kabul army, there was obviously no intention to let up. Both the United States and the Soviet Union, therefore, were determined, from a safe distance, to perpetuate the war irrespective of the pain and uncertainty it caused. The *mujahideen* and the Afghan government sustained their struggle even if they were less enthusiastic about the eventual outcome. Pakistan alone seemed to hold the key to the situation, and the

---

[1] *The New York Times,* 17 July 1989.

government of Benazir Bhutto was faced with an impossible set of choices.

If Prime Minister Bhutto had a clear hand in this matter she no doubt would call for the recognition of the Najibullah Government, cease supplying the *mujahideen*, and arrange with Kabul for the return of the Afghan refugees to their ancestral homes.[1] Such action would terminate American assistance to the *mujahideen*. It would also cause the United States to reduce its military commitment to Islamabad. But Benazir does not have a clear hand, and she is not likely to acquire one. The Pakistan military establishment remains the dominant institution in the country and none of the above is in its interest. The war in Afghanistan may wind down, the flow of supplies may diminish, but this will only add to the condition of stalemate that already permeates the mountain kingdom. The Soviet involvement in Afghanistan spanned nine years; it is likely the current phase of the contest will continue for at least the next five. If this is an accurate assessment, Benazir will find her tenure as Prime Minister of Pakistan even less rewarding than she or her followers bargained for.

VI. Pakistan, the Islamic World and the Future

Immersed in conflict within and across its borders, Pakistan finds little relief in its association with the Muslim nations. They too are rocked by crisis and challenged by conflicts that refuse to yield to solution. The Iranian revolution held out the promise of a new beginning but the situation there has been more destabilizing than anything experienced during the long reign of the Shah. The Arab world is no better. The war in Lebanon is now a decade and a half in duration and a once flourishing country has been wilfully and deliberately transformed into a classic hell on earth. No agency or power would seem to have an answer to the anarchy that has destroyed the civilized character of that Mediterranean community. The Israeli-Palestinian struggle entered the phase of the *intefada* in 1987 but that violent recourse has only piled more new tragedy on the old. The Iraq-Iran War, after eight savagely destructive years yielded to a ceasefire in 1988, but the fires of that contest still burn red in Baghdad and Tehran. Official and clandestine terror is a fact of life in the majority of Muslim states and none can adequately project the cause of human freedom. Even in Turkey, where the military again allowed civilian government to resume its managerial

---

[1] *Pakistan Progressive*, 8, 3, Winter 1987, pp. 3-18.

ways, ethnic and sectarian tensions prevent a full-blown experiment in democratic expression.

Pakistan under Benazir Bhutto is something of an exception when viewed in the context of the contemporary Middle East. The promise of democracy is now a practical reality, albeit under tight constraints, and not without significant limitations. But there is more free expression in Pakistan today than at any time since the first months of independence. This fragile experience needs nurturing if it is to be sustained, but the source of that succour will not be found in the external world. Pakistan's quest for fulfillment is within itself, where it has always been.[1] If the country can perpetuate the current experiment and give it strength and substance; if it can bridge ethnic differences and ease sectarian strife; if its government proves more responsive to the material needs of its many publics and can improve their quality of life; Pakistan stands a chance of doing what no other Muslim country in southwest Asia has done, that is, establish a working democracy.

The challenge of democracy is also the challenge of Pakistan's foreign policy.[2] A democratic Pakistan in the twenty-first century holds out the possibility of a new political model for the Islamic world. When Pakistan was formed in 1947 some observers believed the country was destined to lead the Muslim nations. That belief remains alive in the last decade of the twentieth century. Of all the Muslim countries Pakistan alone seems likely to set a pace for the others. But before this can be realized there still remains the matter of Pakistan's immediate neighbours, and no one has suggested that resolving the Indian, Afghanistan and Iranian questions will be easy.

[1] *The Nation*, 1 June 1989.
[2] *Pakistan Progressive*, 10, 1, Spring 1989, pp. 3-19.

Bibliography of Sources Cited

Books

Abdur Rahman Amir of Afghanistan, The Life (Autobiography) of, I, II, John Murray, London, 1900.

Acheson, Dean, *Present At the Creation*, W.W.Norton, New York, 1969.

Afzal, M. Rafique (ed.), *Selected Speeches and Statements of the Quaid-i-Azam Mohammad Ali Jinnah*, Research Society of Pakistan, Lahore, 1966.

——, *Speeches and Statements of Quaid-i-Millat Liaquat Ali Khan, 1941-1951*, Research Society of Pakistan, 1967.

——, *Guftar-i-Iqbal*, Research Society of Pakistan, 1969.

Ahmad, Jamil-ud-Din, *Speeches and Writings of Mr. Jinnah, I*, Muhammad Ashraf, Lahore, 1960.

——, *Some Recent Speeches and Writings of Mr. Jinnah, II*, Muhammad Ashraf, Lahore, 1947.

Ahmad, Mushtaq, *The United Nations and Pakistan*, Pakistan Institute of International Affairs, 1955.

Ahmed, Col. Mohammad, *My Chief*, Longmans, Green, Lahore, 1960.

Ali, Akhtar, *Pakistan's Nuclear Dilemma*, Economist Research Unit, Karachi, 1984.

Ali, Chaudhri Muhammad, *The Emergence of Pakistan*, Columbia University Press, 1967.

Ambedkar, B.R., *Pakistan or the Partition of India*, Thacker and Co., Bombay, 1946.

Azad, Maulana Abul Kalam, *India Wins Freedom*, Longmans, Green, 1960.

Balabushevich, V.V., and Dyakov, A.M. (eds.), *A Contemporary History of India*, People's Publishing House, New Delhi, 1964.

Banuazizi, Ali and Weiner, Myron, *The State, Religion, and Ethnic Politics: Afghanistan, Iran, and Pakistan*, Syracuse University Press, Syracuse, 1986.

Barnett, A. Doak, *Communist China and Asia*, Vintage Books, New York, 1961.

Bazaz, Prem Nath, *The History of Struggle for Freedom in Kashmir*, Kashmir Publishing Co., New Delhi, 1954.

——, *Kashmir in Crucible*, Pamposh Publications, New Delhi, 1967.

——, *Whither India After Independence?* Pamposh Publications, New Delhi, 1970.

Note: The bibliography for the period 1972-1989 is only a partial list. No attempt has been made to include periodical articles or government documents and publications. It represents a cross-section of the monographs and edited volumes released on Pakistan since the first edition of the book.

Berkes, Ross N., Bedi, Mohinder S., *The Diplomacy of India*, Stanford University Press and Oxford University Press, London, 1958.

Bhutto, Zulfiqar Ali, *Important Press Conferences Held in 1965*, Ministry of Foreign Affairs, Govt. of Pakistan,1965.

———, *The Myth of Independence*, Oxford University Press, London, 1969.

———, *'If I am Assassinated...'*, Vikas Publishing House, New Delhi, 1979.

Birdwood, Lord, *Two Nations and Kashmir*, Robert Hale, London, 1950.

Bolitho, Hector, *Jinnah,* John Murray, London, 1954.

Bose, S. C., *The Indian Struggle*, Asia Publishing House, London, 1964.

Bowles, Chester, *Ambassador's Report*, Harper & Row, New York, 1954.

Braibanti, Ralph, *International Implications of the Manila Pact*, American Institute of Pacific Relations, Inc., New York, 1957.

Brecher, Michael, *Nehru: A Political Biography*, Oxford University Press, London, 1959.

———, *India and World Politics: Krishna Menon's View of the World*, Oxford University Press, London, and Frederick A. Praeger, New York, 1968.

Bright, J. S. (ed.), *Before and After Independence* (Nehru's Speeches, 1922-1957), Indian Printing Works, New Delhi, n.d.

Brines, Russell, *The Indo-Pakistani Conflict*, Pall Mall Press, London, 1968.

Bulganin, N. A., and Khrushchev, N. S., *Visit of Friendship to India, Burma and Afghanistan*, Foreign Languages Publishing House, Moscow, 1956.

Burki, S. J., *Pakistan Under Bhutto*, St. Mardin's Press, New York, 1980.

———, *Pakistan: A Nation in the Making*, Westview, Boulder, Colorado, 1986.

Campbell, John C., *Defence of the Middle East*, Frederick Praeger, New York, 1961.

Campbell-Johnson, Alan, *Mission With Mountbatten*, Robert Hale, London, 1951.

Caroe, Sir Olaf, *The Pathans*, Macmillan, London, 1958.

Central Office of Information, London, Reference Division, Central Treaty Organization, R.5296/64,1964.

Chakravarti, P. C., *India's China Policy,* Indiana University Press, 1962.

Chatham House (A Report by a Study Group), *Collective Defence in South-East Asia*, Oxford University Press, London, 1958.

Choudhury, G. W., *Pakistan's Relations with India, 1947-1966*, Pall Mall Press, London, 1968.

———, *India, Pakistan, Bangladesh, and the Major Powers*, The Free Press, New York, 1975.

———, *The Last Days of United Pakistan*, Indiana University Press, Bloomington, Indiana, 1974.

Churchill, Winston S., *The Second World War* (six volumes), Bantam Books, New York, 1962.

Clubb, Oliver E., Jr., *The United States and the Sino-Soviet Bloc in South East Asia*, The Brooking Institution, Washington, D.C., 1962.

Connell, John, *Auchinleck*, Cassell, London,1959.

Coupland, R., *The Indian Problem, Report on the Constitutional Problem of India, Part I*, Oxford University Press, London, 1943.

———, *India: A Re-Statement*, Oxford University Press, London, 1945.

Critical Issues Council, *Critical Issues Paper No.10,* 'The U.S. Position in the Far East' (sponsored by Republican Citizens' Committee of the United States), 1964.

Current Problems in Afghanistan, The Princeton University Conference, Princeton, 1961.

de Toledano, Ralph, *Nixon*, Henry Holt, New York, 1956.
Dupree, Louis, *First Reflections on the Second Kashmir War*, American Universities Field Staff Reports Services, South Asia Series Vol. IX, No. 5, 1965.
Dutt, R. Palme, *India Today and Tomorrow*, Lawrence and Wishart, London, 1955.

Eden, Sir Anthony, *Full Circle*, Cassell, London, 1960.
Embree Ainslee T. (ed.), *Pakistan's Western Borderlands*, Carolina Academic Press, Durham, NC, 1977.

Fletcher, Arnold, *Afghanistan: Highway of Conquest*, Cornell University Press, 1965.
Foreign Languages Press, China, *The Truth About How the Leaders of the CPSU Have Allied Themselves with India Against China*, 1963.
Fraser-Tytler, W. K., *Afghanistan*, Oxford University Press, London, 1967.

Galbraith, John Kenneth, *Ambassador's Journal*, Houghton Mifflin, Boston, 1969.
Gardezi, Hassan, and Rashid, Jamil, *Pakistan: The Roots of Dictatorship*, Zed Publishers, London, 1983.
Garratt, G. T., *Legacy of India*, Clarendon Press, Oxford, 1951.
Griffiths, John C., *Afghanistan*, Pall Mall Press, London, 1967.
Gupta, J. B. Das, *Indo-Pakistan Relations (1947-1955)*, Djambatan, Amsterdam, 1960.
Gupta, K., *Indian Foreign Policy*, The World Press Private Ltd., Calcutta, 1956.
Gupta, Sisir, *Kashmir*, Asia Publishing House, London, 1966.

Haque, Azizul, *Trends in Pakistan's External Policy*, Asiatic Society of Bangladesh, Dhaka, 1985.
Harrison, Selig S.(ed.), *India and the United States*, The Macmillan Co., New York, 1961.
Hasan, K. Sarwar, *The Strategic Interests of Pakistan*, Pakistan Institute of International Affairs, 1954.
Hasan, K. Sarwar (ed.), *Documents on the Foreign Relations of Pakistan: The Kashmir Question*, Pakistan Institute of International Affairs, 1966.
Hodson, H.V., *The Great Divide*, Hutchinson, London, 1969.

India, Govt. of, *Notes, Memoranda and Letters Exchanged between the Governments of India and China, White Papers Nos. I to XIII*.
——, *Report of the Officials of the Governments of India and the People's Republic of China on the Boundary Question, 1961*.
——, *Summary of the Report of the Governments of India and the People's Republic of China on the Boundary Question (undated)*.
Iqbal, Javed, *The Ideology of Pakistan and its Implementation*, Sh. Ghulam Ali & Sons, Lahore, 1959.
Iqbal, Sir Muhammad, *The Reconstruction of Religious Thought in Islam*, Sh. Muhammad Ashraf, Lahore, 1960.
——, *Letters of Iqbal to Jinnah*, Sh. Muhammad Ashraf, Lahore.

Jafri, Rais Ahmad, *Ayub, Soldier and Statesman,* Mohammad Ali Academy, Lahore, 1966.

Jain, Girilal, *Panchsheela and After,* Asia Publishing House, Bombay, 1960.

Jinnah, Quaid-i-Azam Mohammed Ali, *Speeches as Governor-General of Pakistan, 1947-1948,* Karachi (undated).

Kahin, George McT., *The Asian-African Conference,* Cornell University Press, 1956.

Karunakaran, K. P., *India in World Affairs, Aug. 1947-Jan. 1950,* Oxford University Press, London, 1952.

——, *India in World Affairs, Feb. 1950-Dec. 1953,* Oxford University Press, London, 1958.

Kaul, Lieut.-General B. M., *The Untold Story,* Allied Publishers, Bombay, 1967.

Kavic, L. J., *India's Quest for Security,* University of California Press, 1967.

Kennedy, Charles, *Bureaucracy in Pakistan,* Oxford University Press, Karachi, 1987.

Kennedy, John F., *The Strategy of Peace,* Harper and Row, New York, 1960.

Khan, Major-General Fazal Muqeem, *The Story of the Pakistan Army,* Oxford University Press, London, 1963.

Khan, Liaquat Ali, *Pakistan: The Heart of Asia,* Harvard University Press, 1950.

Khan, Field Marshal Mohammed Ayub, *Speeches and Statements, I, II, III, IV, V, VI, VII, VIII* (1958-66), Pakistan Publications, Karachi.

——, *On the Crisis Over Kashmir,* Govt. of Pakistan, 1965.

——,*Friends Not Masters,* Oxford University Press, London, 1967.

Khan, Mohammed Zafrulla, *Pakistan's Foreign Relations,* Pakistan Institute of International Affairs, 1951.

——, *Reminiscences,* (unpublished), Oral History Research Office, Columbia University, New York, 1962.

Kiernan, V. G., (translated by), *Poems from Iqbal,* John Murray, London, 1955.

Kissinger, Henry A., *Nuclear Weapons and Foreign Policy,* Harper and Brothers, New York, 1957.

Korbel, Josef, *Danger in Kashmir,* Princeton University Press, and Oxford University Press, London, 1954 (2nd edn., 1966).

Korson Henry (ed.), *Contemporary Problems of Pakistan,* Brill, Leiden, 1974.

Kundra, J. C., *Indian Foreign Policy, 1947-1954,* J.B. Wolters, Groningen, Netherlands 1955.

Lakhanpal, P. L., *Essential Documents and Notes on Kashmir Dispute,* International Publications, New Delhi, 1958.

Lamb, Alastair, *The China-Indian Border,* Oxford University Press, London, 1964.

——, *The Kashmir Problem,* Frederick A. Praeger, New York, 1966.

La Porte, Robert, *Power and Privilege: Influence and Decision Making in Pakistan,* University of California Press, Berkeley, 1975.

Lenczowski, George, *The Middle East in World Affairs,* Cornell University Press, 1962.

Mahajan, Mehr Chand, *Looking Back,* Asia Publishing House, New York, 1963.

Mohamood, Safdar, *The Deliberate Debacle,* Sh. Muhammad Ashraf, Lahore, 1976.

Mansergh, Nicholas, *Documents and Speeches on Commonwealth Affairs, 1931-1952, I, II,* Oxford University Press, London, 1953.

Maxwell, Neville, *India's China War,* Jonathan Cape, London, 1970.

Mende, Tibor, *Nehru: Conversations on India and World Affairs,* George Braziller, Inc., New York, 1956.

Menon, V.P., *The Transfer of Power in India,* Princeton University Press, 1957.

——, *The Story of the Integration of the Indian States,* Orient Longmans, 1961.

Michel, A. A., *The Indus River,* Yale University Press, 1967.

Modelski, George, *SEATO,* F.W. Cheshire, Melbourne, 1964.

Molesworth, G. N., *Afghanistan 1919,* Asia Publishing House, New York, 1962.

Moody, Piloo, *Zulfi My Friend,* Paramount Publishers, Karachi, 1974.

Mosley, Leonard, *The Last Days of the British Raj,* Weidenfeld and Nicolson, London, 1961.

Mountbatten of Burma, Earl, *Time Only to Look Forward,* Nicholas Kaye, London, 1949.

Nadvi, R. A. J. (ed.), *Selections from Muhammad Ali's Comrade,* Muhammad Ali Academy, Lahore, 1965.

Nehru, Jawarharlal, *Eighteen Months in India,* Kitabistan, Allahabad, 1938.

——, *The Unity of India,* The John Day Co., New York, 1942.

——, *Jawaharlal's Discovery of America,* East and West Publishers, Delhi, 1950.

——, *An Autobiography,* The Bodley Head, London, 1958.

——, *Discovery of India,* Meridian Books, London, 1960.

——, *India's Foreign Policy* (speeches, Sept. 1946-Apr. 1961), Govt. of India, 1961.

——, *India's Freedom,* Unwin Books, London, 1962.

——, *India and the World* (Nehru, Toynbee and Attlee), Allied Publishers, New Delhi,1962.

——, *Speeches, I, II, III, IV, V,* Govt. of India, 1963, 1958, 1964, 1968.

Nixon, Richard M., *U.S. Foreign Policy for the 1970s, The Emerging Structure of Peace, A Report to the Congress, Feb. 9, 1972.*

Noorani, A. G., *Our Credulity and Negligence,* Ramdas G. Bhatkal, Bombay, 1963.

Nyrop, Richard, (ed.), *Pakistan: A Country Study,* US Government Printing Office, Washington, DC, 1984.

Overstreit, Gene D., and Windmiler, Marshall, *Communism in India,* University of California Press, 1960.

Pakistan, Govt. of, *No-War Declaration and Canal Waters Dispute, Correspondence between the Prime Ministers of Pakistan and India,* Karachi (undated).

——, *The Bajaur Incident* (undated).

——, *India's Threat to Pakistan, Correspondence Between the Prime Ministers of Pakistan and India, 15 July-11 Aug. 1951,* Ministry of Foreign Affairs and Commonwealth Relations, Karachi, 1951.

——, *Negotiations Between the Prime Ministers of Pakistan and India Regarding the Kashmir Dispute, June 1953-Sept. 1954.*

——, *Prime Minister's Statement on Foreign Policy,* 1956.

——, *Reports on Kashmir by United Nations Representatives,* Karachi, 1958.

Palmer, Norman D., *South Asia and United States Policy,* Houghton Mifflin, Boston, 1966.

Panikkar, K. M., *In Two Chinas,* George Allen & Unwin, London, 1955.

Panjabi, K. L., *The Indomitable Sardar*, Bharatiya Vidya Bhavan, Bombay, 1964.

Pazhwak, Rahman, *Pakhtunistan*, London (undated).

Pirzada, Syed Sharifuddin, *Evolution of Pakistan*, The All-Pakistan Legal Decisions, Lahore, 1963.

Prasad,Bimla, *The Origins of Indian Foreign Policy*, Bookland Private Ltd., Calcutta, 1962.

Pyarelal, *Mahatama Gandhi, The Last Phase, I, II*, Navajivan Publishing House, Ahmedabad 1956, 1958.

Radhakrishnan, S., *Eastern Religions and Western Thought*, 2nd. edn., Galaxy Book, Oxford University Press, New York, 1959 (also Clarendon Press, Oxford).

Rahman, Ataur, *Pakistan and America: Dependency Relations*, Young Asia Publication, New Delhi, 1982.

Rahman, Sheikh Mujibur, *6-Point Formula: Our Right to Live*, Pioneer Press, Dacca, 1966.

Rajan, M. S., *Indian World Affairs, 1954-56*, Asia Publishing House, London, 1964.

Rajkumar, N.V. (ed.), *The Background of India's Foreign Policy*, Delhi, Navin Press, 1952.

Razvi, Mujtaba, *The Frontiers of Pakistan*, National Publishing House, Karachi, 1971.

Richardson, H. E., *Tibet and Its History*, Oxford University Press, London, 1962.

Rizvi, Hasan-Askari, *The Military and Politics in Pakistan*, Progressive Publishers, Lahore, 1986.

Saxena, K. C., *Pakistan and Her Relations with India, 1947-1966*, Vir Publishing House, New Delhi, 1966.

Sayeed, Khalid B., *Politics in Pakistan*, Praeger, New York, 1980.

Schlesinger, A. M., Jr., *A Thousand Days*, Houghton Mifflin, Boston, 1965.

Schofield, Victoria, *Bhutto: Trial and Execution*, Cassell, London, 1979.

Schonlfield, Hugh J., *Suez Canal in World Affairs*, Yale University Press, 1967.

Shahi, Agha, *Pakistan's Security and Foreign Policy*, Progressive Publishers, Lahore, 1988.

Shamloo (ed.), *Speeches and Statements of Iqbal*, Al-Manar Academy, Lahore, 1948.

Sheean, Vincent, *Nehru: The Years of Power*, Victor Gollancz, London, 1960.

Sherwani, Latif Ahmed (and others), *Foreign Policy of Pakistan*, The Allies Book Corporation, Karachi, 1964.

Siddiqi, Aslam, *Pakistan Seeks Security*, Longmans, Green, Pakistan Branch, 1960.

Sitaramayya, Pattabi, *The History of the Indian National Congress, I, II*, Padma Publications Ltd., Bombay, 1946.

Stebbins, R. P., *The United States in World Affairs, 1954*, Harper & Brothers, New York, 1956.

Stephens, Ian, *Pakistan*, Ernest Benn, London, 1963.

——, *Horned Moon*, Ernest Benn, London, 1966.

Syed, Anwar H., *Pakistan: Islam, Politics, and National Solidarity*, Praeger, New York, 1982.

——, *China and Pakistan: Diplomacy of an Entente Cordiale*, University of Massachusetts Press, Amherst, 1974.

Sykes, Sir Percy, *Sir Mortimer Durand*, Cassell, London, 1974.

Talbot, Phillips, and Poplai, S. L., *India and America, A Study of Their Relations*, Harper and Brothers, New York, 1958.

Tendulkar, D. G., *Mahatma* (8 vols.), Publications Division, Govt. of India, 1960-3.

Thien, Ton That, *India and Southeast Asia*, Librairie Droz, Geneve, 1963.

Van Eekelen, W. F., *Indian Foreign Policy and the Dispute with China*, Martinus Nijhoof, The Hague, 1964.

Venkataramani, M. S., *Undercurrents in American Foreign Relations*, Asia Publishing House, London, 1965.

Walker, Patrick Gordon, *The Commonwealth*, Mercury Books, London, 1965.

Waseem, Mohammad (ed.), *Politics and the State in Pakistan*, Progressive Publishers, Lahore, 1989.

Wilcox, Wayne, A. (ed.), *Asia and the United States*, Prentice Hall, Englewood Cliffs, 1967.

——, Leo Rose, Gavin Boyd (eds.), *Asia and the International System*, Winthrop, Cambridge, 1972.

Williams, Francis, *Twilight of Empire: Memoirs of Prime Minister Clement Attlee, as Set Down by Francis Williams*, A.S. Barnes & Co., New York, 1962.

Wriggins, Horward (ed.), *Pakistan in Transition*, University of Islamabad Press, Islamabad, 1975.

Ziring, Lawrence (ed.), *Asian Security Issues*, Institute of Government and Politics, Kalamazoo, Michigan, 1988.

——, *Pakistan: The Enigma of Political Development*, Dawson, Kent, 1980.

——, *The Subcontinent in World Affairs*, revised edition, Praeger, New York, 1982.

Articles

Abdullah, Sheikh Mohammad, 'Kashmir, India and Pakistan', *Foreign Affairs*, April 1965.

Baqai, I. H., 'Relations Between Afghanistan and Pakistan', *Pakistan Horizon*, Sept. 1948.

Barton, Sir William, 'Pakistan's Claim to Kashmir', *Foreign Affairs*, Jan. 1950.

Bowles, Chester, 'A U.S. Policy for Asia', *New Leader*, 22 Feb. 1954.

Burke, S. M., 'The Sino-Indian Conflict', *Journal of International Affairs*, vol. XVII, no. 2, 1963.

——, 'Sino-Pakistani Relations', *ORBIS*, vol. 9, no. 2, Summer 1964.

Chaudhri, M. A., 'Pakistan and East Asia'. *Pakistan Horizon*, March 1959.

Cunningham, Sir George, 'Pakistan's Frontier and the Tribes', *Statesman*, 28 May 1949.

da Costa, E. P. W., 'India's New Five Year Plan', *Foreign Affairs*, July 1965.
Daultana, Mumtaz Muhammad, 'Reflections on Pakistan's Foreign Policy', *Dawn*, 10 Dec. 1965.
Dyakov, A., 'Partitioned India', *New Times*, no. 3, 1948.

Gupta, B. S., 'A Maoist Line for India', *The China Quarterly*, Jan.- March 1966.

Harrison, Selig S., 'Case History of a Mistake', *New Republic*, 10 Aug. 1959.
——, 'Troubled India and Her Neighbours', *Foreign Affairs*, Jan. 1965.
——, 'America, India and Pakistan', *Harper's Magazine*, July 1966.
Hasan, Sarwar, 'The Background of American Arms Aid to Pakistan', *Pakistan Horizon*, 2nd Quarter 1967.

Indian Official, An, 'India as World Power', *Foreign Affairs*, July 1949.
Ispahani, M. A. H., 'The Foreign Policy of Pakistan, 1947-64', *Pakistan Horizon*, 3rd Quarter 1964.

Kalyagin, B., 'India's Ultras', *New Times*, no. 28, 1970.
Kennan, George, 'The Sources of Soviet Conflict', *Foreign Affairs*, July 1947.
Khan, Haffez-ur-Rahman, 'Pakistan's Relations with the U.S.S.R.', *Pakistan Horizon*, 1st Quarter 1961.
——, 'Pakistan's Relations with the People's Republic of China', *Pakistan Horizon*, 3rd Quarter 1961.
Khan, Mohammad Ayub, 'Pakistan Perspective', *Foreign Affairs*, July 1960.
Kripalni, Acharya J. B., 'For Principled Neutrality', *Foreign Affairs*, Oct.1959.

Lockwood, David E., 'Sheikh Abdullah and the Politics of Kashmir'; *Asian Survey*, May 1969.

Markov, M., 'After San Francisco', *New Times*, no. 39, 1951.
Montagno, George L., 'Pak-Afghan Detente', *Asian Survey*, Dec. 1963.

Narain, Jayaprakash, 'The Need to Re-Think', *Hindustan Times*, 15 May 1964.
Nehru, Jawaharlal, 'Changing India', *Foreign Affairs*, April 1963.
Nixon, Richard M., 'An Interview with the President: "The Jury Is Out"', *Time*, 3 Jan. 1972.

Orestov, O., 'The War in Kashmir', *New Times*, no. 40,1948.

'P' (Panikkar, K. M.), 'Middle Ground Between America and Russia: An Indian View', *Foreign Affairs*, Jan. 1954.
Palmer, Norman D., 'India's Position in Asia', *Journal of International Affairs*, no.2, 1963.
——, 'India and Pakistan: The Major Recipients', *Current History*, Nov. 1965.
Qureshi, Khalida, 'Diplomacy of the India-Pakistan War', *Pakistan Horizon*, 4th Quarter 1965.

Rahman, Tunku Abdul, 'Malaysia: Key Area in Southeast Asia', *Foreign Affairs*, July 1965.

Rana, A. P., 'The Nature of India's Foreign Policy', *India Quarterly*, April-June 1966.

Sayeed, K. B., 'Southeast Asia in Pakistan's Foreign Policy', *Pacific Affairs*, Summer 1968.

Shahabuddin, Khwaja, 'King Feisal As I Knew Him', *Dawn* (Supplement), 19 April 1966.

Sheean, Vincent, 'The Case for India', *Foreign Affairs*, Oct. 1951.

Shepley, James, 'How Dulles Averted War', *Life*, 16 Jan. 1956.

Spain, J. W., 'Military Assistance for Pakistan', *American Political Science Review*, Sept. 1954.

Suhrawardy, Husein Shaheed, 'Political Stability and Democracy in Pakistan', *Foreign Affairs*, April 1957.

Tourellot, A. B., 'Kashmir: Dilemma of a People Adrift', *Saturday Review*, 6 March 1965.

News Media
A. *Radio*
   B.B.C. Monitoring Service
   Department of State Press, Radio and TV News Briefing
   Radio Mecca

B. *Television*
   Channel 13, WNDT, New York
   Independent Television Network (UK)
   N.E.T. Network

C. *Newspapers*
   Al-Gamhouria; Christian Science Monitor; Daily Telegraph; Dawn; Evening Star(Washington, D.C.); Hindu; Hindu Weekly Review; Hindustan Times; Jin Min Jin Pao; Manchester Guardian; Minneapolis Tribune; Morning News (Karachi); New York Herald Tribune; New York Times; Observer; Pakistan Times; Peshawar Times; Pravda; St. Paul Dispatch; Statesman; Statesman Weekly; Sunday Star (Washington, D.C.); Sunday Times; The Times; Times of India; Tribune (Lahore); Washington Post; Zamindar.

D. *Press Releases and News Agencies*
   Govt. of Pakistan Handouts
   New China News Agency

E. *Press Digests*
   Asian Recorder
   Indian Press Digests (University of California)
   Pakistan News Digest
   Survey of Mainland China Press

Periodicals
  American Political Science Review; Asian Review; Asian Survey; Asiatic Review; Aviation Week and Space Technology; China Quarterly; Current History; Current Notes; Economist; Foreign Affairs; Harper's Magazine; India News; India Quarterly; International Affairs; International Studies; Journal of International Affairs; Life; Listener; New Leader; New Republic; Newsweek; New Times; New York Times Magazine; Pakistan Affairs; Pakistan Document Series; Pakistan Horizon; Pakistan News; Parade Magazine (St.Paul Sunday Pioneer Press); Peking Review; People's China; Round Table; Saturday Review; Soviet News; United States Department of State Bulletin (USDSB); U.S. News and World Report.

Parliamentary Publications
Congressional Record and Hearings before House and Senate Committees.
Constituent Assembly of India Debates.
Constituent Assembly of Pakistan Debates.
House of Commons Debates.
House of Lords Debates.
Lok Sabha Debates.
National Assembly of Pakistan Debates.
Parliament of India Debates.
Rajya Sabha Debates.
Report of the Indian Statutory Commission, Vol.I, Cmd.3568 of 1930, and Vol.II,Govt. of India, 1930.
Report on the Eighth Session of the General Assembly of the United Nations, House Report 1695, 83rd Congress, 2nd Session, Washington, D.C., 1953.
Report of Special Study Mission to Asia, House Report 1386, 86th Congress, 2nd Session, Washington, D.C.,1960.
Report of the Special Study Mission to the Far East, South Asia and the Middle East of the Committee on Foreign Affairs, House Report 1946, 87th Congress, 2nd Session, Washington, D.C., 1962.

United Nations Documents
General Assembly Official Records.
Security Council Official Records.
Security Council Official Records, Fourth Year, Special Supplement No.7, UNCIP, Third Report, S/1430, 9 Dec.1949.
Report of the Secretary-General to the Security Council on the Situation in Kashmir, S/6651, 3 Sept. 1965.
Introduction to the Report of the Secretary-General on the Work of the Organization, New York, 1965.
Report Submitted by the United Nations Representative for India and Pakistan, Sir Owen Dixon, to the Security Council, S/1791, 15 Sept 1950.
Reports Submitted by the United Nations Representative for India and Pakistan, Mr. F.P. Graham, to the Security Council, S/2375, S/2448, S/2611, S/2783, S/2967, S/3984, dated 15 Oct. 1951, 19 Dec. 1951, 22 April 1952, 19 Sep.1952, 27 March 1953, and 31 March 1958.
Report Submitted by the President of the Security Council for the month of February 1957, Mr. Gunnar Jarring, to the Security Council, S/3821, 29 April 1957.

Index

Abbas, Chaudhri Ghulam, revives Muslim Conference, 20

Abdullah, Sheikh Muhammad, founds All-Jammu and Kashmir Muslim Conference, 20; converts Muslim Conference into All-Jammu and Kashmir National Conference, 20; Head of Government, 25; favours Kashmir's accession to India, 42-3; independence for Kashmir, 42, 46, 381; agreement with Nehru, 44; upset at rise of Hindu Communalism 45; dismissal and imprisonment, 46; provisional nature of Kashmir accession to India, 230, 380; released and rearrested, 230; released and sent to Pakistan, 321; proposes confederation 321; travels abroad, 326; meets Chou En-lai, 326; rearrested, 327; released, 380; convenes convention, 380; barred from Kashmir, 381; writes in *Foreign Affairs*, 380; on Indian secularism, 385

Acheson, Dean, praises Nehru, 120; replies to Nehru on Korean issue, 128; statement on Far East, 156; article on US foreign policy, 250

Afghanistan, relations with Pakistan, 68, 205, 376, 427-8; opposes Pakistan's admission to UN, 73; resignation of Daud, 207; attitude towards Indo-Pakistani September 1965 war, 355; Bhutto's visit, 422; improvement in relations, 427-8; Daud's visit to Pakistan, 428, 438-40; Zia's visit to Kabul, 441-2; Afghan politics preceding Soviet invasion, 443-4; Soviet invasion, 444; *mujahideen* begin operating from Pakistan, 444; stand of Islamic Conference on Afghan issue, 448-9; UN mediation efforts, 452, 453, 459; Afghan refugees as a threat to Pakistan,

454-5; border attacks, 457; spill-over effect of Afghan war on Pakistan, 459; Gorbachev signals desire to terminate Soviet role in Afghan conflict, 459; Geneva Accords, 460; impact of accords on *mujahideen*, 460-1; Benazir's handling of Afghan question, 471-4; Jalalabad fiasco, 472; factional fighting among the *mujahideen*, 472-3; see also Pakhtunistan

African-Asian Conference (Second), proposed, 310; postponed, 311

Algeria, Pakistan supports independence of, 141; supports Pakistan in Sept. war, 355

Ali, Chaudhri Muhammad, offers no-war pact to India, 51; why Pakistan remained in Commonwealth, 116

Ali Bogra, Muhammad, desires good relations with India, 39; negotiates with Nehru, 39; suggests joint defence with India, 55; role in Colombo Conference, 174; role in Bandung Conference, 175-80; praises Chou En-Lai, 178; defends receipt of US Military aid, 220-1; statement on foreign policy, 272

Ali, Syed Amjad, Pakistan's bias towards the U.S.A., 148; Pakistan's economic difficulties, 259

All-India Muslim League: see Muslim League

All-Jammu and Kashmir Muslim Conference: see Muslim Conference

All-Jammu and Kashmir National Conference: see National Conference

Asian-African Conference (1955): see Bandung

Attlee, Clement, modifies British stand on Kashmir dispute, 31; suggests arbitration of Kashmir dispute, 34; dis-